The
INTERNATIONAL CRITICAL COMMENTARY
on the Holy Scriptures of the Old and New Testaments

GENERAL EDITORS

J. A. EMERTON, F.B.A.
Fellow of St. John's College
Emeritus Regius Professor of Hebrew in the University of Cambridge
Honorary Canon of St George's Cathedral, Jerusalem

C. E. B. CRANFIELD, F.B.A.
Emeritus Professor of Theology in the University of Durham

AND

G. N. STANTON
Lady Margaret's
Professor of Divinity in the University of Cambridge

FORMERLY UNDER THE EDITORSHIP OF

S. R. DRIVER
A. PLUMMER
C. A. BRIGGS

THE SECOND EPISTLE TO THE CORINTHIANS

VOLUME II

A CRITICAL AND EXEGETICAL
COMMENTARY

ON

THE SECOND
EPISTLE TO THE
CORINTHIANS

BY

MARGARET E. THRALL

*Former Reader in Biblical Studies in
the University of Wales, Bangor*

IN TWO VOLUMES

VOLUME II

Commentary on II Corinthians VIII–XIII

T & T CLARK INTERNATIONAL
A Continuum imprint
LONDON • NEW YORK

T&T Clark LTD
A Continuum Imprint

The Tower Building   15 East 26th Street
11 York Road   New York, NY 10010
London. SE1 7NX   USA

www.tandtclark.co.uk
Copyright © T&T Clark Ltd, 2000

First published 2000
This edition 2004

ISBN 0 567 08543 0 (hardback)
0 567 08435 3 (paperback)

British Library Cataloguing-in-Publication Data
A catalogue record for this book is available from the British Library

Typeset by Fakenham Photosetting Ltd, Fakenham, Norlfolk
Printed and bound in Great Britain by The Cromwell Press, Wiltshire

Dedicated to my colleagues, past and present, academic and secretarial, in the Department of Religious Studies and the School of Theology in the University of Wales, Bangor, in gratitude for their support and encouragement.

CONTENTS OF VOLUME II

PREFACE

I should like to express my sincere thanks to all the authors whose works have assisted me in the preparation of the second volume of this commentary, and to reiterate my gratitude to the other colleagues and friends mentioned in the preface to the first volume. Especially, again, my warmest thanks go to Professor Charles Cranfield, for his wise advice and continuous interest. In addition, I am very grateful indeed to Mr Kevin Stuart-Banks, research student in the School of Theology in the University of Wales Bangor, who has typed the MS of this volume with great care and promptitude. I am most grateful to Mrs Beti Llewellyn, Secretary of the School of Theology and Religious Studies in the University of Wales Bangor, who has kindly typed the indexes. Finally, I am very much indebted to the publishers of the ICC series, for their initial invitation to contribute to it and for the patience with which they have awaited the completion of my work.

As in Vol. I, some biblical quotations are taken from the Revised Standard Version of the Bible, copyright 1946, 1952 and 1971 by the Division of Christian Education of the National Council of the Churches of Christ in the USA. Used by permission. All rights reserved. Others are taken from the New Revised Standard Version of the Bible, copyright 1989 by the Division of Christian Education of the National Council of the Churches of Christ in the USA. Used by permission. All rights reserved. These quotations from the RSV and NRSV are acknowledged on the pages where they occur. Further quotations, similarly acknowledged, are taken from the Jerusalem Bible, published and copyright 1966, 1967 and 1968 by Darton Longman & Todd Ltd (London) and by Doubleday, a division of Random House, Inc. (New York), and are used by permission of both publishers. Other brief biblical quotations, acknowledged where they occur, are taken from the following translations: the New English Bible (Oxford University Press and Cambridge University Press, 1970); the Revised English Bible (Oxford University Press and Cambridge University Press, 1989); and Y Beibl Cymraeg Newydd (BFBS, Swindon, 1988). I am again indebted to Professor J. H. Charlesworth for permission to quote from *The Old Testament Pseudepigrapha*, published by

Darton Longman & Todd Ltd (London, 1983–85). Translations of classical and hellenistic texts are usually taken from the Loeb Classical Library, published by William Heinemann Ltd (London) and Harvard University Press (Cambridge, Massachusetts), and are acknowledged where they occur.

Margaret E. Thrall

SUPPLEMENTARY ABBREVIATIONS AND BIBLIOGRAPHY

BBB: Bonner Biblische Beiträge
BHTh: Beiträge zur Historischen Theologie
CAH: *Cambridge Ancient History*
JRLB: *John Rylands Library Bulletin* (Manchester)
KD: *Kerygma und Dogma* (Göttingen)
MBPS: Mellen Biblical Press Series
NIGTC: New International Greek Testament Commentary
Baird, W., 'Visions, Revelation and Ministry: Reflections on 2 Cor 12:1–5 and Gal 1: 11–17', *JBL* 104 (1985), pp. 651–62.
Barnett, P., *The Second Epistle to the Corinthians*, NICNT, Grand Rapids, 1997.
Barrett, C. K., 'Cephas and Corinth', pp. 1–12 in *Abraham unser Vater* (see main bibliography under Friedrich), 1963; reprinted in *Essays on Paul*, London, 1982, pp. 28–39; references are to the pages in *Essays*.
Barrett, C. K., 'Christianity at Corinth', *JRLB* 46 (1964), pp. 269–97; reprinted in *Essays*, pp. 1–27; references are to the pages in *Essays*.
Barrett, C. K., 'ΨΕΥΔΑΠΟΣΤΟΛΟΙ (2 Cor 11.13)', pp. 377–96 in *Mélanges Bibliques en Hommage au R. P. Béda Rigaux*, ed. A. Descamps and A. de Halleux, Gembloux, 1970; reprinted in *Essays*, pp. 87–107; references are to the pages in *Essays*.
Barrett, C. K., *The Signs of an Apostle*, London, 1970.
Barrett, C. K., 'Paul's Opponents in II Corinthians', *NTS* 17 (1971), pp. 233–54; reprinted in *Essays*, pp. 60–86; references are to the pages in *Essays*.
Baumgarten, J., *Paulus und die Apokalyptik. Die Auslegung apokalyptischer Überlieferung in den echten Paulusbriefen*, WMANT 44, Neukirchen-Vluyn, 1975.
Benz, E., *Paulus als Visionär*, Wiesbaden, 1952.
Berger, K., 'Almosen für Israel: Zum Historischen Kontext der Paulinischen Kollekte', *NTS* 23 (1977), pp. 180–204.
Betz, H. D., 'Eine Christus-Aretalogie bei Paulus (2. Kor. 12, 7–10)', *ZTK* 66 (1969), pp. 288–305.
Betz, H. D., *Der Apostel Paulus und die sokratische Tradition*, BHTh 45, Tübingen, 1972.
Bietenhard, H., *Die himmlische Welt im Urchristentum und Spätjudentum*, WUNT 2, Tübingen, 1951.
Black, D. A., *Paul, Apostle of Weakness. Astheneia and its Cognates in the Pauline Literature*, New York, 1984.
Bruce, F. F., *The Epistle of Paul to the Galatians*, NIGTC, Exeter, 1982.
Buck, C. H., and Taylor, G., *Saint Paul: A Study of the Development of His Thought*, New York, 1969.

Burton, E. de W.,   *A Critical and Exegetical Commentary on the Epistle to the Galatians*, ICC, Edinburgh, 1921 (reprint 1962).

Clavier, H.,   'La Santé de l'Apôtre Paul', pp. 66–82 in *Studia Paulina* (see main bibliography under Manson).

DiCicco, M. M.,   *Paul's Use of Ethos, Pathos, and Logos in 2 Corinthians 10–13*, MBPS 31, Lewiston, 1995.

Dittenberger, W., ed.,   *Sylloge Inscriptionum Graecarum*, Leipzig, 1915–24.

Dungan, D.,   *The Sayings of Jesus in the Churches of Paul*, Oxford, 1971.

Ebner, M.,   *Leidenslisten und Apostelbrief. Untersuchungen zu Form, Motivik und Funktion der Peristasenkataloge bei Paulus*, FB 66, Würzburg, 1991.

Fee, G. D.,   *The First Epistle to the Corinthians*, NICNT, Grand Rapids, 1987 (reprint 1993).

Fraikin, D.,   'The Rhetorical Function of the Jews in Romans', pp. 91–105 in *Anti-Judaism in Early Christianity* I (see below, under Richardson).

Haenchen, E.,   *Die Apostelgeschichte*, Meyer K 3, Göttingen, [14]1965.

Hahn, F.,   'Der Apostolat im Urchristentum: seine Eigenart und seine Voraussetzungen', *KD* 20 (1974), pp. 54–77.

Heckel, U.,   *Kraft in Schwachheit. Untersuchungen zu 2. Kor 10–13*, WUNT 2. Reihe 56, Tübingen, 1993.

Hengel, M.,   *The Pre-Christian Paul*, London, 1991, translated by J. Bowden from 'Der vorchristliche Paulus', in *Paulus, Missionar und Theologe und das antike Judentum*, WUNT 58, eds. M. Hengel and U. Heckel, Tübingen, 1991.

Himmelfarb, M.,   *Ascent to Heaven in Jewish and Christian Apocalypses*, Oxford, 1993.

Hock, R. F.,   *The Social Context of Paul's Ministry: Tentmaking and Apostleship*, Philadelphia, 1980.

Holladay, C. H.,   *Theios Aner in Hellenistic-Judaism*, SBLDS 40, Missoula, Montana, 1977.

Horrell, D. G.,   *The Social Ethos of the Corinthian Correspondence: Interests and Ideology from 1 Corinthians to 1 Clement*. Studies of the New Testament and its World, Edinburgh, 1996.

Horsley, G. H. R.,   *New Documents Illustrating Early Christianity* I, Macquarie University, 1981.

Jervell, J.,   'Der schwache Charismatiker', pp. 185–98 in *Rechtfertigung*, FS E. Käsemann, eds. J. Friedrich, W. Pöhlmann and P. Stuhlmacher, Tübingen, 1976.

Judge, E. A.,   'Paul's Boasting in Relation to Contemporary Professional Practice', *AusBR* 16 (1968), pp. 37–50.

Kennedy, G. A.,   *The Art of Persuasion in Greece*, London, 1963.

Klauck, H. J.,   *2 Korintherbrief*. Die Neue Echter Bibel 8, Würzburg, 1986.

Lambrecht, J.,   'Philological and Exegetical Notes on 2 Corinthians 13,4', chap. 20 (pp. 589–98) in R. Bieringer and J. Lambrecht, *Studies in 2 Corinthians*, BETL 112, Leuven, 1994.

Leivestad, R.,   ' "The Meekness and Gentleness of Christ". II Cor.x.1', *NTS* 12 (1966), pp. 156–64.

Lightfoot, J. B.,   *The Epistle of St. Paul to the Galatians,* London, 1865, (reprint[3], Grand Rapids, 1962.)

Lincoln, A. T., ' "Paul the Visionary": the setting and significance of the rapture to Paradise in II Corinthians xii.1–10', *NTS* 25 (1979), pp. 204–20.

Lohse, E., ed.   *Verteidigung und Begründung des Apostolischen Amtes (2 Kor 10–13)*, Monographische Reihe von 'Benedictina: Biblisch-Ökumenische Abteilung', Rome, 1992.

Lüdemann, G.,   *Paul, Apostle to the Gentiles: Studies in Chronology*, London, 1984, translated by F. S. Jones from *Paulus, der Heidenapostel I: Studien zur Chronologie*, FRLANT 123, Göttingen, 1980.

Lüdemann, G.,   *Paulus, der Heidenapostel II: Antipaulinismus im frühen Christentum*, FRLANT 130, Göttingen, 1983.

Malherbe, A. J.,   'Antisthenes and Odysseus, and Paul at War', *HTR* 76 (1983), pp. 143–73.

Menoud, P. H.,   'L'écharde et l'ange satanique (2 Cor 12,7),' pp. 163–71 in *Studia Paulina* (see main bibliography under Manson).

Metzger, B. M.,   *A Textual Commentary on the Greek New Testament*[2] ([1]1971), Stuttgart and New York, 1994.

Morray-Jones, C. R. A.,   'Paradise Revisited (2 Cor 12:1–12): The Jewish Mystical Background of Paul's Apostolate. Part 1: the Jewish Sources; Part 2: Paul's Heavenly Ascent and its Significance', *HTR* 86 (1993), pp. 177–217, 265–92.

Murphy-O'Connor, J.,   *Paul: A Critical Life*, Oxford, 1996.

Nickle, K. F.,   *The Collection: A Study in Paul's Strategy*, SBT 48, London, 1966.

Ogg, G.,   *The Chronology of the Life of Paul*, London, 1968.

Peterman, G. W.,   *Paul's Gift from Philippi: Conventions of Gift-exchange and Christian Giving*, SNTSMS 92, Cambridge, 1997.

Pratscher, W.,   'Der Verzicht des Paulus auf finanziellen Unterhalt durch seine Gemeinden', *NTS* 25 (1979), pp. 284–98.

Richards, E. R.,   *The Secretary in the Letters of Paul*, WUNT 2. Reihe 42, Tübingen, 1991.

Richardson, P., ed.,   *Anti-Judaism in Early Christianity I: Paul and the Gospels*. Studies in Christianity and Judaism 2, Waterloo, Ontario, 1986.

Riesner, R.,   *Die Frühzeit des Apostels Paulus: Studien zur Chronologie, Missionsstrategie und Theologie*, WUNT 71, Tübingen, 1994.

Rowland, C.,   *The Open Heaven. A Study of Apocalyptic in Judaism and Early Christianity*, London, 1982.

Sanders, E. P.,   'Paul on the Law, His Opponents, and the Jewish People in Philippians 3 and 2 Corinthians 11', pp. 75–90 in *Anti-Judaism in Early Christianity* I (see above, under Richardson).

Savage, T. B.,   *Power through Weakness: Paul's Understanding of the Christian Ministry in 2 Corinthians*, SNTSMS 86, Cambridge, 1996.

Schmithals, W.,   *The Office of Apostle in the Early Church*, London, 1971, translated by J. E. Steely from *Das kirchliche Apostelamt*, FRLANT 79, Göttingen, 1961.

Schreiber, S.,   *Paulus als Wundertäter: Redaktionsgeschichtliche Untersuchungen zur Apostelgeschichte und den authentischen Paulusbriefen*, BZNW 79, Berlin, 1996.

Schütz, J. H.,   *Paul and the Anatomy of Apostolic Authority*, SNTSMS 26, Cambridge, 1975.

Seesemann, H., *Der Begriff KOINΩNIA im Neuen Testament*, BZNW 14, Giessen, 1933.

Shaw, G., *The Cost of Authority*, London, 1983.

Sherwin-White, A. N., *Roman Society and Roman Law in the New Testament*, Oxford, 1963.

Spittler, R. P., 'The Limits of Ecstasy: an Exegesis of 2 Corinthians 12.1–10', pp. 259–66 in *Current Issues in Biblical and Patristic Interpretation*, ed. F. G. Hawthorne, Grand Rapids, 1975.

Stanley, C. D., *Paul and the Language of Scripture: Citation Technique in the Pauline Epistles and Contemporary Literature*, SNTSMS 74, Cambridge, 1992.

Stone, M. E., *Fourth Ezra*, Hermeneia, Minneapolis, 1990.

Sundermann, H.-G., *Der schwache Apostel und die Kraft der Rede: Eine rhetorische Analyse von 2 Kor 10–13*, Europäische Hochschulschriften XXIII 575, Frankfurt, 1996.

Tabor, J. D., *Things Unutterable; Paul's Ascent to Paradise in its Greco-Roman, Judaic, and Early Christian Contexts*. Studies in Judaism, Lanham and London, 1986.

Taylor, J., 'The Ethnarch of King Aretas at Damascus: A Note on 2 Cor 11.32-33', *RB* 99 (1992), pp. 719–28.

Taylor, N., *Paul, Antioch and Jerusalem: A Study in Relationships and Authority in Earliest Christianity*, JSNTSS 66, Sheffield, 1992.

Theissen, G., *The Social Setting of Pauline Christianity,* Studies of the New Testament and its World, Edinburgh, 1982; Essays on Corinth, translated and edited by J. H. Schütz.

Thrall, M. E., 'Super-Apostles, Servants of Christ, and Servants of Satan', *JSNT* 6 (1980), pp. 42–57.

Thrall, M. E., 'Paul's Journey to Paradise. Some Exegetical Issues in 2 Cor 12, 2–4', pp. 347–63 in R. Bieringer, *The Corinthian Correspondence*, BETL 125, Leuven, 1996.

Travis, S. H., 'Paul's Boasting in 2 Corinthians 10–12', TU 112 (1973), pp. 527–32.

Trench, R. C., *Synonyms in the New Testament*[8], London, 1876.

Verbrugge, V. D., *Paul's Style of Church Leadership Illustrated by his Instructions to the Corinthians on the Collection: To Command or not to Command*, San Francisco, 1992.

Vliet, H. van, *No Single Testimony. A Study on the Adoption of the Law of Deut. 19:15 Par. into the New Testament*. Studia Theologica Rheno-Traiectina 4, Utrecht, 1958.

Wedderburn, A. J. M., *The Reasons for Romans*. Studies of the New Testament and its World, Edinburgh, 1988.

Weima, J. A. D., *Neglected Endings: The Significance of the Pauline Letter Closings*, JSNTSS 101, Sheffield, 1994.

Winter, B. W., *Philo and Paul among the Sophists*, SNTSMS 96, Cambridge, 1997.

Witt, R. E., 'ΥΠΟΣΤΑΣΙΣ', pp. 319–43 in *Amicitiae Corolla*, FS J. R. Harris, ed. H. G. Wood, London, 1933.

Zerwick, M., *Biblical Greek*, Rome, 1963.

Zmijewski, J., *Der Stil der paulinischen 'Narrenrede': Analyse der Sprachgestaltung in 2 Kor 11, 1–12, 10 als Beitrag zur Methodik von Stiluntersuchungen neutestamentlicher Texte*, BBB 52, Bonn, 1978.

V

THE COLLECTION CHAPTERS
(8.1–9.15)

1. INTRODUCTION

At the beginning of this discussion it will be useful to recall the critical decisions made in Vol. I which may have some relevance to our understanding of the success or otherwise of Paul's collection project. We have argued that chap. 8 belongs to the same letter as chaps. 1–7, which are themselves a unity.[1] Thus, chaps. 1–8 constitute a single letter which we regard as the second extant letter Paul wrote to the Corinthians. We take chap. 9 to be a separate letter which followed that of chaps. 1–8.[2] The letter of chaps. 10–13 we see as the final letter in the series.[3] If this is the correct sequence, the last explicit picture we have of Paul's relationship with the Corinthians is one of conflict. And this in turn might suggest that, although Corinth did make some contribution to the collection (Rom 15.26), it was not as substantial as Paul might have originally hoped. Whilst there could have been some renewal of support during his final stay in the city, this might not have been sufficient to make up for the initial loss of contributions from those members of the congregation who only earned (and doubtless spent) a weekly or a daily wage, and who had given up saving anything during the period of conflict. There is also the possibility that the contents of the letter of chaps. 10–13 might have become more widely known, and might have affected the attitude of the Jerusalem church towards the gift from the Pauline churches.

This scenario would change somewhat if we were to accept the different sequence of events proposed by Verlyn Verbrugge.[4] He argues that it is chaps. 1–8 that constitute the last extant Pauline letter to Corinth: chaps. 10–13 are to be identified with the

[1] Vol. I, pp. 20–38, 77.
[2] Vol. I, pp. 38–43, 77.
[3] Vol. I, pp. 5–20, 77.
[4] Verbrugge, *Collection*, pp. 115–18.

preceding Painful Letter, and chap. 9 is a separate communication, written just prior to that of chaps. 1–8.[5] Thus, the period of conflict would lie further back in the past, and some degree of reconciliation and support for the collection could have preceded Paul's arrival in Corinth, resulting in a larger contribution. But we find the identification of chaps. 10–13 with the Painful Letter difficult to accept, for the reasons already given,[6] and prefer to see this letter as the last of the series.

In content, chaps. 8 and 9 belong together. Consequently, before embarking on the detailed exegesis, we shall begin with a general discussion, relevant to both chapters, of various questions related to Paul's project. First, what is the connection (if any) between this project as we see it in the Corinthian correspondence (1 Cor 16.1–4; 2 Cor 8; 9) and Romans (Rom 15.25–28) and the request of the 'pillar'-apostles at the Jerusalem Conference that Barnabas and Paul should 'remember the poor' (Gal 2.10)? Secondly, who, exactly, within the Jerusalem church, were to be the recipients of the money collected? Thirdly, what did Paul see as the purpose and significance of the project? Fourthly, was it a success or failure? Fifthly, what do we learn from these chapters about Paul's relationship with the Corinthians?

(i) *Connection with the Jerusalem Conference*

It is often taken for granted that Paul's collection was the direct outcome of the Jerusalem agreement. Furnish, for example, whilst allowing that the agreement is not specifically mentioned either in the Corinthian letters or in Romans, would see it nevertheless as the 'historical origin' of the collection project, which is 'directly related' to it.[7] Other scholars, however, reject any direct equation of Paul's project with the agreement he refers to in Gal 2.10. According to Georgi, Paul was initially enthusiastic for the implementation of the Jerusalem agreement. But as a result of the Antioch incident (Gal 2.11–16) he distanced himself from Jerusalem and lost his earlier enthusiasm as he embarked on a completely independent mission. Some four or five years later he

---

[5] Verbrugge, *Collection*, pp. 97–104.
[6] Vol. I, pp. 13–18.
[7] Furnish, p. 410. See also Carrez, p. 179; Martin, p. 251; Bruce, pp. 157–8; less definitely, Barrett, pp. 26, 217. Nickle, *Collection*, pp. 59–62, whilst offering a somewhat complex analysis of the situation, likewise sees fundamental continuity between Gal 2.10 and the project mentioned in 1 Corinthians and Romans and discussed at length in 2 Cor 8–9.

revived the enterprise (see 1 Cor 16.1), but this was not because his attitude to the Jerusalem church had altered. Rather it was for the spiritual benefit of the Corinthians. They had tendencies towards individualism, and saw Christian existence as constituted by a mystical identity of experience with the risen Christ, here and now. Paul aims to counteract these tendencies. In 1 Cor 15.5–7 he directs attention to the first witnesses to Jesus's resurrection, who belonged for the most part to the Jerusalem church, and in 16.1–3 introduces the collection as an outward expression of this essential link with the first Christian community.[8] This is an ingenious scenario, but more than a little improbable. Whatever may have been the religious tendencies of the Corinthians, it is scarcely likely that so elaborate an enterprise (involving considerable travel on the part of a number of people) would have been reactivated for the sole purpose of their spiritual reform. Georgi is probably right, however, in suggesting that Paul's confrontation with Peter in Antioch (Gal 2.11–14), and his subsequent departure on an independent missionary enterprise,[9] produced at least an hiatus in his original commitment to the raising of money for Jerusalem. It is in any case improbable that he would have solicited financial aid for the Jerusalem church before his new Gentile communities in N. Galatia, Macedonia and Achaia were firmly established. But it is likely that there were other factors in the situation as well. The Antioch incident may have caused Paul to regard the Jerusalem agreement as suspended, since in his view the other side would seem to have broken it.[10] It is in fact probable that this event effected a more radical break still between the original agreement and the Pauline collection with which chaps. 8–9 in 2 Corinthians are concerned. Taylor argues that the agreement was an agreement between the two churches—that of Jerusalem and that of Antioch. Paul attended the conference (as junior colleague to Barnabas) only as a representative of the Antiochene church. In consequence, when

[8] Georgi, *Kollekte*, pp. 30–40.

[9] Lüdemann, *Paul: Apostle to the Gentiles*, pp. 75–7, proposes a different chronological scheme. The start of the European mission preceded the Antioch confrontation, and the confrontation itself preceded the Jerusalem conference. Jewett, *Dating Paul's Life* (end-graph), also claims that the European mission began before the apostolic conference. This is not probable. Paul attends the conference with his Antiochene colleague Barnabas; his concern in respect of the Antioch incident is more understandable if it was as a representative of that church that he went to Jerusalem, and the incident itself provides a plausible reason for his decision to inaugurate an independent mission. See Taylor, *Paul, Antioch and Jerusalem*, pp. 98, 138–9, who also argues that in Gal 2 Paul will have retained the correct chronology; see p. 54.

[10] See Wedderburn, *Reasons for Romans*, pp. 38–9.

he left Antioch after the confrontation with Peter and his supporters, he was no longer involved in the original agreement. Thus he was no longer involved with the collection which expressed Antioch's recognition of their obligation to the Jerusalem church and consolidated the κοινωνία between the two communities.[11] Both Wedderburn[12] and Taylor[13] draw attention to Gal 2.10 ὃ καὶ ἐσπούδασα αὐτὸ τοῦτο (remembrance of the poor) ποιῆσαι: the aorist tense of ἐσπούδασα suggests that Paul's original keenness has waned,[14] or even that he now has no commitment at all to the initial collection project.[15]

Paul's collection, then, is a fresh start. Nevertheless, since it is a collection for Jerusalem, it is difficult to suppose that there is no relation whatsoever between this project and the earlier one. What the connection may have been will be discussed when we consider the purpose of Paul's enterprise.

(ii) The recipients

When Paul refers in Gal 2.10 to the beneficiaries of the action promised on Antioch's behalf he terms them οἱ πτωχοί The recipients of his own collection, however, are called οἱ ἅγιοι in six out of the seven instances (1 Cor 16.1; 2 Cor 8.4; 9.1, 12; Rom 15.25, 31). It is only in Rom 15.26 that οἱ πτωχοί occurs again, this time with οἱ ἅγιοι and with specific reference to Jerusalem: τοὺς πτωχοὺς τῶν ἁγίων τῶν ἐν Ἰερουσαλήμ. Were this last expression the only reference to the recipients, the matter would be very straightforward. They are the materially poor members amongst the Jerusalem Christians, who are called ἅγιοι in precisely the same way that Paul applies the term to all Christians. The other instances, however, where οἱ πτωχοί and οἱ ἅγιοι stand unqualified, prompt the question of whether the two terms are self-explanatory titles, designating the members of the

---

[11] Taylor, *Paul, Antioch and Jerusalem*, pp. 102–3, 115–22, and chap. 4 as a whole; pp. 137–9.
[12] Wedderburn, *Reasons for Romans*, p. 39.
[13] Taylor, *Paul, Antioch and Jerusalem*, p. 198.
[14] Wedderburn, *Reasons for Romans*, p. 39.
[15] Taylor, ibid. D. R. Hall, 'St Paul and Famine Relief: A Study in Galatians 2.10', *Exp Tim* 82 (1970–71), pp. 309–11 argues that Paul here refers to the Famine Relief project of Acts 11.27–30, prior to the Jerusalem agreement: to refer ἐσπούδασα to post-conference activity would be a confession of obedience to Jerusalem, thus vitiating Paul's defence of his independence. But Paul goes on to point out that he had forcefully opposed Cephas. And if vv. 10–11 are taken together, the point is made that he kept his side of the bargain, whilst Cephas did not.

Jerusalem church, and all the members (whatever their financial status).

Since we have argued that Paul's collection is to be differentiated from the 'remembrance of the poor' to which he had assented as a representative of the church in Antioch, we need to discuss the meaning of οἱ πτωχοί in Gal 2.10 without reference to Rom 15.26. In the context it is clear that these people are members of the Jerusalem church.[16] But are they some members only, i.e., the materially disadvantaged? Or is 'the poor' to be understood as a titular designation of all the Christians of Jerusalem? The second alternative is maintained by Holl and by Georgi on the ground of the term's absolute use.[17] Georgi sees the titular use prefigured in the OT, especially in the Psalms, and claims that when, in later Judaism, the word πτωχός became synonymous with 'pious' and 'righteous', those groups which adopted these titles saw themselves as the true Israel, the holy remnant,[18] and as those who would share God's dominion in the age to come.[19] This concept was taken over by the Jerusalem church, whose members claimed to constitute the eschatological people of God in the holy city.[20] They shared with their fellow Jews the expectation that God would manifest himself in Zion, but for them this meant that Jerusalem would be the locus of the Parousia. They themselves were the watchers who were to look for and proclaim Christ's advent.[21] Thus, for Georgi, 'the poor' was both a title and an indication of function.

This interpretation is difficult to assess. In view of the Jewish background it is certainly not impossible that πτωχοί[22] might have been a titular designation of the Jerusalem church, whose members thought of themselves in the way Georgi suggests. In Gal 2.10 Paul is virtually quoting their leaders' request to the Antiochene representatives. At the same time, however, he would use precisely the same word, were he to wish to refer simply to

---

[16] The Jerusalem conference was concerned with the relationship between the two churches of Jerusalem and Antioch, and what might be required on either side from the other to maintain and consolidate this relationship (see Taylor, *Paul, Antioch and Jerusalem*, pp. 106–10). If the delegates from Antioch are required, as their part of the bargain, to 'remember the poor', the allusion is not to general charity but to some obligation undertaken for the benefit of Jerusalem.

[17] Holl, *Gesammelte Aufsätze* II, pp. 58–61, with discussion also of οἱ ἅγιοι; Georgi, *Kollekte*, p. 23.

[18] Georgi, *Kollekte*, p. 23, with reference (n. 53) to Ps. Sol. 10; 15; 18.1–5; 1 Qp Hab 12.3, 6, 10; 14.7; 1QM 11.9, 13; 13.14; 1QH 5.13, 14, 16, 22.

[19] Georgi, *Kollekte*, p. 23, n. 54.

[20] Georgi, *Kollekte*, pp. 23–4.

[21] Georgi, *Kollekte*, pp. 26–7.

[22] Or rather, its Aramaic or Hebrew equivalent.

those who were economically poor.²³ And it could be significant that πτωχός occurs nowhere in Acts, despite the fact that the author does know several terms for the early Christians, and that this word would have fitted his picture of the early church where the better off gave up their wealth for the sake of the community as a whole.²⁴ Hence, it seems unlikely that in the sphere of the Pauline mission οἱ πτωχοί was a titular designation of the Jerusalem Christians, and since there is no evidence that Luke knew it as such either, the import of the word in Gal 2.10 remains ambiguous.

What, then, of οἱ ἄγιοι? Is this usage titular? It is certainly probable that the term 'the holy ones' originated in Jerusalem as a self-description of the Christians of that city, and an indication of their privileged status as the elect eschatological community.²⁵ But this is not quite to say that it develops into the title of the Jerusalem church, used by other Christians with this obvious reference. Certainly the term remains without further definition in the Corinthian references (1 Cor 16.1; 2 Cor 8.4; 9.1, 12). If it is not a title, how are Paul's correspondents to know whom he has in view? But since he has in general extended its use so as to refer to any or all believers,²⁶ anywhere or everywhere, how could he now use it in a restricted titular sense? Windisch, commenting on 2 Cor 8.4, would answer the first of these questions with the claim that the εἰς τοὺς ἁγίους is a self-explanatory abbreviation arising out of previous correspondence.²⁷ The only previous reference in the Corinthian letters, however, is in 1 Cor 16.1, where the term remains similarly undefined. Nevertheless, there are several indications in 1 Cor 16.1–3 that definition is unnecessary, since the Corinthians know of the project already. The opening Περὶ δέ implies that this is something they had asked about in their own letter to Paul (cf. 7.1). It may be that he had told them of it in his previous letter (1 Cor 5.9).²⁸ And in v. 3 the almost casual reference to the conveyance of the proceeds to Jerusalem is significant. That the money was to go to the Christians of Jerusalem was well known: the undecided question was whether Paul himself should assist in conveying it there.²⁹ Lastly, as Fee

---

²³ It is used in a literal sense in 2 Cor 6.10, and probably also in Rom 15.26, where 'the poor' are a smaller group within the larger group of the whole Christian community of Jerusalem.

²⁴ L. E. Keck, 'The Poor among the Saints in the New Testament', *ZNW* 56 (1965), pp. 100–29; see pp. 103–4.

²⁵ Vol. I, pp. 85–6.

²⁶ Vol. I, ibid.

²⁷ Windisch, p. 246.

²⁸ Fee, *First Corinthians*, p. 811; cf. Furnish, p. 409.

²⁹ Cf. Fee, ibid., who notes the indirectness of the reference to the destination of the collection.

notes, the very fact of the comparative lack of further information, e.g., about the purpose of the collection, shows that the Corinthians were well informed about it.[30] If, then, they were so informed, the failure to specify the location of 'the saints' for whom the collection is intended loses significance. It does not mean that οἱ ἅγιοι is a recognised title for the Jerusalem church, but refers simply to this particular group of Christians on whose behalf Paul has embarked on his project.

We conclude that in Paul's independent usage neither οἱ πτωχοί nor οἱ ἅγιοι functions as a title for the Jerusalem church. In that case, it seems, according to Rom 15.26, that the recipients of the collection are simply the economically poor members of that church. But this may be an over-simplification. First, according to Acts (2.44–45), the whole community was responsible for the economic needs of its members. And, secondly, it is likely that Paul had purposes, or a purpose, in view in addition to the relief of poverty. Hence, it would be to the whole church, represented by its leaders, that the collection was to be delivered.

(iii) *Purpose and significance*

From what has been said already, it will be clear that we need to consider separately the obligation mentioned in Gal 2.10 and the project with which Paul is concerned in 2 Cor 8–9. Whilst the purpose of the one may turn out to have some connection with that of the other, this cannot be taken for granted at the outset.

(a) *Gal 2.10.* To begin with, it is obvious that, whatever the precise meaning of πτωχοί, what is in view is not a spontaneous impulse of charity but something required of the Antiochene delegation by the Jerusalem church. In return, Jerusalem will recognise the authenticity of the missionary preaching stemming from Antioch, and the freedom of that church to accept Gentile converts without requiring circumcision.[31] Moreover, whilst in the first instance it is financial aid that is required, this financial support may have been seen as the expression of a more fundamental obligation and the acceptance of an unequal relationship. According to Georgi, it expresses the recognition by the Antiochenes of the unique position and function of the Jerusalem church, as the eschatological people of God *par excellence* who await Christ's parousia in the holy city. This function required the

---

[30] Fee, ibid.
[31] Taylor, *Paul, Antioch and Jerusalem*, pp. 115–22.

economic viability of the church, hence the financial aid, but this was subordinate to the theological aspect of the recognition.[32] For Berger the arrangement has a different significance. The financial contribution is parallel to the practice in Judaism whereby Gentiles who converted to the God of Israel and the keeping of his commandments, but who did not wish to undergo circumcision, brought 'alms for Israel' to indicate the seriousness of their conversion and their desire to belong to the Jewish community. The apostolic conference had agreed that circumcision and ritual observance were not to be imposed upon Gentiles converted by the Antiochene mission. In consequence, the one obligation imposed upon the Antiochene delegation must refer to something on the same plane and of comparable import, i.e., something relevant to the relationship between the two groups of Christians, which would have similar value for their mutual integration. The model would be the relationship of Gentile godfearers to the congregation of Israel.[33] Of these two suggestions, that of Berger is the more plausible, since it is related more directly to the question at issue in the apostolic conference, i.e., the terms on which non-Jewish converts should be admitted into the Christian community. Taylor, however, argues against it. Almsgiving was not seen in Judaism 'as a complete substitute for circumcision', and Berger has produced no evidence that a righteous Gentile who gave 'alms for Israel' was ever regarded as integrated into the 'covenant community'. Hence, this model scarcely works for the Jerusalem agreement, unless the Gentile Christians of Antioch and elsewhere were not to be regarded, after all, as full and equal members of the Christian church.[34] But it is surely possible that the Jerusalem church did not so regard them, thinking instead to create a class of Christian godfearers. The ensuing dispute in Antioch shows that the implications of the agreement could be understood in different ways. Berger's suggestion could still have some validity. Taylor himself sees the monetary offering simply as an indication that Antioch recognised the dominant position of the Jerusalem church and its right 'to regulate Christian life in Antioch'.[35] This could well have been the purport of the Jerusalem requirement, but one

---

[32] Georgi, *Kollekte*, pp. 23–9. The argument is based on his understanding of οἱ πτωχοί in a titular sense (see above, p. 507). We have suggested that this interpretation is doubtful. But the term οἱ ἅγιοι though likewise non-titular, does express the same idea and probably originated with the Jerusalem church (see above, p. 508).

[33] Berger, 'Almosen', pp. 183–92, 195–204.

[34] Taylor, *Paul, Antioch and Jerusalem*, p. 119.

[35] Taylor, *Paul, Antioch and Jerusalem*, pp. 117–22; the phrase quoted is on p. 120.

aspect of this regulation could have been the eventual imposition of the godfearer model upon converted Gentiles.

(b) *Paul's collection.* The material in the Corinthian letters and in Romans has suggested to exegetes various ways of understanding Paul's intentions.

1. The collection was intended chiefly, if not entirely, as an act of charity, to benefit those who were economically needy.[36] It is spoken of as a χάρις (2 Cor 8.7), a gracious gift,[37] and as a project in which churches which have a present surplus may afford relief to those who are in want (2 Cor 8.13–14). It is clear that there was poverty in the Jerusalem church, and there could have been various reasons for this state of affairs. A growth in numbers would have increased the number of dependants, such as widows,[38] and possibly also the number of victims of economic ostracism.[39] This church in particular may also have been called upon to provide hospitality for Christian visitors from elsewhere.[40] In addition, it had a proportionately larger number of leaders to support.[41] Lastly, its financial situation may well have been weakened by the sharing of resources attested in Acts (2.42–47; 4.32–37; 5.1–11), since this had led to the disposal of capital assets.[42] Hence, we can say that the need of the church may in itself have evoked a charitable response from Paul himself and from those to whom he communicated his collection plan. At the same time, most exegetes agree that there may have been other reasons for the project as well. After all, the Jerusalem church may not have been the most impoverished amongst the Christian communities Paul had knowledge of. What about the Macedonian churches (2 Cor 8.2)?[43]

2. Was the collection a response to an obligation imposed upon the Pauline churches by the leaders in Jerusalem? And, if so, did

---

[36] Barrett, p. 27, who comments that this is the only explicit reason given by Paul himself.

[37] BAGD s.v. χάρις 3.a.

[38] Martin, p. 256.

[39] Hughes, p. 284.

[40] Nickle, *Collection*, p. 24 n. 43.

[41] Nickle, ibid, n. 44.

[42] Nickle, *Collection*, pp. 23–4; Martin, p. 256.

[43] Cf. Windisch, pp. 246–7, commenting on 2 Cor 8.4. Verbrugge, *Collection*, pp. 327–30, argues that Paul, fundamentally, did not regard the collection as a voluntary act of gracious generosity at all. He observes that χάρις is not used of it in Romans, where Paul is writing more freely, without the constraint of his relationship with the Corinthians. It is a word he uses 'to motivate the Macedonians and Achaians' (p. 329). Basically, he regarded the collection as 'a duty for his churches to participate in' (p. 330). This viewpoint will be discussed further under (v) below.

these authorities see it, as Holl suggests, as analogous to the Jewish temple tax collected in the Diaspora and conveyed to the city annually?[44] The suggestion of an imposed donation is to be rejected: it derives from Gal 2.10, which refers to the obligation undertaken by the Antiochene delegation and does not relate directly to Paul's later project.[45] But might Paul himself have been influenced by the Jewish institution? Some parallels, as Nickle notes, can be seen: money is paid to Jerusalem as the significant centre of the faith; representatives of local communities accompany the delivery; the regular setting aside of funds is encouraged; care is taken for the good reputation of those directly concerned with the funds; lastly, the operation is seen as a visible expression of unity.[46] But he observes also that there are significant differences: the temple tax was for the maintenance of the sacrifices; it was paid annually, whilst Paul's collection was not intended as a recurrent event; the Jewish tax was compulsory and the amount fixed by legislation, but the Pauline collection was voluntary, and he nowhere hints at any norm for contributions.[47] Nevertheless, it is possible that he borrowed some aspects of organisation from the Jewish model, and the symbolism of unity.[48] Any too obvious borrowings, however, might have vitiated the whole enterprise. The collection, Taylor points out, could have been misunderstood as a diversion of the Jewish tax, and the Romans might have supposed that Paul was making illegitimate use of the protection they afforded to the conveyance of donations to the Temple. And this in turn would have endangered the Jerusalem church rather than assisting it.[49]

3. Did Paul attach eschatological significance to the delivery of the collection in Jerusalem? This view is forcibly argued by Munck, as follows. Paul is to be accompanied to Jerusalem by a comparatively large body of church representatives.[50] Now the defraying of their travel expenses would cut down more than somewhat the amount of money that could eventually be handed

---

[44] Holl, *Gesammelte Aufsätze* II, pp. 58–62.
[45] See above, pp. 511–12; and see Verbrugge, *Collection*, p. 314, for further cogent arguments to this effect.
[46] Nickle, *Collection*, pp. 87–8; see pp. 74–87 for a detailed account and discussion of the Jewish tax.
[47] Nickle, *Collection*, pp. 90–3.
[48] Nickle, *Collection*, p. 99.
[49] Taylor, *Paul, Antioch and Jerusalem*, pp. 214–15.
[50] See the list in Acts 20.4, usually seen as listing Paul's companions on the collection journey to Jerusalem: there are seven names, to whom must be added Paul himself. If Titus and the two anonymous 'brothers' of 2 Cor 8:16–24 are to be added as well, the maximum total would be eleven.

over to the Jerusalem church. Hence, there must be some good reason for their number. Munck suggests that this journey of Paul to Jerusalem 'with a representative company of believing Gentiles' who bring gifts is seen by him as a fulfilment of such OT passages as Isa 2.2–3; 60.5–7; Mic 4.1–2: i.e., passages which speak of the pilgrimage of the nations to Zion, bringing thither the riches of the world. This will produce an effect on the whole Jewish nation. Israel will be saved by being moved to jealousy of the Gentiles, as they see this fulfilment of the Scriptures in process.[51] This suggestion has met with some acceptance.[52] The fact remains, however, that Paul nowhere refers to the relevant OT passages,[53] nor does he make express mention of this eschatological motif when speaking of the collection. Furthermore, it is not clear whether this connection of Paul's project with the theme of the eschatological pilgrimage of the nations to Zion actually fits what he says in Romans. The collection journey, according to that theory, is intended as the demonstration of the salvation of the Gentiles, which is to move the Jews to envy and bring about their own salvation (Rom 11.11–12, 25–27). This journey to Jerusalem, we must suppose, is the initial end-event, to be followed at once by the expected consequences. Now the final conversion of Israel waits upon the completion of the Gentile mission (Rom 11.25). If the collection journey is to be equated with the eschatological pilgrimage to Zion, we must suppose that Paul believes the full evangelisation of the Gentiles to be, in principle, accomplished. But this is not so. For in Rom 15.24, 28 he indicates that he is about to begin work in a totally new area, i.e., in Spain.[54] Consequently, he must have expected Israel to remain 'hardened' at least until his new mission in the West had been completed. In that case, the collection delegates can scarcely be seen as representative in any comprehensive sense, and we cannot suppose Paul thought that their arrival in Jerusalem would trigger off the expected conversion of the Jews.[55]

4. What of the suggestion, already considered, that the model for the collection was the Jewish custom whereby converts brought

[51] Munck, Salvation, pp. 302–4, with reference to Rom 9–11.

[52] See Nickle, Collection, pp. 129–42, and Georgi, Kollekte, pp. 72–3: both draw attention to the quotation of Isa 55.10 in 2 Cor 9.10, and note that in the context of this verse in Isaiah (see 55.4–5) we find the motif of the coming of the nations to Israel, glorified by God. See also Fallon, pp. 68–9; Furnish, p. 412; Martin, p. 251.

[53] See Wolff, p. 166.

[54] Cf. Verbrugge, Collection, p. 327.

[55] Verbrugge, Collection, pp. 325–6, notes that in Rom 15, where Paul speaks of the collection, there is no reference to the eschatological timetable (as we have remarked above), whilst in Rom 11 there is no reference to the collection. Nor is there any hint in Romans that Gentiles will accompany Paul to Jerusalem.

'alms for Israel'?[56] We have allowed that for the Jerusalem church this could have been the model for their request to the Antiochene delegation that they should 'remember the poor'. But the subsequent Antioch incident (Gal 2.11–14) would have exposed, for Paul, the possible adverse implications of such a model, and he would scarcely have adopted it for his own purposes.

5. It is probable that Paul saw the collection as a means to church unity. Nickle suggests that he hoped thereby to heal the schism that had opened up as a result of the Antioch incident. He wished to prove to the Jerusalem church the genuineness of God's grace at work in the Gentile churches, grace which was producing in them a sincere love for their fellow Christians in Jerusalem. In 2 Cor 9.13–14 he indicates the effect he hopes for. The Jewish Christians would be moved to praise God for the faith of the Gentile believers, and for the reality of the fellowship between the Gentile congregations and themselves.[57] At the same time the collection is the acknowledgement and payment of a debt (Rom 15.27). The Jerusalem church is the original repository of the message of Christ's death and resurrection, and of the other Jesus-traditions, and is the original source of the Christian mission.[58] The Gentile Christians have no intention of cutting loose from this source and establishing some sectarian religious cult of their own. More particularly, whilst Paul's collection is not to be identified with that of the Jerusalem agreement,[59] his purpose in initiating the project, it is suggested, may nevertheless have some connection with the earlier enterprise. Taylor argues that Paul may have wished to create a relationship between his Gentile churches and the church of Jerusalem which would be similar to that established between Jerusalem and Antioch as a result of the apostolic conference. He may have repaired his own relationship with Antioch through the visit mentioned in Acts 18.22, and may then originally have hoped to rejoin the Antioch collection which was still in process of implementation. This would have secured the desired association with Jerusalem for the churches of his Gentile mission. As it turned out, there

---

[56] See above, p. 510.

[57] Nickle, *Collection*, pp. 118–19, 128. See also Hughes, p. 286; Martin, p. 251.

[58] See Cranfield, *Romans*, p. 773. We may add that despite Paul's insistence in Gal 1.11–12 upon his own reception of the gospel independently of human contact, it is obvious that he would have been unable to interpret his experience of Christophany, had he not been able to relate it to the Christian message which originated in Jerusalem. See also Verbrugge, *Collection*, pp. 316, 318: Paul recognises the significance of the Jerusalem church, and intends the Gentile Christians to do the same.

[59] Taylor, *Paul, Antioch and Jerusalem*, p. 198; and see above pp. 504–6.

were delays, which meant that Paul's collection would have to be delivered separately, but the aim would have been the same.[60] Taylor allows, however, that on the part of Jerusalem the extension of their relationship with Antioch to include the Pauline churches would have required some measure of subordination on Paul's side, and that this would have been 'an unlikely eventuality'.[61] It remains possible, nevertheless, that Paul did recognise the desirability of establishing a formal relationship with Jerusalem of some kind, and that in that sense the Jerusalem-Antioch bond may have served as a precedent. The Antioch incident had given warning that representatives of the Jerusalem church were prepared to travel elsewhere to exert their influence on church practice. And if that had happened even after the conclusion of an agreement, it would be even more likely to happen in areas where no such agreement was in place. If this was Paul's thinking, it would account for the comparatively large number of Gentile delegates,[62] who would be able to assure their churches of the terms of association with Jerusalem, should itinerant members of that church attempt to cause trouble.

It is not, perhaps, very likely that the Corinthians would be aware of all these possible ramifications. In general, however, the collection project would be acceptable within their own cultural milieu. According to Verbrugge: 'financial aid of a benevolent nature between various town [sic] and cities appears to have been a regular phenomenon in the Greek-speaking world, particularly when some natural disaster struck a community.' Such help, moreover, could have a unifying effect, where there had previously been discord.[63]

Paul's purpose in initiating the collection remains a matter of conjecture. It seems likely, however, that he saw the project both as an act of charity (1. above) and as a means of establishing a satisfactory association between the church of Jerusalem and his Gentile churches, and hence as promoting Christian unity (5. above).

(iv) Success or failure?

There are two questions here. First, how successful was the collection in the churches involved in the project? Secondly,

---

[60] Taylor, *Paul, Antioch and Jerusalem*, pp. 199, 204–5, 206–7.
[61] Taylor, *Paul, Antioch and Jerusalem*, p. 199.
[62] The evidence that they accompanied him to Jerusalem comes, of course, not from Paul himself, as Verbrugge has observed, but from Acts 20.4. There is no reason, however, to reject its historicity.
[63] Verbrugge, *Collection*, p. 183.

granted some degree of success, did it meet with acceptance in Jerusalem?

(a) How successful was the collection in Corinth? Here the evidence is uncertain. What Paul says in 2 Cor 8 shows that originally the Corinthians had been enthusiastic, but that later they had lost their keenness. He needs to revive their interest and their activity. His efforts, however, may not have been altogether successful. The general situation in the church worsened (from Paul's point of view) after the dispatch of the letter of 2 Cor 1–8, owing to the influence of the itinerant missionaries castigated in chaps. 10–13.[64] These people, moreover, received financial support from the congregation, thus reducing the amount of money to be spared for the collection. In addition, doubts were cast on Paul's own integrity in financial matters (2 Cor 12.16). Lastly, no one from Corinth is mentioned in the list of Paul's travelling companions in Acts 20.4. Nevertheless, in Rom 15.26 we are told that Achaia, as well as Macedonia, has contributed to the collection. Since, in all probability, Romans was written in Corinth, the Corinthians must be known to have made a contribution of some sort.[65] It remains possible, as we have already suggested, that it was not as large as he had originally hoped.[66] The Macedonians, by contrast may be presumed to have contributed generously in proportion to their financial ability (2 Cor 8.1–4), but they were poor to start with.

It is more doubtful whether the project had any ultimate success in the churches of Galatia. There is no mention of them either in 2 Cor 8–9 or in Rom 15.26. According to Nickle, there is a reference to Galatian representatives in Acts 20.4, i.e., Gaius of Derbe and Timothy (associated with Lystra in Acts 16.1).[67] But in the first case there are textual problems and Timothy is Paul's personal assistant, not a church representative. The silence in Romans and 2 Corinthians may not, of course, be especially significant. In 2 Cor 8–9 it is natural that Paul should refer to the Macedonians, since he is writing from Macedonia and knows what is happening there, whilst the state of affairs in Galatia might not be known to him. It is similarly natural that in Romans,

---

[64] For this reconstruction of the sequence of events see Vol. I, p. 77.

[65] This interpretation is questioned by Buck, 'Collection', p. 10, who rejects the view that Romans was written from Corinth and that the collection from Macedonia and Achaia was complete at the time of writing. Romans could have been written from Macedonia, 'at a time when Paul still hoped that the collection in Achaia would be successful'. See Cranfield, *Romans*, p. 12, however, for the argument that the epistle was written in Corinth.

[66] See above.

[67] Nickle, *Collection*, p. 68.

written from Corinth, he should mention Achaia as well: he may still not yet know of the situation in Galatia. Nevertheless, it is equally possible that the trouble which evoked Paul's letter may have put an end to the project. Even less can be said about other participating churches. According to Acts 20.4, Tychicus and Trophimus from the province of Asia, presumably from Ephesus, were amongst Paul's companions on the delivery journey, which would suggest some contribution from the province. And in view of the length of time Paul had spent in Ephesus it would be strange had he not attempted to organise a collection there. But we cannot know for certain.

(b) Was the collection accepted by the Jerusalem church? From Paul himself we have no information. In Acts the only possible reference is an obscure allusion in Paul's speech before Felix (24.17), where he says that he came to bring alms and cultic offerings to his nation. To a reader unacquainted with his letters this would in no way convey any idea of the collection project. Now there would seem to be only two possible reasons why the author of Acts should say nothing about the reception of the collection. Either he was genuinely ignorant, having at his disposal only some defective piece of tradition which he reproduces in 24.17. Or else he did know about the collection and knew that it had either been rejected altogether or not been accepted in such a way as to further Paul's purpose in organising it. Was he, then, totally ignorant of what had happened in Jerusalem? This seems unlikely. Lüdemann argues that in Acts 21, which tells of Paul's meeting with James and the elders, Luke is redacting an historically reliable source which must have contained the requisite information about the collection.[68] Furthermore, it may well be that he does intend an indirect allusion in 24.17. It may well not be pure coincidence that the reason Paul is made to give for his visit to Jerusalem is of a monetary character.

If, then, Luke did know of the collection and of the reaction of the Jerusalem leaders to Paul's offering, what can be deduced from his silence? Nickle suggests that the collection was in fact accepted. Luke says nothing about it because he is concerned to present Christianity in a favourable light to the Roman authorities. At the time of writing it had become clear that Christianity was separate from Judaism, and this meant that Paul's collection would have been regarded as illegal, since no longer covered by the special concessions granted by Rome to the Jews.[69] But it is not clear that the giving of alms and offerings was

---

[68] Lüdemann, *Heidenapostel* II, pp. 84–98; see especially pp. 94–8.
[69] Nickle, *Collection*, pp. 148–51.

illegal.[70] (If this were so, it would not have been mentioned.) And if the collection had been well received, Luke could surely have presented the occasion in terms of the gift of charitable donations and offerings and its grateful acceptance. It is more likely that this was not so. Dunn suggests that the Jerusalem Christians were unwilling to accept the gift immediately and outright because by doing so they would signal their approval of Paul's law-free mission and this in turn would damage their position with their fellow Jews, and this in a time of nationalist fervour. They may not have intended an absolute rejection. If Paul could prove himself a good Jew, the gift might later become acceptable. But since things went wrong, the rejection remained in force.[71] Or perhaps, as Georgi suggests, the collection was accepted, but only in private, and after Paul had agreed to pay the expenses of the Nazirite vow, so as to clear both himself and the Jerusalem Christians from the charge of opposition to the (Mosaic) law.[72] Whichever of these suggestions may be correct, we have to conclude that Paul's collection did not achieve its aims. If received only with reservation or not received at all it would have failed of the purpose expressed in 2 Cor 9.12–14. The Jerusalem Christians would scarcely glorify God for a gift which might put their own community at risk. Still less would they either give thanks for it as a symbol of fellowship with Paul's law-free Gentile congregations, or accept it as a means to establish some regular association with them. Their own position was too vulnerable. Furthermore, as we have already suggested, Paul's bitter castigation of the rival missionaries might have become public knowledge. We shall argue that these people represent the Petrine mission, and in consequence have close connections with Jerusalem. Paul's harsh treatment of them would not have commended his offering to the Jerusalem church, even had the church's general circumstances been more favourable. Within a decade or so, in any case, Paul's objective had become irrelevant, with the fall of Jerusalem and the dispersal of the Jerusalem church.

(v) The collection and Paul's relationship with the Corinthians

A final study of the apostle's relationship with the church in Corinth must wait until the exegesis of the remaining chapters

---

[70] Nickle does not suggest this.

[71] J. D. G. Dunn, *Unity and Diversity in the New Testament*, London, 1977, p. 257.

[72] Georgi, *Kollekte*, pp. 88–9.

has been completed. At this point we shall simply consider what we might learn from the collection chapters, primarily from chap. 8.

Verbrugge draws a contrast between Paul's manner of expression in 1 Cor 16.1–2, on the one hand, and 2 Cor 8–9 on the other. In the first extant allusion to the collection, in 1 Cor 16.1–2, we find two direct imperatives.[73] In effect, the apostle is giving orders to his readers: 'You are to do (ποιήσατε)' as he has directed the Galatian churches and 'each of you is to put something by (τιθέτω)' every Sunday, as a contribution. This, Verbrugge argues, follows the style of a form of letter which may be designated a 'commanding letter': 'Its key feature is the use of a second person imperative, with no attempt to justify the action or to motivate the recipient.'[74] It is expected that the recipient will acknowledge the authority of the writer and comply with the command.[75] In 2 Cor 8–9, however, the style has changed. It has become that of a 'requesting letter'. In this type of letter the actual request is made indirectly, and with emphasis on the freedom of the recipient to comply or not to do so.[76] In 8.7, the request is expressed in a ἵνα-clause which may implicitly depend on an understood verb of wishing.[77] This change of style reflects a changed relationship. It is true that in 8.11 we do find an imperative (ἐπιτελέσατε). Here, however, Paul is simply urging his readers to complete what they have already begun.[78] And in 8.24 a final request is expressed by a participle.[79] These various characteristics of chap. 8, Verbrugge claims, indicate 'extreme hesitancy' on Paul's part,[80] by contrast with the confidence of 1 Cor 16.1–2.

Why, then, the change of attitude? Verbrugge notes that the interval between 1 Corinthians and 2 Cor 8 and 9 was the period of stress which led to the writing of the Painful Letter. This is to be identified, he claims, with 2 Cor 10–13. During this time, money was one of the chief causes of conflict. Hence the change of style, from a 'commanding letter', to 'rhetorical letters of request'.[81] Paul's authority had been weakened, and, in order to persuade the Corinthians to persist with the collection, he 'had to use more subtle means to motivate them'.[82] We should not

[73] Verbrugge, *Collection*, p. 210.
[74] Verbrugge, *Collection*, pp. 25–67, 69; the quotation is on p. 69.
[75] Verbrugge, *Collection*, p. 69.
[76] Verbrugge, *Collection*, pp. 196, 209–10.
[77] See the exegesis, p. 529.
[78] Verbrugge, *Collection*, pp. 252–4.
[79] Verbrugge, *Collection*, p. 254.
[80] Verbrugge, *Collection*, p. 259.
[81] Verbrugge, *Collection*, p. 294.
[82] Verbrugge, *Collection*, p. 367.

wholly agree with this scenario, since we have rejected the identification of the Painful Letter with 2 Cor 10–13. This is not essential, however, to Verbrugge's argument. The main point holds good. The trouble that evoked the Painful Letter may well have caused Paul to adopt a less authoritative attitude in respect of the collection, especially if (as we have suggested[83]) the offence which caused the letter was in some way itself connected with the collection.

2. THE COLLECTION IN CHAPTER 8

(i) *The zeal of the Macedonians; further encouragement* (8.1–15)

[1]And now, brothers, we have information for you about the grace of God which has been bestowed amongst the congregations of Macedonia: [2]that is, that in the midst of a great ordeal of affliction[84] their abundance of joy and their deep poverty have abundantly resulted in their wealth of generosity. [3]For in accordance with their means, I testify, and beyond their means, they gave of their own volition, [4]with many pleas begging of us the favour of partnership in the charitable service to the saints, [5]and not simply as we expected, but they first gave themselves to the Lord and to us through God's will; [6]with the consequence that we have urged Titus that, as he had previously launched it, so he should also finalise for you this gracious enterprise also. [7]So now, just as you are prolific in everything—faith and speech and knowledge and all zeal, and the love deriving from us and present in you—do become prolific also in this gracious enterprise. [8]I am not speaking by way of command, but as putting to the test, through the zeal of others, the genuine quality of your love also. [9]For you know the grace of our Lord Jesus Christ, that, rich as he was, for your sake he became utterly poor, so that by means of his poverty you might become rich. [10]And I give my opinion on this matter for this is beneficial for you, you who had previously made a start a year ago, not only to take action but also to prove willing. [11]Now, then, bring the action also to completion, so that its completion may correspond with your ready willingness—completion in accordance with what one has. [12]For if readiness is present, the gift is acceptable in accordance with what a person possesses, not with what he does not possess. [13]For the aim is not relief for others, hardship for you, but action on the basis of equality. [14]At the present time your abundance will meet their insufficiency, so that also their abundance may meet your insufficiency, so that there may be equality. [15]As it is written, 'he who gathered much had no surplus, and he who gathered a small amount did not have too little.'

Paul turns to the last topic of the letter contained in chaps.

---

[83] Vol. I, pp. 68–9.
[84] For this phrase, see BAGD s.v. δοκιμή 2.

1–8.[85] The spontaneous enthusiasm for the collection shown by the Macedonians has moved him to urge Titus to go to Corinth to complete the contribution there. He himself attempts to encourage the Corinthians to renew their efforts, both by his description of the zeal of the Macedonians and by instancing the supreme example of Christ's self-impoverishment for the enrichment of humankind. In addition, he points out that what he is asking for is simply equality between the contributors to the collection and its recipients.

1. Γνωρίζομεν δὲ ὑμῖν, ἀδελφοί, τὴν χάριν τοῦ θεοῦ τὴν δεδομένην ἐν ταῖς ἐκκλησίαις τῆς Μακεδονίας, We move finally[86] to a matter, the collection, less immediately related to the main themes of the present letter, which has been concerned so far with Paul's apostolic ministry and his personal relationship with the Corinthian church. The collection project plays a part, of course, in his general missionary strategy, and in 7.2 there is a hint of suspicious criticism of his financial probity in respect of this enterprise.[87] But his main lines of defence in the earlier chapters do not address these issues. Nevertheless, there are two points of connection with chap. 7: in both chapters Paul refers to the situation in Macedonia, and in both he speaks of visits to Corinth by Titus (the one past, the other prospective). In the Macedonian churches there is enthusiastic involvement in the collection, and this is seen as a manifestation of divine grace.[88] The participants may come from any or all of the towns of Philippi, Thessalonica, and Beroea.[89] These are 'Romanized' centres. Philippi was a Roman colony, and the other two possessed the status of *municipia*.[90] The Roman province of Macedonia in which the three towns are located lies in northern Greece, bordering on Achaia in the south.

2. ὅτι ἐν πολλῇ δοκιμῇ θλίψεως ἡ περισσεία τῆς χαρᾶς αὐτῶν καὶ ἡ κατὰ βάθους πτωχεία αὐτῶν ἐπερίσσευσεν εἰς τὸ πλοῦτος τῆς ἁπλότητος αὐτῶν· This verse either explains why Paul has spoken of the manifestation of divine grace in the Macedonian congregations,[91] or else (more probably) it gives the further content of the information he is passing on to his

[85] The δέ is simply transitional, as in, e.g., 1 Cor 7.1; 8.1. See BAGD s.v. δέ 2.
[86] See n. 85 above.
[87] See Vol. I, p. 482.
[88] Perhaps it is simply the impulse to generosity which is so bestowed: cf. Windisch, p. 243. But perhaps Paul has also in view the ability to put the impulse into practical effect: see Barrett, p. 218.
[89] Barrett, p. 218. See Acts 17.10–12 for Paul's contact with Beroea.
[90] Betz, p. 50; see pp. 49–53 on Macedonia in general.
[91] Furnish, p. 398; ὅτι = 'for'.

Corinthian readers about what is happening there.[92] There is little difference in sense. More importantly, this grace has been at work whilst the Macedonians were suffering 'a great ordeal of affliction'.[93] According to Acts 16.11–17.15 the original preaching of Christianity in Macedonia had provoked hostility from both the Jewish and the non-Jewish population. After Paul and his assistants had left the province the original hostility may have persisted, directed now against the newly-established churches. When he returned, it may have increased in force. Nevertheless, these believers were experiencing abundant joy. In 1 Th 1.6 Paul speaks of the Spirit-inspired joy evoked by the Christian message itself. Here he may be thinking also of joy derived from their experiencing divine support in the midst of persecution.[94] This joy is coupled with extreme poverty.[95] Opinions differ as to why the Macedonian Christians were so poor. On the one hand, it is suggested that poverty may have been general in the province. Livy's account of the Roman settlement of Macedonia after the battle of Pydna in 168 B.C.E. is cited as evidence. The Romans had forbidden the mining of gold and silver and the cutting of timber for ship building, and the Macedonians were not allowed to trade in land or buildings outside the region to which each belonged.[96] The life of a Macedonian peasant, it is said, was usually one of poverty.[97] On the other hand, commentators point out that Livy is referring to conditions which obtained some two centuries before Paul is writing.[98] And in any case the picture he gives is not one of unrelieved financial oppression, since the Romans had halved the amount of taxes the Macedonians had

---

[92] Barrett, p. 216; Martin, pp. 248, 253. According to this reading of the verse, ὅτι = 'that', and the clause is in apposition to χάριν. Some commentators suppose there are two sentences here, supplying a verb after τῆς χαρᾶς αὐτῶν. (Meyer, p. 341, suggests ἐστί, while Osiander, pp. 298–9, prefers ἦν or ἐγενήθη.) The verb ἐπερίσσευσεν is singular and so might seem to refer only to the immediately preceding ἡ κατὰ βάθους πτωχεία. But the use of a singular verb following a composite subject presents no syntactical problem. See MHT, pp. 313–14, and Mt 6.19; Mk 4.41; Jn 1.17; 1 Cor 15.50.

[93] BAGD s.v. δοκιμή 2. The suffering in the churches of Macedonia is attested also in Phil 1.29–30 and 1 Th 1.6; 3.3–4.

[94] Cf. Amstutz, ΑΠΛΟΤΗΣ, p. 104.

[95] On the phrase κατὰ βάθους see BAGD s.v. κατά I.1.b. for the use of the preposition, and for the rendering of the present phrase as 'extreme' or 'abysmal poverty'. A few witnesses (𝔓[46] D* pc bo) read κατὰ βάθος. This appears to be a scribal error, occasioned by the accidental omission of Υ, which would still leave a grammatically acceptable prepositional phrase.

[96] Livy XLV 29; see Plummer, p. 233.

[97] Betz, pp. 50–1, n. 87; see also p. 43.

[98] Barrett, p. 219; Furnish, p. 413.

previously paid to their kings.[99] Furthermore, since the major Christian communities were located in the urban centres,[100] their members might have been better off than the average peasant in the rural areas. In that case, it is more probable that their poverty was due to social ostracism and harassment on account of their new faith.[101] At all events, it has not caused them to be mean with what few financial resources they possess. Rather, an abundance of both joy and poverty has led to what Paul describes as a wealth[102] of ἁπλότης, 'liberality'.[103] That poverty should produce generosity is something of a paradox, but the point may be that those who are themselves poor are better able to understand and sympathise with others in the like situation.[104] Additionally, as Betz suggests, it could be that the Macedonians saw themselves as conforming to a 'cultural ideal' in which simple people were traditionally generous with what they had.[105]

The meaning of ἁπλότης. In 2 Cor 8.2 and 9.11, 13 it appears obvious from the context that ἁπλότης ought to mean 'generosity'. The difficulty is, however, that this sense is uncertainly attested. When the term is applied to persons, the usual meaning is 'simplicity', 'frankness', or 'sincerity'.[106] Certainly the lexicons do also give 'liberality', but it is the Pauline occurrences in 2 Corinthians and in Rom 12.8 that provide the basic evidence.[107] These apart, there are a few other isolated occurrences which might perhaps support this sense, when seen in context, and possibly translated with a degree of paraphrase. An instance cited by various authorities[108] occurs in Josephus. He recounts that when David went to buy the threshing floor of Oronnas the

---

[99] Livy, XLV 18, 19; see Furnish, p. 413. See also *CAH* VIII, pp. 273–4, where it is suggested that the restrictions on mining and the felling of timber may have been advantageous to the populace in general. Barrett, p. 219, cites *CAH* X, p. 403, on the general prosperity of Macedonia. In the period of the early empire this province was apparently more prosperous than the rest of Greece.

[100] See above, p. 521.

[101] Cf. Barrett, p. 219, who concludes that the poverty Paul speaks of was largely 'a Christian phenomenon'.

[102] There is a textual variant in respect of the gender of πλοῦτος. Some witnesses (𝔓46 ℵ* B C P 0243. 6. 33 .81. 104. 1175. 1739. 2464 pc) read τὸ πλοῦτος, whilst others (ℵ2 D F G Ψ 𝔐) have τὸν πλοῦτον. Paul uses the masculine in Romans (2.4; 9.23; 11.33) but the neuter in Phil 4.19 (cf. Col 1.27). The consistent masculine in Romans might count in favour of the masculine here. But the MS evidence suggests that it is a secondary correction to the more classical gender.

[103] See below, pp. 523–4.

[104] Schlatter, *Paulus*, p. 593; Barrett, p. 219.

[105] Betz, pp. 44–5.

[106] LSJ s.v. ἁπλότης II.2.

[107] LSJ s.v. II.3; BAGD s.v. ἁπλότης 2.

[108] See, e.g., Amstutz, *ΑΠΛΟΤΗΣ*, pp. 42–3; O. Bauernfeind, on ἁπλότης, in *TWNT* I, pp. 385–6; see p. 386.

Jebusite, Oronnas said that he would present it as a gift, along with his plough and oxen for a sacrifice, and that David then said that he admired the man for his ἀπλότης.[109] Here, according to Amstutz, the word indicates unconditional giving.[110] Similarly, in the *Testament of Issachar* the patriarch says that he gave to the poor in the ἀπλότης of his heart.[111] To give unconditionally is to give generously, with sincere, single-minded concern for the recipients: it is to give with inward integrity. This complex of ideas, in a context concerned with giving, could give rise with relative ease to the equation of sincerity, single-mindedness, with generosity.[112] Outside such a context, however, ἀπλότης would not be likely to carry this sense.[113]

3–4. ὅτι κατὰ δύναμιν, μαρτυρῶ, καὶ παρὰ δύναμιν, αὐθαίρετοι μετὰ πολλῆς παρακλήσεως δεόμενοι ἡμῶν τὴν χάριν καὶ τὴν κοινωνίαν τῆς διακονίας τῆς εἰς τοὺς ἁγίους, Paul explains further what he has just said about the extreme generosity of the Macedonians.[114] (In his eagerness to stress the extent and the spontaneity of their response to the needs of the Jerusalem church, he has omitted a main verb.[115]) In what may be somewhat formulaic language, he tells the Corinthians that they contributed according to their means,[116] and also, indeed, somewhat beyond[117] their financial powers. And this was altogether of their own accord.[118] This last assertion is perhaps something of an exaggeration, since it was presumably Paul or

---

[109] Jos., *Ant* VII 332; the Loeb translator does here render ἀπλότης as 'liberality'.

[110] Amstutz, *ΑΠΛΟΤΗΣ*, p. 42. In BAGD s.v. ἀπλότης 1. this reference is given under the heading of 'simple goodness, which gives itself without reserve'.

[111] In BAGD s.v. 2. the meaning in this reference is given as 'generosity'. In *OTP* I, p. 803, however, the phrase is rendered, 'In the integrity of my heart.'

[112] Bauernfeind, on ἀπλότης (n. 108 above), p. 386, rather differently, relates the word to the concept of generosity by means of the idea of a sufficiency (presumably indicating simplicity of lifestyle) which has something over to give to others.

[113] Amstutz never quite gets to the point of rendering ἀπλότης simply as 'generosity', not even in 2 Cor 8–9.

[114] The ὅτι is causal: see, e.g., Barrett, p. 216; Furnish, p. 399; Martin, p. 248.

[115] We need to supply 'they gave', probably before αὐθαίρετοι. Meyer, p. 343, and Hughes, p. 290, however, claim that vv. 3–5 are a syntactical unity, and that the main verb is the ἔδωκαν of v. 5. Furnish, pp. 399, 402, takes the same view, commenting that this verb 'has been anticipated since the beginning of the sentence, 8:3, but delayed' until v. 5. When it does appear, however, it is not related to vv. 3–5 as a whole, but stands within the οὐ καθὼς . . . ἀλλά antithesis. Within this antithesis, moreover, it has its own object ἑαυτούς. This makes it even more difficult to suppose that it has any syntactical relation to the implicit financial object in v. 3.

[116] Betz, p. 45 n. 44, observes that in the papyri, and especially in marriage contracts, κατὰ δύναμιν often means 'in accordance with one's financial capability'.

[117] The correct reading is doubtless παρὰ δύναμιν (ℵ B C D F G 0243. 6. 33. 81. 1175. 1739. 1881. 2464 *pc*). The reading ὑπὲρ δύναμιν (Ψ 𝔐) is a scribal correction to the more usual form of expression.

[118] The adjective αὐθαίρετος occurs in the NT only here and in v. 17. It is good classical Greek.

one of his assistants who told them about the collection in the first instance. And to inform them of it would in itself at least suggest that a contribution would be welcome.[119] Perhaps it is to counter possible Corinthian suspicions that the Macedonians' eagerness for the project might, after all, owe something to apostolic pressure that Paul ascribes to them the technical language of official petitions,[120] thus underlining the seriousness of their own determination. He represents them, moreover, as petitioning for a favour, a χάρις,[121] rather than as simply performing a duty. This χάρις is then itself defined in official language as a κοινωνία in the collection project.[122] The collection itself is termed the διακονία for the Jerusalem Christians. Furnish translates 'the relief work', and claims that in Greek-speaking Judaism the διακον-words were used 'in a technical sense for supplying the needs of the poor'.[123] The only references cited, however, are found in the *Testament of Job*.[124] Collins, by contrast, would render διακονία here by 'mission', and sees the basic idea as that of the management and delivery of a gift:[125] it is a 'sacred task' because it is a commission carried out on behalf of churches which are 'assemblies of God'.[126] The basic difference between these two interpretations is that in the first the service is done to other people, whilst in the second it is ultimately service 'under God'.[127] The question here, however, does not turn so much on this distinction (since the collection could be seen in both lights) as on a rather simpler point. The Macedonians begged the favour of participation in the διακονία. If the word here stands for the supplying of the needs of the Jerusalem Christians, it is easy to speak of their sharing in this project. But if διακονία refers

---

[119] Cf. Windisch, p. 245, who observes that the Macedonian offer must have been evoked by Paul's description of the need of the Jerusalem church.

[120] See Betz, p. 46 and nn. 47, 49, on the use of technical terms. See also Vol. I, p. 437, n. 1729, on the use of δέομαι in petitions.

[121] Commentators differ on the precise sense of χάρις. Windisch, p. 246, and Barrett, p. 220, take it to mean 'gracious work', i.e., the gracious act of giving to relieve the need of the Jerusalem Christians. As the object of δέομαι, however, it possibly makes better sense when rendered 'favour', or 'privilege': see Plummer, p. 235; Betz, p. 46; Martin, p. 248.

[122] See Betz, p. 46, for κοινωνία as an administrative and legal term for 'partnership'. As noted by Furnish, p. 401, and others, the phrase τὴν χάριν καὶ τὴν κοινωνίαν constitutes an hendiadys, i.e., the co-ordination, with καί, of two nouns, one of which is dependent on the other, so as to avoid a sequence of genitives (which here would be τὴν χάριν τῆς κοινωνίας τῆς διακονίας). See BDF 442(16).

[123] Furnish, pp. 399, 401, with reference to Berger, 'Almosen', pp. 189, 199–200.

[124] Furnish, p. 401, cites the following: *T. Job* 11.1–3; 12.2; 15.1,4,8; with reference to Berger, 'Almosen', p. 189 n. 45.

[125] Collins, *Diakonia*, p. 218.

[126] Collins, *Diakonia*, p. 336.

[127] Collins, ibid. For further bibliography on διακονία see Cranfield, *Romans*. pp. 622–3 n. 4

526 COMMENTARY ON II CORINTHIANS

instead to the administration and delivery of the money raised, it makes much less sense to speak of their participation. Even though some Macedonians were to accompany Paul on the journey to Jerusalem, there would not be many of them, and he himself remains the chief organiser and courier. The διακονία, then, is more probably to be understood in the first of the two senses noted above. That the ἅγιοι for whom this act of service is undertaken are the Christians of Jerusalem is known to the Corinthians from earlier communications of one kind or another.[128]

5. καὶ οὐ καθὼς ἠλπίσαμεν ἀλλ᾽ ἑαυτοὺς ἔδωκαν πρῶτον τῷ κυρίῳ καὶ ἡμῖν διὰ θελήματος θεοῦ. The Macedonians, further, surpassed Paul's expectations,[129] in that, as he puts it, they gave themselves. But what does he mean, not only by this but also by the additional phrase πρῶτον τῷ κυρίῳ[130] καὶ ἡμῖν? There is some support for the view that the Macedonians are seen as putting themselves at the disposal first of Christ and then of the apostle. The phrase would then be similar to those in Rom 1.16 and 2.9 which speak of 'the Jew first and also the Greek'.[131] The parallel is not exact, however.[132] Moreover, the word order tells somewhat against this interpretation. The ἑαυτούς is in an emphatic position, and this suggests that the contrast implicit in the πρῶτον has ἑαυτούς as one of its terms. Hence, the other term must be the monetary donation. The Macedonians gave themselves before they gave their money.[133] Or, what was of prime importance was that they put themselves at the Lord's disposal.[134] Or perhaps both thoughts might be combined.[135] This self-giving will have been demonstrated in the complete enthusiasm with which the Macedonians responded to the collection project. It was self-giving to the Lord because the care for one's fellow Christians exemplified in the collection is care for other members of Christ's body.[136] And it was self-giving to Paul because he was

---

[128] See above, pp. 508–9. The odd addition, in a few minuscules (6 945 *al*), of δέξασθαι ἡμᾶς after εἰς τοὺς ἁγίους can scarcely be original.

[129] It is noted in BAGD s.v. ἐλπίζω that the verb can mean 'expect', 'foresee', as well as 'hope'. Paul says, 'not as we expected', but this has to be taken in a positive sense: the Macedonians did not fall below his expectations but far exceeded them.

[130] A few witnesses (𝔓⁴⁶ *pc* a f r vg^ms Ambst) read τῷ θεῷ for τῷ κυρίῳ. This is not likely to be original. It is not probable that Paul would have written τῷ θεῷ ... διὰ θελήματος τοῦ θεοῦ· the θεοῦ would have been replaced by αὐτοῦ, had the reading of 𝔓⁴⁶ been correct.

[131] Windisch, p. 247 and n. 1; cf. Allo, p. 214; Furnish, p. 399.

[132] In both instances in Romans the two nouns are co-ordinated with τε ... καί.

[133] Barrett, p. 221.

[134] Meyer, p. 346; Plummer, p. 236.

[135] Hughes, p. 292.

[136] Windisch, p. 247.

the initiator and organiser of the project. Some exegetes suggest
that the phrase διὰ θελήματος θεοῦ adds a further nuance of
meaning. The phrase is associated in Paul's mind with his
vocation as an apostle.[137] He may therefore intend to indicate that
the Macedonians have recognised him as the authoritative representative of Christ, and recognised his collection likewise as
divinely authorised.[138] The phrase in question does, of course,
refer to the response of the Macedonians, and not to the activity
of Paul.[139] Nevertheless, the divine authorisation of this response
does imply the complementary authorisation of Paul himself.

This verse is of further interest because, again,[140] it raises
implicitly the question of the voluntary nature of the collection. In
one sense, of course, it was wholly voluntary. Paul had no legal
powers to compel contributions. But in another sense there
may have been some element of compulsion, i.e., of a moral kind.
Paul had hoped, or even expected, that the Macedonians
would participate in the collection, and it seems unlikely that
these hopes or expectations would have been completely
concealed when they were informed about the project. Moreover,
this lavish praise of the Macedonians in 8.1–5 is clearly designed
to exert moral pressure on the Corinthians. Betz notes that
there was ethnic and political rivalry between Corinth and
Macedonia. He suggests that this enabled Paul to use the
rhetorical technique of comparison to engender a state of competition in respect of the collection, with ultimate benefit for the
Jerusalem Christians.[141]

**6. εἰς τὸ παρακαλέσαι ἡμᾶς Τίτον ἵνα καθὼς προενήρξατο
οὕτως καὶ ἐπιτελέσῃ εἰς ὑμᾶς καὶ τὴν χάριν ταύτην.** In consequence[142] of the Macedonian enthusiasm for the collection, Paul
has now made a request[143] to Titus that he should assist the

---

[137] Windisch, p. 248, who suggests that Paul adds the phrase to justify and
moderate his placing of himself side by side with Christ. Martin, p. 255, relates it to
1.1.

[138] See Martin, p. 255.

[139] Cf. Bachmann, p. 314.

[140] See above, pp. 524–5, on vv. 3–4.

[141] Betz, p. 48.

[142] In Pauline usage, εἰς with the articular infinitive usually expresses purpose
(MHT, p. 143). But the construction can in itself also express consequence (MHT,
ibid.). This is the better interpretation here: so Barrett, p. 221. The following ἵνα-
clause gives the content of the request: see BDR 402(2) 2 for ἵνα with παρακαλέω
as an alternative to an infinitive.

[143] Betz, p. 54, claims that παρακαλέω is used here 'with the technical meaning
"to summon", or even "to appoint"'. The verb 'is commonly found in administrative writings, where it refers to the appointment of legal or political
representatives'. Wolff, p. 169 n. 43, however, rejects this interpretation in the
present verse, in view of the sense of the cognate noun παράκλησις in v. 4 and of
the absence of this use of the verb elsewhere in Paul. We have allowed, however,

Corinthians to complete their own contribution.[144] The main point is clear. Queries arise, however, in respect of the καί which precedes τὴν χάριν ταύτην and of the significance of the double compound προενήρξατο. The καί before τὴν χάριν must mean 'also'. This might seem to suggest that Titus will be coming to Corinth primarily to complete some other task, previously begun, to which the work for the collection will be an addition. This other task would be the restoration of a good relationship between the congregation and Paul, begun during the visit to which Paul refers in chap. 7.[145] Against this line of argument, however, it must be said that, in the context, the primary object of both προενήρξατο and ἐπιτελέσῃ must be the collection. The first five verses of the chapter have been wholly concerned with it, as is the remainder. Perhaps, when writing (or dictating) ἐπιτελέσῃ, Paul thought again of the successful mission Titus had already concluded in Corinth (chap. 7), and this did cause the addition of the καί. Titus is to complete the Corinthian collection also, just as he has already completed the renewal of good relations between the apostle and the congregation. He is to finalise the collection in Corinth, just as he had previously made a start on the project there. When was this? The use of προενάρχομαι must have some special significance since the two occurrences here (i.e., in the present verse and in v.10) are the only examples given in LSJ.[146] The force of the prefix προ- must certainly be taken into consideration, since it seems to suggest a time more remote in the past than that to which chap. 7 refers.[147] It is possible that this visit took place before the writing of 1 Corinthians,[148] with the purpose of acquainting the Corinthians with the collection project and soliciting their participation. This timing is not precluded by the fact that Paul needs to give instructions about the practicalities in 1 Cor 16.1–2.[149] The practical questions may not have arisen on the occasion of Titus's original visit.

7. ᾿Αλλ᾿ ὥσπερ ἐν παντὶ περισσεύετε, πίστει καὶ λόγῳ καὶ γνώσει καὶ πάσῃ σπουδῇ καὶ τῇ ἐξ ἡμῶν ἐν ὑμῖν ἀγάπῃ, ἵνα καὶ ἐν ταύτῃ τῇ χάριτι περισσεύητε. Having explained the

---

that Paul may be using official language to some extent in v. 4, and so would not preclude the possibility here also.
[144] The word χάρις here obviously refers to the collection, seen as a gracious gift: see BAGD s.v. 3.a.
[145] Bachmann, pp. 314–15; cf. Allo, pp. 214–15; Wolff, p. 169.
[146] LSJ s.v. προενάρχομαι.
[147] See Plummer, p. 237; Windisch, p. 249. Betz, p. 55, and Vielhauer, *Geschichte*, p. 145, also suppose that Titus had visited Corinth before the visit of chap. 7.
[148] Hughes, pp. 293–4.
[149] *Pace* Windisch, p. 249.

purpose of Titus's present visit, Paul now urges his readers to respond.[150] What was implicit in v. 6 is now made explicit. The Corinthians are exhorted to contribute generously to the collection. Is this, in effect, an order? Both Furnish and Martin regard the ἵνα-clause as possessing the force of an imperative.[151] Verbrugge, however, argues for caution. This use of ἵνα, though beginning to become current during the first century C.E., would be 'one of the least direct ways' of expressing a command. It is more indicative of a wish. Verbrugge would supply θέλομεν, and points to v. 8 in confirmation.[152] This would seem consonant with the beginning of the verse, where Paul seems to encourage his readers by expressing his recognition of the spiritual graces he knows them to possess. Those of 'speech' and 'knowledge' are especially mentioned in 1 Cor 1.5. The former, in that context, will include, according to Barrett, prophecy, glossolalia, and general Christian discourse. The latter, in an equally general sense, may refer to 'intellectual apprehension and application of Christian truth'.[153] The σπουδή, 'zeal', or 'devotion', is obviously mentioned because of the recent favourable reaction to Paul's letter (7.11)[154] The gift of πίστις could be that of 'wonder-working faith',[155] or simply faith in a more general sense.[156] It is the last of these gifts or qualities, i.e., ἀγάπη, that is problematic, in part because there is a textual variant. What is not clear is the preceding phrase which describes the origin and direction of the love. According to one reading, Paul refers to 'the love which derives from me and dwells within you/your community': τῇ ἐξ ἡμῶν ἐν ὑμῖν ἀγάπῃ (𝔓46 B 0243. 6. 104. 630. 1175. 1739. 1881 pc r sy^pco Ambst). According to the other viable option,[157] he speaks of 'the love which derives from you and dwells within me': τῇ ἐξ ὑμῶν ἐν ἡμῖν ἀγάπῃ (ℵ C D F G Ψ [33] 𝔐 lat sy^h). In favour of this second alternative there is the fact that it is qualities belonging to the Corinthians that Paul is listing here. But to

---

[150] The opening ἀλλά may have a double function. It marks a point of transition: see, e.g., Denniston, *Particles*, p. 14; Wolff, p. 170 n. 51; Betz, p. 56. It is probably used also to strengthen the virtual command which follows: see BAGD s.v. ἀλλά 6. (citing this reference); also Furnish p. 403; Theobald, *Gnade*, p. 279 n. 7. As indicating 'a break-off in the thought' (Denniston, ibid), it might theoretically retain some weak adversative force, but there is no substantial contrast in content with the previous verse.

[151] Furnish, p. 403, with reference to BDF 387(3), and MHT, p. 95; Martin, p. 262.

[152] Verbrugge, *Collection*, p. 251.

[153] Barrett, *First Corinthians*, p. 37.

[154] Windisch, p. 250.

[155] As in 1 Cor 12.9; cf 13.2 See Hughes, p. 296; Furnish, p. 415.

[156] Plummer, p. 238.

[157] The third reading τῇ ἐξ ὑμῶν ἐν ὑμῖν ἀγάπῃ (326. 629. 2464pc) makes no sense and is an obvious scribal error.

present Paul's Christian love as originating from the Corinthians would be contrary to the facts of history.[158] And what is said in 6.11–13 and 7.3 suggests that, in his view, the Corinthians do not have much real love for him. The first alternative makes the better sense. Since Paul is the founder of the community he is, humanly speaking, the originator of the spirit of Christian love by which the community is characterised. He has shown what love is through the manner of his own work in Corinth.[159] The reading ἐξ ἡμῶν ἐν ὑμῖν is preferable.[160]

In respect of all these gifts the Corinthians are lavishly endowed. Let them, then, show themselves equally lavish in the matter of the collection, ἐν ταύτῃ τῇ χάριτι. As in the previous verse, χάρις primarily means 'gracious deed', 'benefaction'. Does it have a further nuance of meaning as well? Barrett suggests that contribution to the collection is seen to be itself a divine gift in much the same way as 'knowledge', 'speech', and the like.[161] On vv. 1–7 as a whole, see Theobald,[162] who elaborates on Georgi's treatment of vv. 1–5.[163] Georgi claims that Paul presents himself as simply a spectator of an event which unfolds without his assistance, as a demonstration of pure divine grace. Theobald stresses the inner dynamism of the process. This is not wholly convincing. Perhaps Paul might regard the Macedonian enthusiasm in this way. But in vv. 6–10 he is far from a mere spectator in respect of the Corinthians' participation in the collection.

8. οὐ κατ' ἐπιταγὴν λέγω, ἀλλὰ διὰ τῆς ἑτέρων σπουδῆς καὶ τὸ τῆς ὑμετέρας ἀγάπης γνήσιον δοκιμάζων· Paul disclaims any intention of giving a direct command. If we interpret the ἵνα-clause of v. 7 as Verbrugge does,[164] the apostle will be emphasising that in v. 7 he is expressing a wish rather than issuing an order. This is the simplest interpretation of v. 8a. Other exegetes, however, who may understand the ἵνα of v. 7 either as more strictly imperatival, or as possessing some other function, have proposed different explanations. Some of these suggestions are unlikely. Paul does not issue his disclaimer because he sees himself as the spectator of a divine activity which progresses of its own accord.[165] He is himself the subject of the participle

---

158 Prümm, *Diakonia Pneumatos* I, p. 510.
159 So Schlatter, *Paulus*, pp. 595–6.
160 So, e.g., Lietzmann, p. 134; Windisch, p. 250; Martin, p. 259; Betz, p. 37; Wolff, p. 169.
161 Barrett, pp. 216, 222.
162 Theobald, *Gnade*, pp. 280–1.
163 Georgi, *Kollekte*, p. 53.
164 See above, p. 529.
165 *Pace* Georgi, *Kollekte*, pp. 60, 53, who interprets the ἵνα-clause as consecutive. This is improbable. In this context, Paul is either expressing a wish, or, more strongly, giving a command. He is not stating that the Corinthians' participation in

δοκιμάζων,[166] and is thus personally involved in the action.[167] Neither is it because charity without spontaneity degenerates into legalism.[168] Legalism was not a problem in Corinth. Conceivably Paul could be pointing out that he has no direct command from Christ in this matter. The phrase οὐ κατ᾽ ἐπιταγήν occurs in 1 Cor 7.6 in the context of a discussion (on marriage) where there is reference to what the Lord has and has not commanded.[169] But there is no such explicit reference in the present context. Perhaps Paul's manner of speaking shows that he seriously respects the independence of the Corinthian congregation.[170] But it is obvious, whether or not we interpret the ἵνα of v. 7 as expressing a wish rather than as an imperative, that he is putting all possible pressure on them to make a substantial contribution. In all probability he is simply aware that a direct command would be counter-productive, since it would be taken as an unjustifiable attempt at dominance (cf. 1.24).[171] In addition, he could be following a social convention that stressed the voluntary character of contributions to public fundraising.[172] Whilst not giving an order, Paul is putting the Corinthians to the test in the confident expectation of a favourable result.[173] It is the genuineness[174] of their love for other Christians in need that concerns him here.[175] The means of testing is described as διὰ τῆς ἑτέρων σπουδῆς. This is generally (and surely correctly) seen as a reference to the

the collection is (already) the result of their possession of the qualities he lists in v. 7a.

[166] There is a textual variant: D* FG read δοκιμάζω. This may be a simple scribal error. Alternatively it could be an intentional 'correction'. Superficially, it might seem more appropriate grammatically that the οὐ ... λέγω should be balanced by ἀλλὰ ... δοκιμάζω. In fact, however, the contrast is not between λέγω and δοκιμάζων but between κατ᾽ ἐπιταγήν and τὸ ... γνήσιον δοκιμάζων, with both expressions dependent upon λέγω: 'I am speaking not by way of command but as testing your genuineness.'

[167] Georgi, *Kollekte*, p. 60, appears to evade the problem by putting the point impersonally: Paul instances the zeal of the Macedonians in the certainty that this comparison will put the Corinthians to the test. But this is not precisely what he says.

[168] *Pace* Tasker, p. 114.

[169] See Furnish, pp. 404, 416.

[170] Barrett, p. 222, following Bachmann, p. 316.

[171] Windisch, pp. 250–1; cf. Furnish, p. 416, who suggests, as one possibility, that, as in 1.24, Paul is indicating his awareness of criticism and sensitivity to it.

[172] Betz, p. 59.

[173] Plummer, p. 240. On δοκιμάζω see BAGD s.v 2.b.

[174] The adjective γνήσιος 'genuine' (BAGD s.v. 2.) is here, in the neuter singular, turned into a noun by the addition of the definite article: see BDR 263(2); also Vol. I, p. 352 n. 1119.

[175] Barrett, p. 222, supposes that he is thinking also of love shown towards himself in that the Corinthians will be falling in with his wishes by contributing generously. This is possible in view of the καὶ ἡμῖν of v. 5, but is scarcely the main point.

Macedonians. Their zeal, Paul hopes, will serve as a spur to the Corinthians, so that they will give practical proof of their own love. An alternative possibility is nevertheless sometimes suggested, i.e., that the zeal is that of the Corinthians, and the 'others' (ἑτέρων) are the Christians of Jerusalem. Paul would be testing the Corinthians' love through observing their zeal for the welfare of the Jerusalem Christians. The genitive ἑτέρων is objective: the 'others' are those to whom the zeal is directed.[176] But this interpretation is less suited to the context.[177] In view of the emphasis on the keenness of the Macedonians, it is much more probable that it is they who are the 'others'. Moreover, there appears to be something of an intentional contrast between the two genitives ἑτέρων and ὑμετέρας. This makes sense if the σπουδή on which ἑτέρων depends and the ἀγάπη to which ὑμετέρας is attached are ascribed to different groups of people. But the point of the contrast is lost if both qualities belong to the Corinthians.[178] Lastly, the καί (= 'also') preceding τὸ τῆς ὑμετέρας ἀγάπης γνήσιον would become redundant if it is only one group of people to whom reference is made.[179]

9. **γινώσκετε γὰρ τὴν χάριν τοῦ κυρίου ἡμῶν Ἰησοῦ Χριστοῦ, ὅτι δι' ὑμᾶς ἐπτώχευσεν πλούσιος ὤν, ἵνα ὑμεῖς τῇ ἐκείνου πτωχείᾳ πλουτήσητε.** Paul's readers are urged to participate generously in the 'gracious work' of the collection (v. 7), because they well know of the archetypal example presented by the 'gracious act' of the Lord Jesus Christ[180] himself, here expressed in the language of self-impoverishment. The point is underlined by the δι' ὑμᾶς:[181] the Corinthians themselves are the beneficiaries of this impoverishment.

In what sense, then, did Paul suppose that Jesus Christ became poor? By voluntarily embracing human, material poverty? By identifying himself, during his historical lifetime, with the spiritual poverty of fallen humanity? Or by the total event of incarnation? The case for the first of these options has been put by G. W. Buchanan. He points out that Paul saw an integral relationship between material and spiritual wealth (Gal 6.6; 1 Cor 9.11; Rom 15.27). Hence the apostle's logic could have accommodated the

---

176 Allo, p. 216, suggests this interpretation as an alternative possibility, and Kümmel, p. 207, thinks it worth considering.

177 Cf. Hughes, pp. 298–9 n. 23; Osiander, p. 309.

178 Hughes, pp. 298–9 n. 23; cf. Osiander, p. 309.

179 Hughes, ibid.

180 Χριστοῦ is lacking in B sa. In view of the scribal tendency to expand divine names this reading cannot be ruled out entirely. But it could well be due to accidental omission, through homoioteleuton, after Ἰησοῦ.

181 A few witnesses (C K 6. 323. 614 al Eus Did Epiph) read ἡμᾶς. This may be a simple error, but could be explained, alternatively, as an intentional correction: Christ's work was for all believers, not just for the Corinthians.

idea that Jesus's financial self-impoverishment had produced spiritual wealth for the Corinthians. In fact, Buchanan argues, Jesus may well have belonged to a higher social class than is usually supposed: many of his parables are concerned with upper-class characters, and he associated with the upper classes himself. Other Jews at that time gave up their wealth to join such groups as the Essenes. Jesus may have acted in a similar way.[182] This suggestion is ultimately unconvincing, however. If Jesus were known to Paul to have acted in the way proposed, it is difficult to believe that the record of it would have been entirely lost from the Jesus-traditions elsewhere.[183] Certainly during his public work Jesus did lead a life of economic poverty: commentators refer to the saying about homelessness in Mt 8.20.[184] Possibly Paul has this in view as a subordinate motif. But it is doubtful whether the change from his original circumstances was so great or so remarkable as to give rise in itself to the assertion here.

The second option again concerns only the historical life of Jesus, but relates to spiritual wealth and poverty rather than to economic circumstances. It is supported by J. D. G. Dunn, who offers two alternative interpretations. It could be that Christ's 'wealth' refers to the richness of communion Jesus enjoyed with God, reflected in his prayer to God as 'Father', and that his 'poverty' is his sense of abandonment by God during his execution (Mk 15.34).[185] This seems unlikely. It is doubtful whether Paul was sufficiently interested in the human Jesus's religious experience to have drawn this kind of contrast. Even if he knew the tradition of the cry of dereliction, from his point of view it was as God's Son that Jesus died. The other suggestion is that Paul's Adam christology provides the exegetical key. The unfallen Adam could be thought of as 'rich'. The fallen Adam would be 'poor', because deprived of his glory and immortality. Jesus freely chose identification with fallen, sinful Adam even to the point of death. This death can be seen as a 'gracious act', since it was not a punishment for Jesus's own sinfulness.[186] The difficulty here, however, is that the πλούσιος ὤν has no real content, but remains a purely hypothetical possibility.[187]

The third option represents the traditional view The phrase

[182] G. W. Buchanan, 'Jesus and the Upper Class', *NovT* 7 (1964–65), pp. 195–209.

[183] Cf. F. B. Craddock, 'The Poverty of Christ: an Investigation of II Corinthians 8:9' *Int* 22 (1968), pp. 158–70; see pp. 164–5.

[184] Grotius, p. 488; Calvin, p. 111.

[185] J. D. G. Dunn, *Christology in the Making*, London, 1980, p. 122.

[186] Dunn, *Christology*, pp. 122–3.

[187] Cf. Martin, p. 263. Unless we presuppose Paul's belief in Christ's pre-existence, there is no point at which riches already possessed would be abandoned.

πλούσιος ὤν refers to Christ's pre-existent state, and the ἐπτώχευσεν to his incarnation. The assertion is seen to be parallel in general sense to Phil 2.6–8, as traditionally interpreted.[188] The aorist verb is understood by some exegetes[189] to refer simply to the initial 'moment' of incarnation. But it may well function ingressively, with the sense 'began to be poor',[190] and so include the whole of Jesus's earthly life and his death by crucifixion.[191] Throughout this period he was self-deprived of his original glory. This self-deprivation was his 'gracious act', his χάρις. Dunn argues, in opposition, that in other Pauline contexts where χάρις occurs in relation to what Christ has done, the thought is of his death and resurrection (see Rom 5.15, 21; Gal 2.20–21): there is no hint elsewhere that his 'gracious act' consisted in his becoming man.[192] This may be so. It does not, however, preclude the possibility of such an allusion here. The fact remains that, to make sense of the present assertion, we need some point of reference for Christ's state of 'wealth' which is 'chronologically prior' to the 'poverty' of his historical life and death, and pre-existent glory is the most likely possibility. The traditional interpretation of the verse is preferable to the other possibilities suggested.

His[193] self-impoverishment in the whole event of incarnation was for the spiritual enrichment of believers. We have the same principle of interchange as in 5.21.[194] The riches are not further defined, and are probably to be understood in a comprehensive sense as all the blessings of eschatological salvation, both those enjoyed already through the gift of the Spirit and those yet to come through final glorification.

10. καὶ γνώμην ἐν τούτῳ δίδωμι· τοῦτο γὰρ ὑμῖν συμφέρει, οἵτινες οὐ μόνον τὸ ποιῆσαι ἀλλὰ καὶ τὸ θέλειν προενήρξασθε ἀπὸ πέρυσι· In what he has been saying, Paul is expressing his judgment[195] as to the correct course of action for his readers. The

---

[188] So, e.g., Meyer, p. 350; Bousset, p. 196; Denney, p. 268; Plummer, p. 241; Wolff, p. 171.

[189] Lietzmann, p. 134; Tasker, p. 115.

[190] Furnish, p. 404; Wolff, pp. 171–2; Martin, p. 263.

[191] Barrett, p. 223, speaks of 'the absolute naked poverty of crucifixion'.

[192] Dunn, *Christology*, p. 121.

[193] The ἐκείνου is emphatic, underlining the contrast with the equally emphatic ὑμεῖς: 'so that *you* might become rich, by means of *his* poverty'. A few witnesses (D F G syᴾ Did) read αὐτοῦ. This might result from a mistaken attempt at correction. The ἐκείνου may have seemed odd, as though referring to some person other than the subject of the ὅτι-clause.

[194] Windisch, p. 253. As in the case of 5.(18–)21, it is suggested that in the present verse Paul is quoting tradition (so Georgi, *Kollekte*, p. 61 and n. 227), or freely adapting 'a traditional theological statement' (Furnish, p. 417). We have argued, however, that it is not a question of quotation in 5.18–21 (Vol. I, pp. 445–9). Here, similarly, it is not clear why Paul himself may not be credited with the formulation of the assertion.

[195] BAGD s.v. γνώμη 2.

ἐν τούτῳ refers to the Corinthians' (generous) participation in the collection. The positive γνώμην δίδωμι complements the negative οὐ κατ᾽ ἐπιταγὴν λέγω of v. 8. It is counsel[196] that Paul is giving, not any kind of order. Nevertheless, it is not quite the case that he is merely drawing attention to the collection as a work solely of divine grace which possesses its own (sufficient) momentum.[197] If he did regard the project as possessing an inner dynamic in this fashion, he would scarcely need to address the Corinthians on the subject at such length. He does so because he believes what he has said[198] and will say to be for their benefit. This appeal to what is advantageous conforms, it would seem, to a convention of rhetorical exhortation.[199] Paul does not explain, however, quite why a favourable response to his exhortations will be expedient for the Corinthians. Is it simply that what has been begun ought to be completed?[200] This may be the idea in part, but one might expect some more specific benefit to be in mind as well. Possibly there is a clue in the εὐπρόσδεκτος of v. 12: by contributing to the collection the Corinthians will be doing something that is well-pleasing to God, which cannot but be beneficial to themselves also. Or perhaps, as v. 14 suggests, there will be some kind of return benefit from Jerusalem.

The chief exegetical problem in this verse is contained in the relative clause. It is odd, at least at first sight, that Paul should describe his readers as having previously begun[201] not only to take action (in the matter of the collection) but also to be willing to do so. The doing (ποιῆσαι) is made to seem inferior to the willingness (θέλειν),[202] and possibly prior to it. Various explanations are proposed. Paul's order of reference may imply, it is suggested, that in his view 'pure activism' was an easier thing than 'sincere

---

[196] Furnish, p. 405, with reference to 1 Cor 7.6, observes that he is giving 'serious, apostolic counsel', guided by the Spirit.

[197] *Pace* Georgi, *Kollekte*, p. 61.

[198] We take the τοῦτο to refer to the content of the γνώμη, and so as probably possessing both a backward and a forward reference.

[199] See Betz, p. 63, who comments that Paul's allusion to expediency is 'a stock argument in deliberative oratory'; in n. 183 he refers to Arist, *Rhet.* I 3.5; 6.1. See also 8.2, 7. Furnish, p. 405, similarly notes that, in Aristotle's description of deliberative rhetoric (i.e., speech designed to persuade to a particular course of action or to dissuade from it), exhortation is seen as the commendation of τὸ συμφέρον (*Rhet.* I 3.3–5).

[200] Betz, p. 63.

[201] Most witnesses read προενήρξασθε ('began beforehand'), but a few (D* F G 629*) have ἐνήρξασθε ('began'). The majority reading could be seen as assimilation to v. 6, but it is more likely that this second occurrence of the unusual προενάρχομαι is also due to Paul himself.

[202] Plummer, p. 242. Windisch, p. 254, draws attention to Phil 2.13, where, by contrast, we find the expected (logical) order καὶ τὸ θέλειν καὶ τὸ ἐνεργεῖν.

motivation'.[203] But v. 11 rather implies the opposite. Or perhaps the προ of προενήρξασθε sets the Corinthians in comparison with the Macedonians: not only the action but also the intention of contributing had had its beginning in Corinth prior to its beginning in Macedonia.[204] But what would be the point of such an assertion? It could surely be taken for granted that if the Corinthians were prior in action they were also prior in intention. Is it, then that the ποιῆσαι and the θέλειν refer to different points in time? Barrett suggests that the beginning of the θέλειν goes further back in time than the beginning of the ποιῆσαι. The Corinthians' intention to contribute pre-dates 1 Corinthians (see 1 Cor 16.1–4), whilst they began to put it into effect only during the visit of Titus to which Paul refers in chap. 7 and also in 8.6.[205] It is as though he had written: οὐ μόνον τὸ ποιῆσαι ἐνήρξασθε ἀλλὰ καὶ τὸ θέλειν προενήρξασθε.[206] There are two difficulties with this solution, however. First, we have ourselves argued that the activity of Titus which is mentioned in v. 6 occurred during a visit prior to that of chap. 7. Secondly, the natural way of understanding the οὐ μόνον ... ἀλλὰ καί correlation in the present verse is to suppose that the verb προενήρξασθε relates to the τὸ ποιῆσαι in the same way as it relates to τὸ θέλειν. Is Paul, perhaps, saying to his readers that it was they who had taken the initiative originally? They had not, that is, simply engaged in preliminary action under pressure from himself. On the contrary, they had themselves expressed, spontaneously, their willingness to take part in the project.[207] This seems the best exegetical option. The initially strange order of 'acting' and 'willingness to act' is due to the desire to emphasise the willingness: τὸ θέλειν, coming in the second half of the correlation, carries the required emphasis.[208] This earlier enthusiasm began ἀπὸ πέρυσι, 'a year ago', or was in evidence from some point in the previous year, 'since last year'.[209] This expression allows some latitude for determining the point of time in view.[210] We suggest that Paul is thinking of the initial interest in the collection to which he refers in 1 Cor 16.1–4, and which he heard of in the letter the Corinthians had written to

---

[203] Betz, p. 64.
[204] Meyer, p. 354; Tasker, p. 116.
[205] Barrett, p. 225.
[206] This would be the Greek that would result from the exegesis suggested by Barrett.
[207] Bachmann, p. 318; Allo, p. 218; Bruce, p. 223. This is Paul's view of the situation, of course.
[208] Bachmann, p. 318.
[209] BAGD s.v. πέρυσι.
[210] Cf. Windisch, p. 255.

him. According to the chronological scheme already proposed,[211] this letter reached him at about the beginning of the Jewish New Year in autumn 54. Writing the present letter in spring 56, he could still refer, in terms of the Jewish calendar, to autumn 54 as 'last year'.

11. νυνὶ δὲ καὶ τὸ ποιῆσαι ἐπιτελέσατε, ὅπως καθάπερ ἡ προθυμία τοῦ θέλειν οὕτως καὶ τὸ ἐπιτελέσαι ἐκ τοῦ ἔχειν. Now,[212] the Corinthians are urged to bring matters to a conclusion. Paul's injunction contains the thought both of doing (τὸ ποιῆσαι) what one has intended and of completing (ἐπιτελέσατε) what one has begun.[213] The completion in action, moreover, should match the initial enthusiasm.[214] Paul stresses the fact of this original enthusiasm by means of the pleonastic expression ἡ προθυμία τοῦ θέλειν, 'zeal of willingness'.[215] But he stresses also that he is not asking his readers to give more than they can afford. The completion[216] is to be in accordance with their means,[217] but not, apparently, beyond their means, as the following verse makes clear. This limitation hardly seems congruent with the earlier account of the zeal of the

[211] Vol. I, p. 77.

[212] The δέ following νυνὶ marks a slight contrast with the preceding ἀπὸ πέρυσι.

[213] Windisch, p. 256.

[214] There is no verb either in the ὅπως-clause or in the καθάπερ-clause. We might supply γένηται in the former (Bachmann, p. 319) and ἐγένετο in the latter.

[215] On the construction, see BAGD s.v. προθυμία where there is a reference to the use of the same phrase in Plato, Leg. (Laws) III 697E: μετὰ προθυμίας τοῦ ἐθέλειν κινδυνεύειν ('[with] readiness to endanger their lives', LCL). In BDF 400(2) the sense is given as 'zeal in willing so that one really wills'; the relationship between the noun and the infinitive is said to 'tend toward the consecutive sense'. Windisch, p. 256, notes a similar expression in Phil 3.21: τὴν ἐνέργειαν τοῦ δύνασθαι.

[216] Betz, p. 65, comments that ἐπιτελέω is used 'of completing an administrative act', and that προθυμία is attested as 'a business term'. See nn. 201-3; also p. 54 n. 122. If Paul was familiar with these uses, he may have thought them appropriate when dealing with a financial matter. But since both terms are current also in more general senses, one cannot be certain. Furthermore, evidence has been produced to show that the verb was widely used in various ways for the performance of religious duties. See R. S. Ascough, 'The Completion of a Religious Duty: the Background of 2 Cor 8.1-15', NTS 42 (1996), pp. 584-99. Investigation of inscriptional evidence reveals instances of ἐπιτελέω in regulations for the performance of various mysteries, for the offering of sacrifices, and for the discharge of other ritual duties by the priests of the different cults. It is found also with reference to the fulfilment of oaths and to benefactions made for religious purposes. Consequently, if in the present verse ἐπιτελέω is used in a more specialised sense, it is to this religious context that we should look more particularly.

[217] For ἐκ in the sense 'in accordance with', see BAGD s.v. 3.i., where the present phrase is rendered 'in accordance with your ability'. This takes ἔχω in the sense 'be able': Hughes, p. 305 n. 3, argues for this meaning of the verb in vv. 11-12. But it would usually be followed by an infinitive, which here is lacking. If it is not so followed, it is just as easy to supply a pronominal object (ὅ or τι), allowing ἔχω to mean 'have', 'possess', as to supply a suitable infinitive.

Macedonians.[218] But it may be, as Furnish suggests, that the Corinthians have excused their dilatoriness on the ground that they would not be able to offer very much, and that Paul is pointing out that what counts is the fact of the contribution, not its size.[219]

12. εἰ γὰρ ἡ προθυμία πρόκειται, καθὸ ἐὰν ἔχῃ εὐπρόσδεκτος, οὐ καθὸ οὐκ ἔχει. Paul spells out the meaning of the ἐκ τοῦ ἔχειν in v. 11. His form of expression, however, is not altogether clear He appears to say that it is the willingness (ἡ προθυμία) that is acceptable.[220] But the whole point of v. 11 has been the necessity for readiness to be translated into action. Perhaps we should suppose an extension of the sense of the 'willingness' so as to include the thought of consequent action.[221] Alternatively, we might understand an unexpressed 'a gift' (χάρις) as the subject of '(is) acceptable'.[222] The subject of ἔχῃ and ἔχει is not specified, but is probably 'someone', 'a person' (τις),[223] i.e., in the context, any Corinthian Christian. Despite the elliptical manner of expression, the basic point is obvious enough. As long as giving is proportionate to one's means, the gift is acceptable whether it be large or small.[224] The thought may well be, 'acceptable to God'. The word εὐπρόσδεκτος is used with sacrificial connotations in Rom 15.16.[225] As regards the idea of proportionality, it is probable that some qualification is necessary. If we were to take the concluding clause οὐ καθὸ οὐκ ἔχει literally, it would imply, strictly speaking, that a gift which was larger than a person's resources would justify would not be acceptable.[226] But Paul can scarcely mean this, since he has praised the Macedonians for giving παρὰ δύναμιν (v. 3), 'beyond their means'. The point must be that the demands of piety do not go beyond what is proportionate to one's resources, not that it

---

[218] See vv. 3–4.
[219] Furnish, p. 419.
[220] So Martin, p. 265.
[221] Windisch, p. 257, claims that the context requires an extension of reference so as to cover the action.
[222] So NRSV. This may be preferable.
[223] Barrett, p. 216, and Furnish, p. 399, translate 'what one has'; Martin, p. 259, has 'what a person has'.
[224] There is a parallel in Tob 4.8, noted by e.g., Plummer, p. 244; Furnish, p. 407; Betz, p. 66 n. 215. The syntax of Paul's assertion is more easily understood if we take καθὸ ἐάν as καθ᾽ ὃ ἄν, i.e., as an indefinite relative clause, 'according to that which (a person may possess)'. In any case, the ἐάν must stand here for the indefinite ἄν, since a conditional ἐάν would not make sense. The second καθό may likewise be divided.
[225] Windisch, p. 257; cf. Betz, p. 66; Martin, p. 265.
[226] Windisch, p. 256, hints at this interpretation when he claims that the verse might be read as containing a concealed reproach directed against Macedonians.

would be displeasing to God to exceed them. All that is asked of the Corinthians is that their donations should match their means. Perhaps Paul has in mind the advice he had given in 1 Cor 16.2 that each person should each week put aside 'whatever profit he makes',[227] so as to have something for the collection. This already has implied that the giving should simply be proportionate to one's means. When resuming the topic, Paul would need to take care that he did not appear to make further demands.

13. οὐ γὰρ ἵνα ἄλλοις ἄνεσις, ὑμῖν[228] θλῖψις, ἀλλ' ἐξ ἰσότητος·[229] The point is put more plainly still. In all this, Paul's purpose[230] is not that relief for others should cause hardship for the Corinthians, but that there should be a state of equality, ἐξ ἰσότητος. This last phrase may appear simple enough, but in fact raises some questions. Georgi claims that there is inherent in it a cosmic and mystical idea of ἰσότης.In Philo, he argues, ἰσότης is treated as a divine power which can be personified and put on a level with God himself.[231] In line with the general tendency of the speculative mysticism of hellenistic Judaism, the communal aspect of the concept (originally so essential in Greek thinking) retreats into the background. Paul is not speaking here of human equality of resources. Rather, ἰσότης is a periphrasis for God: the phrase ἐξ ἰσότητος has a causal function and is the equivalent of ἐκ θεοῦ.[232] This would require us to take the phrase with v. 14, and the sense would be: 'But, through divine causality, your abundance will

---

[227] Barrett, *First Corinthians*, p. 385.

[228] Some witnesses (ℵ² D F G Ψ 𝔐 lat syʰ Cl Ambst) add δέ, to point up the contrast between ἄλλοις and ὑμῖν. It should be omitted (with ℵ* B C 048. 0243. 33. 81. 323. 1739. 1881 *pc* d Cyp). The lack of δέ is consonant with the elliptical style of the context.

[229] Some translators and commentators attach ἀλλ' ἐξ ἰσότητος to the following verse: so, e.g., REB; Plummer, p. 244; Allo, p. 220; Barrett, p. 226. In favour of this interpretation, as Barrett, ibid., points out, there is the fact that otherwise v. 14 would begin abruptly without a connecting particle. Others attach the phrase to the end of v. 13: see, e.g., Windisch, p. 257; Martin, p. 259; Furnish, p. 399; Betz p. 37. This is preferable on two counts. First, as Windisch, ibid., notes, it gives a better rhythm to combine this third succinct expression with the two preceding, equally succinct phrases. And secondly, if ἀλλ' ἐξ ἰσότητος belongs with what follows we have a double reference to ἰσότητος within the same sense-unit, which is at least awkward. Furnish, p. 407, supports the attachment of the phrase to v. 13 for this reason.

[230] The expression is elliptical, but ἵνα may still be taken in its final sense. C. J. Cadoux, 'The Imperatival Use of ἵνα in the New Testament', *JTS* 42 (1941), pp. 165-73, suggests, pp. 170-1, that it might be imperatival. But this would surely require ἵνα μὴ ἄλλοις ἄνεσις. The verb γένηται has to be supplied: see BAGD s.v. ἵνα III.3.

[231] Georgi, *Kollekte*, p. 62, refers to Philo, *Rer. Div. Her.* 141-206.

[232] Georgi, *Kollekte*, pp. 62-5. This is in line with his claim that the collection project, in Paul's view, is a work of divine grace, with its own dynamic. See above, p. 530.

meet their insufficiency so that there may be equality.' This interpretation has not met with general acceptance. Paul, it is noted, was not the same type of thinker as Philo: the point in the present passage is 'fair dealing'.[233] In any case, is the required interpretation of Philo correct? According to Theobald, it is doubtful whether he puts ἰσότης on the same level as God. The personification is most likely a stylistic device, since it can be used also for the opposite concept ἀνισότης.[234] Furthermore, if ἀλλ' ἐξ ἰσότητος is to be contrasted with the two previous phrases (taken as one sense-unit), it must mean 'on the basis of equality'. The opposite of inequality is not 'caused by God'. But if the phrase is to be attached to v. 14, we should have the one word ἰσότης used in the same sentence in two quite different senses. This is not impossible, but the usual exegesis seems more likely.

What Paul has in view, then, is the concept of communal equality as this had developed in Greek law and politics.[235] He is appealing to it as something which would be familiar and congenial to his readers.[236] It is less clear, however, what he means in precise terms. He is not concerned to promote a state of general financial equality between all Christian churches, since in that case he would surely have been asking for assistance for the Macedonians, rather than accepting a donation from them. In v. 14 he attempts further explanation, though not, perhaps, with entire success.

14. ἐν τῷ νῦν καιρῷ τὸ ὑμῶν περίσσευμα εἰς τὸ ἐκείνων ὑστέρημα, ἵνα καὶ τὸ ἐκείνων περίσσευμα γένηται[237] εἰς τὸ ὑμῶν ὑστέρημα, ὅπως γένηται ἰσότης, The initial assertion seems clear enough, despite the need to supply a verb after περίσσευμα (γίνεται or γενήσεται to correspond with the γένηται of the two following clauses). At the present time,[238] when the Corinthians have something of a material surplus, this surplus will be available to supply the material deficiency in the Jerusalem church. We should then expect that the following ἵνα-clause would refer to the converse process in the future:[239] the Christians of Jerusalem will come to the assistance of the Corinthians,

[233] Barrett, p. 227.
[234] Theobald, *Gnade*, p. 288 and n. 69. See *Rer. Div. Her.* 162, where 'equality' gives birth to peace, whilst 'inequality' gives birth to all kinds of war. The maternal image applies to both.
[235] See G. Stählin, on ἰσότης, in *TWNT* III, pp. 343–56; Furnish, p. 407; Betz, pp. 67–8 and nn. 229, 230.
[236] Stählin, ἰσότης pp. 348–9.
[237] The verb is omitted in a few witnesses (𝔓[46]. 0243. 630. 1175. 1739. 1881 *pc*), probably by accident, in unconscious conformity to the structure of the previous sentence.
[238] See Furnish, p. 408, who supports a literal, rather than a theological, interpretation of ἐν τῷ νῦν καιρῷ.
[239] The καί following ἵνα suggests the equivalence of ideas in the two clauses.

should they, in turn, find themselves in material need. This interpretation has some support.[240] Other commentators, however, reject it. Paul would not have been so unrealistic as to suppose that the Jerusalem Christians would be able in the near future to make some monetary return to the Corinthians.[241] If that is so, there are two alternative possibilities. The first, suggested by Furnish, is that the verse is simply 'a formal statement of the principle of equality'. Paul does not have in mind any specific future response on the part of Jerusalem.[242] But since the first half of the statement relates to real action (by the Corinthians, for the Jerusalem church), would not a purely formal, unreal, suggestion of converse action (by Jerusalem, for Corinth) tend to be misleading, if not somewhat dishonest? (There is nothing in the text to show the readers that the prospect is envisaged as unreal.) The second possibility is that Paul is thinking of spiritual benefits to be imparted to the church in Corinth by the mother church. This interpretation goes back to Chrysostom, although he is not very specific as to the particular nature of these benefits.[243] The idea would be the same as the thought in Rom 15.27 Again, however, the suggestion is problematic. Certainly in the past the Corinthians had been spiritually indebted to the Jerusalem church, but by now 'they were spiritually wealthy, both in their own regard and in that of Paul'.[244] Furthermore, whatever the function of Jerusalem as the original source of the Christian gospel, Paul himself had suffered unpleasant experiences of the spiritual influences deriving therefrom:[245] the dispute in Antioch had been followed in due course by trouble in Galatia. It might seem impossible that he could hope for spiritual sustenance for his own converts from the church in Jerusalem.[246] It could be, of course, that the spiritual blessing he has in mind relates to the prayer of thanksgiving which he believes the Jerusalem Christians will offer for the collection (see 9.12–15), which he sees as beneficial for the donors.[247] If the 'surplus' of the Jerusalem Christians relates to spiritual benefits, this is the most probable interpretation. Martin proposes a more elaborate hypothesis. The whole verse is to be interpreted in the light of Rom 9–11. The

---

[240] Meyer, p. 358; Plummer, p. 245; Hughes, p. 306; Barrett, p. 226.

[241] Prümm, *Diakonia Pneumatos* I, p. 523.

[242] Furnish, p. 420, with reference to Héring (see p. 70).

[243] Chrysostom, *PG* 61 col. 519 (NPNF XII, p. 361).

[244] Betz, p. 68.

[245] Windisch, p. 260.

[246] Lietzmann, p. 135; Barrett, p. 226.

[247] So Theobald, *Gnade*, p. 286, with reference to D. Zeller, *Juden und Heiden in der Mission des Paulus. Studien zum Römerbrief* FBI, Stuttgart, 1973, p. 234. See also Wolff, pp. 173–4.

present time is the era of law-free grace exemplified in Paul's Gentile churches, and the περίσσευμα of the Corinthians is precisely this rich endowment with grace (i.e., not their material surplus as such). They are able, therefore, 'to demonstrate concern for ethnic Israel in her want, both in physical distress but also in her parlous condition *extra Christum*'. Conversely, Israel's future reconciliation will enrich the Gentiles by hastening the 'final homecoming of the nations' and the end of the age.[248] This is an interesting suggestion, but unlikely to be correct. The equality is between two groups of Christians, not between Gentiles in general and Israel as a whole, and the Corinthian gift, similarly, is in no way directed to non-Christian 'ethnic Israel'.

It is not easy to reach a satisfactory conclusion. But it might be useful to reconsider the possibility that Paul does, after all, have in mind material benefits in both cases. Perhaps rejection of this interpretation is due in part to our own knowledge of events in the years almost immediately following the Corinthian correspondence. We are aware that the Jewish war with Rome broke out within a decade or so. The Christians of Jerusalem could not have remained unaffected, moreover, by the disturbed state of affairs prior to its outbreak. These conditions would scarcely have been conducive either to their economic welfare or to concern for fellow Christians elsewhere. But Paul did not know all this in advance. If Christian poverty was sometimes the result of persecution, he could have envisaged a time when the Jerusalem church might be free of it whilst the Corinthians were suffering. Again, poverty might result from poor harvests: the Corinthians might be affected whilst the inhabitants of Judaea were not. The theoretical prospect of future aid from Jerusalem to Corinth might well seem realistic. It remains possible that this is what Paul had in mind.

15. καθὼς γέγραπται· Ὁ τὸ πολὺ οὐκ ἐπλεόνασεν, καὶ ὁ τὸ ὀλίγον οὐκ ἠλαττόνησεν. The concept of equality has scriptural warrant in the story of the manna in Exod 16,[249] where each had

---

[248] Martin, pp. 267, 269; the quotation is on p. 267.

[249] The quotation is from v. 18. In the LXX this reads: [καὶ μετρήσαντες τῷ γομορ] οὐκ ἐπλεόνασεν ὁ τὸ πολύ, καὶ ὁ τὸ ἔλαττον οὐκ ἠλαττόνησεν. On the differences between the Pauline text and the LXX, see C. D. Stanley: *Paul and the Language of Scripture: Citation Technique in the Pauline Epistles and Contemporary Literature*, SNTSMS 74, Cambridge, 1992, pp. 231–3. The initial phrase καὶ μετρήσαντες τῷ γομορ 'becomes an irrelevant and intrusive detail': the basic point is 'the equality of Yahweh's provision for his people'. The change in word order, whereby ὁ τὸ πολύ now precedes οὐκ ἐπλεόνασεν, serves to heighten the antithesis in relation to the following sentence. Commentators note that both texts require that a participle be supplied after τὸ πολύ (and understood after τὸ ὀλίγον). Barrett, p. 227 (with reference to Robertson, p. 1202), supplies ἔχων. But Furnish is more probably correct in suggesting, p. 408, 'gathered', συλλέξας, from the previous συνέλεξαν (v. 17).

enough, no more and no less. Paul takes it for granted that the Corinthians have some general familiarity with the narrative.[250] Is this all? Or does he expect his readers to be aware of the context in Exodus and to draw further conclusions from it? Plummer suggests that he does. He notes that the equality of supply was imposed upon the Israelites. Paul, by contrast, is to be seen as encouraging a voluntary and joyful acceptance of the principle by the members of 'the new Israel'.[251] For Windisch, he is implying that what took place by means of a miracle for the Israelites should be brought about voluntarily in the case of the two Christian churches.[252] But both these interpretations require that, in using the verse from Exodus, Paul is drawing a contrast in some way between the situation of the Israelites and that of the Christian communities. There is nothing in the text to suggest this. To the contrary, the καθὼς γέγραπται implies the opposite. The verse should not be overloaded with significance. The exegesis proposed by R. P. C. Hanson tends in this direction. Paul, he claims, sees the manna miracle as 'a foretaste or prophecy of the self-adjusting love of Christ in His members which supplies the need of each without deficiency or embarrassment'.[253] But Paul does not use the idea of the church as the body of Christ in his collection appeal. The point of the quotation is simply to validate the principle of equality.

(ii) *The mission and commendation of Titus and two colleagues* *(8.16–24)*

[16]And thanks be to God, the giver of the same zeal on your behalf within the heart of Titus. [17]For he accepted our request, but, being yet more zealous, of his own accord he set off to you. [18]And with him we have sent the brother whose praise in the sphere of the gospel pervades all the churches. [19]And not only this. On the contrary, he was also elected by the churches to travel as our companion with this benefaction, which on our part is in process of organisation, resulting in the glory of the Lord himself and in our own enthusiasm. [20]We are making this preparation lest anyone should cast blame upon us in respect of this lavish gift organised by us. [21]For we take thought for what is morally good not only in the sight of the Lord but also in the sight of men. [22]And we have sent with them our brother, whom we have frequently, in many respects, proved to be zealous, but now much more zealous by reason of his substantial confidence in you. [23]If anyone should inquire about Titus, he is my partner and with respect to you our fellow worker: if about our brothers, they are

[250] Stanley, p. 231.
[251] Plummer, p. 245.
[252] Windisch, p. 259.
[253] R. P. C. Hanson, *The Second Epistle to the Corinthians*, London, 1954, p. 71.

church delegates, Christ's glory. [24]Show them then, before the churches, a proof of your love and of our boast about you.

Paul emphasises Titus's eagerness for this present mission to complete the collection in Corinth, and designates him his partner. But the chief point in this paragraph is the introduction and commendation of the two colleagues who will travel with him and assist him. The one is well known for his Christian work, perhaps as an evangelist, and he has been specifically appointed by a group of churches. The other appears to be a member of Paul's own staff, although similarly acting on behalf of the contributing churches. The purpose of these appointments is to guarantee the financial integrity of Paul himself.

16. Χάρις δὲ τῷ θεῷ τῷ δόντι[254] τὴν αὐτὴν σπουδὴν ὑπὲρ ὑμῶν ἐν τῇ καρδίᾳ Τίτου, The expression of thanksgiving which opens this paragraph probably needs no further explanation than that every aspect of the collection is seen by Paul to be due to divine grace, including the zeal of Titus on the Corinthians' behalf.[255] In the context, this zeal must relate to the benefits that will accrue to them from their participation in the collection.[256] But it is also said to be 'the same' eagerness. With whose zeal is Titus's own enthusiasm compared? With that of the Corinthians? In v. 7 they are said to abound in zeal.[257] Or with that of the Macedonians, to which Paul has referred in v. 8?[258] The difficulty with both these suggestions is that the phrase τὴν αὐτὴν σπουδήν seems closely connected with the following ὑπὲρ ὑμῶν: it is zeal on the Corinthians' behalf. This rules out the first suggestion and also excludes the second, since the enthusiasm of the Macedonians was for the welfare not of the Corinthians but of the church in

---

[254] There is a textual variant here. Some witnesses (𝔓46 D F G L 6. 323. 326. 1241. 2495 al lat bo Ambst) read δόντι, followed by the N-A text and preferred by Furnish, p. 421. Others (ℵ B C Ivid Ψ 0243 𝔐 sa) have the present participle διδόντι, preferred by, e.g., Meyer, p. 340; Windisch p. 261; Prümm, *Diakonia Pneumatos* I, p. 525; Martin, p. 271; Wolff, p. 174 n. 76. The present participle is the more difficult reading (Prümm, Windisch, Wolff), since its result is described in the two aorists (in v. 17) ἐδέξατο and ἐξῆλθεν (Windisch). Hence, the aorist δόντι could easily be explained as a scribal correction to amend this odd sequence of tenses. (Windisch; cf. Wolff). Alternatively it could have arisen from a scribal error in which a scribe's eye passed from the first to the second Δ of ΔΙΔΟΝΤΙ. The reverse change, from δόντι to διδόντι, is less easy to account for.

[255] *Pace* Windisch, pp. 260–1, who suggests that Titus's zeal was a surprise to Paul, who concluded that it was only to divine grace that it could be due. Windisch supposes that when Titus visited Corinth on the occasion to which chap. 7 refers there had not been much enthusiasm for the collection, and that he might have been reluctant to return in connection with it.

[256] See above, pp. 540–2.

[257] Betz, p. 70, suggests this.

[258] Also suggested by Betz, ibid.; this interpretation is supported by Windisch, p. 261.

Jerusalem. The comparison, then must be with Paul's own zeal for his readers' wellbeing, despite the fact that there has been no explicit mention of it.[259] Betz notes that σπουδή 'is commonly found in Hellenistic administrative letters as the most important qualification of the administrator'.[260] This is interesting in relation to the commendation of Titus.[261] But since the word has been used already (vv. 7, 8) with quite different points of reference, the fact may not have much significance.

17. ὅτι τὴν μὲν παράκλησιν ἐδέξατο, σπουδαιότερος δὲ ὑπάρχων αὐθαίρετος ἐξῆλθεν πρὸς ὑμᾶς. Paul amplifies what he has said about Titus's eagerness.[262] He acceded to Paul's request, and also showed spontaneous keenness for the task referred to in v.6. Barrett sees the use of παράκλησις as a significant indication of the apostle's relationship with his associates. He is their leader, but a leader who makes requests rather than giving orders.[263] But this is, of course, inherent in the situation. Paul does not employ his assistants for wages, as far as we know, nor are they, in legal terms, his slaves. They co-operate with him because of personal attachment, or because of their devotion to the Christian mission, or perhaps on both counts. Nevertheless, it must say something for his style of leadership that people like Titus stayed with him. Betz, rather differently, claims that the reference in τὴν ... παράκλησιν ἐδέξατο is to the acceptance of a 'legal mandate'. The 'mandate' was an institution in Greek and Roman law whereby someone was commissioned by 'a binding declaration' to perform some item of business on another's behalf. A contract was drawn up noting the specific provisions of the commission. Chapter 8 of 2 Cor is the document which contains Paul's contract with Titus, and he is using technical language when he says that Titus accepted his παράκλησις[264] It is doubtful,

---

[259] This is the majority view: see, e.g., Rückert, p. 256; Meyer, p. 359; Bachmann, p. 321; Plummer, p. 247; Lietzmann, p. 135; Barrett, p. 227; Wolff, p. 176; Martin, p. 273. Furnish, p. 421, also supports it, whilst allowing that Paul may refer to the Macedonians, and also suggesting comparison with the Corinthians' zeal for Paul himself.

[260] Betz, p. 70.

[261] Betz, ibid., claims also that the reason Titus is mentioned here as though there had been no previous reference to him in v. 6 is that a formal commendation requires that he be so mentioned. See n. 252 for references to Graeco-Roman documents containing commendations of envoys. It is by no means clear, however, that there is anything unusual in the reference to Titus here. The immediately preceding paragraph has been concerned with the Corinthians. How else could Paul have made the transition to the topic of the present section without mentioning Titus by name?

[262] The ὅτι is causal: so Barrett, p. 217; Furnish, p. 420; Martin, p. 271.

[263] Barrett, p. 228.

[264] Betz, pp. 70–1. The document, he says (p. 71), 'is identical with chapter 8'.

however, whether there is sufficient warrant in the text for this interpretation.[265] Titus is commended as σπουδαιότερος. Does this mean 'more zealous', as in v. 22? If so, 'more zealous' than whom, or what? More zealous than Paul himself?[266] Or more so than Paul had hoped?[267] Neither suggestion is wholly satisfactory, since the σπουδαιότερος δέ of v. 17b is set in contrast with the τὴν μὲν παράκλησιν ἐδέξατο of v. 17a, so that the contrast is not between Titus and some attitude on Paul's part but between two degrees of response on Titus's own part. The alternative is to suppose that the comparative σπουδαιότερος is used in an elative sense, as though it were the superlative form, 'very zealous'.[268] This may be right. But since the same word in v. 22 is clearly comparative, it might be desirable to give some comparative force to it in the present verse as well. The sense might be: 'more enthusiastic than the mere acceptance of a request implies'.

This is further described as acting (or about to act) αὐθαίρετος, 'of his own accord'. But how could he visit Corinth both of his own accord and in response to Paul's request?[269] One suggestion is that Titus has already left for Corinth, whilst Paul himself had not required that he should take up this fresh mission with such instantaneous zeal.[270] But it is most unlikely that he has already started on his journey. Alternatively, the meaning is that the request was unnecessary: 'Titus was already anxious to go.'[271] This is a better explanation. The idea that Titus has already left for Corinth at the time of writing derives from the aorist tense of the verb ἐξῆλθεν. If this is understood as a true aorist, it could mean that the delegation is already in Corinth and that they have begun to fulfil their mission.[272] But it would surely be an extraordinary procedure on Paul's part to send a letter commending his envoys, not with the delegation but at some later stage when they had already arrived. If the letter was necessary, they would need to

---

[265] First, chap. 8 is not simply the record of a mandate given by Paul to Titus: it is primarily an appeal to the Corinthians to renew their collection activity. Secondly, Betz provides no explicit citation of the Greek terminology employed in such mandates. In consequence, no clear comparison is possible. Thirdly, in discussing v. 4, we have accepted the claim that Paul uses the technical vocabulary of petition (see above, p. 525). On the face of it, the making of a petition is not the same as the bestowal of a mandate.

[266] Bachmann, p. 322.

[267] Barrett, pp. 227–8.

[268] Windisch, p. 261; Furnish, p. 422, with reference to BDF 244(2) and MHT p. 30.

[269] Cf. Barrett, p. 228.

[270] Bachmann, p. 322; Wendland, p. 221; Allo, p. 223.

[271] Barrett, p. 228.

[272] Allo, p. 223.

have it with them on arrival. The aorist is epistolary,[273] referring to what will have happened by the time the letter is read in Corinth.

18. συνεπέμψαμεν δὲ μετ' αὐτοῦ τὸν ἀδελφὸν οὗ ὁ ἔπαινος ἐν τῷ εὐαγγελίῳ διὰ πασῶν τῶν ἐκκλησιῶν, With the use of a further epistolary aorist συνεπέμψαμεν[274] Paul begins his introduction of the first of Titus's companions. The choice of verb may be significant. He has 'requested' Titus to undertake this mission, but he 'sends' this 'brother'. The suggestion may be that this person is in a more subordinate position by comparison with Titus.[275] Does the designation ὁ ἀδελφός indicate that he has a specific function as a missionary or as a church worker of some other, particular, kind?[276] The following description would fit this interpretation.[277] But if, for some reason, Paul does not wish to name him,[278] to call him 'the (Christian) brother' in a general sense would be the simplest form of reference.

This man is the object of praise. In what respect, and in how wide an area? The phrase ἐν τῷ εὐαγγελίῳ has had various interpretations. It means 'in the sphere of [279] the gospel', but that in itself is ambiguous. It seems that in the early centuries some took εὐαγγέλιον to mean 'written gospel'. Chrysostom, whilst not himself preferring this view, refers to some who identify the ἀδελφός as Luke because of the gospel he wrote.[280] This interpretation cannot be correct. It is not probable that any written gospel was already in existence.[281] In any case, there is no evidence that the word εὐαγγέλιον was used to refer to any such written

---

[273] Meyer, p. 360; Plummer, p. 247; Tasker, p. 119; Furnish, p. 422.

[274] Wolff, p. 177; Martin, p. 274.

[275] Windisch, p. 263.

[276] So Ellis, *Prophecy*, p. 15 and n. 55.

[277] So would the use of the definite article, although this is in any case natural in view of the following relative clause.

[278] See below, pp. 558–9.

[279] For ἐν with this sense see MHT, p. 262.

[280] Chrysostom, *PG* 61 cols. 523–4 (NPNF XII, pp. 363–4). See also Wordsworth, pp. 169–70, who argues in favour of this view.

[281] The point is made by Grotius, p. 490, with reference to the Gospel of Luke. He thinks Luke could be the ἀδελφός, but it is not on account of his book that he is praised, since at that time it was not yet published. Denney, p. 276, makes the same comment. See further Estius, p. 616. Paul is speaking of a preached gospel. And it is not certain that the Gospel of Luke was written before 2 Corinthians. Acts (not written until after Paul's two-year stay in Rome) seems to follow immediately upon the Gospel as its second volume. Wordsworth, p. 170, is compelled to argue for an early date for Acts (no later than 63 C.E.). He claims, p. 169, that this brother's praise could scarcely have spread through all the churches as a result of his oral teaching alone. But this is to take a modern view of the rapidity of circulation of published works.

document at this early stage.²⁸² It is possible that Paul has in view Christian service in a broad sense.²⁸³ Probably, however, he is referring more specifically to the preaching of the gospel.²⁸⁴ Out of the five other Pauline examples of ἐν τῷ εὐαγγελίῳ, four (Rom 1.9; 1 Cor 9.18; 2 Cor 10.14; 1 Th 3.2) have this reference, and the fifth (Phil 4.3) would allow it. As famed for his preaching, this man may have been chosen to emphasise the fact that the collection was integrally related to the gospel itself.²⁸⁵ Alternatively, or in addition, he might have been selected for his skill in persuasion. The first reason one might ascribe to Paul. But this person is primarily a church delegate, as v. 19 shows, so that the second consideration might have had more weight. It is clear, however, from what follows that his main function was to guarantee the financial integrity of the whole project. In that case it would have been his own moral probity that was the chief factor in his appointment. Betz suggests that Paul could be speaking ironically when he refers to the man's high reputation, since in the apostle's view it is only the praise that comes from God that counts for anything (Rom 2.29; 1 Cor 4.5).²⁸⁶ But Paul presumably wanted this delegation to succeed in their mission to Corinth, and, if so, he must surely have intended that his commendation should be taken seriously. This aim would not have been achieved by his speaking ironically. It is likely, however, that he does exaggerate somewhat when he says that this delegate is praised throughout all the Christian congregations.²⁸⁷ Which, then, does he have in mind? The appointing churches (v. 19) will, of course, be included, but their identification is a matter of debate.²⁸⁸ Perhaps Paul simply knows that the man has been active as an evangelist in other areas as well, and supposes that the churches in these areas will have an equally high opinion of him.

19. οὐ μόνον δὲ ἀλλὰ καὶ χειροτονηθεὶς ὑπὸ τῶν ἐκκλησιῶν συνέκδημος ἡμῶν σὺν τῇ χάριτι ταύτῃ τῇ διακονουμένῃ ὑφ' ἡμῶν πρὸς τὴν [αὐτοῦ] τοῦ κυρίου δόξαν καὶ προθυμίαν ἡμῶν, This brother has been elected²⁸⁹ by the churches as Paul's

---

²⁸² See BAGD s.v. εὐαγγέλιον 3. and 4. The meaning 'written gospel' occurs in Justin, *Apol.* I 66; *PG* 6 col. 429 (mid-second century) and in *Diognetus* 11.6 (second or third century). The transition to this sense is reflected in 2 Cl 8.5 (mid-second century), where 'the Lord says in the gospel' is followed by an exact quotation of Lk 16.10a. See also Martin, p. 274.

²⁸³ Barrett, p. 228; Furnish, p. 422; Martin, p. 274.

²⁸⁴ So Chrysostom, *PG* 61 col. 524 (NPNF XII, p. 364); Lang, p. 321; Wolff, p. 177.

²⁸⁵ Wolff, p. 177, with reference (n. 97) to Georgi, *Kollekte*, pp. 54–5.

²⁸⁶ Betz, p. 74.

²⁸⁷ Windisch, p. 262.

²⁸⁸ See below, pp. 559–61.

²⁸⁹ On the sentence construction, see BDF 468(1). We have here an example of

travelling companion for the purpose of the collection. Since the apostle is not, at this moment, about to go to Corinth, it looks as though he has in mind the final journey with the collection to Jerusalem. If so, the appointment post-dates 1 Corinthians, since in 1 Cor 16.3–4 he is uncertain whether he himself will travel to Jerusalem with the proceeds. The election may well have been a comparatively formal process, in line with customary Greek democratic procedures.[290] Betz sees this as standing in some contradiction to Paul's belief in his own apostolic authority, and suggests that he endorsed the process in this instance because he may have been advised that it might be risky to entrust the task to Titus alone.[291] In fact, whether or not he felt there to be a contradiction, he has shown already in this letter (7.2) that he is aware of the need to defend himself against the suspicion of fraud. He may have initiated the election process himself.[292] The identity of the electing churches is uncertain: the more likely possibilities are the congregations of Asia or Macedonia, or both.[293]

The collection, in process of organisation by Paul, is again termed χάρις (as in v. 7), perhaps with reference to the actual gift[294] and in respect of its conveyance to Jerusalem. Its arrangements, here especially the election of Paul's travelling companion, will result in[295] the glory of the Lord himself,[296] since the whole enterprise is the product of divine grace. This is straightforward. It is the final phrase, καὶ προθυμίαν ἡμῶν, that is debatable. The προθυμίαν ἡμῶν is dependent on the preceding πρός, but in this

---

Paul's fondness for continuing a construction begun with a finite verb (here, συνεπέμψαμεν in v. 18) with a participle (here, χειροτονηθείς, which the sense requires to be related to the preceding τὸν ἀδελφόν), which does duty as a second finite verb.

[290] On χειροτονέω see BAGD s.v.: see also, e.g., Bachmann, p. 323; Windisch, p. 263; Betz, pp. 74–5 (see p. 75 nn. 289, 290, for references to procedures in the Greek *polis* and in religious organisations).

[291] Betz, p. 75.

[292] *Pace* Betz, p. 73.

[293] See below, pp. 559–61.

[294] The preposition preceding τῇ χάριτι is textually uncertain. Some witnesses (𝔓⁴⁶ ℵ D F G Ψ 𝔐 a b p) read σύν (B C P 0225. 0243. 6. 33. 81. 104. 365. 630. 1175. 1739. 1881. 2464 *al* f vg co Ambst) have ἐν. Whilst σύν could be an assimilation to the συνέκδημος, it is the more difficult reading, since it is the less usual preposition. See Metzger, *Textual Commentary*¹, pp. 581–2, where σύν is the preferred reading of the majority of the Committee. On σύν with things, see BAGD s.v. 4.a.

[295] On πρός as indicating result, see BAGD s.v. III.3.b.

[296] There is a variant following τήν. Some witnesses (ℵ D¹ Ψ 𝔐 sy [𝔓⁴⁶ 33]) read αὐτοῦ, others (P 0243. 630. 1739. 1881 *pc* vgᵐˢ) have αὐτήν, yet others (B C D* F G L 81. 104. 326. 365. 629. 1175. 2464 *al* lat co Ambst) omit the pronoun. The reading αὐτήν, weakly attested and most likely due to assimilation to the preceding τήν, can be discounted. The omission of the pronoun has good support, but why would it then have been inserted? The reading αὐτοῦ is probably correct.

instance the force of the preposition is uncertain. There are two possibilities. The first is that πρός means 'in accordance with'.[297] The appointment of this delegate has been in accordance with Paul's own willingness that it should be made.[298] The difficulty is that when a single preposition is followed by two dependent nouns, one would expect it to have the same force in both cases. The second (more likely) possibility is that πρός expresses result in the case of this second noun as well.[299] The result of the appointment has been an increase in Paul's own eagerness for the project. Perhaps he has been freed from anxiety lest his motives might be mistrusted,[300] or the prospects for the success of the enterprise have been increased on account of this extra assistance.[301]

20. στελλόμενοι τοῦτο, μή τις ἡμᾶς μωμήσηται ἐν τῇ ἁδρότητι ταύτῃ τῇ διακονουμένῃ ὑφ' ἡμῶν· The general sense is clear. The dispatch[302] of this envoy was intended to prevent or avert adverse criticism of Paul himself in the matter of the collection. What is in doubt is the precise sense of στελλόμενοι. There are three possibilities.[303]

(i) στέλλομαι means 'avoid', 'try to avoid', 'keep away from': it is used in this last sense in 2 Th 3.6 (στέλλεσθαι ὑμᾶς ἀπὸ παντὸς ἀδελφοῦ ἀτάκτως περιπατοῦντος).[304] One might expect, however, that the verb would then be followed by an ἀπό-phrase.[305]

(ii) Perhaps στέλλομαι, here, is the equivalent of φοβοῦμαι,

---

[297] BAGD s.v. πρός III.5.d.
[298] Bachmann, p. 324; Lietzmann, p. 137; Barrett, pp. 217, 229.
[299] Plummer, p. 249.
[300] Cf. Meyer, p. 363, although he takes πρός as expressing purpose rather than result.
[301] Plummer, p. 249.
[302] With Plummer, p. 249, and Windisch, p. 264, we take it that στελλόμενοι is related grammatically to συνεπέμψαμεν in v. 18.
[303] See Wettstein, pp. 198–9, Wordsworth, p. 170, and Hughes, p. 318 n. 46, for a fourth suggestion. This is that the participle is a naval metaphor in which the shortening of sails to avoid danger becomes a figure for a general taking of precautions. See LSJ s.v. στέλλω IV. for the verb (active and middle) as a nautical term; the middle can be used absolutely, with ἱστία ('sails') to be understood. There is no indication, however, that any metaphorical use emerged. This would be plausible in the present instance only if there were to be no other possible interpretation.
[304] Chrysostom, PG 61 col. 325 (NPNF XII, p. 364); Meyer, p. 364; BAGD s.v. στέλλω 2.
[305] Héring, p. 71 (with reference to 2 Th 3.6). One would expect ἀπὸ τούτου instead of τοῦτο. But in any case, if the demonstrative points forward ('this, i.e.') it has to receive its content from the following μή-clause, and there does not seem to be any other Pauline example of this construction. One would more naturally expect: στελλόμενοι τοῦτο (ἀπὸ τούτου), τὸ (τοῦ) τινα ἡμᾶς μωμᾶσθαι. If the τοῦτο points backwards ('avoiding this difficulty just mentioned'), there would be no problem with the μή-clause, but what would the demonstrative pronoun refer to?

'fear'.[306] There is a verse in Malachi where the two verbs stand parallel: καὶ ἔδωκα αὐτῷ ἐν φόβῳ φοβεῖσθαί με, καὶ ἀπὸ προσώπου ὀνόματος μου στέλλεσθαι αὐτόν (Mal 2.5).[307] This would be somewhat easier grammatically, but not wholly satisfactory.[308] Moreover it is not clear that the two verbs in Malachi do have equivalent meanings.[309] And would it have been appropriate for Paul to speak of fear? The general tone is one of confidence.

(iii) The meaning of στέλλομαι is 'prepare', 'organise'.[310] In classical Greek the initial sense of the active verb is 'make ready',[311] and in NT Greek it happens not infrequently that the middle voice of a verb is found instead of the active.[312] In fact in the LXX there is one clear instance of στέλλομαι with the sense 'prepare': πλοῦν τις πάλιν στελλόμενος (Wisd 14.1). Giving a further example to prove his case, the writer refers to someone 'getting ready to sail'.[313] This interpretation is the best option. The τοῦτο, as the direct object of στελλόμενοι, refers back to the appointment and dispatch of the envoys, and the μή-clause expresses the precautionary reason for the procedure, 'lest'.

The need to forestall criticism by the appointment of independent witnesses to Paul's financial integrity and that of Titus may have arisen for two reasons. First, Betz notes that the apostle had to distinguish himself from the great number of 'religious charlatans' abroad in the Mediterranean world who solicited money for good causes and then embezzled it: see 1 Th 2.3-12.[314] Secondly, because he had refused financial maintenance whilst working in Corinth, he was peculiarly vulnerable to the suspicion that the collection was a means whereby he intended to enrich himself, directly or via such associates as Titus (cf. 12.16-18[315]). He refers to the project here as ἁδρότης 'abundance'. The word is hapax legomenon in biblical Greek, and may be intended both as a compliment to the

---

[306] Windisch, p. 265; Hesychius, cited by Wettstein, p. 198; Betz, p. 76 n. 297; BAGD s.v. στέλλω 2.

[307] Windisch, p. 265; BAGD ibid. A fairly literal translation would run: 'And I granted him to reverence me with fear, and to shrink in awe from the presence of my name.'

[308] The μή-clause follows more naturally after a verb of fearing, but an ἀπό-phrase (present in Mal 2.5) is lacking.

[309] See K. Rengstorf, on στέλλω, in TWNT VII, p. 589.

[310] Héring, p. 71; Martin, p. 276; Furnish, p. 423; Rengstorf, on στέλλω, p. 590.

[311] LSJ s.v. στέλλω I.1.

[312] MHT, pp. 54-6.

[313] Noted by Rengstorf, on στέλλω, p. 589. See also Wisd 7.14, where Rengstorf, ibid., sees a further example of the sense 'prepare'.

[314] Betz, p. 76.

[315] Cf. Windisch, p. 265. We take these verses to refer to Titus's first visit to Corinth: see below, p. 854.

prospective givers in Corinth and also as an encouragement to them to give generously in actual fact.[316]

21. προνοοῦμεν γὰρ[317] καλὰ οὐ μόνον ἐνώπιον κυρίου[318] ἀλλὰ καὶ ἐνώπιον ἀνθρώπων. Paul's words are an adaptation and an expansion of Prov 3 (LXX).4: προνοοῦ καλὰ ἐνώπιον κυρίου καὶ ἀνθρώπων ('Take thought for what is good in the sight of the Lord and of men').[319] The added οὐ μόνον ἀλλὰ καί emphasises, for obvious reasons, the need for conduct to be seen to be honourable by one's fellow men and women as well as by the Lord.[320] The collection arrangements will secure that this is so in Paul's case

22. συνεπέμψαμεν δὲ αὐτοῖς τὸν ἀδελφὸν ἡμῶν ὃν ἐδοκιμάσαμεν ἐν πολλοῖς πολλάκις σπουδαῖον ὄντα, νυνὶ δὲ πολὺ[321] σπουδαιότερον πεποιθήσει[322] πολλῇ τῇ εἰς ὑμᾶς. This second ἀδελφός has been more closely associated with Paul than the first,[323] and the ἡμῶν may suggest that it was Paul who nominated him.[324] Whilst the apostle has frequently found him a keen associate,[325] he is now even keener in respect of this mission to Corinth, by reason of his considerable trust[326] in the Corinthians. Does this imply that he had visited Corinth before?[327] Not necessarily. His enthusiasm and confidence may have been kindled by Titus's account of the church there (7.13b–15).[328] At the same time, the reference to his confidence in the congregation would make even better sense, had he already made their acquaintance at some earlier time.[329] The question as

[316] Hughes, pp. 318–19 n. 47.

[317] The reading προνοοῦμεν γάρ (𝔓46 ℵ B D F G P 0243. 6. 630. 1175. 1739. 1881 pc latt) is the original. The secondary προνοούμενοι γάρ (C 0225. 33. 81. 326. 2495 pc) is probably an assimilation to the participle at the beginning of v. 20, and would then in other witnesses (Ψ 𝔐) produce the omission of γάρ as superfluous.

[318] A few witnesses (𝔓46 (pc) lat syP Ambst) read τοῦ θεοῦ instead of κυρίου, perhaps because θεός seemed the more natural counterpart to ἄνθρωποι.

[319] Cf. Rom 12.17.

[320] Cf. Furnish, p. 424, who notes that it is the second phrase that carries the emphasis. Wolff, p. 178, deduces from the allusion to Prov 3.4 and from Paul's use of ἐνώπιον in assertions about God (Rom 3.20; 14.22; 1 Cor 1.29; 2 Cor 4.2; 7.12; Gal 1.20) that κυρίου refers to God. This could be correct.

[321] 𝔓46 appears to omit πολύ, presumably in error.

[322] B adds δέ after πεποιθήσει, but the latter word is probably causally attached to σπουδαιότερον rather than forming the beginning of a new phrase.

[323] Allo, p. 227; cf. Windisch, p. 266.

[324] Betz, p. 78.

[325] For the construction with δοκιμάζω see BDR 416(2), and for the use of ἀδελφός in the sense 'colleague' 'associate', see LSJ s.v. I.3.

[326] The dative πεποιθήσει will be a dative of cause: see BDR 196.

[327] Klöpper, p. 394, thinks this is the most natural explanation; cf. Allo, p. 227; Wendland, p. 221.

[328] Windisch, p. 266; Wolff, p. 179.

[329] Had he, perhaps, accompanied Titus on the earlier visit to which Paul refers in 12.18?

to why, if this is so, Paul does not name him will be considered below.

23. εἴτε ὑπὲρ Τίτου, κοινωνὸς ἐμὸς καὶ εἰς ὑμᾶς συνεργός· εἴτε ἀδελφοὶ ἡμῶν, ἀπόστολοι ἐκκλησιῶν, δόξα Χριστοῦ. Paul summarises the basic credentials of his three envoys, distinguishing somewhat between Titus, who is named and described in a separate clause, and the other two, who remain anonymous and are grouped together.[330] Betz claims that the use of the preposition ὑπέρ also serves to distinguish Titus from the others. It is usually understood to mean simply 'with reference to', 'concerning'.[331] Betz, however, gives it a more specialised interpretation. It is used frequently, he observes, in legal, administrative and business contexts, with reference to 'a legal statement on someone's behalf', to denote 'the act of authorized representation'. Hence, in the present verse, Paul makes 'an official statement on behalf of Titus, authorising him to be his legal and administrative representative'.[332] Perhaps so. But the examples Betz actually cites do not appear to substantiate his interpretation. In these instances, ὑπέρ is followed by the name of the person who authorises, not by that of the one who is authorised. Nevertheless, Titus is differentiated from the other two envoys by virtue of the description of him as Paul's 'partner', κοινωνός,[333] and as his 'fellow-worker', συνεργός[334] Whilst both terms were in general use,[335] the second is of special interest, in that in the NT, with implicit reference to another person,[336] it is exclusively Pauline, and appears to be something of a technical term. The συνεργός is someone who works in the common task of missionary preaching, as one who is himself directly commissioned by God.[337] The other two delegates are Paul's

[330] The construction is elliptical, since a verb needs to be supplied following each εἴτε (Perhaps ἐπιζητεῖ τις, 'anyone should inquire'). The use of εἴτε … εἴτε ('if … if', or 'whether … or') without a finite verb is classical, however: see BDF 446. In the second clause here one would expect ὑπὲρ ἀδελφῶν ἡμῶν, to match the phrase in the first clause. The nominative ἀδελφοί is presumably an assimilation to the preceding κοινωνός and συνεργός.
[331] BAGD s.v. ὑπέρ 1f.: ὑπέρ acts as the equivalent of περί.
[332] Betz, pp. 79–80.
[333] Wolff, p. 179. Furnish, p. 437, comments that the use of the singular pronoun ἐμός 'suggests that Titus was especially esteemed by Paul, and regarded as a particularly valuable associate'.
[334] On the preceding εἰς ὑμᾶς see BAGD s.v. συνεργός: the εἰς indicates 'the field in which the coöperation took place'. The present phrase is translated 'fellow-worker among you'.
[335] See LSJ svv. See also BAGD s.v. κοινωνός 1.d. and b.α. for the combination of the two terms in Plutarch: see *Mor.* 45E; 819C.
[336] Outside the Pauline corpus, the word occurs once only, in 3 Jn 8: συνεργοὶ … τῇ ἀληθείᾳ ('fellow-workers with the truth').
[337] Ollrog, *Mitarbeiter*, pp. 67–9.

colleagues, ἀδελφοὶ ἡμῶν,[338] and in one sense they travel to Corinth at his behest (vv. 18, 22). But their primary function is to act as delegates of the contributing churches,[339] to guarantee the integrity of the collection proceedings (see v. 20). They are further designated ἀπόστολοι, but they are to be distinguished from 'apostles of Christ' (such as Paul himself and the Jerusalem apostles). These people are church delegates who attend to a task which is limited in content and which lasts for only a limited period of time. There is another example of this type of apostle in Phil 2.25, where Epaphroditus, who has brought a gift to Paul from the Philippian church, is described as ὑμῶν ... ἀπόστολον.[340] They are not representatives of a central authority. Hence, there is no connection with the later Jewish institution whereby the central authorities sent out emissaries to the Diaspora, even if there may be some small degree of evidence that the system was in operation before 70 C.E. In any case, there is no warrant for supposing that the Greek word ἀπόστολοι was applied to them.[341] Moreover, in the period prior to 70 C.E. the bearers of the Temple tax to Jerusalem were called by Philo ἱεροπομποί,[342] not ἀπόστολοι. The simplest explanation of the word in the present context is that it derives from the occasional (though infrequent) use of ἀπόστολος in Greek sources in the sense 'emissary'.[343]

These delegates are finally described as δόξα Χριστοῦ. Some commentators take the phrase in a deeply theological sense. The two men reflect the glory of Christ,[344] or, they come as bearers of the authority of Christ.[345] They are, in fact, apostles of Christ, who has himself commissioned them so that they will belong to the

---

[338] Ellis, *Prophecy*, p. 14 and n. 47, includes this reference as an instance of what he claims is the specialised use of 'the brothers' for a particular group of church workers. The presence of the article, he maintains, p. 15 n. 54 (with reference to p. 21 n. 81), is not essential to this meaning of the term. But would Paul have had his own group (ἡμῶν) of such people? And if he did have, would they have been appointed, as here, as church delegates? (In the sense, 'our brother Christians [already mentioned]' the phrase does not have the implication of possession which attaches to 'our group of specialised church workers'.)

[339] *Pace* Nickle, *Collection*, pp. 18–22, and Holmberg, *Paul and Power*, p. 47, it is highly unlikely that they were, instead, agents of the Judaean churches. As Martin, p. 279, points out, Paul was by no means certain whether the Jerusalem church would accept the offering (Rom 15.31).

[340] Hahn, 'Apostolat', p. 56.

[341] On the dating and nomenclature of the Jewish institution see Barrett, 'Shaliaḥ', pp. 95–7.

[342] Schmithals, *Office of Apostle*, p. 102 and n. 32, with reference to Philo, *Leg. Gai.* 216; *Spec. Leg.* I 77–8; cf. Furnish, p. 425, who cites the latter reference (as I 78).

[343] Schmithals, *Office of Apostle*, pp. 97–8; see also BAGD s.v. ἀπόστολος.

[344] Bachmann, p. 326.

[345] Windisch, p. 267, suggests this interpretation as a possibility.

wider apostolic circle to which Paul refers in 1 Cor 15.7. The claim that they are 'Christ's glory' corresponds with the description in chap. 3 of the glory of the apostolic office.[346] This is improbable. Persons of this stature would not be subordinated to Titus, who was not an apostle,[347] nor would they be designated apostles of churches. Betz offers a different suggestion. He observes that the motif of glory was connected in the hellenistic world with the sending and reception of envoys, and supposes that Paul's expression may owe something to this diplomatic terminology. His envoys will represent 'a kind of glory ... consistent with that of Christ'. As in the relevant hellenistic contexts the expression is vague, but will presumably relate to 'the brothers' appearance, conduct, and speech, as well as to their privileges as guests in Corinth'.[348] But would Paul want to stress in this way what would be, in effect, a personal splendour attaching to the delegates? And in any case, how would this fit in with Betz's other claim that in some sense he is down-grading them?[349] It is more likely that the sense of the phrase δόξα Χριστοῦ is 'promoting the glory of Christ'.[350] That Paul could sometimes use δόξα followed by a genitive in the sense 'promote the glory of' is shown in 1 Th 2.20: ὑμεῖς γάρ ἐστε ἡ δόξα ἡμῶν. Participation in the administration of the collection promotes the glory of Christ because the whole enterprise is the work of divine grace (cf. v. 19).

24. τὴν οὖν ἔνδειξιν τῆς ἀγάπης ὑμῶν καὶ ἡμῶν καυχήσεως ὑπὲρ ὑμῶν εἰς αὐτοὺς ἐνδεικνύμενοι[351] εἰς πρόσωπον τῶν ἐκκλησιῶν. Having concluded this very lengthy commendation of the delegates he is sending to Corinth, Paul ends with an exhortation. Before we note its contents, we need to pay some attention to its grammatical form. It is expressed by means of the participle ἐνδεικνύμενοι, used with imperatival force. This usage is noted by the grammarians,[352] with reference to such NT passages as Rom 12.9-17. There, and in similar passages of paraenesis, it may be

---

[346] Wendland, p. 222.
[347] See above, p. 547 on v. 18, and below, p. 558.
[348] Betz, pp. 81-2.
[349] See below, p. 558.
[350] So Chrysostom, PG 61 col. 526 (NPNF XII, p. 365). See also, e.g., Filson, p. 373; Héring, p. 71; Bruce, p. 225; Wolff, p. 179.
[351] The textual witnesses are divided between the participle ἐνδεικνύμενοι (B D * F G 33 pc b p vgᵐˢ) and the aorist imperative ἐνδείξασθε (ℵ C D² Ψ 0225.0243 𝔐 lat). The decisive argument in favour of the participle is that it is the more difficult reading. The verse constitutes a fresh and a complete sentence, but its sole verb is the participle, which one might more usually expect to find only in a subordinate clause. Hence, it would be susceptible to scribal alteration, whilst the reverse change would be most unlikely. See Metzger, *Textual Commentary*¹, p. 582.
[352] See, e.g., BDR 468(2); MHT, p. 343; Moule, *Idiom Book*, pp. 179-80.

attributed to Semitic influence,[353] and the present instance is likewise, on occasion, so attributed.[354] Verbrugge, however, observes that the theory of Semitic influence does not fit this particular case. Daube had pointed out that the Hebrew participle is used imperativally with reference to rules and customs,[355] but never to commands 'addressed to a specific person on a specific occasion'.[356] The latter type of context, however, is precisely what we find in 2 Cor 8.24. Consequently, we need some other explanation of the participle ἐνδεικνύμενοι. Verbrugge, who has argued that 8.24 is the conclusion of a letter consisting of chaps. 1–8, suggests that it was originally connected grammatically 'with a conventional epistolary conclusion similar to ἔρρωσθε'. The redactor of the Corinthian correspondence omitted the imperative ἔρρωσθε (or its equivalent), leaving the participle dangling, and thus required in itself to provide the imperative force grammatically, as it does in fact in content. As Verbrugge notes, this explanation provides further support for the view that one of the letters of which the canonical epistle is composed ended at this point.[357]

In this concluding exhortation Paul urges his readers to give proof both of their own Christian love and also of the validity of his boasting about them. This proof will be provided by the way they receive and treat his delegates. And it is to be given εἰς πρόσωπον τῶν ἐκκλησιῶν. Possibly this means rather more than that the delegates will eventually report back what they have seen of the Corinthians to the churches that elected them.[358] Windisch draws attention to the idea in Ignatius that whole congregations may in some way be actually present in the persons of their delegates: see Ign., Mg 2; 6.1; I Tr 1.1. There may be the same notion here.[359] Betz, rather similarly, interprets the phrase in terms of the concept of 'legal personality'. The two ἀδελφοί were the legal and political *persona* of the churches they represented. The treatment the Corinthians gave to them would be treatment directed towards the churches which had sent them.[360] The behaviour Paul here requests is not, of course, concerned with legal activity. Nevertheless, the general idea of legal personality might well be transferable to the relationship between the brothers, those who sent them, and the Corinthians who received them.

---

[353] See David Daube, in E. G. Selwyn, *The First Epistle of St Peter*, London, 1946, pp. 467–88 (cited by subsequent scholars).
[354] Furnish, p. 425; Martin, p. 272.
[355] Daube, in Selwyn, *First Peter*, pp. 474–5.
[356] Daube, in Selwyn, *First Peter*, p. 474; cited by Verbrugge, *Collection*, p. 256.
[357] See Verbrugge, *Collection*, pp. 254–8, for the discussion of the verse.
[358] *Pace* Plummer, pp. 251–2.
[359] Windisch, p. 268.
[360] Betz, pp. 85–6. The meaning 'legal personality' for πρόσωπον is given in LSJ s.v. IV.2., with reference to Diog. Laert. IV 46.

EXCURSUS VIII

The ἀδελφοί of 8.16-24

There are several questions for discussion. First, why are they not named? Secondly, what churches do they represent? Thirdly, is it possible to offer any suggestions as to their identity?

(i) Why are the 'brothers' not named?

It seems obvious, on the face of it, that one would not recommend anonymous persons.[361] Hence, commentators have felt some obligation to provide reasons for the omission of names in this instance. Plummer points out that Titus would be able to introduce the two men,[362] and suggests that, since they were not known personally in Corinth, there would be no point in naming them.[363] In reply to this, however, Furnish argues that one would not commend so well-known a person as the ἀδελφός of v. 18 in this anonymous fashion.[364] And elsewhere Paul does name those he recommends.[365] So some explanation is needed of the present anonymity of these two people. Either Paul did originally name them and the names were later deleted, or he went against his usual custom and for some reason left the ἀδελφοί anonymous.[366]

(a) If the names were originally in the text, why were they later deleted? Had these two people been involved in some unpleasant incident in Corinth?[367] If this was so, perhaps the editor of Paul's correspondence had 'followed Ignatius's practice of refusing to name certain heretics so as not to increase their notoriety'.[368] At this point the suggestion remains vague. Nickle, however, proposes a reconstruction of the situation which both leads to a specific identification of the two delegates and also explains why the Corinthians later struck their names out of Paul's letter. The two ἀδελφοί, he argues, were appointed

---

[361] Lietzmann, p. 136, followed by Betz, p. 73.

[362] Plummer, p. 248; cf. Barrett, p. 228.

[363] Plummer, ibid.

[364] Furnish, p. 435.

[365] Betz, p. 73 n. 276, draws attention to Rom 16.1; 1 Cor 16.10–15; he refers to Plummer, p. 248, who cites these examples. But he notes, p. 73 n. 275, that in the study by C.-H. Kim, *Greek Letter of Recommendation* (see Vol. I, p. 218 n. 218), there are four examples where no names are given.

[366] *Pace* Allo, p. 224, it is unlikely that names were not needed because the whole delegation had arrived in Corinth and started work there before the present letter was written. See above, pp. 546–7. In any case, even were the situation to have been as Allo supposes, the anonymity remains unexplained. The omission of names would be even more strange if the ἀδελφοί were already known by name to the Corinthians.

[367] Lietzmann, p. 137; cf. Windisch, p. 262.

[368] Betz, p. 73, with reference (n. 274) to Ign., Sm 5.3.

by the Jerusalem church, and two likely candidates would be Judas and Silas. These two are mentioned in Acts 15.22 as charged with the conveyance of the Apostolic Decree to Antioch. Nickle accepts their connection with the Decree and sees it as significant, but thinks that the Decree itself was not formulated until the meeting recorded in Acts 21.25. At the earlier stage of the aftermath of the conference of Acts 15, he suggests, Silas worked with Paul both in evangelising and in furthering the collection. The latter activity evoked particular hostility from Jewish communities, since it seemed to be competing with the temple tax. Consequently, Paul and Silas visited Jerusalem for further consultation (Acts 18.22). On this occasion, Silas and Judas were specifically appointed to assist in the gathering of the collection, as a means of guaranteeing that the project would not impinge upon the payment of the temple tax by those from whom this was required. These same delegates, however, were later appointed to convey the Apostolic Decree to the Pauline Gentile churches. But to the Corinthians the provisions of the Decree were particularly unwelcome. The names of its promoters, therefore, were excised from the apostolic letter.[369]

This reconstruction would certainly provide a very plausible reason for the deletion of the names of the envoys, had they been originally included. There are two difficulties, however. The first is the claim that it was the Jerusalem church that had appointed the envoys.[370] The second, admitted by Nickle himself,[371] is that the hypothesis would require the rejection of the usual identification of the Silas of Acts with the Silvanus of the Pauline letters. For in 2 Cor 8 Paul appears to be introducing people as yet unknown to the Corinthians, whereas Silvanus had taken part in the initial evangelisation of the city (2 Cor 1.19).[372] Moreover, if his name was deleted from chap. 8, why was it not deleted also at 1.19? In any case, there is no positive evidence for the deletion of the names.[373]

(b) In view of these difficulties, it may be better to suppose that it was Paul himself who, for some reason, had purposely omitted to name the two delegates. But why? Betz suggests that it was not originally Paul's own idea that these additional envoys should be appointed to accompany Titus, and that they were not his own nominees. The initiative came from the appointing churches. Paul agreed to their appointment after some negotiation and thereafter fully supported them. At the same time, he was concerned to make clear that it was Titus alone who was fully authorised as his representative. Hence, he did not name the two extra envoys so as to authorise them as individuals. He did not intend that they should have opportunity to act independently in Corinth, and consequently,

[369] Nickle, *Collection*, pp. 21–2, 55, 61–2.
[370] See below, p. 559.
[371] Nickle, *Collection*, p. 22 n. 35.
[372] It is at this point, moreover, that the Silas of Acts and the Silvanus of the Pauline letters merge into one. In Acts 18.5 we are told that Silas and Timothy joined Paul in his evangelistic work in Corinth, whilst in 2 Cor 1.19 he refers to the gospel preached in that city by Silvanus, Timothy, and himself.
[373] Betz, p. 73.

perhaps, occasion conflict.[374] Basically, this is a plausible explanation of the anonymity of the envoys. It conflicts to some degree with the implications of 8.20–21, where Paul gives the impression that the initiative was his own. But a tentative warning of suspicion, coming from one or more of the participating churches, may have been sufficient to spur him into action to organise safeguards himself, or, rather, to encourage the congregations to make such provision.

(ii) *Which were the appointing churches?*

It is improbable, *pace* Nickle,[375] that the delegates were appointed by the Jerusalem church. Furnish points out that when Paul elsewhere has the Judaean churches in view he says so: Gal 1.22; 1 Th 2.14.[376] Furthermore, it is doubtful whether he would have either instigated appointment by Jerusalem or agreed to it. To do so would give the impression that this church was demanding a kind of tax, whilst Paul himself was determined to maintain (at least in theory) the voluntary character of the collection. Lastly, it is likely that the authorities in Jerusalem were doubtful about receiving it, which would seem strange if they had actively participated in its arrangement.

What are the other possibilities? Taylor suggests that the first envoy (8.19) was nominated by the church in Antioch. If Paul's intention (originally at least) had been to organise the collection in his own churches in some sort of conjunction with the Antioch collection which was still in process, it would be quite likely that the church in Antioch would have appointed one of their own members to assist him.[377] There is no hint of any such assistant, however, in 1 Cor 16.3–4. Either Paul, at that point, saw fit to conceal the appointment of the συνέκδημος, or else the appointment had not yet taken place. But there would be little point in concealment if the man was to make his appearance in Corinth eventually. If, then, the arrangement had not yet been made, it seems somewhat unlikely on geographical grounds that the delegate was elected from the Antiochene church. Paul himself was based in Ephesus in the period following 1 Corinthians, and subsequently travelled to Troas and then to Macedonia. Seemingly, there would have been no opportunity for a visit to Antioch to make the arrangement. Paul could, of course, have communicated with Antioch through one of his aides. On the whole, however, Antioch is less likely than some other possibilities.

Because Paul was based in Ephesus during the period following

---

[374] Betz, pp. 72–4. Taylor, *Paul, Antioch and Jerusalem*, pp. 201–3, with reference to Betz, takes a similar view. The omission of the names may be due to Paul's desire to 'enhance Titus' standing and authority' (p. 201), and to prevent the other two envoys from interfering in church affairs outside the sphere of the collection.

[375] See above, p. 554 n. 339.

[376] Furnish, p. 434.

[377] Taylor, *Paul, Antioch and Jerusalem*, p. 202.

1 Corinthians it may have been the Asian churches who sponsored the delegates.[378] And since it was during this time that his relations with the Corinthian church deteriorated, it is at least probable that it was precisely then, whilst he was in Asia, that he came to realise the need for independent guarantors of his financial integrity (cf. 7.2).[379] The more usual identification of the sponsoring congregations, however, is that they are the churches of Macedonia.[380] Paul is in Macedonia when he writes the present letter, so that the conclusion is in one sense natural. Or possibly the electing churches were other than those of Macedonia but it was the Macedonians who confirmed the election.[381] These are likely possibilities, but they are rejected by Nickle, who denies any involvement of the Macedonian churches in the appointment. He points out that in 8.18 'all the churches' cannot refer only to the Macedonians. In consequence, he argues, if in 8.19 the Macedonian congregations were the appointing churches one would expect Paul to specify, as he does in 8.1. It is not clear, moreover, how 'two unknown Macedonians' would be seen by the Corinthians as guaranteeing Paul's integrity. The point, presumably, is that the Macedonian churches are Pauline foundations, and thus cannot be regarded as independent witnesses to his conduct. Lastly, the reference in 9.3–4 to the later arrival of Macedonians in Corinth makes no sense, Nickle claims, if the delegates who come with Titus are themselves Macedonians.[382] These arguments are not altogether convincing. In v. 19 the lack of specification, after the διὰ πασῶν τῶν ἐκκλησιῶν, is odd anyway, but no more odd if the churches are those of Macedonia than if they are some other Christian communities. That Paul found his guarantors only in churches of his own foundation may have been due to geographical necessity.[383] And this very fact might account for his insistence that these people are church delegates, not his private assistants. Finally, in 9.3–4 the point is not that no other Macedonians have visited Corinth (or are still in the city) but that these Macedonians, accompanying Paul himself, will bear obvious testimony to the successful conclusion of the collection in the Macedonian churches, and thus put to shame their rivals, the Corinthians, if the latter are not ready with their own contribution.

A definite conclusion is not possible. We can say, however, that, of the options discussed, the Jerusalem church and the congregations of Judaea are the least likely to have sponsored the delegates. The church of Antioch is just possible, but improbable. It is more likely that the envoys

---

[378] Allo, p. 224, who would include the Macedonians also.

[379] It is of some interest, perhaps, that in Acts 20.33–34, in the course of Paul's speech to the Ephesian elders at Miletus, the apostle protests his innocence in financial dealings as well as vindicating his conduct in general. This might reflect a recollection that the question of guaranteeing Paul's probity as regards the collection had been a matter of interest amongst the Christian communities in Asia.

[380] Rückert, p. 261; Meyer, p. 362; Bachmann, p. 322; Windisch, p. 263; F. Lang, p. 321; Furnish, p. 436, allows this is a possibility.

[381] So Georgi, *Kollekte*, p. 54.

[382] Nickle, *Collection*, pp. 19–20.

[383] See above, p. 559.

were appointed either by the churches of Asia or by those of Macedonia, or, perhaps, by the two groups in combination, whereby the election took place in the Asian congregations and was then confirmed in the Macedonian churches.

(iii) Can the delegates be identified?

There have been numerous suggestions. Most may claim some indirect support from the text of the present passage or from Acts, or from both sources, but in all cases the evidence is minimal. Sometimes it relates to only one of the ἀδελφοί, sometimes to both. The main proposals for their identification are these.

(a) The ἀδελφός of v. 18 was an actual blood-brother of Titus.[384] This is highly improbable. Paul would scarcely have sent two actual brothers to deal together with a matter of such financial delicacy.[385] Furthermore, the ἀδελφοὶ ἡμῶν of v. 23 shows that the term ἀδελφός does not, in the present context, refer to a blood relationship.[386]

(b) The delegate of vv. 18–19 is Barnabas. He shone as a preacher of the gospel, so fitting the description in v. 18, and was chosen as Paul's partner in mission, i.e., as the συνέκδημος of v. 19.[387] This identification is likewise improbable. Barnabas would not have been subordinate to Titus, as this 'brother' seems to be.[388] And he was known by name to the Corinthians (1 Cor 9.6), so why would Paul have referred to him anonymously?[389] In addition, this ἀδελφός was appointed as the apostle's travel-companion not to preach (by contrast with Barnabas, according to Acts 13.2–5), but to guarantee the probity with which the collection was administered and to assist in its safe conveyance to Jerusalem.

(c) The delegate of vv. 18–19 is Luke. This view has more support,[390] and the evidence, whether or not convincing, appears slightly more substantial. The identification depends on the traditional view that the 'we' of the 'we'-passages in Acts refers to the author of Luke-Acts, who is to be identified, further, with the Luke of Col 4.14 and Phm 24. It depends also on the (tenable) hypothesis that in Acts 20.3–6 we have a report of the departure from Greece of a group who will eventually travel with Paul to Jerusalem for the presentation of the collection. It is apparent from vv. 5–6 that the writer of the 'we'-passages is one of this

---

[384] Rückert, p. 259; Plummer, p. 248, cites Souter as supporting this view.
[385] Meyer, p. 360; cf. Hughes, p. 315; Bruce, p. 224.
[386] Cf. Meyer, p. 360.
[387] The suggestion of Chrysostom, *PG* 61 col. 524 (NPNF XII, p. 364).
[388] Rückert, p. 258; Meyer, p. 360; Hughes, p. 313. Estius, p. 616, observes that Barnabas, in view of his apostolic status, would not have been 'sent' by Paul himself.
[389] Alternatively, if the names of the delegates were later deleted, one would have expected Barnabas's name to have been deleted in 1 Cor 9.6 as well.
[390] Chrysostom, *PG* 61 col. 523 (NPNF XII, p. 363), observes that some hold this view, and Hughes, p. 312, refers to Origen, Jerome and other patristic writers who support it. Grotius, p. 490, allows it as a possibility. Amongst modern commentators we may cite Bachmann, pp. 325–6; Plummer, p. 248; and Hughes, p. 313.

group,[391] and we see from Acts 21.15, 17 that he did reach Jerusalem with Paul.[392] Here we do have a logical chain of evidence. Its basis, however, is somewhat fragile. The use of the first plural in Acts may be a literary convention rather than a pointer to authorship, and the identification of the author with the Luke of Col 4.14 is again hypothetical.

(d) It may be correct to suppose that the names of both delegates are to be found in the list in Acts 20.4. These are:

Sopater from Beroea in Macedonia
Aristarchus from Thessalonica in Macedonia
Secundus from Thessalonica in Macedonia
Gaius from Derbe in Galatia, or just beyond the frontier with Commagene[393]
(Timothy Paul's personal assistant)
Tychicus from Asia
Trophimus from Asia.

If we should agree with those exegetes noted above[394] who argue that the envoys cannot be Macedonians, we should then eliminate the first three. This would leave us with the Asians, Tychicus and Trophimus, and Gaius. Otherwise any two of the group, bar Timothy, might be identified as the ἀδελφοί. No definite decision is possible.

---

[391] Tasker, p. 120.
[392] Hughes, p. 313.
[393] On the location of Derbe, see Bruce, *Galatians*, p. 5.
[394] See above, p. 560.

3. THE COLLECTION IN CHAPTER 9

Anxiety about progress in Corinth and plea for generosity

¹For as regards the charitable service to the saints, my writing to you is superfluous. ²For I know your willingness, which I am boasting about on your behalf to the Macedonians, that is, that Achaia has been prepared since last year; and your zeal has given a stimulus to the majority of them. ³But I sent the brothers so that our boast about you in this respect should not come to nothing, so that, as I was maintaining, you would be prepared; ⁴lest perhaps, if some Macedonians should come with me and should find you unprepared, we should be put to shame—to say nothing of you¹—in respect of this project. ⁵So I thought it necessary to request the brothers to go on to you beforehand, and to make arrangements in advance for your generous gift, previously promised, so that this may be ready in such a way as to be (really) a generous gift, and not a reflection of (your own) covetousness.² ⁶The point is this. He who sows sparingly will also reap sparingly, and he who sows bountifully will also reap bountifully. ⁷Each should do as he has made up his mind³ to do, not regretfully, nor under compulsion, for 'God loves a cheerful giver.' ⁸And God is able to supply you abundantly with all grace, so that, always possessing all sufficiency in every respect, you may be prolific in every good work, ⁹as it is written:

He scattered abroad, he gave to the poor,
his righteousness lasts for ever.

¹⁰And he who provides seed for the sower and bread for food will supply and multiply your seed and will increase the products of your righteousness, ¹¹whilst you are in process of enrichment in every way for all generosity which, through our agency, is bringing about thanksgiving to God; ¹²because the administration of this service is not only supplying the wants of the saints but is also abundantly productive through multitudinous thanksgivings to God. ¹³Through the proof provided by this act of service, they will be glorifying God for the obedience consisting in your confession of the gospel of Christ, and for the genuineness of your sense of fellowship with them and with all. ¹⁴And in their prayer for you they will be longing for you because of the abundant grace of God bestowed on you. ¹⁵Thanks be to God for his indescribable gift.

Despite his opening words, Paul is more than a little apprehensive about the adequacy of the Corinthians' activity in respect of the collection. There is a further reason, it seems, for the dispatch of the envoys: they are to make sure that the Corinthian contribution is ready before Paul arrives in person. He hopes it will be a generous gift, and he encourages generosity, quoting from Scripture to reinforce his exhortations. God himself will abundantly provide the resources they require. And the final

---

¹ Cf. Furnish, p. 421, who renders the phrase: 'to say nothing of yourselves'.
² The ὡς πλεονεξίαν is very difficult: see the exegesis.
³ See BAGD s.v. προαιρέω 2.

result will be abundant thanksgiving to God from the recipients. They will glorify God, furthermore, for the proof the gift provides of the Corinthians' conversion to the gospel of Christ. **1. Περὶ μὲν γὰρ τῆς διακονίας τῆς εἰς τοὺς ἁγίους περισσόν⁴ μοί ἐστιν τὸ γράφειν ὑμῖν·** In the Introduction in Vol. I we have tentatively agreed with the view that chap. 9 is a separate letter. It will have been addressed to the same readership as the letter contained in chaps. 1–8, but will have been sent a little later.⁵ Against this view it is argued that the phrase Περὶ μὲν γάρ is never elsewhere used at the beginning of a document.⁶ We have maintained, however, that the γάρ here could well be redactional, and have observed that we do find Περὶ μέν at the beginning of a letter of Demosthenes.⁷ Whichever view is correct, Paul begins this letter or section of a letter with a rhetorical device intended to show some sensitivity to his readers' feelings.⁸ Perhaps he realises that they may be bored with the topic of the collection,⁹ or that his resumption of the subject may suggest to them that he lacks confidence in their generosity. Consequently, he appears to allow that it is unnecessary for him to write about the matter.

2. οἶδα γὰρ τὴν προθυμίαν ὑμῶν ἣν ὑπὲρ ὑμῶν καυχῶμαι Μακεδόσιν ὅτι Ἀχαΐα παρεσκεύασται ἀπὸ πέρυσι, καὶ τὸ ὑμῶν ζῆλος ἠρέθισεν τοὺς πλείονας. Paul explains why it is really unnecessary for him to write about the collection. The explanation, in terms of his readers' willingness to participate, appears simple enough, but in fact is more than a little problematic when this verse is considered in relation both to 8.10–11 and to 9.3–4. The difficulty is this. Paul says that he is boasting to the Macedonians that Achaia has been ready with its contribution 'since last year'. But how can he make this claim when in 8.10–11 he has indicated that the Corinthians, 'last year', had done little more than show willingness and make some sort of

---

⁴ 𝔓⁴⁶ g read περισσότερον for περισσόν. This must be an unconscious scribal error.

⁵ Vol. I, pp. 38–43.

⁶ See S. K. Stowers, 'Peri men gar and the Integrity of 2 Cor. 8 and 9', *NovT* 32 (1990), pp. 340–8. He points out that the only other occurrence in the NT (Acts 28.22) is not introductory in character, and that in a study of some 90 instances elsewhere he has found no example of any such introductory function.

⁷ Vol. I, pp. 42, 39. In addition, we may note that Stowers does not discuss the oddity of the full description of the διακονία nor the related point that if chap. 9 follows on from chap. 8 one would expect to find a demonstrative pronoun (τῆς διακονίας ταύτης): see Vol. I, p. 39.

⁸ Meyer, p. 370. Betz, p. 91 n. 10, notes that the rhetorical figure is a paralipsis or praeteritio: see BDF 495(1). This is a figure in which a speaker 'pretends to pass over something which he in fact mentions' (BDF ibid.).

⁹ Betz, p. 90.

a beginning?[10] The problem is scarcely eased if we regard chap. 9 as a letter separate from that of chaps. 1–8, since there would be no great lapse of time between the two items of correspondence.[11] In any case, in 9.3–4 he goes on to express the fear that his correspondents might *not*, after all, be ready with their contribution when he himself finally arrives in Corinth. Is he more or less admitting that he is not telling the Macedonians the truth? And, if so, how were his readers to know whether what he had previously said in 8.1–6 about the generosity of the Macedonians was true?[12]

Various ways of resolving the difficulty have been proposed. First, it is argued that Paul customarily presented his converts in the best possible light when speaking of them to others. Hence his optimistic picture of the Corinthian response in the present verse, i.e., the picture he was presenting to the Macedonians.[13] This may be so, but it is not an entirely satisfactory solution to the problem. To make clear contradictory statements about the Corinthian situation ἀπὸ πέρυσι, even if in two separate letters, could still look more like untruthfulness than anything else, and evoke suspicion concerning the praise of the Macedonians in 8.1–6. Secondly, stress may be laid on the term Ἀχαΐα. The letter of chap. 9, it is claimed, is not intended for Corinth but is directed to the other groups of believers in the province. The Corinthians themselves, as 8.10–11 implies, had not been ready the previous year, but these other Achaians, unaffected by the troubles in Corinth, had progressed with the collection, and it is about these people that Paul was boasting to the Macedonians.[14] We have argued, however, that the letter of chap. 9, like that of chaps. 1–8, is addressed to Corinth itself, though also to other Christians in the province.[15] Thirdly, it is suggested that the perfect tense of παρεσκεύασται does not necessarily mean that preparations are complete and that the Corinthian collection is now ready. The sense may be, 'since last year Achaia has begun preparation, and is still engaged in this activity'.[16] The difficulty here is that vv. 3–4 clearly imply that the verb in the perfect tense means 'to have

[10] The question is put by Windisch, p. 270.

[11] See the chronological outline in Vol. I, p. 77.

[12] Rückert, p. 270, and Windisch, pp. 270–1; Windisch comments that the raising of this question would scarcely have a favourable effect on the progress of the collection in Corinth.

[13] Bruce, p. 226; Barrett, pp. 233–4.

[14] Betz, pp. 91–3.

[15] Vol. I, p. 42. Wolff, p. 181 n. 120, finds Betz's view highly unlikely, since Corinth was the capital city of Achaia. Furnish, p. 431, is surely correct in suggesting that the term 'Achaia' may be used here because of the reference to the 'Macedonians'.

[16] Allo, p. 230.

completed one's preparations': see the παρεσκευασμένοι ἦτε of v. 3. Paul is not, here, expressing apprehension lest the Corinthians should not have begun their preparations. The apparent contradiction remains. None of these solutions to the difficulty is wholly satisfactory. All the same, Paul would scarcely intend to give the impression of untruthfulness. In his own mind, that is, there must have been some compatibility between what seem to us to be incompatible assertions about the state of the collection in Corinth. It is reasonable to suppose that when writing the letter which concludes with chap. 8 he was anxious lest the disruption of good relations which had evoked the Painful Letter should also have undone whatever preparations had been made in respect of the collection, hence his exhortation in 8.10-11. When he begins to write the letter of chap. 9, however, he might recall that when he initially arrived in Corinth for the Interim Visit preparations for the Corinthian contribution appeared to be well in hand, in accordance with the instructions he had given in 1 Cor 16.1-2. It is this state of affairs he now boasts of to the Macedonians. And he hopes that the unfortunate incident which marred that visit will *not* have changed the situation. Nevertheless, he cannot be sure: hence the apprehension reflected in vv. 3-4.

The apprehension will have been the more acute in that the apostle's boasting about the Corinthians has had· an encouraging result in Macedonia. Their zeal[17] has stimulated τοὺς πλείονας. The expression οἱ πλείονες, whether it means 'the majority'[18] or 'the others', 'the rest'[19] suggests that it was not all the Macedonians, who had been thus affected by Paul's description of the Corinthians. What, then, of the remainder? Perhaps these are the ones who had quite spontaneously shown enthusiasm for the collection (8.3), whilst the πλείονες had been moved to participate by what they heard of the Corinthians' zeal. Alternatively, they could be a minority who for some reason

---

[17] The brief phrase τὸ ὑμῶν ζῆλος is subject to textual variation. The gender of ζῆλος is uncertain. In some MSS(𝔓⁴⁶ ℵ B 33. 1175 *pc*) it has the neuter article τό, whilst in others (C D F G Ψ 0243 𝔐) it has the masculine ὁ. Allo, p. 230, accepts the latter reading, since ζῆλος is always masculine in classical Greek and always (he claims) elsewhere in Paul, with the possible exception of Phil 3.6: see Rom 10.2; 13.13; 2 Cor 7.7; 11.2. In Rom 13.13 and 2 Cor 11.2, however, the word is in the dative, and hence ambiguous. But if the masculine form is in general the more usual, it is also the more likely to have resulted here from a scribal correction. Another variant consists in the addition of ἐξ before ὑμῶν (D F G Ψ 0209 𝔐 vg^ms). This looks like scribal elaboration. The reading without the preposition (𝔓⁴⁶ ℵ B C P 0243. 6. 33. 81. 326. 630. 1175. 1739. 1881 *pc* lat co Ambst) is preferable.

[18] See BAGD s.v. πολύς II.2.a.α.

[19] Ibid., II.2.a.γ.

remained doubtful about the project.[20] If so, however, this need not have been due to any kind of suspicion about its purpose or about Paul's motives.[21] Some of the Macedonian Christians had already assisted Paul financially (11.8–9). Perhaps they simply felt that they could not do more.

3. ἔπεμψα δὲ τοὺς ἀδελφούς, ἵνα μὴ τὸ καύχημα ἡμῶν τὸ ὑπὲρ ὑμῶν κενωθῇ ἐν τῷ μέρει τούτῳ, ἵνα καθὼς ἔλεγον παρεσκευασμένοι ἦτε, The opening δέ serves to correlate vv. 3–4 with vv. 1–2, introduced by μέν, and to indicate that Paul is now putting the other side of the picture. On the one hand (μέν in v. 1), he does not need to go on writing about the collection, being aware of the keenness his readers have shown, but on the other hand (δέ in v. 3) he sent[22] the envoys in advance of his own arrival to make sure that everything would be in order. The envoys are collectively termed 'the brothers', i.e., 'the colleagues'. It is natural to suppose that Titus is included in the term, even though it is not applied to him in chap. 8.[23] (Paul does, however, refer to him as his ἀδελφός in 2.13.) Clearly Paul was worried lest one of his major churches should fail him in the matter of[24] the collection. But he does at least attempt to express his anxiety in a form complimentary, to some degree, to his readers. He fears lest his *praise* of them should lose its justification,[25] and implies by the use of the imperfect ἔλεγον that the praise was reiterated.[26]

4. μή πως ἐὰν ἔλθωσιν σὺν ἐμοὶ Μακεδόνες καὶ εὕρωσιν ὑμᾶς ἀπαρασκευάστους καταισχυνθῶμεν ἡμεῖς, ἵνα μὴ λέγω ὑμεῖς, ἐν τῇ ὑποστάσει ταύτῃ. He also expresses the content of his fear in a tentative manner: 'lest perhaps, if ...'[27] There is just this remote possibility, he suggests, that his Macedonian companions might arrive with him only to witness the unprepared state of the Corinthians. We may presume that these Macedonians will bring with them the Macedonian contribution to the

---

[20] So Betz, p. 93, who suggests that it was these people who insisted on the sending to Corinth of the church representative to whom Paul refers in 8.18–21.

[21] *Pace* Betz, p. 93.

[22] If chap. 9 is a separate letter, the aorist is not epistolary here.

[23] Bruce, p. 226, and Barrett, p. 234, think that all the three people mentioned in 8.6, 16–24 are in view here. Bachmann, p. 328, argues that Titus is not included, since he went to Corinth as a result of his own decision (8.17), and so was not 'sent' by Paul. Windisch, p. 271, points out, however, that the prefix σύν in the συνεπέμψαμεν of 8.18 implies that πέμπω can be loosely applied to Titus. Betz, p. 93, excludes Titus, noting, p. 94, that in 12.18 he is mentioned by name (which, presumably, one would expect here also). But this is another letter, referring (probably) to a different occasion.

[24] The phrase ἐν τῷ μέρει τούτῳ means 'in this case', 'in this matter'. See BAGD s.v. μέρος 1.b.θ.

[25] On this sense of κενωθῇ see BAGD s.v. κενόω 3.

[26] Cf. Filson, p. 375.

[27] Cf. Osiander, p. 338.

collection.[28] Consequently, failure on the part of the Corinthians would be all the more humiliating for Paul, and indeed for his readers themselves.[29] The general sense of the verse is obvious. The debatable point is the precise meaning of the final phrase ἐν τῇ ὑποστάσει ταύτῃ.[30] We take the sense to be: 'in respect of this project'. This is not the traditional rendering of ὑπόστασις, but it has some support elsewhere, and fits the context well. The word ὑπόστασις has in general a great variety of meanings.[31] Within the NT, however, since it occurs only five times (2 Cor 9.4; 11.17; Heb 1.3; 3.14; 11.1), its range is more limited. In BAGD s.v. three meanings are proposed: 1. 'substantial nature, essence, actual being, reality' (Heb 1.3); 2. 'situation, condition', also 'frame of mind' (2 Cor 9.4; 11.17; Heb 3.14); 3. 'realization' (Heb 11.1). It is noted that Köster, in *TWNT*, prefers 'plan, project' for the two instances in 2 Corinthians. It will be immediately apparent to those who consult the earlier edition of this lexicon that there has been a considerable change of mind concerning this item during the two or three decades which have separated the one from the other. BAG gives the same first meaning as BAGD but the other two definitions are missing, and, more importantly, the second meaning proposed is that of 'confidence, conviction, assurance, steadfastness', with references in Polybius, Diodorus Siculus, Josephus and the LXX, followed by 2 Cor 9.4; 11.17; Heb 3.14; 11.1. This is in line with the traditional understanding of ὑπόστασις in 2 Cor 9.4[32] as denoting the 'confidence' in the Corinthians Paul has expressed in boasting of them to the Macedonians.

This traditional interpretation has not gone unchallenged. Windisch observed that the ἵνα μὴ λέγω ὑμεῖς would count against it, since the confidence would be that of Paul only, not of his readers as well.[33] But it is obviously the discussion by Köster in *TWNT* which has influenced the revised definition in BAGD.[34]

---

[28] Windisch, p. 272.

[29] Furnish, p. 427, with reference to BDF 495(1) and Robertson, p. 1199, observes that the ἵνα μὴ λέγω ὑμεῖς is a good example of paralipsis. The singular λέγω (𝔓46 C* D F G 048 a p vgmss sams Ambst) is preferable to the plural λέγωμεν (ℵ B C² Ψ 0209. 0243 𝔐 f vg sy samss bo). See Metzger, *Textual Commentary*[1], p. 582: the reading λέγωμεν is a scribal assimilation to the preceding καταισχυνθῶμεν; the first singular is predominant in the context.

[30] Some witnesses (ℵ² D¹ Ψ 0209 𝔐 sy(p)) add τῆς καυχήσεως. This is obviously a scribal addition, resulting either from an attempt to clarify the sense, or, as Furnish, p. 427, suggests, from assimilation to 11.17.

[31] See LSJ s.v.

[32] See, e.g., KJV, RSV, NEB, REB, BCN; Calvin, p. 120; Meyer, p. 372; Bachmann, p. 328; Lietzmann, p. 137; Plummer, p. 255; Allo, p. 231; Witt, 'ΥΠΟΣΤΑΣΙΣ', p. 330.

[33] Windisch, p. 273.

[34] H. Köster, on ὑπόστασις in *TWNT* VIII, pp. 571–88.

He claims that the biblical passages adduced in support of the sense 'confidence' should be differently interpreted. In Ruth 1.12, for example, where Naomi speaks of the possibility of her having a husband and bearing sons, the LXX has: ἔστιν μοι ὑπόστασις τοῦ γενηθῆναί με ἀνδρὶ καὶ τέξομαι υἱούς. The sense of the Hebrew is: '(Even if I said) there is still hope for me, even if I were to have a husband ... and bear sons' (JB). Here it would seem natural to render ὑπόστασις as 'hope'. Köster, however, argues that it expresses 'the reality which gives a firm guarantee'.[35] In Heb 3.14 and 11.1, also, the meaning of ὑπόστασις is 'reality'.[36] He points out, further, that the sense 'plan' or 'purpose' emerges in hellenistic Greek.[37] Polybius uses the word for the 'plan' of his historical presentation.[38] Diodorus Siculus uses it similarly in connection with historians: οἱ δὲ τὴν ὑπόστασιν τῆς ἐπιβολῆς οὐ συνετέλεσαν ('while others have failed to complete the plan to which they had set their hand').[39] Köster argues that 'plan' or 'project' would make good sense in 2 Cor 9.4 likewise. If the collection is delayed because the Corinthians are unprepared, Paul's whole project will be thrown into confusion. His readers also will be affected, since they have themselves become closely involved in it.[40]

Köster's argument is not, perhaps, quite as strong as it may appear. It has to be said that his interpretation of the LXX passages is somewhat forced, requiring, as it does, a good deal of explanation and paraphrase, and the same is true of his understanding of Heb 3.14 as referring to 'the reality on which the existence of the community rests'.[41] It would not be wholly impossible for Paul to have taken ὑπόστασις to mean 'hope' in the verses in the LXX, given his knowledge of the Hebrew text. At the same time he could scarcely expect his readers to be so familiar with them (or familiar at all) that they would understand such a usage on his part. They are at least somewhat more likely to be acquainted with the sense 'plan' or 'purpose'. Moreover, support of a more negative kind for Köster emerges when we examine some of the references given in BAG which are held to substantiate the traditional rendering 'confidence'. Two of these,

---

[35] Köster, on ὑπόστασις, p. 580. See also his exegesis of Ezek 19.5 and Ps 38 (LXX).8, pp. 580–1.

[36] Köster, on ὑπόστασις, pp. 584–6.

[37] Köster, on ὑπόστασις, p. 577; see also LSJ s.v. ὑπόστασις, B.II.3. 'plan, purpose'.

[38] Polyb. IV 2.1, cited by Köster, ibid.

[39] Diod. Sic. I 3.2, LCL; cited by Köster, ibid.

[40] Köster, on ὑπόστασις, pp. 582–3. See also Furnish, pp. 427–8, 439; Betz, p. 95, agrees with Köster.

[41] Köster, on ὑπόστασις, in *TDNT* 8, p. 587.

i.e., Polyb. IV 50.10 and VI 55.2, are certainly listed in LSJ s.v. ὑπόστασις under B.II.4, 'confidence, courage, resolution, steadiness', but with the significant addition 'of soldiers'. The first refers rather generally to standing firm in a war situation: οἱ δὲ 'Ρόδιοι θεωροῦντες τὴν τῶν Βυζαντίων ὑπόστασιν, 'The Rhodians seeing that the Byzantines stood firm' (LCL). The second speaks of the steadfastness of Horatius in keeping the bridge against enemy onslaught: οὐχ οὕτως τὴν δύναμιν ὡς τὴν ὑπόστασιν αὐτοῦ καὶ τόλμαν, 'less [astonished] at his physical strength than at his endurance and courage' (LCL). Likewise in Jos., *Ant.* XVIII 24, also cited in BAG s.v. 2., ὑπόστασις is used of 'resolution', in respect of indifference to pain, submission to death, and the like. It is quite clear that in these contexts, if ὑπόστασις were to be rendered 'confidence', its synonyms would be 'steadfastness', 'resolution', and the like. In 2 Cor 9.4, however, the required synonym would be something like 'hopeful trust'. Consequently, the extra-biblical passages claimed as supporting 'confidence' in fact do no such thing. We agree, therefore, with Köster's interpretation of ὑπόστασις in 2 Cor 9.4.

5. ἀναγκαῖον οὖν ἡγησάμην παρακαλέσαι τοὺς ἀδελφοὺς ἵνα προέλθωσιν εἰς[42] ὑμᾶς καὶ προκαταρτίσωσιν τὴν προεπηγγελμένην εὐλογίαν ὑμῶν, ταύτην ἑτοίμην εἶναι οὕτως ὡς εὐλογίαν καὶ μὴ ὡς πλεονεξίαν. Paul further explains the purpose of his dispatch of the envoys to Corinth. As in v. 3, Titus will be included in the term τοὺς ἀδελφούς. In commenting on 8.16–18, we have suggested that Paul draws a subtle distinction in status between Titus and the other two delegates, in that Titus accepts a 'request', παράκλησις, from him, whilst he simply 'sends' the other envoys. Here, however, the verb παρακαλέω is used in relation to all three, without distinction. It may be that the language in chap. 8 is more precise, since there Paul is officially introducing the delegates, whilst in the present (separate) letter there is now no need for such precision. That their function is to make sure that the Corinthians' preparations are complete before Paul's own arrival is stressed by the repetition of verbs beginning with the prefix προ-.[43] In addition, the readers are reminded that their gift has been pledged beforehand.[44] It would not be

---

[42] For εἰς ὑμᾶς a few witnesses (B D F G 365. 1175. 2495 *pc*) read πρὸς ὑμᾶς. This is probably a stylistic correction, since πρός would be the usual preposition when a writer is speaking of coming to a group of people: see BAGD s.v. πρός III.1.a.

[43] Meyer, p. 373; cf. Plummer, p. 255.

[44] According to Meyer, p. 373, it was Paul who had promised the contribution from the Corinthians. But even if Paul himself might possibly have reverted in thought to his original acceptance of the request made at the Jerusalem conference (Gal 2.10), it is scarcely likely that he would have indicated to the Corinthians that he had promised their support for 'the poor' without having first secured their agreement. In any case, we have accepted the view that Paul's own collection was

unreasonable (Paul may intend to imply) that he should expect
them to have it ready when he arrives. The gift itself is here designated εὐλογία: it is a 'benefit', a
source of 'blessing',[45] 'a generous gift'.[46] Thus defined, it is
something deriving from a human source. Theobald, however,
would give it more content than this. It indicates, he claims, the
spiritual as well as the material dimension of the Corinthians'
contribution. The gift mediates a blessing, and in OT thought all
blessing comes ultimately from Yahweh, so that the one who
gives it functions as God's intermediary. This line of thinking can
be presupposed for Paul also. Thus, the bestowal of the blessing
is more than simply an imitation of the divine action (*contra*
Windisch): it is the divine blessing itself which takes shape in the
Corinthians' gift.[47] But to read this much into the present use of
εὐλογία may be to over-interpret its significance.[48] Paul's allusion
to the collection in Rom 15.27, moreover, may count against any
such view, since there it is the Jerusalem Christians who are seen
as bestowing spiritual gifts upon the Gentiles, and the latter's
service is in terms of material benefits.

The delegates are to organise this gift in advance, for it to be
ready, or, so that it is ready,[49] and in such a way as to be ὡς εὐλογίαν καὶ[50] μὴ ὡς πλεονεξίαν. It is the last phrase of all, μὴ ὡς
πλεονεξίαν, which constitutes the chief exegetical difficulty. It is
easy enough to see how the promised Corinthian contribution can
be seen as a means of blessing or as a bountiful gift. It is much less
easy to understand the further qualification 'and not as (an
expression of) avarice', or 'and not as covetousness'.[51] Why
should any such qualification be thought necessary? How can a
charitable donation possibly be seen in this light? There would
seem to be two possible ways of resolving the difficulty. The first
supposes that the Corinthians are the subject of the attitude or

in some sense a fresh venture. It is the Corinthians who have previously promised
their gift: see Windisch, p. 274, and Furnish, p. 428.
   [45] BAGD s.v. εὐλογία 3.b.β.
   [46] BAGD ibid, 5.
   [47] Theobald, *Gnade*, pp. 290–1. He puts the final point (p. 291) as follows: 'Die
Gabe der Korinther ist derart, daß Gottes Segen selbst in ihr Gestalt gewinnt.'
   [48] It is not clear that, when εὐλογία is used in the LXX of a blessing bestowed by
man, there is always a reference to divine blessing as well. There is nothing to
support this in, e.g., 1 Kgdms 25.27 or 4 Kgdms 5.15.
   [49] The clause ταύτην ἑτοίμην εἶναι ... μὴ ὡς πλεονεξίαν may be either final or
consecutive: see Moule, *Idiom Book*, p. 141. The infinitive without ὥστε can be
used to express result: see BDR 391(4).
   [50] Some witnesses (𝔓46vid ℵ* F G latt syp) omit καί. This could be correct, in view
of the similar linguistic pattern in Col 3.2. But there are other verses in 2
Corinthians itself (4.7; 5.12) which would suggest that καί is original.
   [51] On πλεονεξία see BAGD s.v.

activity implicit in the word πλεονεξία,[52] whilst the second takes Paul as the implicit subject.

(i) The word has the sense given it in BAGD s.v.: 'a gift that is grudgingly granted by avarice'. The donors would really prefer to keep their money.[53] In favour of this interpretation there is the fact that the Corinthians are obviously the subject of the action implicit in the preceding ὡς εὐλογίαν. Also, since ὡς πλεονεξίαν must be seen as the equivalent of the φειδομένως in v. 6, it must refer to the attitude of the giver of the gift: in v. 6 the ἐπ᾽ εὐλογίαις can be seen as the equivalent of the ὡς εὐλογίαν of v. 5, which shows the degree of parallelism between the two verses.[54] Despite the support from BAGD, however, this exegesis is not altogether easy to accept. It does seem to distort the natural meaning of πλεονεξία.[55]

(ii) The hypothetical avarice is Paul's. If he has to compel the Corinthians to give, he will seem to be exacting the money in a greedy spirit.[56] One could argue that the occurrence of the cognate verb πλεονεκτέω in 12.17–18 is decisive evidence for this view: Paul has been charged with extorting money from the Corinthians on the pretext of raising funds for the collection.[57] And it gives more point to his concern that the Corinthians' contribution should be ready. If it is , then the Macedonians will see that it is motivated by love. But if it is not, Paul will have to plead for it and this will look like 'extortion'. It will be 'money obtained from reluctant donors by inappropriate means'.[58] Furthermore, this interpretation gives a more natural sense to πλεονεξία. Its disadvantages are the mirror image of the advantages of (i). The subject of the action implied by πλεονεξία is different from that of the action of the εὐλογία, and there is a less complete parallel with v. 6. The exegesis of v. 6 will show that it does refer back to v. 5, so that an interpretation of v. 5 that preserves the parallelism would be preferable.

Decision between the two alternatives is not easy. Since, however, the advantage of retaining the same subject for ὡς πλεονεξίαν as for ὡς εὐλογίαν is, in our view, a strong argument for the first interpretation, it may be useful to offer a somewhat different version of it, which would mitigate the force of the claim that it distorts the natural sense of πλεονεξία.

[52] As in the questions above.
[53] Windisch, p. 275; see also Hughes, pp. 327–8.
[54] Plummer, p. 256.
[55] Bachmann, p. 328.
[56] Filson, p. 375; see also Bruce, p. 226, and Furnish, p. 439.
[57] Barrett, p. 235. He translates, p. 231: 'as a gift and not as something wrung from you'.
[58] Furnish, p. 439.

It is not impossible that Paul could have been thinking back to what he had said in 8.13–15 in his earlier letter. He would also have expected his readers to be able to grasp such a possible allusion: his letter of chaps. 1–8 would still be available, he would suppose, and in any case no great length of time would have separated the two items of correspondence. In 8.15 he has quoted, from the story of the manna, Exod 16.18, part of which runs: οὐκ ἐπλεόνασεν ὁ τὸ πολύ. The meaning of πλεονάζω in this context is 'have too much'.[59] In the story, those who gathered large quantities of manna clearly intended to 'have too much' in the sense of having more than they needed. Now the literal meaning of πλεονεξία is 'a desire to have more'.[60] There could be a connection, therefore, in Paul's mind between his use of the Exodus story in 8.13–15 and the ὡς πλεονεξίαν of 9.5. The latter phrase could refer to a possible attitude on the Corinthians' part which would be similar to that of the Israelites in Exodus. What would this mean? In the Exodus story, the desire of some Israelites to have more than they needed was frustrated by the divine miracle of equalisation, and Paul uses this item in the story to give scriptural backing to his plea for equality of financial resources as between the Corinthians and the Jerusalem church. The Corinthians are not to 'have too much' by comparison with the Jerusalem Christians, i.e., to 'have more' than the latter. If this is what is being said in 8.13–15, this may throw light on the μὴ ὡς πλεονεξίαν of 9.5. The Corinthian contribution to the collection is not to be an expression of any such 'desire to have more' than their fellow Christians of the mother church. In other words, it is not to be a sparing contribution. It is to be ὡς εὐλογίαν, i.e., 'as a bountiful gift'.

6. **Τοῦτο δέ, ὁ σπείρων φειδομένως φειδομένως καὶ θερίσει, καὶ ὁ σπείρων ἐπ᾽ εὐλογίαις ἐπ᾽ εὐλογίαις καὶ θερίσει.** Paul has just made an implicit plea for generosity. Now he embarks on a more extensive encouragement to liberality, supported by a number of scriptural allusions. He begins with the elliptical Τοῦτο δέ,[61] which both connects v. 6 with v. 5 and also introduces what follows. Hence, the meaning is something like ' "the point is this" '.[62]

---

[59] BAGD s.v. πλεονάζω 1.b.

[60] BAGD s.v. πλεονεξία.

[61] See BDR 481. Here, it is suggested, we are to supply φημί (cf. 1 Cor 7.29; 15.50); it is noted that the use of ellipsis in letters may be due to imitation of ordinary speech.

[62] Hughes, p. 328 n. 61. See also Martin, p. 287: 'To enforce the point'. Betz, p. 102, claims that Τοῦτο δέ is a ' citation formula', with the sense ' "consider the following" '. But Paul's use elsewhere of καὶ τοῦτο, τοῦτο δέ φημι, λέγω δὲ τοῦτο and τοῦτο (δὲ) λέγω (Rom 13.11; 1 Cor 7.29; 15.50; 1.12; 7.6, 35; Gal 3.17) suggests that the τοῦτο will refer backwards as well as forwards.

In itself, the point is made very generally, by means of an image familiar both in Jewish and in Graeco-Roman culture.[63] One 'reaps' what one 'sows'. Here, the 'reaping' is lavish or the reverse in proportion to the extent of the 'sowing':[64] the image is to be applied to the Corinthians' contribution to the collection, so that it is a matter not so much of the quality of the 'seed' sown (which will clearly be good) as of its quantity (plentiful or sparse). Paul's readers should 'sow' lavishly, i.e., make a generous contribution. This is obvious. It is less obvious, however, what the second half of the image means. What does the 'reaping' signify for the Corinthians? For some commentators the harvest stands for the final judgement at the end of the world.[65] Supporting evidence for this interpretation would be found in Gal 6.7–8,[66] where the harvest a person may reap is either φθορά or ζωή αἰώνιος, and in the use of the image elsewhere in the NT (Mt 13.39[67]; Rev 14.14–20[68]) and in other eschatological contexts (4 Ezra 4.26–32[69]; 3 *Apoc. Bar.* 15.2[70]; see also Joel (LXX) 4.13[71]). It has to be said, however, that the context in 2 Cor 9 gives no positive support for this line of exegesis. There is nothing to indicate that Paul is thinking of the reward of eternal life (which could scarcely be bestowed in a quantitative fashion) or of particular blessings of the world to come.

The alternative is to suppose that the rewards of 'harvest' come about in this present life. What we have here, according to Georgi, is simply a gnomic saying in the Wisdom tradition.[72] The notion in itself, then, is a general one: the consequences of one's actions are consonant with, and proportionate to, the actions themselves. The image is used in a wide variety of contexts.[73] For its common application to morality, see Prov 22.8[74]: ὁ σπείρων φαῦλα θερίσει κακά ('He who sows evils will reap ills'). In the present context the 'harvest' Paul has in view may be what he promises his readers in vv. 8–10, i.e., God's abundant provision

[63] See the references to be given below.

[64] Note the chiastic formulation in both halves of the verse, which emphasises the adverbial expressions 'sparingly' and 'bountifully', and the contrast between them. For the phrase ἐπ᾽ εὐλογίαις see below, p. 575 n. 76.

[65] Meyer, pp. 374–5; Plummer, p. 258.

[66] Cited by Plummer, ibid.

[67] Cited by Plummer, ibid; also by Windisch, p. 276, though he does not definitely support this interpretation.

[68] Cited by Georgi, *Kollekte*, p. 68, n. 268, though he does not accept this interpretation in the present verse.

[69] Cited by Georgi, ibid.

[70] Cited by Barrett, p. 236.

[71] Cited by Georgi, *Kollekte*, p. 68, n. 267.

[72] Georgi, *Kollekte*, pp. 68–9.

[73] See below for some examples cited by commentators.

[74] Cited by Windisch, p. 276; Furnish, p. 440; and others.

for their needs, together with the prospective thankful prayers of
the Jerusalem church on their behalf and affectionate longing for
them (vv. 13–15).[75] In this way they will reap generously[76] the
results of their own generosity.
The following selection of examples will illustrate the use of the
metaphor of sowing and reaping.
Aristotle, *Rhet.* (*Rhetoric*) III 3.4:
σὺ δὲ ταῦτα αἰσχρῶς μὲν ἔσπειρας, κακῶς δὲ ἐθέρισας
'you have sown shame and reaped misfortune' (LCL).[77]
Cicero, *De Or.* (*Orator*) II lxv (II 261):
'Ut sementem feceris, ita metes'
'You shall reap your sowing' (LCL).[78]
Philo, *Conf. Ling.* (*Confusion of Tongues*) 152:
ἀδικίαν μὲν σπείραντες, ἀσέβειαν δὲ θερίσαντες
'having sown injustice, they reaped impiety' (LCL).[79]
Mut. Nom. (*Change of Names*) 269:
ἀλλὰ γὰρ τῷ σπείραντι καὶ θερίζειν ἔθος
'But note that the sower generally reaps' (LCL).[80]
See also Plato, *Phaedr.* 260C–D; Philo, *Conf. Ling.* 21; *Leg. Gai.*
293; *Test. L* 13.6.[81]

7. ἕκαστος καθὼς προῄρηται τῇ καρδίᾳ, μὴ ἐκ λύπης ἢ ἐξ
ἀνάγκης, ἱλαρὸν γὰρ δότην ἀγαπᾷ ὁ θεός. Each should give[82] as
he has inwardly determined[83]. Georgi would see here an echo of
Stoic discussion of freedom of decision, as found, for example, in
Epictetus. He refers to *Diss.* I 17.21.[84] The context in which the
question of freedom of moral choice arises is, of course, very
different. In Epictetus, the point is that the Stoic is inwardly free
from any constraint which might prevent him from assenting to
the truth or might force him to accept what is false. Paul is talking
about freedom from compulsion to participate generously in a
good work. His terminology, nevertheless, has some similarity to
that of Epictetus. Whilst the verb προαιρέομαι does not occur in

75 Theobald, *Gnade*, p. 293, connects the harvest with Jerusalem. Furnish, p. 447,
sees it as the further resources God will provide to enable further generosity.
76 On the phrase ἐπ᾽ εὐλογίαις see BAGD s.v. ἐπί II.1.b.ζ. It corresponds to an
adverb, with the meaning 'generously'. Betz, p. 103, renders it 'bountifully'.
77 Cited by Barrett, p. 236, and by Georgi, *Kollekte*, p. 68 n. 266.
78 Cited by Plummer, p. 258, and by Georgi, ibid.
79 Cited by Georgi, *Kollekte*, p. 68 n. 266.
80 Cited by Georgi, ibid.
81 Cited by Georgi, ibid.
82 Plummer, p. 259, notes the ellipsis of the main verb, and suggests that it makes
the sentence more forcible.
83 For προῄρηται (א B C F G P 0243. 6. 33. 104. 365. 1175. 1739. 1881 *pc* lat co
Cyp) some witnesses (D Ψ 048 𝔐) have προαιρεῖται, which may be a scribal error
due to similarity in pronunciation.
84 Georgi, *Kollekte*, p. 69.

the discussion in I 17.20–29, we find the cognate terms προαίρεσις and τὸ προαιρετικόν.[85] And Paul's ἐξ ἀνάγκης is paralleled by the three cognate words ἀναγκάζω, ἀναγκαστός and ἀνανάγκαστος in Epictetus. It is not impossible that Paul might consciously be employing some of the language of popular philosophy as likely to have some appeal to his readers. His μὴ ἐκ λύπης, however, is reminiscent of Deut 15.10,[86] where, in reference to giving, it is said: οὐ λυπηθήσῃ τῇ καρδίᾳ, ('you shall not become sad at heart'). It may be that the μὴ ἐκ λύπης and the ἢ ἐξ ἀνάγκης are two ways of making the same point: giving under compulsion is regretful giving.[87] The compulsion which Paul here hopes to avoid could come either from his envoys or from himself when he arrives. It could, however, take the form only of this very kind of moral persuasion which he is employing in this letter itself.[88]

The plea that the Corinthians' donations should not be made regretfully is then reinforced by means of an allusion to Prov 22 (LXX).8a: ἄνδρα ἱλαρὸν καὶ δότην εὐλογεῖ ὁ Θεός ('God blesses a cheerful man and giver'). One might ask why Paul has ἀγαπᾷ instead of εὐλογεῖ, which might have seemed the more suitable in view of v. 6.[89] It may be that he is quoting from memory,[90] or perhaps from a version of the Greek text different from that of the LXX.[91] A further suggestion is that he may be consciously introducing a new thought: to desire God's love is a higher motive than to expect reward.[92] This is not impossible. In any case we need to ask how Paul understood his assertion, whether a conscious alteration or not. It might very well seem to conflict with his deeper theological principles. Barrett, arguing that the sense of 'love' is 'approves' or 'values', suggests that otherwise there would be a contradiction of Paul's belief in God's love for the sinner, 'the man who will not give at all, cheerfully or otherwise'.[93] Georgi, differently, does accept the meaning 'loves'.

---

[85] Both are rendered 'moral purpose' in the LCL translation.
[86] Noted by Plummer, p. 259.
[87] Plummer, p. 259.
[88] It is not very likely, as Héring, p. 75, notes, that he would be thinking of the imposition of a fixed contribution on the individual members of the congregation. In the first place, he would have no means of enforcing payment. And, secondly, any such attempt would surely rupture yet again his good relationship with the Corinthians, only lately restored.
[89] See Windisch, p. 277.
[90] Plummer, p. 259; Betz, p. 107. Paul presumably could not count on access to the actual text of the Scriptures wherever he might be. Did he have the greater part of them roughly by heart? Or did he, when texts were available, take pains to memorise such sections as would be useful for his current preoccupations—here the collection?
[91] Hughes, p. 331 n. 65.
[92] Windisch, p. 277.
[93] Barrett, p. 236.

He claims, however, that what is in view is God's love as the atmosphere in which the cheerful giver moves. It is not the consequence of human giving but its ground. This must be Paul's meaning, since all his other references to God's love are concerned with the saving love manifested in the death of Christ.[94] This second interpretation is certainly too elaborate.[95] But whether, with Barrett, we need to give a reduced sense to ἀγαπᾷ is also questionable. Paul is not saying that God loves *only* the cheerful giver: he is giving his readers positive encouragement, not a negative warning. And whilst he certainly regards the love of God as prior in a fundamental sense to human attitudes and activities, this need not exclude the possibility that it could be seen also as a response on particular occasions to such activities or attitudes. He does not suppose that the behaviour of believers has no effect on God: he speaks elsewhere of pleasing God (1 Th 4.1) or the Lord (1 Cor 7.32), and also of provoking the Lord's jealousy (1 Cor 10.22).

The general idea of giving cheerfully is widespread.[96] Some similarity to the language of Paul's quotation may be seen in Ecclus 35.8(11): ἐν πάσῃ δόσει ἱλάρωσον τὸ πρόσωπόν σου ('with every gift show a cheerful face', NRSV).[97] See also Philo, *Spec. Leg.* IV 74, where he urges the rich man to alleviate the hard life of the poor by means of ἱλαραῖς μεταδόσεσιν ('cheerful distributions of benefits').[98]

8. δυνατεῖ[99] δὲ ὁ θεὸς πᾶσαν χάριν περισσεῦσαι εἰς ὑμᾶς, ἵνα ἐν παντὶ πάντοτε πᾶσαν αὐτάρκειαν ἔχοντες περισσεύητε εἰς πᾶν ἔργον ἀγαθόν. Paul adds some further encouragement, in the form of the promise of abundant divine grace. The basic point is clear, but there is some difference of opinion as to the precise connection with what he has already said. One suggestion is that he is returning to the notion of recompense which has appeared in v. 6 and which is amplified in v. 7, in that the recompense is

---

[94] Georgi, *Kollekte*, p. 70.

[95] Wolff, p. 185 n. 155, comments that Georgi fails to take sufficient account of the character of the saying as belonging to the Wisdom tradition. Furnish, p. 441, disagreeing with Georgi and agreeing with Barrett, notes examples from the Wisdom literature where there are similar references to those whom God loves: Wisd 7.28; Prov 22 (LXX).11; Ecclus 4.14 (the first two are also cited by Windisch, p. 277).

[96] See Plummer, pp. 259–60; Windisch, p. 277; Barrett, p. 236; Furnish, p. 441; Betz, pp. 107–9.

[97] Cited by Barrett, p. 236; and by Furnish, p. 441.

[98] Cited by Georgi, *Kollekte*, p. 69; also (in translation) by Furnish, p. 441.

[99] The verb δυνατέω, which here means 'be able' (BAGD s.v. 2.), although used twice elsewhere by Paul (Rom 14.4; 1 Cor 13.3), is very infrequent. Hence δυνατεῖ (𝔓46 ℵ B C* D* F G 104 t vg Ambst) is replaced in some witnesses by δύναται (33 *pc* f g p vg^ms) and in others by δυνατός (C² D² Ψ 048. 0243 𝔐 b).

shown to derive from God's appreciation of Corinthian giving.[100] In opposition to this view, however, it is argued that Paul, here, is not formulating God's response to the activity of the Corinthians, but rather is indicating the condition, i.e., God's grace, which makes such activity possible.[101] Lastly, there is an intermediate position proposed by Furnish. The grace is indeed the 'harvest' of v. 6, but Paul does not view it as any kind of reward or payment. Furthermore, it is given for the promotion of 'specific acts of Christian service', like that of the collection.[102] Which of these three suggestions is most suited to the context? The first should not be ruled out on *a priori* dogmatic grounds: Paul does speak elsewhere of reward (1 Cor 3.8, 14). And if it should prove plausible, i.e., if he does see the promised divine grace as in some sense the result of Corinthian generosity, it is difficult, *pace* Furnish, altogether to eliminate the notion of reward.[103] Nevertheless, the second suggestion makes the best connection with v. 7.[104] If we take πᾶσαν χάριν in a comprehensive sense,[105]we can see Paul as amplifying or elucidating his scriptural quotation: God is able most abundantly to bestow both the spiritual quality of cheerful generosity and the practical resources for its implementation, so that the individual Corinthian may truly fulfil the role of the ἱλαρὸς δότης.

That the content of πᾶσαν χάριν may include spiritual blessings is in one sense obvious. In relation to the collection the point is reinforced by the way Paul has spoken in 8.1–4, where the Macedonians' urgent desire to participate in the project is seen as the result of the divine grace bestowed upon them.[106] Here he assures his readers that God is able also in their case to endow them with abundant liberality. At the same time both the context and the following reference to αὐτάρκεια suggest that material blessings are also in view. Windisch supposes that Paul is anticipating questions as to how his readers are to be expected to find money for their contribution, and their own means of livelihood

---

[100] Windisch, p. 277.
[101] Theobald, *Gnade*, p. 294. See also Georgi, *Kollekte*, p. 70, who similarly rejects the idea of recompense.
[102] Furnish, p. 447.
[103] A further difficulty inherent in Furnish's interpretation is that he appears to relate the divine activity of v. 8 wholly to some post-collection activity on the part of the Corinthians, whereas v. 14 shows that it is participation in the collection itself that Paul primarily has in view when he speaks of the grace God is able to bestow on them.
[104] And with v. 14.
[105] See below, pp. 578–9.
[106] The parallel is noted by Hughes, p. 331. In his view the whole canonical letter is a unity, but the point holds good also if chap. 9 is a separate letter, since what Paul says in 8.1–4 shows his way of thinking.

as well.[107] Hence the content of the χάρις is both spiritual and material.[108] Its comprehensive and unlimited character is emphasised by the repetition of πᾶς in various forms in the second half of the verse,[109] and also by the recurrence of περισσεύω. It will enable the Corinthians to be prolific in every kind of good work, and especially, as v. 9 will show, in contributing to the collection. This is because they will be possessed of αὐτάρκεια in the highest degree.[110] How is this gift to be defined? In BAGD s.v. two basic meanings are given: 1. 'sufficiency', 'a competence'; 2. 'contentment', 'self-sufficiency'. The first of these, however, itself comprises two different senses. The lexicon notes that from Plato onwards the word 'means the state of one who supports himself without aid from others', but that in one of the papyri (P Oxy 729:10) it has the sense 'sufficient supply'. Under 2. there is the observation that self-sufficiency was 'a favourite virtue of the Cynics and Stoics'. The person who possesses this virtue, of contentment 'in relation to his own inner possibility', is independent of others, Kittel notes—he needs no one.[111]

Which meaning does Paul have in view? The sense 'inward self-sufficiency' is strongly supported by Meyer: God is able to bestow upon believers a complete inward contentment that desires nothing from anyone else.[112] But this is scarcely the point in the present context. As commentators remark, there is a substantial difference between the Stoic αὐτάρκεια and what is meant here. The Stoic virtue is an end in itself, whilst, for Paul, the purpose of the αὐτάρκεια is to enable one to assist the needy.[113] For Paul, it is something which facilitates relationship with others, not withdrawal from them.[114] It is unlikely that he is thinking of the inner quality, even in a reduced, non-philosophical, sense.[115] Most exegetes understand him to use αὐτάρκεια in the sense rendered in BAGD as 'sufficient supply'.[116] The Corinthians will have a sufficient income, a sufficient livelihood, sufficient material goods

---

[107] Windisch, pp. 277–8.

[108] So, e.g., Plummer, p. 260; Windisch, ibid.; Allo, p. 234.

[109] Theobald, *Gnade*, p. 294.

[110] See BAGD s.v. πᾶς 1.a.δ. The παντὶ πάντοτε probably qualifies the participial phrase: 'in every respect, at all times, possessing the highest degree of αὐτάρκεια'.

[111] G. Kittel, on αὐτάρκεια, in *TWNT* I, pp. 466–7; the quotation is from *TDNT* I, p. 466.

[112] Meyer, p. 377.

[113] Windisch, p. 278; see also Barrett, p. 237.

[114] Furnish, p. 448.

[115] Meyer does not specifically mention the Stoics. Bachmann, p. 331 makes the general point that the inward quality provides no certain motivation to do good works.

[116] This would also imply the possession of αὐτάρκεια in the sense 'state of being self-supporting'.

to enable them to share with others, and, in particular, to contribute generously to the collection.[117] In the latter respect, practically speaking, Paul must mean that, if they do not yet have this surplus, they are nevertheless to give liberally, in the confidence that divine grace will make up the deficit later. **9. καθὼς γέγραπται, Ἐσκόρπισεν, ἔδωκεν τοῖς πένησιν, ἡ δικαιοσύνη αὐτοῦ μένει εἰς τὸν αἰῶνα.** Paul quotes exactly the first two lines of Ps 111 (LXX).9,[118] except for the omission of the final τοῦ αἰῶνος,[119] with the intention of substantiating from Scripture what he has just said. How exactly is the quotation to be understood in its present context? The answer depends, in turn, upon the answers to three other, interrelated, questions. Whom does Paul see as the subject of ἐσκόρπισεν and ἔδωκεν? What is the meaning of δικαιοσύνη? And what is meant by saying that this δικαιοσύνη 'endures forever'?

(i) In the original psalm the subject is the pious, beneficent man. It would be natural, therefore, to suppose that Paul applies the words to the typical Corinthian who contributes to the collection.[120] Certainly quotations can be used with a change of application. One might, therefore, see the ὁ Θεός of v. 8 as the subject of v. 9 as well, especially as in the preceding psalm (LXX 110.3 [MT/EVV 111.3]) the assertion that 'his righteousness remains for ever' is made with reference to God.[121] Nevertheless, it is argued, the context favours the view that the righteous man is the subject:[122] it is a matter of giving alms for the poor.[123] The alternative interpretation, however, has also attracted support: it is God, or Christ, who is the chief subject, and it is only as a man is incorporated within the divine activity and righteousness that he can function as joint subject. Thus, Georgi points out that God is the subject both in v. 8 and in v. 10, which would suggest that he is the subject also in the intervening verse. The objection that the pious man is the subject in Ps 111 (LXX).9 can be met by pointing to the close connection of this psalm with the preceding one where God is the subject. There is also the striking fact that Paul avoids specifying the subject of his quotation, which must necessarily suggest that it is God who is the proper author of human compassion, and that it is his righteousness which is the origin of

[117] See, e.g., Windisch, p. 278; Bachmann, p. 331; Barrett, p. 237; Georgi, *Kollekte*, p. 71; Furnish, pp. 447–8.
[118] Hebrew/English versions Ps 112.9.
[119] Added in some witnesses (F G K 0243. 6. 326. 629. 630. 1241. 1739. 1881 *al* a vg[cl] bo[mss]).
[120] Meyer, p. 378; Plummer, p. 261; Strachan, p. 143; Allo, pp. 234–5; Barrett, p. 238.
[121] Plummer, ibid., notes this possibility.
[122] Plummer, ibid.
[123] Allo, p. 235.

man's righteousness. At the same time, it appears that for Georgi there is a human subject as well: the generous Corinthian will be joint subject with God.[124] For A. T. Hanson, somewhat differently, the subject is Christ-in-the-Christian. The psalm from which the quotation comes could have been seen by Paul, he suggests, as referring to Christ. The allusion in v. 4 to light which has arisen in darkness and in v. 9 to exaltation in glory would be taken as references to Christ's resurrection (or, in the first case, to the appearance of the Messiah in history). Hence, whilst Paul does relate his quotation to the giving of the Corinthians, this is secondary. Their giving is something which Christ is doing in them. Hanson claims that this is the only interpretation that can be reconciled with Paul's theology as a whole. The righteousness to which he refers must be 'Christ's righteousness in Christians': it cannot be some quality of the Corinthians, independently displayed in, or achieved by, their own almsgiving to the poor.[125]

The first of these alternatives is obviously the simpler, and the very fact that the thought of the Corinthians' activity has itself to be incorporated into the second interpretation may suggest that it is, after all, they who are the implicit subject of the quotation. The only argument of any substance which would count against the first alternative is the attribution of δικαιοσύνη to this subject. The remaining such arguments, which would favour the second alternative, are not strong. Whilst ὁ Θεός is the subject of the main clause in v. 8, the Corinthians are the subject of the subordinate clause which is immediately followed by the quotation of v. 9, and the quotation can be seen as giving content to the abundance of beneficent activity to which Paul refers at the end of this subordinate clause. The alleged connection with the previous psalm, where God is the subject, is by no means obvious (there is no specific reference there to the poor and needy), and Paul's failure to specify the subject of his quotation is in no way significant, since the subject is not specified in the verse he cites. And the context in 2 Cor 9 does not suggest a christological use of the psalm.

(ii) For those who understand God or Christ as the primary subject of ἐσκόρπισεν and ἔδωκεν the δικαιοσύνη is the righteousness of God into which man is incorporated,[126] or Christ's righteousness active within the believer.[127] But if one sees the

---

[124] Georgi, *Kollekte*, pp. 71–2. Furnish, pp. 448–9, appears to favour this line of exegesis. Giving generously to the needy is a part of the 'larger righteousness of God' by which the beneficent live and in which they will forever remain.

[125] A. T. Hanson, *Studies in Paul's Technique and Theology*, London, 1974, pp. 179–80.

[126] Georgi, *Kollekte*, p. 72.

[127] A. T. Hanson, *Paul's Technique and Theology*, p. 180.

Corinthian contributor as the subject of these verbs, then 'his righteousness' could refer to the justified status of the man who gives to the poor,[128] or to that person's moral righteousness,[129] or, more particularly, to his benevolence as expressed in almsgiving.[130] Of these three possibilities the first is the least likely in the context and the third the most probable.

(iii) How are we to understand the claim that this righteousness remains 'for ever'? It is obvious that, in Paul's view, the righteousness of God and Christ is everlasting, but the answer is not so clear if 'his' refers to the Christian. There are two possible types of interpretation in this case.[131] First, Paul may be seen as saying that the righteous acts of the good man continue as long as he lives, since God always supplies him with the means, or that the prosperity which is the reward of righteousness lasts throughout his life. Secondly, the thought could be that the righteous man's goodness will always be remembered, by humankind or by God, or that its effects will influence generation after generation. But this second type is less likely, at least if it is a matter of perpetual human remembrance or of lasting influence on future generations. Whilst the thought of the imminent Parousia is not present in 2 Corinthians, it is improbable that the expectation had so totally receded in Paul's mind that he would now be looking positively to generations to come amongst whom the Corinthians' acts of charity would be recalled. The most probable interpretation of 'remains for ever' is the first of those we have noted: the acts of the righteous man continue throughout his life. Whether or not there might also be the thought of reward in mind, and, if so, what kind of reward, would depend on the understanding of v. 10. The primary assertion that the pious person's righteous deeds are continual follows naturally upon the 'always' and 'every good work' of v. 8, to which it gives scriptural substantiation.

How, then, are we to understand the application of the quotation? The discussion has produced two basic exegetical options. Paul may be saying that the divine righteousness which meets the needs of the poor is everlasting. Or he may intend to substantiate from Scripture his assurance in v. 8 that his readers will always be sufficiently supplied with the wherewithal for their own almsgiving: Scripture itself speaks of the man whose beneficence to the poor is perpetual. This second option both fits the context and is a more natural use of the verse from the psalm, where the subject is the pious man. Furthermore, the δέ which

---

[128] Bachmann, p. 332.
[129] Allo, p. 235.
[130] Strachan, p. 143; Tasker, p. 127; see also Windisch, pp. 278–9, and Lietzmann, p. 138, who refers to Mt 6.1.
[131] Noted by Plummer, p. 262.

introduces v. 10, where it is God who is the subject of the action, might well suggest that we have here a change of subject from that of v. 9. In addition, the ἔδωκεν of the quotation surely refers back to the 'giver' of v. 7, who is the model for the Corinthian contributor to the collection. The only difficulty is the claim by some commentators that Paul would not speak of δικαιοσύνη as something apparently possessed and exercised by man. But this is to take too rigid a view.[132] In any case, this righteousness, in the sense of benevolence, is not self-generated, since v. 8 shows that it is engendered by the abundant gifts of divine grace. There is, moreover, the striking fact that in v. 10 Paul speaks plainly of 'your righteousness', i.e., the δικαιοσύνη of his readers.[133] We conclude that the representative Corinthian contributor is the implicit subject of ἐσκόρπισεν and ἔδωκεν, and the point of reference of αὐτοῦ.

10. ὁ δὲ ἐπιχορηγῶν σπόρον τῷ σπείροντι καὶ ἄρτον εἰς βρῶσιν χορηγήσει καὶ πληθυνεῖ τὸν σπόρον ὑμῶν καὶ αὐξήσει τὰ γενήματα τῆς δικαιοσύνης ὑμῶν. With the assistance of a further scriptural allusion,[134] Paul continues to emphasise, as in v. 8, God's abundant provision of resources. He will provide for the Corinthians just as certainly as in general he provides the means for the production of food.[135] But what, exactly, will this provision consist of? Would it be possible to take the σπόρος of τὸν σπόρον ὑμῶν in a literal sense? A good harvest would be the condition of being able to give away a surplus to others.[136] In the context of the collection, however, one would presumably have to think of a cash sale of the surplus crop. It is simpler to see material wealth

---

[132] See Ziesler, *Meaning of Righteousness*, p. 162, who notes this verse, and the instances of δικαιοσύνη in v. 10; 6.7, 14; 11.15 as Pauline examples of reference to 'the Christian's uprightness' without any allusion to the thought of 'righteousness-in-Christ'.

[133] Wolff, p. 186 n. 160, notes that this counts against taking God as subject in the psalm quotation.

[134] There is a probable reference (*pace* Betz, p. 113) to Isa 55 (LXX).10: καὶ δῷ σπέρμα τῷ σπείροντι καὶ ἄρτον εἰς βρῶσιν. In the context the subject is the earth, but in Paul's usage the subject must be the ὁ θεός of v. 8. Did he change σπέρμα to σπόρον or not? Some witnesses (ℵ C D² Ψ 048. 0209. 0243 𝔐) have σπέρμα here, whilst σπόρον is read by others (𝔓⁴⁶ B D* F G 1175 *pc*). The reading σπέρμα could be an assimilation to the text of the LXX, but σπόρον (according to Plummer, p. 264) might be assimilated to τὸν σπόρον ὑμῶν. The first alternative is more likely: in view of the virtual repetition of ἐπιχορηγῶν we might expect the σπόρον ὑμῶν also to be a repetition.

[135] Betz, p. 112, sees here a close similarity to Greek religion 'where the concept of God as provider was fundamental'. Paul uses both the simple χορηγέω and the compound ἐπιχορηγέω. It is very probably correct to take them as synonymous (so Windisch, p. 279, and Betz, p. 114 n. 193). Allo, p. 235, sees the compound as adding a note of abundance, but the simple verb may have this connotation, according to BAGD s.v.

[136] Windisch, pp. 279–80, notes the possibility, but rejects it.

in general as the 'seed'.[137] God will provide the Corinthians with the means to contribute to the collection and will even multiply the financial resources at their disposal.

Paul adds, 'and increase the products of your righteousness'.[138] Is he simply repeating in different words what he has said already? If so, these 'products' are the monetary contributions which will result from the Corinthians' active benevolence.[139] But he may be saying something more. He could intend to refer to divine blessings and spiritual benefits which will be bestowed on the Corinthians as a result of their generosity.[140] This is preferable. There is surely a natural contrast between σπόρος and γενήματα, sowing and yield, which makes it unlikely that the two nouns have precisely the same reference. It is possible that the remaining verses of the chapter give some indication of what these spiritual blessings may be.

All three finite verbs in v. 10 are subject to textual variation, as follows.

χορηγήσει
πληθυνεῖ   ℵ* B C D* P 33. 81. 326. 1175. 2464 *pc* latt
αὐξήσει

χορηγήσει
πληθυνεῖ   𝔓46 D² 104
αὐξήσαι

χορηγήσαι
πληθύναι   F G
αὐξήσει

χορηγήσαι
πληθύναι   ℵ² Ψ 0209. 0243 𝔐
αὐξήσαι

Thus, ℵ* with its companion witnesses has Paul making three statements: God will supply, will multiply, will increase. This

---

[137] Betz, p. 114, who has earlier, however, claimed, pp. 111–12, that Paul is using this terminology in its literal sense.

[138] This appears to pick up the phraseology of Hos 10 (LXX).12 ἕως τοῦ ἐλθεῖν γενήματα δικαιοσύνης ὑμῖν (Plummer, p. 263, and others; the allusion is rejected by Betz, pp. 114–15). As we have noted (see above, p. 513 and n. 52), Nickle and Georgi regard both of the scriptural allusions in this verse as substantiating the 'eschatological' understanding of the collection: the γενήματα δικαιοσύνης then refers to the conversion of Israel (Nickle, *Collection*, p. 137), or to the participation of Gentiles in God's salvation, i.e. in the divine covenant and blessing (Georgi, *Kollekte*, p. 73). We have argued against this interpretation of the collection, however (see above, p. 513), and on the present verse would agree with Furnish, p. 450, that Paul would hardly allude so obliquely to so important a concept.

[139] Windisch, p. 280; Tasker, p. 127.

[140] Filson, p. 378; Hughes, p. 335.

contrasts with the reading of ℵ² and its companions, where we have three optatives: may God supply, multiply, increase. The other two groups of witnesses alternate between indicative and optative. The optative is in general rare in the NT, and the probability is that Paul's original text contained all three verbs in the indicative. The change to the optative may have come about through scribal error, or atticising tendencies on the part of scribes, or both.

11. ἐν παντὶ πλουτιζόμενοι εἰς πᾶσαν ἁπλότητα, ἥτις[141] κατεργάζεται δι' ἡμῶν εὐχαριστίαν τῷ θεῷ·[142] The thought of God's[143] provision for the Corinthians is repeated: it is in every respect that they are in process of enrichment,[144] i.e., there is an increase in both their economic and their spiritual wealth,[145] resulting in every kind of generosity.[146] This generosity in turn produces thanksgiving to God:[147] Paul moves on to the effect of the collection upon its recipients.[148] The present tense of κατεργάζεται may be significant. Paul is so certain of a successful outcome that he can speak of the results of his project as though they are coming about already (by contrast with his attitude in Rom 15.30–31).[149] As the following verses show, the content of the thanksgiving is not confined to the monetary assistance brought to the Jerusalem Christians.[150]

[141] A few witnesses (𝔓⁴⁶ D* 326 b Ambst) read εἴ τις which is obviously a scribal error.

[142] D* omits the article, as does B which has θεοῦ: these readings, again, must be due simply to error.

[143] Wolff, p. 187, notes that πλουτιζόμενοι is a divine passive.

[144] Barrett, p. 239, and Furnish, p. 443, regard the participle πλουτιζόμενοι as the equivalent of a finite verb, so that Paul is making a further, independent statement: see BDR 468(2) on this use of the participle in Paul. Plummer, p. 264, and Wolff, p. 187 n. 168, would attach it loosely to the preceding ὑμῶν. There is not, perhaps, any great difference between these two interpretations, but the lack of a connecting particle at the beginning of the verse would tend to support the second of them.

[145] Windisch, p. 281; Wolff, p. 187. The content of πλουτιζόμενοι could include the δικαιοσύνη of v. 9 and the πᾶσαν χάριν of v. 8, as well as the σπόρον of v. 10. Furnish, p. 450, sees v. 11a as summarising the main points of the preceding five verses.

[146] On ἁπλότης see above, on 8.2.

[147] The εὐχαριστία τῷ θεῷ is formed by analogy with εὐχαριστέω τῷ θεῷ: see BDR 187(5).

[148] Windisch, p. 280. He comments, p. 281, that the notion of thanks to the human donors is almost wholly suppressed, receiving oblique mention only, in v. 14.

[149] Theobald, Gnade, p. 298. See also Furnish, p. 450.

[150] The definition of its further content will depend on one's understanding of the purpose of the project. Martin, p. 292, sees the reason for the thanksgiving to be the fact that the gift to Jerusalem 'moves God's age-old plan of universal salvation to its appointed goal (Rom 11:30–32)'. We have seen reason, however, to reject the eschatological interpretation.

12. ὅτι ἡ διακονία τῆς λειτουργίας ταύτης οὐ μόνον ἐστὶν προσαναπληροῦσα τὰ ὑστερήματα τῶν ἁγίων, ἀλλὰ καὶ περισσεύουσα διὰ πολλῶν εὐχαριστιῶν[151] τῷ θεῷ. Paul repeats and amplifies what he has said in v. 11b about the thanksgiving which will ensue when the donation is received, and implies that this is of even more importance than the meeting of need in the Jerusalem church. His phrase ἡ διακονία τῆς λειτουργίας ταύτης is a new description of the collection project, and raises the question as to whether the use of λειτουργία in this connection tells the reader anything more about its significance.[152] This term in secular Greek was used of public services of various kinds, and of services in general.[153] It might also have a cultic sense, relating to service of the gods,[154] and in the LXX the word and its cognates are always cultic, with reference to the functions of the priests and Levites.[155] Some commentators suppose that Paul has in mind the secular, 'political' usage: the λειτουργία is a service done for the benefit of the community.[156] Others see the background as sacral: the collection is a priestly offering,[157] a cultic event of the highest order.[158] Yet others suggest that the word may have both secular and sacral connotations.[159] Strathmann, however, by contrast with all these suggestions, argues that Paul uses λειτουργία in its popular sense of service in general, with no further implications. It occurs in Phil 2.30 to denote the Philippians' financial gift to the apostle himself, i.e., in a private and non-cultic sense.[160] But Strathmann himself allows

---

[151] A few witnesses (𝔓46 (d g r) Cyp Ambst) read εὐχαριστίαν by assimilation to v. 11: see Metzger, *Textual Commentary*[1], pp. 582–3.

[152] The relationship of the two nouns is also a matter of debate. If διακονία means 'service' (BAGD s.v. 1.–3.), then it would be synonymous with λειτουργία (BAGD s.v.), and the genitive λειτουργίας would be epexegetic: 'the ministry consisting in this service' (see Windisch, p. 281). But this interpretation is less likely. First, it would be odd that both nouns should have exactly the same sense (Barrett, p. 239; Furnish, p. 443). Secondly, the semantic range of διακονία is much wider than this (Collins, *Diakonia*, p. 335, who sees the 'service' terminology as unsuitable) and it is more probable that some such word as 'execution' (Barrett, p. 232), 'rendering' (RSV), or possibly 'performance' (cf. Collins, p. 335; Furnish, p. 443) would be preferable. The genitive would then be objective.

[153] LSJ s.v. I., II.; H. Strathmann, on λειτουργέω, λειτουργία in *TWNT* IV, pp. 221–9, 232–6; see pp. 223–4.

[154] LSJ s.v. III.; Strathmann, on λειτουργέω, pp. 224–5.

[155] Strathmann, on λειτουργέω, pp. 225–8; BAGD s.v. λειτουργία 1.

[156] Plummer, p. 265; Betz, p. 117. Verbrugge, *Collection*, p. 149, however, notes that a λειτουργία was no longer a voluntary service, and so would not provide a parallel to Paul's collection.

[157] Meyer, p. 382.

[158] Bachmann, p. 333.

[159] Lietzmann, p. 139; Windisch, pp. 281–2; Allo, p. 236.

[160] Strathmann, on λειτουργέω, p. 234.

that in Phil 2.17 the connection of λειτουργία with θυσία indicates that the word may have a cultic connotation in Pauline usage.[161] Similarly, λειτουργός, figuratively, has a cultic sense in Rom 15.16 (λειτουργὸν ... ἱερουργοῦντα).[162] In the present context it is noticeable that the thought of thanksgiving to God concludes both v. 11 and v. 12, that v. 13 speaks of glorifying God and v. 14 of prayer, and that the whole paragraph concludes with a final expression of thanksgiving. In view of this setting it is at least highly probable that Paul here sees the collection as a cultic act. As Furnish suggests, it can be regarded as such both because its delivery will evoke thanksgiving and praise and also because it is part of the apostle's 'priestly task' in relation to the Gentiles (Rom 15.16).[163]

Hence, whilst it will supply the wants[164] of the Jerusalem Christians, it will do more than that. There will be an abundance of good effects. What does this 'abundance' consist of? Chrysostom suggests that the contributors to the collection will furnish its recipients with even more than they need,[165] but this is unlikely in view of what has been said in 8.13–15. Might Paul have in view the 'fulness of blessing' to be accorded to his missionary labours (Rom 15.29)? The following verses might suggest this, if for the Jerusalem Christians the collection is to be an expression of the obedience of the Gentiles to the gospel.[166] This is possible perhaps.[167] But if the introductory ὅτι be taken seriously, v. 12 is explanatory of v. 11, and v. 11 concludes with the assertion that the Corinthians' generosity produces thanksgiving to God. Consequently, the most likely content of the 'abundance' or 'surplus' will be this thanksgiving itself.[168] It is 'by means of' (διά)[169] this expected multitude of thanksgiving prayers that the collection will surpass, in its effects, the simple supply of aid. According to Boobyer, the praise and thanksgiving envisaged in vv. 12–13 are thought of as increasing God's glory in a completely

---

[161] Strathmann, ibid.

[162] Furnish, p. 443.

[163] Furnish, p. 451. The goal towards which Paul is called to work is the integration of the Gentiles into the holy people of God (Rom 11.25), and the acceptance of the Gentile churches' gift by the Jerusalem church would further that end. See the discussion above, pp. 514–15 on the purpose of Paul's collection.

[164] According to Plummer, p. 265, προσαναπληροῦσα means 'fill up in addition', 'help to fill', with reference to the other contributors to the collection. But the verb can simply mean 'supply someone's wants' (BAGD s.v. προσαναπληρόω).

[165] Chrysostom, PG 61 col. 537 (NPNF XII, p. 373).

[166] Theobald, Gnade, pp. 299–300.

[167] But see below on v. 13.

[168] Windisch, p. 282; Georgi, Kollekte, pp. 74–5; Furnish p. 444.

[169] On this use of διά see BAGD s.v. A.III.1.a.

realistic sense.[170] Whether or not, however, Paul adopted this hellenistic understanding of thanksgiving is debatable.[171]

13.[172] διὰ τῆς δοκιμῆς τῆς διακονίας ταύτης δοξάζοντες τὸν θεὸν ἐπὶ τῇ ὑποταγῇ τῆς ὁμολογίας ὑμῶν εἰς τὸ εὐαγγέλιον τοῦ Χριστοῦ καὶ ἁπλότητι τῆς κοινωνίας εἰς αὐτοὺς καὶ εἰς πάντας. Here there is further elaboration of the consequences of a successful conclusion to the collection project. But there are differences of opinion as to the precise nature of these consequences. Who are those who are glorifying God? What is the meaning of δοκιμή, and, more importantly, of ὁμολογία? And what is the point of the final εἰς πάντας?

How is the participle δοξάζοντες to be understood? To find a preceding nominative plural with which it might be co-ordinated we should have to look back to the πλουτιζόμενοι of v. 11. The subject of this participle is the Corinthians, so that, if δοξάζοντες is to be correlated with it, it will be the Corinthians who, in v. 13, are seen as glorifying God. Hence the rendering of the RSV: 'Under the test of this service you will glorify God by your obedience . . .'; cf. NRSV. But this interpretation is unlikely. First, v. 12, with substantial content, intervenes between v. 11 and v. 13.[173] Secondly, in vv. 11b–12 the focus of interest has shifted from the Corinthians as donors to 'the saints' as recipients. Since it is clearly the latter who give thanks, it is only natural to suppose that they are the subject of δοξάζοντες as well.[174] The participle functions as a finite verb,[175] and it is the Jerusalem Christians who are envisaged as glorifying God. The cause[176] of their activity is expressed in the opening phrase διὰ τῆς δοκιμῆς τῆς διακονίας ταύτης. With Barrett and Furnish, we take this to mean 'the proof provided by this διακονία'.[177] The collection project, seen as a

---

170 Boobyer, '*Thanksgiving*', pp. 78–80; see p. 70 for a summary of the general idea. Boobyer is followed in his interpretation of the present verse by Georgi, *Kollekte*, pp. 74–5; Furnish, p. 451; and Betz, pp. 118–20. If it should be accepted, one could regard the τῷ θεῷ as dependent upon the whole participial phrase, with the sense 'to the benefit of God', i.e., as a dative of advantage (see BDR 188). Otherwise it would depend only on εὐχαριστιῶν (cf. v. 11).
171 See Vol. I, pp. 126–7.
172 B sa insert καί before διά.
173 Meyer, p. 383, commenting on Hofmann, who takes the view reflected in RSV and NRSV.
174 See, e.g., Lietzmann, p. 139; Plummer, p. 266; Barrett, p. 240; Furnish, p. 440.
175 See BDR 468(2).
176 On διά with the genitive with a causal function see BAGD s.v. A.IV.
177 Furnish, p. 440; Barrett, p. 232. The genitive is epexegetic, and δοκιμή has the same sense as in 13.3: see BAGD s.v. 2. The alternative is 'quality of being approved': see BAGD s.v. 1., with the present reference, translated 'the approved character of your service'. The genitive would then be possessive. But the first possibility gives more point to the use of the word here.

'mission'[178] from the Gentile churches to the church of Jerusalem, will 'prove' to the Jerusalem Christians something about these other congregations. What is this 'something'? The answer comes in the lengthy ἐπί-clause, running to the end of the verse, which further explains[179] the glorifying of God. But the nature of the answer largely depends, in turn, upon the sense given to ὁμολογία, and here the divergence of views may affect the understanding of the whole relationship between Gentile Christians and Jerusalem. It is usually supposed that ὁμολογία means 'confession', in the sense of a confession of religious faith, and that the following εἰς τὸ εὐαγγέλιον is dependent upon it: 'confession of the gospel'. Plummer and Windisch note a similar use of ὁμολογία εἰς in Justin: τὴν εἰς τὸν χριστὸν τοῦ θεοῦ ὁμολογίαν.[180] In the present verse, the genitive τῆς ὁμολογίας is itself dependent upon ἐπὶ τῇ ὑποταγῇ, and would probably be an epexegetic genitive: 'because of the obedience which consists in your confession of the gospel of Christ'.[181] The Jerusalem Christians glorify God because of the conversion of the Gentiles whose gifts are delivered to them. The collection is proof that these Gentiles too have been brought to 'the obedience of faith' (Rom 1.5).[182] Betz, however, proposes a quite different interpretation. The term ὁμολογία has the sense of 'contractual agreement', and this agreement would regulate the relationship between the contributors and Jerusalem. The preceding ὑποταγή refers to the contributors' obedient acknowledgement of it.[183] Hence, it was an agreement which would establish the dominance of the Jerusalem church in relation to the Gentile Christian communities. At the same time, the raising of the collection and its reception would create a partnership between the contributing churches and the recipients. The language of the verse, Betz claims, is, legal, not confessional. The phrase εἰς τὸ εὐαγγέλιον τοῦ Χριστοῦ is not immediately dependent on τῆς ὁμολογίας ὑμῶν, but means 'for the purpose of Christ's gospel'.[184] This interpretation has some attraction. In the

---

[178] See Collins, *Diakonia*, p. 219.

[179] For ἐπί with the sense 'because of', see BAGD s.v. II. 1. b. g.

[180] Justin, *Try.* 47; *PG* 6 col. 577; cited by Plummer, p. 266; see also Windisch, p. 283.

[181] On the epexegetic genitive see MHT, pp. 214–15. Georgi, *Kollekte*, p. 76 n. 302, takes ὁμολογίας in this sense; Furnish, p. 445, similarly sees it as 'identifying that of which the obedience consists'.

[182] For this general understanding of Paul's meaning see, e.g., Barrett, pp. 240–1; Bruce, p. 228; Furnish. p. 451.

[183] The genitive ὁμολογίας would thus be objective: see Betz, p. 123. The whole phrase would then have to mean something like 'your obediently accepting the agreement'.

[184] See Betz, pp. 122–5, for the details of his interpretation of the whole verse.

introduction to chap. 8 we have allowed that the purpose of Paul's collection was somewhat similar to that of the original Antiochene project, i.e., the creation of a relationship between Gentile churches and Jerusalem which would involve some recognition of the dominant position of the Jerusalem church (albeit with an acknowledgement by Jerusalem of the law-free character of the Gentile communities.). This would fit Betz's view of 9.13.[185] In its favour also is the linguistic fact that the verb ὁμολογέω, of a confession of faith, is nowhere in the NT followed by εἰς with the accusative of the content of faith. In Rom 10.10 the ὁμολογεῖται εἰς σωτηρίαν means confession *resulting in* salvation. On the other side of the argument, however, it could be urged that the other NT occurrences of ὁμολογία (1 Tim 6.12–13; Heb 3.1; 4.14; 10.23) in no way support the sense Betz wishes to give to it in the present verse, nor do the two Pauline instances of ὁμολογέω suggest it.[186] In all these cases the reference is to confession of faith. In addition, the phrase in Justin at least points to the possibility that ὁμολογία εἰς might mean 'confession of' in the religious sense. We may note also that ὁμολογέω is followed by ἐν in Mt 10.32 = Lk 12.8, and that in hellenistic Greek there was some interchange of εἰς and ἐν.[187] Hence, the more usual interpretation of ὁμολογία noted above, remains a possibility, linguistically. If we have to choose, then, between a 'technical' legal sense for ὁμολογία (Betz) and a 'technical' religious sense (most, if not all, other commentators), the NT use of ὁμολογία and ὁμολογέω would tip the balance in favour of the latter.[188] We take it that Paul is, after all, speaking of 'confession of the gospel of Christ'. The submission, or obedience,[189] to the gospel[190] consists in the confession of faith in it, and it is for this surrender to the gospel on the part of the Corinthians that the Jerusalem church, which had acknowledged the validity of Paul's mission to the Gentiles (Gal 2.9), will offer praise and thanksgiving to God.

They will praise God also because of the ἁπλότης of the κοινωνία εἰς αὐτοὺς καὶ εἰς πάντας. The precise meaning of this phrase depends largely upon the sense given to κοινωνία, but also upon the ease or difficulty with which this sense can accommodate the concluding εἰς πάντας. It is likely that two of the possible

185 See above, pp. 514–15.
186 Wolff, p. 188 n. 175. The Pauline examples of the verb occur in Rom 10.9–10.
187 MHT, pp. 254–6.
188 See above for the instances of ὁμολογία. The verb ὁμολογέω in a confessional sense occurs in Mt 10.32 = Lk 12.8; Rom 10.9–10; Heb 13.15; 1 Jn 2.23; 4.2, 15. This use of the word-group was clearly familiar in various circles in early Christianity, and would most likely suggest itself to Paul's readers in Corinth.
189 See BAGD s.v. ὑποταγή.
190 For the idea of response to the gospel as obedience see Rom 10.16.

interpretations of κοινωνία can be ruled out on that account. Meaning 3. in BAGD s.v. is 'sign of fellowship', 'proof of brotherly unity', 'gift', 'contribution'. The appropriate sense of ἁπλότης would then be 'liberality': 'the liberality of your contribution'.[191] Quite apart from the question of whether ἁπλότης can actually have the meaning 'generosity',[192] this interpretation becomes doubtful when its connection with εἰς πάντας is considered. The monetary contribution was for the Jerusalem church alone. In view of the Corinthians' tardiness in raising money simply for Jerusalem it would scarcely have been tactful or productive for Paul to have implicitly suggested that they might be required to give financial assistance to other churches as well.[193] The same objection would militate against meaning 4. 'participation', 'sharing', if this is understood in the sense implied by the translation offered by Furnish: 'the generosity of your sharing with them and with all'.[194] The other two meanings of κοινωνία are 1. 'association', 'communion', 'fellowship', 'close relationship' (the most usual sense, it would appear), and 2. 'generosity', 'fellow-feeling', 'altruism'.[195] The first, in the present verse, would mean 'state of fellowship', the second 'feeling of fellowship': the two senses would tend to merge.[196] The preceding ἁπλότης would then mean 'sincerity' or 'genuineness'. There would be no problem in either case as regards the εἰς πάντας. The Corinthians' state or sense of fellowship with the Jerusalem church, attested by the collection, could readily be supposed to extend to all other Christian communities.[197] Perhaps Paul would intend the additional phrase to be seen as expressing praise of the Corinthians for their 'ecumenical' outlook.[198] In that case, 'sense of fellowship' would be the better rendering of κοινωνία.

Here, then, Paul looks forward with some optimism to the

[191] Plummer, pp. 257, 266–7; see also Filson, p. 379.
[192] See above, pp. 523–4.
[193] Plummer, p. 267, suggests that Paul had in mind the thought of the church as the body of Christ (1 Cor 12.26): 'a benefit conferred on the brethren at Jerusalem is a benefit to the whole body of Christians.' But there is no indication elsewhere that this idea played any part in his thinking about the collection. Georgi, *Kollekte*, p. 77, nevertheless supposes that Paul sees the collection as a 'Selbstdarstellung des leibes Christi'.
[194] Furnish, p. 440.
[195] For 1., see Windisch, p. 284; for 2., Lietzmann, p. 139; Tasker, p. 129.
[196] Windisch, pp. 284–5, appears to alternate between them.
[197] Lietzmann, p. 139.
[198] Martin, p. 294, thinks Paul is praising his readers for the generosity they show in the collection and will show wherever the need arises. In our view the point is not financial generosity; however, the general point about praise may be valid. He draws attention to the view of J. Hainz, *KOINONIA*, p. 144, that the εἰς πάντας is intended as a relativisation of the authority of Jerusalem.

reception of the collection in Jerusalem.[199] The recipients will glorify God both for the Corinthians' conversion and for their sense of solidarity with the Christians of Jerusalem and elsewhere. For the first time Paul reveals what the objective of the collection is in terms of ecclesiastical politics, i.e., his intention of securing some formal recognition of his Gentile churches on the part of Jerusalem.[200]

14. καὶ αὐτῶν δεήσει ὑπὲρ ὑμῶν ἐπιποθούντων ὑμᾶς διὰ τὴν ὑπερβάλλουσαν χάριν τοῦ θεοῦ ἐφ' ὑμῖν. He turns finally to consider the more direct response of the recipients to the donors, in the form of prayer and longing for them.[201]

The syntax of the verse is debatable. It is possible to connect καὶ αὐτῶν δεήσει with the preceding verse: the δεήσει would function as an instrumental dative,[202] and the participle ἐπιποθούντων would stand in apposition to αὐτῶν. This would give the sense reflected in the KJV: [13]'they glorify God for your ... subjection ...; [14]And by their prayer for you, which long after you.'[203] Alternatively, we have a fresh assertion, unrelated grammatically to the previous verse. The participle ἐπιποθούντων replaces a finite verb, and in addition constitutes an example of the looser use of the genitive absolute in NT Greek.[204] The dative δεήσει would be either instrumental, indicating the means by which the Jerusalem Christians express their affection, or modal,[205] indicating attendant circumstances: 'in their prayer', or 'as they pray'. The majority of commentators separate the two verses syntactically, as in this second alternative,[206] and this interpretation is preferable: in v. 14 there is a slight change of direction, in that the attitude of the Jerusalem Christians towards the Corinthians becomes more prominent. The opening καί is connective. It is unlikely that it means 'also', indicating that *like Paul himself* the recipients of the collection are longing for the

---

[199] Windisch, p. 284, notes the contrast with Rom 15.30–31.

[200] Windisch, pp. 283–4. For Windisch, it is a matter of the Christian status of these communities. We have suggested that the point is their law-free status as Christian churches. But this would amount to the same thing, since doubts concerning Christian morality in a law-free church would lead to doubts about the genuineness of Christian conversion.

[201] A few witnesses (א* B 1881. 2495 *pc* vg^ms) read ἡμῶν for ὑμῶν. This is obviously a scribal error: in the context it is prayer for the Corinthians (not for Paul) that is relevant.

[202] BDR 195.

[203] See Hughes, pp. 340–1 n. 77, who regards this as a possibility. Bachmann, p. 335, attaches v. 14 to v. 13, but takes δεήσει as expressing attendant circumstances. Bengel, *Gnomon*, p. 804, also connects the two verses, but takes δεήσει as dependent upon the ἐπί of v. 13.

[204] BDR 468, 423.

[205] BDR 198.

[206] See, e.g., Plummer, p. 257; Barrett, p. 232; Martin, p. 287.

Corinthians.[207] This would require a different word-order, e.g., ἐπιποθούντων ὑμᾶς καὶ αὐτῶν. The anticipated longing on the part of the Jerusalem Christians may be a longing to see the Corinthians.[208] At any rate, it indicates a wish for personal fellowship of some kind.[209] But its motivation is theological.[210] They would wish to witness, or at least to know more about, the wealth of divine grace at work in the Corinthian church. Is this, perhaps, a somewhat exaggerated description of the Corinthians' response to the collection project? As it eventually turned out, this may be so. But Paul's aim here is to encourage generous giving, and to that end he creates a hopeful picture in which he sees his aim realised.[211] In any case, as this verse shows, his basic confidence rests not in the Corinthians but in the power of God to bring the enterprise to a successful conclusion.[212] This may account also for his optimism about the response of the recipients. God's grace will operate in Jerusalem just as much as in Corinth. At the same time, there is a noticeable contrast with the more doubtful tone of Rom 15.31. Whilst it is true that Paul would not have mentioned misgivings about the collection's reception to any of the contributing churches,[213] one wonders whether he could have spoken with such positive enthusiasm, had he harboured misgivings of substance at the time of writing 2 Cor 9. Perhaps it was when he finally arrived in Corinth that he heard unfavourable news about the situation in Jerusalem[214] and that his attitude changed somewhat. It seems likely that news about Jerusalem would reach Corinth more readily than Macedonia. If the trouble which evoked Galatians had been contemporaneous with the Corinthian correspondence, Paul's vehement response might have become known in Jerusalem. It would scarcely have endeared him to the Jerusalem church, and it would become obvious that a project which he sponsored might be doubtfully received.

---

[207] *Pace* Allo, p. 237, and Furnish, p. 445. Meyer, p. 386, who likewise takes καί as 'also', sees a reference to the Corinthians: the recipients of the collection reciprocate the fellow-feeling of the donors.

[208] Chrysostom, *PG* 61 col. 538 (NPNF XII, p. 373); Barrett, p. 241.

[209] Windisch, p. 285.

[210] Barrett, p. 241.

[211] Cf. Plummer, p. 267, who adds (p. 267 n.) that in 1 Cl 2.1 we have evidence that his hopes were fulfilled. Clement praises the Corinthians because they give more gladly than they receive, 'which he would hardly have done had the historic collection been a failure at Corinth'. Furnish, p. 453, however, thinks that this reference should not be pressed.

[212] Windisch, p. 286.

[213] Bruce, p. 228.

[214] Bruce, p. 228, suggests that the misgivings may have arisen as a result of news that came later than the writing of the present letter.

15. χάρις τῷ θεῷ ἐπὶ τῇ ἀνεκδιηγήτῳ αὐτοῦ δωρεᾷ. Since in the last few verses Paul has been speaking of prayer, of thanksgiving, and of glorifying God, it is not surprising that he should conclude with a climactic and liturgical-sounding[215] expression of gratitude to God for his indescribable gift. The debatable point is the nature of the gift. Is it, specifically, the grace of God operative in the collection? Or is it the gift of Christ, and God's whole work in Christ? In favour of the more restricted reference it may be said that there is no suggestion in the immediate context that Paul is thinking of the gift of Christ,[216] that similar exclamations elsewhere (2.14; 8.16; Rom 6.17; 1 Cor 15.57) refer to something which is clearly specified,[217] and that the thought of promoting the unity of Gentile and Jewish Christians by means of the collection is a perfectly sufficient explanation of the hyperbolic language.[218] But on the other side of the argument, and with reference to the last point above, the claim is made that the adjective ἀνεκδιήγητος, meaning something 'that cannot be adequately expressed in words' is too hyperbolical simply to refer to the collection and its anticipated effects.[219] It is the supreme gift of Christ that is meant (cf. 8.9).[220] This may be preferable. Arguably, the αὐτοῦ stands in a somewhat emphatic position: 'his gift', i.e., God's unique gift of his own Son, not the grace by which men and women are enabled to give.

---

215 On the liturgical use of ἀνεκδιήγητος see Betz, pp. 126–7. On the χάρις-formula, see Deichgräber, *Gotteshymnus*, p. 43. It has occurred in 2.14. See Vol. I, p. 191 and n. 14.
216 See e.g., Plummer, p. 268; Windisch, p. 286; Furnish, p. 452.
217 Furnish, p. 452.
218 Plummer, p. 268.
219 Tasker, p. 130.
220 Tasker, ibid. This general line of interpretation is supported also by Chrysostom, *PG* 61 col. 538 (NPNF XII, p. 373), and Bruce, p. 228.

VI

THE LAST LETTER TO CORINTH
(10.1–13.13)

The last four chapters of the canonical 2 Corinthians have aroused critical attention for more than two centuries.[1] The original and longstanding focus of investigation has been the relation of these chapters to the first nine, and in Vol. I we have adopted the view that they constitute a separate letter, written later than chaps. 1–9.[2] More recently, the growing interest in the application of rhetorical theory to the NT documents has produced several monographs which approach the text from this perspective. A full rhetorical study is not possible here, but we shall take note of three of these investigations. In 1978, J. Zmijewski published a detailed stylistic study of the Fool's Speech (2 Cor 11.1–12.10): *Der Stil der paulinischen „Narrenrede".* Almost two decades later, in 1995, M. M. DiCicco has produced a discussion of the three rhetorical means of persuasion denoted by the terms ἦθος, πάθος, and λόγος, and the way Paul uses these methods in 2 Cor 10–13 (to convince his readers of his good moral character, to arouse emotions favourable to himself, and to prove his case logically): *Paul's Use of Ethos, Pathos, and Logos in 2 Corinthians 10–13.* The insights offered by these two scholars will be noted in the course of the exegesis. In the case of the work by DiCicco we shall also select, for each of the three methods of proof, a section of text which illustrates its use more particularly. The third monograph, published in 1996 by A.-G. Sundermann, and entitled *Der schwache Apostel und die Kraft der Rede,* is a structural analysis of the four chapters. Again, his specific exegetical suggestions will be considered as they become relevant. It will be useful at this point, however, to take note of his overall rhetorical scheme. He supports, with caution, the view that chaps. 10–13 are separate from, and later than, chaps. 1–9[3] and sees them framed as a defence speech. A simplified version[4] of his

---

[1] This approach begins with J. S. Semler, in his commentary of 1776.
[2] See Vol. I, pp. 5–20.
[3] Sundermann, *Kraft der Rede,* pp. 29–30.
[4] See Sundermann, *Kraft der Rede,* p. 45, for a more detailed analysis.

proposed structural outline of the whole speech would run as follows:

	Apology[5]
(i) Exordium	10.1–11
(ii) Narration and proposition	10.12–18
(iii) Argument (Fool's Speech)	11.1–12.18
(a) refutation	11.1–15
(b) proof	11.16–12.18
(iv) Transfer	12.19–21
(v) Peroration	13.1–10

The Fool's Speech is seen as made up of two units ((a) and (b) above) which can each be divided into four parts (exordium, proposition, argument, and peroration).

This structure, and the critical theory which sees chaps. 10–13 as a separate epistolary item, receives confirmation from the parallels noted by Sundermann between 10.1–11 and 13.1–10.[6] The peroration is the counterpart to the exordium. One would therefore expect to find points of contact between them, and this is in fact what we do find. The ἀπών / παρών contrast of 10.1–2 recurs in 13.10. The wording of 10.8 is virtually identical with that of 13.10: 10.8 τῆς ἐξουσίας ἡμῶν, ἧς ἔδωκεν ὁ κύριος εἰς οἰκοδομὴν καὶ οὐκ εἰς καθαίρεσιν ὑμῶν ‖ 13.10 τὴν ἐξουσίαν ἣν ὁ κύριος ἔδωκέν μοι, εἰς οἰκοδομὴν καὶ οὐκ εἰς καθαίρεσιν. See also 10.10 ‖ 13.9; 10.11 ‖ 13.10.[7] These correspondences between 10.1–11 and 13.1–10 would support the view of the four chapters 'as a separate and distinct compositional unit'.[8] And this, in turn, allows for, and may favour, the theory that they constitute a separate letter. As the exegesis proceeds, we shall note and comment on Sundermann's analysis section by section. This should not be understood to imply prior acceptance of it. The method is adopted as the simplest and fairest way of presenting and examining the author's theory.

---

[5] Sundermann uses the Latin terminology, which will be noted in the exegesis.
[6] *Kraft der Rede*, p. 47.
[7] Ibid., n. 3.
[8] The quotation is from DiCicco, *Ethos, Pathos, and Logos*, p. 30, indicating his own perception of this section of the canonical letter. He does not make a decision on its unity or otherwise.

1. PAUL AND THE OPPOSITION IN CHAPTER 10

(i) *Paul's response to criticism of himself (10.1–11)*

¹Now I, Paul, I myself, appeal to you by the meekness and clemency of Christ, I who am subservient in your midst, face to face, but bold towards you when absent, ²and what I ask is, not to be bold when present with the confidence I reckon to dare to employ against certain people who reckon we conduct our lives in a merely human fashion. ³For though we live in the human world, we do not campaign in merely human ways, ⁴ᵃfor the weapons of our warfare are not merely human, but powerful for God, to destroy strongholds, ⁴ᵇdestroying intellectual arguments ⁵and every arrogant attitude raised in opposition to the knowledge of God, and taking every intention prisoner for obedience to Christ, ⁶and being ready to punish every act of disobedience when your obedience is brought to completion. ⁷Look at what is before your eyes. If anyone is convinced in his own mind that he belongs to Christ, let him conversely reflect to himself on this: that just as he is Christ's, so also are we. ⁸For if I should boast in some further respect about our authority which the Lord gave me, for constructive purposes and not for your destruction, I shall not be put to shame. ⁹(I say this) so that I may not seem to be effecting your intimidation, so to speak, by means of my correspondence. ¹⁰Because the letters, someone says, are weighty and powerful, but his personal presence is feeble, and his speech contemptible. ¹¹Let such a person take account of this: that such as we are in word, by correspondence, when absent, such also we shall be, when present, in deed.

Both explicitly and by implication Paul details the criticisms to which he knows he is subject in Corinth. He is subservient in manner when present, and obviously lacks the power of the Spirit. His letters may give an impression of strength, but his feeble personal presence has quite the opposite effect. And as an orator he is pathetic. In response, he insists that, to the contrary, he wages a spiritual war with powerful weapons against all that he sees to be opposed to God, that his authority comes from the Lord, and that when he arrives in Corinth he will be as effective in person as he is by letter.

10.1–11 as exordium. As we have indicated, Sundermann sees these verses as constituting the exordium of Paul's speech for the defence in chaps. 10–13. It takes the form of an *insinuatio*.[9] In vv.

---

[9] Cicero (*Inv.* [on invention] I 15.20) defines the *insinuatio* as the second type of exordium (the first being the *principium* in direct language), and describes it as follows: 'Insinuatio est oratio quadam dissimulatione et circumitione obscure subiens auditoris animum.' ('Insinuation is an address which by dissimulation and indirection unobtrusively steals into the mind of the auditor', LCL). See Sundermann, *Kraft der Rede*, p. 47.

1–6, Paul is seeking to gain the interest and the agreement of his audience.[10] The rhetorical strategy accounts for the clear contrast, noted by Windisch,[11] between the moderate tone of the exordium and the sharpness of the following debate.[12] The moderation is to be recognised, Sundermann claims, as a *dissimulatio*,[13] that is, as a form of irony. The ironical tone is likewise manifested in Paul's pretence of appropriating his opponents' representation of him (v. 1b). Furthermore, there is an implicit irony which derives from the context. The apostle is said by his critics to be bold when absent from Corinth but abject when present. Here, by contrast, he begins his letter in a mild and friendly fashion, but in respect of his forthcoming presence in the city he expresses (v. 2) his confidence of bold action if such should be necessary.[14] In another aspect of his strategy (vv. 4–6), he aims to distance the Corinthian congregation from the opponents who come from elsewhere. The λογισμοί of the latter are effectively contrasted with the hoped-for obedience of the former.[15] Sundermann then points to v. 7 and to vv. 10–11 as forming a *partitio*, i.e., a division of the ensuing speech into parts:[16] v. 7 points to the *probatio* in 11.16–12.18 and vv. 10–11 to the *refutatio* in 11.1–15.[17]

This is to a large extent plausible. The mild opening, the apparent acceptance of the view of Paul current in Corinth, and the expectation that the Corinthians will nevertheless be amenable to his authority (and that it is the visiting missionaries, consequently, whom he is basically castigating)– all these aspects of the passage could function as means of securing the goodwill of the audience, as would be appropriate to an exordium. To what extent, however, the term 'dissimulation' would be appropriate to Paul's intention is perhaps another question. It does suggest some degree of misrepresentation, at least (if not deception). Is this congruent with the fact that Paul begins by calling Christ in aid to support his appeal?

1a. Αὐτὸς δὲ ἐγὼ Παῦλος παρακαλῶ ὑμᾶς διὰ τῆς πραΰτητος καὶ ἐπιεικείας τοῦ Χριστοῦ, We have argued in the

---

[10] Sundermann, *Kraft der Rede*, p. 49.

[11] Windisch, p. 292.

[12] Sundermann, *Kraft der Rede*, p. 50.

[13] Sundermann, *Kraft der Rede*, p. 51 n. 14, with reference to Cic. *Inv.* I 15.20 (see n. 9 above).

[14] Sundermann, *Kraft der Rede*, pp. 51–2. The ironical contrast he claims to see, however, is not in fact complete. It is only, again, in a letter that Paul promises strong action.

[15] Sundermann, *Kraft der Rede*, p. 56; see also n. 47 where he observes that Furnish, p. 459, correctly points to the emphatic ὑμῶν in v. 6.

[16] LS s.v. II.B.

[17] Sundermann, *Kraft der Rede*, p. 58. The passages in question constitute the two main sections of the Fool's Speech.

Introduction to Vol. I that chaps. 10–13 of the canonical 2 Corinthians constitute a separate letter, sent to Corinth later than the letters of chaps. 1–8 and chap. 9.[18] Here we have the beginning of the letter-body. The redactor of the Corinthian correspondence will have deleted the opening greeting, and also any further preliminary material such as an opening thanksgiving period. It is likely, however, that, as in Galatians, Paul passed straight from the greeting to the substance of what he had to say. The contents of this letter would make an introductory thanksgiving (or blessing) less than appropriate. There is in addition a sense of urgency.[19] The intruding missionaries must be expelled before money raised for the collection is diverted to their upkeep. The letter must reach Corinth before Paul himself does (13.10), and he must get there in person before the onset of winter.[20]

His opening words are a combination of authority and personal appeal. The Αὐτὸς δὲ ἐγὼ Παῦλος appears to be a conflation of two similar expressions found elsewhere: ἐγὼ Παῦλος (Gal 5.2; Col 1.23; 1 Th 2.18; Phlm 19), and αὐτὸς ἐγώ (Rom 7.25; 9.3; 15.14; 2 Cor 12.13). The ἴδε ἐγὼ Παῦλος of Gal 5.2 is seen by some commentators as the closest parallel to the present verse:[21] here Paul is asserting his authority,[22] or at least is putting the whole weight of his influence behind what he is about to say.[23] Similarly, in all three of the occurrences of αὐτὸς ἐγώ in Romans what is stressed is full personal involvement.[24] And since Paul is essentially an apostolic person, in a context such as the present one, where his apostolic authority is in question, his personal involvement will imply the assertion of his authority.[25] The combination of the two phrases which separately occur elsewhere gives particular emphasis. At the same time, it is an appeal that is made, not an apostolic directive that is issued in an authoritative manner. The verb Paul uses is παρακαλέω, 'appeal to', 'entreat'.[26]

He supports the appeal he is about to make in v. 2 by means of a reference to the character of Christ. The formal structure of the παρακαλῶ ... διά- clause has parallels elsewhere in his letters.

---

[18] See Vol. I, pp. 5–13.

[19] See Furnish, p. 47, on these points.

[20] See the chronological table in Vol. I, p. 77. He would see a further delay as disastrous, both for the collection project and for the general state of affairs in Corinth.

[21] Plummer, p. 272; Lietzmann, p. 140; Furnish, p. 455.

[22] Lightfoot, *Galatians*, p. 203.

[23] Burton, *Galatians*, p. 273. See also Bruce, *Galatians*, p. 229.

[24] See Cranfield, *Romans*, pp. 369 n. 4, 458, 752.

[25] Commentators who see some stress on Paul's authority here include: Lietzmann, p. 140; Hughes, p. 344; Bultmann, p. 184; Bruce, p. 229; Furnish, p. 455; Martin, pp. 300, 302.

[26] BAGD s.v. παρακαλέω 3.

See, for example, Rom 12.1; 15.30; 1 Cor 1.10.[27] In these instances the διά-phrase adds weight to the request,[28] as it does in the present verse.[29]

This said, however, this same phrase presents several exegetical questions. For whom is Christ a model? And in what respect? Also, what are the connotations of ἐπιείκεια? The first question is readily answered. Theoretically, Paul's reminder of the character of Christ could be understood in two different ways: either he is appealing to his readers to behave in a Christ-like manner towards himself, or else he is begging them not to compel him to abandon the Christ-like manner which he would wish to maintain towards them.[30] The general context, concerned as it is with the personal impression Paul makes by his presence and by his letters, would support the second alternative.[31]

The second question requires more discussion. When Paul refers to these characteristics of Christ, does he have in view the historical life of Jesus, or is he thinking of the heavenly Christ? Evidence in favour of the first possibility may be found, it is argued, in Mt 11.29, where Jesus says of himself: πραΰς εἰμι καὶ ταπεινὸς τῇ καρδίᾳ.[32] This, however, may not be an authentic Jesus-saying. Furnish notes that it has 'clear affinities with the Jewish Wisdom tradition', and suggests that it was the influence of this tradition which caused the saying to be attributed to Jesus.[33] If so, one would have to ask at what point it entered the Jesus-tradition. It is Matthean only, so that one could not say with any confidence that it would have been present in the tradition as received by Paul.[34] It is in any case more probable, in view of 8.9 and Phil 2.7-8, that Paul is thinking of the 'meekness' of the pre-existent Christ, who freely took upon himself the lowly condition of humanity and died an humiliating death.[35]

---

[27] Noted by, e.g., Windisch, p. 291, and Furnish, p. 455. On this use of διά, see BDR 223(5), and BAGD s.v. A.III.1.f. ('in urgent requests').

[28] In Rom 15.30 and 1 Cor 1.10 it does so by appealing to the authority of Christ (in Rom 15.30 also the love produced by the Holy Spirit), and in Rom 12.1 by appealing to an attribute of God.

[29] Here by appealing to attributes of Christ.

[30] Windisch, p. 292, thinks the phrase has meaning for both parties.

[31] See Bruce, p. 229, and Leivestad, ' "Meekness" ', p.161, for the view that the phrase relates to the behaviour of Paul.

[32] Klöpper, p. 424; Plummer, p. 273; Allo, p. 242; Kümmel, p. 208; Schmiedel, p. 270.

[33] Furnish, p. 455, with reference to Ps 131 (LXX).1 and Ecclus 45.4; see also p. 460.

[34] Barrett, p. 246, however, thinks that Paul did know some tradition which depicted Jesus as possessing these characteristics. See also G. N. Stanton, *Jesus of Nazareth in New Testament Preaching* SNTSMS 27, Cambridge, 1974, p. 108, for the claim that 2 Cor 10.1 refers to the character of the historical Jesus.

[35] See Leivestad, ' "Meekness" ', pp. 163-4; Bultmann, p. 184; Furnish, p. 460.

The third question, concerning the precise sense of ἐπιείκεια, likewise exposes a difference of scholarly opinion. The meanings given in BAGD are 'clemency', 'gentleness', 'graciousness'. There is some overlap with its companion term πραΰτης, which can also mean 'gentleness' (as well as 'humility', 'courtesy', 'considerateness', meekness'),[36] and the two words are found together elsewhere.[37] What is debated is whether ἐπιείκεια itself means here the clemency displayed by someone of authority. It is certainly used in this sense in other contexts. Plutarch, for example, speaking of Caesar, says: καὶ τό γε τῆς Ἐπιεικείας ἱερὸν οὐκ ἀπὸ τρόπου δοκοῦσι χαριστήριον ἐπὶ τῇ πραότητι ψηφίσασθαι.[38] In the LXX, God is said to judge ἐν ἐπιεικείᾳ (Wisd 12.18), and to discipline sinners μετὰ ἐπιεικείας (2 Macc 10.4).[39] Consequently, it is suggested that in the present verse the word indicates the graciousness of Christ who possesses heavenly authority, and in that authoritative capacity exercises clemency.[40] Against this line of argument, however, it is urged that there is at least one significant use of the word in the LXX where it has no such connotation, but refers rather to the gentleness of the righteous man which is to be tested at the hands of his violent adversaries (Wisd 2.19).[41] In the NT there is only one occasion when ἐπιείκεια is attributed to someone in authority (Acts 24.4), and one instance where the adjective ἐπιεικής is applied to masters of domestic slaves (1 Pet 2.18). In other occurrences (Phil 4.5; 1 Tim 3.3; Tit 3.2; Jas 3.17) the adjective has different connotations.[42] In addition, it may be associated (as in the present verse) with the virtue of πραΰτης, a word which 'denotes the humble and gentle attitude which expresses itself in particular in a patient submissiveness to offence'.[43] In the present instance, the combination of ἐπιείκεια with πραΰτης may be seen as an hendiadys, in which the sense is defined by πραΰτης, which is the more familiar of the two words.[44] Note also that the key word in

---

[36] BAGD s.vv. ἐπιείκεια and πραΰτης.

[37] Windisch, p. 292, draws attention to 1 Cl 30.8; Plut., Per. 39; Sert. 25; Philo, Opif. Mundi 103; cf. Wettstein, p. 202, who notes the reference in Plut., Per.

[38] Plut., Caes. 57: 'and certainly it is thought not inappropriate that the temple of Clemency was decreed as a thank-offering in view of his mildness' (LCL). (Windisch, p. 292, notes the reference, but without citation.)

[39] Windisch, p. 292.

[40] H. Preisker, on ἐπιείκεια, ἐπιεικής in TWNT II, pp. 585–7; see p. 586 on 2 Cor 10.1. See also Spicq, Lexicographie Néo-testamentaire I, pp. 263–7.

[41] Leivestad, ' "Meekness" ', pp. 157–8.

[42] Leivestad, ' "Meekness" ', p. 158.

[43] Leivestad, ' "Meekness" ', p. 159.

[44] Leivestad, ' "Meekness" ', pp. 159-60. This interpretation, he argues, p.160, is supported by the other occasions in early Christian texts where these terms are found together (Tit 3.2; 1 Cl 21.7; 30.8), and describe 'a gentle, humble and modest attitude as a general Christian ideal'.

the second half of the verse is ταπεινός, 'lowly', and that Paul must intend some connection between this term, as applied to himself, and the qualities of Christ to which he appeals.[45] Hence, when he refers to Christ's πραΰτης and ἐπιείκεια he has in mind 'the fact of the kenosis, the literal weakness and lowliness of the Lord'. The term ἐπιείκεια does not allude to the clemency of Christ as 'heavenly judge'.[46] Which of these interpretations is preferable? The linguistic evidence is scarcely decisive. There are too few instances of ἐπιείκεια and ἐπιεικής in the NT to indicate which alternative is the more probable, and outside the NT there is as much evidence of the one sense as the other. The answer, then, must derive from the context. It is clear that Paul does see a connection between his own conduct and the characteristics of Christ to which he appeals,[47] and that he would wish to preserve the attitude which his opponents describe as ταπεινός (v. 2), and which in his view is consonant with the 'meekness' of Christ. Nevertheless, in the context of vv. 1–11 what is at issue is the question of apostolic authority, and what Paul seeks to avoid is the need to exercise this authority harshly when he arrives in Corinth.[48] An allusion to the 'clemency' of Christ would fit the context very well. There is no need to interpret ἐπιείκεια in terms of πραΰτης· it can equally well refer to the divine mercy which Paul himself has experienced (1 Cor 7.25), and which should be reflected in the attitude of Christ's apostle. This interpretation seems the better one.

1b. ὃς κατὰ πρόσωπον μὲν ταπεινὸς ἐν ὑμῖν, ἀπὼν δὲ θαρρῶ εἰς ὑμᾶς· Before coming to the content of his appeal, Paul elaborates upon his self-introduction in a description which appears to reflect the adverse criticism of his opponents: although the wording is different, the substance is similar to that of v. 10, where there is an actual quotation of what his critics are saying about him. Some commentators suppose that in the present verse also he is using his opponents' language.[49] By contrast with v. 10, however, we do not have an exact quotation of what they may have said since the main verb is in the first person.[50] Is it possible, then, that it is Paul himself who has introduced the terms ταπεινός and θαρρῶ into the controversy?[51] It may be so, but there is also a third option, at least in respect of ταπεινός. In 7.6 Paul has seen

[45] Leivestad, ' "Meekness" ', pp. 161–2.
[46] Leivestad, ' "Meekness" ', p. 163.
[47] Leivestad, ' "Meekness" ', pp. 164–5.
[48] Cf. Preisker, on ἐπιείκεια, p. 586.
[49] Chrysostom, *PG* 61 col. 542 (NPNF XII, p. 375); Meyer, p. 391; Plummer, p. 273.
[50] Betz, *Tradition*, p. 46.
[51] So Betz, *Tradition*, p. 52.

the word as applicable to himself when he says ἀλλ' ὁ παρακαλῶν τοὺς ταπεινοὺς παρεκάλεσεν ἡμᾶς ὁ θεός. If, as we suppose, this is said in a letter earlier than that of chaps. 10–13, it is possible that the opponents he is now confronting had taken up the description for their own pejorative purposes, and that he, in turn, is responding to their use of it.[52] In 7.6 it simply meant 'downcast'.[53] Here, however, it must have a derogatory sense as far as Paul's opponents are concerned, whilst there is the further possibility that Paul himself is attempting to rehabilitate the term. Hence its nuances of meaning require more extended discussion.

In the mouth of the critics, what did ταπεινός signify? English equivalents proposed are 'pliant', 'subservient', 'abject',[54] or 'servile', 'ineffectual', 'inferior'.[55] Barrett claims that here it has the same sense as in a passage in Xenophon, where it is paired with (τὸ) ἀνελεύθερον, 'servility', and means 'self-abasement'.[56] This disparaging use of ταπεινός would be thoroughly in line with the vast majority of its occurrences in Greek literature.[57] The primary basis for its application to Paul was doubtless his failure to master the situation in Corinth at the time of his painful visit.[58] On this occasion, he had been unimpressive, to say the least. It is possible that one or two representatives of the rival mission had already arrived, to assess their own prospects of success in the city, and had witnessed his ineffectiveness. If not, they will have learnt of it from the resident congregation. The visiting missionaries themselves do create a powerful personal impression, and exercise authority in an obvious way (11.20). They will have emphasised Paul's apparent lack of authority by applying to him a term which in general usage had connotations of subservience or outright servility.[59] Paul reproduces their criticism. At the same

---

[52] In that sense Paul is quoting his critics. In the context of vv. 1–2 the change from the third to the first person would come about quite naturally.

[53] See Vol. I, p. 486.

[54] BAGD s.v. ταπεινός 2.

[55] See the translation, p. 19, by G. W. Bromiley, in *TDNT* VIII, pp. 1–26, of W. Grundmann, on ταπεινός, in *TWNT* VIII, pp. 1–27; see p. 20.

[56] Barrett, p. 247, with reference to Xen., *Mem.* III 10.5. The rendering 'self-abasement' comes from the LCL translation. See also Furnish, p. 456, who suggests that ταπεινός conveys the sense of the loss of 'one's dignity and personal sense of worth'.

[57] See Grundmann, on ταπεινός, pp. 1–4.

[58] Lietzmann p. 140; Windisch, p. 293.

[59] According to P. Marshall, *Enmity in Corinth*, pp. 323–4, the use of ταπεινός is one of the indications that Paul's critics charge him with being a flatterer, since in Greek literature the word is popularly used in denigration of such characters. But such a connotation has no obvious connection with the situation during Paul's interim visit to Corinth, and if he is replying here to a charge of this kind one would expect him to be more specific, as he is in 1 Th 2.5 (οὔτε γάρ ποτε ἐν λόγῳ κολακείας ἐγενήθημεν).

604   COMMENTARY ON II CORINTHIANS

time, however, he sets it in a context which throws a new light on its apparently negative content. He has just appealed to the 'meekness' of Christ, in a way which implies a correspondence between Christ and himself as an apostle. Thus, his own ταπεινότης is based on the πραΰτης of Christ himself. Furnish suggests he is saying that if, to the Corinthians, he seems to have been demeaned among them, this is because he is a true apostle of the Christ who demeaned himself (Phil 2.8).[60]

Rather differently, Betz, who does not attribute the use of ταπεινός to Paul's opponents, nevertheless supposes that his introduction of the term does serve as a response to his critics. The whole complex of thought regarding ταπεινότης belongs to the debate about the outward bearing and appearance of the genuine philosopher. The image of the unimpressive outward appearance of Socrates had become part of the Cynic tradition, and it was held that the true philosopher will always be defamed on account of his poor external showing. Paul stands within this intellectual tradition, and intends to indicate that the charges brought against him need no refutation, since they correspond to those contrived against the genuine philosopher.[61] It is doubtful, however, whether this is the point in the present verse, where the contrast is with boldness; Cynic philosophers were not precisely lacking in this quality. Betz claims that for Paul the two attitudes were not contradictory, but this is scarcely the way the verse naturally reads. In addition, he provides no clear evidence that the word ταπεινός was in frequent currency as a standard description of the true philosopher.[62]

Subservient or ineffectual when present, his critics say, Paul is bold towards the Corinthian congregation when absent. The obvious reference is to the letters mentioned in v. 10, and more particularly to the Painful Letter (2.3–4; 7.8) which had temporarily reasserted his authority in Corinth.

2. δέομαι δὲ τὸ μὴ παρὼν θαρρῆσαι τῇ πεποιθήσει ᾗ λογίζομαι τολμῆσαι ἐπί τινας τοὺς λογιζομένους ἡμᾶς ὡς κατὰ σάρκα περιπατοῦντας. Having indicated in the previous verse that he is making a personal appeal to his readers, Paul now

---

60 Furnish, p. 460; cf. Martin, p. 303.
61 Betz, *Tradition*, pp. 47–50, 55.
62 Betz, *Tradition*, pp. 53, 49 n. 36. He gives only one reference for this use of ταπεινός, i.e., Luc., *Somn.* 9, 13, and its relevance is obscure. The word ταπεινός is applied to a career as a sculptor, which Lucian is advised to reject. Should he choose it, he will be 'humble-witted', ταπεινὸς τὴν γνωμήν—indeed, 'altogether humble', πάντα τρόπον ταπεινός (the quoted English phrases are taken from the LCL). Socrates was himself brought up to this career (*Somn.* 12), but forsook it for education (ibid.). Whatever the point of the parody as a whole, it scarcely seems to prove the point about the use of ταπεινός.

introduces its content with the more neutral verb δέομαι, 'I ask'.[63] In doing so, he shows that he clearly distinguishes between the Corinthians themselves and the rival (and, in his view, intruding) missionaries. The former he does not want to have to treat in a bold, assertive manner: as far as the latter are concerned he counts on being able to do just that.[64]

These critics, it appears, consider Paul as someone who conducts himself, or lives, κατὰ σάρκα. What did they mean by this? The suggestions are numerous.

(i) It is an accusation in rather general terms that Paul's conduct is not directed by the Holy Spirit.[65]

(ii) This general suggestion may be put more strongly, and in various ways may be defined more precisely. The phrase may be a slogan of gnostics who denied that Paul was 'spiritual', πνευματικός: his weak personal presence would be due to this lack of πνεῦμα.[66] It may refer to lack of visionary and ecstatic experiences,[67] or to deficiency in 'demonstrable, charismatic gifts of leadership'.[68] If the opponents are would-be θεῖοι ἄνδρες, they may be claiming that the 'spiritual' person 'should transcend all

---

[63] According to Rückert, p. 290, Bachmann, pp. 341–2, and Prümm, *Diakonia Pneumatos* I, pp. 568–9, δέομαι is addressed to God, so that what we would have here would be a prayer-report. It would not be within the power of the Corinthians to control the τινες (Bachmann), and since, if Paul were addressing the Corinthians, it would be only the more loyal of them to whom he would be speaking, one would have expected him to make this clear (Prümm). But this interpretation would leave the παρακαλῶ ὑμᾶς of v. 1 standing on its own in a very abrupt fashion (Meyer, p. 392), and the arguments adduced to support it are scarcely convincing: Paul's concern is to detach all the Corinthians from their support for the rival missionaries, and thus indirectly to destroy their power. On the construction following δέομαι see BDR 399(3).

[64] As Windisch, p. 294, notes, the two verbs θαρρέω and τολμάω are synonymous. Betz, *Tradition*, pp. 67–8, investigating the background, observes that τολμᾶν in a good sense is the daring of the philosopher who is not afraid to speak the truth, and especially that of the Cynic preacher-philosopher (Betz refers, p. 67 n. 163, to Epict., *Diss.* II 16.42; III 1.41; Luc., *Cat.* 13; *J. conf.* 5.19); in a bad sense the τολμα-word group may be used against the sophists, and is a favourite anti-sophist insult in the early Christian period. It would appear, then, that the connotations of τολμάω are determined by the context in which it occurs. All that one might deduce, perhaps, is that it is a term suited to confrontation and controversy. (Not all Betz's references are wholly relevant, moreover: see Epict., *Diss.* II 16.42.) The use of λογίζομαι also, according to Furnish, p. 456, may be related to Paul's confrontation of his critics, in that its repetition (together with the λογισμοί of v. 4) suggests that it is one of their terms which he redirects against them. But since 33 of the 41 NT instances of the verb occur in the Pauline letters the suggestion is scarcely compelling.

[65] Rückert, p. 292; Meyer, p. 393; Bruce, p. 229.

[66] The suggestion comes from Windisch, p. 295, although he does not finally adopt this view.

[67] Barrett, p. 250.

[68] Martin, p. 304; cf. Barrett, p. 250; Sundermann, *Kraft der Rede*, pp. 53–4.

human weakness and give evidence of his adherence to the divine sphere by an exalted manner of existence'.[69]

(iii) The claim is that Paul is prone to human fears and failings, and hence to the inconsistent behaviour described in v. 1 (see also 1.12–17).[70]

(iv) The charge may be more disparaging. Paul is an apostolic swindler with worldly motives, who employs all the tricks against which he defends himself in 1.12; 2.17; 4.2. He is an impostor, and his 'weak' behaviour will have been urged as proof.[71]

(v) The charge is based on Paul's affliction by the 'Satanic messenger' (12.7), understood as an illness. This shows that he remains in the unredeemed condition, has no part in Christ, and cannot, therefore, be a legitimate apostle.[72]

(vi) Paul is too concerned with securing his own means of support by working at his craft, and has too little trust in Christ. His way of life is in sharp contrast to that of the rival missionaries. These people, it is claimed, were itinerant charismatics for whom support by the community was a means of legitimating their apostleship, since it was in accord with the command of Jesus that preachers of the gospel should live from the gospel. Such a manner of life would perhaps commend itself to the Corinthians as similar to that of the Cynic itinerant preacher who was in principle free from concern about his means of support.[73] Paul's insistence on self-support may have appeared to degrade the office of apostle.[74]

(vii) Perhaps the Corinthians were turning against him his own proof that they themselves were only 'infants in Christ' (1 Cor 3.1–3). He himself was introducing contention and rivalry into the situation in their church, and was thus behaving in a worldly, purely human manner.[75]

Which of these possibilities is the most likely?[76] Since the opposite of σάρξ is πνεῦμα (see Rom 8.3–9), the charge could in

---

[69] Jewett, *Anthropological Terms*, p. 128. Jewett follows Georgi in seeing the intruding missionaries as 'divine men'.

[70] Bachmann, pp. 342–3; Plummer, p. 275; Hughes, p. 348.

[71] See Windisch, p. 295, and cf. Tasker, p. 133.

[72] Betz, *Tradition*, p. 96.

[73] Theissen, *Social Setting*, pp. 42–8.

[74] Furnish, p. 461, with reference to Theissen, sees this as a possibility: Paul's work would have been seen both as humiliating and as a sign of worldliness.

[75] Reitzenstein, *Mystery-Religions*, p. 459.

[76] In discussing the question we shall assume that the Pauline phrase κατὰ σάρκα was actually itself used by his critics. Whilst Paul might have expressed in this way some criticism which had been otherwise formulated, the way in which the σάρξ-motif is taken up in a repetitive fashion in vv. 3–4 does tend to suggest that it is his own words that have been used against him. We have observed that v. 1 may reflect the same situation.

theory relate to 'unspiritual' personal behaviour (see above under (i), (iii), (iv), (vi), (vii)), or to personal weakness of some sort which would seem inconsonant with the gift of the Spirit (see above under (ii), (v)). The phraseology is general enough to cover a number of supposed defects in Paul's apostolic character, and may have been used by his opponents for precisely that reason, so as to unite in opposition to him different members of the congregation who criticised him on various grounds. His own understanding of the basic charge, however, is apparent from v. 4. The primary issue is that of power: his weapons are not σαρκικά but powerful. The charge is that he lacks the charismatic power necessary to effective apostolic leadership (see above under (ii)), and this may be supplemented by reference to his recurrent illness (see above under (v))—if this is the correct interpretation of 12.7. We need not necessarily see any specifically gnostic group in the background, nor suppose the rival missionaries to have presented themselves as θεῖοι ἄνδρες. Paul's apparent weakness during his interim visit could in itself have been seen as proof of his deficiency.

3. ἐν σαρκὶ γὰρ περιπατοῦντες οὐ κατὰ σάρκα στρατευόμεθα. Paul has already implied that his opponents' criticism is without foundation. Here he begins to explain why this is so. He allows that he lives ἐν σαρκί. Although in Rom 8.8 this phrase is used in a pejorative sense scarcely distinguishable from the κατὰ σάρκα of vv. 4–5, it must here have some different meaning, since activity κατὰ σάρκα is what Paul denies. At the same time the word σάρξ itself must have some basic sense which would be applicable in both phrases. Furnish suggests that in both the word 'stands for what is finite, worldly, limited and limiting'.[77] Hence ἐν σαρκί will mean 'in the sphere of earthly life',[78] 'in the human world' which all men and women inhabit, which imposes its limitations upon them, and in which particular conditions of weakness may become apparent. For Paul, however, there is a further dimension of existence. The life which derives from the indwelling Spirit of God interpenetrates earthly life. Those who possess this dimension of existence do not go about things κατὰ σάρκα, in a purely human way, for whilst the gift of the Spirit does not eliminate human limitation and weakness it enables the recipients to experience the operation of divine power within these conditions.

Jewett argues that this Pauline concept of an earthly sphere which is open to the spiritual realm is possible only on the basis of apocalyptic assumptions, since it means that there is a 'confluence of the two aeons'. The theme of vv. 1–6 is the campaign to bring

[77] Furnish, p. 457.
[78] Cf. BAGD s.v. σάρξ 5.

about the submission of the world to Christ, and in the background there lies the apocalyptic notion of the final battle between good and evil.[79] This is not wholly convincing, since it is unlikely that Paul ever thought of the material world as impervious to the operation of God's Spirit. It is true, however, that for him the bestowal of the Spirit upon believers is an anticipation of the eschatological existence of the age to come,[80] so that in this sense there is a 'confluence' of the two ages. Whether or not Paul sees himself as participating in the final battle between good and evil depends on the significance of the military imagery here and in the following verses. Windisch supposes that he has transposed the concept of the Jewish messiah who conquers on the field of battle into that of the apostolic campaign for the world's subjection to Christ, and has combined the prospective punitive visit to Corinth with this wider purpose.[81] We shall see, however, that this is not a necessary interpretation.

4a. τὰ γὰρ ὅπλα τῆς στρατείας[82] ἡμῶν οὐ σαρκικὰ ἀλλὰ δυνατὰ τῷ θεῷ πρὸς καθαίρεσιν ὀχυρωμάτων. The military image is developed, as Paul describes his 'weapons', first negatively, then positively. The negative description, 'not merely human', must primarily mean that his instruments of spiritual warfare are not weak or ineffective, since σαρκικά is opposed to δυνατά, 'powerful'. Possibly this is the only content that needs to be given to οὐ σαρκικά. Some commentators suggest that it indicates a rejection of various apparent assets such as wealth, eloquence, forcefulness of personality, and the like.[83] But this scarcely fits the context. The denial that Paul's weapons are σαρκικά is part of his rejection of his opponents' charge that he goes about things κατὰ σάρκα, i.e., in an all too human way. By this, his critics clearly do not mean that he relies on eloquence or a forceful personality—rather the contrary (v. 10).[84] More plausibly, if σαρκικά has further connotations, Paul might have in

[79] Jewett, *Anthropological Terms*, pp. 129–30.
[80] Barrett, p. 80, commenting on 1.22.
[81] Windisch, pp. 295–6.
[82] The reading στρατείας is that of a number of minuscules (33. 81. 104. 365. 630. [1175]. 1739. [2464]. 2495 *pm*). Other witnesses have στρατιᾶς (K L 1241. 1881 *al.*) or the unaccented στρατιας (𝔓[46] ℵ B C D F G P Ψ). Clearly Paul is referring to a campaign, στρατεία, and not to an army, στρατιά. The other two readings, therefore, could result from scribal error due to itacism, i.e., the identical pronunciation of ει and ι: see BAGD s.v. στρατεία. But it is possible that Paul himself originally wrote στρατιας, which has good support. The word στρατιά was occasionally used in the sense of στρατεία. See BAGD s.v. στρατιά 2.
[83] Chrysostom, *PG* 61 col. 543 (NPNF XII, p. 376), cited by Meyer, p. 394 n. 1; Tasker, p. 134.
[84] The same objection would apply to the suggestion by Theissen, *Social Setting*, p. 45, that σαρκικά is reminiscent of 1 Cor 9.11, where Paul describes the support to which he is entitled, but which he rejects, as τὰ σαρκικά, 'material benefits'.

mind the discreditable, 'all too human', methods of missionary propaganda which in 4.2 he claimed to have renounced.⁸⁵ This is a possibility if the image of warfare relates to his apostolic mission in general, but if it refers only to the assertion of his authority amongst the Corinthians it would be less appropriate. He does not explain what his means of operation consist of, but simply comes to the main point: they are powerful.⁸⁶ Why, however, does he add τῷ θεῷ? There are three suggested grammatical explanations of the force of the dative.

(i) It is the dative of advantage.⁸⁷ Paul wields his weapons 'for God',⁸⁸ fights 'in God's cause'.⁸⁹

(ii) It may be an hebraistic use of θεός as an intensive, as in Jon 3.3, where πόλις μεγάλη τῷ θεῷ simply means 'a very great city'.⁹⁰ Paul's weapons would be 'very powerful indeed'. It is doubtful, however, whether the Corinthians could be expected to understand such an idiom.⁹¹

(iii) It is 'a dative of subjective judgment',⁹² with the sense 'in God's eyes'.⁹³

The first of these options is the easiest grammatically and makes perfectly good sense. Paul fights in God's service, to destroy opposition to knowledge of God and to secure obedience to Christ. It is noticeable, however, that some of the proponents of both (i) and (ii) tend to make Paul say not that his weapons are powerful for God or that they are exceedingly powerful but that they are divine, filled with God's power, and the like. Thus Martin takes (i) to mean: 'God can work powerfully through these weapons.'⁹⁴ Windisch likewise detects in the background the Israelite tradition whereby the weapons of God's people are

---

⁸⁵ See Furnish, p. 462, and Martin, p. 305.

⁸⁶ According to Schütz, *Apostolic Authority*, pp. 241–2, Paul uses δυνατός here because he is responding to opponents who have arrogated to themselves the description πνευματικός, who claim to possess power, and who accuse him of weakness. Since he wants to differentiate himself from these people he does not use πνευματικός (the natural converse of σαρκικός) at all, and he speaks of his weapons, not of himself, because he does not wish to base his defence on personal attributes. But it is not necessary to suppose that Paul's critics themselves claimed the description πνευματικός to explain either his own non-use of the term or the charge of weakness. The charge itself is explicable on the basis of the interim visit, and the non-use of πνευματικός on the basis of the charge. And since Paul is the subject of vv. 4b–6 the distinction between his weapons and himself is rather fine.

⁸⁷ See BDR 188(2).

⁸⁸ Lietzmann, p. 141.

⁸⁹ JB, cited by Furnish, p. 457; see also Barrett, p. 251, and MHT, p. 238.

⁹⁰ Moule, *Idiom Book*, p. 184.

⁹¹ Barrett, p. 251.

⁹² The defining phrase comes from Furnish, p. 457, though he prefers option (i).

⁹³ Noted by Plummer, p. 276, as a possibility, with reference to RV 'before God'.

⁹⁴ Martin, p. 305, with reference to Plummer, p. 276, and to Barrett, p. 251.

effective because they are filled with divine power.[95] Similarly, Hughes, favouring (ii), has 'divinely powerful'.[96] The REB, more explicitly, translates the phrase 'strong enough with God's help'. But these interpretations effectively turn τῷ θεῷ into a dative of agent. This use does exist,[97] but probably occurs only once in the NT,[98] and in any case would be used with a passive verb, which is not what we find here.

Perhaps the force of this 'for God', i.e., 'in God's service' is to be understood with reference to the later description of the apostle's opponents as intermediaries of Satan (11.14–15).

Paul's 'weapons' are for the purpose of demolishing strongholds, πρὸς καθαίρεσιν ὀχυρωμάτων. This phrase is thought by several exegetes to provide a clue to the origin and consequent significance of the military imagery employed in these verses. There are various suggestions.

(i) A. T. Hanson sees a possible link with the LXX version of Zech 9.12: καθήσεσθε ἐν ὀχυρώματι, δέσμιοι τῆς συναγωγῆς, which he translates: 'you shall dwell in the fortress, prisoners of the synagogue'. If Paul has this verse in mind, he may be thinking of non-Christian Jews who 'insist on remaining in their fortress of unbelief'. It is this 'stronghold' that the apostle proposes to destroy.[99] This interpretation is highly unlikely. The only point of contact with Zech 9.12 is the word ὀχύρωμα, which is fairly common elsewhere in the LXX.[100] Furthermore, Paul's apostolic mission, if this is in view, is directed primarily to Gentiles, whilst, if he is thinking of the rival missionaries, these people, although Jews, are not unbelievers in their own eyes or in the eyes of the Corinthians.

(ii) Paul has in mind a verse in Proverbs (21.22) where the wise man is said to attack strong cities and destroy the stronghold which the ungodly trusted in:

πόλεις ὀχυρὰς ἐπέβη σοφὸς
καὶ καθεῖλεν τὸ ὀχύρωμα, ἐφ'ᾧ
ἐπεποίθεισαν οἱ ἀσεβεῖς.[101]

Perhaps the apostle saw in this verse a reflection of his own task, and believed himself to have inherited the calling of 'the wise' of

[95] Windisch, p. 296.
[96] Hughes, p. 351 n. 6.
[97] BDR 191.
[98] Lk 23.15.
[99] Hanson, *Paradox*, pp. 100–1.
[100] Plummer, p. 276; Martin, p. 305, who notes its frequency in 1 Maccabees (Plummer refers simply to 'Maccabees'). In 1 Macc 5.65 and 8.10 it is the object of καθαιρέω. There are other occurrences of the word in e.g., 4.61; 5.10, 11, 27, 29, 30; 6.61, 62.
[101] Noted by Plummer, p. 276, Windisch, p. 297, and others.

the OT period.[102] Here we have not only the word ὀχύρωμα but also the verb καθαιρέω (cf. the noun καθαίρεσις in Paul's phrase). Hence, if some particular OT verse is in view, this is a likely possibility. At the same time, the combination of the two words would appear to be something of a stock phrase,[103] which Paul could have been familiar with quite apart from its occurrence in Prov 21.22. (iii) The suggestion under (ii) may be further developed with reference to a parallel in Philo. In his spiritual interpretation of the Tower of Babel his theme is the destruction of arguments designed to deflect the mind from honouring God and pursuing holiness.[104] He refers to a 'stronghold' (ὀχύρωμα) constructed through the persuasiveness of such arguments,[105] and then speaks of preparation for its destruction: πρός γε τὴν τοῦ ὀχυρώματος τούτου καθαίρεσιν.[106] According to Windisch, Philo, like Paul, starts from Prov 21.22. He then uses the imagery as part of his attack on the sophists.[107] Paul himself takes up the anti-sophistic terminology for use against the Corinthian gnostics.[108] Perhaps, then, he is himself involved here in a campaign against sophists? According to Betz, in hellenistic Judaism battle against the sophistic movement was already the task of the Wise, whilst Paul transfers it to the Christian apostle.[109] Again, however, the argument is tenuous, in view of the wide currency of the vocabulary of siege warfare.[110]

(iv) The imagery of which the present phrase is a part originates simply in the tactics of Graeco-Roman siege warfare. Its use was common amongst the philosophers, and Paul could have been influenced by this general philosophical tradition.[111] This is perhaps the most likely explanation. It does not in itself necessarily imply that Paul was engaging in specifically anti-sophistic polemic.

4b–5a. λογισμοὺς καθαιροῦντες καὶ πᾶν ὕψωμα ἐπαιρόμενον κατὰ τῆς γνώσεως τοῦ θεοῦ, Paul begins to interpret the imagery. The 'strongholds' marked out for demolition[112] are

---

[102] Windisch, p. 297.
[103] See, e.g., 1 Macc 5.65; 8.10.
[104] Philo, *Conf. Ling.*, 128–32.
[105] Ibid., 129.
[106] Ibid., 130.
[107] Windisch, p. 297, with reference to the passages noted above.
[108] Windisch, ibid.
[109] Betz, *Tradition*, pp. 68–9.
[110] See above p. 610; cf. Malherbe, 'Antisthenes', pp. 143–4.
[111] Furnish, p. 458, with reference to Malherbe, 'Antisthenes', pp. 148–56.
[112] The participle καθαιροῦντες takes up the previous καθαίρεσιν (Lietzmann, p. 141), and is to be seen as an example of Paul's absolute use of the nominative participle as a finite verb, with no grammatical relation to what precedes (BDR 468; See Plummer, p. 276; Allo, p. 244). It is not likely, *pace* Bachmann, p. 344, that it is to be attached anacoluthically to the ἡμῶν of v. 4a, which hardly carries much emphasis. Nor is it to be connected with the στρατευόμεθα at the end of v. 3. As Windisch, p. 297, notes, this would leave v. 4a as a parenthesis, which it is not, since vv. 4b–5 constitute its continuation and explication.

λογισμοί,[113] 'thoughts', 'reasonings', perhaps here, specifically, 'sophistries'.[114] There could be an allusion to intellectual forms of resistance to the apostolic preaching in general.[115] In the context, however, Paul must primarily have in view the forms of argument used by the rival missionaries and their Corinthian supporters.[116] Malherbe, rather differently, supposes that the λογισμοί are not the arguments produced by the reason but the reasoning faculties themselves.[117] The singular, however, would seem more likely in this sense.[118]

It is debatable whether the following καὶ πᾶν ὕψωμα ἐπαιρόμενον adds a further item to the military imagery or whether it also is part of the interpretation of the ὀχυρώματα. According to Chrysostom, Paul continues with his metaphor. The word ὕψωμα is the equivalent (so Chrysostom implies) of πύργωμα.[119] The general meaning of ὕψωμα is 'height', 'exaltation',[120] whilst πύργωμα means 'that which is furnished with towers', 'fenced city'.[121] No doubt many such in the ancient world were established on heights, so that the transition to the use of ὕψωμα as a synonym would not be inconceivable. Plummer, taking the participle as middle, thinks that the metaphor derives 'from walls and towers standing defiantly'.[122] If, however, Paul is already interpreting his metaphor, ὕψωμα will refer to psychological exaltation in a bad sense, i.e. to pride, arrogance, and the like.[123] The word has this meaning in Job 24 (LXX).24.[124] If this is the sense in the present verse it is parallel to the preceding λογισμούς and the following πᾶν νόημα,[125] as constituting a direct, non-figurative, reference to the mental attitude of Paul's opponents and critics. This

---

[113] Furnish, ibid.

[114] See BAGD s.v. λογισμός 1., where 'sophistries' is given for the meaning in the present verse.

[115] Plummer, p. 276; cf. Grotius, p. 495; Windisch, p. 298, supposes such an allusion to be included in the term.

[116] Lietzmann, p. 141; Windisch, p. 298; Barrett, p. 252; Bultmann, p. 187; Furnish, p. 458.

[117] Malherbe, 'Antisthenes', p. 147.

[118] See BAGD s.v. λογισμός 2.

[119] Chrysostom, PG 61 col. 543, after quoting the phrase and commenting on the continuation of the metaphor, says: κἂν γὰρ ὀχυρώματα ᾖ, φησί, κἂν πυργώματα ..., εἴκει καὶ παραχωρεῖ τοῖς ὅπλοις τούτοις (' "For though there should be strongholds," he saith, "though fortifications, ... they yield and give way before these weapons." ' NPNF XII, pp. 376–7). See also Windisch, p. 298, and BAGD s.v. ὕψωμα 2., where the possibility is noted.

[120] BAGD s.v.

[121] LSJ s.v.

[122] Plummer, p. 277. Furnish, p. 458, sees an allusion to high defensive fortifications.

[123] See BAGD s.v. ὕψωμα 2.

[124] G. Bertram, on ὑψόω, ὕψωμα, in TWNT VIII, pp. 604–14; see p. 612.

[125] Lietzmann, p. 141.

parallelism counts in favour of a non-metaphorical sense for ὕψωμα,[126] and the whole phrase will mean 'every arrogant attitude raised in opposition …'[127] This would in any case be what Paul intends to convey: the question is simply whether he conveys it directly or figuratively.

To whom, then, are these arrogant attitudes attributed, and what is the significance of the claim that they are directed against the knowledge of God? Primarily the people in view must be the rival missionaries (the same verb ἐπαίρω is used of them in 11.20), but their Corinthian supporters may also be included (as v. 6 implies). This is the more likely since γνῶσις was something the Corinthians prided themselves upon (1 Cor 8.1–2), and which they seem now to be denying to Paul (11.6).[128] If it is to the intruding missionaries that the term ὑπερλίαν ἀπόστολοι in 11.5 refers, then the implication of 11.5–6 would be that these people claim to possess some superior knowledge. In Paul's eyes all such attitudes would be contrary to, and destructive of, the genuine knowledge of God, because those who adopt them do so in opposition to himself as the true propagator of divine knowledge (2.14; cf. 4.6). It is uncertain whether there is any wider reference. According to Windisch, the phrase γνῶσις τοῦ θεοῦ is missionary terminology (2.14), and the ὕψωμα stands for any town in which idolatry flourishes. Paul has in mind the hostility of unbelievers as well as the Christian opposition in Corinth.[129] But how likely is this, in a letter so concentrated on the defeat of the latter?

5b. καὶ αἰχμαλωτίζοντες πᾶν νόημα εἰς τὴν ὑπακοὴν τοῦ Χριστοῦ, Paul's military metaphor has been that of a siege. First, the fortifications of the city have been destroyed, and now its inhabitants are taken prisoner,[130] captured 'for obedience to Christ'.[131] The debatable question here is the precise sense of νόημα. According to BAGD, it is used in this verse to mean 'design', in a pejorative sense.[132] Allo takes it in a more neutral sense, 'thought'.[133] Essentially, however, this is the same interpretation, in that in both cases νόημα stands for the result of the activity of the mind, νοῦς.[134] By contrast, some commentators

---

[126] In terms of the military imagery as a whole, that is.
[127] See BAGD s.v. ἐπαίρω 2.b.a. for the figurative 'rise up', 'offer resistance', 'be in opposition'.
[128] Bultmann, p. 187.
[129] Windisch, p. 298.
[130] Windisch, pp. 297–8.
[131] The genitive τοῦ Χριστοῦ is objective (Windisch, p. 298, and Barrett, p. 253), and εἰς expresses purpose (BAGD s.v. 4.f.).
[132] BAGD s.v. νόημα 2.; cf. Barrett, p. 252.
[133] Allo, p. 245; see LSJ s.v. νόημα I. 2., 3.
[134] See J. Behm, on νόημα, in *TWNT* IV, pp. 958–9; see p. 959.

understand it to mean 'mind' itself.[135] Jewett argues as follows. In both 3.14 and 4.4 the sense of the word must be 'mind', or 'understanding'. In the present verse, moreover, the translation 'thought' would make πᾶν νόημα simply a repetition of the λογισμοί of v. 4. And 'mind' makes better sense: 'If Paul aims to destroy all sophistic thoughts, how could he take such thoughts captive?' The usual translation 'every device', with its pejorative connotation, derives (not from linguistic or contextual necessity but) from the reaction against Luther's rendering 'alle Vernunft', 'all reason', seen as having 'anti-intellectual implications'.[136] These arguments are scarcely persuasive. In 3.14 and 4.4 νόημα is plural, and the plural would lend itself fairly readily to the transition to the sense 'mind', as standing for the sum total of the mind's contents, but it is less certain that the singular could do so, even when qualified by πᾶν. There is no repetition of v. 4 if νόημα means 'design' or 'device', and in any case the logic of Paul's imagery should not be pressed too rigorously. Lastly, in 2.11 the plural νόηματα is used in a bad sense of the 'designs' of Satan. In view of the polemical context of the present occurrence of the word it is not necessary to postulate a reaction against Luther's rendering to explain the usual translation(s).[137]

At the same time, it may be a mistake to suppose that πᾶν νόημα has an inherently bad sense, for each such is to be (not destroyed but) made obedient to Christ. The meaning 'purpose'[138] may be preferable to 'design'. If we then ask whose purposes Paul has in mind we find the same difference of opinion as before. He may be referring to his general apostolic task of winning the Gentiles to obedience to the gospel.[139] Or he may be thinking chiefly of those who oppose the proper understanding of Christ's gospel, and oppose himself as Christ's apostle, within the Christian congregations and especially in Corinth.[140] A definite decision, if such is possible, will depend in part on the interpretation of v. 6, where the theme of obedience recurs.

6. καὶ ἐν ἑτοίμῳ ἔχοντες ἐκδικῆσαι πᾶσαν παρακοήν, ὅταν πληρωθῇ ὑμῶν ἡ ὑπακοή. It is clear that there are two groups of

[135] Hughes, pp. 353–4, n. 10, suggests that it may denote the 'intellective centre of man's being'.
[136] Jewett, *Anthropological Terms*, pp. 380–2.
[137] See BAGD s.v. νόημα 2., where 2 Cor 10.5 and 2.11 are seen as using νόημα in the same sense.
[138] See BAGD s.v. νόημα 2.
[139] Furnish, p. 463, with reference to Rom 1.5; 10.16; 15.18.
[140] See Martin, p. 306, who comments that, practically speaking, the 'obedience to Christ' which is in view 'involves a submission to Paul's kerygma which is in danger of losing its credibility at Corinth (11:4) as a result of the rival mission there'. If v. 6a refers to the representatives of the latter, in v. 5b it will be the Corinthians themselves whom Paul has in mind.

people with whose obedience or disobedience Paul is concerned. He hopes, positively, that the Corinthians' obedience will be brought to completion. Obedience to Christ must be meant, in view of v. 5,[141] and what is required will be their detachment from the influence of the rival missionaries whom Paul later castigates as intermediaries of Satan (11.14–15), the opponents of Christ and the gospel. At the same time it is likely that renewed obedience to Paul himself is also included,[142] since he saw himself as Christ's representative,[143] at least as far as the Corinthians were concerned (cf. 1 Cor 9.2). Negatively, he is prepared [144] to punish every act of disobedience. Whose? Presumably that of the intruding missionaries,[145] but does the πᾶσαν παρακοήν have a wider reference as well? Windisch thinks it includes disturbances in other churches, and also Paul's prospective missionary campaign in new territory (10.15–16; cf. Rom 15.23, 28).[146] This is unlikely. In view of the crucial nature of the crisis in Corinth it is improbable that at this point Paul was concerned with opposition in other churches. As regards his mission in general, whilst he does speak of securing obedience to Christ, he nowhere suggests that he will himself directly punish those who reject his preaching.[147] It is only the rival missionaries, therefore, who are to be the object of punishment for disobedience. If they are delegates of Satan, they are clearly disobedient to Christ.[148] But are they seen as disobedient to Paul as well? Those who were neither his converts nor his assistants were under no general obligation to obey him.[149] If, however, in vv. 13–16 there is an oblique allusion to the agreement in respect of missionary territory which is mentioned in Gal 2.9 and in which Paul was a prime participant, then the 'disobedience' of his opponents would relate to this arrangement, which they had disregarded, and would in some sense count as disobedience to Paul.[150]

The nature of the threatened punishment remains undefined. Doubtless it would mean the total exclusion of the rival

[141] Furnish, p. 459; see also Bachmann, p. 345.

[142] Plummer, p. 278.

[143] See Vol. I, pp. 199–200.

[144] See BAGD s.v. ἕτοιμος 2. for the usage of ἐν ἑτοίμῳ ἔχειν in the sense 'be ready'. Furnish, p. 459, takes it as a continuation of the military image, with reference to 1 Macc 7.29.

[145] So Chrysostom, PG 61 col. 544 (NPNF XII, p. 377); Meyer, p. 397; Wendland, p. 228; Barrett, p. 254; Furnish, p. 464.

[146] Windisch, p. 299.

[147] According to Rom 2.8, punishment will come from God, at the final judgement.

[148] See above.

[149] Barrett, p. 254.

[150] Ibid. See further the exegesis of 11.15.

missionaries from the Corinthian church. For this Paul would require the support of the congregation, hence the reference to the prior completion of the Corinthians' obedience.[151] But something more than this might be intended. Perhaps Paul has in mind some exercise of a miraculous power that belonged to him as an apostle, something comparable, it might be, to the 'handing over to Satan' of 1 Cor 5.5,[152] resulting in physical suffering or even death. According to Holmberg, he must have regarded his divinely-given power as something perceptible and real, since this is the only interpretation which tallies with his 'expressions of power-consciousness' in 1.23; 10.1–6; and 13.10.[153] In favour of this suggestion it could be said that Paul's language does seem to be too strong if all that is meant is the barring of access to the Corinthian congregation. (He cannot 'excommunicate' the intruders in any meaningful sense, since he does not have jurisdiction over the whole Christian church, and as they are itinerants there are other congregations to which they can go.) The early church, moreover, did believe in the possibility of miraculous infliction of punishment by an apostle. If it should be asked why the infliction of such a punishment should depend upon the restoration of the Corinthians' obedience to Paul, one answer could be that, unless they had already been won back to their proper allegiance, punishment of the rival missionaries to whom they had become attached would further alienate them from Paul himself.

When we view vv. 1–6 as a whole it seems clear that Paul's main target is the τινές of v. 2 and that these people are the rival missionaries who have intruded into Corinth. In v. 6b, however, it appears that some of what is said must apply to the Corinthians themselves. It is likely that the capture of every purpose or thought for Christ in v. 5b is directed towards them, whilst the punishment of v. 6a relates to the intruders. Possibly Paul's use of non-personal nouns and imagery, rather than direct references to the personal objects of his attack, may be due to the fact that he suspects some of the Corinthians may have become so attached to the rival missionaries that they are to be virtually counted in with them, but does not wish to spell this out because he must still hope that the whole congregation can be restored to its proper allegiance. It is a further question whether he has in view the wider apostolic task as well as the necessity of dealing with the situation in Corinth. On the one hand, the allusion to 'knowledge of God' could suggest a mission context, and elsewhere Paul's concept of mission is expressed in terms of securing obedience. In

151 Wendland, p. 228; Filson, p. 385.
152 Meyer, p. 398; see also Holmberg, *Paul and Power*, p. 79.
153 Holmberg, *Paul and Power*, pp. 78–9.

addition, the very use of military imagery has suggested to some exegetes that he has in mind the apocalyptic notion of the final battle between good and evil, which again widens the scope of his thinking beyond that of the immediate Corinthian crisis. But on the other hand 'knowledge' is a matter of great interest to the Corinthians, and this may well be the only reason for Paul's allusion to it. It is doubtful, moreover, whether he saw himself as inflicting specific punishment on those who rejected his missionary appeal. Lastly, military imagery of the kind found here was widely used in the hellenistic philosophical tradition, and Paul's figurative use of the terminology of siege warfare could simply derive from some general acquaintance with this tradition.

This raises a further question. Paul is seen here by Betz[154] as taking upon himself the task of the struggle against the sophists. By the first century C.E. the sophists were basically practitioners and teachers of rhetoric, the skill essential to success in public and professional life. They made a great impact on city life and won considerable admiration, but came under criticism from philosophers. Philo, like Plato several centuries earlier, claimed that they used rhetoric to beguile the hearers, rather than to give expression to the truth.[155] It may be that the rival missionaries in Corinth did stand in the sophistic tradition, and this possibility will be explored as the exegesis proceeds. It is doubtful, however, whether Paul's attack is here consciously anti-sophistic in the sense that he takes the side of anti-sophistic philosophers. This could scarcely be deduced from his use of the metaphor of siege warfare. The fortified city stands for something that Paul attacks, whereas in Stoicism the image is used to describe the sage's impregnability, not something which he assails.[156]

At this stage, then, our provisional conclusions must be, first, that these verses contain no necessary reference to Paul's wider apostolic task, and, secondly, that there is no clear evidence that he is a conscious participant in the wider conflict between philosophers and sophists, although his opponents may have sophistic characteristics. In fact, a third point which emerges from the consideration of these verses is that in one sense Paul may have some affinity with the sophists. We have already noticed that 10.1–11 can be seen structurally, in rhetorical terms, as an exordium. To this we may add the suggestion offered by DiCicco that in 10.3–5 Paul is using the rhetorical technique of πάθος, the arousal of emotion, to exert influence over the Corinthians. He wishes them 'to feel the situation as he experienced it'.

154 Betz, *Tradition*, pp. 68–9. See also Furnish, p. 462.
155 Winter, *Sophists*, pp. 3–5, 92–3.
156 Malherbe, 'Antisthenes', p. 155.

Consequently he gives full expression here to the anger he feels towards the visiting missionaries. Thus, if the latter make use of the devices of rhetoric to sway the Corinthian congregation, so, now, does Paul himself, despite his apparent disclaimer in 11.6.[157] This is a plausible suggestion.

7. Τὰ κατὰ πρόσωπον βλέπετε. εἴ τις πέποιθεν ἑαυτῷ Χριστοῦ εἶναι, τοῦτο λογιζέσθω πάλιν ἐφ' ἑαυτοῦ ὅτι καθὼς αὐτὸς Χριστοῦ οὕτως καὶ ἡμεῖς. Paul continues directly to address the Corinthians. His opening words, however, are ambiguous. Perhaps he is uttering a reproach: all that they seem to be able to see is the purely superficial aspect of things. The phrase κατὰ πρόσωπον is used in a pejorative sense, and the verb is in the indicative, either making a statement or asking a question. Alternatively he may be issuing a command: let them merely look at the obvious facts that are staring them in the face. The κατὰ πρόσωπον is used in a neutral sense, and the verb is in the imperative. In favour of the first possibility[158] it is argued that, were βλέπετε an imperative, it would have come first, and that the κατὰ πρόσωπον relates to v. 1, i.e., to the unfavourable impression made by Paul when personally present in Corinth.[159] In favour of the second,[160] commentators note that Paul's characteristic use of βλέπετε is as an imperative,[161] that if here it were indicative one would expect to find some kind of adversative particle at the beginning of v. 7b,[162] and that, although the other Pauline instances of imperative βλέπετε do stand at the beginning of the sentence, it may be placed later here because it is the item which carries the emphasis.[163] As regards the nuance of meaning to be attached to κατὰ πρόσωπον, no contrast is drawn with realities of an inward nature (as one might have expected, were it used pejoratively),[164] and it does not necessarily possess adverse implications.[165] In v. 1 it is simply the opposite of the ἀπών in the following clause.[166] Of the other Pauline uses of πρόσωπον (18 or

[157] DiCicco, *Ethos, Pathos, and Logos*, pp. 164, 169, 176; quotation on p. 164.
[158] Supported by Chrysostom *PG* 61 col. 547 (NPNF XII, p. 379); Meyer, pp. 398–9.
[159] Meyer, ibid.
[160] Supported by, e.g., Bachmann, p. 347; Barrett, p. 256; Furnish, p. 465; Allo, p. 246; Windisch, p. 300; Bruce, pp. 230–1; Wolff, p. 200.
[161] Barrett, p. 256; Furnish, p. 465.
[162] Héring, p. 79; Furnish, ibid.
[163] Windisch, p. 300.
[164] Bachmann, p. 347.
[165] Barrett, p. 256.
[166] Alternatively, if there is a reference back to v. 1 and κατὰ πρόσωπον is seen as having pejorative force there, the interpretation proposed by Wolff, p. 200, may be correct. Supposedly, when Paul is with the Corinthians he is as v.1 describes him. But he bids them consider how matters really stand. This, however, would require more emphasis on βλέπετε than its position seems to warrant.

19[167]), 16 (or 17) have no pejorative undertone, and in the two remaining examples it is the remainder of the phrase which imparts the adverse sense.[168] On balance, the second alternative is preferable. The verb βλέπω occurs 27 (or 28[169]) times in Paul's letters, amongst which there are 9 (or 10) examples[170] of βλέπετε as an imperative, but none as indicative.[171]

What the obvious facts are that the Corinthians are bidden to look at has then to be deduced from what follows. The positive assertion which concludes the verse is that Paul himself is 'Christ's person'. But precisely what this means, and why it is said, requires elucidation in the light of the rest of v. 7b.

The assertion is made in response to the claim of 'someone' else, who is convinced[172] in his own mind[173] that he is 'Christ's'.[174] The change to the third person suggests that Paul is referring to the external opposition and not to any representative of the Corinthian congregation. There is a similar use of τὶς at 11.20, where allusion to the rival missionaries is without doubt.[175] Whether any particular one of the opponents is in view is uncertain. Barrett suggests that it may be some leading figure amongst them to whom Paul refers.[176] Furnish, however, points out that in the Pauline letters εἴ τις has usually a general sense.[177] It may be that a decision on the meaning of Χριστοῦ εἶναι may indicate which is the more probable point of view. Whichever it may be, there is still the difficulty that Paul here appears to allow that his opponent(s) and he are on the same level in respect of their relationship to Christ, which is very strange in view of what he says about the opposition in 11.13–15.[178] His form of expression is to be noted, however. Windisch observes that the verb πέποιθα often has a connotation of unjustified self-

---

[167] The number is 19 if 2 Th 1.9 be included.

[168] In 2 Cor 5.12 ἐν προσώπῳ is contrasted with ἐν καρδίᾳ, whilst in Gal 2.6 Paul employs the biblical expression πρόσωπον λαμβάνω for showing partiality.

[169] These figures exclude the present verse. The higher figure includes Eph 5.15.

[170] 1 Cor 1.26; 8.9; 10.18; 16.10; Gal 5.15; Phil 3.2 (3 times); Col 2.8; (Eph 5.15).

[171] Barrett, *First Corinthians*, p. 56, suggests that 1 Cor 1.26 is indicative, because it is followed by γάρ. See, however, Fee, *First Corinthians*, p. 79 and n. 3.

[172] B reads δοκεῖ πεποιθέναι, 'seems to be convinced', or 'thinks he is convinced'. Here we must have an intentional alteration, perhaps because Paul appeared to be conceding too much to his opponents (see Windisch, p. 301).

[173] For 'convinced in his own mind' see BAGD s.v. πείθω 2.b.

[174] Some witnesses (D* F G a vg^mss Ambst) read δοῦλος after χριστοῦ. This appears to be a scribal attempt to clarify Paul's meaning.

[175] Noted by Plummer, p. 280.

[176] Barrett, p. 256, with reference to his exegesis, pp. 260–1, of vv. 10–11. All three verses make it probable that it is 'a leader of the opposition' who is in view.

[177] Furnish, p. 466, with reference to Rom 8.9; 1 Cor 3.12; Phil 3.4.

[178] The difficulty of this concession is noted by Windisch, p. 300, and by Wolff, pp. 200–1.

assurance,[179] and that the ἑαυτῷ likewise stresses the subjective aspect of the confidence.[180] Paul describes a viewpoint: he does not vouch for its truth. But he does provisionally accept it for the sake of his own defence. What, then, did he suppose was meant by the claim to be 'of Christ'? There are various possibilities.

(i) Does it mean 'belong to Christ' as all Christians do, i.e., 'be a Christian'?[181] Does Paul, that is, have to insist on his own Christian standing because his opponents, confident of their own such standing, were denying it to him? Perhaps this is what they meant when they charged him with living κατὰ σάρκα.[182] Or perhaps it would be the logical consequence of some other criticism. If he is seen as lacking apostolic power and authority, this would mean that he lacks the Spirit, and to Paul himself this would cast doubt not only upon his apostleship but upon his Christian existence as such.[183] But this interpretation is improbable. Throughout chaps. 10–13 Paul is defending his authority, not his Christianity,[184] and there is no evidence that he had specifically drawn out the suggested implication of an attack on the former in the direction of an assault upon the latter. It is not likely either that 'be a Christian' was what the opponents meant by Χριστοῦ εἶναι. As Barrett observes, this would be too tame and modest a claim for them to make.[185] And in a situation where self-professed Christian missionaries are at work in an existing Christian community what would be the point of it?

(ii) Is there some connection with the Christ-group of 1 Cor 1.12? Possibly this original group have made common cause with the rival missionaries and thus the phrase Χριστοῦ εἶναι may have come to be associated with the latter as well.[186] The basic suggestion is elaborated by Schmithals. The Christ-group consists of gnostics. These people saw their own spiritual selves as fragments of the cosmic Christ, whom they identified with the Spirit. Thus, 'to be Christ's' meant, for them, to be πνευματικός, possessing the divine Spirit, indeed a part of the Christ who is this Spirit. And it is only the one who is πνευματικός who would count for anything as an apostle. At the time of the writing of 2 Cor 10–13 it is still these people who constitute the opposition to Paul. In response to the objection that in 1 Cor 1.12 the phrases parallel

[179] Windisch, p. 302, with reference to Rom 2.19 and Phil 3.4.
[180] Windisch, ibid; see also Wolff, pp. 200–1.
[181] Oostendorp, *Another Jesus*, pp. 18–19.
[182] Oostendorp, *Another Jesus*, p. 19.
[183] Käsemann, 'Legitimität', pp. 34–6.
[184] Kümmel, p. 208. See also Windisch, pp. 301–2.
[185] Barrett, p. 257.
[186] Allo, pp. 246–7, 272–4.

to ἐγὼ δὲ Χριστοῦ do not mean 'I am a fragment of Paul / Apollos / Cephas', Schmithals claims that these other slogans are Paul's own creation, to characterise those who supported the apostles against the gnostics.[187] This, however, is improbable. Moreover, there are two other objections to any interpretation of 2 Cor 10.7 which relates it to 1 Cor 1.12. First, in 1 Cor 1.12 the Christ-group consists of members of the Corinthian church, whilst in the present verse the context suggests that Paul is alluding to visitors from elsewhere.[188] Secondly, one has to take into account the οὕτως καὶ ἡμεῖς. It is hardly likely that Paul would suggest that he is himself a member of the Christ-party.[189]

(iii) Perhaps those who are confident that they belong to Christ are claiming to have had a personal knowledge of Jesus during his historical lifetime.[190] Paul's own credibility as an apostle could have been challenged by people who made a claim of this kind.[191] But, first, the subjective nature of the εἰ-clause goes against this (since personal acquaintance with the human Jesus would have been an objective fact), and, secondly, the nature of Paul's relationship to Christ must be the same as that claimed by his opponents[192] (which would rule out personal contact with the historical Jesus).

(iv) It may be that, although the people Paul has in view are not to be identified with the Christ-group of 1 Cor 1.12, they do nevertheless claim some special spiritual relationship with Christ which bestows a special power and authority.[193] Héring suggests that they are gnostics who repudiate apostolic authority on the pretext of their possessing direct inspiration by Christ himself.[194] This specific form of the theory, however, is surely implausible. The τις who claims to be Christ's represents visiting missionaries who themselves claimed to be apostles of Christ. And the theory as put more generally is somewhat vague. It could well be incorporated into (v) below.

(v) To be 'Christ's' means to be Christ's servant,[195] and his servant in some special sense, i.e., as an apostle.[196] In v. 8 it is apparent that it is apostolic authority that is in question.[197] Thus, Χριστοῦ will be a kind of shorthand for ἀπόστολος Χριστοῦ or

[187] Schmithals, *Gnosticism*, pp. 199–201, 192, 113–14, 205.
[188] Bruce, p. 231; Barrett, p. 257.
[189] Plummer, p. 280; Barrett, ibid.; Wolff, p. 200.
[190] Klöpper, p. 433; Denney, p. 301; Hughes, p. 356.
[191] Furnish, p. 476.
[192] Windisch, p. 301–2; see also Bultmann, p. 189.
[193] Bultmann, ibid.
[194] Héring, p. 79.
[195] Plummer, p. 280.
[196] Windisch, pp. 301–2; cf. Barrett, pp. 257–8.
[197] Windisch, p. 302; see also Heckel, *Schwachheit*, p. 14.

διάκονος Χριστοῦ: it is clear from 11.13, 23 that Paul's opponents styled themselves ἀπόστολοι Χριστοῦ and διάκονοι Χριστοῦ.[198] Possibly, also, the formula Χριστοῦ εἶναι developed originally in the way suggested below, under (vi). This fifth interpretation may be called in question on two grounds: that nowhere in chaps. 10–13 does Paul appeal to his own calling to be an apostle,[199] and that it would represent him as ready to allow his opponents' claim to apostolic authority to be valid.[200] But in fact there is probably an allusion to his initial call in v. 8,[201] and we have already seen that his acceptance of his opponents' claims is only provisional.[202]

(vi) According to Theissen, the phrase Χριστοῦ εἶναι was a slogan of itinerant charismatic preachers who claimed to belong to Christ's family. He draws attention to Mk 9.41, where Jesus's disciples may be given a cup of water because they 'are Christ's'. As 'belonging to Christ' in this sense, the original disciples reckoned to be able to count on finding people to provide them with board and lodging, and their itinerant successors in mission, including the rival missionaries in Corinth, followed the same policy.[203] Furnish thinks this a plausible suggestion. Paul himself might be under criticism for failing to trust solely in 'belonging to Christ' for the supply of his material needs.[204] But how could he then claim that he does 'belong to Christ' in this sense? In 11.7–11 he makes it quite clear that at least in Corinth this is not how he conducts his mission. It might be possible to suppose, however, that the formula Χριστοῦ εἶναι originated in the way Theissen postulates, and that it then developed into a more general expression for a special representative of Christ with claim to authority. The rival missionary, or missionaries, in view in the present verse may use it in its original sense, whilst Paul would understand it as a more general term.

Which interpretation, then, is the most likely? The first four have various disadvantages. Of the remaining two the fifth is the better one, but it could be that in the language of the rival missionaries, though not in that of Paul, Χριστοῦ εἶναι was a claim to be Christ's agent and to be such in the sense suggested by Theissen, i.e., the sixth option above. For Paul, it is simply the claim to be Christ's apostle.

This means that the reference to 'anyone', εἴ τις, is not as completely general as in some other Pauline examples (Rom 8.9; 2 Cor 5.17; Phil 3.4). But it does not necessarily mean that it is a

198 See Barrett, p. 257.
199 Bultmann, p. 189.
200 Windisch, p. 302, notes this difficulty.
201 See below, p. 624.
202 See above, p. 619.
203 Theissen, *Social Setting*, pp. 46–7.
204 Furnish, p. 476.

leader of the opponents who is in view: at a later point (11.13) Paul calls the whole group 'false apostles'. The τὶς here could be representative rather than specific. The rival missionaries are thus representatively requested to consider that, even granted the validity of their own claim to be 'Christ's',[205] Paul himself, conversely,[206] can make precisely the same claim. The request, however, is really directed at the Corinthians, as v. 7a shows. It is they who are to look at the plain facts and to recognise the validity of Paul's own claim to apostolic authority. The facts in question are not specified. In v. 8, however, he refers to the authority given him for 'building up', εἰς οἰκοδομήν. Consequently, he may have in mind the Corinthians' first-hand experience of his power to build up a Christian community, both as regards its original foundation and in relation to the subsequent nurture of its members.[207] He thus reinforces the plea for the restoration of their loyalty to himself which he has made in vv. 1–6.

This interpretation of Χριστοῦ εἶναι, we may note, would support the claim by Sundermann that v. 7 constitutes, rhetorically speaking, the first item of a *partitio* which points to the lengthy proof of apostleship in 11.16–12.18.[208]

8. ἐάν τε γὰρ περισσότερόν τι καυχήσωμαι περὶ τῆς ἐξουσίας ἡμῶν, ἧς ἔδωκεν ὁ κύριος εἰς οἰκοδομὴν καὶ οὐκ εἰς καθαίρεσιν ὑμῶν, οὐκ αἰσχυνθήσομαι. The introductory τε[209] γάρ shows that Paul now offers some validation of the claim in v. 7b that he is the agent of Christ. If he should boast[210] to a greater

---

[205] The subjective nature of their conviction is again stressed in the ἐφ᾽ ἑαυτοῦ, 'based on himself' (see BAGD s.v. ἐπί I.1.b.β.). Some witnesses (C D F G H Ψ 0209 0243 𝔐 sy) read ἀφ᾽ ἑαυτοῦ, 'of himself'. But ἐφ᾽ ἑαυτοῦ (𝔓46 ℵ B L 1175. 2495 *pc*) is well attested and makes better sense. The variant is probably caused by the similarity in pronunciation. The reading in 𝔓46 of ὁ Χριστός for the second Χριστοῦ is a scribal error, perhaps caused by the preceding αὐτός.
[206] For this sense of πάλιν see BAGD s.v. 4., where, with the present reference given, the word is rendered 'on the other hand'.
[207] See below, pp. 624–5. Cf. also 3.1–3 and 1 Cor 9.1–2.
[208] Sundermann, *Kraft der Rede*, p. 58.
[209] There is substantial evidence both for the inclusion of τε (ℵ C D Ψ 𝔐 f (r) vg sy Ambst) and for its omission (𝔓46 B F G H 0209. 0243. 6. 33. 365. 630. 1175. 1739. 1881 *pc* it vgmss). Its inclusion is probably correct. It is unlikely to be a scribal addition, since this combination of particles is infrequent. But it does occur elsewhere, as in Rom 7.7. Denniston, *Particles*, p. 536, observes that τε γάρ is used by Aristotle as the equivalent of γάρ or καὶ γάρ. Or perhaps here the explanation is that a second ἐάν τε (i.e., the second half of a τε … τε correlation) has been suppressed (see BDR 443(3)), though this does not seem very plausible. It may be that no explanation is necessary. According to MHT, p. 339: 'τε before γάρ appears to be a superfluous affectation.'
[210] There is a variant at this point. The reading καυχήσωμαι (B C D F G Ψ 𝔐) is the only one which both makes sense and is grammatically correct. The alternative καυχήσομαι (ℵ L P 0209. 0243. 6. 104. 326. 1175. 1241. 2495 *al* (g)) is easily understood as a scribal error. An attempt to harmonise the two (indicating the early date of the error) results in the reading καυχήσωμαι, καυχήσομαι of 𝔓46.

extent of his authority, or boast of some additional aspect of it,[211] it will not be an empty boast: he will not be disgraced. What, then would this further boasting consist of? In v. 7a Paul has implied that his readers already possess some evidence that he is 'Christ's'. Perhaps now he may conditionally allow himself to boast of future evidence which he is confident of providing when he actually arrives in Corinth, i.e., that his personal presence will match the weight and power of his letters (vv. 10-11). To some extent he has already hinted (v. 2) that this will be so, but has not made the point explicitly. He might also be looking ahead to what he will say in v. 13, where he speaks of boasting (with the necessary qualification of v. 17) in a way proportionate to the task and territory assigned to him by God.

In the present verse Paul is concerned to indicate the general nature and scope of the authority to which this particular boasting relates. First, it was the Lord who gave him[212] his ἐξουσία. The κύριος, according to Furnish, is Christ, since it was through Christ that Paul received his apostolic commission (1 Cor 9.1-2; Gal 1.1).[213] In fact, he speaks also of God as the initiator of his calling (Gal 1.1, 15-16), although Christ alone may be mentioned elsewhere (1 Cor 1.17; 9.1-2). But since in the present context the authority is that of one who claims 'to be Christ's', it is doubtless Christ who is seen as the κύριος. That Paul does have his initial calling in view is probably indicated by the aorist tense of ἔδωκεν.[214] Secondly, this authority was given for constructive purposes, εἰς οἰκοδομήν.[215] Furnish notes that the noun οἰκοδομή in Paul's usage commonly refers to the building up of the existing Christian community, but that here he will be thinking in addition of the original founding of the church in Corinth.[216] That

---

[211] Grammatically, the περισσότερόν τι could be adverbial in both its elements: see BAGD s.v. περισσότερος 3., and LSJ s.v. τις A.II.11.c. The meaning would be '(boast) somewhat more'. Alternatively, the τι may be the direct object of καυχήσωμαι. Meyer, p. 370, notes that the verb καυχάομαι is followed by a direct object in 7.14; 9.2; 11.30. The περισσότερον would then be adjectival, and the meaning '(boast of) something more'. This second interpretation may seem preferable. Paul may use περισσότερον as an adverb in 1 Cor 15.10, but he uses the true adverbial form περισσοτέρως more frequently (2 Cor 1.12; 2.4; 7.13,15; 11.23; 12.15; Gal 1.14; Phil 1.14; 1 Th 2.17). The first alternative, however, appears to make easier sense.

[212] Some witnesses (ℵ² D² F G (0209) 𝔐 syʰ; also P 629. 1881. 2495 pc it) read ἡμῖν at different points in the relative clause. This is an obvious addition, to be omitted (with 𝔓⁴⁶ ℵ* B C D* H Ψ 0243. 33. 81. 365. 630. 1175. 1739. 2464 pc b vgˢᵗ).

[213] Furnish, p. 467.

[214] Plummer, p. 281.

[215] See BAGD s.v. οἰκοδομή 1.b. Schütz, *Apostolic Authority*, p. 224, notes that the motif of building up and destroying is common in the OT, with both God and his prophets as the agents of these processes: see, e.g., Jer 24.6; 31.28; 42.10; 1.9-10. (The verbs οἰκοδομέω and καθαιρέω are used in the second and third of these examples: Jer 38 (LXX).28, and 49 (LXX).10.)

[216] Furnish, p. 467.

he could use the word in this more comprehensive sense is suggested in 1 Cor 3.9–10, where, having spoken of the church as God's οἰκοδομή,[217] he goes on to say that it was he himself who laid its foundation. Hence, as Christ's accredited agent, Paul possesses the power and authority[218] both to create a new community of believers and also to promote, guide and nurture the development of their spiritual life. This second aspect of his work of spiritual 'construction' he does by means of his letters, as well as by his personal presence. Sometimes it must entail severity and discipline, as in the case of the Painful Letter.

But any such disciplinary use of his authority is still πρὸς οἰκοδομήν: it is not, thirdly, for purposes of destruction, οὐκ εἰς καθαίρεσιν ὑμῶν. It is this last phrase which is somewhat problematic. What is the point of the remark? And does it not appear to contradict what was said in v. 4 about the 'destruction' of 'strongholds'? Various possibilities are proposed.

(i) Perhaps Paul is countering a charge that his own teaching is destructive of faith, or that he abuses his authority.[219] But this does not fit the charges specifically mentioned in vv. 1 and 10.[220]

(ii) He is implicitly criticising his opponents, the rival missionaries.[221] *Their* activity *will* have a destructive result in Corinth. What he says in 11.3–4 about the corruption of the Corinthians' minds would support this exegesis. But can he entirely escape the same charge himself, in view of v. 4?

(iii) Perhaps his use of the OT (and especially Jeremianic) motif of building and destroying[222] is sufficient to account for the occurrence of the phrase.[223] This is possible, but we should note that Paul's specific phraseology is his own: he is not automatically quoting the second half of a verbatim citation. And if so, the phrase must be intended to have some meaning. We are then back with its apparent contradiction of v. 4.

(iv) Does the οὐκ εἰς καθαίρεσιν ὑμῶν refer only to the final destiny of the church? In that case there would be no conflict with v. 4. The destruction of obstacles to the knowledge of God could be seen, in fact, as part of the constructive process which would

---

217 See BAGD s.v. οἰκοδομή 2.b.

218 On this verse as an example of Paul's use of the rhetorical argument (λόγος) from authority, see DiCicco, *Ethos, Pathos, and Logos*, p. 244.

219 Plummer, p. 281, notes the first of these suggestions as a possibility, and Furnish, p. 477, notes both.

220 Bachmann, p. 351.

221 Meyer, p. 401; Bachmann, ibid; Windisch, p. 303; Héring, p. 79 n. 6; Wolff, p. 201.

222 See above, p. 624 n. 215.

223 Furnish, p. 477.

preserve the church at the eschaton.[224] There is no indication, however, that the rejected καθαίρεσις is located at some point in time different from that of the οἰκοδομή: both are possibilities for Paul's present apostolic task.

(v) Is he replying to opponents who criticise him for failing to employ the kind of negative, punitive discipline they claim to expect of a genuine apostle?[225] This is certainly a possible reading of v. 8: Paul's understanding of apostolic authority does not include any such purely negative approach. But what of v. 4?

Of these five possibilities, (ii) and (v) can be combined. Paul can at the same time criticise what he sees to be the destructive effects of his rivals' influence and assert that his own exercise of apostolic authority is of a positive nature. In the Corinthian situation, the one implication of the οὐκ εἰς καθαίρεσιν is the obverse of the other. This may be what Paul intends to be understood. There remains the apparent difficulty of the discrepancy between this verse and v. 4. It is to be noted, however, that here it is a question of 'your' destruction, whilst in v. 4 it is to be inimical thoughts and attitudes that are to be destroyed. If it is to some of the Corinthians that these attitudes belong (as well as to the rival missionaries), their elimination will not mean the spiritual destruction of these people themselves—rather the contrary. Paul's use of καθαίρεσις in both verses at first glance suggests some contradiction, but there is, after all, no real difficulty.

9. ἵνα μὴ δόξω ὡς ἂν ἐκφοβεῖν ὑμᾶς διὰ τῶν ἐπιστολῶν. At this point the line of thought becomes more obscure, as does the syntax. It will be simplest to set out our preferred interpretation first, before discussing the other possibilities. We take it that this verse is connected with v. 8, but by means of some intermediate thought that remains unexpressed. (The connection can scarcely be direct. It would make no sense to say: 'If I should boast ..., I shall not be ashamed, in order that I may not seem to frighten you ...'). The exegesis of v. 8 has suggested that Paul has in view some boasting related to future evidence of his apostolic standing that he will give his readers *in person*.[226] The connecting link with v. 9 would then be: 'I say this'. And the meaning of the verse would

[224] Chrysostom, *PG* col. 548 (NPNF XII, pp. 379–80), and Hughes, p. 360, without reference to the eschaton, see an initial process of destruction as necessary to that of edification.

[225] Bultmann, p. 191.

[226] In respect of v. 8, we have to assume that this thought is present. But the assumption is justified by v. 11, and the fact (we shall argue) that vv. 8–11 form an integrated line of argument.

be: 'so that I may not seem to be operating, so to speak,[227] an epistolary "terror-campaign" '.[228] The other exegetical possibilities fall into three groups:

(i) The present verse is to be attached syntactically to v. 11, with v. 10 as a parenthesis. The line of thought would run as follows: 'So that I might not appear to terrify you by correspondence only (for it is said that my letters are powerful but my personal presence is weak and my manner of speech contemptible), let the person who takes this view consider that I shall be just as formidable when I arrive in person.'[229] But it is difficult to regard v. 10 as parenthetical, since the subject of φησίν is in all probability the τοιοῦτος of v. 11. Moreover, as Allo observes, one would expect some connecting particle to follow the ἵνα.[230]

(ii) Verse 9 is an independent sentence. The ἵνα has the force of an imperative: 'Let me not seem, as it were, to scare you by my letters.'[231] This is easy as regards syntax, but does it convey the appropriate nuance of meaning? It would imply that Paul is trying to minimise the forceful impression his letters have made. But this is not what he intends. What he wants to get across is that he will make *just as forceful* an impression in person.

(iii) Verses 8 and 9 are connected by some intermediate thought other than the one we have suggested.

(a) We should supply something like 'but I refrain from

---

[227] There is some difference of opinion concerning the force of ὡς ἄν. With BAGD s.v. ὡς ἄν we take it to mean 'as if', 'as it were', 'so to speak'. See also Moulton, *Prolegomena*, p. 167; BDF 453(3). An alternative interpretation is proposed by Moule, *Idiom Book*, p. 152, who suggests that there is a conflation of two forms of expression: ἵνα μὴ δόξω ἐκφοβεῖν ὑμᾶς ('lest I should seem to frighten you') and ἵνα μὴ δόξω ὡς ἐὰν ἐκφοβεῖν ὑμᾶς βούλωμαι ('lest I should seem as if I wished to frighten you'). This interpretation is supported by Barrett, p. 259 (from whom I have taken the English translations), and by Furnish, pp. 465, 467. But this surely raises more problems than it solves, since the second item is grammatically unclear. The expected construction following δοκέω in this sense would be an infinitive, not a subjunctive clause (see BAGD s.v. δοκέω 2.a.), and ὡς ἄν / ἐάν followed by the subjunctive would mean 'when', 'as soon as' (see BAGD s.v. ὡς IV.1.c., and the references to Rom 15.24; 1 Cor 11.34; Phil 2.25).

[228] Plummer, p. 281, comments that ἐκφοβέω has a 'strong meaning', but that the ὡς ἄν may mitigate the effect. Hughes, p. 361 n. 17, suggests that the verb may ironically echo what the opponents are saying.

[229] See, e.g., Chrysostom, *PG* 61 col. 548 (NPNF XII, p. 380); Rückert, pp. 302–3; Ewald, p. 295.

[230] Allo, p. 248. He notes that the Vulgate adds 'autem'.

[231] Both the NEB and the REB appear to take the clause this way, since these translations begin, 'So you must not think of me ...' On imperatival ἵνα see Moulton, *Prolegomena*, pp. 178–9; MHT, pp. 94–5. Martin, p. 298, translates: '[Do not think] that I am trying to frighten you ...'

boasting'.[232] But this would turn v. 8 into an unfulfilled condition[233] which is not the way Paul expresses himself.[234]

(b) Plummer would supply 'I will not say more than that'.[235] But could such a thought have remained unexpressed?[236] The same objection would apply to the proposal to supply the thought 'assertive though this may sound',[237] and also to the insertion 'but I shall know how to use my power'.[238]

(c) Furnish, instead of supplying some link in thought before the ἵνα, prefers to supply βούλωμαι with the ἵνα-clause itself, and translates: 'lest I should seem as if I wanted to be scaring you with my letters'.[239] This is one way in which he will not be disgraced as a result of his boasting. 'His authority is not something about which he can only write to them, as if he wanted to frighten them into accepting his apostleship (v. 9); it is a real authority which he can and does also demonstrate when he is with them.'[240] But the addition of an implicit βούλωμαι is doubtful grammatically.[241] And why should 'writing' be synonymous, of necessity, with 'frightening'? Furthermore, Paul is not making a distinction between a frightening epistolary assertion of authority and a non-frightening personal assertion. The point in v. 11 is that he will be exactly the same in person as in his letters.

Returning, then, to our preferred interpretation, we can see Paul as negating (somewhat obscurely, it is true) the impression of his intentions he fears he may have given—and may still be giving. He does not intend to (continue to) inspire fear by means of *correspondence*. Here he obviously has in view the Painful Letter,[242] but perhaps also, paradoxically, this very letter he has now begun to compose. In making this denial he is looking ahead to his actual presence in Corinth. It is this prospective, on-the-

---

[232] Lietzmann, p. 142; Barrett, p. 255.

[233] This is apparent from the rendering offered by Lietzmann: 'ja wenn ich ... noch mehr von mir rühmen wollte ... so würde ich nicht zuschanden werden.' This is translated by Barrett, p. 259: 'if I wished to go beyond this claim ... I should not be put to shame.'

[234] Bachmann, p. 352, notes this as a reason for rejecting this interpretation.

[235] Plummer, p. 279.

[236] Windisch, p. 305, and Furnish, p. 467, find this improbable.

[237] Proposed by Hughes, p. 361.

[238] Proposed by Bultmann, p. 191.

[239] Furnish, p. 465.

[240] Furnish, p. 478.

[241] See above, p. 627 n. 227.

[242] In the Introduction, Vol. I, pp. 13–18, we have argued against the view that chaps. 10–13 themselves constitute the Painful Letter, or part of it. Plummer, p. 282, who does take this view, refers here to the Previous Letter (1 Cor 5.9) and to one part of 1 Corinthians (5.3–5). Barrett, however, points out, pp. 259–60, that it is not easy to account for vv. 9–10 unless the Painful Letter had already been sent to Corinth and read there.

spot, display of personal authority that is the implicit subject of his hypothetical boasting in v. 8, which he is confident will be validated (v. 11), and he begins to raise the point in order to dispel the misleading impression created by some parts of his correspondence with Corinth.

10. ὅτι Αἱ ἐπιστολαὶ μέν,[243] φησίν, βαρεῖαι καὶ ἰσχυραί, ἡ δὲ παρουσία τοῦ σώματος ἀσθενὴς καὶ ὁ λόγος ἐξουθενημένος. Paul now explains why he has brought up the matter of his letters. It is because in the eyes of his critic(s)[244] the effectiveness of his correspondence only serves to throw into stronger relief the ineffectual impression he makes in person. He quotes what is actually being said in Corinth. It is unlikely that the subject of φησίν is an imaginary opponent or an hypothetical objector after the (alleged) idiom of the 'diatribe'.[245] Quite apart from the questions both of the existence of any such definite literary genre and also of the nature of the interlocutor in those works said to belong to it,[246] it is clear, as Barrett points out,[247] that in the present instance Paul is responding to a criticism that is already current. He would scarcely himself gratuitously create a charge of this kind, for the use of his detractors. The φησίν might then be used as an impersonal expression, 'it is said'.[248] But the τοιοῦτος of v. 11 (obviously identical with the subject of φησίν) suggests that some specific

243 The word order ἐπιστολαὶ μέν (ℵ* B H 326. 1175 pc) is reversed in some witnesses (ℵ² D F G I Ψ 0209 0243 𝔐 syʰ). The reversal is probably a scribal correction, since μέν would normally come as second word in the first of the two correlated sentences, though its later position is not incorrect (see Denniston, *Particles*, pp. 371–3).

244 Most witnesses read φησίν, 'he says', but a few (B lat sy) have φασίν 'they say' (the verb is omitted altogether in 1881 b boᵐˢˢ Ambst). Scribal error could account for a change either way, if an H or A were carelessly written, and such an error would not necessarily be corrected, since both singular and plural could make sense in the context. The τοιοῦτος of v. 11, however, does strongly suggest that Paul wrote φησίν in v. 10, since the point of reference of both seems to be identical.

245 *Pace* Moule, *Idiom Book*, p. 29; BDR 130(3) n. 7; Bultmann, *Stil*, pp. 10, 67.

246 Bultmann and other representatives of an older viewpoint spoke of 'the diatribe' as a definite literary genre. The view is open to question. See S. K. Stowers, *The Diatribe and Paul's Letter to the Romans*, SBLDS 57, Chico, Cal., 1981, pp. 49, 75–6; and T. Schmeller, *Paulus und die „Diatribe"* NTAbh n.f. 19, Münster, 1987, pp. 53–4, 428. The most that can be said is that there is a set of shared characteristics found in those writers said to use the form: see Stowers, p. 48–9; cf. Schmeller, p. 54, who refers to a 'diatribal kind' of literature. Dialogue is one of the characteristics, but the interlocutor is not always fictitious. Schmeller, p. 436, observes that in Paul's writing the actuality or otherwise of the dialogue has to be determined in each individual case.

247 Barrett, p. 260.

248 BAGD s.v. φημί 1.c.; cf. Windisch, p. 305; Allo, p. 248.

individual is in view,[249] probably a representative of the rival mission.[250] What exactly does this critic mean when he allows that Paul's letters are βαρύς? It is not very probable that the sense of the adjective is 'burdensome' (as in Mt 23.4 and 1 Jn 5.3)[251]: the word here must be used in a good sense, to point the contrast with the contemptuous reference to the apostle's speech in what follows. Nor is it altogether likely that the letters are seen as displaying 'righteous indignation'. This interpretation is proposed by Forbes, who observes that the noun βαρύτης can refer to the rhetorical stance in which the speaker reproachfully complains that he has been badly treated.[252] Whilst this attitude might have been displayed in the Painful Letter, it is doubtful whether 1 Corinthians would appear βαρύς in this sense, and the Previous Letter, as far as is known, was not concerned with the treatment of Paul personally. It is true that 2 Cor 1–8 is in large part a defence of himself as an apostle, but the tone is not noticeably indignant.

In the present context βαρύς more probably means 'weighty' in the sense of 'impressive'.[253] It is contrasted with ἐξουθενημένος, 'contemptible'.[254] It may also have some connotation of rhetorical impressiveness.[255] The other adjective ἰσχυρός means 'effective',[256] in a strong sense,[257] again, perhaps, as inclusive of an oratorical quality.[258]

Over against this apparently complimentary description of Paul's letters there is set the highly derogatory representation of

---

[249] Barrett, p. 260. Furnish, p. 468, disagrees, on the ground that in such a case (of the use of φησίν) one would expect the person's name to be mentioned (he refers to Epict., *Diss.* IV 8.17, 25). But since the φησίν here is resumed by the following τοιοῦτος this is not a necessary conclusion: in 1 Cor 5.5 and 2 Cor 2.5–7 Paul uses the anonymous ὁ τοιοῦτος where it is clear that he has a particular individual in view. It might be relevant in addition to note the convention of the 'non-naming' of enemies (see P. Marshall, *Enmity in Corinth*, pp. 341–8, although he does not cite this passage as an example).

[250] This would probably require us to suppose that the man was present in Corinth at the time of Paul's interim visit.

[251] *Pace* Furnish, p. 468.

[252] Forbes, 'Comparison', pp. 12–16; see also LSJ s.v. βαρύτης IV.

[253] Martin, p. 298, has 'weighty' with LSJ s.v. βαρύς I.4.; cf. Wolff, p. 202, 'gewichtig'; Plummer, p. 282, suggests 'impressive', as one possibility.

[254] Furnish, p. 465.

[255] P. Marshall, *Enmity in Corinth*, pp. 385–6, notes that Dionysius of Halicarnassus uses the noun βάρος in this way, in *Th.* 23.360.10; *Comp.* 11.37.16; *Dem.* 34.204.14. See also Winter, *Sophists*, p. 207, who notes that Lucian uses βαρύς of rhetorical technique (*D Mort.* 373).

[256] BAGD s.v. ἰσχυρός 2.

[257] Furnish, p. 468, gives the sense as powerful and 'effective'.

[258] See P. Marshall, *Enmity in Corinth*, pp. 385–6, who cites H. Dion., *Th.* 55.417. 17–18 for the use of the noun ἰσχύς as a quality of orators.

his personal presence, ἡ παρουσία τοῦ σώματος. This expression is to be understood in a comprehensive sense, of the apostle's whole outward character and personality, not only his personal appearance in the narrower sense.[259] It is worth noting, however, that physical appearance may have had some importance for the Corinthians.

Winter draws attention to Epictetus's discourse on 'personal adornment' as evidence that students of rhetoric were greatly concerned about their appearance as a means of making an impact on their audience,[260] and Furnish similarly notes that according to Epictetus physical appearance was a matter of importance to the Cynic philosopher.[261] Consequently, criticism of Paul's own appearance may well have constituted a minor aspect of the adverse judgement cited here. What, then, did the critic mean by saying that the apostle's bodily presence was ἀσθενής? In view of what we have just said, the thought of physical infirmity may be included in the description,[262] as something which detracted from Paul's appearance. But the basic thrust of the criticism must be directed at the apostle's personality. When required to take action, he appears feeble and vacillating.[263] In all probability this means also that he is seen as lacking the power of the divine Spirit, i.e., 'the essential traits of the gnostic πνευματικός'.[264] This weak state, moreover, may similarly be seen as indicating his distance from Christ. The presupposition would be that to belong to Christ (v. 7) is to share his power. Hence, the legitimacy of the apostle can be recognised by the power of his personal presence.[265]

Is there, in addition, any reference to Paul's practice of his craft as a further sign of weakness? Furnish, taking up a suggestion proposed by Windisch,[266] thinks that this may be so. If there is an allusion to the weakness of social status reflected in the apostle's function as a craftsman, then its combination with the designation of his speech as 'contemptible' would produce the same conjunction of ideas as in 11.6–11, where his remarks on his

---

[259] Cf. Barrett, pp. 260–1: 'what he is when he arrives in the body'.

[260] Winter, *Sophists*, pp. 116–17, with reference to Epict. *Diss.* III 1. See also P. Marshall, *Enmity in Corinth*, pp. 333–4.

[261] Furnish, p. 468, with reference to Epict., *Diss.* III 22.86–89. The philosopher has to show that his simple way of life does no detriment to his body.

[262] So, e.g., Furnish, pp. 478–9; Martin, p. 312. Furnish draws attention to the probability that in 12.7 Paul alludes to a physical malady which may have hindered his work. For the opposite viewpoint see Lietzmann, p. 142; Hughes, p. 362; Barrett, p. 261; Bultmann, p. 192.

[263] Black, *Astheneia*, p. 137; cf. Savage, *Power through Weakness*, pp. 65–6.

[264] Martin, p. 312, with reference to Schmithals, *Gnosticism*, pp. 176–9.

[265] Heckel, *Schwachheit*, p. 16. Paul thus has to show that as an apostle he belongs to Christ precisely in his state of weakness.

[266] Windisch, p. 306; see Furnish, p. 479, for what follows.

custom of refusing maintenance follow immediately upon the reference to his amateur status as a rhetorician. The low status of artisans is illustrated, as we have seen, in Lucian, who uses the term ταπεινός,[267] applied to Paul by his critics (10.1). Hock, similarly, argues for a connection in Paul's mind between his weakness and the practice of his craft.[268] He observes that an artisan's life was hard, and suggests that some of the hardships Paul lists in the Corinthian correspondence may be attributed to his practice of his craft.[269] Hence, it might not be impossible that some representative of the opposition should have stigmatised him as ἀσθενής in this social sense.[270] There are two reasons for caution, however. First, it can be argued that this interpretation of the status of craftsmen depends only on the literary evidence, disregarding epigraphic evidence that tells a somewhat different story.[271] Secondly, it is in any case doubtful whether it is social status as such which is the issue in the present context. The crucial question concerns Paul's power of effective action (v. 11), and his possession of apostolic authority (v. 8).

The further assertion that Paul's speech is contemptible appears simple enough, but is somewhat problematic on further consideration. In itself, it may mean one or both of two things. First, the critic may be saying that the apostle's spoken discourse is unsophisticated and ineffective from the rhetorical point of view.[272] In that case, however, why should there be so strong a contrast with his letters? For the letters do show some effective use of rhetorical devices such as antithesis,[273] and 'diatribal' dialogue,[274] and we have already noted recent interest in the rhetorical features which may be detected in chaps. 10–13 of 2 Corinthians.[275] Perhaps a partial answer might be that Paul was somewhat deficient in the capacity for extempore oral rhetoric that was so much prized by the sophists.[276] Perhaps also Savage may have a point when he suggests that it was an abusive kind of rhetoric popular in Corinth that he refused to indulge in.[277] A

---

[267] Luc., *Somn.* 13. See above, p. 604 n. 62.

[268] Hock, *Social Context*, p. 60.

[269] Hock, *Social Context*, p. 35.

[270] For this use of ἀσθενής see LSJ s.v. 4., where it is noted that the word can be applied to weakness in respect of property. See Xen., *Cyr.* VIII 1.30, where οἱ ἀσθενέστεροι, 'the weaker sort', refers to 'the poor'.

[271] Savage, *Power through Weakness*, pp. 84–5: see the discussion below, pp. 703–4.

[272] Windisch, p. 306; Allo, p. 249; Hughes, pp. 362–3.

[273] Weiss, *Paulinischen Rhetorik*, pp. 175–81.

[274] Bultmann, *Stil*, pp. 64–74.

[275] See above, pp. 595–6.

[276] See G. A. Kennedy, *The Art of Rhetoric in the Roman World*, Princeton, 1972, p. 560; Winter, *Sophists*, pp. 214–16, 223.

[277] Savage, *Power through Weakness*, pp. 70–1.

second, though related, criticism may have been that Paul lacked
the kind of spontaneity which would indicate to the religious
observer that he possessed the power of the divine Spirit.[278] But
how would this fit the assertion in 1 Cor 2.4 that his discourse and
proclamation proved itself through his possession of the Spirit
and power?[279]

Probably various factors played a part, however illogically, in
the Corinthians' adverse judgement on Paul's oral skills. But in
each case one basic question remains unanswered. The apostle
must originally have established the nucleus of the Corinthian
church precisely through his power of effective speech employed
in the proclamation of the gospel. How else? Why is it, now, that
his speech is said to be contemptible? Perhaps we might postulate
the following phases in his relationship with the church. His
original preaching did indeed possess a spiritual power which
would amply compensate for some lack of spontaneous rhetorical
fluency. This oratorical deficiency (as it would seem to the
Corinthians) may not at the time have appeared of great
importance. Moreover, it eventually became obvious that Paul's
letters, by contrast, did display at least some degree of rhetorical
aptitude,[280] as well as spiritual authority. But there has been a
gradual change in attitude. On the one hand, the Corinthians have
experience of other Christian missionaries, i.e., Apollos, and
those now present in Corinth as rivals to Paul. These others have
shown that their calling is not, after all, incompatible with the oral
skills of the rhetor. On the other hand, Paul himself, on his recent
visit to the city, has signally failed to display the spiritual power
and authority evident during his first visit. Hence there is now
nothing to compensate for lack of professional competence in
extempore rhetoric. Consequently, criticism of him on both
counts, offered by some representative of the opposition, will find
a ready response.

11. τοῦτο λογιζέσθω ὁ τοιοῦτος, ὅτι οἷοί ἐσμεν τῷ λόγῳ δι'
ἐπιστολῶν ἀπόντες, τοιοῦτοι καὶ παρόντες τῷ ἔργῳ. This representative is designated ὁ τοιοῦτος. The form of expression is
probably intended to indicate contempt,[281] rather than to function
as a vague reference to anyone who would criticise Paul in the
manner reflected in v. 10.[282] As in v. 10 we have the formal
opposition between the absent letter-writing Paul and Paul as

[278] Reitzenstein, *Mystery-Religions,* pp. 460–1; Lietzmann, p. 142; Käsemann,
'Legitimität', p. 35.
[279] Windisch, p. 306.
[280] See above, p. 632.
[281] Allo, p. 248, with reference to 1 Cor 5.5, 11.
[282] *Pace* Plummer, pp. 283–4.

personally present in Corinth.[283] But the substantive contrast of v. 10 is negated. The same Paul will be[284] as powerful in personal presence and action[285] as he is impressive and forceful in his letters.[286] Threats, if unheeded, will be put into effect. But we are not told either how this is to be done or why Paul should be so confident that this time, by contrast with the occasion of his earlier visit, he will find himself able to act forcefully. If he has to inflict punishment, what does he have in view? The question takes us back to the exegesis of v. 6,[287] where we have suggested that, in addition to the exclusion from Corinth of the external opposition (and the exclusion, perhaps, of any remaining Corinthian dissidents from the church?) there may be the idea of a miraculous infliction of suffering.[288] But it is worth noting also that the forceful action Paul proposes may include the more positive element of powerful persuasive speech, i.e., in a broad sense, 'rhetoric'. For unless all the disaffected Corinthians are to be consigned to punishment, he will need to *persuade* them to return to their proper allegiance (10.6). Why, then, is he so sure that he will be able to act in this effective way? Perhaps it is simply that various hindrances to action at the time of the interim visit are no longer operative. He himself might have been troubled by illness, and in addition he might have been cautious about attempting to exercise punitive spiritual power in a situation which was somewhat obscure.[289] Now, however, that particular matter which had caused trouble has been resolved, and the apostle himself may have become more confident that occasions of physical weakness will not prove an ultimate hindrance to his exercise of spiritual authority. On his third visit to Corinth, moreover, he will

[283] The statement is carefully constructed, with οἷοι balanced by τοιοῦτοι, and a chiastic arrangement (τῷ λόγῳ ... ἀπόντες ..., παρόντες τῷ ἔργῳ) which gives some rhetorical force to the claim.

[284] Some exegetes would supply the present tense ἐσμέν in the second of the two clauses, since it occurs in the first clause: so, e.g., Bachmann, p. 354; Plummer, p. 284; Allo, p. 248; Furnish, p. 469. From the viewpoint of structural balance there is much to be said for this. But if the present tense be supplied, Paul responds to criticism simply by issuing a flat denial of its truth. Would his readers be convinced? Also, the future οὐκ αἰσχυνθήσομαι of v. 8 points to some future occasion when his authority will be vindicated. Hence, we prefer to supply the future ἐσόμεθα (cf. KJV, NEB, REB, BCN; see also Martin, p. 313).

[285] For this sense of ἔργον see BAGD s.v. 1.a. and LSJ s.v. I.4. It is noted in LSJ that the opposition of ἔργῳ to λόγῳ is frequent in Attic Greek, as in, e.g., Th. II 65. In BAGD there are references to Xen., *Cyr.* VI 4.5 and to Luc., *Tox.* 35.

[286] Furnish, p. 469, notes that whilst in v. 10 λόγος signifies Paul's spoken utterance, here it means what he writes.

[287] See above, pp. 614–16.

[288] Martin, p. 313, commenting on v. 11, sees a possible allusion to the idea of consignment to Satan. As we have noted above, p. 616, this may carry with it the thought of physical suffering.

[289] See Vol I, pp. 61–9.

have had due advance warning of the difficulties he may have to confront, whereas it would seem that he was taken by surprise previously.

(ii) *Paul and the rival missionaries (10.12–18)*

[12]For we do not dare to rank ourselves or to compare ourselves with some of those who commend themselves. On the contrary, they lack understanding, measuring themselves with themselves as the criterion, and comparing themselves with themselves. [13]But we shall not boast beyond measure, but in accordance with the measure of the territorial schedule[290] which God assigned to us as our measure of interest, to reach even as far as you. [14]For it is not that, as though not yet reaching you, we are over-extending ourselves. For we arrived even as far as you with the gospel of Christ. [15]We are not boasting beyond measure, of the labours of others, but we have a hope that, as your faith increases, we may, with your help, grow abundantly in achievement in accordance with our schedule, [16]so as to preach the gospel in the regions beyond you, not to boast with regard to things already accomplished in another's scheduled area. [17]But let the one who boasts, boast of the Lord. [18]For the person who is proved genuine is not the one who commends himself but the one whom the Lord commends.

Paul has already (vv. 7, 10) made allusive reference to the external opposition he faces in Corinth. Now he plainly refers to these people. They are stupid: they subject themselves to no external standard of assessment, but simply compare themselves with each other.[291] Then, by describing his own apostolic practice largely in terms of what he refrains from doing, he suggests by implication the reprehensible behaviour his rivals indulge in: they boast excessively, and they boast of what has been achieved in Corinth, where it is Paul himself who has done all the groundwork, not they. He insists that this area is his own missionary territory, whilst expressing the hope that the Corinthian situation may soon be such as to allow him to embark on some further evangelistic enterprise. This would break new ground, and would not allow boasting of work done by others. But in any case it is of the Lord that one should boast, for it is only the Lord's validation that counts, not the self-commendation practised by the rival missionaries. By implication, Paul believes himself to possess this validation, since he has achieved success in the mission area assigned to him by the Lord as his sphere of work.[292]

---

[290] See the exegesis for this understanding of κανών.

[291] We have translated 'with themselves', but the sense may be nearer to 'with each other'. See the exegesis.

[292] Sundermann, *Kraft der Rede*, p. 71.

10.12–18 as narratio. According to Sundermann,[293] these verses function as the section of the speech next to be expected, the *narratio*, in which the facts of the case are stated.[294] It clarifies what for Paul is the real point of the conflict, i.e., the dispute as to what constitutes a legitimate claim to the title 'apostle'. What is the appropriate criterion? For the opponents, Sundermann claims, it is letters of recommendation and performance of the apostolic signs. For Paul it is the Lord's validation. He does not meet his opponents' criteria, nor can he prove his own apostleship, since recognition of it depends on faith. Hence, he contests not only the specific charges against him, but also the 'trial' process itself. This intention is summed up in vv. 17–18, which thus constitute, in rhetorical terms, the *propositio*, i.e., the central idea of the *narratio*, expressed at its conclusion.[295]

How convincing is this characterisation of the second half of chap. 10? On the one hand, it is correct to say, in general terms, that the basic issue in chaps. 10–13 is the dispute concerning claims to legitimate apostolic authority. Also, it is clear from 12.12 that apostolic 'signs' have something to do with it. Likewise, Paul's conviction that he is validated by the Lord is one of 'the facts of the case', mentioned both in 10.8 and in 13.10, as well as in 10.13–14. On the other hand, it is doubtful whether commendatory letters are still an issue, and the claim that recognition of apostolicity is dependent on faith is not certain as exegesis of 10.15.[296] If, however, it proves to be in general plausible to understand these four chapters to be constructed according to the conventions governing a rhetorical speech, then 10.12–18 would perform the function of the *narratio* well enough. That Paul throughout chaps. 10–12 is confronting, and is confronted by, rival claimants to what he regards as his own missionary territory gives support to the view that the mention of such people in 10.12–18 is intended as the initial setting out of the facts of the situation.

10.12–13 The Text. There is a major textual variant in vv. 12–13 which radically affects the sense and consequently requires

[293] Sundermann, *Kraft der Rede*, pp. 68–74.
[294] Cicero, *Part.Or. (Classification of Oratory)* 9.31: 'narratio est rerum explicatio' ('the statement is an explanation of the facts', LCL).
[295] Sundermann, *Kraft der Rede*, p. 74. See n. 128 for this definition of the *propositio*, derived from H. Lausberg, *Handbuch der literarischen Rhetorik²*, München, 1973. This differs somewhat from Cicero, *Inv. (On Invention* I) I 37.67: 'Propositio, per quam locus is breviter exponitur, ex quo vis omnis oportet emanet ratiocinationis,' ('major premise which sets forth briefly the principle from which springs the whole force and meaning of the syllogism,' LCL).
[296] See below, pp. 650–1.

separate and prior discussion. Basically there is a longer text with variations and a shorter text.

The longer text, in its best attested form, runs as follows:

οὐ γὰρ τολμῶμεν ἐγκρῖναι ἢ συγκρῖναι ἑαυτούς τισιν τῶν ἑαυτοὺς συνιστανόντων· ἀλλὰ αὐτοὶ ἐν ἑαυτοῖς ἑαυτοὺς μετροῦντες καὶ συγκρίνοντες ἑαυτοὺς ἑαυτοῖς οὐ συνιᾶσιν. ἡμεῖς δὲ οὐκ εἰς τὰ ἄμετρα καυχησόμεθα...[297]

For we do not dare to rank ourselves or to compare ourselves with some of those who commend themselves. On the contrary, they lack understanding, measuring themselves with themselves and comparing themselves with themselves. But we shall not boast beyond measure...

According to this reading, those who measure and compare themselves with themselves are Paul's opponents, and this is a bad thing to do.

The shorter text runs:

οὐ γὰρ τολμῶμεν ἐγκρῖναι ἢ συγκρῖναι ἑαυτούς τισιν τῶν ἑαυτοὺς συνιστανόντων· ἀλλὰ αὐτοὶ ἐν ἑαυτοῖς ἑαυτοὺς μετροῦντες καὶ συγκρίνοντες ἑαυτοὺς ἑαυτοῖς οὐκ εἰς τὰ ἄμετρα καυχησόμεθα...[298]

For we do not dare to rank ourselves or to compare ourselves with some of those who commend themselves. But we ourselves, measuring ourselves with ourselves, and comparing ourselves with ourselves, shall not boast beyond measure...

The omission of the οὐ συνιᾶσιν. ἡμεῖς δέ of the longer text changes the sense. Here it is Paul himself who measures and compares himself with himself, and this process must obviously be seen as good.

What are the arguments for and against each text?
(i) In favour of the shorter text:
(a) The sentence beginning ἀλλὰ αὐτοί looks like the expected positive statement which balances the preceding negative οὐ γὰρ τολμῶμεν. If so, it must have the same personal reference, i.e., the subject must be Paul:[299] He does *not* dare to compare himself with

[297] 𝔓46 ℵ* B Hvid 0243. 33. 81. 104. 330. 451. 1739. 1881 Aug Euth Th. Variations: (1) οὐ συνίουσιν. ἡμεῖς δέ Dᶜ K P Ψ 0209vid. 181. 326. 436. 614. 629. 630. 1241. 1877. 1962. 1984. 1985. 2127. 2492. 2405 Byz Lect Chr Th John-Dam; (2) (versions reading either of the above) οὐ συνιᾶσιν / οὐ συνίουσιν. ἡμεῖς δέ itrl syrp h copsa bo goth arm eth; (3) οὐ συνίσασιν. ἡμεῖς δέ ℵ* 88; (4) συνίουσιν. ἡμεῖς δέ l603; (5) ἡμεῖς δέ 429 itdem xz vg Ephr Pel.
[298] D* G it a r d e f g Ambst Vig Sed-Scot.
[299] Windisch, p. 309; see also Bultmann, p. 194.

his rivals, *but rather* acts as his own standard. The objection to this argument would be that the αὐτοί becomes superfluous.[300] It must indicate a new subject.[301] It could refer to Paul, however, if it is seen as an example of the Attic strengthening of the reflexive pronoun.[302]

(b) The οὐ συνιᾶσιν of the longer text is flat and obscure.[303] And if it is original, how did it come to be omitted?[304] These arguments are, however, unconvincing. Precisely in view of its obscurity it is difficult to account for the scribal insertion of οὐ συνιᾶσιν into a text which originally lacked it.[305] By contrast, it is easy enough to explain its accidental omission. The eye of a scribe might easily have passed from the οὐ before συνιᾶσιν to the οὐκ before εἰς τὰ ἄμετρα, thus omitting the intervening words.[306]

(c) What Paul reproaches his opponents with is not (as in the longer text) mutual comparison but their elevation of themselves as superior to others—notably, to himself.[307] It is this superiority that they boast about.[308] In addition, the phrases ἐν ἑαυτοῖς ἑαυτοὺς μετροῦντες and συγκρίνοντες ἑαυτοὺς ἑαυτοῖς may well indicate the charges made against Paul. If so, they must have Paul as their subject, as in the shorter text.[309] In the background there might be the view, sponsored by the opponents, that in a situation of missionary competition authenticating standards were required, with consequent comparison of one missionary with another. Paul would have held aloof from this area of comparison, since his own standard was of a wholly different order.[310] These more general exegetical arguments are of some interest, but they are not wholly conclusive. There is no necessary contradiction between mutual comparison on the part of the rival missionaries and their boasting of their superiority to Paul. Having established their own criteria of missionary authenticity, they could both

[300] Bachmann, p. 356 n.1.
[301] Kümmel, p. 208; Furnish, p. 470; Martin, p. 315.
[302] See BDR 283(5).
[303] Windisch, p. 309; Bultmann, pp. 194–5.
[304] Bultmann, p. 195.
[305] Cf. Prümm, *Diakonia Pneumatos* I, p. 585.
[306] Metzger, *Textual Commentary*², p. 514. See also Barrett, p. 264, for an alternative explanation. He notes that the witnesses to the shorter text are all Latin or Graeco-Latin, and that Latin distinguishes between the plural persons of the reflexive pronoun in a way that hellenistic Greek does not. In the middle of v. 12 the Latin translator would have to make a choice, and might wrongly have chosen 'ourselves' instead of 'themselves'. The third plural verb συνιᾶσιν would become unintelligible, and the following ἡμεῖς δέ superfluous. The verb would be omitted, and in some witnesses the other two words would drop out.
[307] Héring, p. 81.
[308] Bultmann, p. 195.
[309] Käsemann, 'Legitimität', pp. 56–7.
[310] Georgi, *Opponents*, p. 236.

engage in comparisons amongst themselves, with a favourable outcome as regards their own validity, and also disparage Paul as failing to conform to their standard. Further, there is no specific indication that the participial phrases reflect what was being said about Paul, by contrast with v. 10.

(ii) In favour of the longer text.

(a) It has superior MS attestation.[311]

(b) The shorter reading produces a contradiction. In v. 12b Paul would be his own standard of comparison, but in v. 13, as the subject of καυχησόμεθα, he conforms to the standard assigned by God.[312] In response, it is suggested that in Paul's case the two standards could be identical. For him to assess himself by reference to himself would mean assessment by means of the standard set by his divine calling.[313] But this is not very probable. It is not easy to find a good sense for self-assessment by reference to self-provided standards.[314]

(c) As already noted under (i) (b), it is easier to derive the shorter from the longer text than vice versa.

Our preference is for the longer text, in view of the weight of the MS attestation and the difficulty of explaining the insertion of οὐ συνιᾶσιν into an original shorter text. There remains, however, the problem of the force of ἀλλά in v. 12b. If it has its usual adversative sense there seems to be no logical connection with the previous sentence. Paul would be saying: I will not engage in comparison with my rivals, *but* they lack understanding. The requisite connecting particle would be γάρ, 'for'. The only way of resolving the problem would be to suppose some ellipsis between v. 12a and v. 12b. Perhaps the clue is to be found in the obvious irony of v. 12a. Paul's line of thought might run as follows: 'I do not dare to compare myself with these people. (This is meant ironically. It sounds as though they are superior to me.) But (in fact) behaving as they do, they lack understanding.'

12a. Οὐ γὰρ τολμῶμεν ἐγκρῖναι ἢ συγκρῖναι ἑαυτούς τισιν τῶν ἑαυτοὺς συνιστανόντων, Paul now embarks on an explicit contrast between himself and the rival missionaries. He has obliquely referred to them already, and in v. 7 has appeared to invite some representative of their mission to engage in a comparison with himself. The immediate connection of thought, however, between vv. 10–11 and v. 12 is not altogether clear. The opening γάρ suggests a causal link. But what might it be? In v. 11 Paul has insisted on the absolute comparability between his

---

[311] Meyer, p. 388; Hughes, p. 365 n. 22; Furnish, p. 470; Wolff, p. 204 n. 74.
[312] Bachmann, p. 356; Martin, p. 315.
[313] Windisch, p. 309.
[314] Barrett, p. 264; Furnish, pp. 470–1.

epistolary *persona* and his imminent personal presence. Perhaps, then, the formal logical connection might be something like this: I make *this* comparison, between *my own* epistolary and personal self, *because* I do not venture to compare myself with these *other* people. The γάρ-clause must, of course, in any case be seen as ironical.[315] Paul does not dare, he claims, to rank himself[316] with his opponents. Taken at face value, this would imply that he sees them as his superiors. But the following assertion in v. 12b that they lack understanding, as well as the whole tenor of the rest of the chapter, negates this interpretation.

The rejection of comparison, however, must presumably be taken seriously, in view of the second half of the verse, where this is something that the opponents engage in, and a practice for which they are criticised. But how consistent is Paul in this respect? For only a few verses previously (v. 7), as we have noted above, he has challenged the opposition to precisely such comparison. And at a later stage (11.21b–23) he compares himself explicitly with his rivals. There, of course, he claims to be speaking 'as a fool'. But the terms of comparison themselves are seriously intended. The same problem arises in respect of self-commendation. On the one hand, this is the practice of the visiting missionaries, and thus suspect. Furthermore, Paul goes on to reject it altogether (v. 18). On the other hand, he has previously (6.4a) represented himself as engaging in it. And the whole letter of chaps. 10–13 could well be seen as a powerful exercise in precisely this practice. Again, much of this is part of his discourse as a fool, and a recourse to which the Corinthians have driven him by their own failure to commend him (12.11). And we shall see that self-praise could be regarded as legitimate when it served a good end, as Paul would hope would be the case with the present letter. Nevertheless, to some of his readers, at least, it might appear as though a particular practice is legitimate when Paul himself engages in it, but when his opponents do the same it is not. In fact, this could well be what Paul himself, in the present situation, is thinking. In v. 18 he asserts that it is only the commendation of the Lord that counts. But he firmly believes that he is himself the apostle appointed by God to establish the Corinthian church (vv. 13–15). Hence, his own self-commendation to the

---

[315] Belser, p. 304; Windisch, p. 308; Bultmann, p. 194; Furnish, p. 480.

[316] This is the only occurrence of the verb ἐγκρίνω in the NT. According to BAGD, s.v., it means here, '*to class … someone w. someone*'. It may be used of the admission of a person to a group. Barrett, p. 262, notes that it is used by Josephus (*Bell.*, II 138) of enrolment in the Essene community; see also Hughes, p. 364 n. 21, and Furnish, p. 469, for other examples. Here it may be virtually synonymous with συγκρίνω, 'compare', as Windisch, p. 308, suggests.

Corinthians is in effect the Lord's commendation, whilst that of his rivals[317] is not such.

12b. ἀλλὰ αὐτοὶ ἐν ἑαυτοῖς ἑαυτοὺς μετροῦντες καὶ συγκρίνοντες ἑαυτοὺς ἑαυτοῖς οὐ συνιᾶσιν. In discussion of the textual variant we have noticed the awkwardness of the initial ἀλλά and have suggested an ellipsis of some kind: (Paul has spoken as though these people are his superiors,) *but* in fact they lack understanding.[318] This verdict is based on the description of the opponents as 'measuring themselves by themselves and comparing themselves with themselves',[319] or, perhaps, we should understand 'themselves' as 'each other'.[320] The second alternative might be preferable, but in general sense there may be no real difference. Paul means that their self-commendation is based on criteria internal to their own group, standards which they themselves have decided upon as appropriate to the authentication and commendation of apostolic missionaries.[321]

What these criteria were concerned with he does not here specify. Theissen suggests that the opponents took as their standard those Jesus-sayings which lay upon the Christian missionary the obligation of a particular lifestyle, i.e., one of poverty, and reliance upon others to meet one's material needs. To appeal to the norm of a lifestyle, he argues, would evoke the charge of using oneself as a standard of measurement.[322] But it is doubtful whether Paul could have characterised reference to the Jesus-tradition in this way—more especially as he had quoted it with approval in 1 Cor 9.14. Furnish thinks that these people were concerned with the ability to display the 'signs of apostleship', i.e., various miraculous phenomena, to which Paul refers in 12.12.[323]

[317] Nowhere in his letter does Paul identify his opponents by name. In this verse and elsewhere they are τινές, τὶς, or described in an anonymous participial clause (11.4, 12). P. Marshall, *Enmity in Corinth*, pp. 341–8, claims that he is making use of a rhetorical convention of the non-naming of enemies illustrated in the *Res Gestae* of Augustus. This device both made one's enemy 'available for caricature', and also shamed him through anonymity, since 'it was the traditional aspiration of a person of rank that his name ... should live on after him' (p. 344).

[318] See above, p. 639.

[319] We understand μετροῦντες and συγκρίνοντες as conjunctive participles, possibly with causal force (BDR 418(1)). Turner, however, (MHT, p. 160), sees them as predicative, and translates: '*they do not realise that they are measuring themselves by their own standards.*' This makes less good sense. The participle συγκρίνοντες must be included in the construction, and the opponents would certainly realise that they were engaged in mutual comparison.

[320] The pronouns are understood as reciprocal in NRSV: 'they measure themselves by one another, and compare themselves with one another.' See also BAGD s.v. μετρέω 1.b. Furnish, p. 470, notes the possibility, but argues that this meaning would usually require πρὸς ἑαυτούς.

[321] Barrett, p. 263.

[322] Theissen, *Social Setting*, p. 52.

[323] Furnish, p. 480, with reference to Käsemann, 'Legitimität', p. 50.

But the tradition of apostolic miracle-working was widely known in the early church. Could competence in it have been seen as a criterion self-generated by one particular group of missionaries? A further possibility, proposed by P. Marshall, is that the opponents' criteria were the topics of the conventional encomium, i.e., the eulogy: 'physical appearance, education and achievements'. The Corinthians would be familiar with the convention, and would recognise it.[324] In view of the connection between the encomium and the practice of comparison,[325] which Paul attributes to his rivals, this last suggestion could well be correct. Whilst conformity to the requirements of encomiastic glorification was scarcely a standard originally generated by the in-group of the apostle's opponents in Corinth, its use as a criterion of apostolic authenticity within the Christian movement could well have originated with them. It will have been a standard which they were confident of having themselves reached (whilst Paul, in their view, did not). Hence, it was simply a mirror of their own *persona* (collective and individual), and it could be said that they indulged in self-measurement and self-comparison.

Their practice of comparison could have been in part a means of individual self-advertisement,[326] and in part a group exercise of 'friendly rivalry and mutual esteem'.[327] But it is likely that 'the real cutting edge of the comparisons was directed against Paul'.[328] As a rhetorical device, comparison could be used to depreciate one's opponents whilst magnifying one's own virtues.[329]

Paul charges them with lack of understanding. In what respect, he does not say. Perhaps it is because the only criteria by which they are willing to be assessed are those which they choose themselves. Hence, it could be said, the process of assessment is a fraud: 'measurement by their own standards meant in effect the use of no standards at all.'[330] Perhaps it is that they fail to comprehend what genuine apostleship means: this is proved by their boastfulness.[331] Or perhaps the clue lies in v. 13: Paul's claim that he does not himself indulge in boundless boasting may suggest that he is charging his rivals with failing to understand the proper limits of behaviour.[332] These possibilities are not mutually

---

[324] P. Marshall, *Enmity in Corinth*, p. 327.
[325] See below, p. 643.
[326] See below, p. 643.
[327] Forbes, 'Comparison', p. 15.
[328] Forbes, ibid.
[329] P. Marshall, *Enmity in Corinth*, p. 325.
[330] Barrett, p. 263.
[331] Forbes, 'Comparison', p. 28 n. 78.
[332] Marshall, *Enmity in Corinth*, p. 200.

exclusive, but in view of the repetition of the reflexive pronoun the first may well have been predominant in Paul's mind.

The concepts of comparison and self-praise (i) Comparison, σύγκρισις, was a fundamental part of rhetoric, primarily as belonging to the encomium,[333] where it functions as a means of showing the excellence of the person praised.[334] It is found also in history writing, as in Plutarch,[335] where, in his 'Lives' of the famous men of Greece and Rome, he arranges his subjects in pairs and then offers a short comparison between the two members of each pair.[336] It is clear from a number of sources that 'comparison' played a significant part in Greek education.[337]

(ii) In the encomium, and in Plutarch, the comparison is made by a third person, the orator or the writer. But first person comparison was also a known convention in Paul's day. In Plutarch, the comparison of oneself with some 'good and perfect man' can be seen as a way to self-knowledge.[338] But self-comparison could also be a hazardous business. As an adaptation of the encomium it would naturally result in self-praise.[339] This was regarded as a dangerous exercise, liable to misuse. Nevertheless, in certain circumstances it might be necessary. For example, one might praise oneself if in doing so one served a good end by telling the truth about oneself, and if it was necessary to counteract harmful and mistaken praise of others.[340] Self-praise was acceptable also if it was 'a direct response to the allegations against the speaker'.[341]

(iii) The popular teachers of rhetoric and philosophy in Paul's day, anxious to attract students, and in competition with each other, resorted to self-promotion, and employed the convention of comparison to this end.[342] The rival missionaries in Corinth, in all probability, used this same convention.[343]

13. ἡμεῖς δὲ οὐκ εἰς τὰ ἄμετρα καυχησόμεθα, ἀλλὰ κατὰ τὸ μέτρον τοῦ κανόνος οὗ ἐμέρισεν ἡμῖν ὁ θεὸς μέτρου,

[333] Forbes, 'Comparison', pp. 2–8; Betz, *Tradition*, p. 119.
[334] Betz, *Tradition*, pp. 119–20.
[335] Betz, *Tradition*, p. 119.
[336] Forbes, 'Comparison', p. 5.
[337] Forbes, 'Comparison', p. 7.
[338] Forbes, 'Comparison', pp. 5, 26 nn. 24, 25. He cites Plut., *Mor.* 84D and notes, pp. 5, 26 n. 27, that for Epictetus also self-comparison may be a valuable tool in the development of self-knowledge: *Diss.* II 18.21; 24.24.
[339] Forbes, 'Comparison', p. 8.
[340] Forbes, 'Comparison', pp. 8–10, with reference to Plut., *Mor.* 539E–47.
[341] Forbes, 'Comparison', p. 8.
[342] Furnish, p. 480; Forbes, 'Comparison', p. 7. Both refer to P Oxy 2190, in which a student complains of an inadequate teacher who nevertheless engages in comparison (σύγκρισις) with others.
[343] Winter, *Sophists*, p. 223.

ἐφικέσθαι ἄχρι καὶ ὑμῶν. The emphatic ἡμεῖς followed by δέ suggests that Paul is contrasting his own conduct with that of his rivals who have been the subject of v. 12b.[344] The behaviour he repudiates for himself is what he ascribes to them. They boast excessively, 'beyond limits'.[345] He thus implicitly charges them with conduct contrary to the Greek ethos of moderation.[346] The cause of this excessive boasting is the opponents' lack of external standards, and the content of it is their apostolic status, according to Meyer[347] and Barrett.[348] Possibly, however, the point may be apostolic accomplishments rather than status as such. Furnish suggests that the implicit reference to Paul's own activity 'within proper limits' could be quite specific: the apostle has in mind the areas where he has worked to plant the gospel.[349]

What Paul himself will say is both moderate and also in accordance with the standard laid down for him by God. His manner of expression, however, is involved, and commentators are not agreed on the nature of the standard to which he believes himself to conform. It will be useful to note first the meanings of the two key words μέτρον and κανών. The term μέτρον, 'measure', has 'instrument of measuring' as its primary meaning, and then 'measure' in the sense of 'the result of measuring', both literally and figuratively.[350] The word κανών means first 'rule', 'standard', and secondly (less certainly, perhaps) 'sphere', 'province', 'limits'.[351] It would appear that the two words stand fairly close together in sense. Hence, some commentators take them as virtually synonymous, whilst others differentiate between them. The division of opinion roughly corresponds to the difference between those who attach no geographical significance to either the κανών or the μέτρον and those who do suppose that the one term or the other relates in some way to geographical boundaries.

(i) Those in the first group give to κανών, 'rule', or 'standard',

---

[344] Wolff, p. 205.

[345] BAGD s.v. ἄμετρος, with reference to the use of ἀμέτρως of self-praise by Epictetus, *Ench.*, 33.14.

[346] Betz, *Tradition*, pp. 130–1, who observes that the Greek ethic is one of 'measure', and claims that Paul is here paying attention to the Delphic maxim μηδὲν ἄγαν, 'nothing too much'. See also P. Marshall, *Enmity in Corinth*, p. 200, on the term μέτρον.

[347] Meyer, p. 408.

[348] Barrett, p. 263.

[349] Furnish, p. 471.

[350] BAGD s.v. μέτρον. The figurative secondary sense is assigned to the present instance; see 2.b.

[351] BAGD s.v. κανών. Apart from the present uses in 2 Cor 10, the only examples given for the second sense are 1 Cl 1.3 and 41.1, where the LCL translation gives 'rule' as the sense.

a content derived from their general interpretation of Paul's thinking, and treat μέτρον as a comparatively colourless term for 'criterion', 'means of measurement'. Paul will speak of his achievements by reference to the criterion consisting of the κανών constituted by his apostolic commission and its validation, by divine grace, in missionary success.[352] Or, the content of the κανών is 'the mind of Christ' (1 Cor 2.15–16), which is possessed by the apostle by virtue of his possession of the Spirit. This means that he is not subject to human assessment, but that nevertheless he is not autonomous, or limitless.[353] There is a criterion by which he is measured. The difficulty, however, with this general line of approach is that, as the two interpretations given above illustrate, the content of the κανών is capable of such varied definition. How were Paul's readers to be expected to grasp what he meant? Moreover, the terms μέτρον and κανών become synonymous, as we have noted, and the sentence thus becomes tautologous. Lastly, as Martin, with reference to Barrett, points out, this unnecessary repetition of words for measuring remains unexplained, as does the concluding ἐφικέσθαι ἄχρι καὶ ὑμῶν, which must surely refer to geographical outreach in some way.[354]

(ii) We turn, then, to consider those forms of exegesis which in one way or another suppose that Paul has geographical limits in view.

(a) The word κανών is understood to mean 'measuring instrument' and the first μέτρον to indicate the result of measuring, the 'space' marked out by the measuring instrument.[355] The μέτρον, then, is the geographical space measured out by God as Paul's area of evangelistic work.[356] See Gal 2.9 and Rom 1.5, 14.[357] The κανών would presumably stand for the initial divine decision concerning his missionary sphere (cf. Gal 1.15–16; 2.7-8). Paul is saying, then, that he will speak of his achievements only in respect of the mission area (μέτρον) defined for him by the divine ruling (κανών), this ruling which God has allotted to him as a μέτρον (οὗ ἐμέρισεν ἡμῖν ὁ θεὸς μέτρου). It is at once apparent, however, that this interpretation requires two different senses for μέτρον within the same sentence: 'area

[352] H. W. Beyer, on κανών, in *TWNT* III, pp. 600–6; see pp. 603–4. See also Wendland, p. 232; Kümmel, p. 209; Prümm, *Diakonia Pneumatos* I, p. 590.

[353] Käsemann, 'Legitimität', pp. 57–8.

[354] Martin, pp. 320–1, with reference. to Barrett, 'Christianity at Corinth', p. 18. Barrett comments that if κανών means 'measuring-rod', then the phrase τὸ μέτρον τοῦ κανόνος 'is absurd'.

[355] The genitive κανόνος is subjective.

[356] Meyer, pp. 409–10; Windisch, p. 310; cf. Bultmann, p. 196.

[357] Windisch, p. 310.

measured' for the first occurrence, and 'measuring instrument' for the second.[358] This is something of a drawback.

(b) The μέτρον is the instrument of measurement, and the κανών is the sphere of Paul's missionary work.[359] The latter defines the former.[360] The point at issue (as under (a)) is the assignment of geographical areas to the apostolic leaders (Gal 2.7–9).[361] Paul will speak of his achievements only with reference to the criterion of his appointed area of activity, i.e., he will speak only of what he has done within this geographical sphere. This interpretation has some attraction. It is criticised, however, on various grounds. Is there anything in the context to suggest that Paul had in mind the meeting of leaders in Jerusalem (Gal 2.1–10)? The key word κανών does not occur in his account of it.[362] What is more, in Gal 6.16 (its only other occurrence in the NT outside 2 Cor 10) it means 'principle (of life)', not 'sphere', or 'province'.[363] And the 'geographical' interpretation of Gal 2.9 is itself problematic, since Jews lived amongst Gentiles almost everywhere.[364] But these objections are not necessarily compelling. The remaining verses of ch. 10 surely indicate, however vaguely, that spheres of missionary interest are in view, as in Gal 2. And whilst Paul does use κανών in Galatians in a sense different from that proposed here, it cannot here, in any case, primarily possess the meaning it has in Gal 6.16: on the contrary, its repetition, here, in vv. 15–16, especially in v. 16 (ἐν ἀλλοτρίῳ κανόνι), strongly suggests that it has some territorial connotation. Lastly, despite the acknowledged difficulty of the precise interpretation of the agreement described in Gal 2.7–9,[365] Paul did believe that he had some special missionary task which necessitated a vast amount of travel within the Mediterranean world. From that point of view, a divinely-appointed criterion of apostolic achievement would necessarily contain some 'geographical' element.

(c) Possibly, however, the term κανών in the present context has a dual meaning. Furnish, who translates it as 'jurisdiction',[366] sees it as referring both to Paul's apostolic authority and to the

---

[358] For an alternative way (sponsored by Furnish, p. 472) of understanding the grammatical construction, which would obviate this difficulty, see BDR 294(6): the relative οὗ is referred back to μέτρον, not κανόνος. This, however, is not the natural way of reading the clause and no parallel examples are given.
[359] Martin, p. 320.
[360] κανόνος is appositive (BDR 167(2)).
[361] Martin, p. 316.
[362] Furnish, p. 472.
[363] Beyer, on κανών, p. 602.
[364] Beyer, on κανών, p. 603.
[365] See, for example, Bruce, *Galatians*, p. 125.
[366] Furnish, p. 465.

area within which it is operative. In support he notes the use of the word in one of the texts published in *New Documents*.[367] The document is concerned with the provision of transport for the official personnel of the Roman Empire by the local communities through whose territories these people passed. The relevant sentence runs: κατὰ πόλιν καὶ κώμην ἔταξα κανόνα τῶν ὑπηρεσιῶν ('I have promulgated in the individual cities and villages a schedule of the services').[368] E. A. Judge, commenting on the text, notes its significance for the understanding of κανών in 2 Cor 10.13, 15–16, since there has been previously a total absence of evidence for the attachment to the word of the geographical connotation which a number of exegetes feel to be present in these verses. According to Judge, the meaning of κανών is 'the official schedule, in this case of the transport services to be supplied by the local community ... The κανών in itself is not a geographical concept, but the services it formulates are in this case geographically partitioned ...' Paul would have been familiar with this type of official edict, and could have taken over the word κανών to express God's scheduling of his own territorial commitment.[369] This territorially-defined schedule of duties is the criterion which will govern what he says about his apostolic achievements. This interpretation does justice both to the 'geographical' demands of the context and to the negative fact that κανών in itself does not mean, *tout court*, 'geographical sphere'. It is the best option of those we have considered.

Paul's territorial schedule was allotted him by God, and the divine purpose[370] was that he should reach even to Corinth. He has implicitly worked round again to the assertion of his God-given apostolic authority over the Corinthian church (cf. v. 8). And the tacit contrast with his rivals which is signalled by the opening ἡμεῖς δέ indicates that he is rejecting, and wishes his readers to reject, any such claim to authority on their part.

14. οὐ γὰρ ὡς[371] μὴ ἐφικνούμενοι εἰς ὑμᾶς ὑπερεκτείνομεν ἑαυτούς, ἄχρι γὰρ καὶ ὑμῶν ἐφθάσαμεν ἐν τῷ εὐαγγελίῳ τοῦ

---

[367] Furnish, p. 471. See Horsley, *New Documents* I, no. 9 (pp. 36–45).

[368] *New Documents* I, p. 37. For τῶν ὑπηρεσιῶν the translation, p. 38, has 'of what I judge desirable to be supplied', but this is based on the original Latin version of the edict, p. 36.

[369] *New Documents* I, pp. 44–5; quotation on p. 45.

[370] The ἐφικέσθαι is most probably to be taken as an infinitive of purpose: see BDR 390(1). In view of the beginning of v. 14, the implied subject must be Paul himself.

[371] B has ὡς γάρ for οὐ γάρ ὡς read by all other witnesses. This would make sense if we punctuate with a question mark after ὑπερεκτείνομεν (see Plummer, p. 288, though he does not accept this reading). But it is more likely to have resulted from an accidental omission of οὐ and a consequent transposition of γάρ as second word in the new sentence.

Χριστοῦ, Paul here substantiates the claim which emerges implicitly from v. 13, i.e., that he will not exceed the acceptable limit when he includes Corinth in the area of apostolic achievements he can boast about.[372] In this he is not over-reaching himself since he was the first to evangelise the Corinthians. He is not over-extending himself, as though not yet arriving in their city. The present participle is somewhat strange. The required sense seems to be such as is reflected in Martin's translation: 'For we are not overreaching our limit, as we should be doing if we had not [already] reached you.'[373] Strictly, however, this would require the aorist participle ἐφικόμενοι.[374] Some would see the present participle as meaning 'reaching so as to have continuing authority over',[375] or 'reaching "with continuing pastoral responsibility" for the Corinthian church'.[376] This type of interpretation is possible, but it does overload the significance of the verb ἐφικνέομαι more than a little. Perhaps the participle is simply attracted into the present tense on account of the present tense of the main verb ὑπερεκτείνομεν.

With several previous commentators,[377] we take the verb ἐφθάσαμεν to mean 'we arrived first'. This is in accordance with the classical use of φθάνω.[378] Against this interpretation, and in favour of the view that the sense is simply 'we arrived', other exegetes point out that the verb means 'arrive' (and not 'arrive first') in Rom 9.31; Phil 3.16; 1 Th 2.16. Had Paul meant that he had arrived before his opponents, he would have said something like ἐφθάσαμεν ἐκείνους (cf. 1 Th 4.15).[379] Furnish observes that in the three examples of φθάνω = 'arrive' which have just been noted the verb is followed by a preposition, as in the present instance.[380] It cannot be denied, however, that the sense 'arrive first' is better suited to the context. Since both Paul and his rivals obviously are, or have been, present in Corinth, this fact alone cannot distinguish between them. The distinction is that he arrived there with the Christian message[381] before they did, so that Corinth, as Barrett points out, 'was part of the virgin territory that Paul claimed as his special mission field': Rom 15.17–20.[382]

---

[372] Cf. Bachmann, p. 358.
[373] Martin, p. 315.
[374] Cf. Windisch, p. 311.
[375] Cf. Barrett, p. 266.
[376] Furnish, p. 472.
[377] See, e.g., Allo, p. 252; Barrett, p. 267; Tasker, p. 141; Bruce, p. 233; Hughes, p. 366 n. 24.
[378] LSJ s.v. φθάνω.
[379] Meyer, p. 411; cf. Bachmann, p. 359; Bultmann, p. 197.
[380] Furnish, p. 472.
[381] See BAGD s.v. ἐν I.4.c.β.
[382] Barrett, p. 267.

Furthermore, the sense 'get there first' is the thought that is
carried on in v. 15.[383] In response to the claim that ἐφθάσαμεν in
this sense, i.e., 'precede', 'anticipate', would require an object (as
it has in 1 Th 4.15), it may be noted that there are classical
examples of the verb's absolute use.[384]

15a. οὐκ εἰς τὰ ἄμετρα καυχώμενοι ἐν ἀλλοτρίοις κόποις,
Here we have further elucidation of the claim in v. 13 that the
apostle's boasting will not exceed acceptable limits: he will not
claim credit[385] for what belongs to others,[386] i.e., for work done by
other missionaries.[387] In all probability his assertion is polemical,
i.e., by implication he criticises his opponents for doing precisely
this.[388] His initial allusion to boasting, in v. 13, has begun with an
emphatic ἡμεῖς δέ, which implies a contrast with some other
person or people, i.e., the rivals who are the subject of v. 12.
Whilst he himself aims to preach the gospel where it is as yet not
known, his opponents abide by no such principle, but claim an
authority equal to his in the church he himself has founded.[389] If
they boast of their success in Corinth, it is Paul's hard work they
are boasting of, not their own. Or should we see the situation in
reverse? Perhaps Paul is defending himself against a criticism
directed against himself by these same opponents. It is he who
poaches on the mission territory of others and boasts about it. As
representatives of the Jewish Christian mission, they might have
claimed that the Jewish Christian leaders, primarily Cephas
(1 Cor 1.12; 3.22; 9.5; 15.5), were responsible for the creation of
the church in Corinth.[390] A third option would be to regard the
accusation of missionary poaching as mutual, and Corinth
as disputed territory. This could well be so, if, as Barrett argues,
this passage in 2 Corinthians reflects the agreement recorded in

---

[383] Martin, p. 322.

[384] See LSJ s.v. φθάνω II.

[385] The participle καυχώμενοι is to be understood as the equivalent of a finite
verb: so, e.g., Plummer, p. 289; Lietzmann, p. 143; Allo, p. 252; Furnish, p. 472; see
also BDR 468(1). Meyer, pp. 411–12, suggests that this clause resumes (grammatically) the beginning of v. 13 (with v. 14 as parenthetical), so that the καυχώμενοι
is dependent upon the καυχησόμεθα of this earlier verse. But this main verb is
rather remote. Moreover, the construction postulated by Meyer would require a
similar subordination to v. 13 of the following participle ἔχοντες and its clause,
which would be unlikely, since this clause is concerned with a rather different
point.

[386] Cf. Windisch, p. 311.

[387] Windisch, ibid., points out that κόπος is used of apostolic labours in 1 Cor 3.8
and in 1 Th 3.5. See also the use of the verb κοπιάω in 1 Cor 15.10.

[388] See, for the view that he has his rivals in mind, e.g., Bachmann, p. 359;
Plummer, p. 289; Windisch, ibid.; Allo, p. 253; Furnish, p. 481.

[389] Furnish, ibid.

[390] Martin, p. 323, with reference to Barrett, 'Cephas and Corinth', pp. 35–6. The
Jewish mission could at least claim an interest.

Gal 2.9. He observes that since there was a 'synagogue of Hebrews' in Corinth the members of the Jewish Christian mission might claim some justification for operating in the city, but 'had no right to invade an existing Gentile church'.[391] It is true that there is no specific reference here to the Jerusalem agreement,[392] and true also that the criterion of territorial responsibility implicit in the ἐφθάσαμεν of v. 14 and explicit in Rom 15.20, i.e., evangelisation of an area previously untouched by the Christian mission, is different from the Jewish-Gentile division of responsibility reflected in Gal 2.9. But it could have been precisely in Corinth that Paul developed this new criterion, as the ambiguities of the original agreement began to cause difficulties. This third option has some attraction.

It is not clear that the Corinthian congregation was, in fact, a wholly Gentile church (*pace* Barrett, above). Whilst Paul's missionary task was concerned primarily with the evangelisation of Gentiles, his preaching could well have attracted some Jews also. There are two verses in 1 Corinthians, i.e., 7.18 and 9.20, which suggest that the church in Corinth may have been mixed. In addition, our exegesis of 2 Cor 3 would imply that there was some substantial Jewish influence within the Corinthian congregation. It seems that some members were troubled by criticism coming from non-Christian Jews. That they should be troubled by it to the extent that Paul realised the need for a strong theological response suggests they were Jews themselves or at least that they had previously had close links with the synagogue. If this was so, the Jewish Christian rival missionaries could have claimed some pastoral responsibility for them, and credit, if not for their conversion, at least for their further instruction. Consequently, since Paul regarded himself as the spiritual father of the whole church (12.14; 1 Cor 4.14–15), he would have to find some way of asserting his own rights which would supplement the earlier agreement.

15b–16a. ἐλπίδα δὲ ἔχοντες αὐξανομένης τῆς πίστεως ὑμῶν ἐν ὑμῖν μεγαλυνθῆναι κατὰ τὸν κανόνα ἡμῶν εἰς περισσείαν εἰς τὰ ὑπερέκεινα ὑμῶν εὐαγγελίσασθαι, After his denial that he exceeds proper limits, by boasting of the work of others, Paul passes to a more positive point. He hopes that, through the increase of his readers' faith, he himself will 'grow'[393] (increase, presumably, in apostolic achievement), so as to evangelise fresh territory. His reference to the faith of the Corinthians may be a straightforward allusion to spiritual growth, or an indirect

[391] Barrett, ibid.
[392] Furnish, p. 481.
[393] See BAGD s.v. μεγαλύνω 1.

suggestion that their toleration of his rivals is due to the inadequacy of their present faith.[394] It is less likely to be a reflection of their confidence that, through instruction by these same teachers, they have 'moved on to a higher level'.[395] Since Paul would not believe any such thing, he would be speaking ironically, but his sentence as a whole is surely to be understood seriously.[396] He is serious, we may presume, when he indicates that his increase in the achievement of his task will be brought about, or at least facilitated, by his Corinthian readers.[397] Once he is convinced that their faith is secure, and that they have progressed to a satisfactory degree of maturity, he will be at liberty to extend his sphere of work, since they will make fewer demands on his pastoral attention. Furthermore, if he can disengage them from the influence of the rival mission, he may secure his own freedom for future evangelism without interference: these same opponents, worsted in Corinth, would be less likely to follow him elsewhere. He hopes for abundant[398] success for his future projects, which will be carried out in accordance with his schedule of territorial responsibilities. The result[399] of his greater scope for action will be the preaching of the gospel in regions further afield.[400] If at this point he has any specific locations in view, he

---

[394] Windisch, p. 312.

[395] *Pace* Barrett, p. 268.

[396] A further suggestion, proposed by Martin, pp. 323–4, is that πίστις here may mean 'faithfulness' rather than 'faith': the faithfulness of the Corinthians to Paul's mission 'will act as a support to his future service'. But the interpretation of πίστις in this less usual sense would require contextual confirmation which here is lacking.

[397] We take the ἐν ὑμῖν as going with the following μεγαλυνθῆναι. Bultmann, p. 198, and others attach it to the preceding phrase, but this would make the expression tautologous: see, e.g., Plummer, p. 289, and Furnish, p. 473. Bultmann argues that attachment in sense to μεγαλυνθῆναι would require that ἐν ὑμῖν should follow the infinitive. Its present position, however, produces a chiastic arrangement (verb of increasing—ὑμῶν—ἐν ὑμῖν—verb of increasing) which serves to emphasise the responsibility of the Corinthians. For the use of ἐν to indicate agency, see BDR 219(1).

[398] See BAGD s.v. περισσεία, where the phrase is taken as adverbial, 'greatly'.

[399] We take the εὐαγγελίσασθαι as an infinitive used in a somewhat free way by itself for the expression of result: see BDR 391(4). Furnish, p. 473, claims that it depends upon ἐλπίδα ἔχοντες. But in that case it would be parallel, grammatically, with μεγαλυνθῆναι, and a connecting καί would be required, as Windisch, p. 313, observes.

[400] In BAGD s.v. εἰς 1.d.β. the εἰς of εἰς τὰ ὑπερέκεινα ὑμῶν is listed as an example of εἰς following 'verbs of saying, teaching, proclaiming, preaching, etc.'. Hence, the sense would be 'preaching to' the regions beyond Corinth. At the end of this section, however, it is noted that in such cases the meaning of εἰς approaches that of ἐν (see εἰς 9.), and in fact translators often prefer the sense 'preaching in': see, e.g., NRSV, BCN; Barrett, p. 255; Furnish, p. 465; Martin, p. 315. But 'preaching to' is preferred by JB, REB. See BAGD s.v. ὑπερέκεινα for the remainder of the phrase. The ὑπερέκεινα is an adverb, 'beyond', used with a following genitive (here, ὑμῶν), and τά requires a following μέρη to be understood: 'the parts (i.e., regions)'.

may be thinking of the missionary enterprise in Spain to which he refers in Rom 15.24, 28.[401] **16b. οὐκ ἐν ἀλλοτρίῳ κανόνι εἰς τὰ ἕτοιμα καυχήσασθαι.** In a clause syntactically parallel to v. 16a,[402] Paul repeats, for emphasis, in negative form the point he has just made about the extension of his evangelistic work beyond Corinth. It will not be done within the area of other missionaries' scheduled responsibilities. He will not boast of[403] results ready to hand, i.e., of work done by others. And whilst the 15b syntactical connection is with v. 16a, with the connection in sense just indicated, the form of expression shows that there is also a reiteration of v. 15a. The dispute over missionary responsibility and the allocation of credit for missionary success was clearly acute.

17. Ὁ δὲ καυχώμενος ἐν κυρίῳ καυχάσθω. Paul has been castigating the immoderate boasting which consists of taking the credit for work done by others and within others' proper spheres of responsibility. He may thus have given the impression that there is a moderate kind of boasting to which one would be entitled. Here he takes care to dispel any such impression. No boasting of human achievement is legitimate, only boasting of what the Lord has done. The point is made by means of what is intended as a scriptural quotation. This is not made explicit, but in 1 Cor 1.31 the identical injunction is introduced with the formula καθὼς γέγραπται: Paul's readers might be expected to remember this.[404] The quotation is a reformulation of Jer 9 (LXX).23, in which boasting of one's understanding and knowledge of the Lord who practises mercy, judgement and righteousness is replaced by the concise ἐν κυρίῳ as the object of boasting.[405] It is possible that Paul might have seen some scriptural justification for this substitution of ἐν κυρίῳ.[406] In the present verse the κύριος is Christ, in all probability.[407] This is most likely so in 1 Cor 1.31, in view of the reference to Christ in the

---

[401] So, e.g., Bachmann, p. 360; Plummer, p. 289; Barrett, p. 268; Martin, p. 324.
[402] The καυχήσασθαι will then be an infinitive expressing result, as is εὐαγγελίσασθαι (see above).
[403] See BAGD s.v. καυχάομαι 1. for καυχάομαι εἴς τι with the meaning 'boast with regard to something'.
[404] Stanley, *Paul and the Language of Scripture*, p. 234 n. 178.
[405] The LXX text runs: ἐν τούτῳ καυχάσθω ὁ καυχώμενος, συνίειν καὶ γινώσκειν ὅτι ἐγώ εἰμι κύριος, ποιῶν ἔλεος καὶ κρίμα καὶ δικαιοσύνην ἐπὶ τῆς γῆς. On its reformulation in the Pauline texts, see Stanley, *Paul and the Language of Scripture*, pp. 186–8, 263.
[406] Furnish, p. 474, draws attention to this suggestion in the article by J. Schreiner, 'Jeremia 9, 22.23 als Hintergrund des paulinischen „Sich-Rühmens"', in *Neues Testament und Kirche* (FS Rudolf Schackenburg), ed. J. Gnilka, Freiburg-Basel-Wien, 1974, pp. 530–42; see p. 540. Ps 43.9, for example, reads ἐν τῷ θεῷ καυχησόμεθα.
[407] So, e.g., Allo, p. 254; Hughes, p. 372; Barrett, p. 269.

previous verse, and one would expect the same application of the term here.[408] In Rom 15.17–18, moreover, Paul refers to boasting of what Christ has done through his agency in respect of the evangelisation of the Gentiles.[409] **18.** οὐ γὰρ ὁ ἑαυτὸν συνιστάνων,[410] ἐκεῖνός ἐστιν δόκιμος, ἀλλὰ ὃν ὁ κύριος συνίστησιν. The negative implication of v. 17 is that no boast of one's own human achievements is legitimate. This is now explicitly substantiated. It is commendation by the Lord which alone provides validation.[411] By contrast with the letter of chaps. 1–8, self-commendation, equated with boasting, is now in itself a bad thing.[412] Paul's statement is made in general terms, but obviously he has the Corinthian situation in view, and the rival missionaries in particular, since in v. 12 he has described them as self-recommenders.[413] By implication, he denies them the seal of the Lord's approval: as apostolic missionaries they are unauthentic (cf. 11.13). His use of the actual term δόκιμος may have been motivated by the agitation in Corinth, since it appears (13.3) that a δοκιμή, a proof of authenticity, was demanded of Paul himself.[414] He believed that his evangelistic work there had already provided the Corinthians with the evidence that his apostolate was validated by the Lord (1 Cor 9.1–2; 2 Cor 3.1–3), but they had presumably remained unimpressed by his claim, at any rate by comparison with the proofs apparently provided by his opponents.

---

[408] Furnish, p. 474.
[409] See Bruce, p. 234, and Furnish, ibid.
[410] The reading συνιστάνων (𝔓⁴⁶ ℵ B D F G H Iᵛⁱᵈ P 0121a. 0243. 6. 33. 81. 104. 365. 1175. 1739. 2464. 2495 *al*) is clearly preferable to συνιστῶν (Ψ 𝔐), probably produced by scribal error, but retained as the equally possible participle of the συνιστάω form of the verb.
[411] See BAGD s.v. δόκιμος 1. for the sense 'approved by testing'.
[412] See above, on v. 12a.
[413] Windisch, p. 314.
[414] Bultmann, p. 199.

2. PAUL THE FOOL IN CHAPTERS 11-12 (11.1-12.18)

Commentators are in general agreement in terming the greater part of these chapters the Fool's Speech. Whether or not this title should carry with it the implication that Paul is conforming to a particular rhetorical genre or to some stereotyped dramatic role, or to both combined, is a question that will be discussed in the course of the exegesis. The more obvious reason for such a title is that in 11.1 Paul asks his readers to indulge him in a little foolishness, and that references to folly occur throughout (11.16, 17, 19, 21; 12.6, 11). There is agreement for the most part that it is at 11.1 that the discourse begins.[1] Martin, however, treats 11.1-15 as a digression from the main argument begun in chap. 10, and supposes the 'Fool's Story' to begin at 11.16.[2] At 11.1, he argues, Paul 'turns aside from his chief theme of missionary service and the dispute of territoriality (in 10:12-18), only to revert to that topic in 11:16'.[3] In opposition to this viewpoint, we might argue that the theme of 'missionary service' is too general to serve as a means of demarcating one section from another, and that the resumption of the territorial debate at 11.16 is by no means obvious. Furthermore, the frequency of the ἄφρων/ἀφροσύνη words in 11.1-12.11 tends to connect 11.1ff. with the remainder of chap. 11 and with chap. 12.[4] Lastly, the πάλιν λέγω at 11.16, followed in vv. 16, 17, 19, 21 by three instances of ἄφρων and two of ἀφροσύνη, likewise connects these later verses with the beginning of the chapter. This opening phrase does not very obviously provide a link with 10.17-18.

There is less agreement about where the speech is thought to end. According to Zmijewski, it ends at 12.10.[5] The γέγονα ἄφρων of v. 11a, taken by itself, could be seen as supporting this interpretation. It is clear, however, that it introduces a short paragraph in which each sentence is connected with what precedes, either structurally (γάρ 11c, d, 13a) or in sense (11b, 12, 13c). This would favour the view of Furnish and Wolff, i.e., that the speech ends at 12.13:[6] the whole paragraph would thus function as the conclusion. In v. 14 Paul then seems to take up the fresh topic of his prospective third visit to Corinth. But

---

[1] Zmijewski, *'Narrenrede'* (see title page); Wolff, p. 208; Furnish, p. 484; Sundermann, *Kraft der Rede*, p. 45.
[2] Martin, p. 356.
[3] Martin, p. 328.
[4] There are 7 instances in this section (11.16-12.11), and thus, with 11.1, 8 in all in 2 Corinthians. Elsewhere in Paul there are only 2 (Rom 2.20; 1 Cor 15.36) or 3 (with Eph 5.17).
[5] Zmijewski, *'Narrenrede'* (see title page).
[6] Furnish, p. 484; Wolff, p. 208.

the substance of what he has to say, in respect of his refusal of maintenance and the suspicions this policy has generated, has already received mention in 11.7–11. Consequently, it would also make sense to see 12.18 as the ending of the discourse, as Sundermann does.[7] The opening of v. 19 could refer to the impression produced by the whole of chap.11 and the preceding verses of chap.12. At this point, we leave the question open.

How might the discourse be seen in terms of the rhetorical divisions of a speech?[8] We have noted that in the scheme proposed by Sundermann chap. 10 can be divided, with some plausibility, into *exordium* and *narratio*. What follows would then be the main argument, in which the positive case is proved and objections are refuted. Sundermann regards the whole of the Fool's Speech as the *argumentatio*, but reverses the order of proof and refutation, so that 11.1–15 constitutes the latter and 11.16–12.18 the former.[9] This main division is in a general way convincing: the reference to folly in 11.16 picks up the similar reference in 11.1, and, as a kind of heading, signals a fresh start. The more detailed analyses of the two sections will be considered at the appropriate points in the exegesis.

Before embarking on the detailed exegesis, however, we must take note of the different type of rhetorical analysis proposed by DiCicco. As we have already observed,[10] he seeks to show that in the letter of chaps. 10–13. Paul can be seen to make use of all three of the basic methods of proof employed in rhetoric. A few instances have been noted already in the exegesis of chap. 10.[11] In the remaining chapters we shall choose a particular example of each proof to illustrate Paul's rhetorical method. The use of ἦθος will be considered in relation to the hardships-list of 11.23–29, that of πάθος in connection with 11.1–15, and that of λόγος with reference to various sections in chaps 11–13. Each proof is, of course, employed throughout chaps. 10–13, but to note each instance in each relevant verse would overload the general exegesis too heavily. In addition, the force of each aspect of persuasion may be better appreciated by treating each separately, as DiCicco himself does.

---

[7] Sundermann, *Kraft der Rede*, p. 45.
[8] The word 'speech' is somewhat ambiguous. In terms of the rhetorical analysis we are considering, chaps. 10–13 constitute the speech as a whole, with the Fool's Speech as its *argumentatio*.
[9] Sundermann, ibid.
[10] See above p. 595.
[11] See above pp. 618, 625.

(i) *Paul's plea for tolerance and his castigation of the rival missionaries* (11.1–15)

[1]Would that you tolerated a little foolishness on my part! Now do tolerate me. [2]For I am jealously concerned for you, with divine jealousy. For I betrothed you to one man, to present you as a pure virgin to Christ. [3]But I fear lest perhaps, just as the serpent deceived Eve in his craftiness, so your minds might be corruptly diverted from single-minded (and pure)[12] devotion to Christ. [4]For indeed, if your visitor preaches another Jesus, whom we did not preach, or you receive a different spirit which you did not receive, or a different gospel which you did not accept, you tolerate him splendidly. [5]For I reckon that I am in no way inferior to the super-apostles. [6]But if in respect of oratory I am indeed a layman, yet I am not such as regards knowledge. To the contrary, we have revealed our knowledge to you in every way and in all its aspects.

[7]Or did I commit a sin, lowering myself so that you might be elevated, in that I preached the gospel of God to you without financial reward? [8]I plundered other churches, taking pay so that I might do you service. [9]And when I was present with you and in want, I did not burden anyone. For the brothers came from Macedonia and supplied my wants. And in every respect I kept myself from burdening you, and will so keep myself. [10]As Christ's truth is in me, this boast shall not be barred to me in the region of Achaia. [11]Why? Because I do not love you? God knows! [12]But what I am doing, and shall do, is done so that I may cut off the opportunity of those who desire an opportunity to be found to be just like us in respect of what they boast of. [13]For such people are false apostles, dishonest workmen,[13] disguising themselves as apostles of Christ. [14]And no wonder. For Satan himself disguises himself as an angel of light. [15]So it is no great wonder if his agents also disguise themselves as agents of righteousness—whose end will accord with their works.

Recognising that his prospective self-defence will be in some sense folly, Paul begs for tolerance: he points to his own concern for his readers, their toleration of his rivals, and the fact that he is in no way inferior to these people. He then turns to one particular cause of contention: his refusal to accept financial assistance from the Corinthians. He implies that in his view this policy was a virtue. Contrary to what the Corinthians are clearly thinking, he claims that he refused the money they offered because he loves them. But he explains in addition that he intends also to frustrate the designs of the rival missionaries. These people are pseudo-apostles. In fact, they are agents of Satan in disguise.

---

[12] See the discussion of the textual variant below, p. 663.
[13] The phrase is taken from BAGD s.v. δόλιος.

11.1–15 as argumentatio (a): refutatio Sundermann further divides
this section:

insinuatio	11.1-6
propositio	11.7
argumentatio	11.8–11
peroratio	11.12–15[14]

11.1–6 as insinuatio
Sundermann claims that these verses serve as introduction to the
whole argument, and also, more immediately, to 11.7–15.[15] Paul
has to meet the opposition on their own ground, but has reservations about their criteria of apostleship. Consequently, he resorts
to a rhetorical ploy. Without denying his own position, he can
meet the views of the Corinthians by playing a part—that of a
fool.[16] We should agree on the introductory function of the
paragraph, and would suggest that it might be seen to have three
aspects: Paul's concern for the Corinthians in v. 2 anticipates his
later assertion of his love in v. 11; his reference to the visiting
missionaries in vv. 4–5 looks ahead to his attack on them in vv.
12–15 and the allusions in vv. 20–23; and the plea for toleration
of folly has relevance for the speech as a whole. The element of
indirection, proper to 'insinuation',[17] if present, would be more
difficult to determine. Perhaps it might be that Paul represents as
'folly' what is really a deadly serious attack on his opponents, or
that the plea for 'toleration' masks his determination to assert
authority. In either case, his self-presentation as a 'fool' would be
a kind of dissimulation: he scarcely thinks of himself in this way.
Or does he? Does *self*-presentation accord with the OT figure of
the *wise* man who does not boast of himself?
   1. Ὄφελον ἀνείχεσθέ μου μικρόν τι[18] ἀφροσύνης· ἀλλὰ καὶ
ἀνέχεσθέ μου. Paul gives warning that in further pursuit of his
self-defence he is going to indulge in 'folly'. What it consists in he
does not explain until he arrives at vv. 16–18. But whatever its

---

[14] Sundermann, *Kraft der Rede*, p. 45.
[15] Sundermann, *Kraft der Rede*, p. 82 n. 15.
[16] Sundermann, *Kraft der Rede*, pp. 77–9.
[17] See above, pp. 597–8.
[18] There is textual confusion at this point. The reading τι has substantial attestation (𝔓46 ℵ B D Ψ 0121a. 0243. 6. 33. 365. 1739. 1881 *al* f t vg sy^h), but is omitted
in some witnesses (F G H 𝔐 it Lcf Ambst). But some of this latter group and other
witnesses (F G 6. 81. 630. 1175 *pc*) add τῆς before ἀφροσύνης, although the article
is lacking in a preponderant number of MSS (𝔓46vid ℵ B D P Ψ 0243. 33. 1739. 1881
pc). A third variation replaces τι ἀφροσύνης with τῇ ἀφροσύνῃ (H 𝔐). It is possible
that a single scribal error might lie at the root of this textual disturbance. It could
be that a scribe wrote TH for TI, thus producing the ungrammatical τῇ ἀφροσύνης.
This would then be remedied in various ways: by omitting τῇ (τι), by changing τῇ
to τῆς, or by changing ἀφροσύνης to ἀφροσύνῃ.

nature, it will require toleration on the part of his readers. Does he expect that it will be forthcoming? In view of the fact that he will proceed to commend himself at some length in a fashion he admits to be foolish, the context might suggest that he regards the wish expressed in the first half of the verse as attainable. Otherwise, why should he embark on his 'Fool's Speech' at all? But his form of expression indicates the contrary. The grammarians are agreed that ὄφελον with a past tense of the indicative (here, the imperfect) indicates that the wish is unfulfilled or unattainable.[19] And yet in the second half of the verse Paul either allows that his readers do tolerate him or urges them to do so. Perhaps the initial negative expectation reflects his awareness of a general lack of tolerance towards himself on the part of the Corinthians. Or there may be some element of implicit irony. Since they are so wise in their own estimation (1 Cor 4.10), he could scarcely hope that they would tolerate folly of any kind. In either case, what follows puts this initial attitude into reverse.

The importance of the notion of 'foolishness' in what follows is indicated here by the placing of ἀφροσύνης in the centre of the sense-unit of v. 1.[20] Consequently, it is the μικρόν τι ἀφροσύνης, 'some small degree of foolishness', that is to be seen as the object of the ἀνείχεσθε,[21] and the μου, despite its position, is to be attached to ἀφροσύνης, 'foolishness on my part', rather than the verb, 'tolerate me'.[22] It may be that Paul is taking up a charge made against him by the rival missionaries. His words in 11.16, μή τις με δόξῃ ἄφρονα εἶναι, might suggest that, for one reason or another, they were calling him 'senseless'.[23] If so, it will become apparent, as he proceeds, that he returns the accusation.

[19] See, e.g., BDR 359(1); MHT, p. 91; Zerwick, *Biblical Greek*, p. 123 n. 15; Moule, *Idiom Book*, p. 137.

[20] Zmijewski, *'Narrenrede'*, pp. 77–8.

[21] So, e.g., Windisch, p. 318; Bultmann, p. 201; Martin, p. 331. The verb ἀνέχομαι with a thing as its object may take either the accusative or the genitive case, although it takes only the genitive when its object is a person; see BAGD s.v. ἀνέχω.

[22] This alternative interpretation has support however, from Bachmann, p. 362, in view of the separation of μου from ἀφροσύνης, and from Plummer, p. 293, who draws attention to the ἀνέχεσθέ μου in v. 1b. See also Barrett, p. 271, and Furnish, p. 485. The μικρόν τι [ἀφροσύνης] would then become either an accusative of reference (Plummer) or a second object of the verb (Bachmann). The argument from word order, however, is indecisive, since, according to Zmijewski, *'Narrenrede'*, p. 77 n. 4, unstressed pronouns tend to stand near the beginning of the sentence. And the ἀνέχεσθέ μου in v. 1b can be seen as an abbreviated version of the longer expression in v. 1a (in which admittedly, the grammatical function of the μου has changed). Full repetition would have been more than a little heavy.

[23] Lietzmann, p. 144. On the apparent conflict with v. 1 see below on v. 16.

There is some ambiguity in the second part of the verse, since the verb ἀνέχεσθε may be either indicative or imperative. There is considerable support for the former of these grammatical possibilities. Paul has just expressed his wish for toleration as though it were unattainable, and is now correcting himself. The indicative, affirming that his readers do bear with him, provides more of a correction than would the imperative.[24] The introductory ἀλλά will possess its usual adversative force, and the καί will emphasise the verb: 'But [I must correct myself] you *do* tolerate me.' One has to ask, however, whether the content does not rather suggest that ἀνέχεσθε is imperative. If vv. 2 and 3 belong together and together substantiate v. 1 (by means of the γάρ of v. 2), the anxiety Paul expresses in v. 3 would more naturally provide grounds for an urgent plea than for a confident assertion.[25] Moreover, the complaint in v. 4 that the Corinthians tolerate (ἀνέχεσθε) an alien gospel and the like would suggest that in v.1 we have a repeated plea for toleration of Paul himself. Lastly, if we look at the more remote context, we see that in 11.16 he is still *asking* for acceptance of his 'folly': here the verb δέξασθε is clearly imperative. Hence, it is preferable to understand the ἀνέχεσθε of v. 1 also as an imperative.[26] The initial ἀλλά may be understood as strengthening the command: 'Now *do* tolerate me'.[27] From the point of view of rhetorical technique, Paul is employing, as Furnish points out, the method of 'prodiorthosis': he asks in advance for his readers' toleration of anything he may say that they might find uncongenial.[28]

2. ζηλῶ γὰρ ὑμᾶς θεοῦ ζήλῳ, ἡρμοσάμην γὰρ ὑμᾶς ἑνὶ ἀνδρὶ παρθένον ἁγνὴν παραστῆσαι τῷ Χριστῷ· His motivation, in begging for this toleration, is his deep concern[29] for their spiritual

---

[24] See Meyer, p. 419, and Plummer, p. 293. Other supporters of this interpretation include Chrysostom, *PG* 61 col. 553 (NPNF XII, p. 383); Windisch, p. 318; Rückert, p. 319; Hughes, p. 373 n. 31; Bultmann, p. 201; Zmijewski, '*Narrenrede*', p. 79.

[25] Cf. Furnish, p. 485, who thinks the imperative more likely in view of the context, and points in particular to vv. 2–3.

[26] With Bachmann, p. 361; Allo, p. 275; Furnish, p. 485; and Martin, pp. 327, 328.

[27] Turner, MHT, p. 330, regards the ἀλλά καί as introducing 'a strong addition', with the meaning 'yes, indeed'. Barrett, p. 270, similarly translates, 'yes, do put up with me!' But since v. 1a, strictly speaking, expresses an *unattainable* wish, the 'yes' of these renderings seems inappropriate.

[28] Furnish, p. 499, with reference to BDF 495(3), where the term is defined as 'anticipatory correction'. We may note that it is used by Chrysostom in his comment on the present verse: Μέλων ἐμβαίνειν εἰς τοὺς οἰκείους ἐπαίνους, πολλῇ κέχρηται τῇ προδιορθώσει. (*PG* 61 col. 553; 'Being about to enter upon his own praises, he uses much previous correction.' NPNF XII, p. 383). Sundermann, *Kraft der Rede*, pp. 83–4, likewise sees an instance of prodiorthosis here, intended to make the readers attentive.

[29] See BAGD s.v. ζηλόω 1.b. for this rendering of the verb.

welfare. It is a jealous concern,[30] inspired by God,[31] or a God-like jealousy.[32] The force of this form of expression then becomes apparent in vv. 2b–3: Paul is anxious lest his readers' exclusive devotion to Christ should be displaced by what he would see as a rival commitment, and he is consequently 'jealous' on Christ's behalf. To get the point across, he uses the analogy of betrothal.[33] He betrothed the Corinthians exclusively to one husband, i.e., having founded the church he committed the congregation to exclusive allegiance to Christ, and then became responsible for maintaining them in a state of chastity, i.e., adherence to the original pure gospel, until the time should come for the presentation of bride to husband for the consummation of the marriage, i.e., for the completion of unity between Christ and his people at the Parousia (1 Th 4.17).[34] The basic analogy is clear enough. The only point for debate concerns the precise role that Paul sees himself as playing within the terms of the imagery. Is he the intermediary who arranges the marriage, or is he the bride's father? Meyer, supporting the first possibility,[35] notes that this is the way Chrysostom understands the analogy: ἑαυτὸν μὲν ἐν χώρᾳ τῆς προμνηστρίας ... στήσας.[36] Other exegetes observe that Paul might have been familiar with the idea (attested only later) that Moses acted as a marriage-broker between Yahweh and Israel.[37] It is by

[30] Several commentators would agree that both the verb and the following cognate noun, in the present context, possess the connotation of 'jealous concern'. See Allo, p. 275; Barrett, pp. 270, 272; and Martin, pp. 327, 332.
[31] Martin, p. 327. The genitive θεοῦ would indicate origin. On genitives of 'origin and cause', see MHT, p. 211.
[32] Windisch, p. 319. The θεοῦ would indicate quality. On this use of the genitive, see BDR 165 and MHT, pp. 212–14.
[33] The middle voice of ἁρμόζω, which, with an object, would normally mean 'become engaged to someone', is here used with the force of the active, 'give in marriage', 'betroth'. This is an isolated instance in biblical Greek, but not wholly unique elsewhere. See BAGD s.v. ἁρμόζω 3., and the reference there given to Philo, Leg. All. (Allegorical Interpretation) II 67: [Moses] ᾧ τὴν Αἰθιόπισσαν ... αὐτὸς ὁ θεὸς ἡρμόσατο ('and it was God Himself who wedded to Moses the Ethiopian woman', LCL). Pace Moulton, Prolegomena, p. 160, who sees it as an indication of Paul's personal involvement, no special significance attaches to his use of the middle, since by this time the distinction between middle and active has become blurred (see Moule, Idiom Book, p. 24). The indirect object is ἑνὶ ἀνδρί, 'to one man' (Barrett, p. 270; Furnish, p. 484; cf. NRSV 'to one husband'), rather than τῷ Χριστῷ (RSV, NEB, REB). The natural division of the sentence comes between ἑνὶ ἀνδρί and παρθένον ἀγνήν.
[34] Plummer, p. 293; Windisch, p. 320.
[35] Meyer, p. 421.
[36] Chrysostom, PG 61 col. 554 ('placing himself in the room of her who promotes a match', NPNF XII, p. 384).
[37] R. Batey, 'Paul's Bride Image. A Symbol of Realistic Eschatology', Int 17 (1963), pp. 176–82; see pp. 176–7. Batey refers (p. 177 n. 2) to Exod. Rab. 46.1; Num. Rab. 12.8; Bruce, p. 234, with reference to Mek. on Exod 19.17; Exod.Rab. 46.1 on Exod 34.1.

no means impossible that he might have seen himself in a similar role, since in chap. 3 there is an implicit comparison (as well as contrast) between his own function and that of Moses. It is more probable, however, that he represents himself as the bride's father. First, in 12.14, as also in 1 Cor 4.15, he regards himself as the parent of the Corinthian church.[38] Secondly, in everyday life it would usually be the parents who arranged a betrothal.[39] Thirdly, as Furnish points out,[40] in Jewish society it would be the father who would be responsible for safeguarding his daughter's chastity.

Paul's analogy belongs to a tradition of androcentric imagery familiar to readers of the OT, where Israel is represented by some of the prophets as the (unfaithful) wife of Yahweh: see Hos 1–3; Ezek 16.[41] The idea of Christ as bridegroom of the church is developed fully in Eph 5.22–33; see also Rev 19.7–9; 21.2.

3. φοβοῦμαι δὲ μή πως, ὡς ὁ ὄφις ἐξηπάτησεν Εὔαν ἐν τῇ πανουργίᾳ αὐτοῦ, φθαρῇ τὰ νοήματα ὑμῶν ἀπὸ τῆς ἁπλότητος [καὶ τῆς ἁγνότητος] τῆς εἰς τὸν Χριστόν. The threat to the fulfilment of Paul's responsibility is introduced in a tentative fashion: he fears 'lest perhaps', μή πως,[42] the Corinthians' single-minded attachment to Christ may be compromised. The seriousness of the potential hazard is emphasised, however, by the comparison of their situation to that of Eve in the story in Gen 3. For in that narrative Eve's capitulation to temptation brought about the disobedience of Adam, and with Adam's disobedience, in Paul's thinking, came the introduction into the cosmos of the hostile powers of sin and death (Rom 5.12). The comparison suggests that he fears a similar corruption of the new creation. Just as the serpent deceived Eve (Gen 3.13: ὁ ὄφις ἠπάτησέν με), so the Corinthians may be deceived by the rival missionaries, with the possibility, as he sees it, that his own work in Corinth may come to nothing, with dire consequences for the church there.[43]

Whether the comparison with the Genesis story goes further

---

[38] Plummer, p. 294; Windisch, p. 319; Tasker, p. 145.
[39] Plummer, p. 294.
[40] Furnish, p. 499.
[41] Noted by Windisch, p. 321.
[42] See BAGD s.v. μήπως (μή πως) 1.b.; Zmijewski, 'Narrenrede', p. 88, sees him as choosing a form of expression which would have a softening effect. There is a textual variant here. Some witnesses (D* lat) omit πως, presumably by accident. Others (F G 630. 1739. 1881. 2495 pc vgⁿⁱˢ) read μήποτε instead of μή πως, perhaps because it was felt that something more emphatic (see BAGD s.v. μήποτε 2.a.) was required. From this reading there presumably derives the μήτε of 0243, which makes no sense, and must be due to a scribe who accidentally omitted ΠΟ when copying a MS which read μήποτε. These readings are all secondary.
[43] Barrett, p. 273.

than this is debatable.[44] The biblical narrative itself suggests only the parallel features already noted. But there were some interpretations of it which may have been known to Paul, and by which he might here have been influenced. There is some indication that in contemporary Judaism Satan was at times seen as operative in the downfall of Eve and Adam. In Wisd 2.23–24, after a reference to the original creation of humankind, the writer says: φθόνῳ δὲ διαβόλου θάνατος εἰσῆλθεν εἰς τὸν κόσμον.[45] And in *2 Enoch* 31.6 the devil is said to have entered the garden and corrupted Eve.[46] Paul's representation of his rivals as deceptive agents of Satan (vv. 13–15) may reflect this idea. It is not wholly out of the question that he might also have had in mind an interpretation of the Genesis story in which the physical seduction of Eve played a part. The figure of the παρθένος ἀγνή in v. 2 might suggest this.[47] In the background material it may be present in *2 Enoch* 31.6, since the reference to the corruption of Eve is followed by the contrasting assertion that the devil did not 'contact' Adam.[48] It is attested in the Talmud in *Yebam.* 103b, where it is said: 'When the serpent copulated with Eve, he infused her with lust.'[49] This last reference is comparatively late evidence.[50] If, however, the general idea was current in Paul's day, it would give greater coherence to his imagery: he fears that the Corinthians may become unfaithful to Christ, the last Adam, just as Eve was unfaithful to the first. There may be a hint of the idea in v. 3b. Their minds may be seduced (φθαρῇ) from[51] single-minded (and chaste) devotion to Christ.[52] The verb φθείρω can be

---

[44] Allo, p. 277, thinks that it does not.

[45] Cited by, e.g., Meyer, p. 422; Furnish, p. 486.

[46] Cited by Barrett, p. 273; Furnish, p. 487.

[47] Windisch, p. 323. Other exegetes suppose that Paul might have thought in this way: see, e.g., Lietzmann, p. 145; Bultmann, p. 203; Furnish, p. 500.

[48] See *OTP* I, p. 154: [The devil] 'entered paradise, and corrupted Eve. But Adam he did not contact.' This is found only in the longer recension of *2 Enoch*. But in the introduction, p. 94, F. I. Andersen observes that 'some of the passages found only in manuscripts of the longer recension could preserve ancient traditions'. See also, however, Ellis, *Paul's Use of the Old Testament*, p. 61.

[49] Noted by Windisch, p. 323, and others.

[50] Ellis, *Paul's Use of the Old Testament*, ibid.

[51] The expression φθαρῆναι ἀπό is unusual, and hapax legomenon in the NT. An almost direct parallel in Hermas is noted in BDR 211: οὐ γὰρ διαφθαρήσεται ἡ διάνοια αὐτοῦ ἀπὸ τοῦ κυρίου (Hs IV 7: 'For his understanding is not corrupted away from the Lord' (LCL)). Martin, p. 333, suggests that Paul's phrase may contain the idea both of corruption that results in ruin and of 'a seduction from what is right and pure'.

[52] The term ἁπλότης indicates the exclusiveness with which the congregation should belong to Christ. See Amstutz, *ΑΠΛΟΤΗΣ*, p. 113. Whether or not Paul added 'and purity', καὶ τῆς ἁγνότητος, to 'single-mindedness', τῆς ἁπλότητος, is debatable. See the discussion of the textual variant below. Two other variants may be mentioned briefly. Some witnesses (D¹ Ψ 0121a. 0243 𝔐 lat sy Ambst) read

used of sexual seduction,[53] and would be metaphorically appropriate to Paul's comparison. In addition to the minor textual variants already noted,[54] there is a major variation which requires more attention. The readings are as follows:

(a) ἀπὸ τῆς ἁπλότητος καὶ τῆς ἁγνότητος	𝔓46 ℵ* B F G 33. 81. 104 (326) pc a r syʰ** co Pel
(b) ἀπὸ τῆς ἁγνότητος καὶ τῆς ἁπλότητος	D*
(c) ἀπὸ τῆς ἁπλότητος	ℵ2 (D2) H ψ 0121a. 0243 𝔐 (b) f* vg syᴾ

The choice is between (a) and (c), since (b) seems to be a variation of (a). In favour of the longer text there is, first, 'the age and character of the witnesses which support it',[55] and, secondly, what could be seen as the pleasing rhetorical effect created by the co-ordination of two virtually synonymous nouns to form an harmonious unity.[56] Thirdly, the shorter reading may be derived easily from the longer text through 'scribal oversight occasioned by homoeoteleuton':[57] the last three syllables of the two nouns are identical. Equally, however, it is possible to argue in favour of the originality of the shorter text. The different order of the two nouns in D* suggests that τῆς ἁγνότητος could be 'a gloss inserted in two different places'.[58] And this gloss could have been occasioned by the reference in v. 2 to the παρθένον ἁγνήν.[59] The difficulty of making a decision is indicated by the translations. The longer text is translated in RSV, NRSV, BCN, and by Furnish, p. 484; the shorter text in JB, NEB, REB, and by Martin, p. 327. If pressed for a decision, however, we should opt for the originality of the longer text for two reasons. First, as we have seen already, the age of the supporting witnesses counts in its favour. Secondly, the longer reading, whilst somewhat verbose, does correlate in sense rather neatly with Paul's image in v. 2, in that the ἁπλότης takes up the ἑνὶ ἀνδρί, whilst the ἁγνότης resumes the motif of the παρθένον ἁγνήν.

οὕτως before φθαρῇ: this is an obvious addition to improve the correlation with the preceding ὡς -clause, and should be omitted (with 𝔓46 ℵ B D* F G H P 33. 81. 1175 pc r Cl Lcf). The τόν before Χριστόν (𝔓46 B D H Ψ 𝔐 Cl Epiph), missing in some MSS (ℵ F G 0121a 0243. 365. 630. 1175. 1739. 1881. 2495 al), is to be retained.

53 See BAGD s.v. φθείρω 1.c.; 2.b.
54 See above, pp. 661 n. 42, 662–3 n. 52.
55 Metzger, Textual Commentary[1], p. 584.
56 Zmijewski, 'Narrenrede', p. 87.
57 Metzger, Textual Commentary[1], p. 583.
58 Plummer, p. 296; cf. Barrett, p. 270.
59 Lietzmann, p. 145; Windisch, p. 325; Barrett, p. 270.

4. εἰ μὲν[60] γὰρ ὁ ἐρχόμενος ἄλλον Ἰησοῦν κηρύσσει ὃν οὐκ ἐκηρύξαμεν, ἢ πνεῦμα ἕτερον λαμβάνετε ὃ οὐκ ἐλάβετε, ἢ εὐαγγέλιον ἕτερον ὃ οὐκ ἐδέξασθε, καλῶς ἀνέχεσθε.[61] Paul explains the fear he has just voiced in v. 3. He is apprehensive lest his readers' devotion to Christ should be corrupted, because they are only too ready to tolerate someone who presents an understanding of the faith quite different from that of his own original proclamation.[62] At the same time he seems also to be giving grounds for his plea for toleration in v. 1. If the Corinthians put up with his rival(s), they ought to extend the like forbearance to their founding apostle.[63] The logical structure of vv. 1–6 supports a link with v. 1: in the γάρ-clauses of vv. 2, 4, 5 we are given three separate reasons for the initial ἀνέχεσθε.

The ultimate source of Paul's anxiety for his readers is designated ὁ ἐρχόμενος, 'the one who comes'. To whom does he refer? A number of commentators understand the expression as generic: 'a person' who comes.[64] Parallels in Gal 5.10 and Col 2.8 are cited: ὁ ... ταράσσων and ὁ συλαγωγῶν.[65] Here, then, if we do have a generic usage, the reference, strictly speaking would simply be to someone (anyone) coming to Corinth from elsewhere, 'a visitor', representative of the whole class of visitors.[66] One might doubt, however, whether this classification is entirely correct. As Barrett notes, the parallel with Gal 5.10 is not exact, since there the ὁ ... ταράσσων is followed by ὅστις ἐὰν ᾖ.[67] Similarly, in Col 2.8 the ὁ συλαγωγῶν is preceded by μή τις. There is no such generalising expression in the present verse. In the context, moreover, one might expect some more specific point of reference.[68] What are the possibilities? Schlatter supposes the arrival of the ἐρχόμενος to be still in the future. The Corinthian congregation are expecting some apostolic

---

[60] The μέν lacks a correlated δέ-clause, and is consequently an example of μέν *solitarium* (see Denniston, *Particles*, pp. 380–1).
[61] On the textual variant see the note below.
[62] Cf. Allo, p. 278.
[63] Bultmann, p. 203, and Tasker, p. 147, connect v. 4 with v. 1; Bultmann claims that the request ἀνέχεσθε dominates the context up to v. 6. Barrett, p. 274, sees a connection with both v. 1 and v. 3. Furnish, p. 488, claims that the primary reference is to v. 1, but allows that there may also be a secondary connection with v. 3.
[64] Furnish, p. 488; see also, e.g., Allo, p. 277; Hughes, p. 377; Bultmann, p. 204; Windisch, p. 326.
[65] Windisch, ibid; Bultmann, ibid; Furnish, ibid.
[66] On the function of the generic article see MHT, p. 180.
[67] Barrett, p. 275.
[68] According to Zmijewski, '*Narrenrede*', p. 99, this could still be regarded as generic (the leader of the opposition as representing the group). But ἔρχομαι does not *mean* 'oppose'.

arbitrator whose authority will put an end to their disputes.[69] This theory is generally rejected. There is no hint of any such arbitrator elsewhere in these chapters, and Paul is dealing with realities, not possibilities.[70] The present tenses κηρύσσει and λαμβάνετε exclude the view that the ἐρχόμενος has not yet arrived.[71] If he is an individual, he must be the leader and spokesman of the rival mission, presently at work in Corinth.[72] Some commentators, however, suppose that Paul is referring to the group of these missionaries as a whole.[73] The use of the singular, instead of the plural οἱ ἐρχόμενοι, may be accounted for in part as corresponding to the ὄφις of v.3 and in part as denoting the exemplar to which the group conforms.[74] This may be the most satisfactory interpretation.

These travelling missionaries[75] are dangerous, in Paul's view, because they promote an alternative understanding of Jesus and, in consequence, a different gospel.[76] And since he sees Christ and the Spirit as inseparably related, the preaching of another Jesus implies a different conception of the Spirit. Since also he appears to indicate that his readers 'receive' this Spirit, it seems that the newcomers claimed actually to bestow it. Precisely what these descriptions of Jesus, gospel, and Spirit mean is an unresolved matter of debate.[77] Two things, at least, seem certain. First, these people and their message had clearly made a favourable impression in Corinth, since Paul fears their influence. But secondly, since he ironically congratulates his readers on their splendid toleration of his rivals, there must have been something in their preaching and activity which he would have expected the Corinthians to find uncongenial.

11.4 The Text. The textual variant here has attracted considerable attention on account of the importance of the verse itself. The MS evidence is as follows.

ἀνείχεσθε   𝔓³⁴ ℵ D² F G H (Ψ *al·* ην) 0121α. 0243 𝔐 lat sy

ἀνέχεσθε   𝔓⁴⁶ B D* 33*pc* r sa

---

[69] Schlatter, *Paulus*, pp. 631–2.

[70] Käsemann, 'Legitimität', p. 38.

[71] Prümm, *Diakonia Pneumatos* I, p. 602; Zmijewski, '*Narrenrede*', p. 98.

[72] So Barrett, p. 275, and Martin, p. 335. Barrett suggests also that Paul uses ἐρχόμενος as the antithesis of ἀπόστολος, i.e., of one who is not sent, but simply comes. See also Hughes, p. 377. This is less probable. Paul speaks frequently of his *own* 'coming' to Corinth (1 Cor 2.1; 4.21; 2 Cor 1.15; 13.1).

[73] Wendland, p. 234; Prümm, *Diakonia Pneumatos* I, p. 602.

[74] Wolff, p. 213.

[75] Wolff, ibid. implies that this itinerancy was their prime characteristic.

[76] The terms ἄλλος and ἕτερος are probably not to be differentiated: see Plummer, p.297; Windisch, p. 327; Barrett, p. 275; MHT, p. 197; Martin, p. 336.

[77] See the excursus below, pp. 667–70, for detailed discussion.

The reading ἀνείχεσθε might seem preferable for two reasons. First it is the more difficult reading, in view of the present tenses (κηρύσσει and λαμβάνετε) in the protasis.[78] An unreal condition, had Paul intended it, would have required the imperfect in the protasis as well as in the apodosis. And a real condition, to make good sense in the context, would seem to require that the verb in the apodosis should be in the present tense.[79] Secondly, it might be easier to derive the alternative reading ἀνέχεσθε from ἀνείχεσθε than vice versa: a scribe could have omitted the iota by accident; or the present tense could be a correction on the basis of v. 20.[80] But if we accept ἀνείχεσθε, we need some explanation of why Paul originally wrote it. Perhaps, as Plummer suggests, he changed the grammatical construction in mid-sentence so as to make the conclusion less harsh, using in the apodosis the tense appropriate to an unreal conditional.[81]

There are, however, good arguments in favour of the originality of ἀνέχεσθε. First, there is its varied and early attestation, which is at least comparable to that of ἀνείχεσθε. Secondly, the analogous statement in v. 20 has the present tense with no variant.[82] Thirdly, as Barrett points out, the reading ἀνείχεσθε weakens the sense.[83] Fourthly, it would detract from the force of v. 4 as giving grounds both for the fear of v. 3 and for Paul's plea in v. 1. Fifthly, it is not impossible to explain the origin of ἀνείχεσθε as a variant. The reading might have arisen through scribal error, owing to the similarity of the two words or to a mechanical recollection and repetition of the ἀνείχεσθε of v. 1. Or it could perhaps be seen as an intentional scribal alteration, 'as an attempt', according to Furnish, 'to free the Corinthians from the stigma of having actually given in to the rival apostles'.[84] The reading ἀνέχεσθε makes better and more forceful sense, and is to be preferred.

---

[78] See Zmijewski, 'Narrenrede', p. 93.
[79] In isolation, a sentence which ran, 'If someone comes and preaches another Jesus . . . , you used to tolerate it', would both be possible grammatically and would make some sense. But not here. Paul is not talking of some past regrettable attitude on his readers' part but of the present crisis.
[80] Windisch, p. 326.
[81] Plummer, p. 297; he does not, however, finally (p. 298) accept this reading.
[82] Cf. Windisch, p. 326. Reference to v. 20 can, of course, work both ways—see above.
[83] Barrett, p. 270 n. 2.
[84] Furnish, p. 489.

EXCURSUS IX

11.4: Another Jesus, Spirit, and gospel

These phrases present a major exegetical problem. That the Corinthians are in danger of defecting to missionaries who propound so radically different a message would seem to be of the greatest importance. Yet Paul makes no attempt to counter their false teaching. Precisely on that account it has been argued that the whole expression is unreal. In fact there is not 'another Jesus' (or Spirit, or gospel). Paul must be understood as speaking ironically.[85] Admittedly, his lack of doctrinal response is strange.[86] Nevertheless, he does not speak purely hypothetically. In the first place, one would expect an unreal conditional if that were so. Secondly, Paul has just referred to the real possibility that his readers may become unfaithful to Christ. Hence, the majority of exegetes attempt to give some plausible content to his enigmatic reference to his opponents' position. The various suggestions may be roughly classified under three heads: the opponents preach a Judaizing gospel; they propound a christology different from Paul's own; the attack on his apostleship implies the advocacy of an alien gospel. When we have discussed these points of view, we shall make one further suggestion.

1. The obvious item of evidence for the Judaizing theory is the parallel with Gal 1.6, where the apostle marvels that his readers have so quickly transferred their loyalties εἰς ἕτερον εὐαγγέλιον. For Windisch, Bruce, and others this would be a message which devalued grace, and presented the appropriation of Christ's salvific work as dependent upon human meritorious achievement.[87] The 'other Jesus' is then seen as a more 'Jewish' character,[88] believed to require the imposition of obedience to the law.[89] The 'alternative Spirit' might be identified with the 'spirit of bondage' of Rom 8.15.[90] More recent interpretation of the situation in Galatia sees the Judaizers' promotion of circumcision as differently motivated. Circumcision would ensure full membership of God's covenant people. It would symbolise acceptance of the obligation to maintain the distinctiveness of the chosen nation.[91] Neither interpretation of Galatians, however, would appear transferable to the situation in Corinth. There is no reference in 2 Cor 10–13 either specifically to circumcision or to the law in general.[92] Lack of reference to the law might also tell, as additional evidence, against a variation of the Judaizing

---

[85] Bachmann, pp. 367, 370.
[86] Bachmann, p. 367, draws attention to the contrast with Galatians.
[87] Windisch, p. 328; Bruce, p. 236.
[88] Windisch, ibid.; cf. Allo, p. 279.
[89] Bruce, p. 235.
[90] Plummer, p. 297.
[91] See e.g., James D. G. Dunn, *The Theology of Paul's Letter to the Galatians*, Cambridge, 1993, pp. 29–31, 39, 77–8, 102–3.
[92] Martin, p. 336; cf. Bultmann, p. 204. These omissions would be very strange, were Judaizing a major characteristic of the opposition.

theory proposed by Oostendorp. He suggests that the rival missionaries, who have links with the Palestinian church, claim that there is soon to be a fulfilment of God's promise to establish his kingdom in Zion. They call their message εὐαγγέλιον, on the basis of Isa 52.7–8, where the participle of the cognate verb (εὐαγγελιζόμενος) describes the activity of the messenger who proclaims this imminent fulfilment.[93] For them, Jesus is the Christ who has 'introduced a new era in which the primacy of Israel over the Gentiles' is to be made evident: see 11.18, 20, 22.[94] The 'other Spirit' refers to a gift of the Spirit which will result in the recipients' observance of the law of Moses, as in Ezek 36.26–27.[95] But nothing can be deduced from the occurrence here of the word εὐαγγέλιον, which is Paul's frequent term for his own apostolic message (1 Cor 4.15; 9.12, 14, 18, 23; 15.1; 2 Cor 2.12; 4.3–4; 8.18; 9.13), and had the opposition been concerned with the primacy of Israel he would surely have broached the subject directly.

2. The second line of exegesis concentrates on the phrase ἄλλον Ἰησοῦν. For Schmithals, this means that the opponents are gnostic 'spirituals' (πνευματικοί) who see 'Jesus' as the accursed earthly dwelling of the heavenly spiritual Christ.[96] Furnish points out, however, that some second-century gnostics esteemed the earthly Jesus as the 'pure vessel' which received the descending Christ.[97] In any case, most exegetes who concentrate on the christological aspect suppose that the 'other Jesus' preached by the opponents is a splendid and impressive figure, by contrast with the crucified Christ of the Pauline proclamation (1 Cor 1.18–24; 2.2). Georgi argues that they presented the earthly Jesus as an outstanding 'divine man', θεῖος ἀνήρ,[98] a miracle-worker of unique power.[99] The 'other spirit' would then be 'the spirit of power and ecstasy' which he possessed, and the 'alternative gospel' the message about this kind of Jesus.[100] Such a message would play down the manner of his death, and proclaim him as the 'Lord of glory', whose wonder-working life on earth was validated by his resurrection.[101] This second line of interpretation has some popularity. But it faces one major drawback, noted indirectly by Theissen, who observes that the Corinthians are represented as 'tolerating' (ἀνέχεσθε) the message of the visiting

---

[93] Oostendorp, *Another Jesus*, pp. 9–10.
[94] Oostendorp, *Another Jesus*, p. 80.
[95] Oostendorp, *Another Jesus*, pp. 35–6, 45–6.
[96] Schmithals, *Gnosticism*, pp. 134, 171–2.
[97] Furnish, p. 501.
[98] Georgi, *Opponents*, p. 274.
[99] Georgi, ibid., and pp. 170–1.
[100] Fallon, p. 94, who likewise sees the 'other Jesus' as a miracle-worker. Martin, p. 341, cites Fallon, but has previously noted, pp. 339-40, that there is doubt as to whether the modern notion of the θεῖος ἀνήρ corresponds to any recognisable type in the Graeco-Roman world. See Holladay, *Theios Aner*, pp. 237–41, to whom Martin refers.
[101] J. Murphy-O'Connor, 'Another Jesus (2 Cor 11.4)', *RB* 97 (1990), pp. 238–51; see pp. 249–50. See also Wolff, pp. 214–15, who doubts whether the opponents promoted a specific 'Jesus-proclamation', but would agree that the crucified Christ was not their central interest and that they emphasised Christ's glory in a one-sided fashion.

missionaries.[102] The proclamation of a glorious Christ would have been highly congenial to them—not something that would require toleration.

3. For Käsemann, it is the questioning of Paul's apostolate which provides the key to the interpretation of the three phrases under discussion. From Paul's viewpoint, Käsemann claims, the disputing of his apostleship carried with it the falsification of the gospel: apostolate and gospel are mutually related. And since the apostolic office has the primacy amongst the gifts of the Spirit (1 Cor 12.28), the apostolate of the rival missionaries must bring with it the bestowal of a different Spirit. The 'other Jesus' may allude to their appeal to a connection with the historical Jesus as a mark of genuine apostolic authority.[103] It does not, however, seem to be a sufficient explanation of these three phrases to regard them simply as expressing the consequences of the primary attack on Paul's apostolic status, as Paul himself deduced them. In the first place, these people are said to preach. This would mean nothing unless they did actually proclaim some kind of gospel message. Secondly, the text suggests that this message had a positive christological content which was of significance in itself, and did not function merely as a means to validate the authority of the messengers. According to Wolff, the sentence structure shows that the 'different Spirit' and 'different gospel' follow as the consequences of the 'other Jesus'.[104] The references to Christ in vv. 2–3 would underline the importance of the christological issue.

Since none of these lines of exegesis appears totally satisfactory, it may be worthwhile to suggest one further possibility.

4. Put briefly, it is that the rival missionaries represent a branch of the Christian mission whose policy has some affinity with the outlook of the final mission charge in Matthew's Gospel: Mt 28.16–20. There are various parallels between this charge and what we may deduce about the outlook and activity of Paul's opponents.

(a) In Mt 28.19 the Eleven are instructed to make disciples of all the nations: μαθητεύσατε πάντα τὰ ἔθνη. In 2 Cor 10–13 we encounter Jewish Christians on itinerant mission to a largely Gentile church in a major city of the Graeco-Roman world. In discussing 10.12–18, we have suggested that the Jewish mission as defined in the Jerusalem agreement (Gal 2.9) may originally have had some (legitimate) interest in the Jewish element of the Corinthian populace.[105] But in Paul's view, its present representatives have now overstepped the boundaries. It is clear that they are attempting to exert a dominating influence over the whole church, and to displace the apostolic authority of Paul himself, who had founded it and was responsible for it.

(b) We should agree with those exegetes who interpret the 'other Jesus' as a figure of splendour, although in our view the opponents would

---

[102] Theissen, *Social Setting*, p. 65 n. 54.
[103] Käsemann, 'Legitimität', pp. 48–9. Bultmann, p. 204, and Furnish, p. 502, both agree that the contesting of his apostolic credentials would suggest to Paul that his rivals promoted 'another gospel'.
[104] Wolff, p. 215, n. 142.
[105] See above, pp. 649–50.

be concerned more with his post-resurrection state of glory than with his appearance as a 'divine man' during his earthly life. The Matthean Jesus in 28.16–20 is a being of power and glory. He appears on a mountain, i.e., in close proximity to heaven, whence he has come. The Eleven worship him. He claims to have received all authority in heaven, as well as on earth.

(c) In this narrative the Eleven are to teach obedience to Jesus's commands. In the Matthean context, this must include obedience to the law of Moses. According to Mt 5.17–19, Jesus has come to fulfil this law, and it is to be kept meticulously by those who would be called great in the kingdom of heaven. Paul's opponents in Corinth preach an 'alternative gospel'. The phrase εὐαγγέλιον ἕτερον suggests a partial parallel with the Galatian situation (Gal 1.6), and this, in turn, would mean that the opponents' gospel involves some measure of Torah-observance.

(d) The Eleven are to baptise. In Mt 3.11, 16 (as in the Synoptic parallels) baptism is connected with the gift of the Spirit. In Corinth it seems that the rival missionaries claimed to bestow this gift. It is not clear whether they denied the Corinthians' original reception of the Spirit or whether they offered some new, more powerful experience of πνεῦμα. In either case, Paul describes their gift as ἕτερον, in parallel to his description of the Jesus they preach as ἄλλος.[106]

(e) The opponents style themselves 'agents of righteousness'—διάκονοι δικαιοσύνης. According to the Matthean tradition of the teaching of Jesus, to which we may suppose 28.20 refers, superlative δικαιοσύνη is required for entrance to the kingdom of heaven: see Mt 5.20.

This interpretation is no less speculative than the other possibilities we have discussed. It has one advantage, however. It resolves the contradiction between the Corinthians' obvious welcome of the visiting missionaries and Paul's reference to their toleration of these people. The gospel of the glorified Christ is highly congenial. But if it includes some degree of Torah-observance it would in this respect become much less congenial: hence the need for toleration. Why, though, is there, in that case, no mention of the law, in strong contrast to Paul's letter to the Galatians? Perhaps there are two reasons. First, the main problem in Corinth was the self-exaltation of the opponents, and the favourable impression they have made thereby. This was all the more damaging because it was consonant with the Corinthian ethos,[107] and was producing a detrimental effect on Paul's own authority. It was this problem that he had chiefly to engage with. Secondly, it would be unlikely that the Corinthians would take to the Torah-enforcing aspect of the opponents' message, in view, of their reluctant response to Paul's own efforts to impose moral discipline.

Finally, we might suggest that connection between this branch of the Petrine mission and some early form of the Matthean tradition is not unlikely. The Gospel does have a particular interest in Peter, since there are four passages relating to him which occur in Matthew alone: 14.28–31; 16.16–19; 17.24–27; 18.21–22.

---

[106] See above, p. 665 n. 76.
[107] See Savage, *Power through Weakness*, pp. 54–7.

5. λογίζομαι γὰρ[108] μηδὲν ὑστερηκέναι τῶν ὑπερλίαν ἀποστόλων. Paul gives his third reason for the appeal in v. 1 that the Corinthians should tolerate him:[109] in no way[110] is he inferior to those whom he terms 'super-apostles' (NRSV). We understand the phrase ὑπερλίαν ἀπόστολοι as an ironical reference to the rival missionaries.[111] The word ὑπερλίαν was most likely coined by Paul himself, since 2 Corinthians shows he is fond of ὑπέρ-compounds.[112]

EXCURSUS X

The ὑπερλίαν ἀπόστολοι

Are these people the Jerusalem apostles? Or is Paul referring to the rival missionaries in Corinth? There is substantial support for both possibilities, but there are also difficulties, whichever option is preferred.

(i) Identification with the Jerusalem apostles

In favour of this interpretation there are the following arguments:
   (a) If Paul is speaking seriously and using ὑπερλίαν as a term of respect, to whom else could the appellation refer? Chrysostom supposes that he is alluding to Peter, James and John as the chief apostles.[113] But even if the phrase is intended ironically (as the majority of commentators suppose), such an allusion would still be conceivable. Barrett draws attention to the ironical reference to the 'pillar' apostles in Gal 2.6, 9.[114]

[108] B reads δέ instead of γάρ. This is an obvious scribal correction, made either because v. 5 does not explain v. 4 (cf. Windisch, pp. 329–30, who points out that the transition from the one verse to the other is unclear), or because a scribe felt it appropriate to provide a δέ-clause in correlation with the μέν at the beginning of v. 4 (see Plummer, p. 299).

[109] Hence, the γάρ has causal force. Zmijewski, 'Narrenrede', p. 115, however, would understand it as affirmative, whilst Furnish, p. 489, sees it as connective.

[110] The μηδέν (an accusative of respect [see BDR 160]) is evidence of the absolute character of the assertion, and Zmijewski, 'Narrenrede', pp. 115–16, comments that the use of the perfect infinitive ὑστερηκέναι with present force emphasises its unqualified validity.

[111] See the discussion below, pp. 674–6.

[112] Plummer, p. 299, suggests this, noting the following occurrences: ὑπεραίρομαι, ὑπερβάλλω, ὑπερβαλλόντως, ὑπερέκεινα, and ὑπερπερισσεύω. On ὑπερλίαν itself, see BAGD s.v. As a combination of ὑπέρ and λίαν it is classed, like its second component, as an adverb, with the meaning 'exceedingly', 'beyond measure', but seen as adjectival in 2 Cor 11.5 and 12.11, where Paul's phrase means 'the super-apostles'.

[113] Chrysostom, PG 61 col. 556 (NPNF XII, p. 385).

[114] Barrett, p. 278. Bruce, p. 237, suggests that the irony is at the expense not of the apostles themselves but of the rival missionaries' portrayal of them.

(b) Paul does not claim superiority to these people, but claims only that he is not inferior to them. Surely he would not speak like this were he comparing himself with those opponents in Corinth whom he castigates (vv. 13–15) as Satan's servants and the like.[115]

(c) Paul's rough and bitter treatment of the visiting missionaries, together with the fact that they had gained an unopposed hearing in Corinth, demands the supposition that they were able, or claimed to be able, to rely on some weighty authority in the background. The Jerusalem apostles would best fit this requirement.[116]

(d) The letters of recommendation brought by the opponents (3.1) show them to be an official delegation from some other church, since documents of a less official kind would not have occasioned the extensive exposition of the apostolic office found in chap. 3. This points to the Jerusalem church as the origin of the letters, and makes it natural to identify the ὑπερλίαν ἀπόστολοι with the Jerusalem apostles.[117]

(e) Barrett sees a latent allusion to the Jerusalem 'pillars' in 10.12–18, where it is a question of who has apostolic rights in Corinth. This recalls the division of labour mentioned in Gal 2.7–10, and Paul appears to blame the rival missionaries for failing to observe this agreement made between himself, on the one hand, and James, Cephas and John on the other. If, then, he has the Jerusalem concordat in mind, it is likely that it is the leaders of the mother church whom here he calls 'super-apostles'.

(f) Barrett further observes that the two allusions to the ὑπερλίαν ἀπόστολοι are followed almost immediately by Paul's defence of his refusal to accept financial support from the Corinthians (11.7–11; 12.13–15). Now we find this same conjunction of themes (defence of apostleship and the matter of apostolic maintenance) in 1 Cor 9, and there a comparison is drawn with Cephas, the Lord's brothers, and the other (Jerusalem) apostles. This parallelism suggests that the ὑπερλίαν ἀπόστολοι were 'high officials' in Jerusalem, as are those with whom Paul compares himself in 1 Cor 9.[118]

Each of these arguments has in turn been countered as follows:

(a) Not only is there general agreement that the appellation is ironical, but there is substantial agreement also that the irony is too strong to allow for an allusion to the Jerusalem apostles. It is described as sarcastic, contemptuous,[119] and derisory.[120]

(b) Paul's claim to simple equality with the 'super-apostles' can be interpreted differently. If the claim is seen as ironical, what he may be insisting on in reality is his absolute superiority to these people, who

---

115 Käsemann, 'Legitimität', p. 42; Barrett, p. 278.
116 Käsemann, 'Legitimität', p. 43; he suggests, however, that the opponents' appeal to the Jerusalem apostles would have been made without their official consent.
117 Käsemann, 'Legitimität', p. 44–5.
118 See Barrett, 'Opponents', pp. 65–6, 74, on points (e) and (f).
119 Plummer, p. 298.
120 Allo, p. 279; see also, e.g., Meyer, p. 427; Lietzmann, p. 146; Hughes, p. 380 n. 41; Prümm, *Diakonia Pneumatos* I, p. 611; Georgi, *Opponents*, p. 39.

must, in consequence, be identified with his opponents in Corinth.[121] The difficulty with this explanation, however, is that it seems not to fit very well with v. 6a, where Paul does concede that he is ἰδιώτης τῷ λόγῳ in apparent contrast to the skills of the ὑπερλίαν ἀπόστολοι.[122] Is his claim, then, an aspect of his boasting 'as a fool' (and so not to be regarded as a serious statement)?[123] But in the 'foolish boasting' that is introduced in vv. 16–21 and begins in earnest in v. 22 it is not that Paul is making *false* claims about himself but rather that it is foolish to *parade* these claims, however true they may be. In the present verse, then, the folly would lie not in the content of the assertion of equality but in the fact of its being made. Does this mean, then, that the 'super-apostles' are, after all, the Jerusalem apostles? This conclusion is not absolutely necessary. Bultmann suggests that, in order to open his readers' eyes to the true nature of the situation, Paul has to do two apparently contradictory things: to demonstrate the real character of his opponents (hence his castigation of them in vv. 13–15), and also to show that he himself has powers equal to theirs (as he indicates in the present verse).[124]

(c) We do not need to postulate the backing of Jerusalem to explain the success of the rival missionaries in Corinth. They could well have made their mark there on the basis of their own impressive manner, eloquence, wonder-working, and the like.

(d) As we have noted in our exegesis of 3.1, there is no parallel to the kind of official document presupposed as the basis of the fourth argument above for the identification of the ὑπερλίαν ἀπόστολοι with the Jerusalem apostles, nor would Paul have designated such an hypothetical communication as a συστατικὴ ἐπιστολή.[125] We have suggested further that it was Jewish criticism in Corinth, primarily, that evoked his exposition of the apostolic office in chap. 3.[126]

(e) We have agreed that in 10.12–18 there is some indirect allusion to the Jerusalem agreement of Gal 2.7–10,[127] and have allowed that the rival missionaries may have been operating in accordance with their own understanding of it.[128] This still does not require, however, the identification of the ὑπερλίαν ἀπόστολοι with the Jerusalem apostles, although it might suggest such an interpretation, other things being equal.

(f) The same might be said in respect of the parallelism in the matter of the connection between apostolic maintenance and defence of apostolic authority. Whilst the parallelism might suggest that the rival missionaries have some connection with the Petrine mission, this does not in itself demand that Paul's phrase in the present verse should refer to Cephas and the other Jerusalem apostles.

121 Zmijewski, *'Narrenrede'*, p. 117.
122 Zmijewski, *'Narrenrede'*, p. 122, does allow that in v. 6 the concession is genuine.
123 Betz, *Tradition*, p. 121.
124 Bultmann, *Probleme*, pp. 26–7. See also Oostendorp, *Another Jesus*, p. 11 n. 16, for a similar point of view.
125 See Vol. I, p. 220.
126 Vol. I, p. 248.
127 See above, pp. 650–1.
128 Ibid.

(ii) *Identification with the rival missionaries*

In favour of this interpretation it might be said:

(a) The term ὑπερλίαν constitutes irony of a fairly powerful kind, and is more appropriate to the direct contest with the opposition in Corinth than to an allusion to higher authorities in the background somewhere else. It relates to the rival missionaries' high opinion of themselves and their exaggerated claims.[129] Betz notes that similar terms are used in philosophical polemic. The platonic Socrates, for example, ironically regards sophists as πάσσοφοι.[130]

(b) In v. 6 Paul concedes that the ὑπερλίαν ἀπόστολοι are superior to him in eloquence. As Furnish observes, this concession would not have been necessary if it is the Jerusalem apostles whom he has in mind: 'They could not have qualified as more polished orators than he—certainly not in Greek (note Acts 4.13).'[131]

(c) The claim of v. 5 and the actual phrase ὑπερλίαν ἀπόστολοι are repeated in 12.11. Here the reference is clearly to the contest with the rival missionaries present in Corinth which begins in 11.21 and continues until 12.11, and in which it is Paul's equality with these people that he is arguing for, not his equality with the Jerusalem apostles.[132] The following verse (12.12), moreover, clearly refers to the apostolic signs which he has performed in Corinth. Consequently, it is in Corinth that the 'super-apostles' have put Paul in the shade through their own activity: their identification with the Jerusalem apostles is thus precluded.[133]

Again, there might be something to be said in reply, at least in respect of the first two arguments above:

(a) It may be that the degree of irony felt to be inherent in the term ὑπερλίαν is to some extent a matter of subjective judgement.

(b) Käsemann finds it possible to suppose that the people to whom Paul refers in v. 5 are different from those with whom he is by implication comparing himself in v. 6. In v. 5 there is a reference to the Jerusalem apostles, whilst in v. 6, as in v. 4, he has the rival missionaries in view. Thus, we cannot use what is said in v. 6 to identify the 'super-apostles' of v. 5. There is a dialectical quality, Käsemann claims, in the polemic of chaps. 10–13. Paul does not respect the intruding missionaries, and attacks them harshly, yet at the same time he is restrained by the thought of the authorities standing behind them, with whom he does not wish to come into conflict, and with whom, also, he wishes simply to assert his equality. He refers to the former group in 11.4, 6, and to the latter in 11.5 and 12.11.[134]

---

129 See Georgi, *Opponents*, p. 39, and Furnish, p. 505, for this interpretation of the term's reference.
130 Betz, *Tradition*, p. 121 n. 570, with reference to Plato, *Protag.* 315E; *Theaet.* 149D.
131 Furnish, p. 504; cf. Windisch, p. 330; Allo, p. 280.
132 Windisch, p. 330.
133 Bultmann, *Probleme*, p. 28.
134 Käsemann, 'Legitimität', pp. 44–8.

(iii) *Conclusion*

The discussion of the arguments which favour identification of the ὑπερλίαν ἀπόστολοι with the Jerusalem apostles has shown that most are indeterminate ((a), (c), (e), and (f)) and that one, i.e., (d), is probably wrong. We are left with (b): the claim that Paul would scarcely assert his equality with rival missionaries whom he later calls servants of Satan, and that he must, therefore, be thinking of Cephas and the other original apostles. We have noted a possible counter-argument, but as it stands it is not altogether strong. Turning to the arguments which support identification with the rival missionaries in Corinth, we should regard (a) as indecisive, but (c) as strongly convincing, for the alternative interpretation proposed by Käsemann of vv. 5–6 is surely wrong. He regards v. 5, with reference to the 'super-apostles', as a parenthesis between v. 4 and v. 6, so that these people are distinct from the opponents to whom vv. 4, 6 refer. But the structure of vv. 5–6 suggests that v. 5 is in fact closely related to v. 6 and cannot possibly be regarded as parenthetical. This claim requires elaboration.

There are two passages in 1 Corinthians which are structurally similar to 2 Cor 11.5–6. They are these:

τοῖς δὲ γεγαμηκόσιν παραγγέλλω ..., γυναῖκα ἀπὸ ἀνδρὸς μὴ χωρισθῆναι,– ἐὰν δὲ καὶ χωρισθῇ ... (7.10–11)

μὴ ζήτει γυναῖκα. ἐὰν δὲ καὶ γαμήσῃς, ... (7.27–28)

In both cases we have an absolute negative, which is then qualified by a conditional clause, introduced by adversative δέ and containing an emphatic καί, which stresses the possible existence of an exception. In 2 Cor 11.5–6 we find the same pattern:

λογίζομαι γὰρ μηδὲν ὑστερηκέναι τῶν ὑπερλίαν ἀποστόλων·

εἰ δὲ καὶ ἰδιώτης τῷ λόγῳ ...

In the instances in 1 Corinthians it is apparent that the content of the conditional clause is closely linked in sense with the content of the previous sentence. We should expect the same to be true in 2 Cor 11.5–6. Paul is not, therefore, making two unrelated assertions, the one referring to his status *vis-à-vis* the Jerusalem apostles and the other to the way his rhetorical skills compare with those of his rivals in Corinth. Rather, he is making one integrated statement. In no way is he inferior to the ὑπερλίαν ἀπόστολοι, except that he may not come up to their standard as regards oratory. The 'super-apostles' are those who have impressed the Corinthian congregation with their rhetoric, i.e., the rival missionaries.[135]

On balance, then, the case for this second interpretation is more convincing than the case for the first. There remains the problem of the apparent conflict between Paul's assertion of his own equality with those whom he later terms false apostles and agents of Satan. But this very

---

[135] See Thrall, 'Super-Apostles', pp. 45–6, for this line of argument; cf. Furnish, p. 504.

same difficulty recurs in v. 23, where these same satanic agents of vv.13–15 are now designated διάκονοι Χριστοῦ. The problem will be discussed further in the exegesis of these later passages. At this point we simply observe that since Paul's duality of attitude towards his rivals is clearly exemplified in this later section of chap. 11, there is no need to deny its existence in vv. 5–6, and no need, therefore, to reject the identification of the ὑπερλίαν ἀπόστολοι with the visiting missionaries in Corinth.

6. εἰ δὲ καὶ ἰδιώτης τῷ λόγῳ, ἀλλ᾽ οὐ τῇ γνώσει, ἀλλ᾽ ἐν παντὶ φανερώσαντες ἐν πᾶσιν εἰς ὑμᾶς. In one respect, Paul has to allow, he may be inferior to his rivals, but he quickly adds a compensatory, and comprehensive, assertion of equality (perhaps, in his view, superiority) in what he may regard as a far more important qualification for apostleship. His concession is that he is not an expert in oratory, but rather an ἰδιώτης, a 'layman'.[136] Alternative interpretations of the phrase ἰδιώτης τῷ λόγῳ are less convincing. For Käsemann, λόγος here is the charismatic gift of spontaneous, inspired utterance which proves the speaker's possession of πνεῦμα.[137] But such a gift is surely not, by definition, a matter of professional training or expertise.[138] According to Bultmann, λόγος refers to gnostic speculation, as it does, in his view, in the phrase πειθοῖς σοφίας λόγοις in 1 Cor 2.4. Paul's opponents, with whom he is contrasting himself, may have engaged in allegorical exegesis in the Alexandrian manner, as Apollos (Acts 18.24) may have done.[139] Again, this is unconvincing. For it is difficult to see how the word λόγος, in and by itself, could convey the sense Bultmann wishes to attribute to it. In 1 Cor 2.4 (if such a meaning is present there) it would be the term σοφία which would give it this connotation. Moreover, Paul contrasts λόγος with γνῶσις, and since he does not here explicate the content

---

[136] See BAGD s.v. ἰδιώτης 1. The word means 'layman, amateur in contrast to an expert or specialist of any kind'. The implicit expert may be, e.g., the physician, the philosopher, the orator, or simply the educated person. See also H. Schlier, on ἰδιώτης, in *TWNT* III, pp. 215–17, and C. Spicq, *Lexicographie Néo-testamentaire* I, pp. 384–6. The nature of the implicit contrasting expertise has to be determined from the context. Here, as the lexicographers comment and as the majority of commentators agree, it is a matter of training in rhetoric. In this respect Paul is inexpert: on the dative of respect, τῷ λόγῳ, see BDR 197; on λόγος in the sense 'utterance', 'speech', see LSJ s.v. IX.1. For examples of ἰδιώτης, in some combination with λόγος, with reference to inexperience in speaking see Dio Chrys. *Or.* XLII 3 (see further below, n. 143) and Isocr. IV 11 (cited by Spicq, p. 385 n. 5). Josephus, *Ant.* II 271 (cited in BAGD s.v. ἰδιώτης 1.), as an ἰδιώτης ἀνήρ, is at a loss how to persuade by his words: πῶς ἂν ἰδιώτης ἀνὴρ … πείσω λόγοις …

[137] Käsemann, 'Legitimität', p. 35. See also Vielhauer, *Geschichte*, p. 147.

[138] Reitzenstein, *Mystery-Religions*, p. 461, asserts the conjunction of rhetoric and πνεῦμα, but with little supporting evidence.

[139] Bultmann, p. 206.

of the latter, it is not clear how the readers would be expected to understand that λόγος refers to some unauthentic 'gnostic' kind of knowledge, whilst γνῶσις denotes the true knowledge disseminated through Paul's preaching of the gospel (2.14). The term λόγος, then, refers here to rhetorical discourse. The more difficult question is how seriously we are to take Paul's assertion that he has no skill or training in it. In discussing 10.10 we have already noted that his letters can be seen to show some use of rhetorical forms,[140] and we have earlier drawn attention to current interest in the application of rhetorical theory to these chapters (10–13) of 2 Corinthians themselves.[141] As the exegesis proceeds, we are considering the structural analysis proposed by Sundermann and taking note of the different rhetorical approach employed by DiCicco.[142] In view of these possible pointers to Paul's rhetorical competence, we are bound at least to ask the question whether the very disclaimer in the present verse may not be itself a rhetorical device. Perhaps we have here an example of asteïsmos, where 'one urbanely displayed one's skill by affecting the lack of it'.[143] This is probably to go too far, however.[144] The context of the disclaimer (vv. 5, 6b, c) is surely to be understood seriously, rather than ironically. It is clear, moreover, from 10.10 that the Corinthians did regard Paul as in some sense oratorically incompetent, and would not themselves perceive any irony in what he says here. In the discussion of 10.10 we noted the probability that his deficiency lay in the sphere of extempore oral rhetoric, and this seems the most likely solution of the problem presented by the present verse.[145] In the art of public delivery

---

[140] See above, p. 632.

[141] See above, pp. 595–6.

[142] See above, p. 595. DiCicco claims, *Ethos, Pathos, and Logos*, p. 23, that Paul may well have been 'acquainted with the rhetorical theory and practice of his day through exposure to formal rhetorical training in his education and to the speeches of his contemporaries ...'

[143] The definition comes from Judge, 'Paul's Boasting', p. 37. He notes the use of ἰδιώτης in an asteistic sense in Dio Chrys. *Or.* XLII 3, where the writer speaks of his oratorical inexperience in an ironic fashion:

τὴν ἀπειρίαν τὴν ἐμαυτοῦ περὶ πάντα μὲν ἁπλῶς

μάλιστα δὲ τὴν περὶ τοὺς λόγους, ὡς ἰδιώτης ὢν διανοοῦμαι

('[Whenever I consider myself] and my inexperience in simply everything, but especially in speaking, recognizing that I am only a layman,' LCL). For the rhetorical term, see LSJ s.v. ἀστεϊσμός. See also G. A. Kennedy, *Art of Persuasion*, p. 91, who comments, with reference to the presentation of the speaker's character, 'Usually, like Socrates in the *Apology*, the speaker claims to be unskilled in speaking ...'

[144] Judge, 'Paul's Boasting', p. 37, does not support this interpretation here. He notes, p. 42, that it would be rejected by the Greek Fathers.

[145] DiCicco, *Ethos, Pathos, and Logos*, p. 15, n. 23, refers to this possibility. He notes that the *Antidosis* of Isocrates provides an example of the separation of literary rhetoric from oratorical delivery. This is 'an eloquent piece of rhetoric on paper but was never delivered to a live audience'.

Paul confesses himself a layman. The rival missionaries, by contrast, appear to be professionals, and for this reason, as well as others, to have gained popularity in Corinth.[146] Allowing, though only conditionally, that in this respect he cannot match their professionalism, Paul nevertheless insists that in respect of knowledge he is their equal, or indeed their superior. This knowledge he has already revealed to the Corinthians.[147] He will have in view the knowledge of God, revealed through the gospel he preaches[148] (2.14) and requiring powerful and positive defence (10.5) in Corinth. Its revelation has been comprehensive. The ἐν παντί will mean 'in every particular',[149] or 'in every way'.[150] The ἐν πᾶσιν is more ambiguous, since it could be either neuter or masculine in gender. In favour of the latter interpretation, 'among all men',[151] there is the argument that as neuter it would be a mere tautologous repetition of ἐν παντί.[152] But perhaps 'tautologous' would be an unsuitable term. Furnish would argue that, as neuter, 'in all things',[153] the ἐν πᾶσιν would emphasise the fact that 'the depth of Paul's spiritual insight should have been clear to the Corinthians in every dimension and detail of his ministry among them'.[154] This is probably right. In any case, the basic point is that since Paul's gospel is fully comprehensive, his readers have no need of the 'other gospel' of his rivals.

---

[146] See below, pp. 679–81, for discussion of the wider cultural background.

[147] The participle φανερώσαντες replaces a finite verb (see BDR 128(2)). It also lacks an object (cf. Rom 1.19): αὐτήν, with reference to the preceding γνῶσιν, may be understood (Barrett, p. 280), or a repeated γνῶσιν (Plummer, p. 300; Windisch, p. 333). The omission of an object may in part account for the textual disturbance in this second half of the verse. Some MSS add ἑαυτούς after the participle (0121a. 0243. 630. 1739. 1881 pc) whilst others turn it into a passive, either φανερωθέντες (𝔓34 ℵ2 D2 Ψ 𝔐 r) or φανερωθείς (D* [lat Ambst]). The whole clause is omitted, presumably by accident, in 𝔓46. Several major witnesses (ℵ* B F 33 pc) attest the text printed for comment.

[148] Bultmann, p. 206.

[149] Plummer, p. 300.

[150] Barrett, p. 270.

[151] Plummer, p. 300.

[152] Plummer, ibid.; Hughes, p. 382 n. 44.

[153] Furnish, p. 484.

[154] Furnish, p. 491.

EXCURSUS XI

11.6: Cultural background

According to H. D. Betz, Paul takes up here a theme which belongs to the longstanding opposition between philosophers and sophists, aligning himself with the former and the rival missionaries with the latter. This opposition is exemplified in the Socrates portrayed by Plato. Socrates, representing the philosophers, renounces the rhetorical techniques of the sophists, and in this connection uses the word ἰδιώτης of himself.[155] The controversy between the apostle and his opponents would thus have its cultural roots, ultimately, in the sophistic movement of earlier centuries.

This movement originated in the Greek world during the second half of the fifth century B.C.E. By this time the term σοφιστής had come to be used of a class of 'professional educators'[156] who took fees for their teaching.[157] Individual sophists may have taught various subjects, and in general they claimed to teach wisdom and virtue.[158] Most importantly, however, they all taught rhetoric,[159] i.e., 'skill in argument and persuasion'.[160] This was essential for success in the political sphere.[161] Consequently, it can be said that the sophists 'were primarily teachers of political excellence',[162] and in this capacity they naturally attracted plenty of pupils. Plato, however, disapproved of them. Wisdom and virtue were not qualities that could be taught.[163] And the sophists' 'philosophical relativism' questioned the existence, or at least the knowability, of 'absolute truth'. Hence there are no universal principles, and the art of persuasion becomes all the more important for the determination of policy.[164] After Plato's day, the opposition between the philosophers and the rhetoricians declined to some extent, although there was sometimes a clash of professional interests in respect of the teaching of rhetoric.[165] Some considerable time later, in the second century C.E., the movement known as the Second Sophistic came into existence. By this time, the sophist could be described as 'a virtuoso rhetor with a big public reputation': in public oratory, such a man had 'reached the peak of rhetorical skill'.[166]

It will immediately become apparent that this brief historical sketch

---

[155] Betz, *Tradition*, pp. 60, 62–3, 66; see Plato, *Phaedr.* 236D; cited by Betz, p. 63 n. 128.

[156] W. K. C. Guthrie, *The Sophists*, Cambridge, 1971, p. 35.

[157] Guthrie, ibid.; G. B. Kerferd, *The Sophistic Movement*, Cambridge, 1981, p. 25.

[158] See the discussion in Hafemann, *Suffering and the Spirit*, pp. 110–13.

[159] Guthrie, *Sophists*, p. 44.

[160] H. D. Rankin, *Sophists, Socratics and Cynics*, London and Canberra, 1983, p. 14.

[161] Rankin, *Sophists*, pp. 15, 24.

[162] Kennedy, *Art of Persuasion*, p. 13.

[163] Hafemann, *Suffering and the Spirit*, p. 113.

[164] Kennedy, *Art of Persuasion*, pp. 13–15.

[165] Kennedy, *Art of Persuasion*, pp. 18–21.

[166] G. W. Bowersock, *Greek Sophists in the Roman Empire*, Oxford, 1969, pp. 13–14.

leaves us with a chronological gap of considerable significance. What was the situation in Paul's own day, in the first half of the first century C.E.? Was there, or was there not, continuing sophistic activity? The evidence provided by Betz is somewhat sparse. From the period of the first century C.E. he notes a few references in Josephus where the word σοφιστής occurs,[167] and a few passages in Philo where cognates of σοφιστής are found in places where the true philosophy is opposed to the false.[168] The only one of the references in Josephus, however, which has even a remote connection with the kind of conflict Betz postulates as the background to the Corinthian situation is that which occurs in *Ap.* (*Against Apion*). II 236, where there is an allusion to ἀδόκιμοι σοφισταί, μειρακίων ἀπατεῶντες ('reprobate sophists and deceivers of youth', LCL). Even here, moreover, the substance of complaint is the attacks of these people on the Jews, rather than conflict with the philosophers. A passage noted in Philo, however, is somewhat more to the point. In *Post. Caini* (*Posterity of Cain*) 101, having said that the royal road is that of philosophy, Philo continues: οὐχ ἦν μέτεισιν ὁ νῦν ἀνθρώπων σοφιστικὸς ὅμιλος, λόγων γὰρ οὗτοι τέχνας μελετήσαντες κατὰ τῆς ἀληθείας τὴν πανουργίαν σοφίαν ἐκάλεσαν ('not the philosophy which is pursued by the sophistic group of present-day people, who, having practised arts of speech to use against the truth, have given the name of wisdom to their rascality', LCL). By itself, this passage does not provide very substantial evidence for the continuity of the sophistic movement between the age of Plato and Isocrates and the time of the Second Sophistic.

B. W. Winter has now shown, however, that there is more evidence to be found in Philo, and also to be found elsewhere, which will serve to bridge this gap. Winter notes that in the first century C.E. the term 'sophist' was used of the outstanding orators who were able both to attract students and also to draw audiences to their public displays. He cites Philo's observation that these sophists, at work in one city after another, were acquiring universal honour,[169] and draws attention to clear evidence of their presence and activity in first century Alexandria: in Dio Chrysostom's Alexandrian oration,[170] in P Oxy 2190,[171] and in numerous passages in Philo,[172] who assumes that his readers are familiar with them.[173] It appears also that Alexandria was not untypical. Dio provides evidence for the existence of the sophistic movement in Corinth,[174] and it would seem that the Corinthians were enthusiastic for it.[175] In addition,

[167] Betz, *Tradition*, pp. 26 nn. 90–4; p. 37 n. 175.

[168] Betz, *Tradition*, pp. 109–10.

[169] Winter, *Sophists*, pp. 3–4, citing *Agr.* 143.

[170] Winter, *Sophists*, pp. 48–54: Dio Chrys. *Or.* XXXII; in 11 and 39 the actual term occurs, used pejoratively; in 10 Dio refers to those who declaim 'display-speeches' (ἐπιδεικτικοὺς λόγους) and in 68 there is an allusion to a sophist's lecture room.

[171] Winter, *Sophists*, pp. 19–39.

[172] Winter, *Sophists*, chaps. 3–5.

[173] Winter, *Sophists*, p. 64, with reference to *Cont.*31.

[174] Winter, *Sophists*, pp. 126–32. He draws attention, p. 128, to Dio Chrys., *Or.* VIII 9, where Dio refers to 'crowds of wretched sophists (πολλῶν μὲν σοφιστῶν) shouting and reviling one another' (LCL) at the Isthmian Games.

[175] Winter, *Sophists*, p. 135.

Winter argues that several passages in 1 Corinthians may be seen as reflecting 'a calculated antisophistic stance' on Paul's part.[176] In 1 Cor 2.1–5, for example, the apostle shows that he had rejected the conventions governing the initial visit of a sophist to a city, which required him to 'establish his reputation as a speaker'.[177] Hence, it is highly probable that Paul's words in 2 Cor 11.6 are to be understood against a background of Corinthian familiarity with the sophistic movement.[178]

Whether we are to suppose, as Betz does, that he is consciously taking sides with 'the philosophers' is a rather different question. It is on specifically Christian grounds, in 1 Cor 2.1–5, that rhetoric is repudiated as the medium for the proclamation of the gospel.[179] Judge, moreover, argues that, if Paul does make use of philosophical ideas, this is not because he adheres to any philosophical tradition as such. Rather, it is because 'in any community there is a fluid and active field of thought-convention which belongs to every intelligent man and in which he shares'.[180] Whatever the truth of the matter, it is as a Christian apostle, not as a philosopher, that Paul has to defend himself, and it is what he believes to be the genuine Christian gospel, not some form of Greek philosophy, that he sees to be endangered. Awareness of the general cultural background may, however, enlarge our hypothetical profile of the rival missionaries. They may well have possessed sophistic characteristics, especially an impressive skill in public speaking, and would on that account have appealed to the congregation in Corinth.

11.7–15: rhetorical structure

According to the analysis proposed by Sundermann, v. 7 functions as the *propositio* governing the *refutatio* (vv. 1–15).[181] This seems to fit well enough. The matter of Paul's refusal of maintenance and the Corinthians' reaction is the theme of vv. 8–11, and his explanation of his 'sin' in v. 12 is connected with the presence of the visiting missionaries and leads to his castigation of them (vv. 13–15).

The following section, vv. 8–11, is then defined as the *argumentatio*.[182] Here Paul contests some accusation made against him.

The *peroratio* then follows in vv. 12–15. This is an interim peroration, according to Sundermann, serving as the conclusion of the refutation.[183] Granted that this whole section can be

---

[176] Winter, *Sophists*, chaps. 8–9; quotation on p. 155.
[177] Winter, *Sophists*, pp. 147–61; quotation on p. 151.
[178] See also Bowersock, *Greek Sophists*, p. 9, for confirmation of sophistic activity at this period.
[179] Zmijewski, 'Narrenrede', p. 122.
[180] Judge, 'St Paul and Socrates', p. 110. I am grateful to Dr Bruce Winter for drawing my attention to this article. For further discussion, see, however, P. Marshall, *Enmity in Corinth*, p. 357, n. 63, and the references given there. Marshall thinks it 'feasible to suggest that Paul was aware of Socrates' apology'.
[181] Sundermann, *Kraft der Rede*, pp. 45, 98–102.
[182] Sundermann, *Kraft der Rede*, pp. 45, 102–8.
[183] Sundermann, *Kraft der Rede*, pp. 45, 108–18.

divided rhetorically in such detail, this would be a fair definition of these four verses, to the extent that in v. 12 Paul reveals the basic reason for his persisting in financial independence of the Corinthian congregation, and then in vv. 13–15 refers to the critical situation in the Corinthian church which makes his refutation of criticism so necessary.

7. Ἦ ἁμαρτίαν ἐποίησα ἐμαυτὸν ταπεινῶν ἵνα ὑμεῖς ὑψωθῆτε, ὅτι δωρεὰν τὸ τοῦ θεοῦ εὐαγγέλιον εὐηγγελισάμην ὑμῖν; We have seen that the section 11.1-6 can function with some plausibility as introduction not only to the immediately following paragraphs in vv. 7–15 but also to the Fool's Speech in its entirety.[184] In themselves, vv. 1–6 form an integrated unit. Consequently, we should not necessarily expect a close logical connection specifically between v. 6, which ends the introduction, and v. 7, where Paul takes up a major complaint against the policy he has pursued in Corinth. Certainly, Zmijewski argues for a connection with v. 6. He supposes that v. 7 substantiates the second half of the previous verse. The preaching of the gospel δωρεάν is an act of self-abasement for the sake of the congregation, and it is precisely in this way that Paul provides concrete proof of his genuine knowledge of the Christ who was crucified, and so can be designated as Christ's representative.[185] The emphasis in v. 7, however, does not lie on this, but on the question of whether he has been guilty of some 'sin' against the congregation by refusing financial support. There is, of course, a general link, in that he is throughout defending himself against criticism.

He has refused their financial assistance, and he asks, rhetorically, whether he has committed a sin in doing so.[186] The form of the question indicates that he expects a negative answer.[187] Had his critics claimed that his refusal was actually sinful, or is he indulging in ironical exaggeration? Betz takes the latter view.[188]

184 See above, p. 657.

185 Zmijewski, 'Narrenrede', pp. 124–5.

186 As regards the construction of the sentence, Zmijewski observes that the short main clause is first expanded by means of a participial construction, which he sees as explicative, i.e., as defining the ἁμαρτία, and then by a ὅτι-clause which gives the reason for the question ('Narrenrede', pp. 122–3). The distinction is rather subtle, however, and he notes that Lietzmann, p. 146, and Bultmann, p. 207, take both clauses as explanatory. This is simpler. The ὅτι-clause gives the factual content of the alleged 'sin', whilst the participial clause explains its subjective intention on Paul's part (the 'exaltation' of the Corinthians) together with its personal cost (ἐμαυτὸν ταπεινῶν), which, from the Corinthian viewpoint, might, paradoxically, be regarded as an aspect of the ἁμαρτία.

187 See the following examples of other rhetorical questions introduced by ἤ: Rom 6.3; 7.1; 11.2; 1 Cor 6.9, 19. The alternative thus introduced is unacceptable (Plummer, p. 302), so that a clear negative answer is expected (see Zmijewski, 'Narrenrede', p. 123).

188 Betz, Tradition, p. 101; cf. Wolff, p. 220.

But there is something to be said for the other alternative. Whilst 'sin' may still be somewhat too strong a term, in Graeco-Roman society the refusal of a proffered benefaction would nevertheless be seen as an insult to the benefactor(s) and as likely to engender hostility.[189] The Corinthians would see it as a rejection 'of their status as a patron congregation'.[190] From the specifically Christian point of view, it could be seen also as a rejection of their importance for the furtherance of mission, since the acceptance of remuneration would facilitate further missionary work in the city.[191] It is less likely that the alleged 'sin' was Paul's transgression of the apostolic norm of charismatic poverty, *pace* Theissen.[192] In view of v. 11 it seems to be some more personal offence that is the point at issue. Lastly, it is also unlikely that the Corinthians were complaining, under the influence of the rival missionaries, that by refusing their support Paul was depriving them of their share in the coming kingdom of God. This is suggested by Oostendorp.[193] He maintains that the rival missionaries have argued, on the basis of various scriptural passages (Jer 12.15–17; Zech 2.11; 8.23; Isa 61.6), that Gentiles must attach themselves to Israelites (such as these visiting missionaries) and give proof of their attachment by material support, if they are to have a place in the kingdom. It is true that this would account for the Corinthians' complaint that Paul did not love them. But it is by Graeco-Roman criteria that he has been found wanting in other respects (10.10; 11.6), and it seems much more probable that it is by these criteria that also his refusal of maintenance has been criticised.

From his own point of view Paul explains the policy to which the Corinthians have objected as his self-abasement[194] for their benefit. In refusing financial support he has humbly renounced the use of his apostolic rights,[195] and accepted deprivation and the need for manual labour.[196] This self-humbling was for the sake of

---

[189] See below, p. 704; also Furnish, p. 508.
[190] Furnish, ibid.
[191] Georgi, *Opponents*, p. 236.
[192] Theissen, *Social Setting*, pp. 42–6. In the Synoptic mission charges the missionaries are obligated to make no provision for themselves but to trust in God's grace to supply their needs. They thus possess a 'charismatic legitimation' based on their life-style.
[193] Oostendorp, *Another Jesus*, pp. 77–8.
[194] Some witnesses (D F G K* L P 365 *pc*) read ἑαυτόν for ἐμαυτόν (𝔓34.46 ℵ B Ψ 0121a 𝔐 sy), but the context requires ἐμαυτόν as the clear and emphatic correlative to the following ὑμεῖς. The variant might have arisen from the accidental omission of M. Once the mistake was made it may not have been subject to correction, in view of the tendency to use the third person reflexive in place of the first/second person (MHT, p. 42).
[195] Osiander, p. 407.
[196] Bultmann, p. 207. See below, pp. 703–4, for discussion as to whether working as an artisan was seen as in itself socially degrading.

his converts and so for the better progress of the gospel. But the Corinthians clearly saw things differently. His policy reflected adversely on their own status.[197] In an attempt to change their minds he claims that in fact he has somehow raised them to a higher level. What does he mean? It is not likely, *pace* Bultmann, that this is an allusion to what Paul says in v. 9 about his care lest he should be a burden to his converts,[198] and thus an indication that their financial standing is higher than would otherwise have been the case. His policy did not, after all, make the Corinthians materially *richer* than they had been before his arrival in the city: it simply prevented their becoming *poorer* as a result of conversion. It makes much better sense to understand the 'exaltation' as spiritual enrichment through acceptance of the gospel Paul preached.[199] As Barrett puts it: 'Paul lives in physical poverty, that his hearers may become spiritually rich (cf. vi.10; ix.11; 1 Cor. i.5); there is no respect in which Paul could be more like the Lord himself (viii.9).'[200]

Finally, although it would no doubt have been obvious what he was referring to, he explains the alleged 'sin' in plain terms: he preached the gospel of God to them without making any financial demands (or accepting any financial assistance from them).[201]

8. ἄλλας ἐκκλησίας ἐσύλησα λαβὼν ὀψώνιον πρὸς τὴν ὑμῶν διακονίαν, The preceding rhetorical question has implied its own negative answer. Of course Paul has committed no 'sin', given no cause for offence to his readers. In fact (he now goes on to say), his acceptance of assistance from other churches, which might seem to dishonour the Corinthians whose aid he had refused,[202] was in reality all done for their benefit.[203] As Furnish suggests, Paul's manner of expression here may be designed to dispel the suspicion that, having rejected would-be benefactors in Corinth, he had willingly become the client of other Christian patrons. The verb ἐσύλησα means, 'I plundered', and this is the opposite of receiving something as a benefaction.[204] The imagery

[197] See above, p. 683, and below, p. 703.
[198] Bultmann, p. 207.
[199] So most commentators. See e.g., Meyer, p. 430; Plummer, p. 303; Windisch, p. 334.
[200] Barrett, p. 282.
[201] See below, pp. 701–2.
[202] See below, p. 704.
[203] As becomes apparent in what follows, Paul aims to persuade his readers to accept his Corinthian policy as a mark of his affection. It is wholly erroneous to suppose, with Chrysostom, *PG* 61 col. 558 (NPNF XII, p. 386), Meyer, p. 430, and Allo, p. 283, that his object is to make the relatively affluent Corinthians ashamed of the fact that, whilst serving them, he allowed himself to be paid by others who were probably less fortunate.
[204] Furnish, pp. 484, 492, 508.

may be military, when ἐσύλησα is taken in conjunction with the following ὀψώνιον, which may be used for soldiers' pay.[205] Which, then, are these 'other churches' that Paul 'plundered'? And in what did the 'plunder' consist? This verse has to be taken in conjunction with v. 9, and most naturally refers to events prior to the apostle's arrival in Corinth itself (since the καὶ παρών of v. 9 suggests the next stage in the sequence of activity).[206] If so, then Paul is most likely speaking here of the provision of money for travel expenses for his journey from Macedonia to Achaia,[207] together with some funding for his first days in Corinth.[208] The itinerary of his travel in Acts (16.11–17.15) would suggest that the congregations which provided this financial support were those in Philippi, Thessalonica, and Beroea. This understanding of the 'other churches' appears simple enough. The difficulty emerges when we try to correlate this reference to two or more Christian congregations with Paul's assertion in Phil 4.15 that when he set out from Macedonia on his continued mission it was *only* the church in Philippi that provided him with financial assistance. Is it the Philippians with whom he is less than honest, or is it the Corinthians? Or is there some alternative explanation of the discrepancy? Peterman suggests that the plural 'churches' might have in view 'house congregations' in the city of Philippi.[209] But there is no positive evidence that any such house-churches existed there. Perhaps the answer could be that the neat distinction which Paul himself in principle made between travel assistance and financial support for residence and subsistence in a new mission area did not in practice always hold good. Money from Philippi to be used for mission in Thessalonica might remain over so as to be available for travel expenses, while conversely money provided by other congregations for travel could be used,

---

[205] In LSJ, s.v. συλάω, the basic meaning is given as 'strip off', with references in Homer to stripping a slain enemy of his arms. It is then used more generally (I.2.) in the sense 'pillage', 'plunder': the more general sense, however, would clearly relate to situations of violence, whether in formal warfare or otherwise (Furnish, p. 492, refers to 'pillaging a captured city'). The primary meaning of ὀψώνιον, according to BAGD s.v. 1., is 'ration-(money)' for soldiers, which then widens into the sense 'pay', 'wages'. In the present verse the military sense is said to have passed into 'a more general one', and the phrase λαβὼν ὀψώνιον is translated 'accepting support'. Reference is made to C. Caragounis, 'ὀψώνιον: A Reconsideration of its Meaning', *NovT* 16 (1974), pp. 37–57. But the combination of ὀψώνιον with συλάω and its use in 1 Cor 9.7 as part of a military image speak in favour of the primary, military, sense here, as Furnish, p. 492, observes. Other exegetes who favour military imagery include Windisch, p. 335; Hughes, pp. 385–6; and Martin, p. 346.

[206] Windisch, p. 335.

[207] Martin, p. 346, with reference to Bultmann, p. 207.

[208] Wolff, p. 220.

[209] Peterman, *Paul's Gift*, p. 146 n. 134.

if there was a surplus, for the first few days of residential mission in Corinth. Writing to the Corinthians, Paul here has the latter situation in view. Writing to the Philippians, he thinks of the original purpose of the funds they had provided for him.

9. καὶ παρὼν πρὸς ὑμᾶς καὶ ὑστερηθεὶς οὐ κατενάρκησα οὐθενός· τὸ γὰρ ὑστέρημά μου προσανεπλήρωσαν οἱ ἀδελφοὶ ἐλθόντες ἀπὸ Μακεδονίας· καὶ ἐν παντὶ ἀβαρῆ ἐμαυτὸν ὑμῖν ἐτήρησα καὶ τηρήσω. Whatever the funds Paul had brought with him to Corinth, they soon ran out, and he began to be in need.[210] Both according to Acts (18.3) and according to his own account (1 Cor 4.12) he practised his trade whilst he was in Corinth, but it seems that this was an inadequate means of securing his livelihood. Artisans were not necessarily affluent: it might take a whole day's work simply to earn enough to buy a meagre ration of food.[211] It might take time for a newcomer to the city to acquire custom.[212] And in any case Paul's concern for his primary task of evangelism must to some degree have limited his earning capacity.[213] In this state of indigence, however, he did not load[214] his financial cares upon the Corinthians.

To the contrary, it was Christians travelling from Macedonia who supplied[215] his wants. Some commentators suggest that these ἀδελφοί are Silvanus and Timothy, who are said in Acts 18.5 to

---

[210] Zmijewski, 'Narrenrede', p. 133, is most likely correct in regarding the aorist participle ὑστερηθεὶς as an ingressive aorist.

[211] See Hock, Social Context, pp. 34–5; also the discussion below, pp. 703–4.

[212] Cf. Hock, Social Context, p. 35.

[213] Cf. Barrett, p. 283.

[214] On the verb καταναρκάω see BAGD s.v. It occurs in Hippocrates with the meaning 'stupefy', 'disable' (LSJ s.v. καταναρκάομαι Pass. has 'grown quite numb'). But this would make little sense here. According to Jerome (Ep. 121:10,4), 'the Cilicians used it for the Latin "gravare" ', i.e., 'weigh down', 'burden'. This is the meaning adopted by Chrysostom and Theodoret, and also by the Latin and Syriac versions. Martin, p. 347, notes that the simple verb ναρκάω is used in Gen 32.25–33 'of numbing by applying pressure', and so when prefixed by κατά 'means "to impose a burden" '.

[215] Exegetical opinions differ as to whether the προσ- of προσανεπλήρωσαν is significant. Plummer, p. 305, suggests that it is: the monetary assistance brought by the brothers was additional, either to the previous gifts of the Macedonians (Phil 4.15–16) or to what Paul earned by his own manual labour. Hughes, pp. 387–8 n. 52 allows either possibility, whilst Prümm, Diakonia Pneumatos I, p. 620, opts for the second alternative. Martin, p. 346, prefers the first. Pratscher, 'Verzicht', p. 289, supports the second (additional to what Paul earned himself) because he claims that vv. 7–8 and v. 9 refer to the same occasion of Paul's acceptance of support. This is the less natural way of reading these verses (see above). By contrast with all these suggestions, however, Furnish, p. 492 (with reference to Windisch, p. 336) doubts whether the προσ has any such significance: the verb may mean simply 'supplied' (see 9.12). This may be right, in view of the hellenistic liking for compound verbs: see BDR 116(1).

have arrived in Corinth from Macedonia.[216] But why would Paul not have named them (as in 1.19)?[217] In any case, the assistance, whether in monetary form or in the form of provisions (or both), came from the Macedonian Christians, whoever were the carriers. Consequently, Paul was able to leave the Corinthians free of the burden of his own financial upkeep.[218] And he is determined so to leave them in the future. Perhaps he wishes to avoid the suspicion that what he has written was covertly designed to obtain maintenance from them during his coming third visit to the city.[219] It is, at any rate, a firm restatement of policy, which he confirms even more strongly in the following verse.

10. ἔστιν ἀλήθεια Χριστοῦ ἐν ἐμοὶ ὅτι ἡ καύχησις αὕτη οὐ φραγήσεται εἰς ἐμὲ ἐν τοῖς κλίμασιν τῆς ᾿Αχαΐας. Paul appeals to the ἀλήθεια Χριστοῦ dwelling within him. Opinions differ as to whether we have here an actual oath formula,[220] but in substance the assertion performs this function.[221] In some way Christ is claimed as guaranteeing the truth or reliability of the following affirmation. The claim in all probability relates to, and derives from, Paul's general belief in the indwelling of Christ within

[216] Plummer, p. 305; Lietzmann, p. 147; Allo, p. 283.

[217] Did they, when present in Corinth, follow Paul's own practice in respect of maintenance? We may presume that Timothy did, as one of Paul's close associates, but perhaps Silvanus followed the practice of Cephas and the other Jerusalem apostles.

[218] The word ἀβαρής means 'not burdensome': see BAGD s.v. It is the context which shows that the burden would have been financial, as is the case also with the use of the cognate ἐπιβαρέω in 1 Th 2.9. See J. G. Strelan, 'Burden-Bearing and the Law of Christ', *JBL* 94 (1975), pp. 266-76; see pp. 268-9. Strelan refers to G. Schrenk, on βάρος, βαρέω, in *TWNT* I, pp. 551-9, where Schrenk notes the use of these words in the papyri in relation to financial matters: see pp. 552, 559. See also Peterman, *Paul's Gift*, pp.168-9. It must be borne in mind, however, that Paul uses this group of words in a varied way (2 Cor 1.8; 2.5; 4.17; 5.4). They are not, necessarily, for him technical financial terms. Chrysostom, *PG* 61 col. 558 (NPNF XII, p. 386), again, as with v. 8, wholly mistakes Paul's meaning, claiming that the apostle implies that he ought to have been supported by the Corinthians.

[219] Windisch, p. 327.

[220] Bultmann, p. 208, and Barrett, p. 283, understand the opening clause as an oath formula. Hughes, p. 389, however, would describe it as an 'asseveration'. This could be the more correct, since it is not quite an explicit invocation of Christ as witness to the truth of Paul's assertion (contrast the invocations of God in Rom 1.9; 2 Cor 1.23; Phil 1.8; 1 Th 2.5). Moreover the similar expression in Rom 9.1 (᾿Αλήθειαν λέγω ἐν Χριστῷ, οὐ ψεύδομαι), frequently cited as a parallel (see, e.g., Meyer, p. 432; Plummer, p. 306; Windisch, p. 337), is seen by Cranfield, *Romans*, p. 452 n. 1, as distinguishable from an oath formula. But the distinction is a fine one, and Stählin, 'Beteuerungsformeln', p. 133, claims that it would be invalid in the case of someone (i.e. Paul) who 'stands before God' with his every utterance.

[221] See n. 220. Cranfield, *Romans*, p. 452, sees the ἐν Χριστῷ in Rom 9.1 as 'an implicit appeal to Christ as the ultimate guarantor of the truth of what Paul is about to say'. The same thing could surely be said of the reference to Christ in the present verse.

himself.[222] If Christ dwells within him, then the truthfulness[223] of Christ will condition his own assertions and guarantee the objective truth[224] of his words. The central position of Χριστοῦ[225] suggests that some theological weight should be attached to it.[226] What is guaranteed is the (present and) future validity of 'this boasting'.[227] What is boasted of must be Paul's independence of the Corinthians in respect of his upkeep (v. 9). But who is it who does the boasting? Bachmann supposes that it is the Achaians, and this interpretation is supported by Prümm.[228] The point is that the recognition of Paul's selflessness has spread throughout Greece.[229] But this is highly improbable.[230] Who are these hypothetical Achaians? There is no evidence that there were groups of believers outside Corinth who were at the same time sufficiently near to the city to be aware of Paul's practice there, sufficiently numerous for their opinion of him to count, and sufficiently independent of the Corinthian church to hold an opinion totally contrary to the point of view current in Corinth itself. The boasting is done by Paul himself.[231]

His determination that it shall continue is clear, but his form of expression has occasioned debate. The verb φραγήσεται is the second future passive of φράσσω, which has two related meanings. The first is 'shut', 'close', 'stop'.[232] It may be literal, but can also be figurative, with the idea of closing someone's mouth, so that the person is silenced.[233] See the expression ἵνα πᾶν στόμα φραγῇ in Rom 3.19.[234] Thus, in the present verse Paul would be saying,

---

[222] Meyer, p. 432, and others. Windisch, p. 337, Lietzmann, p. 147, and Martin, p. 347, refer in particular to 13.3, where Christ is said to speak in the apostle; and Windisch and Lietzmann note 1 Cor 2.16. See also Allo, p. 284, and Zmijewski, 'Narrenrede', p. 139.

[223] BAGD s.v. ἀλήθεια 1.

[224] BAGD s.v. ἀλήθεια 2.

[225] See Zmijewski, 'Narrenrede', p. 137.

[226] Pace Moule, Idiom Book, p. 112, who appears to reduce Χριστοῦ to the status of an adjective, since he renders the clause 'I am speaking Christian truth ...'

[227] For this sense of καύχησις see BAGD s.v. 1.

[228] Bachmann, p. 375; Prümm, Diakonia Pneumatos I, p. 622; see also Zmijewski, 'Narrenrede', p. 139.

[229] Prümm, Diakonia Pneumatos I, p. 622.

[230] Furnish, p. 493, comments that 'in the context of this letter (chaps. 10–13) it is primarily Paul's own boasting that is in view'.

[231] So, e.g., Windisch, p. 337; Lietzmann, p. 147; Barrett, p. 283.

[232] BAGD s.v. φράσσω 1.

[233] BAGD s.v. φράσσω 1.b., with reference to 1 Macc 9.55 (ἀπεφράγη τὸ στόμα αὐτοῦ) and to Rom 3.19.

[234] Noted by Windisch, p. 337, who claims that in the present verse the combination στόμα φράσσειν is presupposed. The term καύχησις, he suggests is a pregnant expression for τὸ στόμα μου καυχώμενον.

'this boasting will not be silenced'.[235] The second sense of φράσσω is 'stop', 'block', 'bar'.[236] In this case Paul's assertion would mean, 'this boasting will not (let itself) be stopped'.[237] And some commentators who adopt this second sense would find in it the presence of a latent metaphor. Chrysostom suggests that the idea of the damming up of rivers lies in the background.[238] But this has no contextual support.[239] Plummer thinks of the blocking of a road.[240] This would be marginally more likely. If Paul is thinking of himself as traversing the whole region of Achaia and maintaining his καύχησις as he does so, then the possibility of the boasting's being checked at some particular point might perhaps conjure up in his mind the thought of a barrier to his progress (εἰς ἐμέ). In any case, the idea of his boasting not being 'barred' to him seems to make the better sense.[241]

In 1 Cor 9.15 Paul has spoken of his free proclamation of the gospel as a cause for boasting—strangely, perhaps, since he had said in this earlier letter (1 Cor 1.31), and has also said in the present communication (10.17), that boasting must be 'of the Lord'. Here this same personal boasting comes into the picture again. His ultimate consistency (or otherwise) is a matter for later discussion.[242] As regards the present verse, it may be sufficient to suggest that he uses the boasting terminology here because, from the Corinthian point of view, he is in competition with opponents who themselves boast to an extreme degree. Perhaps he speaks of Achaia here (rather than Corinth) because he thinks the rival missionaries might have extended their operations further into the province.[243]

11. διὰ τί; ὅτι οὐκ ἀγαπῶ ὑμᾶς; ὁ θεὸς οἶδεν. It is likely that

[235] BAGD s.v. φράσσω 1.b.

[236] BAGD s.v. φράσσω 2.

[237] BAGD s.v. φράσσω 2.

[238] Chrysostom, *PG* 61 col. 559 (NPNF XII, p. 387); see also Allo, p. 284; Zmijewski, *'Narrenrede'*, p. 139. Plummer, p. 306, whilst not himself understanding Paul in this sense, draws attention to two similar uses of φράσσω in Prov 25.26 (ὥσπερ εἴ τις πηγὴν φράσσοι) and Jdt 16.3 (τὸ πλῆθος αὐτῶν ἐνέφραξεν χειμάρρους).

[239] Meyer, p. 433.

[240] Plummer, p. 306, with reference to Hos (LXX) 2.8 (φράσσω τὴν ὁδὸν αὐτῆς ἐν σκόλοψιν) and Lam 3.9 (ἐνεφραξεν τρίβους μου).

[241] It is the better fit with the εἰς ἐμέ, though other interpretations of the phrase are possible (the εἰς could be the equivalent of ἐν ['... silenced within me']—see BAGD s.v. εἰς 9., or it may have the general meaning 'for'—see BAGD s.v. εἰς 4.g ['... silenced for me',' blocked for me']).

[242] See below, pp. 706–8.

[243] Plummer, p. 306. Or perhaps he would have in view 'the saints in the whole of Achaia' to whom he referred in 1.1 in the earlier letter of chaps. 1–8, i.e., members of the church in Cenchreae and perhaps smaller groups under the influence of the Corinthian church (see Vol. I, pp. 88–9). He may wish to strengthen his assertion by stressing its comprehensive scope.

before the arrival of these other missionaries the Corinthians had taken Paul's refusal of maintenance as an unfriendly act.[244] This reaction will no doubt have been encouraged by the rival apostles.[245] Paul's response is a vehement denial that he does not love his readers: 'God knows I do!' (RSV, JB, REB). Stählin, followed by Furnish, sees the affirmation as an abbreviated form of the 'oath formula' (Furnish) in 11.31: ὁ θεὸς καὶ πατὴρ τοῦ κυρίου Ἰησοῦ οἶδεν... ὅτι οὐ ψεύδομαι.[246] Strictly speaking, the complete expression of Paul's thought would require μὴ γένοιτο to follow the question. The considerable degree of abbreviation adds force to his response.

12. ῾Ο δὲ ποιῶ καὶ ποιήσω, ἵνα ἐκκόψω τὴν ἀφορμὴν τῶν θελόντων ἀφορμήν, ἵνα ἐν ᾧ καυχῶνται εὑρεθῶσιν καθὼς καὶ ἡμεῖς. Having forcibly denied that his refusal of maintenance is due to lack of affection for his correspondents, Paul proceeds to offer a positive reason for the continuation of his practice, with specific reference to the present situation in the Corinthian church. His line of action has as its purpose the prevention of some advantage his opponents are desirous of gaining.[247] His manner of expression is forceful, indicating his deep emotional involvement in the issue.[248] It is also, from our own point of view, allusive. What is this advantage, this base of (hostile) operations,[249] that Paul is determined to excise?

According to Meyer, it is the opportunity to accuse Paul of greed, and the second ἵνα-clause, dependent on the first, indicates

---

[244] See below, pp. 703–4.

[245] Plummer, p. 306, and Hughes, pp. 389–90, suggest that it was the opponents who had put the idea into the Corinthians' heads, but existing conventions would have suggested it already.

[246] Stählin, 'Beteuerungsformeln', pp. 132–3; Furnish, p. 493.

[247] We understand ὃ δὲ ποιῶ καὶ ποιήσω as a unified relative clause which most probably functions as the subject of an implicit γίνεται (so Osiander, p. 413) or ἐστιν: 'What I am doing and shall do is in order that ...' (See Allo, p. 285, who has: 'Mais ce que je fais et continuerai à faire, [c'est] pour retrancher l'occasion ...'). Or the clause may be the object of an omitted ποιῶ (cf. Zmijewski, 'Narrenrede', p. 145) : 'What I am doing and shall do, I do in order that ...' An alternative interpretation which has substantial support is to understand καὶ ποιήσω as the main clause: 'But what I am doing, that I will also continue to do, in order to cut off opportunity ...' (Barrett, p. 270; see also, e.g., Plummer, p. 307; Hughes, p. 390; Bultmann, p. 209; Furnish, p. 484; Martin, p. 327; RSV, BCN.) The advantage here is that nothing needs to be supplied in order to produce a grammatically coherent structure. The drawback is that the stress is shifted somewhat from Paul's motivation (the issue in v. 11) to his practice (see Zmijewski, ibid.).

[248] See Zmijewski, 'Narrenrede', p. 151. He notes that the compound ἐκκόπτω is stronger than the simple verb, and hence more vivid. The image is that of cutting down a rotten tree, or of amputating a diseased limb. (The latter use, according to G. Stählin, on ἐκκόπτω, in *TWNT* III, pp. 857–60, see p. 858, is not attested outside the NT, where it occurs in Mt 5.30; 18.8.)

[249] Zmijewski, ibid., notes the use of ἀφορμή in the sense of a base for (military) operations. See LSJ s.v. 1.

his further intention to compel the rival missionaries to adopt his own policy in respect of financial support, so as to prove the unselfishness they have been boasting about themselves.[250] This is improbable. It would require the inherently unlikely assumption that Paul wished to set his opponents on the same level as himself.[251]

It is much more likely that the ἀφορμή is defined by the second ἵνα-clause (by which it is immediately followed), and that this clause, therefore, expresses the intention not of Paul but of his opponents. It is they who wish to equalise their own status with his. Most commentators prefer this alternative. The nature of the intention is then variously explained.

(i) According to Plummer, the rival missionaries wish to deprive Paul of an advantage which he enjoys, but they do not, in the eyes of the Corinthians. In their own view, their acceptance of maintenance validates their claim to apostolic office, and Paul's refusal indicates his awareness that he lacks this status. But at the same time they realise that to the Corinthians they themselves might appear greedy, and Paul, by contrast, unselfish. Hence, they aim to make him accept financial support himself.[252] There are, however, three difficulties in the way of acceptance of this interpretation. First, there is the obvious fact, plain from the context, that the Corinthians thought less, not more, of Paul because he refused their offer of financial help. Secondly, it would make little sense for his opponents to compel him to adopt a practice which they themselves saw as a mark of that same apostolic status which they claimed for themselves and wished to deny to him. Thirdly, if this is what Paul means, he ought to have said, not that his rivals aimed to put themselves into the situation that he was in, but that they intended to put him himself into their own situation.[253]

(ii) A similar, though not identical, interpretation is suggested by Barrett and Furnish. Paul's opponents desire an opportunity to deprive him of a basic essential of apostolicity, an essential which, in fact, they lack themselves. The real criterion of apostolic status is readiness for self-sacrifice. The opponents boast of their own apostolicity, but as long as they accept financial support from the Corinthians, whilst Paul does not, they fail to satisfy this criterion, by striking contrast with Paul himself.[254] They show that 'they are

[250] Meyer, p. 435.
[251] Bachmann, p. 376; Plummer, p. 307; Windisch, p. 340.
[252] Plummer, pp. 307–8. See also Hughes, p. 390.
[253] Meyer, pp. 436–7. He makes the point with general reference to this exegetical option in which the second ἵνα-clause expresses the intention of the opponents.
[254] Barrett, pp. 284–5.

not in fact true apostles of the Christ who became poor that others might be enriched'.[255] They aim, therefore, to abolish the criterion itself, as it is exemplified in Paul. Here, again, there are difficulties. This interpretation suggests that the Corinthians had already accepted Paul's understanding of apostleship and that it was his rivals who were under pressure to defend their practice of receiving maintenance as compatible with their claim to be apostles. But it is Paul who is on the defensive, and precisely in relation to this matter of financial support. Moreover, whatever his understanding of his own calling and of apostolicity in general, he did not, and could not, regard rejection of maintenance as a *sine qua non* of apostolic vocation (1 Cor 9.4–14).[256]

(iii) The intention of the rival missionaries is to preserve their own form of apostleship by putting pressure on Paul himself to conform to it. Theissen sees these people as 'itinerant charismatics', who, when first claiming material support from the Corinthian church, had been met with the information that this had not been required by Paul. Hence, in addition to quoting Jesus (1 Cor 9.14) in their own defence, they were trying to convert Paul to their own manner of life. The continuation of 'the primitive Christian institution of the itinerant charismatic' is what was at stake, since getting one's living by preaching the gospel was foundational to this tradition.[257] This interpretation, however, foreshortens the course of events in Corinth. By the time Paul writes the present letter it would seem that it is the opponents' conception of the apostolic lifestyle that has become dominant and Paul's which is under threat.[258]

(iv) According to Martin, the intention of the opponents was to take over Corinth as their own missionary territory, and it is their rights specifically in Corinth that they boast of. But their activities will be held in check, and their intention to replace Paul frustrated, so long as he continues to preach 'a crucified Jesus', and offers the gospel free of charge.[259] Martin is probably right in seeing the opponents' boasting as referring to their claim to apostolic oversight in Corinth. Moreover, this makes sense of the formulation of the second ἵνα-clause: they would be aiming to elevate their own status to a level of equality with Paul. But there is no real explanation of how Paul should have supposed that the continuation of his manner of preaching and mode of living would

---

[255] Furnish, p. 509.
[256] Barrett, p. 285, allows this to be a problem.
[257] Theissen, *Social Setting*, p. 53.
[258] And again, Paul does not say that their aim is to assimilate *his* status to *theirs*, but the reverse. See above, under (i).
[259] Martin, pp. 348–9.

circumvent such an attempt on the part of his rivals. All apostolic missionaries preached of the death of Jesus (1 Cor 15.3–4), and this message did not of necessity entail the refusal of material support. Cephas both accepted support (1 Cor 9.5) and is also included amongst those who, Paul says (1 Cor 15.5, 11), preach the same gospel as he does.

How then, in conclusion, may we suppose that Paul's rejection of maintenance served, in his view at least, to set his own authority in Corinth above that of his rivals? He gives us one answer himself, in 12.14. By refusing material assistance he shows that he is the parent, the founding father, of the Christian community in the city. And as the father of the church, as he indicates in 1 Cor 4.14–16, he exercises an authority superior to that of later missionary workers in the community. Presumably, when writing the present letter, he hopes that his Corinthian readers will remember what he has said earlier, and draw the right conclusion. There may be a further answer (additional rather than alternative). Theissen observes that in the Corinthian correspondence we see the meeting of 'two types of missionaries ..., types which can be distinguished by reference to their position on this issue of the right of support'.[260] Now if Cephas appears to represent the non-Pauline type (1 Cor 9.5), it would seem that it is the Petrine mission to the Jews which is primarily distinguished by the acceptance of maintenance on the part of its members. And since the information in Acts 18 suggests that there may have been a considerable Jewish presence in Corinth, it could be that Paul's opponents had come to the city initially in furtherance of the Petrine mission.[261] In any case, their acceptance of support will have aligned them with that mission in the minds of those Corinthians familiar with its ethos.[262] But if Paul himself changes his practice, then he also will align himself with the Petrine mission, and concede, symbolically, that Corinth is Petrine territory. And in that case, if the rival missionaries belong to this alternative mission, their authority in Corinth will equal that of Paul himself. This he is determined to prevent.

13. οἱ γὰρ τοιοῦτοι ψευδαπόστολοι, ἐργάται δόλιοι, μετασχηματιζόμενοι εἰς ἀποστόλους Χριστοῦ. Paul explains the basic reason for his declared intention (v. 12) to prevent the rival missionaries from assuming apostolic control in Corinth: they are not genuine apostles at all. The οἱ τοιοῦτοι, 'such people', whilst theoretically capable of a generalising interpretation,

---

[260] Theissen, *Social Setting*, p. 41.
[261] See above, pp. 649–50.
[262] In 1 Cor 9.5 Paul assumes some such knowledge.

'people like this',[263] is almost certainly specific, with definite reference to the subject of the preceding καυχῶνται and εὑρεθῶσιν.[264] Paul is not engaged in an objective discussion of the criteria of apostleship or his rivals' claims to it. Rather, he insists that *these* specific people *are* pseudo-apostles. The term ψευδαπόστολος itself may be his own coinage,[265] formed, perhaps, by analogy with ψευδοπροφήτης.[266] On what grounds, then, does he apply it to these other missionaries at work in Corinth? One reason, perhaps, is that in his view they bring a different gospel (11.4).[267] We have suggested above some ideas as to the content of this alternative gospel, and it may be interesting to observe that what we have proposed there could be correlated with some of Barrett's suggestions, to explain Paul's use (creation?) of the word ψευδαπόστολος in the present context. Within Jewish Christianity, Barrett suggests, there may have been those such as the rival missionaries in Corinth who disapproved so strongly of Paul that they termed him an antinomian ψευδοπροφήτης, thus classing him with the 'false prophets' who appear in the Matthean tradition (Mt 7.15). Paul, in his turn, regards his opponents as 'pseudo-apostles'.[268] This suggests that his coinage of the term ψευδαπόστολος may be a response to the use of ψευδοπροφήτης in some early form of the tradition later found in Matthew's Gospel, in which these people are characterised as antinomian, and this possibility would fit in with our own theory that the opponents' 'different gospel' could have consisted in a presentation of Christ as a 'Matthean' divine law-giver.[269]

In addition, they would be seen by Paul as false apostles because they were trespassing upon his own missionary territory and contesting his own apostolic authority.[270] It is he who has

---

[263] Lietzmann, p. 148, suggests that the expression describes 'the sort of people the opponents are', and Bultmann, p. 210, agrees that this is a possibility. This comes very near to a specific reference. Schlatter, *Paulus*, p. 646, however, thinks it possible that Paul does not go so far as to label his rivals as already 'false apostles'. Rather, he points out that such false apostles do exist, and that if the rival missionaries persist in their claim to leadership of the Corinthian church this is what in the end they will become.

[264] See, e.g., Zmijewski, '*Narrenrede*', p. 155; Furnish, p. 494; Martin, p. 350. The other occurrences of ὁ τοιοῦτος in 2 Corinthians (2.6,7; 10.11; 12.2, 5) all refer to specific people. In 1 Corinthians it is specific in 5.5 (though general in 5.11; 7.28; 15.48).

[265] Furnish, p. 494, with ref. to Kümmel, p. 211.

[266] Furnish, ibid.

[267] Bultmann, p. 210; cf. Barrett, 'ΨΕΥΔΑΠΟΣΤΟΛΟΙ', pp. 93–4.

[268] Barrett, 'ΨΕΥΔΑΠΟΣΤΟΛΟΙ', p. 91.

[269] See above, p. 670 The phrase 'early form of the tradition' should be emphasised. It is not suggested that Matthew himself held views identical with those of Paul's opponents.

[270] Furnish, p. 510.

been sent by God as apostle to Corinth. These people have not, therefore, been sent to the city, and their claim to be fulfilling an apostolic commission there is false.[271] They are deceitful (mission) workers,[272] disguising themselves as Christ's apostles, when (in Paul's view) they are really emissaries of Satan (v. 15).[273] **14.** καὶ οὐ θαῦμα, αὐτὸς γὰρ ὁ Σατανᾶς μετασχηματίζεται εἰς ἄγγελον φωτός. Such a radical transformation as v. 13 indicates should not be a matter for wonder.[274] Satan is said to transform himself in an equally thoroughgoing fashion. The argument makes some sense as it stands here. But it is given further, biting, point in the following verse, where the pseudo-apostles of v. 13 are described as themselves servants of Satan.

The motif of Satan's disguising himself as an angel is found in Jewish sources. In the *Life of Adam and Eve*, in the story of Satan's second temptation of Eve, after the Fall, we read: 'Then Satan was angry and transformed himself into the brightness of angels and went away to the Tigris River to Eve.'[275] And in the *Apocalypse of Moses* he appears to Eve over the wall of paradise, 'in the form of an angel'.[276] Windisch suggests that Paul will have known the legend somewhat in the form in which it occurs in the *Life of Adam and Eve*.[277] Other commentators likewise suppose that some form of it lies in the background of the apostle's thinking in this verse.[278] Plummer, however, claims that it is unnecessary to suppose Paul to be referring to any such legend. He argues that the use of the present tense μετασχηματίζεται

[271] Martin, p. 350.
[272] Windisch, p. 341, notes that ἐργάτης belongs to the terminology of mission (see Mt 9.37 = Lk 10.2). According to Sundermann, *Kraft der Rede*, p. 113, the opponents are deceitful because they claim 'wages' due only to apostles (1 Cor 9.1–18), whilst they are *fake*-apostles.
[273] Windisch, p. 341.
[274] There is a textual variant. The reading θαῦμα (𝔓46 ℵ B D* F G P 098. 0243. 6. 33. 81. 326. 365. 630. 1175. 1739. 1881 2464 *pc*) has obviously substantial attestation, and is most likely to be given preference over θαυμαστόν (D² Ψ 0121a 𝔐). Plummer, p. 310, suggests that the change to θαυμαστόν may have been occasioned by the extreme rarity of θαῦμα in the LXX and the NT (in the NT only here and in Rev 17.6) and the frequency of θαυμαστός in the LXX (6 instances in the NT). He notes also, p. 309, an instance in Plato of a similar combination of θαῦμα with a negative: the unwillingness of the crowd to be persuaded by what is said is θαῦμα οὐδέν—no (cause for) wonder' (*Rep.* VI 498D). The similar combination of θαυμαστόν with οὐδέν in Philo (*Agr.* 71; *Vit. Mos.* I 156) is noted by Windisch, pp. 341-2.
[275] *Life of Adam and Eve* (*Vita*) 9.1 (*OTP* II, p. 260).
[276] Cited by Windisch, p. 342. See *Life of Adam and Eve* (*Apoc.*) 17.1 (*OTP* II, p.277).
[277] Windisch, ibid.
[278] Lietzmann, p. 149, Héring, p. 86, Bruce, p. 239, Barrett, p. 286, Bultmann, p. 211, and Furnish, p. 495, all refer to the *Life*; Barrett and Furnish mention also the *Apocalypse*.

points to Satan's habitual activity, not to any specific instance of it, and that the Corinthians (few of whom were Jews) could not be expected to understand such an allusion to Jewish legend.[279] But reference to Satan's habitual activity may well have been extrapolated from the story of a particular occasion of it, and the force of what Paul is saying does not absolutely depend upon his readers' knowledge of its legendary background. The precise expression ἄγγελος φωτός appears to be unique to this context, although it derives, no doubt, from the general idea that angels make their appearance in a state of radiant glory: see, e.g., Lk 2.9; 24.4.[280] The phrase could be Paul's own formulation,[281] but this is not certain.[282]

15. οὐ μέγα οὖν εἰ καὶ οἱ διάκονοι αὐτοῦ μετασχηματίζονται ὡς διάκονοι δικαιοσύνης, ὧν τὸ τέλος ἔσται κατὰ τὰ ἔργα αὐτῶν. If Satan adopts such a disguise, it is then 'no great surprise'[283] if his agents likewise disguise themselves, masquerading as agents of righteousness.[284] As Windisch observes, we have here a new pejorative description of Paul's opponents which goes even further than those in v. 13: they are now designated servants of Satan, by whose agency the devil seeks to destroy Paul's own work (cf. 2.11 and 1 Th 2.18, for Paul's sense of satanic opposition).[285]

Their disguise as 'agents of righteousness' is variously interpreted:

(i) The genitive δικαιοσύνης is seen as the equivalent of an adjective: the rival missionaries present themselves as 'upright servants of Christ'.[286] The implicit parallel, however, with the ἀποστόλους Χριστοῦ of v. 13 and the contrast with the διάκονοι αὐτοῦ of the present verse make it unlikely that δικαιοσύνης is simply descriptive.

---

[279] Plummer, p. 309; see also Allo, p. 287; Tasker, p. 153; Hughes, pp. 393–4, n. 57.

[280] Windisch, p. 342. Furnish, p. 495, with reference to Moule, *Idiom Book*, p. 175, suggests that the genitive φωτός may be the equivalent of the adjective φωτεινός, 'shining', 'radiant', following the Semitic idiom.

[281] Zmijewski, '*Narrenrede*', p. 161.

[282] Furnish, p. 495, thinks it unlikely, on account of the Jewish background of thought at this point.

[283] Furnish, p. 484, and Martin, p. 327, adopt this rendering: Martin, p. 352, notes that the μέγα refers back to the θαῦμα of v. 14. For parallels to the construction, see the references in BAGD s.v. μέγας 2.b.b.

[284] According to Bultmann, p. 211, the form of argument is that of 'from the less to the greater', 'a minori ad maius'. But this is surely incorrect. The point is precisely the reverse; the character of the master, the greater, determines the character of the servant, the less. Wolff, p. 224, correctly notes that it is an argument 'a majori ad minus'.

[285] Windisch, p. 343.

[286] Barrett, p. 287.

(ii) Paul's rivals were themselves promoting his own gospel of righteousness through faith, in competition with him, we may suppose, and for their own deceitful ends. Evidence for this interpretation is found in 3.9, where Paul's own apostolic ministry is termed ἡ διακονία τῆς δικαιοσύνης[287] This is highly improbable. What Paul says about them (11.4) is that they preach a different gospel.

(iii) The opponents are Judaizers in the traditional sense. They advocated a legalistic righteousness whereby men achieve their own justification.[288] According to Windisch and Barrett, this is incorrect because Judaizers would not be in disguise in presenting teaching of this kind.[289] Agents of legal righteousness is precisely what they would actually be.[290] But this objection is hardly valid. What these people really are, according to Paul, is agents of Satan. Hence, as agents of the personified power of evil, they do disguise themselves if they claim to promote righteousness.[291] Judaizing in the strict sense, however, is not an issue in this letter.

(iv) No great emphasis is to be laid on the content of δικαιοσύνη. The phrase is an apostolic title, synonymous with ἀπόστολοι Χριστοῦ (v. 13) and διάκονοι Χριστοῦ (v. 23).[292] But in these similar phrases the comparable genitive Χριστοῦ is surely of highly significant content.

(v) There remains a further possibility. The phrase ἡ διακονία τῆς δικαιοσύνης in 3.9 may have some relevance to the present verse, though not in the way suggested under (ii) above. According to our analysis of the Corinthian correspondence, the letter of chaps. 1–8 precedes that of chaps. 10–13.[293] The rival missionaries, therefore, would in all probability be aware of its contents (cf. 10.10). They would then be likely to claim for themselves this διακονία of righteousness, and would claim also that it is they who exhibit the abundant glory by which it is characterised: Paul, in their view would possess none of it. Their claim to serve righteousness would be substantiated by their promotion

---

[287] Meyer, p. 439.
[288] Tasker, p. 154. Plummer, p. 310, and Hughes, p. 395, also see some allusion to Judaizers.
[289] Windisch, p. 343; Barrett, p. 287.
[290] Barrett, ibid.
[291] This would be so even if the righteousness is legalistic. There is no suggestion in 2 Corinthians that the law is demonic. If there might be hints to that effect in Galatians, even these hints do not add up to an understanding of the law as the creation of Satan. Bruce comments: 'Even in Galatians the law is ultimately *God's* law.' (Bruce, *Galatians*, p. 175.)
[292] Windisch, p. 343; Bultmann, p. 211; Wolff, p. 224.
[293] See Vol I, pp. 5–20.

of some degree of Torah-observance, required, in their tradition, by Christ himself.[294] To Paul, they are satanic agents in disguise. The verse concludes with an ominous, though unspecified, threat of judgement,[295] similar to those found elsewhere in Paul's letters; see Rom 3.8; 1 Cor 3.17; Phil 3.19; 1 Th 2.16.[296] Martin suggests, with reference to Käsemann,[297] that what we have here is 'a "statement of sacred law", of the order "destruction to the destroyer" (1 Cor 3:17; ...)'.[298] Käsemann does not cite this verse, however, nor does it appear to fit the structure of the examples he does quote.

Paul can use strong language about Christian opponents and subversives elsewhere (Gal 5.12; Phil 3.18–19), but this is the only extant occasion of his stigmatising such people as agents of Satan. Why does he go to such lengths here? Perhaps it is because it was only in Corinth that he was confronted with opponents who claimed equal or superior *apostolic* rights over a congregation of his own founding. As he has shown in 10.13–16, he is confident that his own apostolic authority in Corinth comes from God. If that is so, then his rivals must be the agents of God's great adversary, Satan.[299] This is not, then, simply intensified abuse. Rather, in Paul's view, it expresses apocalyptic fact. These people are the adversaries in the eschatological warfare which God wages against the power of Satan, whilst Paul himself fights on God's side.[300]

The use of πάθος in 11.1–15.[301] This means of rhetorical proof consists in persuasion through the arousal of emotion. The speaker aims in this way to induce the audience to identify with him, and to support his case, by stirring up in them the appropriate feelings, negative and positive, which he himself experiences (or affects to experience).[302] In 2 Cor 10–13 it is in large part a matter of arousing in the audience Paul's own strong negative emotions towards the visiting missionaries, as well as

---

[294] See above, pp. 670, 694.
[295] The syntactical structure has parallels in Rom 3.8 and Phil 3.19. Whilst, strictly speaking, these assertions are in the form of dependent relative clauses, as regards sense, they function as independent sentences.
[296] The similarity is noted by Windisch, p. 343.
[297] E. Käsemann, *New Testament Questions of Today*, London, 1969, pp. 66–81.
[298] Martin, p. 353.
[299] As Professor Cranfield notes, there would be a contrast here with Paul's attitude in 1 Cor 15.9–11, which might cast doubt on this exegesis. But the basic reference there is to the original apostles, and in any case the Corinthian situation has changed.
[300] Kleinknecht, *Der leidende Gerechtfertigte*, p. 293; cf. Martin, ibid.
[301] See above, p. 655.
[302] See DiCicco, *Ethos, Pathos and Logos*, pp. 113–31.

causing them to feel his own hurt and indignation on account of the welcome given to these people.[303] In 11.1–15 there are various examples of this technique, noted by DiCicco. This section is 'a key passage for understanding Paul's use of invective'.[304] Paul aims to make the Corinthians share his own anger towards his rivals. Hence, he denounces the visiting missionaries as deceitful false apostles, and thus as agents of Satan, the prime deceiver (vv. 13–15).[305] He displays his indignation at the thought of comparison (11.12) between 'their alleged ministry' and his own.[306] Whilst he could be accused of exaggeration in castigating his rivals as satanic, this is comprehensible: 'Paul's anger is such that he has to reach the Corinthians at a deep emotional level to jar them into awareness.'[307] DiCicco notes the significance of the threefold use of the verb μετασχηματίζω in 11.13–15: 'The verb has clearly negative connotations with its overtones of duplicity and spuriousness.'[308] It functions also as an oblique reproach to the Corinthians for having been taken in by these people, and having insulted Paul's own dignity by regarding his own outward appearance, i.e., his σχῆμα, as contemptible.[309] At the same time, he is anxious to show his readers that he loves them, and desires their own love in return; 'he has exalted them at his own expense and that of other churches (11.7); he has loved them as God is his witness (11.11).' Thus:'Paul articulates these feelings of deep love for the Corinthians to persuade them that he has only their best interests at heart, that he is their faithful friend who has always acted with unselfish love toward them.'[310] We find these examples of the use of πάθος convincing.

EXCURSUS XII

Paul and apostolic maintenance

Paul's means of economic support had quite soon become a matter of contention between the Corinthian congregation and the apostle himself.

[303] DiCicco, *Ethos, Pathos and Logos*, pp. 164–87.
[304] DiCicco, *Ethos, Pathos and Logos*, p. 170.
[305] Ibid.
[306] DiCicco, *Ethos, Pathos and Logos*, p. 171.
[307] DiCicco, *Ethos, Pathos and Logos*, p. 172.
[308] Ibid.
[309] DiCicco, *Ethos, Pathos and Logos*, p. 173.
[310] DiCicco, *Ethos, Pathos and Logos*, pp. 182–3; quotations on p. 183.

We shall discuss, first, the precise kind of support that was in view, secondly, the evidence of 1 Cor 9, thirdly, the evidence in the letter of 2 Cor 10–13, and fourthly, the question as to whether Paul was altogether consistent in his practice.

(i) *Types of economic support and Paul's custom in regard to each*

Conventions in the Graeco-Roman world concerning economic support for those in situations similar to Paul's can be broadly divided into two categories. First, there is the custom of short-term hospitality. This was intended as a provision lasting for no more than a week, and probably no more than three days. It included 'bath, board, and bed', together with necessities for the next stage of the traveller's journey.[311] Paul may well have taken advantage on occasion of this form of hospitality. In any case, it is clear from his use of the verb προπέμπω (Rom 15.24; 1 Cor 16.6; 2 Cor 1.16) that he was ready to accept, indeed that he expected, travel assistance in one form or another[312] from the Christians of the town or city he was leaving. This was not the matter at issue between himself and the Corinthians. Secondly, there was the question of long-term provision. How might those free citizens who lacked means of their own, but did not essentially belong to the labouring or trading classes, obtain a livelihood? How might philosophers, as a prime example, secure provision for their needs? There were various answers: begging, fee-charging, entering a patron's household, resorting to manual labour.[313] In the Christian communities there was a rough parallel to the need for long-term provision in the case of the missionary apostles. Like philosophers, they were teachers of a kind, and when founding a new congregation would stay in one place for some period of time. It is apparent from 1 Cor 9.3–7 that in these circumstances they could expect, indeed had a right to, economic support from their converts. In effect, this would be somewhat similar to the acceptance of patronage. It is this form of support that Paul rejected, and it was this refusal that caused trouble for him in Corinth. The trouble was compounded by his acceptance of a third kind of assistance, peculiar, it seems, to himself, i.e., financial support from an existing congregation for missionary work in some other city or region.[314]

---

[311] Hock, *Social Context*, p. 29.

[312] See BAGD s.v. προπέμπω 2.; also Vol. I, p. 74. See further Holmberg, *Paul and Power*, p. 89. Pratscher, 'Verzicht', p. 289, appears doubtful whether Paul did receive support of this kind. He does not, however, consider the implications of 1 Cor 16.6 or 2 Cor 1.16.

[313] Hock, *Social Context*, pp. 52–9.

[314] See Peterman, *Paul's Gift*, pp. 163–7, for a clear distinction between these three forms of support: maintenance whilst with a congregation, which Paul refused; travel expenses and the like, which he accepts; support for mission elsewhere, which he accepts (see Phil 4.16; 2 Cor 11.9).

(ii) *The evidence of 1 Cor 9*

Here we have evidence for Paul's policy, in respect of provision for his economic needs, during his founding visit to Corinth, and implicitly for the adverse reaction it had provoked; also, he gives some measure of explanation for its adoption. It seems clear that right from the start he had refused to accept economic support, for what, in his view, were good reasons. In addition, it is probable that his experience during his prolonged stay in the city (Acts 18.11) had reinforced his determination to maintain his economic independence.

(a) In 1 Cor 9.12 Paul states his basic reason for refusing maintenance. He does not wish to place any obstacle in the way of the progress of the gospel. This intention will have conditioned his policy from the beginning. But why, exactly, would he have supposed that accepting economic support would have proved detrimental to his mission? Commentators offer various suggestions.

(1) Perhaps some potential converts might be deterred from joining the church if membership appeared to entail a financial obligation.[315] This is a possibility.

(2) Paul did not wish to be seen as a fee-charging sophist.[316] There was an 'ingrained ironical mistrust of sophists', which would have militated against the acceptance of his message.[317] This suggestion is rather more problematic. It might be true to say that Paul would not wish to be regarded as a sophist, since he had rejected sophistic rhetoric as a medium for the primary presentation of the Christian gospel (1 Cor 2.1, 4). But the acceptance of monetary reward (or its equivalent) would not of necessity have identified him as a sophist. Some philosophers also charged fees.[318] They were not criticised for this practice in itself, but only if it degenerated into greed, and began to determine the nature of their teaching.[319] Furthermore, it is not probable that the Corinthians distrusted sophists, in view of their later welcome of the rival missionaries with their rhetorical skills.

(3) It may be better to suppose, more simply, that Paul wished to avoid suspicion of his personal motives, i.e., the suspicion that his missionary career was nothing but a means of living at other people's expense.[320]

(4) At a deeper level, Paul believed that the apostolic lifestyle should reflect the essence of the apostolic gospel. This gospel is based on the sacrifice of the Christ who impoverished himself for the spiritual enrichment of others (2 Cor 8.9), and so a similar impoverishment is

---

[315] Barrett, *First Corinthians*, p. 207; cf. Holmberg, *Paul and Power*, p. 92.

[316] Goudge, p. 106 (cited by Barrett, p. 281); see also Winter, *Sophists*, pp. 163–6.

[317] Holmberg, *Paul and Power*, p. 93.

[318] Hock, *Social Context*, p. 52, notes that although the practice had been rejected by Socrates, it was taken up later by various philosophers, 'especially by Stoics, but also by Platonists and Aristotelians'.

[319] Georgi, *Opponents*, p. 238.

[320] Cf. Theissen, *Social Setting*, p. 51, who draws attention to 1 Th 2.5, where Paul insists that his preaching is not to be considered as 'a cover for trying to get money' (JB). See also Plummer, p. 305: Paul wished to avoid the suspicion that his preaching was conditioned by the need to say 'what would please the people who housed and fed him'.

required of Christ's apostle.[321] A strong inward motivation would thus reinforce the more practical considerations mentioned under (1) and (3).[322]

(b) Paul is concerned primarily with his own practice. But it seems that Barnabas's custom was the same (1 Cor 9.6). Was there, then, some guide to apostolic conduct which both followed? In 2 Cor 9.14 Paul quotes the Jesus-saying which sanctions, indeed commands, the acceptance of economic provision (see Mt 10.10).[323] But was there, perhaps, some different, alternative regulation? Furnish, commenting on 1 Cor 9.16–18, suggests that there lies in the background of these verses a 'missionary rule' that the gospel should be preached 'without cost to the hearers'.[324] In the synoptic tradition this would be represented in Mt 10.8: δωρεὰν ἐλάβετε, δωρεὰν δότε.[325]

(c) It is possible that, as the situation in Corinth developed, further reasons emerged for maintaining the initial policy of refusal of economic provision which Paul had embarked on.

(1) It is apparent from 1 Corinthians (1.12; 3.3–4) that the Corinthians were prone to factionalism. Whilst by this stage the different groups are claiming allegiance to apostles whose contacts with the congregation came after Paul's first visit to the city, the general tendency may well have been visible quite early during his stay in Corinth. Peterman suggests that there may have been 'power struggles between the wealthy in the Corinthian congregation'.[326] In these circumstances, acceptance of financial support would have involved Paul in the struggle on one side or the other.[327]

(2) According to 1 Cor 3.1–2, the Corinthians are still 'babes' in respect of Christian behaviour—even after Paul's prolonged stay in Corinth. If it is essential, still, that he should maintain his role as their spiritual father (1 Cor 4.14–15), it must have been even more essential that he should do so throughout his founding visit. He would need, that is, to maintain the parent-child relationship in which he is the superior member. To accept financial support, by contrast, would place him in a situation of 'social dependence', according to the social conventions of the day: it would mean a lowering of status and a loss of apostolic authority.[328]

---

[321] Barrett, p. 282.

[322] See also Horrell, *Social Ethos*, pp. 215–16. He suggests that, in adopting this way of life, Paul aimed to avoid hindrance to the (socially) 'weak', whom he was attempting to gain. 'He lowers himself in order to gain those who are themselves of lower status' (p. 216).

[323] See Dungan, *Sayings of Jesus*, p. 79.

[324] Furnish, p. 506.

[325] Furnish, ibid.; cf. Dungan, *Sayings of Jesus*, p. 79 n. 6, who suggests there may be an echo of the saying in 2 Cor 11.7. On the apparent contradiction between the two sayings, see Furnish, ibid., who suggests that Mt 10.10 could be a rule for congregations and Mt 10.8 could apply to church leaders.

[326] Peterman, *Paul's Gift*, p. 211.

[327] Ibid.

[328] Peterman, *Paul's Gift*, pp. 171–4.

(d) The Corinthians reacted adversely to Paul's refusal of economic support, for various reasons which may be deduced from the text, and from knowledge of the social background.

(1) A major cause of their criticism becomes apparent in 1 Cor 9. They had become aware that other apostolic missionaries did receive support from those they evangelised (9.3–7). Cephas is particularly mentioned, as are Jesus's brothers. It is debatable whether Cephas had ever visited Corinth,[329] and there is no evidence that any of the others had ever done so. But in view of the frequency of travel in the Graeco-Roman world and the key position of Corinth itself it is easy to see how information about them may have reached the Corinthian church via Christian travellers from elsewhere. If, then, it became clear that Paul's missionary practice was not that of these other apostles, the suspicion may have emerged that he was not himself a genuine apostle,[330] or at least that he was of inferior standing. This, in turn, would reflect adversely on the status of the churches he had founded, including the church in Corinth.[331]

(2) Their status might be imperilled also in a more general way. The impoverishment of their leader, consequent upon his refusal of financial assistance, would put them in an ignominious situation in a society where affluence was important and leaders were expected to be sound financially.[332]

(3) Since Paul's rejection of maintenance entailed his working as an artisan,[333] he might perhaps have attracted disapproval on this account, and in consequence would have been seen to cast further dishonour on the church. In 1 Cor 4.10 he refers to himself as 'weak', and two verses later speaks of labouring with his own hands. Hock sees the two things as connected. In Corinth, Paul would be seen as 'a weak figure, without power, prestige, and privilege', and this would be due in part to his working at his trade.[334] Savage, however, argues that this view depends too much on the literary sources for its presentation of attitudes to work in the first century, and that the epigraphic evidence, by contrast, shows that tradesmen and artisans saw their work as a cause for pride.[335] Perhaps the truth of the matter, in Paul's case lies somewhere in between. Those tradesmen who left inscriptions and funerary reliefs on their tombstones must have been reasonably well-to-do. Savage comments

---

[329] Barrett, *First Corinthians*, p. 204, thinks that he had; see also 'Cephas and Corinth', pp. 28–39. Fee, *First Corinthians*, p. 404, is doubtful.

[330] Lietzmann, p. 147; Barrett, p. 282; Fee, *First Corinthians*, p. 400; see also Holmberg, *Paul and Power*, p. 95.

[331] Georgi, *Opponents*, pp. 239–40, and p. 292 nn. 86, 87; cf. Lietzmann, pp. 157–8.

[332] Savage, *Power through Weakness*, pp. 86–8.

[333] In Acts 18.3 he is described as a σκηνοποιός, 'tentmaker'. Hock, *Social Context*, p. 21, suggests that this precise description is due to a preference for 'specialized titles' on the part of artisans, and that Paul would probably make other leather products as well.

[334] Hock, *Social Context*, p. 60. He has already claimed, pp. 35–6, that the practice of a trade was seen as slavish (since workshops were usually manned by slaves), and thus humiliating. See also R. MacMullen, *Roman Social Relations*, New Haven, 1974, p. 115.

[335] Savage, *Power through Weakness*, pp. 84–6.

that many of them 'had moved high up the social ladder'.[336] This says nothing about the status of those who worked for them (slaves, in all probability). It says nothing either about the ambiguous position and social image of Paul himself, who engaged in manual labour, not to accumulate wealth and thus to achieve status elevation, but to keep himself in economic necessities whilst he pursued his main tasks of evangelism and pastoral nurture.

(e) Paul's response in 1 Corinthians to disapproval of his refusal of maintenance is to defend his authentic apostolic status. This he does on two grounds. First he asserts that he has seen the risen Christ (9.1; cf. 15.8): thus, he is able to perform the essential apostolic function of bearing witness to Jesus's resurrection (cf. Acts 1.22). Secondly, he points to his foundation of the Corinthian church itself (9.1–2): 'its existence is a visible sign of his apostleship.'[337] It seems that this defence had little lasting effect, if much effect at all. Paul was not able to assert his authority at the time of his interim visit to Corinth, and although his severe letter following that visit seemed to achieve its object, the advent and activity in force of the rival missionaries rapidly weakened his apostolic position afresh. His further explanation that he aimed to prevent hindrance to the gospel (9.12) likewise will have had little impact.

(iii) *The evidence of 2 Cor 10–13*

(a) It becomes obvious that the Corinthians' criticism of Paul has sharpened rather than diminished. His refusal of maintenance has now become a 'sin' (11.7), and an indication of his lack of love (11.11). This language is best explained in terms of the Graeco-Roman conventions relating to the giving and receiving of gifts. The acceptance of proffered gifts and benefits was usual, and refusal engendered hostility. Moreover, since the one who conferred the benefit was seen as superior to the recipient (at least until the latter had reciprocated), a refusal might be seen not only as a rejection of friendship but also as an insult to the status of the would-be giver. In Corinth, it is likely that it was congregational members of some social standing who had made Paul an offer of financial aid. They would have been affronted by his refusal.[338] Their sense of injury would have been increased, furthermore, by the fact that whilst he was working in Corinth Paul did accept assistance from the Macedonian churches (11.8–9). It is this that will have been the major cause of offence: refusal of aid from Corinth but acceptance of support from other churches.[339] The implication would be that he regarded the Corinthians as inferior to these other Christian congregations.[340]

Reactions of this kind may well have been latent from the beginning,

---

[336] Savage, *Power through Weakness*, p. 86.
[337] Barrett, *First Corinthians*, pp. 200–1; the quotation is on p. 201.
[338] P. Marshall, *Enmity in Corinth*, pp. 8–17, 174, 221–32.
[339] P. Marshall, *Enmity in Corinth*, p. 175.
[340] P. Marshall, *Enmity in Corinth*, p. 177, commenting on the use of ἡσσάομαι in 12.13.

and present, if not overtly voiced, at the time when Paul was made aware of the criticism to which he responds in 1 Cor 9. But by the time he writes 2 Cor 10–13 they will have been exacerbated by the arrival in Corinth of other missionaries who do accept financial aid (11.12)[341] and who are intent on discrediting Paul. They may have drawn particular attention to his inconsistency in respect of acceptance or refusal of aid from different churches. Since consistency of character and conduct was a prime virtue in Greek eyes, this would especially count against him.[342]

(b) Paul is compelled, therefore, to offer further defence of his policy, in respect of financial maintenance, in the letter of chaps. 10–13, and he gives two further reasons for his refusal to accept the offer made to him: he did not and does not wish to impose a burden on the Corinthians (11.9; 12.13–14a), and his relationship to them is parental (12.14). There is yet a third reason, which has emerged since the rival missionaries have taken up residence in Corinth. Paul's refusal of maintenance distinguishes him from these others (11.12).

(1) Acceptance of gifts might cause hardship to the benefactors. In such circumstances the conventions allowed refusal.[343] If Paul supposed that the Corinthian offer of financial support would prove economically burdensome to them, he might have expected his refusal to be understood as a sign of his affection (11.11). Conversely, however, the Corinthians themselves might have expected that he would show affection by acceptance.[344] But it may be that the situation was yet more complex, in respect of Paul's motivation. Peterman draws attention to the Greek and Roman use of 'burden'-language with reference to social obligations as well as to financial responsibilities, and notes their close connection. Seneca, for example, can use the word *onus* with reference to someone who is his dependant both financially and socially.[345] In both respects that person is 'a burden' to him. In Graeco-Roman society 'financial dependence yielded social dependence' and a consequent state of social inferiority.[346] Paul's own awareness of this ethos is apparent in 1 Thessalonians. In 2.9 he points to his own practice: he worked hard (i.e., to earn money) so as not to 'burden' (ἐπιβαρῆσαι) any of them. Then in 4.11–12 he urges his readers to do likewise, so that they may not be dependent on anybody. The combination of these two passages shows that: 'Paul desires to avoid being a *burden* so that he will not be *dependent* on anybody'.[347] Thus, his motivation in refusing support from the Corinthians may be somewhat ambiguous. On the one hand, he thus acts because he loves them (11.11): it is for their sakes. But on the other hand, it may be because he wishes to avoid dependence (perhaps also social inferiority?): it is for his own sake, or, as he would see it, for the sake of his apostolic calling.

(2) As we have already observed, Paul's parental role *vis-à-vis* the

[341] P. Marshall, *Enmity in Corinth*, p. 176.
[342] P. Marshall, *Enmity in Corinth*, pp. 256–7.
[343] P. Marshall, *Enmity in Corinth*, pp. 244–5.
[344] P. Marshall, *Enmity in Corinth*, p. 245.
[345] Peterman, *Paul's Gift*, p. 169; see Seneca, *Ep.* 50.2.
[346] Peterman, *Paul's Gift*, p. 168.
[347] Peterman, *Paul's Gift*, p. 170; the point is made, in effect, by Furnish, p. 508.

church in Corinth requires, in his view, that he should maintain the (superior) position of benefactor.[348] This he insists on (12.14–15): 'parents should make provision for their children, not children for their parents' (REB). Again (cf. 11.11) he presents his practice as a demonstration of love: again, however, he may have his own position in mind as well.

(3) Paul's opponents aim to usurp, or at least to equal, his own authority over the Corinthian church (11.12). Whilst he maintains his unique parental role they cannot achieve their ambition. He must, therefore, maintain this role, and so his consequent status as benefactor, to prevent the congregation from falling into the clutches of missionaries whom he appears seriously to regard as dangerous apostates (11.12–15).

(iv) Was Paul inconsistent?

(a) He must have seemed so to the Corinthians. He had refused their own offer of financial assistance and yet he accepted it from the Macedonians. Why was this? There have been various suggestions, aimed at restoring some measure of consistency to his policy as regards maintenance.

(1) It might be natural to suppose that he took account of the financial circumstances of his converts and prospective converts. Dungan suggests that Paul had been reluctant to make use of his apostolic prerogative in Thessalonica and Corinth because these two congregations were too poor to support him.[349] But this is an improbable explanation. As Holmberg points out, Mediterranean cities such as Corinth were in a flourishing condition, and Paul implies in 2 Cor 8.1–5 that the Macedonians were poorer than the Corinthians.[350]

(2) It is more likely that he refused support from his converts whilst still engaged in evangelism within their own city but felt free to accept financial assistance for work elsewhere.[351] This does not, nevertheless, appear to account adequately for Paul's insistence in 2 Cor 11.9–10 and 12.14–15 that he will never accept aid from the Corinthians.[352] These assertions, especially the first, would surely include the refusal of assistance for evangelism elsewhere.[353]

(3) Perhaps his practice was conditioned by the state of the personal relationship between himself and some particular congregation. He would accept money, only if the relationship was one of mutual trust.[354] In this case there would be an inner consistency in Paul's attitude and practice, but scarcely something that could be communicated to congregations whose assistance he had refused. In the case of Corinth, it could

---

[348] See above, p. 702.

[349] Dungan, Sayings of Jesus, p. 30.

[350] Holmberg, Paul and Power, p. 94; see also P. Marshall, Enmity in Corinth, pp. 233–4.

[351] Plummer, p. 305; Furnish, p. 507.

[352] Horrell, Social Ethos, p. 212.

[353] P. Marshall, Enmity in Corinth, p. 176, comments that 'Corinth, like Philippi, was long established by this time'.

[354] Holmberg, Paul and Power, p. 94.

be that he mistrusted a particularly strong attachment, on the part of the Corinthians, to the Graeco-Roman conventions of benefaction and the kind of relationships which they created.[355] Those who offered the apostle monetary support may have wished to establish themselves as his patrons, so tacitly promoting themselves as his superiors and placing Paul himself under obligation.[356] We may note that his counter-claim of spiritual paternity (2 Cor 12.14) would scarcely have impressed his readers in respect of his consistency. Were not the Christians of Philippi also his spiritual children? He had not, on that account, refused their support. Again, this explanation does not account for his refusal of financial aid for evangelistic work in other areas when he leaves Corinth.

(b) The second and third suggestions above are plausible, and are not mutually exclusive. Both, however, encounter the same obstacle: Paul's downright assertion in 2 Cor 11.9–10 that he will *always* remain financially independent of the Corinthians. This must mean that when he finally leaves Corinth he will not accept assistance from them even for mission in other parts of the Mediterranean world. This would conflict with his policy towards the Christians of Philippi. Hence, there remains at least an apparent inconsistency in his practice.

Perhaps it might be reduced, if not eliminated, in the following ways.

(1) We should consider whether the force and absolute quality of the assertion in 11.9–10 might be in part conditioned by the presence in Corinth of the rival missionaries. Paul needs clearly to distinguish himself from these people and to maintain his superiority. His refusal of financial help is seen as one way of doing this.[357]

(2) Perhaps we should take more notice of the limiting phrase (v. 10) 'in the regions of Achaia'. What does it limit? Does it limit the congregations *from whom* Paul is willing to receive financial assistance? Or does it limit the area *within which* money provided by the Corinthians for further evangelism might be used? If the first, then Corinth is totally excluded from giving him financial support, and the disparity of treatment between Corinth and Philippi remains absolute. If the second, however, Paul does not in principle rule out assistance from the Corinthians for evangelism outside this region. Within it there would be the danger of further trouble from the rival missionaries, and so further reason for his determination to maintain his distinction from them.

(3) Possibly he did not foresee a future situation in which the Corinthians might assist with money for evangelism elsewhere. After he has made his third visit to Corinth he expects to go to Jerusalem with the proceeds of the collection, and then to Rome, *en route* for Spain. The visit to Rome was not for primary evangelism, and if Paul then progressed further west, it would be unrealistic to expect help from Corinth.

(4) It is possible that Paul was not quite so inconsistent as he appears—or as the Corinthians probably thought him to be. There remains a further question. When he eventually arrived in Corinth for the

---

[355] For detailed discussion of these conventions and their relationship to the Corinthian situation see P. Marshall, *Enmity in Corinth*, chap. 6 (pp. 165–258).

[356] Marshall, *Enmity in Corinth*, p. 233; see also Horrell, *Social Ethos*, pp. 203, 213–14.

[357] See above, pp. 690–3.

long-promised third visit, did he maintain his practice of refusing maintenance? According to Acts 20.2–3, he remained 'in Greece', i.e., most probably, in Corinth, for some three months. And in all probability it was here, during this period of time, that he wrote the Epistle to the Romans.[358] Now in Rom 16.23 Paul sends greetings from 'Gaius my host'. This suggests the acceptance of long-term hospitality, and, consequently, something of a change of mind.[359] If his letter in 2 Cor 10–13 had achieved its effect and destroyed the influence of the rival missionaries, and if his close relationship with the Corinthian church was about to be loosened, continuing consistency might have come to seem less important, and a desire to make up differences may have prevailed. In any case, one might still argue for a basic consistency in principle. The Epistle to the Romans is a presentation of Paul's gospel—a means of at least secondary evangelisation—produced with the aid of facilities afforded Paul in Corinth. There is a kind of parallel here with the evangelisation of Corinth with the help of financial provision from Philippi.

(ii) *Presentation of apostolic credentials* (11.16–12.18)

In this extensive section of the letter Paul counters the boasting of the rival missionaries with his own boasting. In many respects it is a paradoxical mirror-image of his opponents' self-glorification, since his conclusion in 12.9 is that what he boasts of are his weaknesses. It is nevertheless not wholly clear that this is consistently the point throughout. Each passage has to be examined to see whether the general principle is carried through.

At this point it will be useful to note the rhetorical structure proposed by Sundermann for the whole section. As we have noted above,[360] it functions as the proof, the *probatio*, which in this analysis forms the second half of the argument of the whole apology of chaps. 10–13. Sundermann divides it further as follows:[361]

11.16–12.18 as argumentatio (b): probatio

insinuatio	11.16–21
propositio	11.22–23a
argumentatio	11.23b–12.10
peroratio	12.11–18

(a) *Renewed plea for toleration of folly* (11.16–21)

[16]Again I say, let no one consider me to be a fool. But if you do, then accept me even as a fool, so that I too may boast a little. [17]What I am

---

[358] See Cranfield, *Romans*, p. 12.
[359] Windisch, p. 337.
[360] See above, p. 655.
[361] Sundermann, *Kraft der Rede*, p. 45.

saying, I am not saying in a Christian way, but as though in a state of folly, in respect of this boasting-project. ¹⁸Since many boast in an unspiritual fashion, I also will boast. ¹⁹For you gladly tolerate the foolish, being wise yourselves. ²⁰For you tolerate it if someone enslaves you, if someone devours you, if someone takes advantage of you, if someone is presumptuous, if someone strikes you in the face. ²¹I say this to my shame. As you say: we have been weak. But in whatever way anyone is bold (I speak foolishly), I too am bold.

Despite Paul's opinion of the rival missionaries as agents of Satan in disguise, he nevertheless finds it necessary to compete with them. Assuming the role of a fool, he will boast as they do. He comments ironically that his correspondents are obviously tolerant of fools, in view of their tolerance of his rivals' behaviour.

11.16–21 as insinuatio
Paul must find a way to gain a hearing, since the congregation has adopted the outlook of the rival missionaries, with the consequence that he cannot appeal directly to his apostolic authority. So he begins with an *insinuatio*: let him at least be heard 'as a fool'.[362] On the surface, appeal is made to a wise audience (φρόνιμοι) to tolerate generously a foolish speaker. Praise of the audience, Sundermann notes, is part of the normal repertoire of introduction. As he also notes, however, it is clear from v. 20 that the praise is highly ironical.[363] Does this, perhaps, tell against the definition of this passage as an *insinuatio*? Ironical praise would be unlikely to induce a favourable attitude on the part of the audience.[364] It might, of course, grip their attention.

Whether v. 21b is part of this exordium or should be attached as a heading to what follows is debatable. Sundermann opts for the former alternative, drawing attention to the resumption of the τις of v. 20.[365] Moreover, the promise (or threat) of bold conduct clearly contrasts with the acknowledgement of weakness in v. 21a, and thus connects the two halves of the verse. At the same time, however, v. 21b provides a suitable introduction to vv. 22–23. As Sundermann allows, the majority of exegetes understand it in this sense.[366]

16. Πάλιν λέγω, μή τις με δόξῃ ἄφρονα εἶναι· εἰ δὲ μή γε, κἄν ὡς ἄφρονα δέξασθέ με, ἵνα κἀγὼ μικρόν τι καυχήσωμαι. This verse clearly points the reader back to v. 1: there is the plea

---

[362] Sundermann, *Kraft der Rede*, p. 119.
[363] Sundermann, *Kraft der Rede*, p. 127.
[364] See LS s.v. insinuatio II.A. The word signifies 'ingratiating oneself' into other people's favour.
[365] Sundermann, *Kraft der Rede*, p. 129.
[366] Sundermann, ibid.

for tolerance, and also the repetition of the phrase μικρόν τι.[367] Paul resumes the Fool's Speech proper (vv. 1–5/6[368]), from which he had diverged somewhat in vv. 7–15, and which in fact he had in substance scarcely begun, since it is only in vv. 5–6 that he makes personal claims which could be related to the boasting which he now proposes to engage in, but which he realises to be foolishness. Martin argues that in this verse and those which follow we have a direct connection with 10.13–18, claiming, as we have seen,[369] that 11.1–15 is a digression. In 11.16ff, as in the earlier section, the issue is the question of legitimate mission; the κατὰ κύριον of 11.17 looks back to 10.17; and in 11.16–21a, as in 10.13–18, the καυχάομαι/καύχησις word-group is frequent.[370] The question of apostolic legitimacy in Corinth, however, has been raised, in all probability, in v. 12,[371] and could be seen as implicit in vv. 4–5. And in v. 12, also, the verb καυχάομαι is used in relation to this same issue. The thought of boasting κατὰ κύριον (or not) is certainly reminiscent of 10.17, but this is not in itself sufficient to mark off the whole of 11.1–15 as a digression.

Although there is clearly a general connection with v. 1, its precise logic is not altogether obvious. In fact, the two verses may appear to contradict each other: in v. 1 Paul begs tolerance of his folly, whilst in v.16 he urges his readers not to regard him as a fool.[372] Hence, the opening πάλιν λέγω, whilst indicating the connection, seems scarcely accurate. It may, however, relate simply to the repeated request for toleration. The more basic difficulty is perhaps to be resolved by means of the suggestion that in v. 16 Paul wishes to indicate that the character of 'fool' is only a role he is playing.[373] Zmijewski sees v. 16a as a kind of 'headline' for what follows, showing the reader how it is to be understood.[374] Should the readers, however, fail to grasp this somewhat subtle point,[375] they are urged even so to accept the Paul they will regard

[367] Wolff, p. 225.
[368] Verse 6 is attached in sense to v. 5 but forms also a loose link to the theme of vv. 7–11: Paul takes up (v. 7) a further Corinthian complaint, in addition to the charge (v. 6) that he is deficient in rhetoric.
[369] See above, p. 654.
[370] Martin, pp. 360–1.
[371] See above, pp. 691–3.
[372] Plummer, p. 313; Windisch, p. 344.
[373] Windisch, ibid.; Bultmann, pp. 211–12. Perhaps also, as we have suggested in commenting on v. 1, he wishes to stress the point because his rivals have termed him a fool. See above, p. 658.
[374] Zmijewski, 'Narrenrede', pp. 193–4.
[375] The possibility is indicated by means of the only Pauline occurrence of εἰ δὲ μή γε (as noted by Plummer, p. 314). The literal meaning is 'but if not', i.e., 'but otherwise'. Strictly, it is an instance of ellipsis in which the verb of the εἰ-clause is left to be supplied. See BDR 376(2), 439(1), and 480(6). This is brought out in the rendering proposed by Furnish, p. 484: 'But should it be otherwise.' It may be,

as (a real) fool,[376] so as to allow also to him[377] some small measure[378] of boasting. The connection Paul makes between boasting and foolishness is scarcely surprising. Already in 1 Cor 1.31 and in 2 Cor 10.17 he has quoted Jeremiah, to show that the only permissible, and therefore right-minded, boasting is boasting of the Lord. To boast about personal advantages or achievements is, in consequence, foolishness. From the Greek standpoint, also, self-praise is a suspect activity.[379] Betz, whilst allowing that Paul's attitude is in line with the OT and with Jewish ways of thinking on the matter of boasting, regards the Greek background as of considerable significance. What the apostle has in mind, he argues, is the familiar Greek concept of ἀλαζονεία, 'false pretension', 'boast-fulness',[380] 'arrogance',[381] and of the ἀλαζών, the 'braggart', 'charlatan'.[382] The latter was a stock character in Attic comedy.[383] And the ἀλαζών, Betz claims, was also regarded as the (man who was) ἄφρων. Hence (so the argument appears to run), when Paul speaks of taking on the character of the fool, it is this notion of the braggart (ἀλαζών) and his arrogance (ἀλαζονεία) that he has in mind.[384] This suggestion might further explain what Paul sees to be the logical connection between foolishness and boasting, if further explanation should be necessary. Betz has to admit, however, that Paul does not, here, use the ἀλαζ- wordgroup

however, that the phrase has become something of a stereotyped formula, in which the omission of an expected verb has been lost to view. See BDR 480(6).

[376] The κἂν ὡς ἄφρονα is seen by some exegetes as elliptical. Thus, Meyer, p. 440, followed by Plummer, p. 313, would suppose the full sentence to be: δέξασθέ με, καὶ ἐὰν ὡς ἄφρονα δέξησθέ με ('Receive me, even if you receive me as a fool'). Moule, *Idiom Book*, p. 151, suggests: δέξασθέ με, καὶ ἐὰν ἢ μόνον ὡς ἄφρονα ('Receive me, even if it be only as a fool'). Zmijewski, '*Narrenrede*', p. 191, however, thinks it equally possible that the κἂν may function as a mere particle, 'at least'.

[377] As Plummer, p. 314, notes, the κἀγώ shows that it is not Paul who has initiated the boasting.

[378] The μικρόν τι is taken by Barrett, pp. 288, 289, to mean 'for a little while'. He allows, however, that in v. 1 it is quantitative, 'some small amount', and that it could have the same meaning here. This is more probable: so Furnish, p. 484, and Martin, p. 356. The latter, p. 362, sees the expression as an example of litotes, 'chosen to poke fun (by understatement) at the large claims the adversaries were making'.

[379] Bultmann, p. 212, however, sees some difference in motivation, suggesting that for the Greeks self-praise was suspect because it was damaging to one's dignity and proper reserve. See also Forbes, 'Comparison', pp. 8–10.

[380] LSJ s.v. ἀλαζονεία.

[381] BAGD s.v. ἀλαζονεία.

[382] LSJ s.v. ἀλαζών II.; BAGD s.v. ἀλαζών 1.

[383] See F. M. Cornford, *The Origin of Attic Comedy*, London, 1914, pp. 136–7. Betz, *Tradition*, p. 79 n. 244, refers to this work.

[384] Betz, *Tradition*, pp. 74–5.

(although he does use ἀλαζών in Rom 1.30).³⁸⁵ Nor is the one specific example he gives of the equation of the ἄφρων with the ἀλαζών altogether convincing.³⁸⁶ He goes on to suggest that the form of the Fool's Speech may have come to Paul via popular philosophy. The platonic Socrates plays the role of an ignorant person, and we have an example of such a discourse in the speech of Alcibiades in the *Symposium*.³⁸⁷ As Barrett rightly remarks, however, this is 'at best an extremely remote parallel'.³⁸⁸ Moreover, it is not clear whether Betz is altogether consistent in his analysis of Paul's Greek background. He claims, on the one hand, that the fool is the ἀλαζών, and, on the other hand, that the platonic Socrates plays the role of the fool. This should mean, then, that Socrates himself is the ἀλαζών. But he is surely portrayed as the direct opposite, i.e., as the εἴρων, the ironical man. The difference, to quote Cornford, is that the ἀλαζών 'claims to possess higher qualities than he has', whilst the εἴρων 'is given to making himself out worse than he is'.³⁸⁹ Finally, as Heckel has pointed out, we need to query the suggestion, implicit or explicit in the work of numerous exegetes, that Paul does present himself as playing the dramatic part of the fool, or as adopting the fool's mask, as though in the theatre.³⁹⁰ It is extremely questionable whether Paul knew the Greek theatre at all in its obscene form of the mime, to which Windisch, followed by others, refers in this context,³⁹¹ or would have imitated it if he did. It is suspicious that none of the Fathers understood him in this sense.³⁹²

17. ὃ λαλῶ οὐ κατὰ κύριον³⁹³ λαλῶ, ἀλλ᾽ ὡς ἐν ἀφροσύνῃ, ἐν

---

³⁸⁵ Betz, *Tradition*, p. 74, n. 210.
³⁸⁶ He refers (p. 75 n. 211) to an incident related by Plutarch (*Mor.* 419B–C). In the course of a discussion of demigods, one of the participants tells a story about a voice heard proclaiming the death of the 'Great Pan', and says he heard the story from a man who was 'neither foolish nor boastful': ἀκήκοα λόγον ἀνδρὸς οὐκ ἄφρονος οὐδ᾽ ἀλαζόνος. But this does not totally identify the two qualities. One may be foolish without being boastful.
³⁸⁷ Betz, *Tradition*, pp. 80–2.
³⁸⁸ Barrett, p. 290.
³⁸⁹ Cornford, *Attic Comedy*, p. 137, with reference to Arist., *NE* IV vii 2: δοκεῖ δὴ ὁ μὲν ἀλαζὼν προσποιητικὸς τῶν ἐνδόξων εἶναι καὶ μὴ ὑπαρχόντων καὶ μειζόνων ἢ ὑπάρχει, ὁ δὲ εἴρων ἀνάπαλιν ἀρνεῖσθαι τὰ ὑπάρχοντα ἢ ἐλάττω ποιεῖν. ('As generally understood then, the boaster is a man who pretends to creditable qualities that he does not possess, or possesses in a lesser degree than he makes out, while conversely the self-depreciator disclaims or disparages good qualities that he does possess' LCL.)
³⁹⁰ Heckel, *Schwachheit*, p. 194.
³⁹¹ Windisch, p. 316; Betz, *Tradition*, pp. 79–82; Wolff, pp. 208–9; Heckel, ibid., nn. 161–2, notes these exegetes and others.
³⁹² Heckel, *Schwachheit*, p. 194.
³⁹³ In place of κύριον, θεόν is read by a few witnesses (a f r t vg^cl Ambst Pel), possibly owing to an unconscious substitution of one divine name for another. The peculiar reading ἄνθρωπον (69) is not easy to account for, but is obviously wrong.

ταύτῃ τῇ ὑποστάσει τῆς καυχήσεως. With reference to what he is about to say,[394] Paul continues to insist that boasting is fundamentally foolish. Negatively, it is not κατὰ κύριον. The preposition κατά, followed by the accusative of the person, indicates that something is done, or occurs, in accordance with the 'will, pleasure, or manner' of that person.[395] Hence, the present phrase could mean, '(not) according to the Lord's will', i.e., 'not on the Lord's authority'.[396] But since Paul must have believed that it was with Christ's authority that he defended his own apostolic standing in Corinth (whatever may have been the means he found it necessary to employ), this is perhaps a less probable interpretation. Alternatively, the κατὰ κύριον could mean 'in the manner of the Lord'. Would Paul then have in mind the thought that one who is 'in the Lord', i.e., one who has died with Christ, can boast no longer?[397] Possibly.[398] But it may well be that no great theological weight is to be attached to the phrase, and that it means simply 'not in a Christian way'.[399] Nevertheless, this still means that from the Christian standpoint Paul will be speaking in a foolish way. And yet in the very process of expressing this thought he appears to qualify it, since he says 'as though (ὡς) in a state of folly'.[400] Why the ὡς? He surely does regard his prospective boasting as folly. It may be, however, that whilst this is so, he knows that his underlying purpose is by no means foolish, in that he intends to show up the folly of his rivals and to re-establish his own authority. Barrett, who draws attention to the ὡς, pertinently comments: 'Paul does not find it easy to make clear how far he is serious, how far ironical.'[401] Heckel similarly provides an analysis of Paul's thought in respect of boasting. In one sense, in the Fool's Speech, he is engaged in folly. Formally speaking, he indulges in egocentric boasting of his own qualities, rather than boasting of the Lord, as enjoined by Jeremiah (9.23–24). But the content of his boasting consists of his weaknesses. And in 12.9 such boasts are christologically grounded, and thus become boasting κατὰ κύριον, after all. This is indicated in the present verse by the ὡς preceding ἐν ἀφροσύνῃ. A final twist is given to Heckel's exegesis by the claim that the

394 Cf. Windisch, p. 345; Furnish, p. 511.
395 BAGD s.v. κατά II.5.a.α.
396 Martin, p. 356; cf. Barrett, p. 290; Heckel, *Schwachheit*, pp. 194–5.
397 Bultmann, p. 212, with reference to 5.12ff. and Phil 3.7ff. See also Gal 3.14.
398 Furnish, p. 485, takes up in his translation the thought of existence in Christ: 'not as one in the Lord'. He sees the point of the phrase, however, as related to that of v. 18, commenting, p. 496, that 'the subject itself is a "worldly" one'.
399 REB has 'not … like a Christian'.
400 See BAGD s.v. ὡς III.3., where the present verse is given as an example of ὡς as indicating 'a quality wrongly claimed, in any case objectively false'.
401 Barrett, p. 290.

apostle's boasting of weakness is intended as a parody of the self-praise of the rival missionaries.[402] In 12.9b, though, it is related to the overshadowing of the power of Christ. Is this compatible with the suggestion of parody? Furthermore, we shall see that the interpretation of the hardships catalogue may not be altogether straightforward.

The chief exegetical problem in the present verse, however, lies in the meaning of ὑπόστασις in the final phrase.[403] The older exegesis took the sense to be 'confidence',[404] and this interpretation is followed by Barrett, who translates the whole phrase, 'in this boastful confidence'.[405] We have seen, however, in discussing the use of the same word in 9.4, that there is little or no evidence for this rendering (now omitted in BAGD, by contrast with BAG).[406] There is some support for the meaning 'matter',[407] although Köster claims that ὑπόστασις has no such sense.[408] And in the present instance, though not in 9.4, the rendering 'situation' would fit tolerably well,[409] as would 'frame of mind'.[410] The best option, however, may be 'plan', 'project', 'intention'.[411] We have followed Köster in adopting this rendering in 9.4, noting that it would fit the present instance as well.[412]

18. ἐπεὶ πολλοὶ καυχῶνται κατὰ[413] σάρκα, κἀγὼ καυχήσομαι. Boasting may be foolish, but Paul is forced to engage in it because his rivals do. Here they are designated πολλοί. Possibly this could be an allusion to their numbers, or could indicate the gravity of the danger (in Paul's view) which they posed.[414] It is more probable, however, that the word is used as a form of contemptuous reference, with the intention of disparaging the

---

[402] Heckel, *Schwachheit*, pp. 194–5, 202–3.

[403] See Zmijewski, *'Narrenrede'*, p. 199, for a list of various suggested interpretations.

[404] So, e.g., Meyer, p. 441; Plummer, p. 314; R. E. Witt, 'ΥΠΟΣΤΑΣΙΣ', p. 330.

[405] Barrett, p. 288; see also Savage, *Power through Weakness*, p. 57; Barnett, p. 530.

[406] See above, pp. 568–70.

[407] Rückert, p. 343; Windisch, p. 346, and Allo, pp. 289–90 see this as one possibility; Furnish, p. 496, supports either this or 'project'.

[408] Köster, on ὑπόστασις, in *TWNT* VIII, p. 583 n. 120.

[409] BAGD s.v. ὑπόστασις 2.

[410] BAGD ibid., citing 2 Cor 9.4; 11.17; Jos., *Ant.* XVIII 24.

[411] Bachmann, p. 379, with reference to Diod. Sic. XVI 32.3; Zmijewski, *'Narrenrede'*, p. 199; Furnish, p. 496, notes 'project' as an alternative to 'matter'.

[412] See above, pp. 568–70, The ἐν which introduces the phrase may have causal force, with reference to the preceding ἐν ἀφροσύνῃ.

[413] Some witnesses (ℵ² B D¹ H Ψ 0121a 𝔐) read τὴν before σάρκα. Paul's invariable usage elsewhere, when using κατά followed by σάρκα, is to omit the article. Hence, the alternative reading (𝔓⁴⁶ ℵ* D* F G 098. 33. 81. 104. 365. 629. 1175. 1739.* 1881.* 2495 *al*) is probably original. See Wolff, pp. 226–7.

[414] Martin, p. 363.

people thus designated.[415] They boast κατὰ σάρκα. Some exegetes take this as an allusion to the content of the opponents' boasting: external advantages such as wealth, birth, or ancestry;[416] human achievements,[417] or 'outward display' and charismatic demonstrations.[418] Others refer the phrase to the manner of boasting. It is in opposition to the κατὰ κύριον of v. 17 and hence in parallel to the ἐν ἀφροσύνῃ of that verse.[419] Zmijewski points out that it is only the beginning of the following boastful discourse which mentions external advantages such as ancestry. If the phrase refers to the manner of boasting, it will denote an egocentric attitude leading to self-praise, and the boast itself can then have diverse contents, including 'spiritual' as well as material advantages.[420] On linguistic grounds the second alternative is preferable,[421] but the difference between them is not so very great, since the one virtually implies the other.[422]

19. ἡδέως γὰρ ἀνέχεσθε τῶν ἀφρόνων φρόνιμοι ὄντες. After a brief parenthesis in vv. 17-18, Paul provides a reason for his plea δέξασθέ με in v. 16.[423] His readers do, after all, gladly tolerate fools, since they are wise themselves.[424] Here he is widely regarded as speaking ironically. He neither thinks of the Corinthians as wise nor wishes to compliment them on their wisdom.[425] And what he speaks of as their ready 'tolerance' of 'the foolish' he knows to be, in reality, a hearty welcome given to rivals[426] whom the Corinthians themselves in no way thought of as

---

[415] Furnish, pp. 496, 511; Zmijewski, 'Narrenrede', p. 202; cf. P. Marshall, *Enmity in Corinth*, p. 344 (Furnish, p. 511, refers to Marshall's original thesis) See also our discussion of οἱ πολλοί in 2.17 (Vol. I, pp. 210–11).

[416] Chrysostom, *PG* 61 col. 565 (NPNF XII, p. 391).

[417] Windisch, p. 346; cf. Allo, p. 290.

[418] Martin, p. 363; Barnett, p. 531, suggests that they boast 'in regard to the elements of ministry in which they regard themselves as "superior" to Paul'.

[419] Meyer, p. 442, arguing against Chrysostom.

[420] Zmijewski, 'Narrenrede', pp. 203–4.

[421] The phrase is used adverbially. When the verb καυχάομαι has an expressed object this is indicated either by ἐν τινι or else by the plain accusative. Hence, in the present case we should expect either ἐν σαρκί or τὰ τῆς σαρκός.

[422] Cf. Bultmann, p. 213. To boast in a self-centred way is to boast of one's own qualities and achievements, and *vice versa*. The concept of boasting in itself suggests both. Note that in the present context boasting of spiritual gifts is included under the first head by Martin and under the second by Zmijewski.

[423] Zmijewski, 'Narrenrede', p. 205.

[424] The verb ἀνέχεσθε is to be taken as indicative, with Zmijewski, ibid., and most commentators. Bachmann, p. 380, takes it as imperative, but this makes little or no sense of the introductory γάρ. The participle ὄντες probably has causal force: see Zmijewski, 'Narrenrede', p. 208; cf. Plummer, p. 315.

[425] Plummer, ibid., singles out the φρόνιμοι ὄντες as a marked example of irony. See also Furnish, pp. 497, 511.

[426] Barnett, p. 532, supposes that Paul is referring to toleration of himself. But v. 20, explanatory of v. 19, clearly refers to the rival missionaries.

'fools'.[427] But it may be that those who heard the letter read would not become fully aware of the irony until they had heard what follows.

20. ἀνέχεσθε γὰρ εἴ τις ὑμᾶς καταδουλοῖ, εἴ τις κατεσθίει, εἴ τις λαμβάνει, εἴ τις ἐπαίρεται, εἴ τις εἰς πρόσωπον ὑμᾶς δέρει. 'Wise' as they are, they 'tolerate' forms of behaviour which sensible people would regard as intolerable.[428] Paul's itemising of it in strong language reveals the irony of his previous description of his readers as φρόνιμοι. The perpetrators of this regrettable behaviour are obviously the rival missionaries.[429] Metaphorically, these people 'enslave' the Corinthian congregation, enforcing their own authority on the church.[430] They thus act in marked contrast to Paul's own behaviour (as he himself sees it, at least), as described in 1.24 and 4.5.[431] And they 'devour' the Corinthians, 'eat them up'. This may well be an allusion to the opponents' acceptance of maintenance. Barrett translates: 'eats you out of house and home'.[432] Or it could refer simply to aggressive behaviour, as it does in Gal 5.15,[433] or to exploitation in some more general sense.[434] But in view of the importance which the financial issue had come to assume, it does seem very probable that financial exploitation is in Paul's mind. Exploitation in some less specific sense may be intended in the following assertion. The verb λαμβάνω, however, has a number of possible senses, and gives rise to various interpretations. Perhaps the λαμβάνει is in effect a repetition of κατεσθίει, both verbs being used in the sense of the appropriation of property.[435] But since the items in the list of charges are not precisely synonymous, it would be better to make some distinction between them. Does this occurrence of λαμβάνω, then, mean 'lay violent hands upon'?[436] This is lexically

---

[427] Zmijewski, '*Narrenrede*', p. 209, sees the combination of the normally positive ἡδέως with the normally negative ἀνέχεσθε as producing an effect of 'estrangement' which gives prominence to the irony.

[428] As Windisch, p. 347, notes, this is not a question of Christian forbearance towards personal enemies (Mt 5.38–44; Rom 12.20): Paul's readers regard these people as authorities, not as enemies.

[429] The singular τις is collective in sense: see Zmijewski, '*Narrenrede*', p. 208.

[430] The same verb is used in Gal 2.4 of the 'false brothers' who attempted to put an end to the freedom from the Mosaic law enjoyed by Paul's Gentile converts, and Barrett, p. 291, suggests that a Judaizing policy may lie in the background in the present verse as well. But Judaizing as such is not the problem in Corinth.

[431] The contrast is noted by Barrett, p. 291; Bultmann, p. 213, and Martin, p. 364, refer to 1.24.

[432] Barrett, p. 288; see also p. 291. Other commentators who see this as a possibility include: Plummer, p. 316; Bultmann, p. 213; Furnish, p. 497; Martin, p. 365; Wolff, p. 227.

[433] Barrett, p. 291, allows this as an alternative.

[434] Furnish, p. 497, thinks this a possibility.

[435] Allo, p. 290.

[436] C. Lattey, 'λαμβάνειν in 2 Cor. xi. 20', *JTS* 44 (1943), p. 148.

possible.⁴³⁷ But, first, it would mean that this item would be virtually identical with the final charge (which in this case would naturally be understood literally), and, secondly, it would not fit what appears to be a similar use of λαμβάνω in 12.16, since to use violence is not the same as to employ trickery. Barrett translates the clause: 'if anyone gets you in his power'.⁴³⁸ This, however, is equivalent to the initial 'if anyone enslaves you'. The best interpretation, in our view, is proposed in BAGD, where it is noted that one meaning of λαμβάνω is 'catch', in relation to hunting and fishing, as in Lk 5.5. This sense can then become figurative: 'take someone in', 'take advantage of someone'.⁴³⁹ This would fit the comparable use of the verb in 12.16.⁴⁴⁰

The next item in the list presents no problem. The Corinthians 'tolerate' a person if he 'is presumptuous', 'puts on airs' (ἐπαίρεται).⁴⁴¹ The last item, however, requires more discussion. Whilst the rival missionaries could scarcely 'enslave' the Corinthians in a legal sense, they could, literally, 'strike them in the face'. Does Paul mean that this was happening? Or is he speaking figuratively? It is difficult to know. Chrysostom supports a figurative interpretation: Paul simply means that his opponents dishonoured the Corinthians.⁴⁴² In the same way, when, in 1 Cor 4.21, he asks his readers whether they would like him to arrive ἐν ῥάβδῳ, 'with a stick', he scarcely means that he would then inflict corporal punishment on them.⁴⁴³ Other commentators, however, think it likely that it is actual physical violence that is in view. Perhaps the rival missionaries do strike the Corinthians as they would strike a slave.⁴⁴⁴ It may not have been unusual for those in ecclesiastical authority to have people struck on the mouth for impious utterances. See Acts 23.2; and compare 1 Tim 3.3 and Tit 1.7.⁴⁴⁵ Nevertheless, in view of the Corinthians' own basic

---

⁴³⁷ See LSJ s.v. λαμβάνω I. 1. b., 'take by violence'.
⁴³⁸ Barrett, p. 288.
⁴³⁹ BAGD s.v. λαμβάνω 1. c. This is the meaning given for the verb in the present verse.
⁴⁴⁰ Plummer, p. 316, and Hughes, p. 400, think that the idea is that of catching or ensnaring. And in BAGD s.v. 1. c. the meaning given for the verb in 12.16 is 'catch someone by a trick'.
⁴⁴¹ See BAGD s.v. ἐπαίρω 2.b.β.
⁴⁴² Chrysostom, PG 61 col. 566 (NPNF XII, p. 392)
⁴⁴³ Windisch, p. 347, notes this parallel, and its possible significance for the exegesis of the present verse. Other supporters of a figurative sense in the latter include: Tasker, p. 158; Bultmann, p. 213; Zmijewski, 'Narrenrede', p. 212; Furnish, p. 497; and Wolff, p. 228.
⁴⁴⁴ Allo, pp. 290–1.
⁴⁴⁵ Hughes, p. 400. Martin, p. 365, likewise thinks it nearly certain that an actual physical blow is implied. He allows, however, that Paul may be using a vivid image for 'the insult that was like a blow'. He then refers to a passage in Philostratus

self-esteem (1 Cor 4.6–10), it does seem improbable that they would really have tolerated this kind of behaviour. In addition, we probably need to recognise that Paul is presenting something of an exaggerated parody of his rivals' conduct.[446] Consequently, even if he should half-intend a literal reference when he speaks of striking in the face, it is unlikely that he really thought that this was what his rivals were doing.

21a. κατὰ ἀτιμίαν λέγω, ὡς ὅτι ἡμεῖς ἠσθενήκαμεν.[447] After his ironical description of his readers' 'wisdom' in 'tolerating' the overbearing behaviour of the rival missionaries, Paul turns back again to his personal defence, with a deprecating comment which itself most probably contains some degree of further irony. Its nature and extent, however, is not entirely easy to determine. There are three questions to be considered. (i) To whose ἀτιμία is Paul referring? (ii) What is the force of the ὡς ὅτι, and how is it related to the preceding λέγω? (iii) What are the connotations of ἠσθενήκαμεν, and does it express the Corinthians' view or his own view of himself?

(i) Paul is saying (or has just been saying) something 'to (someone's) shame'.[448] Chrysostom supposes that it is the Corinthians' disgrace that is in view: they have no excuse for their shameful toleration of the rival missionaries.[449] Similarly, Lietzmann supposes that Paul is responding to his readers' criticisms of his own weakness. Let them look at what the powerful impact of his opponents really amounts to, and let them be ashamed.[450] It is more natural, however, to suppose that the 'disgrace' is Paul's.[451] Otherwise, one would need the addition of ὑμῶν,[452] and the ἡμεῖς in the following clause indicates that the apostle has himself in view.[453]

---

where such an image occurs. The speaker is talking about the suspicion raised by a person's excessive wealth. It is thought to engender insolence, and it hinders obedience to provincial rulers: 'they say indeed that it is very nearly tantamount to giving them a box on the ears (μόνον οὐκ ἐπὶ κόρρης παίει), because they grovel to wealthy men ...' (LCL); see Philostr., *Vit. Ap.* (*Life of Apollonius*) VII 23. The passage was previously noted by Lietzmann, p. 149, with reference to Heinrici, *Das zweite Sendschreiben*, p. 466 n. 4., who comments, on ἐπὶ κόρρης παίει, 'wie einem Sklaven'. Barnett, p. 533, thinks that the allusion may be literal.

446 Zmijewski, '*Narrenrede*', p. 230; Furnish, p. 511.
447 The reading ἠσθενήκαμεν has good support ($\mathfrak{P}^{46}$ ℵ B H 0243. 33. 81. 1175. 1739*. 1881 *pc*). The alternative ἠσθενήσαμεν (D F G I^vid Ψ 0121a 𝔐) is probably secondary, and the result of scribal error.
448 For the use of κατά in this phrase, see BAGD s.v. II.4.
449 Chrysostom, *PG* 61 col. 566 (NPNF XII, p. 392).
450 Lietzmann, p. 149.
451 Windisch, p. 348.
452 Plummer, p. 317; Kümmel, p. 211.
453 Zmijewski, '*Narrenrede*', p. 213. Others who see the ἀτιμία as Paul's include Bachmann, p. 381, Allo, p. 290, Furnish, p. 497, and Martin, p. 366.

(ii) The force of the ὡς ὅτι is more difficult to determine. There are various possibilities. First, one might regard the ὡς as dominant, and as possessing a causal sense, as though Paul had written ὡς ἡμῶν ἀσθενησάντων, '*since* we have been weak'.[454] Or, again with ὡς as dominant, the sense could be '*as if* we have been weak'.[455] Either of these renderings has the advantage of separating the ὡς ὅτι clause from the preceding κατὰ ἀτιμίαν λέγω (see below). But the dominance of ὡς would perhaps seem somewhat strange, in view of the fact that in later Greek ὡς ὅτι becomes simply the equivalent of ὅτι.[456] The second possibility is to take ὡς ὅτι as directly dependent on the preceding λέγω, and thus as introducing indirect speech: 'to my shame I say *that* we have been weak'.[457] This interpretation has more support.[458] Some who adopt it feel the need to give some specific value to the ὡς-component also. Thus, Furnish translates: 'I am ashamed to say that we seem to have been weaklings in comparison.'[459] He comments that the 'seem to have been' is intended as an attempt to represent the force of ὡς.[460] This second option would fit better with the later use of ὡς ὅτι. But there are stylistic difficulties. Bachmann points out that whilst Paul frequently uses formulations similar to the present κατὰ ἀτιμίαν λέγω (i.e., short phrases with λέγω or λαλῶ as the verb, combined with a prepositional phrase), he never attaches a subordinate declarative clause.[461] Neither option, then, is wholly satisfactory. But there is a further possibility. This same combination of ὡς with ὅτι has occurred previously in 5.19. In our exegesis of that verse we took ὡς to mean 'as', assumed an ellipsis of a verb of saying between ὡς and ὅτι, and interpreted ὅτι as recitative.[462] This is how Furnish translates in 5.19: 'As it is said:'[463] The reason that he does not adopt the same rendering in the present verse seems to be that in explaining 5.19 he accepts the view that Paul is quoting

---

[454] Bultmann, p. 214, allows this as a possibility; see also Bachmann, pp. 381–2, and Wolff, p. 228. For this function of ὡς, see BAGD s.v. III.1.b.

[455] See BAGD s.v. ὅτι 1.d.β., where it is noted that the Vulgate renders ὡς ὅτι here as 'quasi'.

[456] Moulton, *Prolegomena*, p. 212; and see other references in Vol. I, p. 432 n. 1683.

[457] This is the interpretation suggested in BAGD s.v. ὅτι 1.d.β.

[458] See, e.g., Plummer, p. 317; Kümmel, p. 211; Hughes, p. 401 n. 68; Barrett, pp. 176, 288; Zmijewski, '*Narrenrede*', pp. 214–15; Furnish, p. 485.

[459] Furnish, p. 485.

[460] Furnish, p. 498. Zmijewski, '*Narrenrede*', p. 215, comments that the ὡς indicates the presence of a subjective 'self-assessment', which is at the same time an ironical agreement with a judgement emanating from the opponents or the congregation. See also Hughes, p. 401 n. 68.

[461] Bachmann, p. 381.

[462] See Vol. I, pp. 431–2.

[463] Furnish, p. 306.

'previously formulated material',[464] which would not be the case here. We would suggest, however, that the apostle could very well be citing what he has been told the Corinthians are saying about him. The force of v. 21a would then be: 'I can say it to my shame. As you say: we have been weak.'[465]

(iii) The division of opinion on the interpretation of ἠσθεν-ήκαμεν turns on the question of whether Paul is reproducing the Corinthians' opinion of him or whether he uses the verb in his own sense. In favour of the first possibility, one could argue that there is a back reference to the assertion in 10.10 that the apostle's personal presence is ἀσθενής.[466] In our exegesis of this verse we have argued that this may be an allusion to physical infirmity, but that basically it refers to weakness of personality, and want of the power of the Spirit.[467] This is what some representative critic has been saying about Paul,[468] and he may have it in mind in the present verse. The alternative is to suppose that we are to understand 'weakness' as Paul himself understands it, i.e., as it is later presented in 12.10. In this case, real weakness is in fact strength in the highest degree. Zmijewski prefers this interpretation, on the ground that it fits the present chapter better: Paul is concerned here with a defence of true apostleship, and the characteristic of the genuine apostle is precisely his 'being weak in the Lord'.[469] I suspect, however, that this is an over-simplification of Paul's rather complex form of defence. Eventually he does intend to show his readers that true strength derives from the power of Christ, and reaches its perfection in the context of human weakness (12.8–10; cf. 4.7). But in vv. 21b–22 he boasts boldly (though foolishly) that he himself possesses the marks of religious status, and hence 'strength', claimed by the rival missionaries. Moreover, the purport of vv. 23–27 is also somewhat ambiguous, in that, viewed from one perspective, Paul's trials could be seen to indicate his (own) superior strength, since he has, after all,

---

[464] Furnish, pp. 317–18, 334. We have not accepted that interpretation (see Vol. I, pp. 448–9).

[465] Barnett, p. 533 n. 23, regards ὡς ὅτι as introducing a quotation of what the opponents are saying.

[466] See, e.g., Bachmann, p. 381; Plummer, p. 317; Hughes, p. 401.

[467] See above, p. 631. Prümm, *Diakonia Pneumatos* I, p. 636, suggests that there is a specific reference in the present verse to Paul's interim visit to Corinth. Zmijewski, 'Narrenrede', p. 215, rejects this view, on the grounds that the perfect tense of ἠσθενήκαμεν precludes an allusion to any specific event. But the accusation of weakness evoked initially by a particular occasion might have been applied more widely, to cover Paul's conduct *vis-à-vis* the Corinthians in general.

[468] This critic, we have suggested, was probably a member of the rival mission, present, in advance of the others, at the time of Paul's interim visit: see above, pp. 629–30.

[469] Zmijewski, 'Narrenrede', pp. 216–17.

overcome them.[470] If, then, in the context, Paul appears to be claiming 'strength' in the Corinthian sense, it is probable that in v. 21a he talks of 'weakness' in their sense as well.

What, then, are we to make of this half-verse as a whole? It may be best seen as spoken from the Corinthian viewpoint. Paul expresses awareness of his own disgrace, disgrace on the grounds (he confesses) that *he* has been a weak character (by comparison, obviously, with the rival missionaries). But what are his readers to make of his confession, after the way he has expressed himself in v. 20? His derogatory description of his opponents' conduct must surely serve as a warning that he cannot seriously mean that his failure to imitate them is a matter of shame. In *this* respect, at least, he must be speaking ironically. He is thus giving a signal that, in what follows, any apparent compliance with Corinthian criteria of apostleship is only limited and provisional.

21b. Ἐν ᾧ δ᾽ ἄν τις τολμᾷ, ἐν ἀφροσύνῃ λέγω, τολμῶ κἀγώ. He begins to turn, nevertheless, to some of these criteria, repeating, in substance, what he has said in v. 18, i.e., that he is going to boast—make bold claims for himself.[471] In this he can match any of his rivals,[472] in whatever aspect of apostolic life and character the boasting may relate to.[473] But why does he use the verb τολμάω instead of the previous καυχάομαι? It may be simply because here, as in 10.2, he is in confrontation with his rivals. Hence, although the grammatical idiom is different (here, the absolute use of the verb, by contrast with 10.2 where it is followed by ἐπί with the accusative), the same sense of underlying conflict may have evoked the use of the same verb. There might be a further possibility also. As we have seen,[474] τολμάω can be used in both a good and a bad sense, and it could be that in the present instance it is used ironically.[475] This would mean that Paul would

---

[470] See below, pp. 755, 758. In addition, in 10.10–11 Paul warns that what the Corinthians regard as his weakness will be replaced, at his next visit, by powerful action, which presumably will be powerful from *their* viewpoint.

[471] Windisch, p. 350.

[472] The τις recalls the repeated τις of v. 20 (Windisch, p. 350), and consequently refers to the rival missionaries in Corinth. Barrett, pp. 292–3, argues, however, that at this point 'Paul's thought has moved beyond his immediate rivals ... to those who stand behind them and whose authority (rightly or wrongly) they appear to have claimed'. The latter group Barrett identifies as the Jerusalem apostles (see p. 294). But this is highly unlikely. As Furnish, p. 533, comments, there is no hint in the context that any group other than the people mentioned in v. 20 is in view here.

[473] Windisch, p. 350: the ἐν ᾧ indicates the sphere in which the daring is exercised. The following ἄν generalises the claim. Hence, it is doubtful whether Zmijewski, *'Narrenrede'*, p. 232 n. 10, is correct when he says that the full form of the expression would be ἐν τούτῳ ἐν ᾧ.

[474] See the exegesis of 10.2, and the note on the different uses of τολμάω in classical and hellenistic literature.

[475] Betz, *Tradition*, p. 67, claims that Paul is speaking ironically here, but does not explain precisely how the irony should be understood.

be castigating his rivals for their *seeming* courage, whilst intending that his own boldness should be seen as genuine.[476] This is not very likely. In the context it is a question of making bold to claim to possess various attributes relevant (so Paul's opponents maintained) to genuine apostleship. An only apparent courage on the part of the rival missionaries would mean that their claims to these attributes were false. But this is not so, as v. 22 indicates.[477] If τολμάω here has a pejorative connotation, it is more likely that it points to the recklessness of boasting,[478] and so enhances the force of the ἐν ἀφροσύνῃ λέγω.

(b) *Comparison with rivals; hardships-list; transitional passage; escape from Damascus* (11.22–33)

[22]Are they Hebrews? I too. Are they Israelites? I too. Are they the seed of Abraham? I too. [23a]Are they agents of Christ? I talk like a madman: I am unequalled; [23b]incomparably abundant in missionary labours, incomparably abundant in spells of imprisonment, exceptionally subject to beatings, frequently in mortal dangers. [24]From Jews I five times received the forty strokes save one; [25]three times I was beaten with rods; once I was stoned; three times I was shipwrecked – I have spent a day and a night in the deep; [26]frequently on journeys, beset by dangers from rivers, dangers from bandits, dangers from my race, dangers from Gentiles, dangers in the city, dangers in the desert, dangers on the sea, dangers amongst pseudo-Christians, [27]with labour and toil, with frequent sleepless nights, in conditions of hunger and thirst, frequent fasting, cold, and near-nakedness. [28]Other things apart, there is the daily pressure upon me imposed by my anxious care for all the churches. [29]Who is weak and I am not weak? Who is led into sin and I do not burn with indignation? [30]If boasting is necessary, I will boast of the instances of my weakness. [31]The God and Father of the Lord Jesus, who is blessed forever, knows that I do not lie. [32]In Damascus, the ethnarch of King Aretas was guarding the city of the Damascenes so as to seize me. [33]And I was let down through a window in a basket through the wall, and I escaped his hands.

By whatever standards of comparison anyone might choose, Paul can prove his equality with the rival missionaries—indeed, his superiority to them. Their equal in respect of race and ancestry, he is incomparably their superior as an agent of Christ. His evangelistic labours have been more numerous. Moreover, in the course of his missionary work he has suffered more varieties of persecution more frequently, and has endured many more potentially fatal dangers. In addition he experiences continual concern for the churches he has founded. Reference to his care

---

[476] This is how Zmijewski, *'Narrenrede'*, pp. 234–5, would understand Betz's suggestion of irony.

[477] Cf. Zmijewski, *'Narrenrede'*, p. 235, with reference to Lietzmann, p. 149.

[478] According to LSJ s.v. τολμάω 2., the verb can mean 'have the effrontery' to do something. Likewise, the noun τόλμα, ibid. s.v. 2., can mean 'recklessness'.

for his converts' weaknesses then brings him to the thought of his own weakness, and to the recollection of one particular incident, i.e., his escape from danger in Damascus.

11.22–23a as propositio: [479] comparison with rivals

The short series of questions and answers reaches a climax with Paul's claim that he surpasses his opponents as an agent of Christ. This is the basis of the following argument.

22. Ἑβραῖοί εἰσιν; κἀγώ. Ἰσραηλῖταί εἰσιν; κἀγώ. σπέρμα Ἀβραάμ εἰσιν; κἀγώ. Paul goes on to specify the bold claims of his rivals, which he can make himself (however foolish the process), and he does this in a series of rhetorical questions which underline the dramatic effect of the exchange with his opponents.[480] It is obvious that the sequence of designations which constitutes the claims emphasises the fact that both the rival missionaries and Paul himself are Jews. But it may be also that each separate term has particular connotations which would tell us something more about the apostle's opponents, and the way they thought of themselves.

In the case of Ἑβραῖοι four possible nuances of meaning have been suggested.

1. Those who can claim the description are Jews by birth as distinct from proselytes.[481] In the OT, 'Hebrew' is used to distinguish the people concerned from those of another nationality: see, e.g., Gen 40.15; 41.12; 43.32.[482] And the sense 'pure-blooded Jew' is attested in Phil 3.5.[483] Perhaps Paul's opponents were suggesting that his own claim to be such was doubtful, since he had been born in Tarsus.[484] This is the simplest interpretation, but there are some difficulties. In some OT contexts the word may be used in a pejorative sense, rather than carrying a sense of national

---

[479] Sunderman, *Kraft der Rede*, pp. 131–3.

[480] Zmijewski, *'Narrenrede'*, p. 236. Plummer, p. 319, notes that some English versions prior to the KJV (such as the Wycliffe NT) suppose Paul simply to be making statements ('They are Hebrews. So am I,' and so on). Prümm, *Diakonia Pneumatos* I, p. 640, also interprets the verse this way. There is no actual obstacle to this rendering. But in view of the forceful way Paul expresses himself throughout his Fool's Speech it is much more probable that the majority reading of the verse as a series of interrogatives is correct. Bultmann, *Stil*, pp. 16, 70, notes that there are similar sequences of questions and answers in Epictetus, and observes, pp. 23, 77, that, in particular, both Paul (here) and Epictetus, *Diss.* II 8.2, employ a series of parallel questions with the same answer: κἀγώ in Paul, μὴ γένοιτο in Epictetus.

[481] Commentators who see this as at least part of the meaning of the word include, e.g., Plummer, p. 319; Windisch, pp. 350–1; Furnish, p. 514; Martin, p. 374.

[482] Plummer, p. 319.

[483] Barrett, p. 293; he sees this as the primary sense.

[484] Hughes, p. 403. See also Windisch, p. 352.

pride: see, e.g., Gen 39.14,17; Exod 1.16; 2.6.[485] This is not a substantial problem, however, since in later literature Ἑβραῖος may become, by contrast, an honorific term, as when, for example, it is applied to the martyrs in IV Maccabees: see 5.2; 8.2; 9.6, 18.[486] But there are two further difficulties which may carry more weight. One is that an ethnic sense for Ἑβραῖος may not fit the use of the word in Acts 6.1, since it is probable that the majority of the (contrasted) 'Hellenists' were as much Jews in the ethnic sense as were the 'Hebrews'. The fact that in 6.5 Nicolaus is expressly said to be a proselyte indicates that the remainder of the Seven were not,[487] which makes it likely that the other 'Hellenists' were not proselytes either, but Diaspora Jews.[488] The other difficulty is that in one instance Philo, undoubtedly a Jew by birth, appears to distinguish himself from a group he terms Ἑβραῖοι.[489]

2. Those who designate themselves Ἑβραῖοι indicate that they speak Hebrew or Aramaic, or both languages. Elsewhere in the NT, it can be argued, the word Ἑβραῖος and its cognates appear to imply the use of Aramaic. That Paul himself, who calls himself Ἑβραῖος (Phil 3.5), was an Aramaic speaker is attested in Acts 21.40; 22.2; see also Acts 6.1; Jn 5.2; 19.13, 17, 20; 20.16.[490] Outside the NT there are two occurrences in Philo where 'Hebrews' are contrasted linguistically with others:

ὡς μὲν Ἑβραῖοι λέγουσι Φανουήλ, ὡς δὲ ἡμεῖς ἀποστροφὴ θεοῦ.

'As Hebrews say, "Phanuel", but as we (say) "turning from God".'[491]

and:

ὡς μὲν Ἑβραῖοι εἴποιεν ἂν Ἀβραάμ, ὡς δ'ἂν Ἕλληνες, πατέρα ἐκλεκτὸν ἠχοῦς.

'As Hebrews would say, "Abraham", but as Greeks (would say), "Elect Father of sound" ' (LCL).[492]

---

[485] G. von Rad, on 'Hebräer', in *TWNT* III, p. 359.
[486] K. G. Kuhn, on Ἑβραῖος, in *TWNT* III, pp. 366–70; see p. 369.
[487] Haenchen, *Apostelgeschichte*, p. 217.
[488] Haenchen, *Apostelgeschichte*, pp. 219–20.
[489] See the first quotation under 2.
[490] Plummer, p. 319, who thinks the word refers to language as well as to nationality. On Acts 6.1, see Haenchen, *Apostelgeschichte*, pp. 213–14.
[491] Philo, *Conf. Ling.* 129, cited by Windisch, p. 351, who comments that Philo seems to exclude himself from the ranks of the 'Hebrews'. In the translation above, the phrase 'turning from God' is taken from the LCL translation.
[492] Philo, *Mut. Nom.* (*On the Change of Names*) 71, cited by Windisch, ibid.

There is also an item of inscriptional evidence. As a number of commentators note, there is an inscription on a building in Corinth which in all probability originally read συναγωγὴ Ἑβραίων. This might have indicated a synagogue where the languages used were Hebrew and Aramaic, rather than Greek.[493] Again, this evidence is not conclusive. That Paul himself was both a 'Hebrew' and an Aramaic speaker does not prove that Ἑβραῖος itself refers to a member of a particular language group. In Acts, moreover, apart from 6.1, it is not the word Ἑβραῖος that is used but the phrase τῇ Ἑβραΐδι διαλέκτῳ, 'in the Hebrew (Aramaic) language', whilst John employs the term Ἑβραϊστί 'in Hebrew (Aramaic)', and the contexts also show that it is a matter of language, which is not so in the present verse. As regards Acts 6.1, Gutbrod argues that the linguistic explanation does not account sufficiently for the neglect of the 'Hellenists' by the 'Hebrews', since in a bilingual country each group would understand the other.[494] This argument, however, tends to overlook the possibly divisive effect of the existence of different language groups for religious or social purposes.[495] And the use of the cognate terms in Acts and John may still strongly suggest that Ἑβραῖος itself has a linguistic connotation. The Corinthian synagogue inscription, however, is perhaps more problematic. Lietzmann and Barrett both suppose that it counts against the linguistic interpretation: Ἑβραῖος must simply mean 'Jew'.[496] This may well be right. Would there have been a sufficient number of Aramaic-speaking Jews permanently resident in Corinth to support a separate institution? The majority of Corinthian Jews, we may suppose, met in a Greek-speaking synagogue. In any case, the purpose of the inscription would be to show people in general the function of the building: the ordinary Corinthian would not, for the most part, be aware of linguistic distinctions within the Jewish community.

3. The word indicates those who have close family ties with Palestine. The 'Hebrews' in Acts 6.1, according to Gutbrod, would then be natives of Palestine, who know each other well but are less familiarly acquainted with the 'Hellenists', who are immigrants from the Diaspora.[497] There is evidence in Pausanias for the use of

---

[493] The inscription is noted by, e.g., Windisch, ibid.; Bruce, p. 240; Carrez, p. 221. See Deissmann, *Light*, pp. 13–14 n. 7, for a reproduction of the inscription. Part of it is missing, but the remaining ΓΩΓΗΕΒΡ appears sufficient for the accepted reconstruction.

[494] W. Gutbrod, on Ἑβραῖος (in the NT), in *TWNT* III, pp. 391–4; see p. 392.

[495] Gutbrod, ibid., does allow that there might be limits to understanding.

[496] Lietzmann, p. 150; Barrett, p. 293.

[497] Gutbrod, ibid. Supporters of this general viewpoint include Wendland, p. 241; Bultmann, p. 215.

'Εβραῖος in a geographical sense.[498] Such Jews would also be Aramaic speakers.[499] Bruce, who agrees with this interpretation, notes that it would appear inapplicable to Paul, who was born, according to Acts 22.3, in Tarsus in Cilicia. He claims, however, that the difficulty can be met if we suppose that the apostle had been brought up in Jerusalem from his earliest childhood.[500] Gutbrod (following J. B. Lightfoot) suggests further that in Phil 3.5 Paul is claiming that he has not been subject to hellenisation.[501] This 'geographical' interpretation may be allowed as a possibility.[502] The phrases in Pausanias show that 'Hebrews' were seen as belonging to a particular locality, and the use of Aramaic would go along with a Palestinian connection. In the present context, however, it is unlikely that Paul would intend any suggestion of freedom from 'hellenisation'. He is competing (however foolishly) with his rivals, and it has become obvious that they pride themselves on their own 'hellenisation', at least in respect of their rhetorical skills.

4. Since the ordinary Greek word for Jews as an ethnic group is Ἰουδαῖος, the term 'Εβραῖος must indicate the special character of the Jewish people. So Georgi.[503] The background, he argues, is the apologetic of hellenistic Judaism, designed to make the special nature of Judaism comprehensible to non-Jews and to present the Jewish faith as universally valid. The adjective 'Εβραῖος, used of the language and script characteristic of Palestinian Jews,[504] comes to be employed more generally of their geographical and cultural distinguishing features,[505] including the past history of the nation,[506] and the whole Jewish way of life.[507]

---

[498] Gutbrod, on 'Εβραῖος (in pagan writers), in *TWNT* III, pp. 374–5; see p. 374. In Pausanias, see V 7.4: ἐν τῇ γῇ ... τῇ 'Εβραίων, and VIII 16.4: ἐν τῇ 'Εβραίων.
[499] Gutbrod, on 'Εβραῖος (in the NT), pp. 392–3.
[500] Bruce, pp. 240–1. He depends here on W. C. van Unnik, *Tarsus or Jerusalem: the City of Paul's Youth*, London, 1962; see pp. 44–5, 52–8. He refers also to Jerome, who, in his commentary on Philemon (v. 23), cites a tradition ('Aiunt') that Paul's parents came from Gischala in Judaea (according to Jerome, though Bruce locates the place in Galilee), after the region had been devastated by the Romans. See *PL* 26 col. 617. It is uncertain, however, according to Bruce, whether much credence should be given to this information.
[501] Gutbrod, on 'Εβραῖος (in the NT), p. 393. See J. B. Lightfoot, *Epistle to the Philippians*, London, 1913 (reprint 1961), pp. 146–7.
[502] Furnish, p. 514; Martin, p. 374.
[503] Georgi, *Opponents*, pp. 41–6.
[504] Georgi, *Opponents*, p. 42. He observes that the *Epistle of Aristeas* shows that the Hebrew script lent the sacred documents of Judaism an exceptional character (*Ep. Arist.* 3,11,30; cf. 176).
[505] Georgi, ibid.
[506] Georgi, *Opponents*, p. 43, notes that according to Artapanus the Jews called themselves 'Hebrews' from the time of Abraham onwards.
[507] Georgi, ibid., refers to Philo, *Jos.* 42; *Abrah.* 251.

. Hence, when the rival missionaries in Corinth claim to be 'Hebrews', they would indicate that they have recent Palestinian connections and a knowledge of Hebrew or Aramaic, and they would also lead people to expect something special of them, grounded in the culture and history they represent.[508] These are interesting suggestions, but raise various questions. First, to what extent had Ἑβραῖος become a composite term, capable of possessing, in a single context, all the various connotations which may be illustrated separately in diverse literary sources? The theory seems to require that this should be so, but it is not clearly evidenced. Secondly, even if the first question should be answered satisfactorily, we should still have to ask whether the Corinthian Christians, if largely Gentile, would have been sufficiently aware of the apologetic of Alexandrian Judaism to catch all these nuances of meaning. Thirdly, granted that they might be aware of some of them, how impressive would the resulting claims seem to be? For example, fluency in a non-Greek tongue such as Hebrew or Aramaic would not necessarily be regarded as an advantage by Greeks, by whom speakers of other languages could be designated βάρβαροι. These questions do not prove Georgi's theory wrong, but they do indicate the need for further discussion.

At this point we postpone a final decision on the best sense to be given, in this verse, to Ἑβραῖος.[509]

The sense of Ἰσραηλῖται, by contrast, is easier to determine. It may have an ethnic connotation, as in passages where it is connected with the thought of genuine descent from Abraham.[510] Primarily, however, it denotes the members of the holy people of God, with all the religious privileges that this implies.[511] As Gutbrod notes, this is clearly apparent in Rom 11.1, where, to the question, 'Can God have rejected his people?', Paul replies, 'Certainly not! For I myself am an Israelite.'[512]

There is more variation of opinion, however, on the significance of the third term, σπέρμα Ἀβραάμ. Three views may be distinguished.

1. The reference is to those who are heirs of the promises made by God to Abraham.[513] But when one asks precisely what promises are in mind, the answer is not very obvious. Plummer

508 Georgi, *Opponents*, p. 45.
509 See below, p. 730.
510 Windisch, p. 351, notes Rom 11.1; 4 Macc 18.1 (῏Ω τῶν Ἀβραμιαίων σπερμάτων ἀπόγονοι παῖδες Ἰσραηλῖται); see also Furnish, p. 514.
511 See, e.g., Plummer, p. 320; Barrett, p. 293; Furnish, p. 514.
512 W. Gutbrod, on Ἰσραηλίτης (in the NT), in *TWNT* III, pp. 385–91; see p. 389. The ethnic connotation is secondary.
513 See, e.g., Bachmann, p. 383; Plummer, p. 320; Allo, p. 293; Bultmann, p. 216.

speaks of promises about the Messiah, but gives no specific references.[514] In fact, none of the OT passages recording a divine promise to Abraham says anything at all about a coming messianic figure. Other commentators refer to various Pauline passages which allude to Abrahamic promises (Rom 4.13–18; 9.6–8; Gal 3.16–18[515]). But in the present context the title σπέρμα Ἀβραάμ is in the first place a designation claimed by Paul's opponents, and this means that we can scarcely go to passages heavily charged with Paul's own theological outlook to determine its meaning. The OT promises concerning numerous descendants might be seen as fulfilled in the numerical growth of Jews in the Diaspora, but this would not single out the rival missionaries in any special way, and the promise of land, in view of the Roman occupation of Palestine, was neither unambiguously fulfilled nor of immediate relevance in Corinth. It could be, however, that the promise of an everlasting covenant between Abraham and his descendants (Gen 17.7) is in some way related to this particular self-designation of Paul's rivals. They were, after all, attempting to supplant the influence in Corinth of the apostle who claimed to be the agent of a new covenant. A claim to be partners in a divine covenant that went right back to the age of the patriarchs, however vaguely this partnership might be understood, might prove a useful counter-weight to Paul's own authority.

2. This designation serves to connect the rival missionaries in some way with the missionary concern of hellenistic Judaism. In this world of thought the figure of Abraham was prominent, as the originator of civilisation and the first monotheist, as engaging in religious and cultural mission, and as the standard of excellence for all proselytes.[516] The implication of the argument seems to be that Paul's opponents took Abraham as their model.[517] This is not impossible. But it has to be remembered that these people are Christian missionaries, not the agents of a mission which aimed to effect full conversion to Judaism, i.e., to persuade Gentiles to become proselytes, with the requisite submission to circumcision. The point of using the figure of Abraham as a model was precisely to facilitate this process of persuasion.[518] This does not seem to have been the situation in Corinth.

3. It is argued that if σπέρμα Ἀβραάμ refers only to some Jewish aspect of the rival missionaries' credentials it would simply be the equivalent of the preceding Ἰσραηλῖται, so that it would make

[514] Plummer, p. 320.
[515] Cited by Furnish, p. 514; Bultmann, p. 216, cites Rom 9.7.
[516] Georgi, *Opponents*, pp. 49–60.
[517] This is how Martin, p. 375, understands Georgi.
[518] Oostendorp, *Another Jesus*, p. 13 n. 24.

better sense to understand it in the way it is used in Gal 3.29, i.e., of Christians as the true 'seed of Abraham'. Thus, whilst the first two titles refer to the opponents' specifically Jewish attributes, the third indicates their new Christian self-understanding.[519] This is not very probable. Structurally, all three phrases run parallel with each other, and one would expect parallelism in sense as well. And again, it is a mistake to use a characteristically Pauline idea to elucidate the self-designation of his opponents.

The first of the three views we have discussed is hence the most probable.

To summarise our discussion of v. 22 is to raise some further questions. We noted initially that, whatever else may be implied, the three designations 'Hebrews', 'Israelites', and 'seed of Abraham' stress the Jewishness of Paul's rivals and of the apostle himself.[520] But why should the intruding missionaries wish to emphasise this fact about themselves? One suggestion, proposed by Plummer, is that they were questioning the genuineness of Paul's own Judaism: he had been born in Tarsus, and seemed to disparage circumcision. Consequently, his rivals could prove their superiority by insisting on their own Jewish pedigree.[521] We might add that ill-disposed critics could also have quoted Paul's own words in 1 Cor 9.20, where he says ἐγενόμην τοῖς Ἰουδαίοις ὡς Ἰουδαῖος. The fact that a few MSS omit the ὡς shows that the sentence as it stands could imply that he was not himself a Jew. But one still has to ask why all this should matter to the Corinthian congregation. The usual view is that its members were mostly Gentile.[522] What difference would it make if the proclaimer of Jesus as universal κύριος (1 Cor 8.6) was a Gentile himself? Perhaps the answer may be that the Jewish component of the church was more substantial than is commonly supposed. And it is possible that these Jewish Christians were subject to ridicule and criticism from their unconverted fellow Jews. How could they have been persuaded by this self-styled agent of a new covenant, when it was doubtful whether he was even a genuine Jew at all? New missionaries who insisted on their own pure Jewish pedigree, and saw themselves (as σπέρμα Ἀβραάμ) as partners in a truly ancient covenant would provide the Corinthian Jewish Christians with needed support. The designation σπέρμα

---

[519] Zmijewski, 'Narrenrede', pp. 239–40.

[520] Barrett, p. 294, thinks there is little more to it than this, and Bultmann, p. 215, suggests that if there are differences between the various titles they are scarcely perceptible.

[521] Plummer, p. 320.

[522] See, e.g., Martin, p. xxix. The discussion of idol meats in 1 Cor 8 may give this impression, as do the sections (1 Cor 5; 6.12–20) which suggest laxity in sexual conduct.

'Αβραάμ may thus have a particular connotation of its own, in addition to its part in reinforcing the basic claim to Jewishness. Similarly the term 'Ισραηλῖται indicates especially membership of God's holy people. What, then, is the specific contribution of the designation 'Εβραῖοι? We have seen that it may contain an honorific nuance, but what else, if anything? The linguistic interpretation has some evidence in its favour, as does the geographical, and if we ask why the Corinthian Christians should have been particularly impressed by Aramaic speakers with Palestinian connections there is probably, after all, a simple answer. These people have a more direct link than Paul seems to have with the original disciples of Jesus, who are the first tradents of his teaching, given in the Aramaic language. If, as we have suggested, the 'other Jesus' whom they preach is the divine law-giver, then the ability to understand his words in their original language would assume considerable significance. Whether the rival missionaries could have invested 'Hebrew' with the whole range of connotations suggested by Georgi is more debatable. This would require that both they themselves *and* a significant proportion of the Corinthian congregation were familiar with hellenistic Jewish apologetic. In the case of Paul's opponents this is likely enough, since their rhetorical fluency in Greek shows them to be at home in the world of hellenistic Judaism. In the case of the congregation, we should have to assume that the Jewish Christian component was larger than is usually supposed. But we have already seen that the emphasis on Jewishness as such may in itself indicate this. It remains then, to consider the significance attached to the designation 'Εβραῖος when Paul claims the title for himself. Like his rivals, he may intend to indicate competence in Aramaic. Whether he wishes also to suggest close family ties with Palestine is less certain. The NT evidence that he did have such connections depends on one particular interpretation of Acts 22.3. But it is not necessary that he should attach to 'Εβραῖος precisely the meaning intended by his rivals. He may simply be making the basic claim that he is fully a Jew by birth and ancestry, as he does in Phil 3.5.[523]

---

[523] According to Betz, *Tradition*, p. 97, Paul is here parodying the encomium motif περὶ εὐγενείας. Wolff, p. 230 n. 240, however, argues that this interpretation fails to take account of the deep significance, for Paul, of being a Jew (see Rom 9.1–5). Moreover: 'parodistisch wäre es, wenn Paulus sich einer niedrigen Herkunft rühmen würde.' That genuine parody of this genre would require Paul to boast of *lowly* origins is in fact attested by Betz himself (ibid), when he gives, as an example, Bion's claim that his father was a fishmonger and his mother a prostitute. See also J. Sánchez Bosch, 'L'Apologie Apostolique', pp. 43–63 in *Verteidigung* (see under E. Lohse, ed.), see pp. 52–3.

23a. διάκονοι Χριστοῦ εἰσιν; παραφρονῶν λαλῶ, ὑπὲρ ἐγώ·
Whatever the difficulty of determining the precise connotations
of the three designations in v. 22, there is no problem in supposing
that they are applicable both to Paul and to his rivals. This is
emphatically not so in the case of the διάκονοι Χριστοῦ of the
present verse. How, in Paul's view, can his opponents function as
agents[524] of Christ, when, some few sentences earlier, he has
stigmatised them as agents of Satan, and as false apostles, whose
presentation of themselves as apostles of Christ is simply a
facade? There is no easy answer to this question. Two possible
ways of mitigating the difficulty have been suggested, however, to
which a third may be added.

(i) As we have noted already,[525] Barrett argues that in vv.
21b–23 Paul has moved away from the thought of his rivals in
Corinth, and has begun to compare himself with the Jerusalem
apostles, whom these 'intruders' claim as their sponsors. This
would certainly solve the present problem, but is inherently
unlikely. As we have seen, v. 21 most naturally refers back to vv.
18–20, which refer to the rival missionaries, and vv. 22–23 clearly
follow v. 21b without a break.[526]

(ii) Perhaps Paul is quoting his rivals' claim without (wholly)
endorsing it: 'for the sake of argument he is willing to assume that
in some sense they are what they claim to be.'[527] But this is a
somewhat unnatural way of reading v. 23 in relation to v. 22. The
question διάκονοι Χριστοῦ εἰσιν; is an exact parallel to the three
preceding questions in v. 22, and in that verse Paul is not denying
that his opponents are genuinely Hebrews, Israelites, and descendants of Abraham, or simply assuming that this is so for the sake
of argument.

(iii) It is just possible that the two categories 'agents of Christ'
and 'agents of Satan' may not have been, in Paul's mind, so totally
exclusive the one of the other as his language suggests. He is not
alone amongst NT writers in his ability to see the same people as
acting now on behalf of God or Christ, now on behalf of Satan. In
the Matthean account of Peter's confession (Mt 16.16–23) Peter

[524] On διάκονος, see Vol. I, pp. 231–2, and nn. 293–5. In both religious and secular usage the basic sense is 'go-between'. Paul sees himself as an intermediary between God and humankind, charged with a message from God that he must transmit.
[525] See above, p. 721 n. 472.
[526] Barrett himself, in fact, seems inconsistent. In his Introduction, p. 30, where he discusses the 'false apostles', he says that these people 'must have been Jews, and Jews who insisted on their Jewishness'. But this assertion must be derived from 11.22. Thus, at this point, by contrast with his later exegesis, pp. 292–4, he sees no transition in v. 21 from the rival missionaries to the Jerusalem apostles.
[527] Plummer, p. 321; see also Windisch, p. 352; Allo, p. 294; Bultmann, p. 216; Furnish, p. 535.

functions both as the spokesman of God (giving expression to the revelation that Jesus is the Christ) and also as the representative of Satan (denying the necessity for the Messiah's suffering).[528] In addition, the possibility that the agreement on division of missionary territory lies in the background may be relevant at this point. On Corinthian territory the rival missionaries are behaving deceitfully when they claim apostolic rights, since this area of mission does not belong to them. And if they are thus deceiving the congregation, then they are doing Satan's work, as agents of the original, archetypal deceiver.[529] But Paul might allow the possibility that these people do have their *own* territory, divinely allocated, in which they might legitimately function as διάκονοι Χριστοῦ. Whilst this description of them does appear to contradict his earlier harsh words, it may be that some such way of thinking as we have outlined here under (iii) could account for the apparent contradiction.

In his following response to this fourth claim of his rivals, Paul is speaking, he confesses, as though he were mad, beside himself, deprived of reason.[530] Why? The answer to this question depends in part on how we understand the ὑπὲρ ἐγώ. This phrase has been interpreted in at least five different ways (although the distinctions are in some cases rather fine).

(i) Paul is saying that he himself is 'more than a servant of Christ'.[531] The 'madness' would then consist in the apparent supposition that there can be any higher status than that of διάκονοι Χριστοῦ.[532] But this interpretation is unlikely. Paul is still engaged in comparison with his rivals.[533] And what would it mean, anyway, to say this?[534]

(ii) The ὑπέρ expresses contrast rather than comparison. Paul is saying, 'Not they, rather I (am it)!'[535] The ὑπέρ is to be taken as the equivalent of μᾶλλον, and as excluding the first alternative.[536] The 'madness' would then, perhaps, relate to the very asking of the question διάκονοι Χριστοῦ εἰσιν; But the structure of v. 23a favours the attachment of παραφρονῶν λαλῶ to what follows. And

---

[528] See Thrall, 'Super-Apostles', p. 52, and note that according to Otto Betz, cited there, a similar way of thinking is found in the Qumran texts: see Betz, 'Felsenmann und Felsengemeinde', *ZNW* 48 (1957), pp. 49–77; I am indebted to Professor Max Wilcox for drawing my attention to this article.

[529] See above, p. 662, for the Jewish equation of the Eden serpent with Satan.

[530] See BAGD, s.v. παραφρονέω.

[531] Meyer, p. 447.

[532] Plummer, p. 321, suggests this as one possibility.

[533] Bachmann, p. 383.

[534] Plummer, ibid.

[535] Zmijewski, '*Narrenrede*', p. 242: '*Nicht sie, vielmehr ich* (bin es)!'

[536] Zmijewski, ibid.

it is more likely that Paul would have used μᾶλλον, were this his meaning.

(iii) Paul is 'more a servant of Christ' than are the rival missionaries.[537] This is a natural interpretation of his words, in their context. He would be speaking 'as a madman', though, in allowing the possibility of comparison.

(iv) The ὑπέρ is to be taken in a superlative sense. Paul is not interested in his rivals' right to the title in question: he himself is διάκονος Χριστοῦ, *par excellence*.[538] The 'madness', then, as in (ii) above, would consist in the very mention of the *opponents'* claim. But it seems unlikely that the sense of comparison has altogether disappeared from view.

(v) A similar but more acceptable interpretation, which takes ὑπέρ as superlative but at the same time retains the notion of comparison would run as follows:'Paul is saying that as a minister of Christ he surpasses the pseudo-apostles altogether, he is beyond their range.'[539] Perhaps then the 'madness' would relate to the impression given of comparison.

Our own exegetical preference is for either (iii) or (v). We shall return to the discussion after considering v. 23b.

11.23b–12.10 as argumentatio
According to Sundermann, this section of the letter is to be divided into three sub-sections: 11.23b–33; 12.1–7a; 12.7b–10. Each ends with a reference to boasting in weakness. This division depends, however, to some degree on the view that 11.30–31 concludes the first sub-section and that 11.32–33 may be a later interpolation (though perhaps by Paul himself).[540] In our view, these verses are part of the original text, and verse 30, whilst having some retrospective reference, acts chiefly as an introduction to what follows. Consequently, we divide this long section of the text into two main passages only: 11.23b–29 and 11.30–12.10. Since, however, 11.30–33 is transitional, and in 12.1 a new topic begins, the translation follows the chapter division. Whatever way the text is to be divided, Paul is throughout presenting a justification of his apostolic calling and activities.

11.23b–29: hardships-list
These verses clearly belong to the Graeco-Roman genre which is labelled *Peristasenkataloge* in German scholarship. As in Vol. I

537 Bachmann, p. 383; Allo, p. 294; Barrett, p. 295; Furnish, pp. 512, 514.
538 Zmijewski, *'Narrenrede'*, p. 242, prefers this.
539 Hughes, pp. 405–6 n. 71.
540 Sundermann, *Kraft der Rede*, pp. 135–6.

we shall use the term 'hardships-lists'.[541] Ebner observes that there are two types: those which give examples of what anyone by mischance might encounter, and those connected with some particular historical or mythological character, such as Alexander or Heracles. He designates the latter 'personal catalogues'.[542] It is this second type that we find in 2 Cor 11.23–29.

Ebner comments further that, in view of the Corinthian situation which provokes Paul's recital, it is of interest that one such personal catalogue, placed by Arrian in the mouth of Alexander, concerns a crisis of authority and a contest between Alexander and his opponents.[543] There are parallels also, however, of a stylistic nature, between Paul's list and the achievements-lists of famous men, in particular the *Res Gestae* of Augustus.[544]

23b. ἐν κόποις περισσοτέρως, ἐν φυλακαῖς περισσοτέρως, ἐν πληγαῖς ὑπερβαλλόντως,[545] ἐν θανάτοις πολλάκις. Paul begins to list the ways in which he can justify his response ὑπέρ ἐγώ to his rivals' claim to be διάκονοι Χριστοῦ, and an effect of intensification is produced as he progresses from 'labours', via 'imprisonments' and 'blows', to 'mortal dangers'.[546] These phrases may be seen to act as headings for what follows,[547] although the second does not appear to have any very obvious counterpart in the later verses. The ἐν may be causal or instrumental.[548] Paul is,

---

[541] See Vol. I, p. 326. Furnish, similarly, uses 'list of hardships' and 'hardships list', whilst Martin refers to 'lists of trials'. The original Greek περιστάσεις initially means simply 'circumstances', 'state of affairs': see LSJ s.v. περίστασις II.1. It is used especially, however, for difficult circumstances: see LSJ ibid., II.1.b., with reference to Epict., *Diss.* II 6.17, where both uses are noted; cf. Ebner, *Leidenslisten*, p. 18.

[542] Ebner, *Leidenslisten*, pp. 115–16, with particular reference to Plutarch on Alexander. See Excursus XIV, below, pp. 755–7; see p. 756.

[543] Ebner, *Leidenslisten*, pp. 118–19: see Excursus XIV, below, p. 756.

[544] See Excursus XIV, below, pp. 756–7.

[545] In the second and third of these ἐν-phrases there are variations in word order in the textual tradition, as follows:

  (i) ἐν φυλακαῖς περισσοτέρως, ἐν πληγαῖς ὑπερβαλλόντως 𝔓46 ℵ¹ B D* (0243) 33. 629. 630. (1739. 1881) *pc* lat Ambst.

  (ii) ἐν πληγαῖς περισσοτέρως ἐν φυλακαῖς ὑπερβαλλόντως ℵ* F G.

  (iii) ἐν φυλακαῖς ὑπερβαλλόντως ἐν πληγαῖς περισσοτέρως P.

  (iv) ἐν πληγαῖς ὑπερβαλλόντως ἐν φυλακαῖς περισσοτέρως D¹ H Ψ 0121a 𝔐 sy^p.

Readings (iii) and (iv) appear to be secondary. Reading (ii) could be due to intentional alteration by a scribe who noted the intensifying effect of the series as a whole, and sought to make it more effective by placing 'imprisonments' (seen as the harsher experience) after 'beatings'. That the latter may have been in fact the more severe hardship is indicated in vv. 24–5, as Zmijewski, '*Narrenrede*', p. 247, observes.

[546] Zmijewski, '*Narrenrede*', pp. 247–8; cf. Martin, p. 376.

[547] Zmijewski, '*Narrenrede*', p. 248.

[548] See BAGD s.v. ἐν III.1. or 3. The final ἐν θανάτοις πολλάκις could be an instance of the use of the preposition to indicate a 'state of being': see BAGD s.v. I.4.d. The general sense would still be causal, however.

or has become,[549] Christ's agent to a superlative degree by reason of his extraordinary labours and so on. These κόποι, which head the list, are most likely to be understood as missionary labours in the strict sense, i.e., the 'arduous evangelistic campaigns' Paul has undertaken.[550] Furnish, differently, sees a reference to his manual labours as a craftsman: this is what κόπος means, he claims, in v. 27, which can be seen as an elaboration of the present phrase; note also the use of the cognate verb in 1 Cor 4.12 for ordinary manual toil.[551] In the latter instance, however, the particular meaning is specified in the following ἐργαζόμενοι ταῖς ἰδίαις χερσίν. Moreover, in 1 Cor 15.10 the same verb is used with obvious reference to apostolic missionary work, whilst κόπος itself, as Barrett notes,[552] occurs in the same sense in 2 Cor 10.15. Paul is saying, then, that he surpasses his rivals, by reason of 'far greater (evangelistic) labours',[553] or, 'very abundantly by reason of his (evangelistic) labours'.[554] The choice between the comparative and the elative force of the adverb makes very little difference to the general sense but does have some slight effect on the interpretation of the preceding ὑπὲρ ἐγώ.[555] The comparative rendering is popular in the English versions,[556] and if it should be accepted would mean that Paul is more a servant of Christ than are his rivals,[557] on account of his far more strenuous work in the service of the gospel. This makes good sense, and may be right. In favour of the alternative, however, there is the fact that the final adverb πολλάκις is not comparative in form, and since the four phrases in v. 23b are parallel in structure one might expect that περισσοτέρως would have a superlative rather than a comparative force.[558] In that case, when Paul says, ὑπὲρ ἐγώ, he would mean that he is altogether out of his rivals' class (although he still has

---

[549] Windisch, p. 354, and Martin, p. 376, would supply ἐγενόμην. In fact it may not be necessary to supply a verb at all (so Plummer, p. 323): the connection of thought is sufficiently intelligible as it is. But if some completion of the sense is required one would need to say, not simply ἐγενόμην, but διάκονος Χριστοῦ ἐγενόμην: so Bultmann, p. 217. See Zmijewski, '*Narrenrede*', p. 244, for more elaborate suggestions.
[550] Tasker, p. 161.
[551] Furnish, pp. 515, 536.
[552] Barrett, p. 295.
[553] RSV. For the comparative sense of περισσοτέρως see BAGD s.v. 1., where the present reference is given. See also Windisch, p. 354; Barrett, p. 288; Furnish, p. 515. Other references in BAGD s.v. 1. include 2 Cor 12.15; Gal 1.14; Phil 1.14.
[554] For the elative force of περισσοτέρως see BAGD s.v. 2.; four other instances in 2 Corinthians are cited: 1.12; 2.4; 7.13, 15.
[555] See above, pp. 732–3.
[556] See, e.g., NRSV, NEB, REB, JB.
[557] Interpretation (iii) above, see p. 733.
[558] Zmijewski, '*Narrenrede*', pp. 246–7.

them in view), 'beyond their range',[559] by virtue of the superlative excellence of his apostolic service. This may be preferable. But the distinction is a fine one. And it has to be noted that the force of the third adverb ὑπερβαλλόντως is also ambiguous, since it can be used in a comparative as well as a superlative sense.[560] Perhaps, in the case both of περισσοτέρως and ὑπερβαλλόντως, what we have here is a subtle combination of comparative and superlative, in which the intensification of the first means that it is virtually transformed into the second. This in fact would best fit the similar interpretation of the ὑπὲρ ἐγώ as indicating that, whilst Paul does see himself in relation to the rival missionaries, there can nevertheless be no valid comparison in respect of the claim to be διάκονος/διάκονοι Χριστοῦ.[561]

We know virtually nothing about the numerous occasions of imprisonment which come next on the list. According to Acts 16.23–40 Paul was incarcerated overnight in Philippi. Perhaps also he may have been imprisoned in Ephesus on the occasion he refers to in 1 Cor 15.32,[562] and in connection with the trouble in Asia mentioned in 2 Cor 1.8–10.[563] To some extent he may be exaggerating here,[564] but there must have been at least several actual instances of imprisonment to serve as a basis for the exaggeration. The mention of beatings which follows is elaborated in vv. 24–25. The occasions of mortal danger[565] could have included these punishments,[566] in addition to the perils of travel and other life-threatening hazards instanced in the following verses.

24. ὑπὸ Ἰουδαίων πεντάκις τεσσεράκοντα παρὰ μίαν ἔλαβον, It may be significant that when Paul comes to speak more specifically of his hardships he begins with his five experiences of punishment by Jews.[567] Is it because this particular hardship was especially unlikely to have come the way of his rivals? And was this because their 'alternative gospel' appeared to involve less of a break with Judaism than what had become known of Paul's own

---

559 Interpretation (v) above, see p. 733.
560 See BAGD s.v. ὑπερβαλλόντως, where, in addition to the meaning 'exceedingly', 'immeasurably', there is given also the comparative sense 'surpassingly', 'to a much greater degree', with two references to Philo (*Plant.* 126 and *Migr. Abr.* 58) and to 2 Cor 11.23.
561 Again, interpretation (v) above; see p. 733.
562 Allo, p. 295.
563 Bruce, p. 242, sees this as more than probable, and Furnish, p. 354, thinks it is a possibility. See also Vol. I, pp. 116–17.
564 According to Furnish, p. 354, this may be an instance of hyperbole.
565 For this sense of θάνατος see BAGD s.v. 1.c.
566 See below, pp. 736–8.
567 The ὑπὸ Ἰουδαίων is emphatic, both because it comes first in the sentence (Windisch, p. 354) and because the agent is specified (Furnish, p. 515).

message and his more radical attitude to the Mosaic law? When we have noted in detail the nature of the penalty, we shall consider the charges that may have been brought against him so as to render him liable to it, and the even more difficult question as to why he submitted in this way to synagogue discipline.

The punishment is based on Deut 25.2–3. If someone is sentenced to be flogged, the number of lashes is to be in proportion to the seriousness of the offence, but must not exceed 40 strokes. More than this, and the guilty person would be degraded. The 'less one'[568] may have been the result of care not to break the law by inadvertence.[569] In addition, it seems that the biblical text could be interpreted to mean 'a number near to forty'.[570] In any case, it must be significant that Paul each time received the maximum penalty, indicating the gravity with which his offence was apparently regarded. Its nature, however, remains a matter of conjecture. Most of the offences listed in *Mak.* 3.1–9 as punishable by flogging would be irrelevant.[571] Of the rest, infringement of the food laws would be the most probable.[572] But it may be a mistake to attempt to identify the charge against Paul by looking through this list of offences. Flogging and ostracism were probably the only forms of punishment which Jews of the Diaspora were able to inflict on fellow synagogue members guilty of transgression and if the ostracised member continued to frequent the synagogue nevertheless, only flogging remained. Hence: 'The penalty ... probably covered so many transgressions that the crime cannot be precisely specified just by learning the punishment.'[573] It could well have been, in any case, Paul's general attitude to the Mosaic law, in relation to his Gentile mission, that exposed him to discipline, rather than any specific personal offence.[574] In particular, there was the fact that he did not require, indeed eventually strongly opposed, the acceptance of circumcision by his male Gentile converts. At a time when the Christian movement seemed still to be part of Judaism, and was

---

[568] See BAGD s.v. παρά III.7, for the use of the preposition to mean 'less' in the sense of subtraction.

[569] See, e.g., Plummer, p. 324; Bruce, p. 242; cf. Chrysostom, *PG* 61 col. 570 (NPNF XII, pp. 394–5).

[570] See *Mak.* 3.10 (cited by Barrett, p. 296; Martin, p. 376; and others). This runs: 'How many lashes do they inflict on one? *Forty less one*, as it is said: *by number forty*—a number that is *near* to forty.' (Cited from Tractate *Makkoth*, translated by P. Blackman, pp. 299–330 in *Mishnayoth* Vol. IV, New York, 1963; see p. 325.)

[571] Windisch, p. 355; Barrett, p. 296, who mentions 'illegal sexual connections, the making of the sacred anointing oil or incense, or tattooing'.

[572] Windisch, p. 355; Barrett, p. 296.

[573] E. P. Sanders, 'Paul on the Law', pp. 86–7; the quotation is on p. 87.

[574] Cf. Wolff, p. 233.

so regarded both by Paul himself and by his fellow Jews, this policy might seem deserving of the most stringent punishment.[575] This understanding of Christianity gives us the answer to our last question. Paul was insistent on maintaining his own Jewish identity, and cared deeply for his own people (Rom 11.17–24), and he hoped and expected that his fellow Jews would in the end be 're-grafted' into this same Israel of God. Hence, he was willing to suffer as a Jew, at the hands of the Jewish synagogue authorities.[576]

25. τρὶς ἐρραβδίσθην, ἅπαξ ἐλιθάσθην, τρὶς ἐναυάγησα, νυχθήμερον ἐν τῷ βυθῷ πεποίηκα· Paul suffered further at the hands of the civic magistrates who represented Roman authority, being beaten on three occasions with the lictors' rods.[577] One of these incidents is recounted in Acts 16.19–24, where Paul's performance of an exorcism has caused a public disturbance. It is likely that the other two occasions were of a similar nature.[578] The stoning may be the incident mentioned in Acts 14.19, where it is recorded that Paul was stoned in Lystra, at the instigation of Jews from Antioch and Iconium. There is no indication, however, that this was done as a punishment for alleged blasphemy (Lev 24.16) on Paul's part.[579] Rather, it will have been an instance of mob violence in which non-Jews may also have been involved.[580] About the three shipwrecks we learn nothing at all from Acts.[581] Paul himself, however, tells us a little more about one of these occasions, i.e., that he spent a whole twenty-four hours[582] 'adrift at sea'[583]—literally, 'in the depth'. Windisch comments that the βυθός, properly speaking, is the deep sea in which one drowns without hope of rescue (see Exod 15.5; Ps 68 (LXX).16). Hence, the idea, strictly, would here be that of a sojourn beneath the

---

[575] Sanders, 'Paul on the Law', pp. 85–7.

[576] Sanders, 'Paul on the Law', pp. 89–90.

[577] The verb ῥαβδίζω means 'beat with a rod': see BAGD s.v. The cognate noun ῥάβδος, in the plural, can refer to the *fasces* of the Roman lictors: see LSJ s.v. ῥάβδος I. 7. These are: 'a bundle carried before … magistrates, and consisting of rods and an axe, with which criminals were scourged and beheaded'. See LS s.v. fascis II. The lictors themselves were the magistrates' attendants: see LS s.v. lictor. In Acts 16.35 the ῥαβδοῦχοι are the lictors who presumably are those who in v. 22 were ordered by the magistrates to beat (ῥαβδίζειν) Paul and Silas. On the relationship between these events and the question of Paul's Roman citizenship, see Excursus XIII below, pp. 739–42.

[578] Barrett, p. 297: Paul's offence would be the creation of public disorder.

[579] *Pace*, Hughes, p. 410, who makes this suggestion.

[580] Furnish, p. 516, with reference to Acts 14.5, where we are told that there was a joint plan by Gentiles and Jews to have the apostles stoned. See also Wolff, p. 234.

[581] See Hughes, p. 411, and Barrett, p. 298, for suggestions as to the voyages on which the shipwrecks might have occurred.

[582] See BAGD s.v. νυχθήμερον.

[583] See BAGD s.v. βυθός for this rendering of Paul's phrase ἐν τῷ βυθῷ.

waters, followed by a miraculous deliverance, as in myth and fairytales.[584] Estius, in fact, does interpret Paul's phrase in this way. The apostle here adds a reference to a further marine peril of a much graver kind: 'he will have been submerged in the depths of the sea as a result of shipwreck; where, however, he will have been preserved unharmed by divine aid for a night and a day, and thence afterwards delivered.'[585] There is a parallel with Jonah, Estius suggests.[586] All that we need to suppose, however, is that Paul managed to keep himself afloat for the best part of a night and day, by clinging to floating wreckage, until help arrived.[587] Was the experience still vividly before the apostle's mind? And is this why the tense of the verb[588] has changed to the perfect?[589] Perhaps so. A concomitant reason could be the desire to show, by the use of a different tense, that the progressive heightening of effect has now reached its climax.[590] In addition, of course, this was an experience of continuing mortal peril, for which the perfect tense might seem a more suitable means of expression.[591]

EXCURSUS XIII

11.25: Paul's punishment and Roman law

1. These beatings with rods were occasions of official punishment meted out by the representatives of Roman authority. This presents a problem. According to Acts (16.37–38; 22.25–29), Paul was a Roman citizen, and there were some legal safeguards against the infliction of this penalty on those who held the citizenship. First, there was the *Lex Porcia*, promulgated in the time of the republic, which forbade the scourging of Roman

---

[584] Windisch, p. 357.

[585] Estius, p. 640: 'demersus fuerit ex naufragio in profundum maris; ubi tamen divina ope fuerit servatus incolumis noctem & diem, atque inde postea liberatus.'

[586] Estius, p. 641.

[587] Meyer, p. 449; cf. Bachmann, p. 384 n. 1; Plummer, p. 325. Windisch, p. 357, notes Josephus's account (*Vita* 3) of a similar incident in which Josephus himself and his companions were forced to swim all night after their boat, on the way to Rome, foundered in the Adriatic.

[588] On the use of ποιέω itself in its present sense, see BAGD s.v. I.1.e.δ.: with an accusative of time it means 'spend'.

[589] So Moulton, *Prolegomena*, p. 144; Plummer, p. 325; Hughes, p. 412 n. 77; Martin, p. 378 (with the alternative suggestion that the tense is used to produce a dramatic effect).

[590] Zmijewski, 'Narrenrede', p. 250.

[591] Hence, in view of these various exegetical possibilities, not mutually exclusive, it does not seem necessary to regard πεποίηκα as an aoristic perfect of no particular significance, *pace* Turner, MHT, pp. 69–70; cf. BDR 343(2); Bultmann, p. 218.

citizens.[592] The law may have originally applied, however, only in Rome itself, as did the right of appeal to it (*provocatio*).[593] Nevertheless, by Paul's time, both the law and the right of appeal may have been extended to cover the provinces.[594] Secondly, there were the provisions of the *Lex Julia*, promulgated early in the imperial period.[595] In summary, they were these. A Roman citizen who invoked his right of appeal to Rome was protected from trial by magistrates in the provinces, and from 'summary punishment, execution or torture without trial'.[596] There were some occasions, however, when a citizen might be beaten legally: if he had not exercised his right of appeal, he might be flogged after being sentenced;[597] in some cases the right of appeal no longer applied;[598] and beating could be legal in matters of minor offences and in cases of 'flagrant disobedience towards a magistrate giving a legitimate order'.[599] These exceptions would fall within the jurisdiction of the provincial governors, although it is a further question as to whether they would be operative in the case of the ordinary municipal magistrates.[600]

2. This apparent contradiction between what happened to Paul and his legal rights as a Roman citizen requires resolution. There are three possible ways of solving the difficulty. First, it may be that the information in Acts is incorrect: Paul did not possess the citizenship. Secondly, he did possess it, but circumstances prevented him from exercising his right of appeal. Thirdly, he himself chose not to make use of his legal rights.

(a) The attribution of Roman citizenship to Paul in Acts could be due to the author's aim to present the apostle as a person of high social standing.[601] The pursuit of this aim does not, however, preclude the possibility that the presentation is based in part on historical fact.[602] At the same time, there are other arguments against the accuracy of Acts. Stegemann finds it noteworthy that Paul has only one name (as far as our information goes), instead of the three names possessed by a citizen.

---

[592] See, e.g., Barrett, p. 297, and Furnish, p. 516. Both refer to Livy, X 9.4–5: 'Yet the Porcian law alone seems to have been passed to protect the persons of the citizens, imposing, as it did, a heavy penalty if anyone should scourge or put to death a Roman citizen' (LCL). Furnish, ibid., gives the probable date of promulgation as 198 B.C.E.

[593] See H. J. Cadbury, 'Roman Law and the Trial of Paul', in K. Lake and H. J. Cadbury, *The Beginnings of Christianity*, Part I Vol. V (London, 1933), pp. 297–338; see p. 314.

[594] Cadbury, ibid.

[595] Héring, p. 89; Lang, p. 344; Sherwin-White, *Roman Law*, p. 58.

[596] Sherwin-White, ibid.

[597] Sherwin-White, *Roman Law*, pp. 71–2.

[598] Sherwin-White, *Roman Law*, pp. 61–2.

[599] Sherwin-White, *Roman Law*, p. 72.

[600] This might depend upon the degree of severity involved. Sherwin-White, *Roman Law*, p. 75, comments: 'It is extremely unlikely that the municipal court even of a Roman colony ... had the power to inflict severe punishments.'

[601] See J. C. Lentz, *Luke's Portrait of Paul*, SNTSMS 77, Cambridge, 1993, pp. 42–51, 58–61.

[602] Lentz allows, *Luke's Portrait*, pp. 59–60, that it is not wholly impossible that Paul possessed Roman citizenship.

Furthermore, that he should have been subjected three times to an illegal beating is surely improbable, even when we consider that the law was occasionally contravened.[603] These difficulties are not insuperable, however. Paul's failure to mention his complete Roman name may not be significant. According to Hengel, the use of the full name 'was seldom customary in Greek-speaking circles',[604] and Cranfield suggests that Paul may have used only the one name by choice 'in view of the fact that most of his fellow Christians only possessed one name'.[605] The fact that the illegal flogging occurred three times is not particularly surprising. It would be strange only if it occurred each time in the same city, twice, after he had had opportunity to prove his citizenship, and even then only if he had chosen to do so.[606] Hence, there is no conclusive reason for rejecting the evidence of Acts on the grounds suggested above. Some further explanation of the apparently illegal beatings seems necessary, nevertheless.

(b) Paul did possess the Roman citizenship, but various external circumstances may have militated against his use of his citizen's rights on the occasions to which 11.25 refers. The magistrates who ordered him to be beaten may have considered the public disturbances caused by his activity to be comparatively minor offences for which they could legally flog him without considering his status. The beating could be seen as 'merely an act of local police *coercitio*'.[607] In any case, as most commentators point out, illegalities are known to have occurred. According to Cicero, Verres, when governor of Sicily, had Roman citizens flogged without regard to their legal rights,[608] and Gessius Florus, when procurator of Judaea, had ordered the scourging and crucifixion of Jews of equestrian rank.[609] But even if, in Paul's case, the magistrates concerned were acting strictly in accordance with the law, his failure to claim his rights as a citizen does not mean that he did not possess the citizenship. Proof would be required, and this would not have been easy to furnish on the spot, in the midst of civic disturbance. As Hengel puts it: 'At that time people did not go around with a personal passport in their pockets.'[610] Paul may have carried a birth certificate with him on his travels, but would probably keep it in comparative safety at the place where he was lodging.[611]

(c) Paul himself may have chosen not to appeal to his citizen's rights, even were he given the opportunity to do so. Perhaps 'he kept quiet

---

[603] W. Stegemann, 'War der Apostel Paulus ein römischer Bürger?', *ZNW* 78 (1987), pp. 200–29; pp. 221–2, 223–4.
[604] Hengel, *Pre-Christian Paul*, p. 8.
[605] Cranfield, *Romans*, p. 50.
[606] See below, under (c).
[607] Hengel, *Pre-Christian Paul*, p. 7.
[608] Cic., *Verr.* II 5. 139–40, cited by Plummer, p. 324, Windisch, p. 356, and others.
[609] Plummer, ibid., Windisch, ibid., both with reference to Jos., *Bell.* II 14.9.
[610] Hengel, *Pre-Christian Paul*, p. 7.
[611] Hengel, *Pre-Christian Paul*, p. 104 n. 61. On the difficulty of proving citizenship see also Ebner, *Leidenslisten*, pp. 136–7 n. 230, and Riesner, *Frühzeit*, p. 132.

about his Roman citizenship deliberately in order to follow Christ in his suffering'.[612] He may also have had his converts in mind. Many of them would not themselves possess Roman citizenship. Conversion to the new faith might well involve them in persecution and, more particularly, in trouble with the civic authorities. Would Paul gain their loyalty to the gospel by exempting himself from suffering which they might themselves have to endure? On a more practical level, as Haenchen points out, an appeal might have involved him in a lengthy legal process of uncertain outcome, during which time he would have been deprived of opportunity for mission.[613]

3. We may conclude that Paul's own mention of the three Roman floggings he has endured does not cast serious doubt on the claim in Acts that he was a Roman citizen. A mixture of various external circumstances and inward motives would be sufficient to account in each case for his silence concerning his possession of the citizenship.

26. ὁδοιπορίαις πολλάκις, κινδύνοις ποταμῶν, κινδύνοις λῃστῶν, κινδύνοις ἐκ γένους, κινδύνοις ἐξ ἐθνῶν, κινδύνοις ἐν πόλει, κινδύνοις ἐν ἐρημίᾳ, κινδύνοις ἐν θαλάσσῃ, κινδύνοις ἐν ψευδαδέλφοις, In the previous verse Paul has mentioned one specific hazard, shipwreck, inherently connected with travel. This leads him on to the general thought of his frequent journeyings, and then to the listing of a number of the particular types of peril they entailed.[614] The repeated κινδύνοις-phrases, following upon the ὁδοιπορίαις πολλάκις, give structure to the verse. Its precise nature, however, is not altogether clear. Since there are eight κίνδυνοι, and since several of them present pairs of contrasts (in the town/in the wilderness, from fellow-Jews/Gentiles), the simplest suggestion is that the whole list is arranged in pairs.[615] This is not altogether satisfactory, however, since the last two items scarcely fit together: dangers on the sea and dangers from pseudo-Christians neither compare nor contrast with each other.[616] It may be preferable to suppose that the structure is somewhat more complex, i.e., that the κίνδυνοι are arranged as two pairs, followed by a triplet, and concluded with the κίνδυνοι amongst pseudo-brothers standing alone to give climactic emphasis:[617]

[612] Hengel, *Pre-Christian Paul*, p. 6. See also Riesner, *Frühzeit*, p. 133.
[613] Haenchen, *Apostelgeschichte*, p. 443.
[614] Barrett, p. 298.
[615] Plummer, p. 326; Lietzmann, p. 151; Zmijewski, '*Narrenrede*', p. 255.
[616] Consequently, Windisch, p. 358, suggests that there may have been some early accidental displacement of the items in the list, and that the dangers ἐν ψευδαδέλφοις should form a triplet with those ἐκ γένους and ἐξ ἐθνῶν.
[617] Plummer, p. 327, suggests that this final phrase may be 'left as a climax at the end'.

ὁδοιπορίαις[618] πολλάκις,
κινδύνοις ποταμῶν, κινδύνοις λῃστῶν,
κινδύνοις ἐκ γένους, κινδύνοις ἐξ ἐθνῶν,
κινδύνοις ἐν πόλει, κινδύνοις ἐν ἐρημίᾳ, κινδύνοις ἐν θαλάσσῃ,
κινδύνοις ἐν ψευδαδέλφοις,

As regards content, there is a similar hardships-list in Epictetus, where some of the same hazards are mentioned, such as 'a brigand', and 'journeys by land and by sea'.[619]

The danger from rivers may be mentioned first because the previous verse has concluded with a reference to shipwreck: hence, danger from waters on land may be the first hazard that comes to mind. Rivers might overflow, and what crossings there were might be difficult.[620] As in the case of shipwreck, these dangers would be the common lot of all travellers, not only those engaged in religious mission, and the same would be true of the danger of attack from brigands.[621] Thus, the first two κίνδυνοι form a pair. The next two, by contrast, are more specifically related to Paul's own missionary experience, and he has partially alluded to them in vv. 24–25. His initial frequenting of the synagogues and his preaching of the Christian message there had provoked hostility from his fellow Jews (cf. Acts 9.23–25; 17.1–5), so that they had subjected him to disciplinary flogging, and had also stirred up general violence against him (Acts 13.50; 14.19; 17.5). This violence would constitute part of what is meant by the 'dangers from Gentiles', although, again according to Acts (16.16–24; 19.23–41), trouble was also sometimes caused not as a result of Jewish instigation but on account of damage to Gentile commercial interests. The following triplet then specifies areas, rather than instruments or agents, of hazard. This sequence is probably added for rhetorical effect, since the associated perils have already received mention: the dangers in the city are those from Jews and Gentiles, those in the uninhabited areas are the dangers from bandits, and dangers at sea have been described in v. 25.[622]

---

[618] What is the grammatical function of the dative ὁδοιπορίαις and the repeated dative κινδύνοις? They could be seen as causal or instrumental, like the ἐν-phrases in v. 23b: see BDR 195, 196. Bultmann, p. 218, takes them as instrumental, still with reference back to v. 23b. By this time, however, the ὑπὲρ ἐγώ is somewhat remote. It may be better to understand the datives, with Furnish, p. 517, as modal. In his translation, p. 512, he indicates the force of the modal dative in this context by rendering it 'risking'. See BDF 198, where this type of dative is described as 'used more or less loosely to designate accompanying circumstances and manner'.

[619] Epict., *Diss.* III 24.28–30; noted by Windisch, p. 357.

[620] Barrett, p. 299; Furnish, p. 517.

[621] See Furnish, ibid, with reference to Hock, *Social Context*, p. 78, and other sources of information.

[622] Windisch, p. 359.

744 COMMENTARY ON II CORINTHIANS

Placed last for emphasis[623] there is the hazard posed by 'pseudo-Christians'.[624] The same term is used in Gal 2.4, where it refers to Judaizers who wished to impose observance of the Torah—specifically, circumcision—upon Gentile converts. In the present verse Judaizers of this sort would certainly be included, but the reference may be somewhat wider. If it includes the rival missionaries in Corinth,[625] it would refer to Jewish Christians who desired to impose at least some degree of Torah observance on Gentile believers,[626] but without the requirement of circumcision. The inclusion of pseudo-Christians in this list of hazards implies that these people had endangered Paul in person. Perhaps they had denounced him on some pretext or another to the civil magistrates or to the synagogue authorities.[627]

27. κόπῳ καὶ μόχθῳ, ἐν ἀγρυπνίαις πολλάκις, ἐν λιμῷ καὶ δίψει, ἐν νηστείαις πολλάκις, ἐν ψύχει καὶ γυμνότητι. After the perils of v. 26 Paul goes on to list other hardships entailed by his missionary work. The opening κόπῳ καὶ μόχθῳ,[628] 'toil and labour', is seen by some exegetes as a heading for what follows.[629] It certainly stands on its own structurally, separated by the lack of a preposition from the following phrases. It does not, however, serve to summarise these phrases, since they appear to relate to the circumstances in which the labour takes place and which it entails, rather than to the various aspects of the labour itself. Nevertheless, this still means that the logical connection is present, and allows the description 'heading' in a somewhat loose sense. The structural arrangement of the verse may then be understood most plausibly in the way suggested by Windisch:

κόπῳ καὶ μόχθῳ
ἐν ἀγρυπνίαις πολλάκις, ἐν λιμῷ καὶ δίψει,
ἐν νηστείαις πολλάκις, ἐν ψύχει καὶ γυμνότητι.[630]

---

[623] See, e.g., Lietzmann, p. 151; Plummer, p. 327; Wendland, p. 242; Barrett, pp. 299–300; Martin, p. 379; Zmijewski, 'Narrenrede', pp. 258–9.
[624] The word ψευδάδελφος is a Pauline creation and used only by Paul in the NT. These are internal enemies (as the apostle regards them): it may be significant that the preposition ἐν is used (by contrast with the preceding ἐκ γένους and ἐξ ἐθνῶν)—see Plummer, p. 327; he allows, however, that this could be accidental, in view of the previous ἐν-phrases.
[625] Hughes, pp. 412–13; Martin, p. 379.
[626] See above, pp. 669–70.
[627] Allo, p. 297; Héring, p. 90.
[628] The dative is to be understood in the same way as the datives of the previous verse. Some witnesses (ℵ² H 0121a 𝔐 lat Ambst) read ἐν κόπῳ, but this is obviously secondary, the ἐν being added to match the ἐν-phrases in the rest of the verse. The plain dative is original (see the reading of 𝔓⁴⁶ ℵ* B D F G Ψ 0243. 1739 pc).
[629] Zmijewski, 'Narrenrede', p. 264; Martin, p. 380.
[630] Windisch, p. 359. For two other possibilities see Zmijewski, 'Narrenrede', p. 264, and Martin, p. 379.

The two opening words κόπος and μόχθος pose two questions. Are they to be distinguished in sense? And do they have a broad, general reference or a narrower, more specific meaning? To the first question the lexicons give an indeterminate answer: there is at least a considerable overlap in meaning, but some distinction might also be possible.[631] According to Plummer, μόχθος has an active force, 'indicating struggle and toil', whilst κόπος has a passive sense, 'indicating the lassitude which results from prolonged exertion'.[632] Zmijewski makes a similar distinction between the more active word (μόχθος) and the more passive (κόπος).[633] But whilst the general usage of the two words would allow this differentiation, it is not clear that we find it elsewhere in Paul. The term κόπος surely has an active sense in 1 Cor 3.8 and 15.58, as also in 1 Th 3.5 and 2 Cor 10.15. Likewise, it seems more natural to understand the cognate verb κοπιάω as indicating positive action in most, if not all, of its Pauline occurrences: see Rom 16.6, 12; 1 Cor 15.10; Gal 4.11; Phil 2.16. Consequently, the two words may here be intended as synonyms.

To what kind of laborious toil, then, do κόπος and μόχθος refer? Some commentators suppose Paul to be referring to his manual labour. When the same phrase is used in 1 Th. 2.9 this explanation is added.[634] Others, however, would understand the phrase in a more general sense, whilst allowing that manual labour may be included. Filson comments: 'Paul describes his heavy load of preaching, teaching, and manual labor.'[635] For two reasons this second view is preferable. First, the word κόπος must surely have the same meaning here as in v. 23, where, we have argued, it refers to evangelistic labours.[636] Both there (explicitly) and here (implicitly) Paul is comparing himself with the rival missionaries in Corinth. Since these people did not, as far as can be seen, engage in manual work at all, an exclusive reference to such

---

[631] In BAGD s.v. κόπος, there are two meanings given: 1. 'trouble', 'difficulty'; 2. 'work', 'labor', 'toil'. The present reference is given under 2., together with 1 Cor 3.8; 15.58; 1 Th 1.3; 2.9; 3.5; 2 Th 3.8. Only one meaning is given for μόχθος· 'labor', 'exertion', 'hardship' (though, of course, the third sense is slightly different from the other two). In LSJ s.v. κόπος II. the options are 1. 'toil and trouble', or 'suffering'; 2. 'fatigue'; 3. 'work', 'exertion'. For μόχθος, we are given 'toil', 'hardship', and 'distress'.

[632] Plummer, p. 327.

[633] Zmijewski, 'Narrenrede', p. 262.

[634] Hughes, p. 413. See also Plummer, p. 327; Tasker, p. 164; Furnish, p. 518.

[635] Filson, p. 402; cf. Martin, pp. 380, 376; Allo, p. 298.

[636] Furnish, p. 518, refers back to v. 23, in apparent support of his view that in the present verse the reference is to manual labour. In his note, p. 515, on v. 23, however, he seems to leave open the possibility of wider reference.

labour would be out of place.[637] Secondly, it is worth asking whether even in 1 Th 2.9 the κόπος and μόχθος do solely refer to Paul's work as an artisan.

For the assertion which explains their meaning runs: νυκτὸς καὶ ἡμέρας ἐργαζόμενοι πρὸς τὸ μὴ ἐπιβαρῆσαί τινα ὑμῶν ἐκηρύξαμεν εἰς ὑμᾶς τὸ εὐαγγέλιον τοῦ θεοῦ. The preaching of the gospel is as much a part of the explanation as is the manual labour. The conditions of the labour and toil are then spelt out. The frequent sleepless nights,[638] mentioned first, may have had various causes. In the exegesis of 6.5, where this hardship has previously been noted, we took up Furnish's suggestion that Paul was deprived (or deprived himself) of sleep because of the demands either of his manual work or of his evangelistic activity or both, with the observation that the members of his congregation would most likely not be free from work commitments during the day.[639] The present reference may be understood in the same way.[640] A further possibility would be to suppose that the sleeplessness was due to Paul's anxiety for his converts.[641] But this is less likely in the present context, since it is to this kind of concern that v. 28 refers, and the beginning of the verse indicates that it is something different from what has gone before. Ebner discounts the idea of involuntary sleeplessness in the present verse. Paul is speaking of vigils consciously endured. In the background, he claims, there lies the philosopher's devaluation of sleep.[642] From a positive perspective, it shows itself in readiness for abstinence from sleep (ἀγρυπνία), and in the use of such abstinence as a means of self-discipline.[643] To watch through the night for the sake of others gives the philosopher an easy conscience.[644] For Cicero, Seneca and Plutarch, vigils (and other toils) are signs of readiness for action, and signs of toughness, and they qualify a man for a position of leadership.[645]

There follows a reference to hunger and thirst. This may relate to hardships encountered in the course of travel,[646] and also,

[637] We have argued that the rival missionaries are in view throughout v. 23b, even though comparison tends to turn into assertion of absolute excellence. See the exegesis.
[638] See BAGD s.v. ἀγρυπνία 1. The force of the ἐν, here and in what follows, is probably to designate accompanying circumstances: BDR 198.
[639] See Vol. I, p. 458, and the references, nn. 1880, 1881, to Furnish, p. 355.
[640] Furnish, pp. 518, 355.
[641] Bruce, p. 243, suggests this; cf. Tasker, p. 164.
[642] Ebner, Leidenslisten, pp. 142–3.
[643] Ebner, Leidenslisten, p. 143, with reference to Epict., Diss. I 7.30; III 15.11.
[644] Ebner, ibid., with reference to Epict., Diss. III 22.95.
[645] Ebner, ibid. See also Excursus XIV, p. 756, below.
[646] Martin, p. 380; cf. Héring, p. 90.

perhaps, deprivation resulting from Paul's insistence on refusing maintenance.[647]

The following hardship also refers to lack of food, but presumably has some difference in meaning from the preceding ἐν λιμῷ. The basic sense given in BAGD s.v. νηστεία is 'fasting', 'abstention from food'. This is then expanded under two heads: 1. 'of hunger brought about by necessity'; the present reference is given, with 6.5 in addition; 2. 'of fasting' as a religious custom. Despite the classification of the present instance under the first heading, however, it is unlikely that Paul is talking of a completely involuntary lack of food. First, the phrase would then become a mere repetition of ἐν λιμῷ.[648] Secondly, elsewhere in the NT the noun νηστεία and the verb νηστεύω are used of fasting as a voluntary religious rite.[649] Allo would suppose that this is the meaning of νηστεία here.[650] The objection would be that disciplinary fasting seems unlikely to figure in a list of apostolic hardships.[651] It is better, perhaps, to adopt an intermediate interpretation. Paul has in mind occasions when he voluntarily went without meals in order to devote more time either to his manual work or to his evangelistic activity.[652] The abstention in the first instance would be caused by his determination not to take money from the Corinthians.[653] It is thus voluntary, but not a matter of private asceticism. The suffering of cold, finally, and lack of adequate clothing is also to be related, according to Furnish,[654] to Paul's practice of manual labour: the phrase may refer to the ill-clad state that was the lot of the craftsman.[655] Possibly Paul does have this in mind. But he could also have in view unpleasant climatic conditions of travel, for which he lacked suitable warm clothes.[656] Finally, Furnish notes that some of these hardships in Paul's list, i.e., cold, hunger and thirst, are regarded by Dio Chrysostom as challenges which are taken on by the 'noble man'.[657] We need to bear this in mind when we consider the interpretation of this section as a whole.

[647] At this point, Furnish's claim that Paul is referring to his hardships as a craftsman would hold good.

[648] Plummer, p. 328; cf. Meyer, p. 451, and Barrett, p. 300.

[649] See Vol. I, p. 458.

[650] Allo, p. 298.

[651] Plummer, p. 328; Héring, p. 90; Zmijewski, 'Narrenrede', p. 263.

[652] Plummer, p. 328.

[653] Barrett, p. 300.

[654] Furnish, p. 519.

[655] Furnish, ibid., with reference to Hock, Social Context, p. 84 n. 94.

[656] Cf. Plummer, p. 328, who refers also to the possibility of being 'stripped by brigands'.

[657] Furnish, p. 518, with reference to Dio Chrys., Or. VIII 16.

28. χωρὶς τῶν παρεκτὸς ἡ ἐπίστασίς[658] **μοι**[659] **ἡ καθ' ἡμέραν, ἡ μέριμνα πασῶν τῶν ἐκκλησιῶν.** From physical hardships Paul turns to the cares he is involved in as founder of churches. The general sense is clear, but various points of detail require discussion. The first of these is whether χωρὶς τῶν παρεκτός is to be connected with what precedes or with what follows. We take it, with the majority of commentators, as belonging to what follows.[660] But what, exactly, does τῶν παρεκτός mean? According to BAGD, the word παρεκτός, when used as an adverb, means either (i) 'besides' or (ii) 'outside'. Hence, in the present verse, the meaning of the phrase would be either 'what I leave unmentioned' or 'what is external'. There is some support for taking παρεκτός in sense (ii): thus KJV has 'those things that are without'; NEB and REB have 'these external things'; and Barrett translates 'such external matters'.[661] The majority of exegetes, however, prefer the alternative (i) 'besides'. Paul would have written τὰ ἔξω, it is argued, or τὰ ἔξωθεν for 'external things'.[662] When he writes χωρὶς τῶν παρεκτός he means 'apart from the other things (things beside)'.[663] What, then, would these 'other things' be? Perhaps they might be other sufferings of the same kind as those mentioned in the preceding list.[664] But what could be left over in the way of deprivations that could be added to the list in v. 27? The question is put by Zmijewski, who suggests instead that what we have here is the use of paralipsis, i.e., the device whereby an orator 'pretends to pass over something which he in fact mentions'.[665] The 'other things', then, would be

---

[658] The reading ἐπίστασις (𝔓46 ℵ B D F G H* 0243. 33. 81. 326. 1175. 1739. 1881 pc) is preferable to ἐπισύστασις (Hᶜ Iᵛⁱᵈ Ψ 0121a 𝔐), as possessing superior attestation. The secondary reading could be due to a two-stage scribal error: an accidental repetition of the first Σ of ἐπίστασις could have produced an incorrect 'correction' by a later scribe who thought that an Υ had been omitted.

[659] The reading μοι (𝔓46 ℵ* B F G H 33. 81. 1175 pc b d) has better support than μου (ℵ D Ψ 0121a.. 0243 𝔐 lat Ambst).

[660] The Moffatt translation (see Strachan, p. 26) sees it as belonging to what precedes: 'cold and ill-clad, and all the rest of it'. Meyer, pp. 451–2, notes that Chrysostom takes it this way (PG 61 col. 571: NPNF XII, p. 395) but rightly argues that this would make the remainder of the verse too abrupt. Translations and commentators who take the phrase with what follows include: RSV, NRSV, NEB, REB, BCN; Barrett, p. 288; Furnish, pp. 512–13; Martin, p. 367.

[661] Barrett, p. 288. The 'external things' would be the physical hardships enumerated in v. 27.

[662] Plummer, p. 329.

[663] This interpretation is supported by, e.g., Windisch, p. 360; Allo, p. 298; Héring, p. 90; Bultmann, p. 218; Furnish, pp. 512–13; Martin, p. 367; see also RSV, NRSV, BCN.

[664] Allo, p. 298; cf. Héring, p. 90, and Filson, p. 402.

[665] Zmijewski, 'Narrenrede', pp. 268–9; for the definition see BDF 495; cf. the similar use of the idiom in 9.4 (see above, p. 568 n. 29). Furnish, p. 519, follows Zmijewski.

precisely what Paul goes on to refer to in the rest of the verse.⁶⁶⁶
This may be right, but it is not wholly obvious. It would seem to
require that the following phrases should stand in apposition to
τῶν παρεκτός, but the change of case from the genitive τῶν to the
nominatives ἡ ἐπίστασις and ἡ μέριμνα does not suggest this.
There could be another possibility. When Paul says 'apart from
the other things', these things would be the items in the previous
list of hardships—and not additions to them. They are, rather,
'other' than, 'additional' to the ecclesiastical problems which he
goes on to mention.

This brings us to the phrase ἡ ἐπίστασίς μοι ἡ καθ' ἡμέραν. The
noun ἐπίστασις has various senses, as the lexicons show. For the
present verse, four possibilities are listed in BAGD s.v.:
'pressure', 'attention', 'oversight', 'hindrance'; the first of these is
noted as 'an outstanding possibility'. Meyer supports the meaning
'attention',⁶⁶⁷ but Plummer is probably right in arguing that this
would be possible only if the reading μου be accepted instead of
μοι.⁶⁶⁸ Otherwise the phrase would mean 'the attention paid to
me' (not, 'my attention to someone else', which would surely be
the sense required).⁶⁶⁹ There could be a similar difficulty with the
meaning 'oversight', and 'hindrance' is probably too restricted.
With the majority of commentators we opt for the sense
'pressure'.⁶⁷⁰

This daily pressure of responsibility is then further defined in
the following ἡ μέριμνα πασῶν τῶν ἐκκλησιῶν.⁶⁷¹ The word
μέριμνα is somewhat negative in its connotations. In BAGD s.v.
the meanings given are 'anxiety', 'worry', 'care', and the present
phrase is rendered 'anxiety about all the churches'. Since Paul is
still cataloguing his apostolic trials, it is this sense that is appropriate,⁶⁷² rather than a more general notion of pastoral care.
Furthermore, the following verse suggests anxiety. From Paul's
point of view, he has had, and at this point has still, ample cause
for anxiety about the Corinthian congregation. It could be also
that the situation in the Galatian churches has not been wholly

⁶⁶⁶ Zmijewski, 'Narrenrede', p. 269.
⁶⁶⁷ Meyer, p. 451.
⁶⁶⁸ Plummer, p. 329.
⁶⁶⁹ The noun ἐπίστασις is a derivative of the verb ἐφίστημι. When the verb is
followed by the dative of a person, this person (obviously) is someone other than
the subject of the verb: see, e.g., Lk 2.9; 24.4; Acts 4.1; 23.11.
⁶⁷⁰ See, e.g., Bachmann, p. 385; Plummer, pp. 329–30; Windisch, p. 360; Barrett,
p. 288; Bultmann, p. 218; Furnish, p. 512.
⁶⁷¹ The natural understanding of the phrase is that it stands in apposition to the
preceding ἡ ἐπίστασις μοι ἡ καθ' ἡμέραν, as various translations suggest: see RSV,
NRSV, REB. The last of these makes the point clearly: 'There is the responsibility
that weighs on me every day, my anxious concern for all the churches.'
⁶⁷² Furnish, p. 519.

resolved by his letter. And he may have feared the infiltration of opponents even into those churches where trouble has not yet occurred. Moreover, there is the state of 'weakness' to which he refers next.

29. τίς ἀσθενεῖ, καὶ οὐκ ἀσθενῶ; τίς σκανδαλίζεται, καὶ οὐκ ἐγὼ πυροῦμαι; With two rhetorical questions Paul brings his list of hardships to an oratorically effective climax.[673] First he speaks of the 'weakness' he shares with everyone (in his churches) thus afflicted. What does he have in mind? There are four main possibilities.[674]

(i) He is referring specifically to those whom he describes as 'weak' in 1 Cor 8.9–11 and Rom 14.1–2, i.e., to those who have scruples of conscience about such things as the eating of idol meats or the contravention of the Mosaic food laws.[675] Whilst he does not himself adopt their standpoint, he feels supportive concern for them.[676] Against this, it could be said that there is nothing in 2 Corinthians to suggest such an interpretation.[677] Furthermore, the ἀσθεν-words occur with some frequency in chaps. 10–13 with different reference.[678] It may be worth noting, however, that the verb σκανδαλίζω occurs in Paul (the present verse apart) only in 1 Cor 8.13 (as a firm reading), i.e., in the context of discussion of idol meats.[679]

(ii) The concept of 'weakness', in a moral and spiritual sense, is comprehensive. Paul expresses his sympathy with any Christian who is weak in faith or conscience, or who has a weak grasp of Christian morality.[680] The general nature of v. 28 would give some support to this interpretation.[681]

(iii) The thought is that of physical weakness. When the apostle speaks of himself as being weak (as in 10.10; 12.5, 9, 10), it may be argued that it is physical illness that he has primarily in mind.[682]

---

[673] Cf. Zmijewski, 'Narrenrede', p. 270. The two questions effectively expect the answer, 'No one'. Martin, p. 382, suggests that in both cases the καί has consecutive force. Zmijewski, p. 271, prefers to see the τίς-clauses as conditional. This, however, turns the interrogative τίς into the indefinite τις, as his rendering ('Wenn jemand schwach ist …') shows. If any such syntactical elaboration is necessary, Martin's suggestion is the better one.

[674] For a fifth suggestion, offered by Barré, see the separate treatment below.

[675] Bruce, p. 244; Plummer, p. 331, includes this as one component of the 'weakness'. On Rom 14, see Cranfield, Romans, pp. 690–6.

[676] Bultmann, pp. 218–19.

[677] Furnish, p. 538, although he allows that this interpretation is possible.

[678] The noun ἀσθένεια occurs in 11.30; 12.5, 9, 10; 13.4; the verb ἀσθενέω in 11.21, 29; 12.10; 13.3, 4, 9; and the adjective ἀσθενής in 10.10.

[679] The point is made, by implication, by Bruce, p. 244.

[680] Meyer, p. 454; Windisch, p. 361, and Prümm, Diakonia Pneumatos I, p. 644, also see 'weakness' as a comprehensive concept.

[681] Furnish, p. 538.

[682] So J. Jervell, 'Charismatiker', pp. 191–3.

Whether or not this is so, however,[683] it is doubtful whether physical weakness is the main idea here. The first half of each question refers not to Paul but to members of his churches, and, in the second half of each, what happens to Paul is a consequence of what happens to these church members for whom he is pastorally anxious. This anxiety, which he speaks of quite generally in v. 28, would not relate only to those who were ill, nor did he see his own physical malady (if it is to such that he refers in 12.7) as a *consequence* of illness in his churches. Hence, his anxious concern may include concern for the physically ill, but must have a wider reference.

(iv) The concept of 'weakness' may be initially physical, but does have a wider sense which may be defined in the following way: 'It is Paul's entire bearing as an unimpressive figure and an outwardly nonpowerful presence at Corinth. Both those ideas—physical weakness and a "non-charismatic *persona*"—interlock, however.'[684] This, it is claimed would fit the understanding of ἀσθένεια, first, 'as a sign of humanity in its earthiness and dependence on God', and secondly, 'as a christological aspect of Paul's apostolic life'—see 13.4.[685] But how does this precisely relate to the actual verse under discussion? For what Paul is saying *here* is that if *any church member* is weak, he himself, in some way, shares their weakness. This concept of weakness is both narrower than the general weakness of humanity as such and also broader than, or different from, the specifically *apostolic* weakness mentioned in 13.4.

What conclusions, then, may we arrive at? If we look at Paul's use of the ἀσθεν-words in relation to other people (which is the point at issue here), it is the first possibility that is best substantiated. There are eight occasions when one or another of these words refers to conscientious scruples of some sort about food (Rom 14.1, 2; 15.1; 1 Cor 8.7, 9, 10, 11, 12). Whilst the letters which make up 2 Corinthians are concerned with other matters, Paul will scarcely have forgotten the issues raised in 1 Corinthians. Scrupulosity in regard to food, moreover, may have been widespread. Paul knows it to exist amongst the Roman Christians, and there had been trouble in Antioch (Gal 2.11–13) as well as in Corinth. Concern on this account may have

---

[683] On 10.10, see above, p. 631. Physical debility may be a part of what is meant, but not the whole of it.

[684] Martin, p. 382.

[685] Martin, ibid., with reference to Black, *Astheneia*, pp. 228–40. Rather similarly, Barrett, pp. 301–2, whilst supposing Paul to refer to any kind of infirmity, sees it as significant that in the general context the apostle speaks of his own weakness ('his humble and humiliated behaviour, his poverty, his unimpressive appearance') as the locus of the revelation of the power of Christ.

752   COMMENTARY ON II CORINTHIANS

constituted a significant aspect of his μέριμνα πασῶν τῶν ἐκκλησιῶν. When he says that in such cases he also is 'weak', he would then mean, not that in principle he shares these scruples, but that, as we have already noted, he gives sympathetic support and respect to those for whom they are important. This same sympathy he would doubtless claim to extend to church members with other difficulties of faith or conduct (perhaps similarly disregarded by the 'strong' in the Corinthian church), to those who were physically ill, and also, perhaps, to those who were seen by other church members as of less importance (1 Cor 12.22).[686] Hence, the concept of 'weakness' may broaden out somewhat, and need not refer exclusively to 'the weak' of 1 Cor 8 and those in other churches with similar scruples. But it is less probable that, in the present verse, it includes the fourth possibility listed above.

It is most probably the thought of 'the weak' in the first sense that leads on to the question of the second half of the verse. For in 1 Cor 8 Paul envisages the possibility that the 'weak' person may be led into serious sin by following the example of the 'knowledgeable' person (1 Cor 8.10–11), and affirms that he himself will never eat meat if by doing so he might cause his brother to sin: διόπερ εἰ βρῶμα σκανδαλίζει τὸν ἀδελφόν[687] μου, οὐ μὴ φάγω κρέα εἰς τὸν αἰῶνα (1 Cor 8.13). The possibility of a believer's being led into sin[688] would, of course, be wider than the specific situation envisaged in 1 Cor 8, and in the present context would include the kind of seduction Paul has in view earlier in the chapter (vv. 1–4). If such a thing occurs, he 'burns' with emotion.[689] The particular emotion in view here is most probably indignation,[690] or even anger,[691] directed against those who are the cause of the seduction to sin.

With whatever variations in detail, therefore, the majority of commentators understand Paul to be speaking of his anxious concern for those in his churches who are in some way 'weak', or even likely to be led into positive sin. There are, however, two markedly different interpretations of the whole

686 See Furnish, p. 538.
687 See BAGD s.v. σκανδαλίζω 1.a., 'cause [someone] to sin'.
688 BAGD, ibid.: the passive, as in the present verse, means 'be led into sin'; the alternative (under 2.), 'have reason to take offence', is less likely.
689 BAGD s.v. πυρόω 1.b.: the passive, in a figurative sense, means 'burn', 'be inflamed'; the possible emotional content is then defined as 'sympathy', as 'readiness to aid', or 'indignation', and references in 2 and 3 Maccabees are noted (2 Macc 4.38; 10.35; 14.45; 3 Macc 4.2).
690 Furnish, p. 513 (cf. p. 520); Bruce, p. 244; NRSV.
691 REB: 'burn with anger'; cf. BCN 'llosgi gan ddicter'. The references in 2 Maccabees (see n. 689 above) concern burning with anger.

verse, one proposed by M. L. Barré,[692] the other by S. B. Andrews.[693]

(i) Arguing that the section vv. 21b–29 displays a chiastic structure, Barré claims that v. 29 corresponds with v. 21b,[694] so that the τίς of v. 21b and the τις of v. 29 will refer, not to some weak church member led astray, but, representatively, to Paul's *opponents*: if any such opponent is 'weak', so is he; and if any such opponent is 'caused to stumble', he himself is subject to πυροῦσθαι. What does all this mean? Barré argues that the background of thought is to be found in Dan 11.33–35, in the version of Theodotion. This passage speaks of the eschatological trials that are to befall 'the wise' before the appointed time of the end, and the language has parallels with 2 Cor 11.29, in that the verb ἀσθενέω occurs three times, and πυρόω once. The wise will become feeble (ἀσθενήσουσιν),[695] but this will happen to refine them (τοῦ πυρῶσαι αὐτούς), i.e., through some fiery trial. Hence, Paul is claiming that if any of his opponents should boast of being 'tripped up' in the eschatological struggle, he himself similarly falls victim, and if any such opponent should boast of 'being ensnared' in this conflict, he himself is 'being tried in the fires of the eschatological ordeal'. The point would be that engagement in this struggle was especially the lot of true apostles—which his opponents claim to be.[696]

This exegesis is ingenious, but can scarcely be accepted. Why should Paul's Corinthian readers be expected to understand the verb ἀσθενέω in this specialised way which differs from his use of the ἀσθεν-words elsewhere?[697] Moreover, as Furnish points out, it is 'precarious' to identify the interrogative τίς (a favourite Pauline idiom) of v. 29 with the indefinite τὶς of v. 21b.[698] Lastly, the theory seems to require not only that Paul himself would have been familiar with a particular Greek recension (or its ancestor) of the book of Daniel (as Barré supposes he may have been), but also that his readers knew of it. This is not very likely.

(ii) For Andrews the weakness in question is a matter of social

---

[692] M. L. Barré, 'Paul as "Eschatologic Person": a New Look at 2 Cor 11:29', *CBQ* 37 (1975), pp. 500–26.

[693] Scott. B. Andrews, 'Too Weak Not to Lead: the Form and Function of 2 Cor 11.23b–33', *NTS* 41 (1995), pp. 263–76.

[694] There are two similarities between these verses: the use of τίς/τὶς and the repetition of the same verb in a different person.

[695] In JB the verb is translated 'be brought down'; in NRSV and REB as 'fall victim'.

[696] Barré, 'New Look', pp. 513–18. The phrases quoted are on p. 518.

[697] We should need to suppose that the opponents had acquainted them with this usage and reference. But how would *this* fit the apparent quotation of the opposition in 10.10 (ordinary pejorative sense of ἀσθενής)?

[698] Furnish, pp. 519–20.

status.[699] He argues that catalogues of hardships, such as the one found in the preceding verses, carry status implication. Those who endure hardships are possessed of noble status, whilst those who succumb to them betray their low status. When Paul speaks of his weakness in v. 29 he is indicating the status that results from the hardships just listed, and is claiming low status for himself as a person who is able to sympathise with others of similar position. Two vocabulary items suggest this. The verb σκανδαλίζω occurs elsewhere in Paul only in Rom 14.21[700] and 1 Cor 8.13, and in both contexts Paul is concerned with the relationship between the weak, i.e., those of low social ranking, and the strong, or powerful, of comparatively high status. The use of πυρόω is to be connected with the fire of 1 Cor 3.15, which 'burns up' weak material. Paul's question, οὐκ ἐγὼ πυροῦμαι; means that he is not strong enough to withstand this testing by fire because he is 'weak' in respect of status. Thus: 'In summary, 11.29 is filled with status implications that result from Paul's inability to master his difficult circumstances.'[701] So what does this mean, in the Corinthian situation? Paul is engaged in a contest with his opponents which concerns leadership. For Paul himself, who reverses upper-class ideals, the genuine leader is one 'whose weak status results from a submission to difficulties'.[702] In his own case he shows cowardice in escaping from Aretas. The whole catalogue, moreover, is to be interpreted in a similar way. Thus, the leadership model Paul adopts is that of the 'populist leader or demagogue'.[703]

This is scarcely convincing. Lambrecht offers some pertinent criticisms.[704] First, 11.29 is not concerned with status. Rather, it gives a specific example of the pressure and anxiety to which v. 28 refers. Secondly, the interpretation of πυροῦμαι is improbable: Paul refers to his sense of indignation. Thirdly, and most significantly, there is no indication that the apostle submissively succumbed to his trials: 'Paul has not overcome the hardships in the sense that he removed them, but he certainly endured them.'[705] We may add that, were the πυροῦμαι of the present verse to be related to the fire of judgment of 1 Cor 3.12–15, Paul would be suggesting that he feared his own work would turn out to be worthless.

---

[699] See p. 270 n. 35, where he refers to Theissen, *Social Setting*, pp. 121–43, on the status connotations of the ἀσθεν-words.
[700] There is a variant, which Andrews fails to note.
[701] Andrews, 'Too Weak', p. 271.
[702] Andrews, 'Too Weak', p. 274.
[703] Andrews, 'Too Weak', p. 275.
[704] J. Lambrecht, 'Strength in Weakness', *NTS* 43 (1997), pp. 285–90.
[705] Lambrecht, 'Strength', p. 289.

The use of ἦθος *in 11.23–29.*[706] 'This proof consists in effecting persuasion in an audience through a presentation of the genuinely good moral character of the speaker.' It serves to create confidence in him.[707] Here, Paul aims to gain the Corinthians' goodwill by his recital of his hardships.[708] In his present situation, projection of his character is crucial, in view of his opponents' attacks on him. His hardships show its quality,[709] and, he hopes, will inspire awe in his readers 'to such an extent ... as to reclaim their allegiance'.[710] For in Graeco-Roman culture, and especially amongst the Stoics, 'adversity best revealed one's character and times of hardship tested the authenticity of one's virtue'.[711] For Paul, his hardships proved that he was truly called by God, since he had been enabled to survive them.[712]

If this is a correct interpretation of the hardships-list, it would confirm the view for which we shall argue below, that the list is not intended as parody. We shall look again at this matter of ἦθος when we discuss Paul's story of his rapture to paradise, which also has been interpreted as parody, but which DiCicco regards as initially part of Paul's claim concerning his quality of character.

EXCURSUS XIV

Cultural background of the hardships-list in 11.23b–29 and discussion of the question of parody

(i) *Cultural background*

As we have observed,[713] Paul's list of his hardships reflects the Graeco-Roman culture of his day. This is apparent in two respects. In content, there are parallels to the personal catalogues which list the difficulties suffered by famous historical or mythological characters. In style, there are affinities with the achievements-lists of famous men. It is doubtful, however, whether, in Paul's case at least, one should make too clear-cut a distinction between the two genres. On the one hand, a recital of

---

[706] See above, p. 655.
[707] DiCicco, *Ethos, Pathos and Logos*, p. 36.
[708] DiCicco, *Ethos, Pathos and Logos*, pp. 78–9.
[709] DiCicco, *Ethos, Pathos and Logos*, pp. 83–4.
[710] DiCicco, *Ethos, Pathos and Logos*, p. 86.
[711] DiCicco, *Ethos, Pathos and Logos*, p. 87.
[712] DiCicco, *Ethos, Pathos and Logos*, p. 91.
[713] See above, pp. 733–4.

hardships by the one who has endured and overcome them could be seen as a demonstration of achievement. On the other hand, the concern for precise information which characterises the achievements-lists is found in the personal catalogues as well.[714] It will be helpful, nevertheless, in this discussion, to say something separately about each type of catalogue.

(a) Personal catalogues. Alexander the Great was clearly a favourite subject of the personal catalogue, and what is said about him in these lists usefully illustrates the nature of the genre. Ebner cites several examples. In one instance, Plutarch says that Alexander never tired of marshalling his forces, was never weary of sieges and pursuits, and dealt with riots and revolts of all kinds. Moreover, he endured all the natural hazards entailed by his campaigns: storms, deep rivers, wild beasts, and the like.[715] In another example, Arrian presents him as confronting the ringleaders of a rebellion, presenting his case before his soldiers as his judges. His style of life has been modest, and what wealth he possesses he holds in trust for those now contesting his leadership. He keeps watch so that they may sleep (προαγρυπνῶν δὲ ὑμῶν οἶδα, ὡς καθεύδειν ἔχοιτε ὑμεῖς). He lists the wounds he has suffered, and asks who amongst them has taken on more labours than he. He has led them to victory over land and sea, through rivers and over mountains.[716] Here, and in the passage noted in Plutarch, there are some obvious parallels to what Paul says of his own care for his churches, of the hazards he has endured in his travels, and of his own privations.

(b) Achievements-lists. The best known example of this type of list is probably the *Res Gestae* of Augustus. On his death in C.E. 14 Augustus left a list of his achievements: it was to be published by inscription on tablets of bronze which would be attached to pillars in front of the mausoleum. Our main source for this catalogue is the copy of it known as the *Monumentum Ancyranum,* found in a temple of 'Rome and Augustus' in Ancyra (Ankara). When the list was published in the provinces it became necessary to provide a Greek paraphrase of the original Latin. The inscription at Ancyra has both versions.[717] In all probability Paul himself would have been acquainted with it.[718] Certainly there are stylistic similarities between his catalogue in 2 Cor 11 and the text of the Augustan list.

---

[714] Ebner, *Leidenslisten,* pp. 117, 120.

[715] Plut., *Mor.* 341E–F; 327C; see Ebner, *Leidenslisten,* pp. 118–19.

[716] Arrian, *Anab.* VII 8.3; 9.8–9; 10.1–2; see Ebner, *Leidenslisten,* p. 120.

[717] For this information, with further discussion, and for the Latin text with English translation and notes, see P. A. Brunt and J. M. Moore, *Res Gestae Divi Augusti: the Achievements of the Divine Augustus,* Oxford, 1967, pp. 1–2 and throughout. According to these editors, the literary genre of such a list is to be seen as a development of the eulogies, 'inscriptions recording their careers and deeds', which some prominent Romans left as their own memorials (*Res Gestae,* pp. 2–3). For the Latin text, Greek paraphrase, and English translation, see E. G. Hardy, *The Monumentum Ancyranum,* Oxford, 1923.

[718] Ebner, *Leidenslisten,* p. 131.

These were pointed out originally by A. Fridrichsen.[719] The most significant parallel to the Pauline passage, in his view, is the use of the first person singular. This he sees as the decisive formal characteristic of the *Res Gestae*.[720] He cites, for example, δὶς ἐνίκησα παρατάξει (*Mon. Anc.* 1.18),[721] εἰκοσάκις καὶ ἅπαξ προσηγορεύθην αὐτοκράτωρ (*Mon. Anc.* 2.10),[722] and δὶς ἐπὶ κέλητος ἐθριάμβευσα, τρὶς ἐφ᾽ ἅρματος (*Mon. Anc.* 2.9).[723] These examples are parallel to the Pauline list also in respect of the numerical information given.[724] Fridrichsen further draws attention to the characteristic use of πολλάκις in the catalogues.[725]

(ii) *The question of parody*

According to Travis, whilst Paul employs here the conventions of the encomium, 'he fills them with material which reverses their effect'. To his opponents, the hardships he catalogues would be discreditable to him. This is a clear indication of parody. He reduces to absurdity 'the whole Graeco-Roman attitude to boasting', as exemplified in the *Res Gestae* of Augustus and similar catalogues of achievements.[726] This interpretation has gained some popularity. Ebner suggests, cautiously, that since Paul must have known Augustus's catalogue, it is conceivable that he parodies the genre, so that his own list becomes an 'anti-list'.[727]

Nevertheless, there seem to be some difficulties in the way of accepting the parody theory, in its complete form at least.

(a) Does the list altogether fit the full definition of parody? According to Heckel, parody is a mocking imitation of a serious genre (or individual work) which retains its outward form but fills it with unsuitable and derisive content.[728] Now it is true that Paul's opponents might have regarded his hardships as a matter for derision. But he himself would see them very differently. For him they would be an aspect of the παθήματα

---

[719] A. Fridrichsen, 'Zum Stil des Paulinischen Peristasenkatalogs 2 Cor 11 23ff.', *Symbolae Osloenses* 7(1928), pp. 25–9; 'Peristasenkatalog und Res Gestae: Nachtrag zu 2 Cor 11 23ff.', *SO* 8 (1929), pp. 78–82.

[720] Fridrichsen, 'Peristasenkatalog', p. 79.

[721] Fridrichsen, 'Stil', p. 28. For the Latin with English translation, see Brunt and Moore, *Res Gestae*, pp. 18-9: 'vici bis acie', 'I twice defeated … in battle.'

[722] Fridrichsen, ibid. See *Res Gestae*, ibid: 'appellatus sum viciens et semel imperator', 'I was twenty-one times saluted as *imperator*.'

[723] Fridrichsen, ibid. See Hardy, *Monumentum Ancyranum*, p. 37: 'Bis ovans triumphavi, tris egi curulis triumphos', 'Twice I received triumphal ovations. Three times I celebrated curule triumphs.'

[724] Fridrichsen, ibid.

[725] Ibid. Fridrichsen cites: πρὸς ἐμὲ ἐξ Ἰνδίας βασιλέων πρεσβεῖαι πολλάκις ἀπεστάλησαν (*Mon. Anc.* 16.16f.). See Hardy, *Monumentum Ancyranum*, p. 143: 'Ad me ex India regum legationes saepe missae sunt', 'From India embassies of kings were many times sent to me.'

[726] Travis, 'Paul's Boasting', pp. 529–30; quotation on p. 530.

[727] Ebner, *Leidenslisten*, p. 131. Other exegetes who to some degree support the parody theory include Sundermann, *Kraft der Rede*, p. 143 and n. 318; Furnish, p. 533; Barnett, p. 534.

[728] Heckel, *Schwachheit*, p. 22.

τοῦ Χριστοῦ (1.5). In the exegesis of 11.22 we noted that Wolff rejects the suggestion that Paul parodies the encomiastic motif of εὐγένεια on the grounds that the apostle is serious about his Judaism.[729] Would not a similar argument apply here? Paul would surely be even more serious about what he believed to be his participation in the sufferings of Christ.

(b) Whilst Paul may imitate the style of the Graeco-Roman achievements-lists, imitation is not, as such, parody. It is interesting to observe that Ebner, despite opting for the possibility of parody, nevertheless argues that Paul presents his hardships as genuinely deserving of fame.[730]

(c) Some of these hardships would in fact correspond with the hellenistic image of the leader, or the man of noble character. As we have seen, for some Greek and Roman writers vigils and other toils may be signs of strength, and qualifications for leadership.[731] Cold, hunger and thirst can be seen as challenges. If taken up as such, they indicated nobility of character.[732]

(d) Travis and Ebner both substantiate their suggestions of parody by reference to vv. 32–33. In these verses it does seem likely that Paul intends a parody of the Roman custom of the wall-crown,[733] But this belongs to the second half of his personal catalogue. It does not necessarily condition the interpretation of the first half. It is not certain, moreover, that it influences in this way even the interpretation of what follows.[734]

All things considered, it is doubtful whether the hardships-list of 11.23b–29 can be seen as consistent parody. There may be a hint of it at one point. Ebner suggests that Paul's references to his being flogged may be intended as parody of the conventional achievements-list: beatings would leave scars on his back (as though he were retreating in battle).[735] Otherwise, the parody theory needs to be treated with caution.

11.30–31: transitional passage

30. Εἰ καυχᾶσθαι δεῖ, τὰ τῆς ἀσθενείας μου[736] καυχήσομαι. Various problems are presented by what is, on the face of it, a straightforward, if paradoxical, statement. What is the structural function of the verse? And what is the meaning of τὰ τῆς ἀσθενείας? These two questions are interrelated. In addition, the

---

[729] See above, p. 530 n. 523.
[730] Ebner, *Leidenslisten*, p. 154. See also F. W. Danker, 'Paul's Debt to the *De Corona* of Demosthenes: A Study of Rhetorical Techniques in Second Corinthians' pp. 262–80 in *Persuasive Artistry*, ed. D. F. Watson, JSNTSS 50, Sheffield, 1991; see p. 272. Danker understands 11.23–27 as an indication of Paul's courage.
[731] See above, p. 746.
[732] Cf. p. 747 above.
[733] See below, p. 765.
[734] See below, pp. 772–3.
[735] Ebner, *Leidenslisten*, p. 130.
[736] Most witnesses read μου, but it is omitted by a few (𝔓[46vid] B H 1175). The omission could be correct, since words of this kind may be added by scribes to make the sense more explicit.

answers to them may affect the way one interprets vv. 23–29, or, alternatively, the answers may themselves be affected by one's general understanding of the previous section. If v. 30 in part forms a conclusion to the preceding hardships-list, then 'weakness' will be related to the hardships and trials therein enumerated, and the list itself will be regarded from this standpoint. But if, with v. 31, it acts as an introduction to the Damascus incident, and is not substantially related to the previous section, then the content of the ἀσθένεια will be seen differently, and the function of the catalogue of hardships may present itself in a different light. Conversely, if it seems plausible that Paul should see his hardships as instances of 'weakness', this would strengthen the case for regarding v. 30 as the list's conclusion. But if 'weakness' appears inappropriate to its contents, then it may be that v. 30 refers only to what follows.

We shall take the question of the structural function of the verse as the lead question, and ask, first, about the arguments in favour of relating it to the preceding section; secondly, about the arguments which would support its relation with what follows; and, thirdly, whether there might be some compromise position whereby the verse might be seen as transitional, and possessing a dual reference. We shall then, fourthly, add some further comments, and lastly, try to reach a conclusion.

(i) This verse may conclude the previous section. The whole catalogue would thus be provided with an effective framework. The key verb καυχάομαι occurs both here and in the introductory section, vv. 16–21, and we may compare the use of ἀσθενέω in v. 21 with the ἀσθένεια of the present verse.[737] Furthermore, the hardships-list can be seen as a demonstration of the human weakness to which v. 30 refers. It is a description of an existence in which one falls victim to human hostility, to the rigours of nature, and to all kinds of hindrances.[738] Paul chooses to speak of trials, i.e., of his weakness, rather than to boast of his miracles.[739]

(ii) There are other arguments, however, which could suggest that vv. 30–31 are to be related to what follows. We find in these two verses motifs which recur in 12.1–10: the phrase καυχᾶσθαι δεῖ is found in 12.1; the future καυχήσομαι in conjunction with 'weaknesses' is repeated in 12.5, 9; and the οὐ ψεύδομαι of 11.31 is reflected in the ἀλήθειαν γὰρ ἐρῶ of 12.6.[740] There is also the

---

737 Zmijewski, 'Narrenrede', p. 276.
738 Windisch, p. 362.
739 Chrysostom, PG 61 col. 572 (NPNF XII, p. 396). Other commentators who would see v. 30 as related to what precedes include Meyer, p. 455; Lietzmann, p. 151; Bultmann, p. 219; and Martin, p. 383.
740 Zmijewski, 'Narrenrede', p. 276.

basic question as to whether the hardships-list is really to be understood, after all, as a catalogue of weaknesses. For if it is not to be seen in this light, then v. 30 would not be related to it. One could well argue that since Paul has overcome these sufferings the list serves to demonstrate his strength.[741] Indeed, in so far as the passage is part of a *Narrenrede*, this could be seen as its intention.[742] More straightforwardly, it may be that before the theme of weakness can be seen in its proper light, Paul has to establish his apostolic authority on other grounds. The list of the trials he endures fulfils this prior function by providing evidence of what he has done as a servant of the gospel.

(iii) Perhaps v. 30 should be seen as both retrospective and prospective. The key terms καυχάομαι and ἀσθένεια denote the motifs which dominate the whole Fool's Speech, and the verse is to be understood as an intentional reminder of the basic principle which determines the whole exposition.[743]

(iv) Some further considerations are worth attention. It is surely significant that in v. 21b, which begins the comparison with opponents which leads into the hardships-list, Paul sets his proposed boldness *in contrast* with 'weakness'. It would then be only natural to suppose that the contrast continues through what follows (cf. the argument under (ii)). But how far does it extend? How far, that is, are we to read Paul's words as a bold assertion of strength? If the contrast continues through to the end of v. 29, one would expect v. 30, which specifically introduces the motif of boasting of weakness, to begin with an adversative particle. Perhaps, then, Barrett is correct in claiming that the list of hardships changes character as it goes along.[744] But the change may not occur as soon as he suggests, i.e. (apparently), at v. 26. For it is perfectly possible to see everything Paul mentions up to the end of v. 28 as illustrating, in one way or another, his capacity for endurance. The change, in fact, may come only in the final verse of the list, v. 29. From the point of view of content, v. 29 may be seen as both retrospective and prospective. Paul's weakness, *here*, is retrospective, in that it relates to the weight of pastoral responsibility he carries (v. 28) (and carries with strength?). But it has a prospective bearing, in that this particular aspect of his

[741] Schmiedel, p. 292: 'die hier genannten Leiden nur uneigentlich ἀσθ. heissen würden und in ihrer Ueberwindung vielmehr die Stärke des P zu Tage kommt'. See also Windisch, p. 362, although he does not ultimately support this view. Also relevant here is the stylistic similarity to the *res gestae* convention: see above, pp. 756–7. This would support Schmiedel.

[742] Windisch, p. 362.

[743] Zmijewski, '*Narrenrede*', pp. 278–9; cf. Furnish, p. 539. Allo, p. 299, also sees vv. 30–31 as transitional.

[744] Barrett, p. 302.

responsibility, concerned with 'weakness', sets off the further train of thought that begins in v. 30 and comes to a climax in 12.10. What conclusions may we come to? From the structural aspect, it makes sense to take v. 30 as the halfway point in the discourse. The presence in it of key terms, as noted under (i) and (ii), provides formal reference both to the beginning of the *Narrenrede* and to its conclusion: we are reminded that its governing motif is that of boasting. Thus, as suggested under (iii), the verse is both retrospective and prospective. As regards content, however, it may be prospective only. If we accept the view of vv. 23–29 outlined under (ii), it does not set out the interpretative principle which is to be applied to the *whole* speech,[745] but rather the principle illustrated in its second half, and in this section only, i.e., boasting of weakness. Thus, together with the preliminary reference to the weakness motif in v. 29, v. 30 marks a substantial point of transition. The assertion in v. 18 that Paul, like his rivals, will boast (κἀγὼ καυχήσομαι) in a worldly fashion is replaced by the resolve to boast (καυχήσομαι) of his weaknesses. If boasting is necessary, it is this second form he will adopt. Since he has already spent some time engaging in the first variety (having indicated in v. 18 his explicit intention to do so), his assertion may seem somewhat self-contradictory. He did, however, indicate at the same time that this earlier boasting was a species of folly, by implication forced upon him by the behaviour of the rival missionaries and the Corinthians' ready acceptance of them. This same compulsion (δεῖ) to prove himself infinitely superior (ὑπὲρ ἐγώ) to his rivals is now recognised again, though more tentatively (Εἰ ... δεῖ), and met differently. It is circumstances of weakness that he will boast of, for the reason that will become apparent in 12.9–10.

31. ὁ θεὸς[746] καὶ πατὴρ τοῦ κυρίου Ἰησοῦ οἶδεν, ὁ ὢν εὐλογητὸς εἰς τοὺς αἰῶνας, ὅτι οὐ ψεύδομαι. Paul here combines elements of doxological and oath formulas to make up a very powerful statement.[747] The doxological ὁ ὢν εὐλογητὸς εἰς τοὺς αἰῶνας has a close parallel in Rom 1.25, ὅς ἐστιν εὐλογητὸς εἰς τοὺς αἰῶνας[748] The oath formula, ὁ θεὸς ... οἶδεν ... ὅτι οὐ ψεύδομαι, is similar to Gal 1.20, ἰδοὺ ἐνώπιον τοῦ θεοῦ ὅτι οὐ

---

745 *Pace* Furnish, p. 539.

746 D* adds τοῦ Ἰσραήλ after ὁ θεός. The whole phrase ὁ θεὸς [τοῦ] Ἰσραήλ is frequent in the LXX, but in the NT occurs only in Mt 15.31 and Lk 1.68. If the addition is intentional, rather than an automatic amplification by a scribe familiar with the LXX, it could have been thought suitable on account of Paul's insistence in 11.22 that he is as Jewish as his opponents.

747 Cf. Windisch, p. 363; Zmijewski, '*Narrenrede*', p. 281.

748 On the Jewish background to the εὐλογητός-expressions, see Vol. I, pp. 100–1.

762   COMMENTARY ON II CORINTHIANS

ψεύδομαι, and to Rom 9.1, ἀλήθειαν λέγω ἐν Χριστῷ, οὐ ψεύδομαι, whilst the opening ὁ θεὸς ... οἶδεν has occurred earlier in the present chapter at v. 11. In 1.3, lastly, we have what is in one respect the nearest parallel: Εὐλογητὸς ὁ θεὸς καὶ πατὴρ τοῦ κυρίου ἡμῶν Ἰησοῦ Χριστοῦ. There the expression is probably to be regarded as a wish,[749] whereas here the εὐλογητός-clause is clearly making a statement. In both cases, however, the same question arises concerning the precise sense of ὁ θεὸς καὶ πατὴρ τοῦ κυρίου (ἡμῶν) Ἰησοῦ (Χριστοῦ). Does Paul speak of God as the God of the Lord Jesus as well as the Father of Jesus? In the discussion of 1.3 we have concluded that this is probably the case.[750] The absence of a second ὁ before πατήρ suggests this,[751] and a number of English translations of the present verse give a literal rendering which would support this interpretation.[752] Furnish, however, translates: 'God, the father of the Lord Jesus'[753] and commenting on the parallel in 1.3 claims that there is no clear allusion in the genuine Pauline letters to the idea of God as Jesus's God (though it does occur in Eph 1.17).[754] Similarly, Barrett translates at 1.3: 'Blessed is God, the Father of our Lord Jesus Christ,'[755] and comments that 'Paul shows no interest in the personal religion of Jesus'.[756] But these arguments are not decisive. There could well be an allusion in Rom 15.6 (τὸν θεὸν καὶ πατέρα τοῦ κυρίου ἡμῶν Ἰησοῦ Χριστοῦ) to 'the God ... of Jesus Christ'.[757] And Paul's alleged lack of interest in Jesus's religion would militate equally (if not more so) against the description 'Father of our Lord Jesus', which clearly he does use.

What, then, is the point of reference of this powerful assertion of Paul's veracity? One suggestion is that he is vouching for the truth of his preceding hardships-list.[758] But if this were the function of v. 31, we should expect it to follow immediately after v. 29.[759] More probably, it emphasises Paul's determination, expressed in v. 30, to restrict himself to the paradoxical type of boasting that will issue in self-humiliation, i.e., boasting of

[749] Vol. I, p. 101.
[750] Vol. I, p. 102. We suggested there that the point might be 'to avoid any implication that Christ, as κύριος, is some kind of independent deity'.
[751] Vol. I, ibid.
[752] See, e.g., RSV, NRSV, NEB, REB, JB.
[753] Furnish, p. 513.
[754] Furnish, p. 109.
[755] Barrett, p. 56; but he translates the present verse, p. 289, 'The God and Father of the Lord Jesus'.
[756] Barrett, p. 58.
[757] Cranfield, Romans, p. 738.
[758] Windisch, pp. 362–3; Tasker, p. 167.
[759] Meyer, p. 456.

weakness.[760] He will thus distinguish himself from the rival missionaries.[761] This kind of boasting is so paradoxical that it may seem to need the confirmation provided by v. 31.

11.32–33: escape from Damascus

With the majority of commentators, we reject the suggestion that these verses are an interpolation. It was proposed by Schmiedel, who argued that Paul's readers would not see the visionary experience of 12.2–4 as an instance of the weakness he speaks of in v. 30. He therefore supposed that an interpolator may have added vv. 32–33 to provide at least one example of such ἀσθένεια.[762] As Windisch points out, however, these verses are not a very obvious example. The escape was successful, after all.[763] It is true that Paul himself does seem to use the story in this way. But would the idea have occurred spontaneously to anyone else?

32–33. ἐν Δαμασκῷ ὁ ἐθνάρχης Ἀρέτα τοῦ βασιλέως ἐφρούρει τὴν πόλιν Δαμασκηνῶν πιάσαι με,[764] καὶ διὰ θυρίδος ἐν σαργάνῃ ἐχαλάσθην διὰ τοῦ τείχους καὶ ἐξέφυγον τὰς χεῖρας αὐτοῦ. There are four questions for discussion: (i) Paul's purpose in narrating this incident; (ii) the general historical background; (iii) the main exegetical item i.e., the meaning here of ἐθνάρχης, and (iv) the relation between Paul's account and the parallel narrative in Acts 9.23–25.

(i) The very fact that interpolation has been suggested requires those who accept these verses as original to explain why Paul should recount this story here. There are a number of suggestions.

(a) The incident was connected in point of time with the event narrated in 12.1–4.[765] But Paul has not been recounting experiences in chronological sequence. Furthermore, the time-gap between his escape from Aretas's ethnarch and the writing of 2 Cor 10–13 was probably longer than fourteen years.[766]

(b) These verses are a supplement to the preceding list of

[760] Furnish, p. 540, sees v. 30 as the primary point of reference; so also Martin, p. 384.
[761] Furnish, ibid.
[762] Schmiedel, p. 291.
[763] Windisch, p. 364.
[764] A number of witnesses (א D² (F G) H Ψ 0121a. 0243 𝔐 syʰ bo) read θέλων after με. The omission (B D* sa) is more probably original. The θέλων may have been added to emphasise the point that Aretas did not succeed in arresting Paul.
[765] Osiander, p. 447.
[766] Jewett, *Dating Paul's Life*, end-graph, places the former event in 37 C.E. and the latter in the period 55–56. Lüdemann, *Paul, Apostle to the Gentiles*, pp. 262–3, would suggest a gap of 17 years.

mortal dangers the apostle has encountered. He mentions the event because it was the first time that, in his apostolic capacity, his life had been endangered.[767] This is not altogether convincing. It could be argued that what is emphasised is not Paul's danger but his escape.[768] Furthermore, the list of hardships shows evidence of careful construction, and it would therefore be somewhat strange to find at this later point a kind of footnote dealing with a matter previously omitted. These verses are not, either, in the style of the list, which deals in a succinct and general itemisation of hazards, rather than in detailed accounts of particular incidents. Lastly, it is separated from the list itself by v. 30.

(c) The incident is intended as an example of weakness, for the means of escape employed were not those of a courageous person.[769] The fact that the story follows vv. 30-31 suggests that 'it is a story about Paul's humiliation, not about his heroism'.[770] This interpretation has substantial support.[771] But might it be possible, instead, to see the apostle's escape as an act of daring?[772]

(d) Is Paul constrained to mention the event because it had been used against him? Perhaps his opponents were saying that he had not been in real danger, and that his flight was due to cowardice.[773] He shows that, on the contrary, there was in fact considerable danger.[774] But was this incident, happening so early in Paul's Christian career, so much a matter of general knowledge as to be used in this way? There is nothing in the way the story is told to suggest that it had been exploited by his critics.[775]

(e) He relates the incident here, rather than within the framework of the hardships-list, so as to provide a contrast with the following account of his ascent to the third heaven (12.2-4). The subject of this latter ineffable experience was the same person as the one who underwent an undistinguished descent in escaping from Damascus. Humanly speaking, he is weak.[776] This suggestion has its attractions. But one would have expected the contrasting relationship between 'descent' and 'ascent' to have been more plainly indicated.[777]

---

[767] Wendland, p. 243; cf. Hughes, p. 422; Strachan, pp. 28-9.
[768] Furnish, p. 540.
[769] Bachmann, p. 387.
[770] Furnish, pp. 541-2; the quotation is on p. 542.
[771] See, e.g., Allo, pp. 300-1; Hughes, p. 422; Barrett, p. 304.
[772] Windisch, p. 363.
[773] Bousset, p. 209; Plummer, pp. 332-3.
[774] Bousset, ibid; Plummer, p. 333; see also Strachan, p. 28.
[775] See Bultmann, p. 220, on this second objection; Furnish, p. 541, is in agreement with him.
[776] Hughes, p. 422.
[777] Cf. Furnish, p. 540: 'One would expect a transitional comment substantially different from the one provided by 12.1.'

(f) What we have here is a reversal of the motif of the Roman 'wall-crown', i.e., the reward given to the man first over the wall in an attack on a city.[778] Paul's intention might then be to ridicule boasting in general[779]—presumably by a kind of parody of the kind of achievement which would usually be regarded as a fit subject for self-congratulation. This is certainly a possibility, although, again, there is no clear pointer to it in the text.[780]

(g) Perhaps Paul has in mind the allusion in Prov 21.22 to the wise man who 'can scale a citadel of warriors' (JB). He could intend a contrast between opponents who regarded themselves as wise (as also did the Corinthians—11.19) and himself: 'They scaled the city walls of the mighty; he only managed to be let down in a fish-basket.' He would use the story to show that it was God who delivered him.[781] But where he has used this verse in Proverbs before (10.4–5) it is he himself who is the one who attacks strongholds.[782] Without specific direction, it is difficult to see how his readers could be expected now to shift their perspective so as to apply the same image to a different referent.

(h) These verses may perform a particular function within the discourse as a whole. Coming after what may be seen as the formal principle governing the whole discourse (vv. 30–31), they provide the point of connection between the first and the second major sections. On the one hand, they take up the content of the hardships-list, providing an especially typical example. On the other hand, the narrative form provides the transition to what follows.[783] But if, as we have argued, v. 30 constitutes the point of transition from the first to the second section of the discourse (rather than expressing the principle applicable to both parts),[784] it is doubtful whether these following verses can be seen, structurally, as the connecting link between them.

It is clear from the variety and number of these suggestions that it is not easy to decide how vv. 32–33 are to be related to Paul's argument as a whole. Some explanations, however, are more likely than others. The most probable, since it best fits the immediate context, is the third, (c), of the possibilities mentioned

[778] The suggestion is noted by Furnish, p. 542, and by Martin, p. 384, both with reference to E. A. Judge, 'The Conflict of Educational Aims in New Testament Thought', *Journal of Christian Education* 9 (1966), pp. 32–45; see pp. 44–5; and to Travis, 'Paul's Boasting in 2 Corinthians 10–12', p. 530. See Furnish for details of the custom.
[779] Martin, p. 384.
[780] Furnish, ibid., points out, however, that the Corinthians, living in a Roman colony, would be familiar with the custom.
[781] Martin, pp. 384–5; the quotation is on p. 385.
[782] See above, pp. 610–11.
[783] Zmijewski, *'Narrenrede'*, pp. 288–9.
[784] See above, p. 761.

above: the incident is an example of Paul's weakness. Had it been intended to illustrate not weakness but daring he would surely have emphasised his own initiative in engineering his escape, whereas the implication of the ἐχαλάσθην is that it was facilitated by fellow Christians in the city. It is possible that he also may have in view what we noted as the sixth possibility, (f): his escape was a parody of the achievement of the 'wall-crown', and hence his story is an implicit denigration of worldly boasting.

(ii) It may be useful next to say something about the general historical background. Aretas is Aretas IV of Nabataea, whose reign lasted from 9 B.C.E. to sometime between 38–40 C.E.,[785] and whose kingdom extended to the neighbourhood of Damascus.[786] His daughter had been married to Herod Antipas, but he had divorced her in order to marry Herodias. Consequently, Aretas took advantage of a frontier dispute to march against the forces of Antipas and inflict a defeat on them.[787] He would initially have feared reprisals on the part of Rome, since military conflict between client kings would have been frowned on. And in this situation he would have been most unfavourably disposed towards the Jews, responsible originally, in the person of Herod Antipas, for Aretas's anxiety.[788] His subjects will have shared his feelings.[789] Whilst the apprehension may have diminished with the passage of time,[790] residual traces of anxiety and anger may well have lingered until the time when Paul came to Damascus, visited Nabatean territory, and returned to the city.

Was Aretas at any time in political control of the city of Damascus? The reference in our text to the activities of his ethnarch may suggest that he was. But the city had been in the possession of Rome from the time of Pompey in 66 B.C.E.[791] If Aretas had gained temporary control of it, how had this come about? It is unlikely that he had seized it by military force, in view of the deterrent presence of the Roman legions stationed in Syria, and unlikely also that he would have been granted control by Tiberius, who viewed client kingdoms with disfavour.[792] But there

---

[785] Jewett, *Dating Paul's Life*, p. 30, who opts for 39 C.E., as does Murphy-O'Connor, *Paul*, p. 5. Furnish, p. 522, and Riesner, *Frühzeit*, p. 67, prefer 40 C.E.

[786] Bruce, p. 244.

[787] J. Taylor, 'Ethnarch', p. 727, and Murphy-O'Connor, *Paul*, p. 82, date this incident in 29 C.E. Both refer to C. Saulnier, 'Hérode Antipas et Jean le Baptiste. Quelques remarques sur les confusions chronologiques de Flavius Josèphe', *RB* 91 (1984), pp. 362–76.

[788] Murphy-O'Connor, *Paul*, pp. 83–4.

[789] Murphy-O'Connor, *Paul*, p. 84.

[790] Murphy-O'Connor, *Paul*, p. 90.

[791] Bruce, *Galatians*, p. 96.

[792] Jewett, *Dating Paul's Life*, pp. 31–2.

might have been a transfer of power on the accession of Gaius in 37 C.E.[793] Gaius initially reversed the policy of Tiberius, and reinstated allied kings in the eastern region of the empire.[794] Moreover, he had some reason to be grateful to Aretas, since the latter had given support to Gaius's father Germanicus.[795] It is possibly significant that Roman coinage has been found at Damascus for the reigns of Augustus and Tiberius and also for that of Nero, but none for the reigns of Gaius and Claudius, the intervening emperors.[796] This, however, could be pure chance.[797] Or was there any need for such a specific transfer of control? Mommsen postulates a system of dual authority which would have been in force prior to the extension of Roman power over Syria. He notes that under the last Seleucids Damascus submitted to the rule of the Nabataean king, and suggests that this state of affairs may have continued. Hence, under Roman authority, the Nabataean king, as 'vassal-prince', may still have possessed considerable autonomy.[798] The fact remains, however, that the Roman coins do not carry any indication of such a system. In the case of other vassal-states, it appears, there would be an allusion on the coins to the client-prince.[799] We are left with a lack of external evidence either way, and compelled to return to the Pauline text itself.

(iii) Within the text, the debatable and key term is ἐθνάρχης. There is external evidence for various uses of the word. It could refer to a tribal chief.[800] Then during the Maccabaean period, under the Syrian regime, it is used of Simon as governing the Jews: he is to be high priest, military commander (στρατηγός), and ethnarch (ἐθνάρχης τῶν Ἰουδαίων).[801] Further, in Alexandria there was a Jewish ethnarch with responsibility for the numerous

---

[793] Plummer, p. 333; Allo, p. 301; Ogg, *Chronology*, p. 22; Jewett, *Dating Paul's Life*, p. 32.

[794] Allo, ibid.; Furnish, p. 522; Jewett, ibid.

[795] Murphy-O'Connor, *Paul*, p. 7, with reference, n. 28, to Tac., *Ann.* II 57; J. Taylor, 'Ethnarch', p. 726 n. 25.

[796] The fact is noted by Plummer, p. 333, Martin, p. 385, and other commentators.

[797] Martin, ibid.; Lietzmann, p. 152; Barrett, p. 303. Riesner, *Frühzeit*, p. 72, observes that there is a shortage of numismatic evidence for the reigns of Tiberius and Nero, and a total lack of Nabataean coins between 37 and 62/3 C.E.

[798] Theodor Mommsen, *The Provinces of the Roman Empire* II, London, 1909, pp. 148–9. A difficulty, for our discussion, is that Roman historians tend to use the present text as itself evidence for Nabataean control: see Mommsen, ibid., and A. H. M. Jones, *Cities of the Eastern Roman Provinces*, Oxford, 1971, pp. 290–1.

[799] Ogg, *Chronology*, p. 21.

[800] Plummer, p. 334, and Windisch, p. 366, with reference to inscriptional evidence.

[801] 1 Macc 14.47. The passage is noted by Plummer, ibid., and by Hughes, p. 424. The latter refers to Jos., *Ant.* XIII 6.7; Plummer cites *Bell.* II 6.3, as an example of the use of the term for the Jewish governor (here, Archelaus).

Jews living in the city.[802] What, then, are the possibilities for the identification of Aretas's ethnarch?

(a) The ethnarch was the Jewish ethnarch in Damascus, parallel to the ἐθνάρχης in Alexandria and other such officials in other cities.[803] This is improbable. Paul would hardly have referred to such a person as 'the ethnarch of Aretas'.[804]

(b) Was the latter a Nabataean chief operating outside Damascus and covering the approaches to the city?[805] Again, there are objections. If the ethnarch's men were outside, Paul would have been safer inside.[806] To quote Jewett: 'it would be absurd to drop over the wall into the hands of an encircling force that could not harm one within the city itself.'[807] And Paul's escape attempt would surely have been spotted.[808] Moreover, it is highly doubtful whether the Romans would have tolerated the presence of a substantial force of Arabs immediately outside the city walls and controlling the approach roads.[809] In addition, Riesner points out that since 2 B.C.E. the Nabataeans were no longer nomads but constituted the hellenised ruling class of the kingdom. The ethnarch would not be the Beduin chief which this theory tends to presuppose.[810] And J. Taylor observes that 'the', rather than 'an' ethnarch sounds like someone who 'held some definite position in relation to the Nabataean ruler',[811] i.e., not simply any tribal chief who had a grudge against Paul.

(c) The ethnarch was the leader and representative of the Nabataean community in Damascus.[812] If he posed a threat to Paul, escape from the city would be a natural expedient. It would not be too difficult to account for the ethnarch's hostility. An attempt on Paul's part to convert the Nabataean Damascenes could very well have led to trouble. It might seem that what he was preaching was a new variety of Judaism, which would not be welcome, if the earlier state of tension between Aretas and the

---

[802] Hughes, ibid., with reference to Strabo, XVII 798, cited by Jos., *Ant.* XIV 7.2.
[803] Thomas Lewin, *The Life and Epistles of St. Paul* I, London, 1890, p. 72 n. 60 (noted by Ogg, *Chronology*, p. 19); Hughes, p. 424, without reference to Lewin.
[804] Ogg, *Chronology*, p. 19.
[805] Bachmann, pp. 387–8, n. 2.; Kirsopp Lake, 'The Conversion of Paul', p. 193, in *The Beginnings of Christianity*, Part I Vol. V, pp. 188–95; see above, p. 740 n. 593.
[806] Windisch, p. 365; Allo, p. 302.
[807] Jewett, *Dating Paul's Life*, p. 31.
[808] Jewett, ibid.
[809] Windisch, p. 365; Jewett, ibid.; Furnish, p. 522.
[810] Riesner, *Frühzeit*, p. 75.
[811] J. Taylor, 'Ethnarch', p. 722.
[812] Bruce, p. 245.

Jews had to some extent persisted.[813] Nevertheless, this interpretation is not without its problems. First, it is unlikely that Paul, as a Jew, would be subject to the authority of the leader of a different ethnic group.[814] To this difficulty there could be an answer if Riesner is correct in his reconstruction of the situation. He suggests that it was the Jews in Damascus who wished to seize Paul, that Paul had taken refuge in the Nabataean quarter, and that the Jews had then solicited the assistance of the Nabataean ethnarch, perhaps by means of bribery.[815] It would seem unlikely, of course, that Paul should seek sanctuary with the Nabataeans, in view of the probability that he had encountered trouble in Arabia. Riesner's reconstruction, however, would meet this objection, at least indirectly.[816] He draws attention to an item of archaeological evidence which suggests that there might have been a small Christian enclave within the Nabataean quarter, where also there was a house located beside the city wall.[817] If this was so, it would account for Paul's presence in this part of the city, and for his escape in the way described. However, there is a second difficulty. It is highly unlikely that such an ethnarch would have the power to guard the city by force.[818]

(d) Damascus at this time was in the possession of Aretas, and his ethnarch is the governor of the city.[819] This is perhaps the simplest interpretation. It certainly explains the ethnarch's authority to use military force to apprehend Paul. The difficulty is that the word ἐθνάρχης appears not to have been used in this sense: the title used for Nabataean governors was στρατηγός.[820] But it is possible that ἐθνάρχης might have been used in conjunction with it. J. Taylor notes a Greek inscription in which the two terms refer to the same person in a dual role: as tribal chief and as commander of auxiliary forces. The στρατηγός of Damascus would himself have been such a chief. Paul simply uses the one title only;[821] and his choice reflects 'the governor's rank as a prince of his own tribe'.[822]

---

[813] Murphy-O'Connor, *Paul*, p. 84, makes the point about opposition to a fresh kind of Judaism with reference to Paul's visit to Arabia following his original arrival in Damascus, but it could be valid for the somewhat later time as well.

[814] Meyer, p. 458; Murphy-O'Connor, *Paul*, p. 6.

[815] Riesner, *Frühzeit*, p. 78.

[816] Riesner, *Frühzeit*, pp. 229–31, rejects the idea that Paul went to Arabia for missionary purposes.

[817] Riesner, *Frühzeit*, pp. 76–7.

[818] Murphy-O'Connor, ibid.; Ogg, *Chronology*, p. 19.

[819] Plummer, pp. 333–4; Allo, p. 301; Martin, p. 385; Murphy-O'Connor, ibid.

[820] Riesner, *Frühzeit*, p. 74.

[821] J. Taylor, 'Ethnarch', pp. 723–4.

[822] Murphy-O'Connor, *Paul*, p. 6; Meyer, p. 458, comments: 'Paul would have had no reason for adding Ἀρέτα τοῦ βασιλέως if at the very time of the flight the Roman city had not been exceptionally (and temporarily) subject to Aretas.'

We accept this fourth interpretation. We are left, then, with a final question. Why did the ethnarch think it necessary to hunt Paul out and arrest him? According to Murphy-O'Connor, he would no longer pose any threat (as perhaps he had seemed to do on his return from Arabia). Did Paul, perhaps, exaggerate the danger he was in?[823] Possibly. But there must have been some reason for the ethnarch's action, and some likelihood of punitive treatment, should the search succeed. It is probable that during his stay in Damascus Paul had attempted to gain converts both amongst the Jews and amongst the Nabataeans, and that this had caused disturbances in both communities. Rome would not take kindly to civic disruption in such an important city, which commanded the trade routes to the East.[824] It might have seemed advisable to seize Paul, administer some harsh punishment, and expel him from the city, in the hope that this would deter him from causing further trouble in Nabataean territory. Paul himself may have feared for his life. But it is possible that the Christians in Damascus might have encouraged his speedy departure, lest, were he found in their midst, they also might come under suspicion. If we were to ask why the hypothetical trouble caused by Paul's evangelistic activities had erupted only after he had been staying in Damascus for two years or so, the answer might lie in the postulated change of control at the beginning of the reign of Gaius. A new, Nabataean, governor would be especially anxious to keep the peace, lest the emperor should change his mind and resume direct rule by Rome.

(iv) We come lastly to consider the relationship between Paul's account of the incident and the parallel story in Acts 9.23–25. The basic narrative is the same, and there is some identical vocabulary (διὰ τοῦ τείχους and the use of χαλάω). There are also some differences. In Paul's account it is the ethnarch of Aretas who is hunting him down, whilst in Acts it is the Jews of Damascus who plot against him. The latter intend to kill him, the former to seize him. The ethnarch guards the city: the Jews keep watch on the gates. In Acts we are specifically told that 'his disciples' assist Paul's escape. Paul does not say this, although he obviously had assistance. He clarifies the manner of his escape with the phrase 'through a window', and, the word for 'basket' differs (σαργάνη in Paul, but σπυρίς in Acts). Acts notes that the escape was 'by night', and also indicates the intensity of the watch, 'by day and by night'.

How, then, is the relationship between these two passages to be explained? In view of the differences, it is unlikely that the author

823 Murphy-O'Connor, *Paul*, pp. 89–90.
824 See Jewett, *Dating Paul's Life*, p. 31, on the strategic location of Damascus.

of Acts is quoting from the Pauline letter.[825] The explanation must be more complex. According to Burchard, Luke derived his account from some part of the Pauline mission tradition which must ultimately derive from the passage in 2 Corinthians. It is only behind Acts 9.24b–25, however, that there stands already-formulated tradition. The remainder is Lucan composition, although dependent on some additional transmitted data.[826] This analysis would seem to account adequately for the similarities and the differences between Paul and Acts. It is noticeable that the major difference, i.e., the identity of Paul's persecutors, stands outside what Burchard sees as formulated tradition. Is Luke's reference to the Jews, then, due entirely to his own redaction, or does it have some basis in transmitted fact? If the latter, is it possible to harmonise the two accounts? Some commentators have made the attempt.[827] It may be more likely, however, that it is Luke himself who has interpreted the threat to Paul as emanating from the Jews. To quote Barrett: 'We must suppose that Paul knew whom he had to fear; Luke probably did not know the source of the threat that led to Paul's escape and was only too ready to blame any bad feeling towards the Christians on the Jews'. It is not likely, Barrett comments further, that there would have been any collusion between Jews and Nabataeans.[828] Nevertheless, the argument may not prove entirely watertight. A Nabataean ethnarch who governed the whole of Damascus would be bound to take notice of Jewish complaints, whatever his own feelings about the Jews,[829] and apprehension as to Roman reaction to civic disorder would amply outweigh any inclination towards disregard of Jewish interests. It is not wholly out of the question to suppose that there might be some truth in Luke's indication of Jewish involvement in the threat to Paul.

---

[825] C. Burchard, *Der dreizehnte Zeuge*, FRLANT 103, Göttingen, 1970, p. 155.

[826] Burchard, *Zeuge*, pp. 153, 158.

[827] See Hughes, p. 424, who relies, however, on the theory that the ἐθνάρχης was the Jewish ethnarch in Damascus, which we have seen to be improbable. See also Allo, p. 301, who suggests the collaboration of the Nabataean governor with the Jews.

[828] C. K. Barrett, *A Critical and Exegetical Commentary on the Acts of the Apostles*, ICC, Vol. I, Edinburgh, 1994, p. 466.

[829] Cf. Allo, p. 301.

(c) Weakness and boasting: ascent to heaven and the infliction of the 'thorn' (12.1–10)

12¹ Boasting is necessary. It is not expedient, but I will come to visions and revelations of the Lord. ²I know a man in Christ—fourteen years ago, whether in the body I do not know or out of the body I do not know (God knows), that such a man was caught up to the third heaven. ³And I know that such a man—whether in the body or apart from the body I do not know (God knows), ⁴that he was caught up to paradise and heard unutterable words, which it is not lawful for a man to speak. ⁵On behalf of such a person I will boast, but on my own behalf I will not boast, except of my weaknesses. ⁶For if I should wish to boast, I shall not be foolish, for I shall speak the truth. But I refrain, lest anyone should credit me with a reputation that exceeds what he sees me to be or anything that he hears from me. ⁷And by reason of the extraordinary quality of the revelations, therefore, lest I should become elated with pride, there was given me a thorn for the flesh, an angel of Satan, to beat me, lest I become elated. ⁸About this I three times implored the Lord that it should leave me. ⁹And he has said to me, My grace is sufficient for you, for power comes to perfection in weakness. Very gladly, then, will I boast rather of my weaknesses, so that the power of Christ may rest upon me. ¹⁰Therefore I take pleasure in weaknesses, in insults, in occasions of distress, in persecutions and difficulties, on behalf of Christ. For whenever I am weak, then I am strong.

Paul appears to realise that he must beat his opponents at their own game, and show that he too can boast of some marvellous experience. So, with hesitation, and speaking objectively as though of some other person, he recounts his rapture to the third heaven. But he goes on to speak of his 'thorn for the flesh', explaining the purpose of this affliction and his own realisation, through a divine revelation, that such conditions of weakness were the necessary context for the manifestation of the power of Christ.

1.¹ Καυχᾶσθαι δεῖ,² οὐ συμφέρον μέν, ἐλεύσομαι δὲ εἰς ὀπτασίας καὶ ἀποκαλύψεις κυρίου. Here Paul makes a fresh start.³ It would be natural to suppose that there is some connection with the εἰ καυχᾶσθαι δεῖ of 11.30,⁴ and, in consequence, with the story of the escape from Damascus told in 11.32–33. But this is not so, if our interpretation of the story is correct. For we have

---

¹ The reading εἰ καυχᾶσθαι δεῖ (ℵ² H 81. 326. 1175 pc a f vg sa Ambst) is clearly an assimilation to the wording of 11.30.

² Of the three variant readings, δή (K 0121a. 945. 2495 pm) is very poorly attested. The reading δέ (ℵ D* Ψ bo) has better support, but could be due to the omission of the final iota of δεῖ (by accident, or in an attempt to avoid asyndeton). The reading δεῖ itself (𝔓⁴⁶ B D² F G H L P 0243. 6. 33. 81. 104. 365. 629. 630. 1175. 1241. 1739. 1881. 2464 pm latt sy sa boᵐˢ) could perhaps come from scribal assimilation to 11.30, but Paul himself is repetitive in this section. The δεῖ is well attested and should be accepted.

³ As the asyndetic opening indicates.

⁴ Zmijewski, 'Narrenrede', p. 325, comments that the opening phrase is a clear intensification of the conditional in 11.30a.

accepted the view that Paul tells it as an example of his determination to boast of his weakness.[5] And it is clear that the narrative of his rapture to paradise does not fall into this category, since in v. 5 the boasting about the rapture is plainly distinguished from boasting about weakness.[6] Hence, there is no tight connection with the concluding verses of chap. 11.[7] The general motif of boasting, however, serves to connect this section with the remainder of that part of the discourse which begins at 11.16 and ends with 12.10. Why, then, does Paul see it as obligatory to boast, as it would appear, about visionary experiences? Presumably it is because the Corinthians regarded such experience as a criterion of apostleship[8] and thought Paul deficient in it. That all this was a matter of discussion in Corinth may be indicated by his manner of expression here, where he says that he is going to 'pass on to', 'come to' this further point.[9] And it is very probable that the topic was under discussion because the visiting missionaries have themselves laid claim to impressive experiences of this kind.[10] Paul now does the same, but with reservations which become more apparent as his discourse progresses. Boasting is not expedient. The point is made succinctly, with the verb ἐστιν left to be understood: οὐ συμφέρον[11] μέν.[12] Although Paul is referring to

---

[5] See above, pp. 764, 765–6.

[6] Windisch, p. 368.

[7] Hughes, p. 429, would dispute this conclusion on the grounds that the narrative of the rapture is essential as an explanation of the 'thorn' of 12.7, Paul's most obvious weakness. But this does not obviate the difficulty that, when v. 1a is taken in conjunction with v. 5a, it is plain that the experience of rapture can be seen as in itself a possible topic of boasting.

[8] Lincoln, 'Visionary', pp. 207–8.

[9] Cf. Barrett, p. 306, who comments that the verb (ἐλεύσομαι) 'suggests turning to a specific point, possibly raised by others'. The reading ἐλεύσομαι δέ (𝔓46 ℵ F G H P 0243. 33. 81. 1175. 1739. 2464 pc lat) has the best attestation, and provides the correct correlation with the preceding μέν-clause. The reading δὲ καί in B may be a stylistic alteration, but adds support for δέ, rather than for γάρ (read by D Ψ 𝔐 sy).

[10] See, e.g., Strachan, p. 30; Tasker, p. 169; Lincoln, 'Visionary', p. 208; Barrett, p. 306; Furnish, p. 543. For the opposite point of view, see Windisch, p. 368, who sees no evidence for these suggestions in the text. But the very fact that Paul acknowledges that his boasting is inexpedient goes to show that it is evoked by external pressures.

[11] The entire verb thus becomes a periphrastic present: see MHT, p. 88. Barrett, p. 307, with reference to Robertson, p. 1130, takes the participle συμφέρον as an accusative absolute (literally, 'it [not] being expedient'). This is less likely. The accusative absolute is comparatively rare, and the μὲν ... δέ correlation leads one to expect a finite verb in both clauses.

[12] There is a textual variant which affects both words. The reading συμφέρον μέν has good attestation (𝔓46 ℵ B F G 0243. 33. 1175. 1739 pc (f vg) co), and in all probability is original. The alternative συμφέρει μέν (D* 81) may be due to a sense that the μέν-clause should have as obvious a finite verb as the corresponding δέ-clause. Other witnesses (D1 H Ψ 𝔐 it vgms syh Ambst Pel), reading συμφέρει, have μοι instead of μέν, perhaps by accident if an exemplar was poorly lettered.

himself, the assertion is probably meant generally as well. In his own case, indeed, and in the present context, it cannot be taken in a completely literal sense, since he hopes that this line of approach will have a beneficial effect, by causing his readers to realise that their attitude to him is mistaken. But the language he uses expresses his distaste for boasting and his feeling that it is a 'suspect emergency measure'.[13] And he makes this reservation in advance of his mention of the actual topic of boasting. This topic is designated 'visions and revelations of the Lord'. The phrase appears to be a general heading for what follows.[14] But in one respect its suitability looks doubtful, since the term ὀπτασία (if not also ἀποκάλυψις) must refer to something seen, and yet in vv. 2–10 there is no specific reference to actual vision.[15] It is true that the agenda, and hence the phraseology, may be determined by Paul's rivals.[16] But unless his response corresponds to some degree with their claims it would have been ineffective. It may be, however, that some element of vision is implicit in what follows, as the exegesis will suggest. At this point we shall consider one aspect of the question only. Did the experience Paul relates here include a vision of Christ? Of relevance to the answer there is, (i) the precise interpretation of the phraseology of the present verse, and, (ii) the evidence, or lack of it, in the letters and in Acts for (other) visions of Christ which the apostle experienced.

(i) The initial linguistic question is whether the genitive κυρίου depends on ὀπτασίας as well as on ἀποκάλυψεις. If it does so depend, then we might be able to conclude that somewhere in vv. 2–10 a vision, as well as an audition (v. 9), of the Lord is presupposed. Several commentators do take 'visions and revelations' as a virtually composite expression upon which, as a whole, κυρίου depends.[17] The fact that the preposition εἰς governs both ὀπτασίας and ἀποκαλύψεις would support this interpretation. This brings us to the main point of linguistic debate. How is the genitive κυρίου itself to be understood? Is it a genitive of origin,[18] which indicates that the visions and revelations come from the Lord as their source? Or is it an objective genitive,[19] designating

---

[13] Filson, p. 405.
[14] Cf. Furnish, p. 524: 'the absence of articles and the use of the plural indicate ... that Paul is taking up a general topic ...' Cf. Heckel, *Schwachheit*, p. 54.
[15] Lincoln, 'Visionary', p. 204, suggests that the plural nouns may imply that Paul had originally intended to relate several such experiences. But even should this be correct (see Furnish, however, as cited in n. 14 above), one would suppose that he would first narrate the most relevant, which leaves us with the same problem.
[16] Zmijewski, 'Narrenrede', pp. 329–30.
[17] Barrett, p. 307; Plummer, p. 338; cf. Wolff, p. 242; see also Furnish, p. 524, who claims (with reference to Windisch, p. 368) that the two nouns are synonymous.
[18] BDR 162. It is not clear, however, whether this use can mean 'deriving from'.
[19] BDR 163.

Christ as the content of vision and revelation? The majority of exegetes favour the first alternative (genitive of origin),[20] basically for the reason that neither in v. 4 nor in the rest of the section, as we have noted already, is it said that Paul has actually seen the Lord.[21] The second alternative (objective genitive), however, would find support from Pauline usage elsewhere, in that in the other instances of ἀποκάλυψις with a following genitive (Rom 2.5; 8.19; 1 Cor 1.7; Gal 1.12) the genitive refers to the content of revelation.[22] Schlatter takes κυρίου as content in the present verse.[23] Zmijewski, more elaborately, thinks it possible that the genitive has a dual function: in respect of Paul's opponents it is objective, since they will have claimed direct visions of the Lord, but in respect of Paul himself it indicates the Lord as the author of the revelations.[24] This would be a neat solution of the exegetical difficulty. It would, however, require us to suppose that Paul means one thing whilst intentionally crafting his language so as to convey something quite different to his readers. For if he is using his rivals' language to counter their claims with his own, he must intend the Corinthians to understand his words in the sense his opponents would attach to them. It would be simpler to allow that he himself shares their meaning (he also is talking about visions of Christ), whilst deprecating their boastful attitude.

(ii) Is there, then, evidence elsewhere that Paul had visionary experiences in which Christ appeared to him? The author of Acts obviously sees him as thus privileged: see 18.9–11 and 22.17–21.[25] In his own letters, however, he mentions only the experience of a resurrection appearance (1 Cor 9.1; 15.8). Nevertheless, in 5.13 he does indicate by implication that he is no stranger to some form of ecstatic experience. At least the question remains open.

Verses 2–10[26]
Verse 1 has been discussed on the assumption that, whatever the precise nature of the rapture to paradise in vv. 2–4 and the revelatory audition of v. 9a, Paul is giving an account of actual

---

[20] See, e.g., Meyer, p. 462; Bachmann, p. 389; Plummer, p. 338; Windisch, p. 368; Wendland, p. 244; Bultmann, p. 220; Furnish, p. 524; Barnett, p. 558.
[21] Bultmann, p. 220; Furnish, p. 524.
[22] Cf. Rowland, *Open Heaven*, p. 380.
[23] Schlatter, *Paulus*, p. 658.
[24] Zmijewski, *'Narrenrede'*, pp. 330–1.
[25] Lincoln, 'Visionary', pp. 205–6. On Acts, see also Benz, *Visionär*, pp. 83–95.
[26] An earlier version of the exegesis of vv. 2–4 has appeared as an article, under the title 'Paul's Journey to Paradise: Some Exegetical Issues in 2 Cor 12.2–4', in R. B. Bieringer, *The Corinthian Correspondence*, BETL 125, Leuven, 1996, pp. 347–63. I am most grateful to the publishers, Leuven University Press, for permission to use this material again in the present commentary. Specific references are given where appropriate.

personal experience. But before considering the details, we need to take notice of the possibility that this is not so. Apart from the suggestion that in the case of the rapture some other person is in view,[27] there are two reasons for raising the question. First, it has been argued that the similar accounts of rapture to heaven in the Jewish apocalypses are literary constructs only. Secondly, it is suggested that Paul's narratives of rapture and audition are to be understood as parody.

(i) Whilst Paul's narrative is very much shorter than the accounts of rapture in Jewish literature,[28] it could be regarded as belonging to the same genre. In consequence, the theory that these apocalypses are simply literary products, with no reference to actual religious experience, might apply, if it is correct, to Paul's account as well. It is claimed that the ascent apocalypses, in modern terms, are simply 'works of fiction'.[29] This is because the life-settings of the visions are those not of the real authors but of the pseudepigraphic heroes,[30] and because the descriptions employ conventional symbolism.[31] The first characteristic does not apply to the Pauline account, but the second does. The motifs of the third heaven and paradise, and that of the condition (bodily or otherwise) of the visionary are all to be found in one or another of the Jewish apocalypses.[32] But this does not of necessity require the conclusion that Paul's story is fictional. Genuine psychological experience of a religious kind may well manifest itself in forms already culturally familiar to the subject of the experience.[33] Some scholars, moreover, would be willing in some cases to argue that the Jewish apocalyptic narratives may have a basis in actual experience.[34] The literary character of Paul's narrative, therefore, does not, in respect of its apocalyptic colouring, militate against its psychological reality.

(ii) The more significant challenge comes from the suggestion that both this and the following account are to be seen as parody. This theory originates with H. D. Betz.[35] He himself claims neutrality on the question of the actuality of the experiences

[27] See the exegesis, and Thrall, 'Journey to Paradise', pp. 347–8.

[28] See, e.g., *2 Enoch* 3–9 (*OTP* I, pp. 110–18); *3 Apoc. Bar.* 2–4 (*OTP* I, pp. 664–6).

[29] Himmelfarb, *Ascent*, p. 113. Baird, 'Visions', pp. 658–9 , raises the question of whether Paul's account is simply a literary exercise, but thinks that 'an actual experience' probably lies behind it. See v. 6, where Paul claims that, if he should boast, he will be telling the truth.

[30] Himmelfarb, *Ascent*, ibid.

[31] Baird, 'Visions', p. 658.

[32] See the exegesis.

[33] Bousset, pp. 210–11.

[34] See Rowland, *Open Heaven*, pp. 215–34; Stone, *Fourth Ezra*, pp. 31–3.

[35] Betz, *Tradition*, pp. 72–3, 82–5, 89–95.

described,[36] but his discussion of 12.2–10 tends towards a negative verdict, and he is so understood by other scholars.[37] Paul, he argues, employs self-parody in order to expose the pretensions of the rival missionaries. He parodies accounts of heavenly journeys and of healing miracles by bringing his own account in each case to an ironical climax: he is unable to communicate the words he heard in paradise, and the divine oracle in the healing story refuses healing.[38] Climax becomes anti-climax, and the whole idea of raptures to heaven and miracles of healing becomes ridiculous. Hence, the pretensions of the pseudo-apostles are exposed as equally absurd.[39] This appears to be the logical conclusion of the treatment of 12.2–10 as parody. It follows that Paul would not intend these stories as accounts of genuine religious experience. And if the contents are fictitious, Paul is not recounting personal experience.

This interpretation has had some influence, albeit in a weakened form.[40] Nevertheless, its tenability is questionable. Paul has begun by indicating that he will speak about visions and revelations that come from the Lord, i.e., Christ, or, indeed, have 'the Lord' as their content. He then describes the subject of the rapture as 'a man in Christ'. Whilst this may simply mean 'a Christian', it is still a theologically significant way of referring to an adherent of the Christian movement: the use of Christ's name in this context is unlikely to have become a mere convention, unthinkingly used. And in the second narrative Christ is himself the central figure. All these allusions to Christ must surely be intended seriously. Is it at all probable that Paul would refer to Christ in the satirical fashion which the parody theory would demand—with the intention, that is, to evoke laughter?[41] But if the parody theory is to be rejected, then what we have here will

---

[36] Betz, *Tradition*, p. 89.

[37] Baird, 'Visions', p. 658; Tabor, *Things Unutterable*, p. 53 n. 79.

[38] Betz, *Tradition*, pp. 84–5, 89–93.

[39] Cf. Lincoln, 'Visionary', p. 209.

[40] Furnish, p. 533, sees 12.2–4 as parody of the motif of the heavenly journey, since Paul's rapture 'yielded no useful religious knowledge', but rejects, p. 547, Betz's claim that vv. 5–10 also are meant as parody. Barnett, p. 562, suggests that Paul is ridiculing his rivals in the rapture story, but says, p. 563, that he is not denigrating his own experience. Then, p. 567, he speaks of Paul as producing 'a revelatory story without a revelation' and 'a healing story without a healing'. This sounds like Betz, but the exegesis hardly suggests that Barnett follows him in regarding vv. 2–10 as parody.

[41] Betz, *Tradition*, p. 84, claims that whilst parody intends to cause laughter, this is not its real aim. But when he provides examples, pp. 84–5, he speaks of derision. See also Wolff, p. 241, who doubts whether Paul would include within a parody the proclamation of divine grace in v. 9a, which he had come to regard as basic to his whole apostolic existence.

be a serious account of real religious experience, and, as the exegesis will show, experience personal to Paul.

2. οἶδα ἄνθρωπον ἐν Χριστῷ πρὸ ἐτῶν δεκατεσσάρων, εἴτε ἐν σώματι οὐκ οἶδα, εἴτε ἐκτὸς τοῦ σώματος οὐκ οἶδα, ὁ θεὸς οἶδεν, ἁρπαγέντα τὸν τοιοῦτον ἕως τρίτου οὐρανοῦ. The usual view is that Paul is speaking here of his own experience. As Chrysostom remarks, the sequence of thought would be lost, were the apostle to introduce reference to some other person in the midst of talking about himself.[42] Moreover, the danger of over-elation (vv. 6–7) makes sense only if it was Paul himself who experienced the rapture to the third heaven.[43] Nevertheless, there have been other suggestions concerning the visionary's identity. According to Herrmann he was Apollos. The account is influenced, he claims, by 2 *Enoch*, and the latter work he believes to have had Apollos as its author.[44] This is an hermeneutical absurdity. The provenance of 2 *Enoch* is obscure,[45] and it is himself whom Paul needs to defend, not a colleague who may well have been more popular with the Corinthians. It is equally unlikely that the ἄνθρωπος who experienced ascent is to be understood as Jesus, with whom the apostle believed himself to be identified.[46] Since he would scarcely speak of Jesus as 'a man in Christ', the beginning of the verse has to be translated as 'I knew in Christ, fourteen years ago, a man …' This is less natural than the usual rendering 'a man in Christ'. If we are to reject the usual view, the only likely alternative would be the interpretation proposed by Goulder: Paul is speaking of the experience of a Christian friend.[47] The main arguments are these. The natural interpretation of vv. 5–6 is that the person in question is someone other than Paul himself, someone who is identified as a Christian with the phrase ἐν Χριστῷ. To this man, caught up to heaven, there was granted a vision, an ὀπτασία. With reference to v. 1, Goulder claims that 'visions' are to be distinguished from 'revelations'. An ὀπτασία is the more sublime experience, an ἀποκάλυψις is less impressive. And when Paul clearly refers to his own states of ecstasy, he 'always' uses ἀποκάλυψις: see Gal 1.12; cf. 1.16; 2.2. It is this word he uses 'for divine communications whether heard or seen (1 Cor 9.2; 15.8)'.[48] Ravishment to heaven

42 Chrysostom, *PG* 61 col. 576 (NPNF XII, p. 399).
43 Furnish, p. 524.
44 L. Herrmann, 'Apollos', *RSR* 50 (1976), pp. 330–6. The similarity lies in the fact that in both works paradise appears to be located in the third heaven.
45 See the introduction by F. I. Andersen in *OTP* I, pp. 95–6.
46 This theory is proposed by Morton Smith, 'Ascent to the Heavens and the Beginning of Christianity', *Eranos* 50 (1981), pp. 403–29; see pp. 425–9.
47 Michael Goulder, 'Vision and Knowledge', *JSNT* 56 (1994), pp. 53–71; see pp. 53–8.
48 Goulder, 'Vision', p. 56.

will have involved a vision of the throne of God, for which the appropriate term would be ὀπτασία, a word not used by Paul with reference to himself. Hence, the visionary was someone other than the apostle. So Goulder. But his linguistic argument is less than convincing. It is incorrect to say that Paul 'always' uses ἀποκάλυψις for divine revelation accorded to him. In 1 Cor 9.2 he says that he has 'seen', ἑόρακα, the Lord, and in 15.8 that the Lord 'appeared', ὤφθη, to him. These words have nothing to do with the ἀποκαλυπ-terms. By contrast, the verb ὤφθη may have at least an indirect link with ὀπτασία: it acts as the aorist passive of ὀπτάνομαι/ὀπτάζομαι, with which ὀπτασία is cognate.[49] Goulder himself observes that in Acts 26.16, 20 [sic] the resurrection appearance to Paul is described by means of this vocabulary (ὤφθην, ὀπτασία). In view of Paul's own use of ὤφθη, it might well be that Luke is using terminology known to be current in Pauline circles and perhaps deriving originally from Paul himself. The stronger argument, of course, would be that of the apparently obvious sense of vv. 5–6. Yet to accept this as decisive evidence against the usual view of the rapture creates other problems. First, if it is Paul's Christian friend that he is boasting about, why should he regard this as 'not expedient' (v. 1)? Elsewhere he has no qualms about boasting of other people: see 2 Cor 1.14; 7.4, 14; 8.24; 9.2–3; 1 Th 2.19. Secondly, why is the description of the rapture so detailed, if intended simply as the preliminary to vv. 5–6? More particularly, why should the note of time (fourteen years ago) be thought necessary? There would be no need to emphasise in this way the factuality of a friend's experience. It is not a friend whom Paul is defending in the Fool's Speech, but himself, in which case emphasis may well be required. Thirdly, if we reject the account of the rapture as a narration of Paul's experience, we have scarcely anything except the brief and unelaborated τῇ ὑπερβολῇ τῶν ἀποκαλύψεων to account for the infliction of the 'thorn'. And yet it is surely necessary that some more adequate explanation should be provided, given that the weakness it caused would be one of the reasons for the Corinthians' questioning of Paul's apostolic status. It is Paul himself who is the ἄνθρωπος, we conclude, despite the apparent difficulty of the third-person style in vv. 2–4 and the problem of vv. 5–6.[50]

This ἄνθρωπος is then further defined by the phrase ἐν Χριστῷ.

---

[49] See BDR 101; LSJ s.v. ὀπτάζομαι.

[50] For criticism of Goulder, see also Morray-Jones, 'Paradise Revisited', p. 272. He points out that no external evidence is offered to support the distinction between 'revelations' and 'visions', and that the argument is circular, since its basis is Goulder's exegesis, itself based on the distinction.

It is not likely that the intention is to describe a Christian in a state of ecstasy,[51] since in Paul's normal usage it is not so restricted, but refers to Christians as such.[52] It is doubtful also, *pace* Furnish, whether its purpose here is to delineate Paul 'as one whose life has been transformed and made new through faith in Christ'.[53] In the present context the argument is not concerned with the general quality of Paul's Christian life. Does he mean, then, that it was ' in the power of Christ' that he was translated?[54] This would be consonant with the view that the ἐν Χριστῷ formula in itself signifies life in the power-sphere of Christ.[55] But had Paul wished specifically to say here that the rapture was effected by the power of Christ, one would have expected to see the ἐν Χριστῷ in somewhat closer proximity to the participle ἁρπαγέντα.[56] More probably, as Lincoln suggests, he may want to indicate that his experience was not the result of 'anything he was in himself', such as the possessor of 'special psychic powers or a unique capacity for mystical experience'.[57] The simplest explanation, lastly, is that of Barrett and others: the phrase means 'Christian'.[58] Those who have become Christ's followers through baptism 'into Christ' then exist 'in Christ'.[59] In view of the third-person narration[60] and the indeterminate force of the colourless ἄνθρωπος, it may have seemed advisable right at the beginning of the account to make clear that it is the experience of a Christian that is narrated.[61] We would therefore take this as the primary sense of ἐν Χριστῷ, whilst allowing that Paul may be indicating in addition that the experience owed nothing to his own spiritual powers.

---

[51] *Pace* Schmithals, *Gnosticism*, pp. 214–15.

[52] Schmithals allows that the restricted interpretation he proposes would be unusual, but suggests that the whole phrase ἄνθρωπος ἐν Χριστῷ was a current technical term, possibly part of the vocabulary of Paul's opponents. But this begs the question as to whether we need to give an unusual sense to the phrase here.

[53] Furnish, p. 524; cf. Allo, p. 304.

[54] Plummer, p. 340. The point would be 'to disclaim all credit for the glorious experience'. See also Martin, p. 399.

[55] For this interpretation of ἐν Χριστῷ see Ziesler, *Pauline Christianity*, p. 63.

[56] For criticism of this general interpretation of the formula see Thrall, Vol. I, p. 425.

[57] Lincoln, 'Visionary', p. 209. This is somewhat similar to the interpretation proposed by Plummer, but fits better the attachment of ἐν Χριστῷ to ἄνθρωπος.

[58] Barrett, p. 308; Héring, p. 93; Wolff, p. 242.

[59] Thrall, Vol. I, p. 425.

[60] See below, pp. 781–2.

[61] Stories of heavenly journeys were popular, after all, both within Judaism and also in the Graeco-Roman world. See the examples noted in the exegesis, and the comprehensive treatment by A. F. Segal, 'Heavenly Ascent in Hellenistic Judaism, Early Christianity and their Environment', *ANRW* II 23/2, pp. 1333–94. Paul himself, moreover, had not always been a Christian. Perhaps he might have been suspected of relating some pre-conversion experience irrelevant to his standing as a Christian apostle.

But why does he speak of it in the third person, as though it had not been his own experience at all? It may be true that this style conveys the solemnity of the event and its exotic character,[62] and also that it has some affinity with stylistic elements in the Jewish apocalypses.[63] But most commentators would see rather more significance in it than this. There are various suggestions.

(i) According to Schmithals, the use of the third person is an aspect of Paul's reaction against rivals who are gnostics. These people will have boasted of experiences of ecstasy in which they became aware of their true form of existence which was already a reality in the present. For Paul, by contrast, an ecstatic state was only an anticipation of the form of existence he would enjoy in the future. He uses the third person to designate his future self, and to distinguish it from his present ego.[64] But the identification of the opponents of 2 Cor 10–13 as gnostics has not gained general agreement.[65] Furthermore, a contrast between first and third persons does not, without further explanation, suggest contrast between present and future.

(ii) Käsemann proposes an interpretation which has gained some popularity. He argues that the effect of the third person style is to distance Paul from the event he describes, and that this shows that his experience of ecstasy is not regarded as in any way relevant to his apostolic service of the church. His function as an apostle is distinct from the events of his private life.[66] But if so, we have to ask why the incident is related here at all. Paul is in the thick of a controversy about criteria of apostleship. The story of the rapture must do more, one would think, than simply register non-applicability to the issue. One would suppose that it has some relevance to the criteria espoused by the rival missionaries and their supporters in Corinth. Paul's opponents must have sought accreditation by means of their own experiences of rapture. But in that case, unless we adopt the parody theory in its full form, Paul himself must intend to show, however unwillingly, that he satisfies this criterion.[67] Hence, this explanation of the third person style would lose its force.

(iii) Perhaps the third person style is used simply to avoid

[62] Bachmann, p. 391; Zmijewski, 'Narrenrede', p. 336.
[63] Baumgarten, Apokalyptik, pp. 143–4.
[64] Schmithals, Gnosticism, pp. 212–13.
[65] See, e.g., Barrett, p. 29; Furnish, p. 53.
[66] Käsemann, 'Legitimität', pp. 64, 66–7. A number of other scholars similarly suppose that Paul here denies that such experience can serve to authenticate apostleship. See, e.g., Baumgarten, Apokalyptik, pp. 143–4; Spittler, 'Limits', p. 261; Furnish, p. 544; Lincoln, 'Visionary', p. 210.
[67] It may even be that for Paul himself the experience did have positive importance in this respect. Tabor, Things Unutterable, p. 37, suggests that it would have confirmed his understanding of his apostolic authority. See also below, p. 797.

giving the impression of egocentric arrogance.[68] This could well be a contributory reason for the choice of style.

(iv) It may be that the third person narration derives originally from the nature of the experience itself, that is, from the ecstatic phenomenon of the displacement of the ego. Furnish notes this possibility. In such experiences there is a 'sense of self-transcendence', illustrated in *3 Apoc. Bar.* 17.3, where, at the end of his visions, Baruch says: 'And when I came to myself, I praised God'.[69] Dunn, similarly, speaks of the ability of the subject, in such states, to 'observe himself undergoing the experience'.[70] This explanation does justice to the psychological reality of Paul's narrative. We accept it as the basic reason for his choice of style, with the desire to avoid apparent arrogance as a contributory cause for its adoption.

Since he is recounting his own experience, he can date the event: πρὸ ἐτῶν δεκατεσσάρων. But is there any particular reason why he should do so? There are these suggestions.

(i) According to Chrysostom, Paul wishes to show that he would not have spoken of the experience at all, had he not been constrained by great necessity. For a long time he had refrained from mentioning it.[71]

(ii) Heckel similarly argues that the temporal interval means that Paul had not previously thought it necessary to speak of the rapture, but goes on to claim that he did not therefore attach any significance to it as a legitimation of his apostleship.[72] This is too sweeping a conclusion. The converse argument could have equal, or greater, force. The fact that Paul speaks of this experience to a church in which his apostleship had now come to be seriously challenged could indicate its importance for him in precisely this respect.

(iii) Another possibility is that the dating constitutes an intentional parallel with the dating of similar events in the prophetic books.[73] In Isa 6.1, Jer 1.2, and Ezek 1.1 the precise dating is given in connection with visions of some kind.[74] The purpose, both of the prophets and of Paul, would be to confirm the historicity of the narrative.[75] It is true, however, that the parallel is not complete.

---

[68] Héring, p. 93 n. 1; cf. Hughes, pp. 429–30; see also Lincoln, 'Visionary', pp. 208–9.

[69] Furnish, p. 543; see *OTP* I, p. 679.

[70] J. D. G. Dunn, *Jesus and the Spirit*, London, 1975, pp. 214–15.

[71] Chrysostom, *PG* 61 cols. 575–6 (NPNF XII, p. 398); cf. Hughes, p. 430.

[72] Heckel, *Schwachheit*, p. 59.

[73] See, e.g., Plummer, p. 341; Windisch, p. 373; Allo, p. 305; cf. Baumgarten, *Apokalyptik*, p. 143; Klauck, p. 91.

[74] These passages are noted by Plummer, ibid.

[75] Windisch, p. 373; cf. also Prümm, *Diakonia Pneumatos* I, pp. 649–50; Lincoln, 'Visionary', p. 211; Furnish, p. 544.

The prophetic datings are related to public events, whilst Paul's dating is personal. Moreover, the genre of the event dated differs: Paul describes a heavenly journey, whilst the prophets speak of their call.[76] And again we are confronted with the insistence that (by contrast with the prophetic accounts) Paul's aim is not to legitimate his commission.[77] But this last claim, we have argued, is doubtful. And, despite the incompleteness of the prophetic parallel, since, in Gal 1.15–16, Paul does see his calling in part in prophetic terms[78] it is not improbable that this self-understanding might have influenced his narrative here as well.

There is, in any case, fairly wide agreement that the basic reason for the precise dating is Paul's concern to underline the factuality of the occurrence,[79] whether or not the prophetic convention is of any relevance. Of course, the dating might also be seen to emphasise the rarity in Paul's experience of this kind of happening.[80] Consequently, it might appear to diminish the force of his response to his opponents' claims to be recipients of visions. Was this event, so long ago in his personal past, the only such experience he could set against theirs?[81] Further on, however, in v. 7a, he does refer to 'revelations' in the plural, with clear allusion to his own experiences. And it may be that the context of this reference provides an explanation of his choice of an event fourteen years in the past as his example of such a revelation. It could be, not only that the rapture was the most outstanding instance of these experiences, but also that it was from the time of this event that the infliction of the 'thorn' (v. 7b) dated. The Corinthians may have got to know that this disability, whatever it was, had afflicted Paul for more than a decade. Yet he claimed to be an apostle, and apostles would be expected to possess charismata of healing and exorcism, and special powers in general. If he was unable to 'heal' himself, after suffering for so long, did this not indicate that he possessed no such apostolic power, and was therefore no true apostle?[82] In tacit response,

---

[76] These objections are raised by Baird, 'Visions', p. 657.

[77] Zmijewski, 'Narrenrede', pp. 340–1, with reference to Bultmann, p. 223.

[78] Bruce, Galatians, pp. 92–3.

[79] See above, p. 782, and n. 75. Other supporters of this view include Baumgarten, Apokalyptik, p. 143; and Zmijewski, 'Narrenrede', p. 334.

[80] See Wendland, p. 245, and Dunn, Jesus and the Spirit, p. 215; see above, p. 782 n. 70, for full reference.

[81] As we have already seen (above, p. 774 n. 15), Lincoln supposes that the plural nouns in v. 1 suggest that Paul's intention originally was to recount several such personal experiences. This is doubtful (see our comment, p. 774 and nn. 14, 15).

[82] Jervell, 'Charismatiker', pp. 191–3, who takes the 'thorn' to refer to chronic illness, claims that to the Corinthians it was a contradiction in terms that Paul should be both a charismatic and afflicted with illness.

Paul would then indicate that the period of his affliction dated from the time of his most remarkable ecstatic experience and was integrally connected with it, as the God-given counterpoise to the temptation it posed. Hence, there was no contradiction between his apostolic claims and his affliction with the 'thorn'. And he would refer to his rapture to the third heaven, not because he had had no revelations since that time but because of its temporal connection with the onset of his painful disability, and because its marvellous nature best accounted for the need for a safeguard against self-exaltation.

Paul is not therefore concerned with precise chronological dating as such, and in view of the different chronologies proposed by various modern scholars it is difficult to make any firm decision on the dating of the event he describes here.[83] We have dated the writing of 2 Cor 10–13 in 56 C.E., following Jewett.[84] This gives 42 C.E. as the date of the rapture, which will then have taken place during the period of Paul's activities in Syria and Cilicia (Gal 1.21).[85] The more interesting question is whether this vision is to be identified with any other event mentioned either by Paul himself or by the author of Acts.[86] There have been three suggestions. First, Belser identified the event with the revelation to which Paul refers in Gal 2.2, i.e., that in which he was directed to go up to Jerusalem to discuss his Gentile mission.[87] As Windisch points out, however, it is unlikely, in view of the 'unutterable words' of 2 Cor 12.4, that any such concrete task as the visit to Jerusalem played any part in the experience at present under discussion.[88] Next, Buck and Taylor argue that Paul has in view his conversion experience.[89] In this section of 2 Corinthians Paul is contesting his rivals' claims to apostolic authority, and is likely to refer to 'the all-important vision' which had 'made him a true apostle'.[90] But there are at least two substantial objections to this identification. The experience narrated here is a rapture to heaven, whilst the conversion vision of the risen Christ, if parallel (as Paul claims) to the experiences of the other apostles

[83] See Martin, p. 399, for references to particular dates proposed by various commentators.

[84] See Vol. I, p. 77.

[85] See the end-graphs in Jewett, *Dating Paul's Life*. Furnish, p. 544, also suggests 'about the year 42' for the date.

[86] It would only be experiences of vision that would be relevant. The suggestion by Zahn, *Introd.* III, p. 462, followed by Bachmann, p. 392, Allo, p. 307, and others, that the rapture took place at the time of Paul's original stay in Antioch (Acts 11.25–26), lacks any such evidence (see Jewett, *Dating Paul's Life*, p. 55).

[87] Belser, p. 346.

[88] Windisch, p. 373.

[89] Buck and Taylor, *Development*, pp. 222–4.

[90] Buck and Taylor, *Development*, p. 224.

(1 Cor 15.5–8), must have been seen whilst Paul knew himself to be here on earth.[91] And what he heard in the conversion vision, at least according to Acts (22.7–8; 26.14–18), was not something he was unable or forbidden to express (as in 2 Cor 12.4), but commands of the Lord which he freely repeats.[92] The last suggestion, proposed by Osiander, is that the rapture is to be identified with the vision of the Lord in the temple in Jerusalem, described in Acts 22.17–21.[93] He points to the suitability of the Acts term ἔκστασις (22.17) for the rapture of 2 Cor 12.2–4. Osiander himself admits, however, that there would be a discrepancy between the 'unutterable words' of 2 Cor 12.4 and the reported words of the Lord in Acts 22.18, 21, and has to argue that the experience may have possessed several different aspects.[94] And the Acts story is not an account of rapture to heaven.[95] We have to conclude that, if these narratives in Acts are authentic, the picture they present does not fit the account in 2 Cor 12.2–4, whilst, if they are unauthentic, they are obviously of no use for its further identification.

From Paul's viewpoint, the form of his experience was ambiguous: εἴτε ἐν σώματι . . . εἴτε ἐκτὸς τοῦ σώματος. He does not know whether he was in a bodily or a non-bodily state. This raises at least three questions. Why would the drawing of the distinction make sense to his readers? Granted that it would make sense, why would he mention it? And does his acknowledgement of ignorance, paradoxically, tell us something positive about the nature of the experience?

(i) In one sense, the answer to the first question is simple, since people in a Greek city would readily see the human person as composed of body and soul, and would accept their separability. And they could be familiar with the notion that the soul might be transported to some extra-terrestrial realm and subsequently return to the body. The example most often cited is Plato's story of Er. After Er had been killed in battle (as it seemed), his corpse

---

[91] Cf. Osiander, p. 453; Furnish, p. 544; Wolff, p. 240, with reference, n. 314, to Klauck, p. 156.

[92] Cf. Jewett, *Dating Paul's Life*, p. 55; Furnish, ibid.

[93] Osiander, p. 453.

[94] Osiander, ibid. See also Jewett, *Dating Paul's Life*, p. 54, who sees the discrepancy as counting against this identification: the content of the vision in Acts has nothing to do with paradise.

[95] Plummer, p. 341; cf. Martin, p. 399. For the opposite viewpoint, see Morray-Jones, 'Paradise Revisited', pp. 285–91. Having argued that Paul's ascent was to the heavenly temple (see below, on paradise), he notes that the Acts vision has allusions to that of Isaiah, and that this narrative (Isa 6.1–8) was important in the Jewish mystical tradition, with which Paul's experience is to be connected. This argument, however, leads Morray-Jones to date 2 Cor 10–13, improbably, at the time of the Jerusalem Conference. I am gratefully indebted to Dr C. H. Williams for drawing my attention to this article.

remained intact. On the day of his funeral he returned to life, and told of the extra-bodily journey of his soul to the entrances of heaven and to the underworld.[96] But would Paul's readers have envisaged the possibility that there could be similar transitions in which the visionary was transported bodily?[97] This might seem less likely. But if we may suppose that the Corinthian church contained a certain number of Jewish Christian members,[98] then it would be probable that the idea of bodily rapture would also be familiar. It could be found in the Scriptures, in the case of the taking up of Elijah in the chariot of fire (2 Kings 2.11), and the brief statement of Enoch's earthly end (Gen 5.24) could be read in the same way.[99] In these two cases there is no return to earth.[100] But in the Jewish pseudepigrapha there are at least two possible examples of the idea of bodily ascent and return. In *2 Enoch*, divine messengers carry Enoch to heaven and bring him back to earth. In heaven, the Lord commands that he should be divested of his earthly clothing and dressed in splendid garments, and he is then given a pen to write with.[101] All this at least suggests bodily translation. Similarly, in the *Testament of Abraham*, the patriarch is taken up in the body, and after experiencing revelations is carried back to earth.[102] Whether there are also examples in the pseudepigrapha of the concept of non-bodily rapture is not so certain.[103]

(ii) Turning to the second question, noted above, we can surely say that Paul refers to the two possible forms of rapture for some reason. Jewett suggests that he is indirectly opposing ideas held by two different groups in Corinth: gnostic members of the

[96] Plato, *Rep.* X 614B–621B; see, e.g., Windisch, p. 374; Furnish, p. 525; Wolff, p. 243; Lincoln, 'Visionary', p. 216; Heinrici, *Das zweite Sendschreiben*, p. 490. Windisch, ibid., draws attention to the fact that in the case of Epimenides of Crete and other Greek seers their souls were thought to be able temporarily to leave their bodies. Plummer, p. 342, notes that Philo speaks of Moses on Mount Sinai as having become bodiless (ἀσώματον γενόμενον): see *Somn.* I 36.

[97] Furnish, p. 525, observes that in Greek thinking 'translation into another realm is almost always a flight of the soul from the body'.

[98] In our earlier exegesis we have suggested that this might be so; see pp. 649–50 above on 10.15a.

[99] Cf. Windisch, p. 375; Plummer, p. 342.

[100] As Tabor, *Things Unutterable*, p. 79, notes.

[101] 2 *Enoch* (J-text), 1.6–10; 3.1 (*OTP* I, pp. 106, 108, 110.); 22.8, 11 (*OTP* I, pp. 138, 140).

[102] *T. Abr* (B-text) 8.1–3; 12.12–14 (*OTP* I, pp. 899, 901); see Plummer, p. 343; cf. Lincoln, 'Visionary', pp. 216–17. Windisch, p. 375, claims that belief in bodily rapture is also attested by the story of the four rabbis who entered paradise and, respectively, died, became demented, apostatised, and (R. Akiba) returned unhurt (*b. Hag.* 14b). Rowland, *Open Heaven*, pp. 309–40, argues that in its earliest form the story was not concerned with ascent to the heavenly paradise, but this is questionable: see Morray-Jones, 'Paradise Revisited', p. 268.

[103] See below, under (iii).

church, for whom ecstatic states would be non-bodily, a means of release from the somatic prison; and the visiting missionaries, whom Jewett identifies as 'divine men' and who believed, it is said, in physical transfiguration through study of Torah, and would therefore emphasise bodily rapture. Paul does not wish to side with either group.[104] He would then be careful to allow both possibilities. This explanation, however, depends for its validity on the correctness of Jewett's analysis of the situation in Corinth. Certainly there may have been some church members who held views of a gnostic kind. What is much less certain is that the rival missionaries held the beliefs here attributed to them. The theory depends upon a particular interpretation of chap. 3, as directed against Christian missionaries who claim some 'Mosaic' experience of transformation. In our view, this interpretation is erroneous.[105] There may be a simpler explanation. Perhaps Paul is expressing his complete lack of understanding of how the rapture occurred.[106] Nevertheless, his repeated allusion to the two forms of translation may tell us something about the nature of the experience, thus providing some answer to our third question.

(iii) In relation to the Jewish apocalypses, regarded as reflecting real religious experience, it has been suggested that the visionaries may have seemed to themselves to be aware, at one and the same time, of being outside the body and yet of experiencing various physical sensations.[107] Some evidence of this state of consciousness may be found in *1 Enoch* 71.1–5. In vv. 1, 5, Enoch says, 'my spirit passed out of sight and ascended into the heavens', and again, 'He carried off my spirit, and I, Enoch, was in the heaven of heavens'.[108] This looks like an extra-bodily experience of ascent.[109] But in the intervening v. 3 we read: 'Then I fell upon my face before the Lord of the Spirits. And the angel Michael ... seizing me by my right hand and lifting me up, led me out into all the secrets of mercy.'[110] Language like this could count as evidence for bodily rapture. It could be that Paul's experience was of this ambivalent character, and that this accounts for his expression of uncertainty.[111]

[104] Jewett, *Anthropological Terms*, p. 278.
[105] See Vol. I, pp. 247–8.
[106] Meyer, p. 465. See also Rowland, *Open Heaven*, p. 383, who suggests that the reference to both types of rapture is to be seen as 'an indication of the overwhelming impact the experience had on the apostle, with the result that he was at a loss to explain adequately how he had experienced the ascent'.
[107] Rowland, *Open Heaven*, pp. 229–32, 384.
[108] *OTP*, I, p. 49.
[109] It is cited as such by Lincoln, 'Visionary', p. 216.
[110] *OTP* I, p. 49.
[111] Cf. Rowland, *Open Heaven*, p. 384.

By contrast, there seems to be some degree of precision in the following assertion that he was snatched away, carried off,[112] to the[113] third heaven: ἁρπαγέντα ... ἕως τρίτου οὐρανοῦ. Nevertheless, there are some points of ambiguity. What was the cosmological scheme Paul had in view? In other words, did he think of the third heaven as the highest, or did he believe that there were more than three heavens, perhaps seven? Also, was this third heaven the location of paradise (v. 4a), or does he imply that his rapture there was a further stage in his experience? These questions are inter-related to some extent, but at this point we shall discuss the first question only (i.e., the number of heavens in Paul's cosmology), leaving the second (the location of paradise) until we consider the exegesis of vv. 3–4a.

The Jewish background material attests a variety of cosmological schemes.[114] One of the most widespread posited the existence of seven heavens.[115] For example, in 2 Enoch (A-text) 3–22 we have an account of Enoch's journeys through six heavens, and what he saw in each, culminating in the seventh, where he sees the Lord himself.[116] By contrast, some exegetes refer to the α-text of the Testament of Levi 2–3, where the third heaven appears to be the highest, since Levi is told that there he will 'stand near the Lord'.[117] The text, however, appears to result from a later recension. Other MSS attest the more usual scheme of seven heavens.[118] There is further variety in other works, where five or ten heavens may be mentioned.[119] Consequently, since in Judaism there was no absolutely fixed view, we are to some extent left with the Pauline text itself.

It could be argued that Paul accepted the more common view

---

[112] See BAGD s.v. ἁρπάζω 2.b. The implication here is that of divine agency. Similar uses of the verb are to be found in Wisd 4.11; Acts 8.39; 1 Th 4.17; Rev 12.5 (references cited by Bruce, p. 246). Betz, Tradition, p. 91, sees it as a technical usage.

[113] The phrase ἕως τρίτου οὐρανοῦ could in theory be translated as indefinite: 'to a third heaven'. And this could suggest that Paul believed in a larger number of heavens. But it is also grammatically correct to translate: 'to the third heaven'. See MHT, p. 178: ordinal numbers usually lack the article (this reference is given).

[114] In addition to the commentators on 2 Corinthians, see, e.g., H. Traub, on οὐρανός, in TWNT V, pp. 496–501, 509–36; Lincoln, 'Visionary', pp. 212–13.

[115] Windisch, p. 371; Traub, on οὐρανός, p. 511.

[116] OTP I, pp. 111–39. This narrative is noted by Windisch, ibid., and Lincoln, 'Visionary', p. 212. The latter refers also to the Apocalypse of Abraham 19.4–5 (OTP I, p. 698), and other works, including rabbinic sources.

[117] OTP I, pp. 788–9. The passage is cited by Windisch, p. 372, and by Lincoln, 'Visionary', p. 212.

[118] See M. De Jonge, 'Notes on Testament of Levi II–VII', chap. XV in Studies on the Testaments of the Twelve Patriarchs: Text and Interpretation. SVTP III, Leiden, 1975, pp. 247–60; see especially pp. 248–50, 258–60. I am gratefully indebted to Dr H. W. Hollander for his assistance on this point.

[119] Lincoln, 'Visionary', pp. 212–13.

that there were seven heavens. The present passage may locate paradise in the third heaven. So does *2 Enoch* in 8.1–8,[120] but in general the work operates with a sevenfold scheme. Perhaps Paul did too.[121] There are other arguments, however, which would favour the alternative view that he had in mind a cosmos containing three heavens only. First, if it is one single experience that is described in vv. 2–4, then the third heaven and the location of paradise are identical. And since paradise, it is argued, is the locality of the presence of God, then the third heaven must itself be the highest.[122] But the background material does not suggest that it is absolutely necessary to see paradise as the location *par excellence* of the divine presence. In *2 Enoch* the Lord certainly walks in paradise (8.3), but it is the seventh heaven where his presence is primarily located (20–22).[123] Secondly, the word ἕως is thought to be more natural if Paul thought of the third heaven as the highest.[124] In the NT it implies, it is said, the reaching of a limit.[125] But this is not certain. It is true that, where a limit is in view, ἕως is seen as a suitable preposition. Does it, however, in itself indicate a limit? In Acts 1.8[126] the idea of limit is provided not by the preposition as such but by the dependent ἐσχάτου τῆς γῆς, and the other instances may be explained similarly.[127] Thirdly, there is the general feeling, expressed by a number of exegetes, that Paul must be speaking of some especially sublime experience, and that this would not be so, were the third heaven, in his view, not the highest.[128] Indeed, within a scheme of seven heavens the third would perhaps possess a somewhat inferior character,[129] and mention of it might even have something of an

---

120 *OTP* I, pp. 115–16.

121 So Bietenhard, *Die himmlische Welt*, p. 166. Lincoln, 'Visionary', p. 213, rejects this argument on the grounds that in two other passages where paradise is connected with the third heaven there is no dependence on a system of seven heavens. But the two works cited fail to prove his point. In *Adam and Eve (Apoc.)* 37.5 paradise is placed in the third heaven, but in 35.2 Eve tells Seth to look up 'and see the seven heavens opened'. (*OTP* II, pp. 291, 289). And in *3 Apoc. Bar.* 4 (*OTP* I, pp. 666–7) there is a similar reference to paradise, but this work employs a scheme of five or six heavens: see Rowland, *Open Heaven*, pp. 81–2.

122 Bachmann, pp. 393–4.

123 *OTP* I, p. 115 (A–text), pp. 135, 137 (A–text). Similarly, in *3 Apoc. Bar.* 11; 14, God's presence seems to be located beyond the fifth heaven, despite the apparent placing of paradise in the third in 4: see *OTP* I, pp. 653, 666–7, 674–7.

124 Plummer, p. 343.

125 Martin, pp. 402–3.

126 Cited by Martin, p. 403.

127 In Mk 13.27 we find ἕως ἄκρου οὐρανοῦ and in Mk 15.38 the whole phrase ἀπ᾽ ἄνωθεν ἕως κάτω indicates arrival at a limit; see also Lk 4.29.

128 Hughes, p. 433; Martin, p. 402; Plummer, pp. 343–4; Lincoln, 'Visionary', p. 212.

129 Plummer, ibid.

adverse effect.[130] There might well be some force in this argument. And it seems likely that the general tendency would be to increase the number of heavens rather than to reduce them: the loftier the heavenly world, the more impressive the greatness of God. If so, the threefold structure would be the earlier, and perhaps the cosmological scheme more familiar to Paul himself.

In any case, how did Paul know that he had reached the third heaven? Was it because he had become aware of passing through two previous heavens?[131] Or did he 'recognise' paradise, which he believed to be located in the third heaven? This second possibility will be discussed in the following exegesis.

3–4a. καὶ οἶδα τὸν τοιοῦτον ἄνθρωπον εἴτε ἐν σώματι εἴτε χωρὶς[132] τοῦ σώματος οὐκ οἶδα,[133] ὁ θεὸς οἶδεν, ὅτι ἡρπάγη εἰς τὸν παράδεισον The striking thing about v. 3 is that to a large degree it consists of repetition of v. 2, and in substance appears to contain no fresh information: this same person[134] undergoes some experience which may or may not have been bodily in character, and which is then described in v. 4a as a rapture. Does the repetition indicate that vv. 3–4 tell of a second rapture, or, at least, a second stage of the experience of v. 2? Or is there a different explanation which would allow us to interpret vv. 2–4 as a description of one single, undifferentiated experience?

In favour of supposing that there was a two-fold, or two-stage, rapture various arguments are adduced:

(i) There is the repetition. Tabor claims that unless the parallel structure of v. 2 and vv. 3–4 is indicative of a two-stage event, there would be an unacceptable degree of redundancy in the style.[135] Other exegetes, however, would see significance in the repetition in various other ways. It may give emphasis to the

---

[130] Lincoln, ibid. See also Heckel, *Schwachheit*, pp. 61–2: Paul's opponents could say that rapture only to the third heaven was an indication of his inferior relationship to Christ, and confirmed their doubts about his apostleship. Similarly, Morray-Jones, 'Paradise Revisited', p. 277, who sees the rapture as basic to Paul's apostolic claim, thinks it could not have functioned in this way, were the ascent 'merely to the third of seven heavens'.

[131] Compare the experiences related in the Jewish apocalypses: *2 Enoch* 3–21 (*OTP* I, pp. 110–36); *3 Apoc. Bar.* 2–11 (*OTP* I, pp. 664–75).

[132] Instead of χωρὶς (𝔓46 B D*), some witnesses (א D2 F G H Ψ 0121a. 0243 𝔐 latt) read ἐκτός probably by assimilation to v. 2: see Metzger, *Textual Commentary*[1], p. 585.

[133] A few witnesses (B sa Ir[lat]) omit οὐκ οἶδα. Its inclusion could be due, as Barrett, p. 310, suggests, to assimilation to the previous verse, but the evidence for omission is not strong.

[134] Bruce, p. 247, notes the use of τὸν τοιοῦτον to mean 'the man in question'; cf. 2.6; 1 Cor 5.5.

[135] Tabor, *Things Unutterable*, p. 115; cf. Meyer, p. 469.

extraordinary nature of the occurrence.[136] Perhaps it expresses Paul's dread of profaning the holy.[137] The effect of hesitancy which it produces supports this possibility. It is only after a further reference to rapture that the apostle is able to speak of the climax of his experience.[138] Perhaps also we are to see the stylistic influence of Semitic synthetic parallelism, in which the second element repeats the first and makes some addition to it, with an intensifying effect.[139] Here, the mention of paradise can be seen as a more precise indication of the part of the third heaven to which Paul was transported, thus clarifying its character.[140]

(ii) The καί at the beginning of v. 3 would be superfluous, it is argued, if one experience only is in view.[141] But the sentence which begins in v. 3 and is completed in v. 4 does introduce a piece of additional information, i.e., the reference to paradise. The καί as a simple connective is natural enough.[142]

(iii) The patristic writers mostly favour this view. Plummer cites Clement of Alexandria, who says that Paul was caught up to the third heaven, 'and *thence* into paradise'.[143] He allows, however, that the patristic writers may quote loosely.[144] Heckel suggests that they are influenced by altered perceptions of the heavens.[145]

(iv) It is not until Paul arrives in paradise that he hears the 'unutterable words'.[146] But if, as in *2 Enoch*, the third heaven is itself the location of paradise,[147] this fourth argument for a two-stage rapture becomes invalid.

It is more likely, then, that it is one, unified, experience that Paul speaks of here. Several commentators draw attention to the fact that there is only one note of time. In view of the emphasis on the dating of the event in v. 2, one would expect a second dating

[136] Bachmann, p. 391.

[137] Windisch, p. 371.

[138] Windisch, ibid.; see also Klauck, p. 92; Benz, *Visionär*, p. 109, sees the repetitive style as due to the impossibility of properly expressing the experience in words.

[139] Zmijewski, '*Narrenrede*', p. 335.

[140] Hughes, p. 437. He suggests that the reference to the third heaven points to the 'distance' of the rapture, and the reference to paradise to its 'depth'.

[141] Plummer, p. 344.

[142] Martin, p. 403.

[143] Plummer, ibid. See *PG* 9 col. 117: οἶδα, λέγων, ἄνθρωπον ἐν Χριστῷ ἁρπαγέντα ἕως τρίτου οὐρανοῦ κἀκεῖθεν εἰς τὸν παράδεισον. See Martin, p. 403, for other patristic references, and Heckel, *Schwachheit*, p. 57 n. 18. Note in particular Heckel's quotation of Theophylact (*PG* 124 col. 929 B): Ἀπὸ τοῦ τρίτου, φησὶν, οὐρανοῦ αὖθις ἡρπάγη εἰς τὸν παράδεισον ('From the third heaven, he says, he was *again* snatched up to paradise').

[144] Plummer, ibid.

[145] Heckel, *Schwachheit*, p. 57 n. 17.

[146] Rowland, *Open Heaven*, pp. 381–2.

[147] See above, p. 789, and the further exegesis below.

in v. 3, were Paul speaking here of a further event.[148] Or, if it is not a question of a fresh date but of a two-stage rapture with the same time reference, one would similarly expect some clearer indication of temporal sequence, such as μετὰ ταῦτα.[149] This argument is perhaps the most compelling. Certainly it precludes the possibility that Paul refers to two quite separate experiences of rapture, and renders less likely the suggestion of a two-stage event. In addition, the second part of such an event would probably be expected to occur in a further heaven, which would most likely be named. Consequently, we opt for the view that it is one single experience that is described.[150] Its culmination is Paul's arrival in paradise.

Paradise. The word derives from old Persian, and in Greek is found first in Xenophon, of parks belonging to the Persian king and his nobles.[151] In the LXX it occurs in Gen 2.8 for the Garden of Eden: καὶ ἐφύτευσεν κύριος ὁ θεὸς παράδεισον ἐν Εδεμ. Hence, it denotes God's garden: Gen 13.10; Ezek 28.13; 31.8.[152] In the NT period it acquires eschatological overtones: the first paradise will reappear at the end. It must therefore exist in hidden form in the present.[153] Clearly it is this notion of the existing hidden paradise which lies in the background in 2 Cor 12.2–4. Its location varies. In several of the Jewish pseudepigrapha, however, it is located in the heavens,[154] and examples can be found of its placing in the third heaven. In the *Apocalypse of Moses* 37.5, God instructs the archangel Michael to take Adam up to paradise, 'to the third heaven',[155] and in *2 Enoch* 8.1, Enoch tells how he was brought to the third heaven and placed 'in the midst of paradise'.[156] Since this hidden paradise can be identified in some way with the Garden of Eden, it can be described in similar terms. In *2 Enoch* 8 it is a garden of fruit trees, with four rivers flowing through it, and the tree of life in its midst.[157] In chap. 9 Enoch is told that it is a place

---

[148] Bachmann, p. 391; cf. Allo, p. 305; Hughes, p. 435; Wolff, p. 244; Lincoln, 'Visionary', p. 211; Barnett, p. 560 n. 21.

[149] Windisch, p. 371; cf. Prümm, *Diakonia Pneumatos* I, p. 649.

[150] Bultmann, p. 223; Barrett, p. 310. See also Morray-Jones, 'Paradise Revisited', p. 278, who observes that a two-stage ascent is nowhere known 'in apocalyptic or Jewish mystical literature'.

[151] J. Jeremias, on παράδεισος, in *TWNT* V, pp. 763–71; see p. 763; also Xen., *An.* I 2.7; II 4.14; *Cyr.* I 3.14.

[152] Jeremias, on παράδεισος, p. 763.

[153] Jeremias, on παράδεισος, pp. 766–7.

[154] Jeremias, on παράδεισος, p. 766, and nn. 30–1. He cites *4 Ezra* 4. 7–8 (*OTP* I, pp. 529–30), and *T. Abr.* (B) 10.1–2 (*OTP* I, p. 900).

[155] *OTP* II, p. 291.

[156] *OTP* I, p. 115.

[157] Bietenhard, *Die himmlische Welt*, p. 162. See *OTP* I, pp. 115, 117.

prepared for the righteous.[158] The idea occurs elsewhere, with some degree of frequency, sometimes with reference to the righteous after their death but at other times of their location after the judgement.[159] A further point of significance, noted by Rowland, is that in the *Life of Adam and Eve* paradise is the location of the presence of God: Adam, caught up to paradise, sees God and his angels.[160]

Further light is cast on this aspect of the Jewish paradise tradition in the two-part article by Morray-Jones.[161] In the first part, which deals with the Jewish sources, there is an extensive discussion of the story of the four rabbis who entered paradise. The conclusion, summarised in the second part, is that in its original version this story spoke of ascent to the heavenly temple, and that the term 'paradise', *pardes*, is used 'as a technical term for the Holy of Holies in the highest heaven, where the Glory of God resides'.[162] In this tradition, 'ascent through the heavenly levels was also a journey "inward" through the temple's concentric areas of increasing holiness to the Holy of Holies at the center'.[163]

We return to the question of Paul's recognition of the place to which he was transported. How did he know it was paradise? The simplest answer would be that this location appeared as a heavenly replica of the biblical Garden of Eden. But there may have been a more compelling reason for the identification, if Morray-Jones is correct in his understanding of the story of the four rabbis and the tradition on which it is based.[164] It could be that Paul experienced a vision of the divine glory, and knew himself to be in the *pardes* of the heavenly Holy of Holies. If the cosmic structure to which this view of paradise belongs was threefold in nature in respect of the heavenly world,[165] this would then confirm in Paul's mind a previous impression of having passed through two previous heavens and so having arrived at the third.

---

[158] Bietenhard, ibid.; *OTP* I, p. 117.

[159] Lincoln, 'Visionary', p. 213. For the former idea he cites, e.g., *T. Abr.* 20 (A), 10 (B); *1 Enoch* 60.7–8, 23; 61.12; for the latter (p. 214), e.g. *T. Levi* 18.10f.; *2 Enoch* (A) 65.9–10. He notes that both concepts occur in the NT: see Lk 23.43 (entrance at death), and Rev 2.7 (the 'paradise of the end-time'). See *OTP* I (references in order of citation above), pp. 895, 900; 40–1, 42; 795; 193.

[160] Rowland, *Open Heaven*, pp. 382–3: see *Adam and Eve (Vita)* 25.3 (*OTP* II, p. 266). Tabor, *Things Unutterable*, p. 118, also cites this passage.

[161] Morray-Jones, 'Paradise Revisited'.

[162] Morray-Jones, 'Paradise Revisited', p. 268.

[163] Morray-Jones, ibid.

[164] See above.

[165] Morray-Jones, 'Paradise Revisited', pp. 268, 278, argues that Paul is using a three-heavens scheme.

4b. καὶ ἤκουσεν ἄρρητα ῥήματα ἃ οὐκ ἐξὸν ἀνθρώπῳ λαλῆσαι. This is all we are told about Paul's experience in paradise. It was auditory, and what he heard was ἄρρητος. Whilst the word can mean 'impossible to express', 'beyond human power of expression',[166] the primary sense here must be 'forbidden to express',[167] on account of the explicit statement following that to utter these words was not permitted.[168] But it could be that the connotation 'impossible to express' hovers in the background as well. The prohibition might rest on the inherently transcendental character of the utterances.[169] The word ἄρρητος is used elsewhere in Greek religious contexts, which will be noted below. First we shall consider various suggestions concerning the likely content of the words heard by Paul himself. These are based on biblical and Jewish religious ideas, which would be more likely to have conditioned Paul's apprehension of what was heard.

Perhaps he heard the songs of the angels. Words forbidden to human speech might be employed by angelic beings for the glorification of God and Christ.[170] But would angelic singing really fall into the category of forbidden utterances?[171] There might be a suggestion to this effect in 2 *Enoch*, where Enoch hears angels' songs which are 'impossible to describe'.[172] As Furnish notes, however, this is ambiguous; perhaps the beauty of the singing was simply beyond words.[173] Did the revelation, then, have to do with 'the depths of God' which Paul speaks of in 1 Cor 2.10?[174] Possibly. In the context, however, the phrase appears to be closely related to the eschatological secrets to which the previous verse refers. Hence, it would be eschatological blessings that would be in view,[175] and, as Windisch points out, Paul did not believe he was forbidden to communicate eschatological mysteries: see

---

[166] BAGD s.v. ἄρρητος 1.

[167] BAGD s.v. ἄρρητος 2.

[168] See, e.g., Meyer, p. 470; Bultmann, p. 224; Zmijewski, *'Narrenrede'*, p. 339; Barnett, p. 561 n. 23 contd.

[169] Zmijewski, *'Narrenrede'*, p. 343, with reference to Prümm, *Diakonia Pneumatos* I, pp. 650–1. See also Windisch, p. 378. In strict logic, of course, the idea of a dual reference can scarcely be maintained: to forbid the communication of a secret revelation is to admit that such communication is possible. But it is questionable whether Paul and his readers would be any more sensitive to the contradiction than the exegetes who suggest a dual meaning.

[170] Bachmann, p. 393.

[171] The question is raised by Windisch, p. 379.

[172] 2 *Enoch* (J) 17 (*OTP* I, p. 130).

[173] Furnish, p. 527.

[174] Windisch, p. 379, and Furnish, p. 545, think this is possible, and perhaps more likely than other suggestions.

[175] So, with hesitation, Bultmann, p. 224, with reference to J. Dupont, *Gnosis*, Louvain, 1949, p. 189.

1 Cor 15.50–55.[176] This is surely the implication also in 1 Cor 2.6–16. A further suggestion is that the 'unutterable words', like the glossolalia of 1 Cor 14, are to be understood as the speech of the new aeon and represent the language of the heavenly realm.[177] But would Paul have spoken of words he was not allowed to divulge, if it was simply ecstatic speech that he had heard?[178] Much more probable is Furnish's tentative suggestion that he heard the utterance of the divine name.[179] This would certainly, in our view, fit the description of the words as 'forbidden to a man to express'.[180] The plural might be used either because Paul heard several, equally unutterable, divine names, or because he heard angelic singing in which the one name was reiterated.[181] At this point a further item of background information becomes relevant. Morray-Jones, in his discussion of the story of the four rabbis, notes that in one version Aqiba heard words which concerned 'the innermost mysteries of God's being, which cannot and may not be described in words, but are only partially known and expressed through the medium of mystical praise'.[182] He sees this as 'a remarkably close parallel' to Paul's ἄρρητα ῥήματα.[183] Combined with the previous suggestion that the apostle heard the divine name, this interpretation appears the most satisfactory.

'Unutterable Words'. Whilst we have argued that the Jewish background is the more significant for our understanding of Paul's auditory experience in paradise, it is worth noting in addition the use of ἄρρητος in Greek religious texts. This may have been significant for the congregation in Corinth.

According to Windisch, Paul has intentionally taken over an element of the cultic terminology of the mystery religions. In these cults, such 'unutterable words' would comprise secret doctrines, formulae, and descriptions of visions that were not to be communicated to the uninitiated.[184] Literary evidence for the use of ἄρρητος in a cultic context is to be found in Herodotus,

[176] Windisch, p. 379.
[177] Käsemann, 'Legitimität', pp. 67–8.
[178] Furnish, p. 545.
[179] Furnish, p. 545, with reference to J. W. Bowker, ' "Merkabah" Visions and the Visions of Paul', *Journal of Semitic Studies* 16 (1971), pp. 157–73.
[180] The dative ἀνθρώπῳ is more naturally to be seen as dependent not on λαλῆσαι ('to utter to a man') but on οὐκ ἐξόν ('not permitted to a man'). See, e.g., Plummer, p. 345; Barrett, p. 311; Furnish, p. 513; Martin, p. 388.
[181] Thrall, 'Journey to Paradise', p. 361.
[182] Morray-Jones, 'Paradise Revisited', p. 281.
[183] Morray-Jones, ibid.
[184] Windisch, pp. 377–8. See also Georgi, *Opponents*, p. 282, who claims that Paul's phrase belonged 'to the repertory of motifs of Hellenistic mysticism'.

where it is applied to religious rites: ἄρρητοι ἱρογίαι,[185] ἄρρητα ἱρά.[186] More particularly, there is in the *Bacchae* of Euripides a clear instance of its use in relation to rites not to be divulged to those not initiated into the Bacchic mysteries:

Τὰ δ᾽ ὄργι᾽ ἐστὶ τίν᾽ ἰδέαν ἔχοντά σοι;
Ἄρρητ᾽ ἀβακχεύτοισιν εἰδέναι βροτῶν.[187]
'And the rites, what form (do you suppose?)
do they have? Not to be divulged to mortals
uninitiate in the Bacchic mysteries, for them to know.'[188]

Plutarch likewise refers to veiled secrets not to be spoken, ἄρρητα, to all and sundry (the πολλοί), nor seen by them.[189] Philo also, Windisch observes, is familiar with the term ἄρρητος as a mystery-concept, used to refer to what the uninitiated are not allowed to hear.[190] In view of these and similar[191] examples, he suggests that Paul was consciously dependent upon the terminology of the mystery religions.[192] This is perhaps doubtful. The appropriation of the language by Philo could point to its currency in more general religious usage.[193] Furthermore the parallel with the mystery cults seems not to be exact, on two counts. First, in these cults the secret formulae and the like were ἄρρητος only in the case of outsiders: to the initiates they were communicated.[194] Secondly, the examples cited do not contain Paul's actual phrase ἄρρητα ῥήματα.[195] It would be simpler, therefore, to

---

[185] Hdt. V 83; cited in LSJ s.v. ἄρρητος III.1. and BAGD s.v. ἄρρητος 2.; cf. Furnish, p. 527.
[186] Hdt. VI 135; cited in LSJ, ibid., and by Windisch, p. 377; see also Lincoln, 'Visionary', p. 216.
[187] Eur., *Bacchae*, ll. 471–2; cited in LSJ and BAGD, ibid.; see also Windisch, p. 377; Furnish, p. 527; Lincoln, ibid.
[188] The LCL translation is not used, as it appears too free here.
[189] Plut., *Mor.* 360F: ὅσα τε μυστικοῖς ἱεροῖς περικαλυπτόμενα καὶ τελεταῖς ἄρρητα διασώζεται καὶ ἀθέατα πρὸς τοὺς πολλούς ('So too all the things which are kept always away from the ears and eyes of the multitude, by being concealed behind mystic rites and ceremonies' LCL). See BAGD, ibid.; Furnish, p. 527; Windisch, p. 377.
[190] Windisch, p. 378, with reference to Philo, *Somn.* (*Dreams*), I 191. The relevant sentence runs: τοῖς δὲ ὡς φίλος ἐπιεικῶς καὶ μετὰ πειθοῦς πολλὰ καὶ τῶν ἀρρήτων ἀναφέρει ὧν οὐδένα τῶν ἀτελέστων ἐπακοῦσαι θέμις. ('Towards others it [the sacred word] acts as a friend with winning condescension imparting to them even many secret truths which are not allowed to reach the ears of the uninitiated' LCL). See also Furnish, p. 527.
[191] Windisch, p. 378, and Lincoln, 'Visionary', p. 216, cite instances where the word used is ἀπόρρητος.
[192] Windisch, ibid.
[193] Barrett, p. 311. In this connection it is worth noting also that in Philo, *Quod Det. Pot.* 175 (cited by Windisch, p. 378, and by Lincoln, 'Visionary', p. 216) the context of the occurrence of ἄρρητος is scarcely cultic in even the broadest sense.
[194] Windisch, ibid., himself allows this.
[195] Spittler, 'Limits', p. 263.

suppose that he was aware of the suitability of the word ἄρρητος in a religious context, that his experience had included a verbal revelation to be kept secret,[196] and that the term ἄρρητα ῥήματα naturally suggested itself as a means of expression.

Paul's experience was auditory, whatever the content of the ἄρρητα ῥήματα. But we have also suggested that it must in addition have been in some way visual, in view of his 'recognition' of paradise. We return, then, to the question already broached.[197] Did Paul see a vision of the divine glory? Did he, that is, see a vision of Christ, who embodies the glory of God (4.6)? That he did 'see' Christ in paradise can be plausibly argued from two different exegetical perspectives. First, Lincoln notes that in Paul's view Christ was the heavenly Adam who restores paradise to fallen humanity. Consequently: 'Paul's anticipation of it should be assumed to be also an anticipation of greater intimacy with his heavenly Lord.'[198] This would very likely imply, we suggest, that his experience included an actual vision of Christ. And such a vision might account for his allusion to the Lord's 'visible form' in 5.7. On earth we do not live διὰ εἴδους, in the sphere of his visible form. But in the state beyond death our situation will be reversed. Paul will have had a foretaste of this reversal.[199] Secondly, there is the suggestion of Morray-Jones. Paul's experience is to be interpreted in terms of the Jewish merkabah (throne-mysticism) tradition. In this tradition the visionary ascended into heaven, and in 'the celestial Holy of Holies' beheld the divine *kabod*, the glory of God. Paul identified the *kabod* with Christ. Thus: 'Paul is describing an ascent to the heavenly temple and a merkabah vision of the enthroned and "glorified" Christ.'[200]

If these suggestions are plausible, either in combination or as alternatives, this experience must have strengthened Paul's conviction of his apostolic calling and authority, for it would have conveyed a sign of Christ's approval, as Tabor argues.[201] As he notes, with reference to Schweitzer, of all the apostles who had seen the risen Christ it is only Paul himself who has experienced rapture to heaven.[202]

This, then, is an account of real experience. DiCicco does so regard it, and sees it as a further example of Paul's argument from

---

[196] The idea of the preservation of secret revelation was familiar in Judaism: see Barrett, p. 311, and Lincoln, ibid.

[197] See above, pp. 775, 793.

[198] Lincoln, 'Visionary', p. 218.

[199] Thrall, 'Journey to Paradise', p. 362.

[200] Morray-Jones, 'Paradise Revisited', pp. 273, 277–8, 283.

[201] See above, p. 781 n. 67.

[202] Tabor, *Things Unutterable*, pp. 37–8.

ἦθος.[203] The apostle may be suggesting that he is a 'messenger of God who, like Isaiah, was privileged to participate in the proceedings of God's court'.[204] But he goes on, DiCicco argues, to 'sabotage' this proof from ἦθος in ironical fashion by means of the 'thorn' narrative, in which divine power comes to fruition in the context of human weakness, and in this way provides Paul with his apostolic legitimacy.[205] The relationship between the two narratives is complex, therefore, according to DiCicco. But the complexity should not, in our view, lead to the discounting of the rapture's serious significance for Paul himself.[206] There is no need to see the two modes of legitimation as mutually contradictory.

5. **ὑπὲρ τοῦ τοιούτου καυχήσομαι, ὑπὲρ δὲ ἐμαυτοῦ οὐ[207] καυχήσομαι εἰ μὴ ἐν ταῖς ἀσθενείαις.[208]** Such a splendid experience would be something, surely about which a person could boast, and in v. 1 Paul has allowed the necessity of boasting. But in accordance with the objectivising, third-person narrative of vv. 2–4 he maintains that it is this 'other' person[209] of whom he will boast, not (in respect of the rapture) of himself. Thus, he avoids the charge of self-praise,[210] and continues to speak in a style which may reflect the sense of displacement of the ego in ecstatic experience.[211] Betz supposes that he has in view the prospect of boasting in the future: καυχήσομαι, after all, is future in tense. This prospect he renounces.[212] But when Paul has said in v. 1, first, that one has to boast, and, secondly, that he is going to deal with the subject of 'visions and revelations', and when, thirdly, the next three verses describe precisely one such

---

[203] DiCicco, *Ethos, Pathos and Logos*, pp. 99–104.
[204] DiCicco, *Ethos, Pathos and Logos*, p. 100.
[205] DiCicco, *Ethos, Pathos and Logos*, pp. 102–4.
[206] DiCicco does not explicitly get to this point, but such expressions as [Paul's] 'maneuver of ironically sabotaging' (p. 104) this proof seem to verge in this direction.
[207] A few witnesses (𝔓[46] lat) read οὐδέν. This is probably an accidental alteration. (Was some scribe absentmindedly thinking ahead to the ἐν preceding ταῖς ἀσθενείαις?)
[208] At this point there is a more substantial division of witnesses. Some (ℵ D² F G Ψ 0121a 𝔐 lat Ambst) read μου after ἀσθενείαις, whilst others (𝔓[46] B D* 0243. 6. 33. 1175. 1739 *pc* sy co) omit it. On balance, it is more likely to have been added, as the expected natural completion of ταῖς ἀσθενείαις, than to have been omitted.
[209] The τοῦ τοιούτου could be neuter in gender, and is so translated in the Moffatt Commentary (Strachan, p. 29): 'of an experience like that'. But the great majority of commentators take it as masculine, 'of such a person'. The preceding τοιοῦτος in vv. 2–3 is masculine (Meyer, p. 471; Bachmann, p. 395; Plummer, p. 345; and others). The contrasting ἐμαυτοῦ in v. 5b suggests a personal object of boasting in v. 5a (the above commentators and others). And Hughes, p. 441 n. 120, points out that in Paul καυχάομαι ὑπέρ is normally used of a person.
[210] Windisch, p. 380; Zmijewski, '*Narrenrede*', p. 350; Martin, p. 406.
[211] See above, p. 782; cf. Plummer, p. 346.
[212] Betz, *Tradition*, p. 95 n. 349.

experience, it is surely obvious that these verses themselves
contain the boasting, i.e., a boasting here and now in the present.
The future tense is probably conditioned by its use in the second
half of the verse, where it appears more natural, as an expression
of Paul's future intentions. His own personal boast will concern
only his weaknesses. This he has indicated already in 11.30. What
it means he will explain more fully in vv. 7–10.

6. ἐὰν γὰρ θελήσω καυχήσασθαι,²¹³ οὐκ ἔσομαι ἄφρων,
ἀλήθειαν γὰρ ἐρῶ· φείδομαι δέ, μή τις εἰς ἐμὲ λογίσηται ὑπὲρ
ὃ βλέπει με ἢ ἀκούει [τι] ἐξ ἐμοῦ. For whilst he could²¹⁴ indeed
boast truthfully of himself in other respects, he nevertheless
refrains: the opening γάρ relates the whole of v. 6 to v. 5b, i.e., to
Paul's determination that personal boasting is to be only of
weakness.²¹⁵ At the same time, he insists that, were he to make
the alternative choice, he would not be a fool. And here there
might seem to be some inconsistency. For in 11.16b–17 he
suggests that all boasting is folly, whilst here he appears to allow
that it would not be foolish to boast (in the ordinary sense of the
word), provided that his claims could be substantiated.
Commentators resolve the problem in various ways. It could be,
perhaps, that Paul has imperceptibly switched to a different
definition of folly. Chrysostom suggests that it is lying that is now
the major folly,²¹⁶ i.e., in the context, boasting without
substance.²¹⁷ But if this is what Paul means, should we not have to
agree with Bultmann that for the moment he does not consider
the implications of what he says? Is boasting no longer κατὰ
σάρκα if it is true?²¹⁸ An alternative interpretation supposes that
Paul distinguishes between *being* a fool and *playing the part* of
the fool. Thus Betz suggests that here for a moment he steps out
of his fool's role to ensure that his conduct will be properly

---

²¹³ The reading of 𝔓⁴⁶, θέλω, καυχήσομαι, is an oddity, and is difficult to explain
except as the result of two scribal errors made independently of each other: the
accidental omission of the ΗΣ of θελήσω and the assimilation of καυχήσασθαι to
the previous καυχήσομαι of v. 5b.
²¹⁴ The θελήσω indicates the possibility of choice. Bultmann, p. 225, comments
that it is not because Paul would have nothing else to boast about that he boasts of
his weaknesses. See also Barrett, p. 312. In form, θελήσω could be either future
indicative or aorist subjunctive (cf. Plummer, p. 346), but is highly unlikely to be
intended as the former. There is no clear instance in the NT of ἐάν with the future
indicative (BDR 373(3)), although it occurs as a variant at Acts 8.31 (MHT, p.
116).
²¹⁵ Windisch, p. 381; Barrett, p. 312; Zmijewski, 'Narrenrede', p. 358. All three
commentators note that an implicit amplification of καυχήσασθαι is required.
Barrett has: 'about things other than my weaknesses'.
²¹⁶ Chrysostom, PG 61 col. 577 (NPNF XII, p. 399).
²¹⁷ So also Bultmann, p. 225.
²¹⁸ Bultmann, ibid.

understood.[219] Zmijewski, lastly, connects this with the previous suggestion. The οὐκ ἔσομαι ἄφρων constitutes an existential assertion. The ἄφρων is a person who boasts of things that do not correspond to the truth, and Paul will *not be* a fool in this sense. There is a back reference to 11.16a, where he has indicated that even when he *plays the part* of the fool, this is not what he really *is*. The οὐκ ἔσομαι ἄφρων of the present verse and the μή τίς με δόξῃ ἄφρονα εἶναι of 11.16a thus stand on a different level from the 'folly-statements' of 11.16b, 17, 21b, 23a, and 12.11, which refer to the role Paul is playing.[220] But it is not really clear how much this helps. For if, according to 11.16b, the *playing of the role* of the *fool* is equated with the facilitation of *boasting*, one must surely conclude that, conversely, boasting, as such, is folly, whether or not it corresponds with the facts. Fundamentally, no doubt, Paul would say that the 'truth', the 'facts', about his apostolic achievements that he would tell of would be that they are not 'his' but the work of Christ (Rom 15.17–19). Hence, this would not, in any ordinary sense, constitute boasting at all. And in consequence he can with a good conscience repudiate the characterisation of himself as essentially a fool.

In any case, he does not propose to speak of his achievements. He refrains,[221] for a reason he goes on to explain. He is concerned lest the Corinthians' opinion of him should be wrongly based and on that account too high. The main point is clear, but some linguistic points require discussion, and we also need to inquire more precisely about the nature of Paul's concern about Corinthian opinion.

The first linguistic item for consideration is the phrase εἰς ἐμὲ λογίσηται. There is substantial support for the view that λογίζομαι is used here, metaphorically, as a commercial technical term, 'place to (someone's) account', 'credit' (something to someone)',[222] and so 'credit to me (too favourable an assessment)'. There is one difficulty, however, in that one would expect the

---

[219] Betz, *Tradition*, pp. 94–5.

[220] Zmijewski, '*Narrenrede*', p. 361; cf. Furnish, p. 527.

[221] Barrett, p. 312, takes the present tense of φείδομαι as conative and the meaning of the verb as 'spare': Paul is trying to spare the Corinthians (Barrett appears to suggest), who 'have only themselves to blame that they have brought upon themselves the story of Paul's rapture'. This suggestion is improbable. It is rightly criticised by Furnish, p. 527, who argues that, on the contrary, the Corinthians would have welcomed boasting by Paul. On the sense 'refrain' for φείδομαι see BAGD s.v. 2., where it is noted that in the present verse one has to supply τοῦ καυχᾶσθαι to complete the sense.

[222] So, e.g., Ewald, p. 306; Windisch, p. 381; Héring, p. 95; Barrett, pp. 305, 312; Bultmann, p. 225; Zmijewski, '*Narrenrede*', p. 359; Furnish, pp. 513, 527. See also BAGD s.v. λογίζομαι 1.a.

dative ἐμοί rather than εἰς ἐμέ.[223] An alternative interpretation would be to take λογίσηται as intransitive, in the sense 'form an estimate', 'make a judgement' and to give εἰς ἐμέ the meaning 'with reference to me'.[224] The following ὑπὲρ ὃ βλέπει κτλ. would then have to be understood as adverbial, 'in a way that exceeds what he sees ...'[225] But since there is some interchangeability between the dative case and εἰς with the accusative,[226] this alternative understanding of Paul's phrase is not absolutely necessary. It could be right, but there is no real grammatical hindrance to our understanding λογίσηται in the 'commercial' sense, with the majority of commentators. If we do so, then the second matter for linguistic comment will be the more exact analysis of the following clause. As a whole, it will function as the direct object of λογίσηται. As regards the precise grammatical relation of the relative pronoun ὃ to the personal pronoun με, we may refer to Zmijewski. He notes two possibilities. The ὃ may be the predicate: 'that which he sees me to be'.[227] Alternatively, we could supply the participle ποιοῦντα after με, and take ὃ as its object: 'that which he sees me doing'. This, Zmijewski claims, fits better with what follows, where an implicitly repeated ὃ acts as the object of ἀκούει.[228] He may be correct; but 'sees me to be' makes perfectly good sense, if a verb is omitted it is most natural to fill the gap with some form of 'to be', and it appears to be Paul's general *persona* (rather than his specific activities) which primarily concerns the Corinthians, together with his

[223] Meyer, p. 473. Note also that in the example quoted in BAGD, ibid, to support the commercial use of λογίζομαι the verb takes the dative of the person: τὰ ἕτερα ἀναλώματα ἑαυτοῖς ἐλογισάμεθα ('we charged the other expenses to our own account'). A further reference (P Fay 21.9) is given, but, as Theobald, *Gnade*, p. 248 n. 36, observes, whilst εἰς with the accusative occurs here, it refers to a thing, not a person: εἰς τὸ δημόσιον ('to the state treasury').
[224] Theobald, *Gnade*, p. 248.
[225] Theobald, ibid.
[226] See BAGD s.v. εἰς 4.g.
[227] Zmijewski, '*Narrenrede*', p. 360, with reference, n. 273, to Bauer, *Wörterbuch*, p. 284.
[228] Zmijewski, '*Narrenrede*', p. 360, followed by Furnish, p. 528. At this point we have to notice that a number of witnesses (𝔓46 ℵ2 D* Ψ 0243 𝔐 f vgcl syh Ambst) read τι as the object of ἀκούει. It is omitted in others (ℵ* B D2 F G I 6. 33. 81. 1175. 1739 *pc* a b vgst co). There is strong attestation for its omission, therefore. And it is not easy to see what its function would be. But precisely on this account, of course, it is the *lectio difficilior*. It would seem 'superfluous and disturbing to the syntax', so that scribes might well 'correct' the text by omitting it. See Metzger, *Textual Commentary*[1], p. 585, for these points. Why any scribe should add τι to a text which lacked it is difficult to understand. Is it, perhaps, original but displaced? It could fit syntactically after λογίσηται as its direct object, with the ὑπέρ-clause then as adjectival in function. Furnish, p. 513, appears to translate the verse this way: 'so that no one can credit me with something beyond what one may see me doing or hear from me'. But he does not discuss the variant as such.

oratorical powers, or lack of them. These considerations tell in favour of the first possibility, which Zmijewski rejects. What Paul's correspondents see him to be goes just as well (better, in fact) with what they hear him say,[229] as providing a basis of assessment.

In any case, it is on this basis, what the Corinthians actually see of him and hear from him, that he wishes them to assess him, not on his own account of himself. Presumably the 'hear from me' will refer to his preaching and teaching.[230] But why does he think it necessary to make the point? In all probability it has some relation to the brief account in vv. 2–4 of Paul's rapture to the third heaven, but commentators interpret the connection in different ways. Some lay emphasis on the unverifiable character of visionary experiences. Paul does not wish his authority to rest on such a basis: a swindler could likewise, though fraudulently, appeal to such visions.[231] And on this account even veridical experiences 'could be challenged by hostile men'.[232] But is there any indication that Paul supposed his account would be doubted?[233] It could be that he has in view those in the Corinthian congregation who will accept his story of rapture without question and will then think him exceptional precisely because of this experience.[234] In fact, he may have in mind both types of response. The ἀλήθειαν ... ἐρῶ in v. 6a could suggest a hint of suspicion that he might not be believed, whilst his knowledge of the general character of the Corinthian church might incline him to fear the opposite reaction. In this latter respect he might be anxious lest the emergence of too high an opinion of himself might obscure the overriding importance of his gospel.[235] And again, lastly, we encounter the insistence that Paul is denying the relevance of his visionary experience to his claim to apostleship.[236] But if he is, why has he mentioned his rapture to heaven at all, in a situation where he is faced with other claimants to apostolic status? The situation is at least more complex than proponents of this argument suggest.

7a. καὶ τῇ ὑπερβολῇ τῶν ἀποκαλύψεων. This phrase requires separate consideration, since it is not clear whether it concludes

---

[229] The ἐξ ἐμοῦ means 'from me'. Plummer, p. 346, notes that the KJV 'of me' is misleading: Paul is not referring to what other people say about him.
[230] Further accounts of ecstatic experience would, of course, likewise come 'from' him.
[231] Lietzmann, p. 155.
[232] Filson, pp. 406–7.
[233] The question is raised by Windisch, p. 381, in opposition to Lietzmann.
[234] Martin, pp. 409–10.
[235] Barrett, p. 313.
[236] Barrett, ibid.; Furnish, p. 546. Both refer to Käsemann, 'Legitimität', pp. 69–70.

v. 6 or begins v. 7. The decision is complicated by the existence of a textual variant at the beginning of v. 7b: some MSS read διό, others omit it. We shall discuss this first, before proceeding to the main question. The two problems are, of course, interrelated, but there are textual criteria which are to some degree independent of the wider exegetical issue.

(i) *The text.* At the beginning of v. 7b some witnesses (א A B F G 0243. 33. 81. 1175. 1739 *pc* sy^h bo) read διὸ ἵνα μὴ ὑπεραίρωμαι, whilst others (𝔓46 D Ψ 𝔐 lat sa Ir^lat) omit the διό. Metzger argues for the retention of διό on two grounds. First, it has the support of several of the Alexandrian witnesses (א A B 33. 81. 1739).[237] We should note, however, that it is lacking in others (𝔓46 Ψ).[238] Secondly, it can be seen as the *lectio difficilior*.[239]

Now, whilst the first reason for the retention of διό is independent of exegetical considerations, this second one is not. Whether or not διό is the more difficult reading depends precisely on the answer given to the main question under discussion. If v. 7a is to be attached to v. 7b, then the διό is certainly odd, but this is not so if it is connected with v. 6. Some connecting word between 6–7a and 7b would be expected. Tasker, therefore, argues that it will have been the lack of διό, or its equivalent, that was felt to be difficult, and that the text will have been 'corrected' by its insertion.[240] Nevertheless, this is not a certainty. The word διό is one of Paul's own favourite conjunctions, and, with the exception of Hebrews (and parts of Acts), not otherwise common in the NT. A scribe 'correcting' asyndeton might have inserted a more usual connective. Tentatively, we accept the inclusion of διό as the original reading, on the basis of MS attestation and Pauline usage.

(ii) *The main question.* (a) In favour of connecting v. 7a with v. 6 there are arguments based on linguistic style and also on sense.

(1) It is thought more likely that v. 7 would begin with διό rather than with καί, since the latter, it is said, would indicate a closer connection with v. 6 than would be warranted.[241] This may be true, but attachment to v. 6 is not without problems.[242]

(2) Connection with the remainder of v. 7 would result in an unacceptable accumulation of datives (τῇ ὑπερβολῇ, μοι, τῇ

---

[237] Metzger, *Textual Commentary*², p. 516.
[238] See *Textual Commentary*², p. 15* for a list of the Alexandrian witnesses.
[239] Metzger, *Textual Commentary*², p. 516.
[240] Tasker, p. 173. Other supporters of the absence of διό in the original text include Bachmann, p. 397 n. 1; Héring, p 95; Bruce, p. 248.
[241] Zmijewski, *'Narrenrede'*, p. 354; Furnish, p. 528.
[242] See below, p. 805.

σαρκί). Also the ἐδόθη would stand rather far removed from the τῇ ὑπερβολῇ τῶν ἀποκαλύψεων with which in sense it would be connected.[243] The first point has little or no weight: the first dative is not adjacent to the other two; μοι is a light form of the pronoun; the three datives are not identical in function. The second point, likewise, is unconvincing: for one could argue that, if v. 7a concludes the sentence beginning with v. 6, the ἐδόθη would, as regards sense, stand even further away from the reference to abundant revelations.

(3) In v. 7b, the double ἵνα μὴ ὑπεραίρωμαι forms an inclusive framework which would lose its effect if v. 7a belongs with v. 7b.[244] But since v. 7a is stylistically awkward whichever way one connects it, this argument is not compelling.

(4) Further structural considerations suggest that v. 7a belongs with v. 6. In v. 6a we have a threefold structure:

Ἐὰν γὰρ θελήσω καυχήσασθαι,
οὐκ ἔσομαι ἄφρων,
ἀλήθειαν γὰρ ἐρῶ.

In vv. 6b–7a there is a similar structure:

φείδομαι δέ,
μή τις εἰς ἐμὲ λογίσηται ὑπὲρ ὃ βλέπει με ἢ ἀκούει [τι] ἐξ ἐμοῦ
καὶ τῇ ὑπερβολῇ τῶν ἀποκαλύψεων.

Thus, we have two threefold assertions set in antithesis to each other.[245] Nevertheless, their grammatical structure differs considerably, as does the length of their component parts.

(5) The most substantial stylistic argument for the connection with v. 6 is that the διό is strangely and awkwardly placed if v. 7a is attached to v. 7b. It should function as an introductory conjunction placed at the beginning of its sentence.[246]

(6) It is argued that the phrase καὶ τῇ ὑπερβολῇ τῶν ἀποκαλύψεων fits v. 6 in respect of content. The dative is causal, and provides an explanation of why Paul should be anxious about the prospect of over-valuation. The καί should be seen as epexegetic: 'namely', on account of his abundant revelations.[247] This certainly would make good sense. But the classification of καί as epexegetic is doubtful. In the other instances of this use

243 Zmijewski, ibid; Furnish, ibid.
244 Zmijewski, ibid; Furnish, ibid.
245 Zmijewski, 'Narrenrede', p. 355–7; Furnish, ibid.
246 Martin, p. 389 n. h.
247 Zmijewski, 'Narrenrede', p. 354–5; see also Heckel, Schwachheit, p. 74. Others who connect v. 7a with v. 6 include Furnish and Martin, as already cited, and Theobald, Gnade, p. 247.

of καί in Paul the particle is followed by some form of οὗτος.[248] The καί in v. 7a is more probably connective. But in that case it would be superfluous, if the phrase is to be attached to v. 6. Of these six arguments, the only one with substantial force is the fifth, i.e., the extraordinary position of διό if v. 7a belongs with v. 7b, not with v. 6.

(b) Other arguments favour the connection of v. 7a with v. 7b.
(1) Stylistically, connection with v. 6 produces a slackness of style.[249]
(2) The 'extraordinary revelations' (BAGD s.v. ὑπερβολή) are most naturally to be seen as the reason for the infliction of the 'thorn'. It would surely be on account of these experiences, primarily, that Paul would be tempted to self-exaltation.[250]
(3) If v. 7a is connected with v. 6b, then the διό of v. 7b must logically relate to the whole of vv. 6b–7a. But this would not make sense. Paul's rejection of boasting (φείδομαι δέ) does not constitute the ground for the infliction of the 'thorn'. Indeed, it might seem to render it unnecessary. And it is in the present that he refrains from boasting, whilst the 'thorn' was inflicted at some point in the past.

(c) What conclusion can we draw? There are good exegetical grounds for attaching v. 7a to v. 7b. But what explanation can we then give of the awkward position of διό? In fact, not all commentators do find it difficult. Barrett, for example, argues that it 'simply anticipates the final clause (for which reason, namely, in order to …)'.[251] Hughes suggests that διό could be regarded 'as an emphatic redundancy', which takes up and emphasises the causal force of the preceding dative τῇ ὑπερβολῇ (τῶν ἀποκαλύψεων).[252] It is quite possible to interpret the διό in some such way. And it is interesting, finally, to observe that Zmijewski, who has argued forcibly for the connection of v. 7a with v. 6, does wish also to relate it to the following διό. In view of this conjunction, the phrase τῇ ὑπερβολῇ τῶν ἀποκαλύψεων has to be seen from a second aspect. Now Paul has to expound the concrete historical consequence which has resulted for him from this very abundance of revelations.[253] But to say so much is in effect to admit that there is a close relationship between v. 7a and v. 7b. We prefer to accept this connection, and to dissociate v. 7a syntactically from v. 6. Hence we are now in a position to discuss v. 7 as a whole.

[248] See Rom 13.11 (καὶ τοῦτο); 1 Cor 2.2 (καὶ τοῦτον); 6.6 (καὶ τοῦτο); 6.8 (καὶ τοῦτο). See MHT, p. 335, for these references.
[249] Prümm, *Diakonia Pneumatos* I, p. 657.
[250] Lincoln, 'Visionary', p. 218.
[251] Barrett, p. 313.
[252] Hughes, p. 449 n. 138.
[253] Zmijewski, *'Narrenrede'*, p. 364; cf. Heckel, *Schwachheit*, p. 75.

7. καὶ τῇ ὑπερβολῇ τῶν ἀποκαλύψεων, διό, ἵνα μὴ
ὑπεραίρωμαι, ἐδόθη μοι σκόλοψ τῇ σαρκί, ἄγγελος Σατανᾶ,
ἵνα με κολαφίζῃ, ἵνα μὴ ὑπεραίρωμαι. The reference to revelations implicitly indicates what would have been the content of
the boasting Paul rejects (v. 6). At the same time it leads into the
explanation, as he has come to understand it, of the infliction
upon him of the condition he metaphorically designates 'a thorn
for the flesh'. Its existence had doubtless played some part in
diminishing the Corinthians' regard for his apostolic status, and
he is anxious that they should realise its true function and significance. He speaks of 'revelations' in the plural, which means that
he is not thinking solely of the unique event he has described in
vv. 2–4.[254] It may well be that such occurrences were not a
frequent feature of his life. He has gone back fourteen years, it
would appear, to find an outstanding example. But there must
have been other such experiences, less striking, but still extraordinary.[255] And it is also possible that the narration of a
fourteen-year-old event is due, not to lack of visionary experience
in the interim, but to the fact that the infliction of the 'thorn'
dated from this point in time. The term ὑπερβολή in any case does
not in itself settle the question of the frequency or otherwise of
the revelations.[256]

Whatever the answer, whether frequent,[257] or (more probably)
simply of extraordinary quality,[258] these experiences were the
cause[259] of the bestowal of the σκόλοψ. Paul might have become
elated with pride on their account: the 'thorn' serves to prevent
any such egocentric reaction. The passive ἐδόθη indicates that
God is the originator of the affliction.[260]

In using (for convenience) the term 'thorn', however, we have
pre-empted the answer to the question of the origin of Paul's
metaphor. The word σκόλοψ can mean '(pointed) stake', or it can
mean 'thorn', 'splinter'.[261] In the first sense it is used in military
contexts in various ways: of stakes placed around a wall, or on

[254] Pace Theobald, Gnade, p. 247.
[255] Plummer, p. 347, suggests that the plural noun could confirm the view that
there are two separate raptures in vv. 2–4. He admits, however, that Acts tells of
other visionary experiences Paul had. Our own discussion has concluded that these
verses refer to one experience only.
[256] On the meaning of ὑπερβολή see BAGD s.v. The sense may be 'excess', or
'extraordinary character', 'extraordinary quality'. The first sense would allow
numerical frequency when the word is followed by a plural noun.
[257] See KJV, 'the abundance of the revelations'; cf. RSV.
[258] See NEB and REB, 'the magnificence of such revelations'; Barrett, p. 305;
Furnish, p. 513.
[259] On the causal function of the dative see BDR 196(1).
[260] See, e.g., Schlatter, Paulus, p. 665; Prümm, Diakonia Pneumatos I, p. 657;
Zmijewski, 'Narrenrede', p. 368.
[261] BAGD s.v. σκόλοψ.

earthworks, or in hidden pits; impalement was used also as a method of execution.[262] Hughes supposes this to be the background thought here. Paul has in view this first sense of σκόλοψ, the image 'of a body helplessly impaled'.[263] D. M. Park likewise adopts it, as more suitable to the severe suffering implied by v. 8.[264] The second sense, 'thorn', 'splinter', is found in the LXX, whilst the alternative, 'stake', is not.[265] In two possibly significant passages the word is used metaphorically with reference to other nations who have been, or who may be, a painful trial to Israel. Thus, in Num 33.55 the Israelites are warned that if they do not drive out the inhabitants of Canaan, these people will be 'thorns in your eyes and javelins in your sides': σκόλοπες ἐν τοῖς ὀφθαλμοῖς ὑμῶν καὶ βολίδες ἐν ταῖς πλευραῖς ὑμῶν.[266] See also Ezek 28.24, and, for a somewhat different metaphorical usage, Hos 2.8.[267] For a number of commentators, this second sense is preferable as the key to Paul's image in 2 Cor 12.7. There are two good reasons for their preference. First, it is the meaning of σκόλοψ in the LXX,[268] where, also, the word is used metaphorically. Secondly, the alternative, 'stake', seems to produce too exaggerated a picture.[269] Whatever its precise reference, the σκόλοψ cannot indicate a condition or circumstance by which Paul was totally and permanently incapacitated. The image of impalement would be out of place.[270]

The 'thorn' is τῇ σαρκί, 'for the flesh'. A few commentators understand σάρξ as a reference to unregenerate human nature.[271] But the word here is part of the image, and must therefore denote the flesh of the physical body.[272] The affliction is further described

---

[262] G. Delling, on σκόλοψ, in *TWNT* VII, pp. 411–15; see p. 411.
[263] Hughes, p. 447.
[264] D. M. Park, 'Paul's σκόλοψ τῇ σαρκί: Thorn or Stake? (2 Cor. xii 7)', *NovT* 22 (1980), pp. 179–83; see pp. 182–3.
[265] Delling, on σκόλοψ, pp. 412–13.
[266] Noted by Plummer, p. 349; see Delling, on σκόλοψ, p. 412.
[267] Plummer, ibid.; Delling, on σκόλοψ, pp. 412–13.
[268] Meyer, p. 475.
[269] Meyer, p. 475; cf. Furnish, p. 529; Martin, p. 412; Heinrici (1883), p. 370.
[270] Other commentators who prefer the sense 'thorn' include Windisch, p. 384; Tasker, pp. 173–4; Barrett, p. 305; Zmijewski, 'Narrenrede', p. 370.
[271] Calvin, p. 159; Tasker, pp. 174–6; cf. Schlatter, *Paulus*, p. 666.
[272] Heckel, *Schwachheit*, p. 78, with reference to E. Schweizer, on σάρξ, in *TWNT* VII, p. 124. The usual translation of the phrase has 'in the/my flesh': see e.g., KJV, JB, REB, NRSV; Barrett, p. 305; Furnish, p. 513; Martin, p. 388. This would strictly require that τῇ σαρκί should be a locative dative, a use absent from the NT, according to BDR 199 (but see Robertson, p. 538, cited by Barrett, p. 314). Allo, p. 310, differently, understands the phrase as parallel to μοι, i.e., as dependent on ἐδόθη, but Martin, p. 413, claims that τῇ σαρκί is too closely tied to σκόλοψ for this interpretation to be plausible.

as 'an angel of Satan'. The idea that the Devil has angels of his own is attested also in Mt 25.41 (τῷ διαβόλῳ καὶ τοῖς ἀγγέλοις αὐτοῦ) and Rev 12.7, 9 (ὁ δράκων ... καὶ οἱ ἄγγελοι αὐτοῦ ... ὁ καλούμενος Διάβολος, καὶ ὁ Σατανᾶς).[273] In the present context the demonic angel's function is to give Paul a beating,[274] repeatedly. As with the 'thorn', the expression ἵνα με κολαφίζῃ is figurative, but perhaps to a lesser degree than the former image. Whereas, if Paul's affliction was of a physical nature, it is highly improbable that it was caused by an actual thorn (surely easily—if painfully—dealt with at the time of injury!), it is possible that he suffered from some illness whose symptoms were analogous to the receiving of blows. In any case, this clause produces an intensification of effect, since it adds the motif of humiliation to the image of pain inherent in the σκόλοψ.[275] It may also indicate in advance what becomes explicit in vv. 8–9, i.e., that the suffering was continuous, or at least recurrent[276]

Its nature has occasioned extensive debate throughout the centuries. In the following excursus[277] we have attempted to summarise the main aspects of the discussion and to arrive at some conclusion. In our view, it is most likely that Paul is referring to some form of physical illness, and that either migraine or recurrent fever would be a possibility. He has come to see it as something bestowed on him by God, and yet at the same time it is inflicted by the agency of Satan. Perhaps there is a parallel to this idea of dual agency, divine and demonic, in Mt 4.1, where we read that Jesus was led into the desert by the Spirit, to be tempted by the Devil. But it remains somewhat strange, even when we take into consideration the notion in Job that the Lord allows Satan to test the integrity of the righteous (Job 1.8–12; 2.3–6): this tale gives the impression that the initiative largely rests with Satan, whereas in the present passage the initiative clearly comes from God. Possibly there could be some truth in the suggestion offered by Güttgemanns that it was the Corinthians who had brought the ἄγγελος σατανᾶ into the picture. In their (gnostic) view, he claims,

---

[273] Cited by e.g., Plummer, p. 352; Windisch, p. 384; Barrett, p. 315. Plummer and Windisch note also the expression ἄγγελοι τοῦ σατανᾶ in *Barn.* 18.1. Furnish, p. 529, refers to *T. Ash.* 6.4, where there is an allusion to 'the angels of the Lord and of Beliar'. See *OTP* I, p. 818.

[274] The verb κολαφίζω means 'strike with the fist', 'beat', 'cuff'. It is used literally in Mt 26.67 and Mk 14.65, and also of 'mistreatment in general' in 1 Cor 4.11 and 1 Pet 2.20: see BAGD s.v. 1.

[275] Zmijewski, '*Narrenrede*', pp. 371–2; Windisch, p. 385.

[276] Meyer, p. 476, draws attention to the present tense of κολαφίζῃ as indicating continuity, and cites Theophylact *PG* 124 col. 933: οὐχ ἵνα ἅπαξ με κολαφίσῃ [aorist], ἀλλ' ἀεί ('Not that once he might buffet me, but all the time'). See also Bachmann, p. 398; Plummer, p. 352.

[277] See below, pp. 809–18.

Paul's illness (to which the 'thorn' refers) was to be attributed to satanic agency, because 'weakness', belonging to the sphere of the *sarx*, was itself a demonic power which held sway within the earthly realm. The genuine apostle should be free from this earthly sphere.[278] We do not need to accept this gnostic scenario *in toto* in order to agree that the basic idea has some plausibility.[279] Paul himself, after all, in 1 Cor 5.5, had spoken of Satan as an agent 'for the destruction of the flesh'. If his own physical constitution appeared threatened by illness, the obvious conclusion might be drawn by readers ill-disposed towards him. As Heckel notes,[280] the charge would be that he is in Satan's power. So he would need to show that this admittedly satanic hindrance lay within the overall purpose of God.[281] That it was important for him to do so is indicated by his repetition of ἵνα μὴ ὑπεραίρωμαι.[282] The 'thorn' was designed for his spiritual benefit, to preserve him from pride.

EXCURSUS XV

12.7: What was the 'thorn'?

The multitudinous theories can be classified under three general headings: (i) an internal psychological state, whether of temptation or of grief; (ii) external opposition; (iii) physical illness or disability.

(i) Identification with some psychological condition

There have been three main suggestions which fall into this category, with a few more which may be mentioned more briefly.

---

[278] Güttgemanns, *Der leidende Apostel*, pp. 164–5.

[279] Heckel, *Schwachheit*, p. 80, also sees an allusion to Corinthian charges. Paul would not introduce the Satan motif of his own accord.

[280] Heckel, ibid.

[281] An alternative possibility is proposed by Zmijewski, '*Narrenrede*', p. 372. It is Paul himself who introduces the figure of Satan, to demonstrate the meaning of his suffering in the context of his apostolic activity: it is by Christ's own adversary, i.e. Satan, that he himself is hindered and threatened. It is not clear, however, that this is quite what Paul has in mind. The purpose of the 'thorn' is not that he should, positively, engage in battle, on Christ's side, with the demonic powers, but that he himself personally should be protected from spiritual arrogance.

[282] The clause is omitted by some witnesses (ℵ A D F G 33. 629* *pc* lat Ir^lat), but retained in others (𝔓46 ℵ2 B I^vid Ψ 0243 𝔐 a sy co Cyp Ambst). In all probability the retention is correct. The clause will have dropped out as unnecessary (Hughes, p. 449 n. 138). Included, it gives the emphasis required (cf. Metzger, *Textual Commentary*[1], p. 585).

(a) For some considerable period of time the 'thorn' was interpreted as sexual temptation. According to J. B. Lightfoot, this view was generally current during the Middle Ages,[283] and he observes that it was adopted by Aquinas, amongst others.[284] In the early seventeenth century, Cornelius a Lapide adopts it, specifically rejecting other interpretations.[285] He refers to Rom 7.23 and 1 Cor 9 (presumably vv. 26–27) in support, and argues that, had the σκόλοψ been anything else, Paul would have explained more clearly.[286] Estius likewise refers to Rom 7 and 1 Cor 9, and sees this interpretation as congruous with the description of the 'thorn' as 'a messenger of Satan', since it is Satan who tempts to sin.[287] Commentators of the modern period, however, voice a number of objections. First, it appears to go against what Paul himself says in 1 Cor 7.7–9 about his possession of the gift of continence.[288] And these verses are explicit, whilst in 9. 26–27 he expresses himself more generally, as he does in Rom 7.[289] Secondly, he would not have regarded sexual temptation as a weakness which he could boast of.[290] Thirdly, in a city such as Corinth, a confession of this kind would be singularly inappropriate.[291] Fourthly, it seems unlikely that this kind of temptation would have come upon Paul suddenly, as a fresh fact of experience, in the course of his missionary career and at some specific point of time.[292] We may add that the reason why he is not more specific may well be that the 'thorn' was some obvious disability visible to his readers, and also that Satan, whilst certainly regarded as the agent of temptation, could be seen in addition as responsible for physical illness.[293]

(b) The 'thorn' is to be understood as pangs of conscience, continually renewed, concerning Paul's earlier persecution of the Christians.[294] It is 'for the flesh' (τῇ σαρκί), not 'in the flesh', and 'the flesh' means the self-seeking impulse which generates pride. The ἄγγελος σατανᾶ is a messenger of the Accuser, and recalls the apostle's bitter memories which have given him a feeling of unworthiness.[295] But Paul does not elsewhere hesitate to speak of the way he persecuted the church (see 1 Cor 15.9; Gal 1.23)[296]—and, indeed, to speak plainly, without employing

---

[283] Lightfoot, *Galatians*, p. 188. He notes that this interpretation is not clearly in evidence before the sixth century. According to Allo, p. 313 n. 1, Pseudo-Primasius is the first to mention it, though he rejects it. See *PL* 68 cols. 581–2.

[284] Lightfoot, ibid. His discussion of the interpretation of the 'thorn' (*Galatians*, pp. 186–91) is arranged chronologically, and illustrates the likely connection between interpretation and the circumstances of the interpreter.

[285] Cornelius a Lapide, pp. 503–4.

[286] Cornelius a Lapide, p. 504.

[287] Estius, pp. 649–50.

[288] So, e.g., Meyer, p. 478; Osiander, p. 473; Heinrici (1883), p. 372; Plummer, p. 350; Windisch, p. 385; Lightfoot, *Galatians*, p. 188.

[289] In any case, the interpretation of Rom 7 both as strictly autobiographical and also as referring to the apostle's Christian existence is debatable.

[290] Lightfoot, *Galatians*, p. 188, Plummer, p. 350; Beet, p. 459.

[291] Allo, p. 310; cf. Osiander, p. 473.

[292] Cf. Menoud, 'L'écharde', pp. 163–4.

[293] See below, p. 814.

[294] Osiander, pp. 474–5; Schlatter, *Paulus*, pp. 666–7.

[295] Schlatter, ibid.

[296] Menoud, 'L'écharde', p. 164.

any such metaphor as we find here. Moreover, one would suppose that pangs of conscience would be felt most keenly immediately after his conversion to Christ, whereas the 'thorn' seems to be connected not with this event but with (later) visionary experiences.[297] Wolff, lastly, rejects this and all other psychological interpretations on the ground that the metaphor must relate to some bodily pain; note the use of κολαφίζω.[298]

(c) A further type of psychological explanation is proposed by Menoud. The 'thorn' must have been the most grievous of Paul's apostolic trials, and its hindrance of his work must be something peculiar to himself. Now his greatest suffering lay in his inability to gain the Jews for the gospel: it was a cause of humiliation. Also, the Jewish failure to believe hindered the mission to the Gentiles: it was more difficult to show them that Christ was the fulfilment of the scriptural promises when their chosen recipients remained incredulous. In the Jewish failure to believe, Paul saw the hand of Satan, the great adversary of the gospel.[299] But this kind of trouble could hardly be classified as one of the 'weaknesses' of v. 10.[300] Moreover, it is difficult to believe that Paul would think of Jewish resistance to the gospel as designed for his own personal spiritual benefit, which is what this theory ultimately implies.

Other interpretations under this general heading would include those of the Protestant reformers, who thought the reference was to spiritual trials such as temptation to despair, or to laxity in apostolic duty (Luther),[301] or indeed to all the various temptations deriving from the unregenerate aspect of the soul (Calvin).[302] More recently, there is the suggestion from Kamlah that Paul was tempted to indulge in rash outbursts of anger.[303] But again there is the question as to whether the apostle would have boasted of temptations.[304] Furthermore, this kind of interpretation does not fit very well either with the singular nouns or with the infliction of the 'thorn' at some particular moment in time.

(ii) *Identification with opponents*

This interpretation goes back to the patristic period, and has support amongst modern scholars. Initially, it may be opposition in general, without especial reference to the Corinthian situation, that is in view. Modern exegetes, however, tend to make this specific connection.[305]

(a) Chrysostom notes that 'Satan' means 'adversary', and claims that the ἄγγελος σατανᾶ, i.e., the 'thorn', refers both to the named opponents

---

[297] See above, pp. 784–5, for the argument against identification with the conversion experience.

[298] Wolff, pp. 246–7.

[299] Menoud, 'L'écharde', pp. 168–71.

[300] Furnish, p. 548.

[301] See Lightfoot, *Galatians*, pp. 188–9.

[302] Calvin, p. 159.

[303] Kamlah, 'Leiden', pp. 218–19.

[304] Plummer, p. 351.

[305] At the beginning of the modern period, Semler, p. 301 n. 339, suggests that the 'thorn' is an adversary belonging to the Judaizing party.

in 2 Timothy (2.17, Hymenaeus and Philetus; 4.14, Alexander the copper-smith) and also to all opponents of the gospel.[306] In the modern period this interpretation finds support from Tasker, on the ground that it is opposition that is most likely to subdue spiritual pride.[307] Meyer objects to it: opposition was something that belonged essentially to Paul's apostolic vocation, and he would not have prayed to be rid of it.[308] In any case, the metaphor suggests something more specific than generalised opposition, whilst the allusions in Chrysostom to particular opponents have no basis in the recognised Pauline epistles.

(b) We turn to the theories which relate the 'thorn' in particular to the situation in Corinth.

On the basis both of context and of usage, Mullins[309] would identify the σκόλοψ with 'a specifically obnoxious member' of the group of opponents whose influence Paul is contesting in chaps. 10–13.[310] The description ἄγγελος σατανᾶ suggests a personal entity, and the verb κολαφίζῃ the activity of a person.[311] The larger context also requires allusion to a personal enemy. In 11.14–15 Paul has referred to Satan's disguise as 'an angel of light' and to the opponents in Corinth as his servants.[312] Now his thought turns to one such particularly. In respect of usage, Mullins claims that Jews would recognise the phrase 'thorn in the flesh' as an allusion to an enemy, in view of its use in Num 33.55 and Ezek 28.24.[313] This last point must be conceded, but the contextual arguments are less convincing. Mullins himself allows that a non-personal σκόλοψ might have been personified.[314] Furthermore, this 'thorn' cannot originally have referred to Paul's present opponents in Corinth, since it appears to have been inflicted at some point in the past, in connection, probably, with the heavenly rapture of 12.2–4.[315] And if this was so, and the singular of σκόλοψ and ἄγγελος is to be taken seriously, the implication would be that Paul has been burdened with one major opponent who has been continually dogging his tracks for some considerable length of time. This is implausible, since no such single opponent makes an appearance either in the letters or in Acts.

Bieder[316] and Thierry[317] similarly relate the 'thorn' to the opponents of chaps. 10–13. For Bieder, it consists in all the humiliations which these people inflict on the apostle. But for him, such humiliation means partici-pation in the sufferings of Christ, and thus, paradoxically, the opponents

---

[306] Chrysostom, PG 61 cols. 577–8 (NPNF XII, p. 400).
[307] Tasker, p. 176.
[308] Meyer, p. 478; Heinrici (1883), p. 372.
[309] T. Y. Mullins, 'Paul's Thorn in the Flesh', JBL 76 (1957), pp. 299–303.
[310] Mullins, 'Thorn', pp. 301–3; the quotation is on p. 302.
[311] Mullins, 'Thorn', p. 301.
[312] Mullins, 'Thorn', p. 302.
[313] Mullins, ibid. See above, p. 807.
[314] Mullins, 'Thorn', p. 301.
[315] Cf. Martin, p. 415. This objection would apply also to the similar exposition by P. Andriessen, 'L'impuissance de Paul en face de l'ange de Satan', Nouvelle Revue Theologique 81 (1959), pp. 462–8.
[316] W. Bieder, 'Paulus und seine Gegner in Korinth', TZ 17 (1961), pp. 319–33.
[317] J. J. Thierry, 'Der Dorn im Fleische', NovT 5 (1962), pp. 301–10.

forward the progress of his gospel. The term σκόλοψ refers to the process of crucifixion with Christ, given by God to safeguard Paul from self-divinisation.[318] This is implausible. The apostolic 'carrying about' of the death of Jesus (4.10) is too fundamental an aspect of Paul's vocation either to be related so particularly to the specific situation of 2 Cor 10–13 or to have been imposed upon him to prevent egocentric exaltation resulting from visionary experience. And again the time factor tells against this view. It is an obstacle also to the theory proposed by Thierry, who suggests that the 'thorn' consists of the opponents' insulting charge that Paul himself is 'a servant of Satan' (a charge he throws back to them in 11.13–15).

Lastly, there is the theory proposed by Barré,[319] which likewise identifies the σκόλοψ and the ἄγγελος σατανᾶ with Paul's adversaries, but from a somewhat different perspective. He sees a parallel between vv. 7–9a and 1QH 2.22, where 'God allows or even instigates the hostile activities of the "congregation of Belial" against the author in order to reveal his power'.[320] In the Pauline passage, the revealing of God's power is the ultimate aim of the infliction of the 'thorn'. It could be, then, that the apostle's own trial was a matter of persecution by adversaries, and that he saw it as divinely intended, as in the Qumran text. Barré notes that 12.7 is framed by two lists of trials, and so should be interpreted in this light. The ἄγγελος σατανᾶ, moreover, is most naturally seen as a personal agent, and the other Pauline occurrence of κολαφίζω (1 Cor 4.11) implies rough treatment at the hands of an enemy. In addition, the effect of the 'thorn' is ἀσθένεια, weakness. Writing on 11.29,[321] Barré has argued that the ἀσθεν-words in these chapters refer to entrapment by the agents of Satan in the eschatological struggle. The ἀσθένεια of 12.9a must also have this connotation, and it follows that the 'thorn' and the ἄγγελος σατανᾶ must allude to Paul's adversaries. We have seen, however, that this interpretation of ἀσθενέω and its cognates is implausible,[322] and we may note that the alleged parallel in 1QH 2.22 is incomplete, since it does not mention weakness.

It seems, then, that the identification of the σκόλοψ with Paul's opponents is less than compelling. Furnish observes that the phrase ἄγγελος σατανᾶ does not sound like a group of people, and also that in 11.14–15 Satan himself is the ἄγγελος, whilst his servants are διάκονοι.[323]

---

[318] See also H. Binder, 'Die angebliche Krankheit des Paulus', *TZ* 32 (1976), pp. 1–13, who agrees with Bieder to some extent.

[319] M. L. Barré, 'Qumran and the "Weakness" of Paul', *CBQ* 42 (1980), pp. 216–27.

[320] Barré, 'Qumran', p. 223.

[321] See above, p. 753.

[322] See above, p. 753, on 11.29.

[323] Furnish, p. 549–50. Since the publication of his commentary, the 'group' identification has been revived by J. W. McCant, 'Paul's Thorn of Rejected Apostleship', *NTS* 34 (1988), pp. 550–72: the 'thorn' is the church in Corinth, and its rejection of Paul's apostolic legitimacy. As R. Penna points out, however, in response to McCant, the affliction was longstanding, and not related, therefore, to the situation in Corinth. See 'La présence des adversaires de Paul', pp. 7–41, and p. 34 n. 78, in *Verteidigung* (see under E. Lohse, ed.).

(iii) *Identification with physical illness or disability*

This is the earliest known explanation of the σκόλοψ, mentioned by Tertullian as an existing tradition.[324] There are several general reasons for this point of view. The metaphor does suggest physical pain—more obviously if the word means 'stake', but still effectively if the meaning is 'thorn'.[325] Satan could be regarded as the agent of physical suffering (Lk 13.16),[326] and the use of κολαφίζω might indicate reference to 'a recurring disability'.[327] Suggestions are numerous.

(a) *Pains in the head.* This is the early tradition noted by Tertullian: 'dolorem, ut aiunt, auriculae vel capitis'.[328] It is mentioned by Jerome,[329] and attested, (though not accepted) by Chrysostom.[330] It would be a reasonable deduction from the fact that κολαφίζω can have the sense 'box on the ear'.[331] And some kind of migraine would do justice to the sense of acute pain conveyed by the metaphor.[332]

(b) *Ophthalmia.* The idea that the 'thorn' was acute and recurrent inflammation of the eyes is based on debatable evidence derived from Galatians. In Gal 4.15, after Paul has noted that it was on account of some bodily infirmity that he first preached in Galatia (4.13), he observes that his welcome had been such that, had it been possible, the Galatians would have 'plucked out their eyes' to give to him. In addition, in 6.11 he refers to the 'large letters' of his own handwriting. Both verses, it is supposed, could allude to some eye disease.[333] But the first argument misunderstands the emphasis in v. 15. Paul is not saying that his readers had been willing to give 'their own eyes' in place of his: the ὑμῶν is not emphatic. Rather, they were ready to give him 'their *eyes*'[334]—their most prized possession.[335] And the 'large letters' of the concluding comments either express the force of his convictions,[336] or are intended to give emphasis.[337] It may be that in 4.13 Paul is alluding to the 'thorn' of 2 Cor 12.7, and that this would count in favour of identifying the latter with a physical ailment. But further identification with a specific disease would

---

[324] See below, and n. 328.

[325] Plummer, p. 349; cf. Furnish, p. 549.

[326] Plummer, p. 352; Windisch, p. 385; Furnish, ibid.; Martin, p. 415. See also Heckel, *Schwachheit*, p. 81.

[327] Bruce, p. 249.

[328] Tertullian, *PL* 2 col. 1004: 'pain, as they say, of the ear or the head'; noted by Lightfoot, *Galatians*, p. 186.

[329] Jerome, *PL* 26 col. 381: 'Nam tradunt eum gravissimum capitis dolorem saepe perpessum.' ('For they relate that often he suffered steadfastly an extremely severe pain in the head.')

[330] Chrysostom, *PG* 61 col. 577 (NPNF XII, p. 400).

[331] See K. L. Schmidt, on κολαφίζω, in *TWNT* III, p. 819.

[332] Windisch, pp. 387–8, sees this interpretation as a possibility.

[333] According to Lightfoot, *Galatians*, p. 191, writing in the mid-nineteenth century, this view had found a considerable number of adherents. He responds specifically to J. T. Brown, 'St. Paul's Thorn in the Flesh', in *Horae Subsecivae*, ed. J. T. Brown, Edinburgh, 1858, in reply to the two points noted above.

[334] Lightfoot, *Galatians*, p. 191 n. 1.

[335] Lietzmann, p. 157; Barrett, p. 315.

[336] Lightfoot, *Galatians*, p. 221.

[337] Bruce, *Galatians*, p. 268.

go beyond the evidence. And is there any form of eye disease productive of symptoms which could be described as being buffeted by an angel of Satan?[338]

(c) *Epilepsy.* According to Krenkel,[339] this interpretation originated with Ziegler.[340] Krenkel himself adopts it and elaborates upon it, and is followed by others.[341] Looking at the brief information given in the text, he claims that the ἄγγελος is an evil spirit, and observes that Jews, Greeks and Romans attributed epilepsy to supernatural forces.[342] The verb κολαφίζω[343] could refer to blows to the head,[344] and Krenkel quotes Galen to the effect that the disease may sometimes produce like symptoms.[345] Further evidence, however, must be looked for elsewhere. Krenkel turns to Gal 4.13–15, and notes Paul's acknowledgement that his readers did not disdain him: literally, 'you did not spit out', οὐδὲ ἐξεπτύσατε.[346] Spitting was (or could be) a preventive gesture to avoid infection by means of averting evil spirits[347] and was particularly connected with epilepsy.[348] This identification, moreover, would be congruous with 2 Cor 12.1, where Paul speaks of 'visions and revelations', since epileptic attacks are often accompanied by visionary experiences.[349] Lastly, the reference in Acts 9.4 to his sudden falling to the ground at the moment of his conversion suggests an epileptic seizure.[350] If it be asked how all Paul's strenuous apostolic activity could be compatible with his being subject to epilepsy, Krenkel would reply that such great men in history as Julius Caesar and Napoleon have themselves been afflicted with this disease.[351]

The case is persuasively argued. Nevertheless, there are difficulties. The image of the σκόλοψ suggests *conscious* acute pain, but the epileptic undergoing a severe attack is unconscious.[352] The testimony of Acts 9.4 is not primary evidence, and may be due simply to the incorporation of a conventional motif in accounts of heavenly visions.[353] Furthermore, according to Paul's account of it, the 'thorn' was inflicted as a consequence of his visionary experiences: the visions were not an inherent part of the experience of the 'thorn'—which is what the epilepsy theory implies. And whilst the οὐδὲ ἐξεπτύσατε of Gal 4.14 would certainly be appropriate as (an unexpected) reaction to epilepsy, it could equally well

---

[338] Lietzmann, p. 157.
[339] Krenkel, *Beiträge*, pp. 66–7.
[340] K. L. Ziegler, in *Theologische Abhandlungen* 2 (Göttingen, 1804), p. 128.
[341] Schmiedel, p. 294; Bousset, pp. 211–12.
[342] Krenkel, *Beiträge*, pp. 49, 58–9.
[343] See above, p. 808 n. 274.
[344] Krenkel, *Beiträge*, pp. 49 n. 3, 64.
[345] Krenkel, *Beiträge*, pp. 64–5, with reference to Galen VIII 173.
[346] Krenkel, *Beiträge*, pp. 69–98, discusses the verb at length.
[347] Krenkel, ibid.; Bruce, *Galatians*, p. 209.
[348] Krenkel, *Beiträge*, p. 98, notes that Plautus, *Captivi* 18, calls epilepsy 'morbus qui sputatur', the 'disease before which one spits'.
[349] Krenkel, *Beiträge*, p. 103.
[350] Krenkel, *Beiträge*, p. 111.
[351] Krenkel, *Beiträge*, pp. 117–24.
[352] Allo, pp. 317–18.
[353] Falling to the ground is seen as a natural response to a heavenly vision: see e.g., Ezek 1.28; 2 Macc 3.27; Rev 1.17.

mean no more than that the illness, of whatever kind, could be seen as the work of demons, and thus likely to evoke some apotropaic gesture.[354]

(d) *Fever.* It has been suggested that Paul suffered from a recurrent malarial fever, which at times had a completely incapacitating effect, and which was accompanied by an extraordinarily severe headache.[355] This has some support,[356] and must be considered a possibility, although it cannot be said that there is any positive evidence for it.[357]

(e) *Other suggestions.* Some exegetes suggest states of depression,[358] or of nervous reaction consequent upon ecstatic experiences.[359] There is little to be said for this idea. If Paul's metaphor refers to an ailment at all, it is more likely to have been something more immediately painful in the physical sense. Barrett thinks it could have been a speech impediment. This would account, he claims, for Paul's expressed fear, in Gal 4.13–15, of making an initial bad impression, and would find support also in 2 Cor 10.1, 9–11; 11.6.[360] This is not very probable, for at least two reasons. First, the metaphor in 12.7, again, implies that the affliction was physically painful. Secondly, this is not an affliction that would have come upon him suddenly, in the middle of his career.[361]

Whilst some of these suggestions have attracted more support than others, it is clear that none is universally accepted. Consequently, we need to consider the view that the whole theory of physical illness or disability is mistaken. The basic reason is simply that the general impression of Paul produced by his letters and also by Acts is that he was 'a man with an exceptionally strong constitution and remarkable powers of physical endurance'.[362] Whilst there may be an allusion to illness in Gal 4.13–15,[363] there is no definite article attached to ἀσθένειαν in v. 13, and so there is no necessary reference to the specific trouble by which Paul was recurrently afflicted.[364] Hence, this passage provides no positive evidence for identifying the recurrent trouble with physical illness, although it does not, of course, exclude the possibility that it was such, and that Paul is referring to it here. The main argument is countered by Furnish with the suggestion that ' a chronic ailment need not have been

[354] Lietzmann, pp. 156–7.

[355] The theory comes from W. M. Ramsay: see *The Church in the Roman Empire*, London, [10]1897 ([1]1893), pp. 62–4, with reference to Gal 4.13.

[356] See, e.g., Gouge, p. 121; Allo, pp. 320–1; Prümm, *Diakonia Pneumatos* I, p. 665.

[357] If κολαφίζω refers to head pains, this could count simply in favour of migraine.

[358] Lietzmann, p. 157; Windisch, p. 387.

[359] Clavier, 'Santé', pp. 77–82.

[360] Barrett, p. 315, with reference to W. K. Lowther Clarke, *New Testament Problems*, (1929), pp. 136–40. Martin, p. 416, appears to allow this as a possibility.

[361] For various further suggestions, see Hughes, p. 446; Furnish, p. 549.

[362] Tasker, p. 175. See also Binder, 'Krankheit' (see above, p. 813, n. 318, for bibliographical details). He discusses Paul's use of the ἀσθεν-words, and argues that they do not refer to sickness (pp. 4–5). The 'weak' of 1 Cor 11.30 (where ἀσθενεῖς would seem most obviously to refer to illness) are simply those whose participation 'in Christ' is minimal: they are lethargic and casual (p. 4). This is improbable: the other terms in the verse clearly suggest physical illness.

[363] So Tasker, ibid.; Binder, 'Krankheit', pp. 5–7, rejects this exegesis.

[364] Tasker, ibid.

debilitating, only aggravating',[365] and by Martin, who argues that in Corinth 'any physical weakness would have seemed a liability'.[366] These comments, however, tend to imply that the affliction was, after all, a fairly minor problem. But this scarcely harmonises with Paul's repeated prayers to be relieved of it. If we conclude that the 'thorn' was physical in nature, we should need to opt for some form of illness which has severe effects when it occurs but allows for periods of intermission in which the sufferer may be engaged in energetic activity. Of the suggestions considered above, migraine or fever would best fit this specification.

All these three categories of interpretation regard Paul's language as in some degree metaphorical. In addition, however, some attention must be paid to a theory which understands the ἄγγελος σατανᾶ in a more literal sense. R. M. Price connects the 'thorn' of 12.7 very directly with the rapture to Paradise in vv. 2–4, and relates both to Jewish merkabah mysticism. With reference to the work of Scholem,[367] he observes that the visionary undergoing experiences of this kind may find himself under attack from angelic or demonic powers. In one instance it is said that angels 'strike his head'. Thus, in the Pauline passage, the ἄγγελος σατανᾶ is quite literally to be understood as 'a demon or malevolent angel, sent to punish Paul's pride at the wonder of his experience'. The whole action of 12.2–10 is seen as taking place during the heavenly rapture.[368] But this, of course, is precisely why the theory is dubious. As Furnish points out, the account of the rapture is quite distinct from that of Paul's prayer and Christ's response. The response is explicitly reported, whilst the words heard in Paradise were not to be repeated.[369] In addition, the two accounts are separated by the interposition of vv. 5–6 and the style has changed from the third to the first person. The present tense of κολαφίζῃ may suggest that the satanic attacks were continuous or recurrent, rather than related to one particular experience (i.e., the rapture). In any case, the whole context indicates that Paul is concerned with some permanent form of weakness.

In view of the abundance of suggestions, it is somewhat difficult to make any definite decision about the nature of the 'thorn', but the preceding discussion suggests the following conclusions. Decisive against the view that it was some temptation there is the point that Paul would not boast of anything of this kind, and other theories concerning some hypothetical psychological state have difficulties peculiar to each. Against the identification of the σκόλοψ with opponents there is the singular ἄγγελος, and other theories present problems. Against the identification with physical illness there is the fact that Paul's basic physical constitution must have been sound. Nevertheless, in our view, this third possibility offers the most probable explanation. Paul may have

---

[365] Furnish, p. 550.

[366] Martin, p. 415.

[367] G. G. Scholem, *Major Trends in Jewish Mysticism*, New York, 1973, pp. 51–3; *Jewish Gnosticism, Merkabah Mysticism and Talmudic Tradition*[2], New York, 1965, p. 77.

[368] R. M. Price, 'Punished in Paradise (An Exegetical Theory on II Corinthians 12:1–10)', *JSNT* 7 (1980), pp. 33–40 (the quotations are on pp. 36, 37). The theory is adopted by Morray-Jones, 'Paradise Revisited', pp. 281–3.

[369] Furnish, p. 550.

suffered from some recurrent malady with comparatively long periods of intermission during which time he was able to engage with energy in his evangelistic and pastoral work. Perhaps this malady was some form of fever, or perhaps it was migraine. If pressed for a decision, we should opt for migraine, in view of the appropriateness of the verb κολαφίζω and of the sense of acute pain suggested by Paul's metaphor.

8. ὑπὲρ τούτου τρὶς τὸν κύριον παρεκάλεσα ἵνα ἀποστῇ ἀπ' ἐμοῦ. It seems that when this affliction overtook him Paul did not immediately realise its purpose, since he prayed for relief.[370] It could be also that the aspect of satanic agency did not originally play a major part in his perception of his trouble, if it was the Corinthians who had brought this issue to the fore.[371] At all events, what he is here concerned with is to describe his reaction in such a way as to lead up to the dominical word in v. 9a, by which, since that time, his whole attitude to his apostolic existence has been shaped. This calls for some detail in respect of his prayer. It was threefold: τρὶς … παρεκάλεσα. For Chrysostom, the τρίς is simply the equivalent of πολλάκις, 'often',[372] and for Barrett, similarly, it is not strictly numerical, but indicates 'earnest and repeated prayer'.[373] If so, however, why did Paul not use πολλάκις itself,[374] perhaps with some such adverb as σπουδαίως? Furthermore, his general cultural background, both Jewish and Greek,[375] would support the ordinary numerical meaning of τρίς. In Judaism the number three is associated with prayer in various ways. Windisch draws attention to the three-member Aaronic blessing (Num 6.24–26), to Elijah's threefold breathing upon the widow's son with the prayer that he might be restored to life (3 Kgdms 17.21), and to the Jewish custom of praying three times a day.[376] The threefold prayer was known in Greek religion similarly, as Windisch, again, observes. He cites a clause from

---

[370] The relief was 'concerning this'. See LSJ s.v. ὑπέρ A.III., and BDR 231(1) for the use of ὑπέρ in the sense of περί, 'concerning'. See n. 371 below on τούτου.

[371] In that case, in Paul's recollection of his original prayer, the τούτου would be less likely to refer, in the masculine gender, specifically to the ἄγγελος σατανᾶ (*pace* Barrett, p. 305). Certainly, such a 'personal' reference would be congruent with the use of ἀφίστημι, since, as Plummer, p. 353, notes, elsewhere in the NT the verb is always used with a personal subject. But it is found with non-personal subjects in Hermas (e.g. 'affliction', *Sim.* VII 7; 'life', VIII 6.4; see BAGD s.v. ἀφίστημι 2.c.). And in v. 7b it is the σκόλοψ (not the ἄγγελος) that is the main designation of Paul's affliction. It is more probable that τούτου is neuter, 'this thing', 'this condition': see RSV, NRSV, JB; Furnish, p. 513; Martin, p. 388.

[372] Chrysostom, *PG* 61 col. 578 (NPNF XII, p. 400); see also Calvin, p. 160.

[373] Barrett, p. 316.

[374] Plummer, p. 353.

[375] Furnish, p. 529, sees both cultural spheres as possible influences.

[376] Windisch, p. 389. See also Furnish, p. 529, who cites Ps 55.16–17; Dan 6.10, 13; 1QS 10.1–7; and 1QH 12.3–9.

Euripides: μηδὲν μάταιον εἰς τρὶς εὔξασθαι θεῷ.[377] Furnish[378] and Betz[379] note that threefold prayers are to be found also in hellenistic healing stories. (The number three has no significance, however, for the records of healings at Epidauros, according to Delling.[380]) The underlying idea in both cultural spheres may be that a prayer can be efficacious only if it has been uttered three times.[381] Within the Christian tradition the most obvious example of the threefold petition is the prayer of Jesus in the Gethsemane narrative (Mt 26.39–44 and parallels).[382] This is recounted as a thrice-spoken prayer uttered on one specific occasion. Was the same true of Paul's prayer?[383] A few commentators prefer to think of three separate occasions,[384] perhaps the first few times he experienced the onslaught of the 'thorn'.[385] Others are indeterminate. But the connotations which Heckel sees attached to τρίς strongly suggest that the apostle's prayer was a repeated petition made at one particular time. The number three allows an action to be seen as complete, since it includes beginning, middle and end, and it serves to effect decision: success or failure. Thus, with the complexive aorist παρεκάλεσα, the τρίς sums up the threefold prayer as a 'rounded-off' event.[386]

As v. 9 shows, the κύριος to whom Paul prayed is Christ:[387] the divine respondent speaks of 'my grace', synonymous with the following 'power' perfected in weakness, and Paul then makes reference to 'the power of Christ'. Windisch comments that this is the only certain testimony in the authentic Pauline letters to prayer to Christ.[388] There is also, as Martin notes,[389] the invocation in 1 Cor 16.22, but this is not an individual, personal petition. Nevertheless, the combination of the congregational invocation and Paul's personal prayer does indicate that for him

---

[377] Windisch, ibid.; see Eur., *Hipp.* 46 ('To ask three things of him [the god], nor pray in vain' [the privilege granted to Theseus by Poseidon], LCL).

[378] Furnish, p. 529; see also p. 17, for an account of the Asclepieium at Corinth.

[379] Betz, 'Aretalogie', p. 293.

[380] G. Delling, on τρεῖς, in *TWNT* VIII, pp. 215–25; see p. 216.

[381] Windisch, p. 389; Zmijewski, *'Narrenrede'*, p. 377 n. 386.

[382] Plummer, p. 353; Windisch, p. 389; and most other commentators. It exemplifies the triple petition, but does not, superficially at least, exemplify its efficacy.

[383] It is not certain whether he knew the Gethsemane tradition. The possibility is rejected by Windisch, p. 389, and regarded as unlikely by Zmijewski, *'Narrenrede'*, p. 380.

[384] Hughes, p. 449; Bachmann, p. 401.

[385] Bachmann, ibid.

[386] Heckel, *Schwachheit*, pp. 84–5. He refers to Delling, on τρεῖς, pp. 216–17, 221. See *TDNT* VIII, p. 222: 'Threefold performance of an action or the threefold occurrence of an event shows that it is complete, finished, definite …'

[387] See, e.g., Plummer, p. 353; Windisch, p. 388; Zmijewski, *'Narrenrede'*, p. 380.

[388] Windisch, p. 388.

[389] Martin, p. 417.

and probably for his churches the risen Christ possessed divine status. Even so, there still remains the question as to why, specifically, he did on this occasion address to Christ his prayer for deliverance. Windisch suggests that it was because he saw Christ as the one who conducts the battle against Satan and his satellites (cf. 1 Cor 15.24),[390] and hence as the one to repel the attacks on Paul of Satan's ἄγγελος. If, however, the thought of satanic agency was not predominant in his initial reaction to the infliction of the 'thorn',[391] there would need to be some other, or additional, reason. This is not far to seek, if, as we have argued, the σκόλοψ was some physical affliction.[392] For the Jesus-traditions present him as a remarkable healer. Granted that Paul had some knowledge of these traditions, prayer specifically to Christ is readily explicable.

He does, in fact, employ one lexical item which is compatible with such knowledge on his part. Plummer draws attention to his use of παρακαλέω, and to the fact that this same verb occurs in several of the gospel narratives, e.g., Mk 1.40; 5.23; 6.56; 7.32; 8.22. It is likely, Plummer thinks, that Paul was influenced by such traditions.[393] In the passages cited, the requests are pleas for healing. We should not, however, discount (pace Plummer[394]) the possible additional influence from the Graeco-Roman cultural sphere. Most exegetes draw attention to the inscription, cited by Deissmann, in which a certain M. Julius Apellas records his cure at the temple of Asklepios in Epidauros, and says of one of his ailments: καὶ γὰρ περὶ τούτου παρεκάλεσα τὸν θεόν.[395] Furthermore, Betz, commenting on the clause ἵνα ἀποστῇ ἀπ᾽ ἐμοῦ, observes that the communication of the prayer's content in indirect speech is typical of the non-Christian healing stories.[396]

9a. καὶ εἴρηκέν μοι, Ἀρκεῖ σοι ἡ χάρις μου, ἡ γὰρ δύναμις ἐν ἀσθενείᾳ τελεῖται. By contrast, Christ's response is cited in direct speech. This suggests, at least, that it was communicated in some revelatory experience characterised by audition. Hence, though this was not part of the experience described in vv. 2–4,[397] there would be a degree of similarity between the one and the other. In addition, the prayer-report thus turns into the report of

---

[390] Windisch, p. 388; cf. Wolff, p. 248.
[391] See above, p. 818.
[392] See above, pp. 814–18.
[393] Plummer, pp. 353–4.
[394] Plummer, p. 354.
[395] Deissmann, *LAE*[2], p. 311 and n. 1, with reference to Dittenberger, *Sylloge*[2], 804. See also BAGD s.v. παρακαλέω 1. c. with reference to *Sylloge*[3], 1170, and note that the verb is used quite generally of calling upon the (a) deity (references in Thucydides, Plato, Xenophon, Epictetus, and Josephus).
[396] Betz, 'Aretalogie', p. 293.
[397] *Pace* R. M. Price: see above, p. 817.

a dialogue, underlined by the personal pronouns, and this emphasises the depth of the personal relationship with Christ which Paul
felt himself to enjoy.[398]
In content, the response is a refusal of the apostle's specific
petition. Moreover, the perfect tense of εἴρηκεν suggests that any
later renewal of the same request would meet with the same
refusal. What Christ said on that occasion remains permanently
valid:[399] the sufficiency of his grace will render unnecessary Paul's
release from the 'thorn' on every occasion of its infliction.[400] This
recording of refusal stands in contrast with the majority of the
narratives with which Paul's account might be compared.
Windisch observes that in the Asklepios stories (which in some
respects he sees as parallel) the answer from the god is
favourable, and brings healing.[401] Betz sees a parallel in Dio
Cassius's account of Antoninus's failure to obtain healing from
any of the healing gods,[402] but the similarity is somewhat remote.
Dio gives no prayer-report. But in any case Paul is writing of his
own actual experience. In consequence, the absence of precise
parallels may not be of much significance.[403]
He is not to be healed of his malady. But his prayer does not go
unanswered, for he is promised the sufficient help of the χάρις of
Christ. The following sentence shows that this χάρις is chiefly to
be defined as divine power,[404] and suggests that this power is not
a static possession, but rather something continually appropriated
and experienced afresh on each occasion of struggle with
weakness.[405] It is not, either, an impersonal power, for it is the

[398] Heckel, *Schwachheit*, p. 87, with reference to Zmijewski, '*Narrenrede*', p. 379.
Heckel suggests also that Paul thereby refutes the doubt as to his belonging to
Christ, harboured by some in Corinth, to which he alludes in 10.7. In our comment
on this verse, however, we have rejected this interpretation of the Χριστοῦ εἶναι:
see above, p. 620.

[399] Meyer, p. 480; see also, e.g., Bachmann, p. 401; Barrett, p. 316; Plummer, p.
354; Zmijewski, '*Narrenrede*', p. 378; Furnish, p. 530.

[400] Bachmann, p. 401. We have argued that the 'thorn' was a recurrent physical
malady.

[401] Windisch, p. 390. For the Asklepios inscriptions at Epidauros see
Dittenberger. *Sylloge*³ Vol. III, pp. 310–31. They end with ὑγίης ἐξῆλθεν or some
similar expression.

[402] Betz, 'Aretalogie', pp. 292, 301, with reference to Dio Cass. LXXVIII 15.6–7;
Betz relates the story to Alexander Severus (father of Antoninus), but this is surely
an error. He offers as a second parallel the story in Philostratus, *Vit. Ap.* I 9, of an
Assyrian youth who was continually disregarded by Asklepios. But since in the end
it seems that the youth was cured this reference appears irrelevant.

[403] And were any records kept of such non-events as non-healings?

[404] Windisch, p. 391; Bultmann, p. 229; Furnish, p. 530. The rather strange
interpretation proposed by Chrysostom, *PG* 61 col. 578 (NPNF XII, p. 400), i.e.,
that the χάρις is the power to work miracles, has not gained acceptance.

[405] Bultmann, p. 229. This would be confirmed by v. 10, which speaks of
'weaknesses' in the plural, along with 'insults', 'persecutions', and the like.

grace of Christ, and so an expression of God's 'movement in love' towards humankind.[406] There is no exact parallel to this grace-element of Paul's prayer-report. But we do find elsewhere a few examples of the motif of refusal to grant a prayer combined with the use of ἀρκέω or some similar verb. Hermas tells of a 'young man' who appears to him, asks why he is constantly praying for revelations, and tells him: ἀρκοῦσίν σοι αἱ ἀποκαλύψεις αὗται.[407] And in the biblical writings we have the example of Moses's prayer in Deut 3.23–26. Moses asks that he may himself be allowed to enter the promised land. He receives a negative reply however, which begins 'Ἱκανούσθω σοι, literally 'Let it be sufficient for you'.[408] Could this have been in Paul's mind? The passage in Deuteronomy does not contain the theme of power working through weakness,[409] nor is the verb the same. And Moses's 'pious resignation to necessity' is rather different from the 'positive accession of δύναμις' promised to Paul.[410] Nevertheless, it was Moses with whom he had compared and contrasted himself in chap. 3. It would not have been impossible for him to have thought of the Deuteronomic passage whilst writing this later letter. There remains the further question of whether the notion of sufficiency in Stoicism has played any part in his prayer-report. Furnish returns a negative verdict: the ἀρκεῖ of Paul is not concerned with the self- sufficiency of the Cynic and Stoic philosophers.[411] But perhaps this is too sweeping a judgement. There is a passage in Epictetus which could be relevant here. He represents Zeus as asking him whether he is content with what he has been given, i.e., the faculty of moral choice and the like. Is he satisfied with these things (ἀρκῇ οὖν αὐτοῖς;)? This is not, then, strictly, a matter of self-sufficiency. For what Epictetus has been given, Zeus tells him, is 'a certain portion of ourself'. The 'faculty of choice and refusal' is in some sense a divine faculty.[412]

We shall return later to the matter of parallels. Christ's

---

[406] Barrett, p. 316.
[407] *Herm. Vis.* III 10.7–8: 'These revelations are sufficient for you' (LCL); cited by Windisch, p. 390.
[408] Cited by Windisch, p. 391.
[409] Windisch, ibid. on this account, regards Paul's use of the passage as uncertain.
[410] Martin, p. 419; cf. Bultmann, p. 228.
[411] Furnish, p. 530.
[412] Epict., *Diss.* I 1.10–13. The passage is cited by Windisch, p. 390. Bultmann, p. 228, observes that what is 'sufficient' for Epictetus is 'the power of the Spirit', and that 'the Spirit' is 'God's gift'. Zmijewski, *'Narrenrede'*, p. 381, thinks that the Stoic concept of God's sufficiency may be in view, as well as that of the OT and Judaism.

response continues: ἡ γὰρ δύναμις[413] ἐν ἀσθενείᾳ τελεῖται.[414] In form, this statement is of a general, proverbial, nature. Windisch comments that the present tense of the verb and the unqualified δύναμις give it the character of a gnomic utterance of universal validity.[415] This claim, however needs qualification. As Heckel points out, had it been a matter of 'everyday wisdom' that it was in weakness that power reached its consummation, the Corinthians would not have objected to Paul's weakness.[416] If the assertion is to be seen as possessing some general sense, this can only be within the sphere of Paul's own theological thought-world and religious experience. In this respect there are various suggestions. For Zmijewski, the primary reference of the unqualified δύναμις is to the power of God, whilst the undetermined singular ἀσθένεια denotes 'the totality of earthly-human existence in its weakness'.[417] The statement is not, it is said, directly limited to the 'thorn' of v. 7.[418] But since it provides the ground for the previous assertion, ἀρκεῖ σοι ἡ χάρις μου, and since there the μου clearly refers to Christ, one would expect that the δύναμις itself is that of Christ. This is made plain, furthermore, by the end of v. 9b. And if so, it is likely that there is a more specific reference to the content of Paul's prayer to Christ than Zmijewski appears to allow. Bultmann links to the exegesis of this verse a general discussion of the difference, as he sees it, between the Pauline and the Stoic understanding of human weakness and divine power. For the Stoics, it is a matter of conditions or qualities, but for Paul of something inherent in events. For him, it is through events that one becomes aware of the human 'nothingness' that he terms ἀσθένεια: this is not some deficiency of a static kind that impairs one's being. Likewise, δύναμις is not a possession, but the transcendent divine power which in events becomes a matter of experience.[419] With this interpretation we may in part agree. Since in v. 10 Paul speaks of 'weaknesses' in the plural, along with 'insults', 'occasions of persecution', and the like, it is plausible to suppose that he has in view, even though propounding a generalisation, specific experiences of weakness, overcome by particular

---

[413] Some witnesses (ℵ² A D² Ψ 0243 𝔐 sy bo^pt) read μου after δύναμις. The evidence for its omission (𝔓⁴⁶vid ℵ* B D* F G latt sa bo^pt Ir^lat) is strong, however, and the word was added, in all probability, to ensure clarity: see Metzger, *Textual Commentary*¹, pp. 585–6.

[414] The reading τελεῖται (ℵ* A B D* F G) has stronger attestation than τελειοῦται (ℵ² D² Ψ 0243 M) and is to be preferred: see Metzger, *Textual Commentary*¹, p. 586.

[415] Windisch, p. 391.

[416] Heckel, *Schwachheit*, p. 91.

[417] Zmijewski, '*Narrenrede*', pp. 382–3.

[418] Zmijewski, '*Narrenrede*', p. 383.

[419] Bultmann, p. 228.

experiences of divine empowerment. If so, however, it is most likely that it is chiefly the occasions of the 'thorn's' infliction that he has in mind, rather than events which evoked in him some existential sense of non-significance.

Other commentators relate Paul's assertion more directly to the Corinthian situation, or to his malady, or to both. For Güttgemanns, he is replying to Corinthian gnostics. These people had attributed his illness to his involvement in the demonic earthly sphere of the *sarx*. It was not in this sphere that the gnostic reached perfection, since in the process of τελείωσις he became wholly spirit and power. Paul, in antithesis to this viewpoint, affirms that the perfecting takes place precisely in the realm of earthly weakness, not in the sphere of the heavenly Pneuma, experienced in visions. This is meaningful only on a christological basis. It was in crucifixion that Jesus was perfected and obtained power, and Paul's own apostolic weakness is the epiphany of this divine power of the crucified Christ.[420] This is scarcely convincing, however, as exegesis of the specific assertion under consideration. By contrast with Phil 3.12, Paul is not here, on the face of it, talking about the perfecting of a person (whether a gnostic or himself),[421] but of the situation in which divine power operates to perfection. It is misleading also to speak, as Güttgemanns appears to do, as though weakness is itself the epiphany of divine power. It is not identical with the δύναμις but the location of its manifestation.[422]

If the assertion that power is perfected in weakness is to be understood, in part, in relation to Paul's, and the Corinthians', hellenistic background, and if it is correct to identify the 'thorn' with some physical malady, then the more relevant material would be the Greek healing narratives to which Betz relates the apostle's prayer-report. He claims that δύναμις (τοῦ θεοῦ) belongs to the technical vocabulary of the aretalogy. In one of the papyri we find the assertion: εἰς πάντα γὰρ τόπον διαπεφοίτηκεν ἡ τοῦ θεοῦ δύναμις σωτήριος[423] (the god is Asklepios). According to this viewpoint, the ἀσθένεια to which the apparently general aphorism refers would be Paul's illness. This is affirmed with

---

[420] Güttgemanns, *Der leidende Apostel*, pp. 164–9.

[421] Paul does not, either, talk of the 'perfecting' of Christ. This is certainly a theme of Hebrews (2.10; 5.9; 7.28), but not of the Pauline letters.

[422] See Jervell, 'Charismatiker', pp. 191, 197 n. 63.

[423] 'For the salvific power of the god has spread to every region': P Oxy XI 1381, ll. 215–18. This is quoted by Windisch, p. 392. In the context of Betz's argument, see 'Aretalogie', p. 300 n. 69. See also Furnish, p. 530. Betz, p. 301, sees a further parallel in Aristides, *Or.* XXIII 16, to Paul's understanding of δύναμις, in that, whilst Aristides does not reject the idea of healing, for him what counts is the experience of the power of his god (Asklepios), not the alternative of sickness or health.

considerable force by Jervell. He also posits, however, a more specific interpretation of δύναμις. This is not simply Christ's divine power in a general sense. Rather, it is an allusion to the charismatic gifts exercised by Paul himself. To the Corinthians, Jervell maintains, the fact that Paul was both a charismatic and afflicted with illness was an offence and a contradiction in terms.[424] Why was he not able to heal himself? To Paul, however, this apparent contradiction was indispensable. His paradoxical situation is crystallised in the present verse. He speaks of something obvious to everyone. Divine power is apparent in the charismata, whilst weakness is visible in his illness. Hence, he supposes that it should be clear that it is not he himself who has effected the apostolic signs: the divine power at work in him is clearly distinguishable as such. He is not, therefore, talking here about human powerlessness in general, but about his individual situation.[425] With this we should agree, and agree also that in the present context it is, primarily at least, his occasions of illness to which the ἀσθένεια refers. But in view of the broader list of weaknesses in v. 10, this primary reference is not to be seen as exclusive. Similarly we would not restrict the content of δύναμις to the charismata. Rather, it should be understood in the light of 4.7–9, as the divine power at work in all of Paul's apostolic activity.

9b. Ἥδιστα οὖν μᾶλλον καυχήσομαι ἐν ταῖς ἀσθενείαις [μου],[426] ἵνα ἐπισκηνώσῃ ἐπ᾽ ἐμὲ ἡ δύναμις τοῦ Χριστοῦ. In view of this mode of operation of Christ's power, weaknesses are a cause for boasting,[427] and this Paul will do very gladly.[428] The general sense is clear. But what is the precise force of the adverb μᾶλλον? Does Paul mean that he now prefers to *boast* of his occasions of weakness *rather than* praying for relief from them?[429] The word order might favour this interpretation.[430] The connective οὖν, moreover, relates the intention of boasting to the prayer-report of vv. 8–9a. Alternatively, however, the meaning

---

[424] Cf. p. 783 n. 82 above.

[425] Jervell, 'Charismatiker', *passim*; see especially pp. 191–5.

[426] A number of witnesses (א A D F G Ψ 𝔐 latt syᵖ) read μου after ἀσθενείαις. It is omitted in others (B 6. 81. 1175*. 1739 *pc* syʰ Ir). The same variant occurred in 12.5, where we have argued that the omission of μου is more likely to be correct. This will be true here as well. Whilst accidental omission is always a possibility, there would be no very obvious reason for it here.

[427] Betz, 'Aretalogie', p. 303, relates καυχήσομαι to the Graeco-Roman healing stories as the equivalent of the healed person's obligation to proclaim the god's beneficial deeds.

[428] The ἥδιστα is an elative superlative: see Zmijewski, '*Narrenrede*', p. 386.

[429] So Bachmann, p. 402; Plummer, p. 355; Zmijewski, '*Narrenrede*', p. 387; Furnish, p. 531; Heckel, *Schwachheit*, pp. 101–2.

[430] Plummer, p. 355.

may be that he will boast of his *weaknesses rather than* of anything else,[431] such as the revelations granted him.[432] The καυχήσομαι ἐν ταῖς ἀσθενείαις is reminiscent of the οὐ καυχήσομαι εἰ μὴ ἐν ταῖς ἀσθενείαις of v. 5,[433] and this earlier verse contrasts boasting about the one who had experienced rapture with boasting about Paul himself. Decision between the alternatives is difficult.[434] But there is in v. 9a some obvious emphasis on ἀσθένεια. Consequently, the recurrence of the word in the first half of v. 9b similarly focuses emphasis on it, and suggests that it is this word which serves as one component of the comparison implicit in the use of μᾶλλον. Hence, we opt tentatively for the second alternative: weaknesses rather than, e.g., revelations.

The remainder of the verse reiterates the correlation of weakness and divine power succinctly expressed in v. 9a. But the syntactical form of this last clause creates a problem. The use of the conjunction ἵνα, whether this be seen as final or as consecutive, suggests that the acknowledgement of one's weakness (the 'boasting' of it) is the prior requirement for the reception of the power of Christ.[435] Paul boasts in *order that* he may experience the δύναμις. Or, it is only *as a consequence* of his boasting that he is able to experience the power. This presents difficulties. Nothing is said in v. 9a of any such requirement, and it is apparent from the context that endowment with the δύναμις has been prior to the apostle's boasting of it.[436] Moreover, this display of divine power is represented as a matter of sheer grace.[437] We may add that the logical sequence implied by the ἵνα would seem to be the direct converse of the sequence in v. 10. For in v. 10 the ὅταν γάρ shows that the contentment expressed in the εὐδοκῶ is the result of the experience of strength in weakness, not its cause or condition. Are there, then, ways of resolving the difficulty? Does Paul, perhaps, have in mind a simultaneous experience of weakness and power?[438] This might be so, but it is not what the conjunction ἵνα indicates. Whatever its precise meaning, it signifies temporal sequence rather than simultaneity. Perhaps,

---

[431] Barrett, p. 317; Martin, p. 421.

[432] Martin, ibid.

[433] The point is made by Windisch, p. 392, although he supports the first alternative.

[434] The difficulty is illustrated in the comments by Black, *Astheneia*, p. 156. He first says: 'rather than pray for the removal of his infirmities, Paul glories in those things which reveal his weakness.' But he then appears to switch to the alternative option: 'Paul intends to boast in weakness rather than strength.'

[435] Windisch, p. 392, draws attention to the logical significance of the ἵνα.

[436] Zmijewski, '*Narrenrede*', pp. 392–3.

[437] Heckel, *Schwachheit*, pp. 104–5.

[438] Heckel, *Schwachheit*, p. 104, citing G. G. O'Collins, 'Power Made Perfect in Weakness: 2 Cor 12:9–10', *CBQ* 33 (1971), pp. 528–37; see p. 536.

then, Paul means that the divine power needs constant renewal, and that the confession of one's own frailty serves to bring this about.[439] But this interpretation does not eliminate the apparent conditionality which is the cause of the difficulty. The same objection would apply to the similar idea, suggested by Heckel, that consciousness of one's weakness 'makes room' for the operation of the grace of Christ.[440] A different solution might be to retain the conditionality but to transpose the implicit location of the condition. It is invariably seen as inherent in the human activity of boasting (καυχήσομαι). But perhaps its logical point of reference is 'the weaknesses' (ταῖς ἀσθενείαις). The sense could then be: 'I will boast of *the weaknesses whose consequence* is to allow the power of Christ to rest upon me'.[441] Similarly, Professor Cranfield (in an editorial comment) suggests that the ἵνα-clause indicates 'the divine purpose behind the weaknesses'. This would give: 'I will boast of the weaknesses whose divine purpose is that Christ's power should rest upon me.' Of the possibilities so far considered, this last proposal seems the best.

There is a further suggestion, however, that deserves consideration. It depends upon the meaning of the verb ἐπισκηνόω. This verb is seen to connote the epiphany of divine glory. Thus, the function of Paul's boasting is to make manifest in speech form the glory of Christ's δύναμις.[442] Paul's boasting is the cause, not of the indwelling of Christ's power in itself, but of its being seen to reside in him.[443] The ground for this interpretation is that the verb ἐπισκηνόω suggests the idea of the *Shekinah*, i.e., the presence of the Lord, dwelling with his people, which may be combined with the concept of the divine glory,[444] visibly perceptible. If this is

[439] Windisch, p. 393, and Bultmann, p. 230 (noted by Zmijewski, *'Narrenrede'*, p. 392 n. 503).

[440] Heckel, *Schwachheit*, p. 103; he refers, p. 106 n. 252, to Calvin. The latter, p. 161, comments: 'we make room for Christ's grace when with a resigned mind we feel and confess our own weakness.' See Heckel, *Schwachheit*, pp. 100–8, for a detailed discussion of v. 9b. He argues forcefully against the view that Paul sees a conditional relationship between weakness and the power of Christ. But it is not at all clear how the alternative (pp. 105–6) of a 'Means-End-connection' ('eine Mittel-zweck-Beziehung') would essentially differ from conditionality.

[441] The suggestion is my own. But I admit that the connection between the two clauses would logically require something like δι' ὦν rather than ἵνα.

[442] Zmijewski, *'Narrenrede'*, pp. 392–3.

[443] Furnish, p. 531.

[444] On the *Shekinah* see M. McNamara, *Targum and Testament*, Shannon, 1972, pp. 98–101. The word means 'presence' and is in origin simply a reverential way of speaking about God himself. In the Palestinian Targum it is combined with Glory to give the phrase 'the Glory of the *Shekinah* of the Lord'. This Glory is revealed on Mount Sinai, goes before the Israelites, and is to dwell in the sanctuary. In the Targum on Isaiah, the prophet is said to have seen 'the Glory of the *Shekinah* of the King of Ages'. The connection with the verb ἐπισκηνόω, according to Hughes, pp. 452–3, would be (a) that the biblical σκην-words evoke the thought of the

right, then Paul is talking of a display of power which is not only felt within himself but which also is open to the perception of others,[445] and to which his boasting of weakness may paradoxically call attention. The general idea that Paul has the concept of the *Shekinah* in mind is supported by several commentators.[446] But Furnish urges caution. The verb ἐπισκηνόω is not common, and elsewhere it always means 'take up residence with'.[447] In fact, the connection with the *Shekinah* is not quite as obvious as it may appear to some exegetes. In the LXX it is the other compound κατασκηνόω that is used for the dwelling on earth of God or his divine name.[448] Granted that Paul may have wanted a word to suggest divine presence, and hence a derivative of the σκην-root, as containing the radicals (S–K–N) of the term *Shekinah*, one would suppose that it would have been κατασκηνόω that would have come more readily to mind. But there could be one possible explanation. If Paul did have the concept of the *Shekinah* in view, he might have recollected the passage in Exod 40.34–35 where the cloud of the divine glory covers the Tent so that Moses is not able to enter it, because: ἐπεσκίαζεν ἐπ' αὐτὴν ἡ νεφέλη καὶ δόξης κυρίου ἐπλήσθη ἡ σκηνή. Might he then have conflated in his mind the verb ἐπισκιάζω[449] and the noun σκηνή, and thus have arrived at the less usual ἐπισκηνόω? This is very speculative. Nevertheless, in chap. 3 Paul has shown his close familiarity with the Exodus theme of the divine glory reflected on the face of Moses, and with the narrative in Exod 34.29–35 which speaks of Moses's entry into the Tent of Meeting. He could well have been equally familiar with Exod 40.34–35. In conclusion, therefore, we accept the view that it is the visibility of Christ's power that is the purpose or the consequence of Paul's boasting. We also accept that the idea of the *Shekinah* lies in the background. It is this that would emphasise visibility as the point,

σκηνή of Exod 25.8–9 (which, 40.34–35, the Lord's glory filled); and (b) that bilingual Jews may have used σκηνή for *Shekinah*. See ibid, n. 141, for the details of this argument and the relevant references to the scholars on whose work it is based.

[445] In the exodus narratives and in Isa 6 the 'glory of the Lord' is visibly perceptible.

[446] See, e.g., Plummer, p. 355; Strachan, p. 33; Héring, p. 97; Martin, p. 421; Zmijewski, '*Narrenrede*', p. 392.

[447] Furnish, p. 531.

[448] See W. Michaelis, on σκηνή and compounds, in *TWNT* VII, pp. 369–96; see pp. 389–90 on κατασκηνόω in the LXX.

[449] This verb is used in the NT of the overshadowing of the divine cloud in the Transfiguration narratives (Mt 17.5 = Mk 9.7 = Lk 9.34) and of the overshadowing of the power of God promised to Mary by the angel of the Annunciation (Lk 1.35). This last occurrence, καὶ δύναμις ὑψίστου ἐπισκιάσει σοι, is not altogether unlike Paul's ἵνα ἐπισκηνώσῃ ἐπ' ἐμὲ ἡ δύναμις τοῦ Χριστοῦ. Was there, perhaps, some sense of the suitability of the ἐπί-verbs to convey the impact of divine presence?

thus avoiding the theological problem otherwise inherent in the
ἵνα-clause.

10. διὸ εὐδοκῶ ἐν ἀσθενείαις, ἐν ὕβρεσιν, ἐν[450] ἀνάγκαις,
ἐν διωγμοῖς καὶ[451] στενοχωρίαις, ὑπὲρ Χριστοῦ· ὅταν γὰρ
ἀσθενῶ, τότε δυνατός εἰμι. Weaknesses give occasion for the
display of the power of Christ. For this reason Paul can take some
pleasure in them.[452] This is probably the best interpretation of the
verb εὐδοκέω here.[453] In view of the reference to boasting in v.
9b something a little stronger than 'I am well content'[454] seems to be
required, whilst the other Pauline occurrences do not give support
to the positive 'I delight in'.[455]

What follows is a short hardships-list.[456] The initial ἐν
ἀσθενείαις appears to function as the general concept, which is
then developed by means of four items in pairs.[457] The term ὕβρις
is found in the plural only here in the NT, although the plural is
found at times elsewhere.[458] Furnish notes that it does not occur in
the other Pauline hardships-lists, and that its inclusion here could
refer to Paul's subjection to slanders originating with the rival
missionaries.[459] The precise function of the concluding ὑπὲρ
Χριστοῦ is debatable. In view of its position one might suppose that
it refers to the hardships: these trials are suffered for the sake of

---

[450] Most witnesses read ἐν before ἀνάγκαις, but 𝔓[46] ℵ* read καί. In favour of this
latter reading one might argue that a scribe would be more likely to continue the
use of ἐν rather than to introduce a καί into the middle of the series. But one could
equally argue that, after the general introductory ἐν ἀσθενείαις, it might seem to a
copyist stylistically neat to have two pairs of specific weaknesses following, with
each member of the pair connected to the other by καί. This would support
the correctness of ἐν, which in any case has substantial support. On balance,
the majority reading is preferable.

[451] Before στενοχωρίαις some witnesses (𝔓[46] ℵ* B 104. 326. 1175 pc) read καί,
others (ℵ² A D F G Ψ 𝔐 latt sy Tert) have ἐν, and yet others (0243. 630. 1739. 1881
pc) read καὶ ἐν. The third option is obviously a conflation. Of the other two, the
reading of 𝔓[46] ℵ* B is preferable, i.e., καί, since the alternative ἐν would derive
naturally from the preceding ἐν-phrases.

[452] Furnish, p. 513, has 'I am pleased'.

[453] The verb can mean 'be well pleased', 'take delight in', 'like', 'approve': see
BAGD s.v. εὐδοκέω 2.

[454] Barrett, p. 306, offers this translation.

[455] See Rom 15.26–27; 1 Cor 1.21; 10.5; 2 Cor 5.8; Gal 1.15; 1 Th 2.8; 3.1. Heckel,
Schwachheit, p. 110, comments that in the present verse the εὐδοκῶ is more than
simple consent, but weaker than the joy depicted by the Church Fathers. Martin,
p. 389, however, translates 'I delight in'.

[456] So, e.g., Windisch, p. 393; Bultmann, p. 230; Zmijewski, 'Narrenrede', p. 387.

[457] Prümm, *Diakonia Pneumatos* I, p. 674, observes that the first and the third of
these items (insults and persecutions) point more clearly to human hostility than
do the second and the fourth (calamities and difficulties). This gives some structure
to the listing of the four items.

[458] Windisch, p. 393. See BAGD s.v. ὕβρις 2.

[459] Furnish, p. 551, with reference to Zmijewski, 'Narrenrede', p. 393, and to the
work of P. Marshall (see now P. Marshall, *Enmity in Corinth*, p. 202).

Christ.[460] Most commentators, however, prefer to relate the phrase to the verb εὐδοκῶ: it is for Christ's sake that Paul can take pleasure in his sufferings.[461] It is through the apostle's weaknesses that Christ has opportunity to bring his power into full operation.[462] This interpretation is preferable, despite the position of ὑπὲρ Χριστοῦ. In the context a major component of the weaknesses must be the 'thorn' of v. 7. If, as we have argued, this is to be identified as some kind of illness, this would not be, in itself, a hardship directly suffered as a result of Paul's specifically apostolic activity.

The following assertion specifically explains his pleasure in weaknesses: paradoxically it is on these occasions that he is strong. In some very general sense there may be parallels elsewhere to the basic idea. Commentators cite Philo, who speaks of the way the divine providence protects Moses and the Israelites on account of their weakness: μὴ ἀναπίπτετε, τὸ ἀσθενὲς ὑμων δύναμίς ἐστιν.[463] Bultmann notes that Stoicism also sees a connection between weakness and strength. Strength is developed through the struggle against weakness. This strength, however, is that of the human rational faculty, and the weakness of suffering does not affect man's essential being. But for Paul, according to Bultmann, it is weakness which precisely characterises man's being, and the power is not a natural human capacity or possession but a gift of divine grace.[464] Certainly Paul may think this way. But it is doubtful whether in the present context he is thus concerned with the general human condition of existential weakness. First, the plurals in v. 10a suggest that what he has in view are particular occasions of weakness which result in specific experiences of divine power. These occasions, moreover, are concerned not with man's inner being but with adverse circumstances such as hostility, illness, and persecution. Secondly, as Heckel observes, in the wider context of the Fool's Speech the final sentence of v. 10 relates not so much to an anthropological problem as to Paul's legitimation as an apostle. He is defending himself against the apparent contradiction expressed in 10.10. Hence, the first person singular is 'the apostolic "I" '. Since his mission success cannot be attributed to his own power, his personal weakness does not stand in opposition to his authority and his affiliation to Christ (10.7b–10).

---

[460] Barrett, p. 306; Tasker, p. 179.
[461] Meyer, p. 482; Bachmann, p. 402; Plummer, p. 355; Windisch, p. 393; Furnish, p. 531; and others.
[462] Bachmann, p. 402; cf. Heckel, *Schwachheit*, p. 111.
[463] Philo, *Vit. Mos.* (*Life of Moses*) I 69: 'Do not flag, your weakness is power' (LCL). This is cited by, e.g., Meyer, p. 483; Plummer, p. 356; Windisch, p. 394; Bultmann, p. 231; Barrett, p. 317; Furnish, p. 551; Wettstein, p. 212.
[464] Bultmann, pp. 231–2.

Rather it commends him as a proven apostle and legitimates him as διάκονος Χριστοῦ (11.23).[465] It follows also that he is not here concerned with the application to all believers of his own claim to be strong in conditions of weakness.[466]

The use of λόγος in chaps 11–13.[467] The third means of persuasion is the presentation of proof consisting of logical reasoning. DiCicco notes, amongst other examples, two instances of syllogistic argument: in 12.1–4, combined with 11.23–29, and 13.4 combined with 12.9.

(i) Initially, Paul argues his claim to authority as follows:
(a) The Corinthians believe that divine 'visions and revelations' authenticate an apostle, and also that endurance of hardships shows divine approval.
(b) Paul qualifies on both counts (12.1–4; 11.23–29).

Therefore:

(c) His apostolic authority derives from God.

This argument, however, is by way of accommodation to the Corinthians' own ways of thinking.

(ii) But from Paul's own viewpoint it is not valid. He himself argues his claim, fundamentally, on a different basis:
(a) Jesus's divine power derives from the weakness of his crucifixion (13.4).
(b) Paul's weaknesses are experienced 'in this same spirit' (12.10).

Therefore,

(c) Christ's power rests upon him (12.9).[468]

This second syllogism 'paradoxically supersedes' the first.[469] Indeed, it may be said to 'contradict' the first.[470]

One has to ask, however, whether this might not put the point

---

[465] Heckel, *Schwachheit*, p. 118.

[466] See further G. G. O'Collins, 'Power Made Perfect in Weakness' (see above, p. 826 n. 438), pp. 528–37. O'Collins maintains that Paul is throughout referring to himself alone. Bultmann, p. 230, argues, on the contrary, that vv. 9a and 10b are intended to be related to all Christians, and Martin, p. 422, similarly disagrees with O'Collins, on the ground that Paul would be nurturing 'an elitist idea' of himself. Nevertheless, we should have to say in response that Paul does suppose himself to possess unique authority in relation to the church in Corinth, whether or not that is 'elitist' in modern terms.

[467] See above, p. 655.

[468] DiCicco, *Ethos, Pathos and Logos*, pp. 242–3.

[469] DiCicco, *Ethos, Pathos and Logos*, p. 243.

[470] DiCicco, *Ethos, Pathos and Logos*, p. 244.

too strongly. To suggest that Paul's experience of rapture had no validity in respect of his apostolic calling is to devalue what for him must have been an event of overwhelming importance. Furthermore, to see a relation of paradox between the two narratives in 12.2–9 is to admit the significance of both equally.

(d) Conclusion of the Fool's Speech: prospective visit to Corinth (12.11–18)

[11]I have become a fool. You it was who forced me into it. For it was I who ought to have received commendation from you. For in no respect did I prove inferior to the super-apostles, even though I am nothing. [12]The apostolic signs were accomplished in your midst with all persistence, by signs and wonders and by deeds of power. [13]In what respect were you devalued by comparison with the other churches, except that I myself did not burden you? Forgive me this injustice!

[14]Look—this third time I am ready to visit you, and I shall not be a burden to you. For I am not seeking your financial assets but you yourselves. For it is not the children who ought to store up resources for the parents, but the parents for the children. [15]And I myself will most gladly spend and be spent for your sakes. Loving you the more, am I loved the less? [16]So be it then. I personally was no financial burden to you. But since I am naturally crafty, I entrapped you by trickery. [17]Surely it was not anyone of those I have sent to you through whose agency I exploited you? [18]I made my request to Titus, and sent the brother with him. Surely Titus did not exploit you in any way? Was our conduct not identical in spirit? Did we not 'walk in the same footprints?'

Paul concludes[471] the Fool's Speech which began at 11.1. He insists again that he is in no way inferior to his rivals, neither has he disadvantaged the Corinthian church in any respect—except that he has spared them his financial support!

Announcing his coming visit to Corinth, Paul reiterates his determination not to be a financial burden, and insists that it is because of his parental love for the Corinthians that he pursues this policy. He repudiates the suspicion that he has made personal financial profit out of them indirectly, through the agents he sent to organise the collection.

12.11–18 as peroratio

Sundermann divides this section into three parts:

(i) v. 11a–c looks back to the beginning of the Fool's Speech in 11.1;

(ii) vv. 11d–12 briefly recapitulate the *probatio* in 11.16–12.10;

(iii) vv. 13–18 recapitulate the *refutatio* in 11.1–15.[472]

---

[471] See the following rhetorical analysis.
[472] Sundermann, *Kraft der Rede*, pp. 182–3.

This is in general a credible analysis. The back reference in v. 11a is obvious, and the matter of Paul's apostolic authenticity, to which v. 12 alludes, is the main topic of 11.16–12.10. In vv. 13–18 the question of Paul's financial policy and its possible implications is taken up again, with obvious reference to 11.7–11. The only doubtful element is the connection of v. 11d, εἰ καὶ οὐδέν εἰμι, with the beginning of v. 12. Attachment to v. 11c creates a neat contrast between the οὐδὲν ... ὑστέρησα and the final οὐδέν εἰμι. If 12.11–18 is to be analysed in this way as peroration it is clear that it is at v. 18 that the Fool's Speech ends, and not at either of the other two points suggested by commentators.[473] It is significant that within these eight verses three important themes of the discourse receive mention: the contest with the rival missionaries, the issue of Paul's financial support, and the related question of his love, or lack of it, for the Corinthians. The crucial theme of strength in weakness has been the subject of the two immediately preceding verses (12.9–10), so that in this case reiteration would be superfluous.

11a. Γέγονα ἄφρων,[474] ὑμεῖς με ἠναγκάσατε. The initial placing of the verb suggests that the Fool's Speech has reached its conclusion.[475] At its beginning (11.1) Paul has begged for tolerance of folly, and at a later point (11.16–17) has indicated that it consists in his boasting.[476] He has indeed remarked twice (11.21, 23) on his foolishness in engaging in this activity,[477] and has also paradoxically restricted its subject matter to his experiences of weakness (11.30; 12.5, 9).[478] Nevertheless, some of what he has said can well be taken as inconsonant with this restriction,[479] and even now he has to add (v. 12) a further item,[480] which appears similarly ambivalent. All this, however, is the fault of the Corinthians,[481] as he goes on to explain.

11b. ἐγὼ γὰρ ὤφειλον ὑφ' ὑμῶν συνίστασθαι· οὐδὲν γάρ[482] ὑστέρησα τῶν ὑπερλίαν ἀποστόλων, εἰ καὶ οὐδέν εἰμι. It was

---

473 See above, pp. 654–5.
474 Some witnesses (Ψ 0243 𝔐 b sy(P)) read καυχώμενος after ἄφρων. This is obviously an explanatory scribal addition to the original text (found in 𝔓46 ℵ A B D F G K 6. 33. 81. 629. 1175. 1739. 2464 al lat co).
475 Windisch, p. 395.
476 Windisch, ibid.; Martin, p. 430.
477 Martin, ibid.
478 Windisch, p. 395.
479 See above, pp. 746–7, 754, 756, 758, 760.
480 Bultmann, p. 232, draws attention to this.
481 The ὑμεῖς is emphatic, as are the following ἐγώ and ὑφ' ὑμῶν in v. 11b. The point is noted by, e.g., Plummer, p. 357; Furnish, p. 552; Martin, pp. 430–1.
482 Two witnesses (𝔓46 B) read τι after γάρ. This might have been added to give emphasis: 'in no way ... in anything'. Alternatively, in the other witnesses it might have been omitted as superfluous.

his correspondents who should have[483] commended him and spoken in his defence over against the hostile criticism of the rival apostles. It was to him that they owed their existence as Christians, and this in itself was sufficient proof of his apostolic status as Paul himself saw it (1 Cor 9.2; 2 Cor 3.2–3).[484] Why, then, had they failed to give him the support he obviously feels was owing to him? Barrett suggests that it was because they were ashamed of him on two counts: first, because they had got him as their apostle on the cheap (since he did not accept maintenance from them), and secondly, because of his lack of eloquence. In both respects he came off badly by comparison with the rival missionaries.[485] In addition, both Barrett and Martin claim that the Corinthians' basic fault lay in their apathy.[486] But perhaps we should consider whether there might be something to be said in defence of the Corinthians. For in Paul's first canonical letter to them, had he not appeared, at one point, somewhat to play down the importance of his own role in the creation of their Christian community? Yes, he had planted the seed, and Apollos had later watered it, but it was God who caused the growth. Neither the planter nor the one who waters the seed is of any consequence (1 Cor 3.6–7). Certainly his continuous efforts to retain pastoral control of the church might suggest that he did not quite mean exactly what he had said, but he *had* said it. Why, then, should the Corinthians feel under any special obligation to produce a testimonial for him, when these other, apparently more professional, ecclesiastical gardeners arrived in the city?

From Paul's viewpoint, however, their failure to do so has created a dilemma. Unless his case is put by someone, the whole congregation may simply fall away, to attach themselves to these other missionaries whom he believes to be pseudo-apostles. And yet for him to put his case himself smacks of self-praise. Those who engage in this practice are regarded as shameless; moreover, they act unfairly, since 'they arrogate to themselves what it is for others to bestow'.[487] Consequently, his Fool's Speech has been precisely that: folly. Nevertheless, seen from another angle it has been legitimate. For the conventions do allow self-praise in certain circumstances, i.e., when an occasion demands that the truth be told about oneself, and especially when this will achieve

---

[483] On the imperfect ὤφειλον see BDR 358(1). It denotes in classical Greek 'something which is or was actually necessary ..., but which does not or did not take place' (BDF 358(1)).

[484] Martin, p. 431.

[485] Barrett, pp. 319–20.

[486] Barrett, p. 319; Martin, p. 432.

[487] Windisch, p. 395, and Furnish, pp. 552, 554, draw attention to Plut., *Mor.* 539–42. See 539D (translation cited from LCL).

some benefit to others.[488] It is not resented if it is in defence of one's good name or in answer to some charge.[489] This would certainly cover what Paul has been doing. He has, after all, remained within acceptable limits, as far as the hellenistic conventions are concerned. Why, then, the dilemma? Why does he speak of himself as ἄφρων? Forbes suggests that this is because Paul himself goes beyond the current conventions. For him, 'self-praise is never legitimate'. The only permissible boasting is to boast of what the Lord has done.[490]

Nevertheless, he has been doing what the Corinthians should have done for him. And they had ample reason to do so. In no way[491] had he proved inferior to the 'super-apostles'. By comparison with 11.5, Paul's assertion here is more decisive.[492] The aorist indicative ὑστέρησα changes the more general previous claim into a specific reference to his past activities.[493] Since, moreover, it is for the Corinthians that these activities should have provided material for his commendation, he must have in view his work in Corinth itself,[494] including the apostolic signs which he mentions in the following verse. Since also there is an implicit element of comparison involved, it is assumed that the Corinthians have direct experience also of the activity of the 'super- apostles'. Hence, the latter must be identified with the rival missionaries.[495]

Paul is their equal, although, he adds, he is 'nothing'. Is he serious, or is he speaking ironically? And does the answer to this question depend upon the identification of the 'super-apostles'? It is certainly true that if, contrary to our previous argument, we were to identify them with the original apostles, it would be more probable that he is speaking seriously, and saying the same as he says in 1 Cor 15.9–10: he is 'the least of the apostles', but by God's

---

[488] Plut., *Mor.* 539E; noted by Furnish, p. 554.
[489] Plut., *Mor.* 540C; cited by Windisch, p. 395.
[490] Forbes, 'Comparison', p. 20.
[491] On the οὐδέν see above, p. 671 n. 110, on the μηδέν of 11.5.
[492] Windisch, p. 395; cf. Bultmann, p. 233.
[493] Bultmann, ibid.
[494] See, e.g., Meyer, p. 483; Plummer, p. 358; Windisch, p. 395; Bultmann, p. 233; Furnish, p. 552. Presumably he has in mind his first visit to the city and comparatively lengthy stay there.
[495] Commentators who identify the ὑπερλίαν ἀπόστολοι with the Jerusalem apostles seem to find it necessary at this point somehow to bring the rival missionaries into the picture as well. Martin, p. 433, suggests that Paul is indirectly attacking the latter, who perhaps had claimed to model themselves on the Jerusalem apostles. Barrett, p. 320, supposes him to be arguing that, if he is in no way inferior to the major apostles, 'he is not inferior to the intruders'. These suggestions are unnecessarily complicated, however, and would have force only if the identification of the ὑπερλίαν ἀπόστολοι with the Jerusalem apostles was certain.

grace he 'worked harder than any of them'.[496] But if, as we have maintained, the ὑπερλίαν ἀπόστολοι are the rival missionaries, in Corinth, the answer is not quite so obvious. For Paul could still be making the same serious point.[497] But it is more likely, perhaps, that he is speaking ironically. The nature of the irony, however, is not altogether easy to define. Three ways of explaining it are possible.

(i) Paul does not really believe himself to be 'nothing', but he makes the ironical concession to score a polemical point against his opponents.[498] How minimal their significance must be, if someone who is 'nothing' is their equal![499]

(ii) The 'nothing' is ironical because Paul knows that 'in Christ's power he is everything and more'.[500] This interpretation becomes almost indistinguishable from the view that the assertion is intended seriously, though it has a different emphasis.

(iii) The οὐδέν εἰμι is to be understood in the light of the classical and hellenistic background of thought. According to Betz, the phrase belongs to the debate between the philosophers and the rhetoricians. Socrates, for example, is represented as referring to his own 'nothingness': ἐπεὶ ἐμέ γε ἔλαθεν ὑπὸ τῆς ἐμῆς οὐδενίας.[501] The οὐδενία becomes a philosophical principle, and ignorance, correspondingly, is shown to be genuine wisdom, by contrast with the alleged wisdom of the rhetoricians.[502] The Socratic οὐδενία, moreover, is to be linked with the ancient Delphic teaching on self-knowledge, which enables man to recognise his own 'nothingness' in face of the power of the divine. The tradition, it appears, was also familiar to hellenistic Judaism, since Philo makes use of it.[503] Hence, it is possible that it was known to Paul.[504] If it is to this type of thought, then, that he is in part indebted, it would seem that the irony has disappeared. He is speaking seriously, for the philosophic and Delphic concept of

[496] Bruce, pp. 249–50.

[497] Hughes, p. 455; see also Furnish, p. 555.

[498] Windisch, p. 396. The basic concept of irony is defined by Forbes, 'Comparison', p. 10, as: 'the use of words or phrases to mean the opposite of what they normally mean'.

[499] Bachmann, p. 404; Allo, p. 324. This conclusion, deriving from the literal sense of οὐδέν, would be rejected by the Corinthians, who would then be forced to acknowledge that the reverse sense, 'something', must be applied to Paul, as well as to the opponents, who had probably applied οὐδέν to the apostle (see, e.g., Barrett, p. 320; Martin, pp. 427, 433–4).

[500] Martin, p. 427.

[501] Betz, Tradition, p. 122 and n. 578; the phrase quoted is from Plato, Phaedr. 234E. The LCL translation reads: 'since because of my stupidity, I did not notice.' But LSJ, for this reference, has 'nothingness', 'worthlessness', for οὐδενία.

[502] Betz, Tradition, pp. 122–3.

[503] Betz, Tradition, pp. 127–30.

[504] Betz, Tradition, p. 130.

human 'nothingness' has some affinity with his own sense that he was 'nothing' *apart from Christ*.[505] In fact, however, this third interpretation, we could suggest, might well combine the features of the first and second possibilities. For the Socratic οὐδενία is ambivalent. On the one hand, it may derive, as Betz suggests, from the Delphic motif of human 'nothingness' *vis-à-vis* the gods. Its profession, from that angle, would be serious. But on the other hand, *vis-à-vis* fellow human beings it has a distinctly ironical connotation and polemical intent. Socrates, after all, is the one who wins the arguments and shows up the intellectual failings of his dialogue partners. In this context he is by no means 'nothing', and in his profession of οὐδενία he is the εἴρων *par excellence*, the ironical man, who affects 'to be less than he is'.[506] Consequently, if Paul's acknowledgement of his 'nothingness' has something of the background claimed for it by Betz, his assertion οὐδέν εἰμι may likewise be ambivalent in its import. It is wholly serious, in that, apart from the power of Christ, he knows himself to be really 'nothing'. But at the same time, in relation to his opponents, he speaks ironically and with polemical intent. His concession is 'mock-modest'. It is shown to be such by his insistence that he is the equal of the rival missionaries. Since neither they themselves nor the Corinthians considered they were 'nothing', Paul does not seriously, in relation to these people, mean it of himself. He affects to do so in order to compel the Corinthians to realise the strength of his own apostolic claims.

12. τὰ μὲν σημεῖα τοῦ ἀποστόλου κατειργάσθη ἐν ὑμῖν ἐν πάσῃ ὑπομονῇ, σημείοις τε καὶ τέρασιν καὶ δυνάμεσιν. Paul is no way inferior to his rivals, since,[507] like them, he has produced the recognised signs of apostleship,[508] or, more exactly, these signs have been performed, i.e., by God through Paul's instrumentality.[509] The actual phrase, τὰ σημεῖα τοῦ ἀποστόλου, will have been coined prior to its use here, and will have been familiar to the Corinthians, since it is to their criticisms that Paul is responding. Perhaps it had been introduced by the rival missionaries, or it may have been in general usage in the early

505 See Betz, *Tradition*, p. 141.
506 See Forbes, 'Comparison', p. 10, for this definition. He notes that in Plato the terms εἰρωνεία and εἴρων are applied overwhelmingly to Socrates.
507 There is no connecting particle to indicate the logical relation to v. 11, but the link is clearly explanatory. The function of μέν is less easy to determine. The probable explanation, as noted in BAGD s.v. μέν 2.a., is that the expected contrasting δέ-clause has been omitted because it would be obvious: the signs were performed (but the Corinthians took no notice).
508 Meyer, p. 484, observes that the definite article preceding ἀποστόλου indicates reference to the general concept.
509 Plummer, p. 358, notes that this is the implication of the passive κατειργάσθη.

congregations.[510] Barrett suggests that both the term and the underlying concept originated with the Corinthians.[511] But the phrase does not occur in 1 Corinthians, even though already Paul's apostleship was questioned (1 Cor 9.1–2; 15.8–10), and at least one other missionary, i.e., Apollos, had worked in Corinth, and so might have raised in the Corinthians' minds the question of apostolic criteria. It will be the advent of these new visiting missionaries that has sharpened the question, and they who may have posed it in terms of 'apostolic signs', whether or not the formula was already known in Corinth.

The remainder of the verse, ἐν πάσῃ ὑπομονῇ, σημείοις τε καὶ τέρασιν καὶ δυνάμεσιν, elaborates upon the performance of the signs. But before we can fully appreciate its force there is a structural question to be addressed. Does the phrase ἐν πάσῃ ὑπομονῇ belong to the preceding statement, or is it to be connected with what follows? Does it, that is, say something about the circumstances in which the apostolic signs were produced? Or is the ὑπομονή to be regarded as itself one of the signs? For various reasons the first alternative appears preferable: ἐν ὑπομονῇ belongs to the preceding statement. If the ὑπομονή were to be connected closely with the following σημείοις, the particle τε[512] would most probably function as a simple connective, rather than as corresponsive, i.e., as connected with the following καί. This is not impossible, since there appears to be an example of single τε in 1 Cor 1.30. But it is not a common Pauline idiom. By contrast, Paul is fond of the τε καί correlation (see Rom 1.12, 14, 16, 20; 2.9, 10; 3.9; 10.12; 1 Cor 1.24; Phil 1.7). Also, in the NT there is a stereotyped connection between σημεῖα and τέρατα[513] which makes it likely that here the two items are bound closely together by means of τε καί, thus separating σημείοις slightly from the preceding ὑπομονῇ. Lastly, ὑπομονῇ is qualified by the adjective πάσῃ, whilst the three following nouns are unqualified, and are thus, again, set somewhat apart from ὑπομονῇ and related more closely to each other. We may therefore discuss the nature of the apostolic signs without immediate reference to the force of ὑπομονή.

Their content is elaborated in the concluding phrase σημείοις τε καὶ τέρασιν καὶ δυνάμεσιν.[514] Similar phrases occur elsewhere

---

[510] Schreiber, *Wundertäter*, pp. 217–18.

[511] Barrett, p. 321; cf. Martin, p. 435.

[512] The reading σημείοις τε has good attestation (𝔓46 ℵ* B (F G) 0243. 33. 81. 326. 630. 1175. 1739. 1881. 2464 *pc* g) and is preferable to σημείοις (A D* *pc* lat Ambst Pel). The third reading ἐν σημείοις (ℵ2 D2 Ψ (2495) 𝔐 vg^cl) looks secondary.

[513] See below.

[514] The datives are instrumental: see Windisch, p. 397; Furnish, p. 553. The repetition of the term σημεῖον appears awkward, but may be due, as Schreiber, *Wundertäter*, p. 217, suggests, to the fact that σημεῖα καὶ τέρατα is a fixed expression. (And the same is true of the σημεῖα τοῦ ἀποστόλου, as we have noted.)

in the NT. All three terms are combined in some way in Acts 2.22;
Rom 15.19; 2 Th 2.9; Heb 2.4. The combination of σημεῖα and
τέρατα is found in Mt 24.24; Mk 13.22; Jn 4.48; Acts 2.19, 43; 4.30;
5.12; 6.8; 7.36; 14.3; 15.12. And the phrase σημεῖα καὶ δυνάμεις is
found once, in Acts 8.13. For Schreiber, as we shall see, it is
significant that the terms σημεῖα and τέρατα are used in combination in the LXX of the miracles that accompanied the
Exodus.[515] See, e.g., Exod 7.3; Deut 4.34; 6.22; 7.19 (cited in
BAGD s.v. σημεῖον 2.a.). The frequency of the combination in the
NT shows its frequency in early Christian usage.[516] In the present
verse all three words have the basic meaning of 'miracle', but each
may possess its own particular connotation.[517] The term σημεῖον
indicates that the miracle is designed to point beyond itself for
some instructive purpose.[518] The τέρας evokes amazement,[519]
possibly numinous awe.[520] And δύναμις shows that the event is an
expression of divine power.[521] It is likely that the miracles in view
are primarily healing,[522] possibly also exorcisms.[523] The plain
sense of Paul's words here is both that he has performed miracles
in Corinth and also that they should be seen as authenticating
signs of his apostleship. As Furnish puts it: 'He clearly shares the
widespread ancient belief, at home as well in the earliest church,
that certain manifestations of divine power will accompany the
propagation of any valid religious truth.'[524] This has been thought
to cause a problem. Before we consider it, however, we need to
attend to the sense of the phrase ἐν πάσῃ ὑπομονῇ.

It indicates the 'circumstances and manner' in which the signs
were performed.[525] The word ὑπομονή has various nuances of
meaning,[526] which give rise here to such translations as 'with
utmost endurance',[527] 'in all persistence',[528] 'in all patience'.[529] All
these renderings are possible. The more interesting question is
what point Paul intended to make by thus describing the manner
of his miracle-working. Martin suggests that he wishes to show the
Corinthian congregation that he has remained loyal to them

515 Schreiber, ibid.
516 Schreiber, Wundertäter, p. 219.
517 Calvin, p. 164; Martin, p. 437.
518 Calvin, ibid.; Trench, Synonyms, p. 330.
519 Calvin, ibid.; Trench, Synonyms, p. 329.
520 Martin, ibid.
521 Calvin, ibid.; Trench, Synonyms, p. 331.
522 Windisch, p. 397.
523 Héring, p. 98.
524 Furnish, p. 555.
525 See BDR 198; Furnish, p. 553; Barrett, p. 321.
526 See BAGD s.v.
527 Furnish, p. 552.
528 Martin, p. 425.
529 RSV.

despite the strain they have imposed upon him by their 'rejection, ridicule, and slander'.[530] This seems implausible. The 'signs' surely belong primarily to Paul's founding visit,[531] when those who now constitute the Corinthian church had been favourably impressed by him, as their conversion makes plain. Furnish, with greater probability, supposes that what is in view is simply the life of hardship which was the context of Paul's missionary labours.[532] But perhaps there is more to it than this. Schreiber would see a connection with the use of this sign-vocabulary in the Exodus traditions. The divine act of salvation in the Exodus was accompanied by signs and wonders. Similarly, such miracles attend the Christ-event as the eschatological saving act. But the time of the church is the interim time between the inauguration of salvation and its consummation. The Christian, in this interim period, must live in a state of ὑπομονή, patience and endurance. Paul has in mind the afflictions and difficulties which hinder the full actualisation of the new creation.[533] In his own case, he may be thinking more particularly of the 'thorn for the flesh' which he has spoken of in v. 7.[534]

We come back to the question of the authenticating function of Paul's miracles. Did he see them as validating his claim to apostleship? Martin would say that in essence he did not. The phrase τὰ σημεῖα τοῦ ἀποστόλου refers primarily, if not exclusively, to quite different indications of apostolic legitimacy. The 'genuine proof' which in Paul's mind distinguishes him from his rivals consists in such things as the 'changed lives' of converts, the foundation of the Corinthian church, and his own life.[535] The miracles are to be seen as the effects of his apostleship, not as proofs of it.[536] This is somewhat unconvincing. It requires Paul's readers in Corinth to find a great deal in the text of the present verse which certainly does not lie on the surface. Moreover, what we have termed 'the plain sense' of his words here, i.e., that he refers to authenticating miracles,[537] would find support in Rom 15.18–19.[538] Nevertheless, this attitude may well appear problematic. In 1 Cor 1.22 the Jews' demand for (miraculous) 'signs' is criticised.[539] And while Martin's interpretation of the

---

[530] Martin, p. 435.
[531] Cf. Prümm, *Diakonia Pneumatos* I, p. 680.
[532] Furnish, p. 555; cf. Plummer, p. 359; Windisch, p. 397.
[533] Schreiber, *Wundertäter*, pp. 219–21.
[534] Especially, perhaps, if the 'thorn' is to be identified as recurrent illness.
[535] Martin, pp. 434–5; see also Hughes, p. 456.
[536] Martin, pp. 437–8. He concludes, however, with a reference to miracles as secondary criteria, which confuses the issue somewhat.
[537] See above, p. 839.
[538] Windisch, p. 397.
[539] See K. H. Rengstorf, on σημεῖον, in *TWNT* VII, pp. 199–260; see p. 258.

apostolic σημεῖα in the present context seems unlikely, it is true that in general we get a different picture of Paul's understanding of apostolic identification. An apostle was such because of his proclamation of the Christian message:[540] see Gal 1.1, 15–16. And it was his missionary success that chiefly authenticated him: see 3.2 and 1 Cor 9.2.[541]

In the present verse there is at least a change of perspective, and this is obviously due to the advent of the rival missionaries, who have forced Paul into unwilling competition. Héring suggests that he is compelled to compete against an ethos deriving originally from the Jerusalem apostles, who attached great importance to miracles: see Acts 2.22; 3.6–8; 4.30; 5.5.[542] If this is plausible, it would have some significance for the identification of the opponents.

13. τί γάρ ἐστιν ὃ ἡσσώθητε[543] ὑπὲρ τὰς λοιπὰς ἐκκλησίας, εἰ μὴ ὅτι αὐτὸς ἐγὼ οὐ κατενάρκησα ὑμῶν; χαρίσασθέ μοι τὴν ἀδικίαν ταύτην.[544] Paul proceeds to give a further reason for his claim in v. 11 that the Corinthians should have commended him. In vv. 11b–12 he has asserted his own equality with the rival missionaries. Now he insists that the church he has founded in Corinth is in no way at a disadvantage by comparison with other churches (although he ironically allows a possible qualification of this assertion). But which are these other churches with which the comparison is made? In view of 11.8–9, it might be natural to suppose that they are the other Pauline churches,[545] especially, perhaps, the churches of Macedonia.[546] This interpretation, however, does not account for the emphatic αὐτὸς ἐγώ. For this phrase does not suggest a contrast between Paul's treatment of Corinth and his treatment of his other congregations. Rather it implies that he is contrasting his own work in the Pauline churches with the work of other apostles within their own spheres of activity. These others may comprise some of the Jerusalem apostles and also the rival missionaries in Corinth.[547] These latter,

---

[540] Schlatter, *Paulus*, p. 670.
[541] Bultmann, p. 234.
[542] Héring, p. 98 n. 1.
[543] F G have two variant readings: ἐλαττώθητε for ἡσσώθητε and ἁμαρτίαν for ἀδικίαν. The latter is an assimilation to 11.7.
[544] There are a few grammatical items to note. The ὅ is an accusative of respect. See Moule, *Idiom Book*, p. 131, who explains that: 'the meaning must be *what is there in regard to which you came off worse* ...?' For ὑπέρ after verbs expressing comparison see BAGD s.v. ὑπέρ 2., where the present reference is cited. The ὅτι is probably elliptical, short for ἐν τούτῳ ὅτι, 'in that': see BAGD s.v. ὅτι 1.c. Or perhaps the whole ὅτι-clause is to be seen as in apposition to the opening τί.
[545] So, e.g., Meyer, p. 485; Bruce, p. 250; Barrett, p. 322; Georgi, *Opponents*, p. 292 n. 86.
[546] Furnish, p. 553.
[547] Windisch, pp. 397–8.

we may assume, will have worked in other Christian communities prior to their arrival in Corinth. They will therefore have been able to inform the Corinthians about current practices in the non-Pauline churches. In particular, they may have emphasised that the agents of the Jerusalem mission accept maintenance (as they do themselves) from the churches they found and work in. The Corinthians have been aware of this already (1 Cor 9.3–7), and, as we have noted,[548] Paul's divergence from original apostolic practice may have seemed to cast doubt on their own status as a genuine apostolic foundation.[549] The advent of the new missionaries will have exacerbated their sense of grievance. From their viewpoint they have indeed been put at a disadvantage vis-à-vis these other churches. Paul does not think so, and his basic question here suggests that he requires the answer οὐδέν, 'in no respect'. But he pays lip-service to the Corinthian outlook with the following qualification. There may be an exception as regards his refusal of maintenance. For this he pleads for forgiveness. Most commentators see irony here. It is not easy to define, however, and one wonders whether the Corinthians would have appreciated it.[550] Its main component is the fact that the 'injustice' (ἀδικίαν) Paul is supposed to have done his readers consists of his refusal to 'burden' (οὐ κατενάρκησα) them financially. Windisch comments that this reduces the Corinthian complaint to absurdity.[551] Paul obviously thought so too. He intensifies what he sees as the irony of the situation by means of his language. The verb καταναρκάω is strange,[552] but is presumably intended as a strong word. This is certainly true of ἀδικία. The cognate verb ἀδικέω is used in 7.12 for the commission of the offence which had caused so much trouble between Paul and the congregation in the period following the writing of 1 Corinthians. The irony of his plea for forgiveness of this 'injustice' is further emphasised by the fact that only a few sentences previously, in v. 11, Paul has clearly shown that in his view the Corinthians have behaved badly towards *him*, in that they have failed to support him in face of hostile criticism from his rivals.

[548] See above, p. 703.
[549] Commentators who make the point in their exegesis of the present verse include Windisch, p. 397; Wendland, p. 252; Lietzmann, p. 158; and Tasker, p. 181.
[550] Perhaps they might not immediately have recognised Paul's qualification as ironical. But if they did, they might well have been annoyed by his apparent failure to see their point of view and by his cavalier manner of reference to it. In fact his very next sentence (v. 14) would show that he was not serious in apparently asking for forgiveness (see below).
[551] Windisch, p. 398.
[552] See the note on 11.9.

14. Ἰδοὺ τρίτον τοῦτο⁵⁵³ ἑτοίμως ἔχω ἐλθεῖν πρὸς ὑμᾶς, καὶ οὐ καταναρκήσω. οὐ γὰρ ζητῶ τὰ ὑμῶν ἀλλὰ ὑμᾶς, οὐ γὰρ ὀφείλει τὰ τέκνα τοῖς γονεῦσιν θησαυρίζειν,⁵⁵⁴ ἀλλὰ οἱ γονεῖς τοῖς τέκνοις. Paul turns to the last main topic of his present letter, i.e., his intended third visit to Corinth. No doubt he would in any case have raised the matter before concluding. There is also, however, a specific connection with what he has just written in v. 13, in that he has some more to say about his custom of refusing maintenance.

With the opening ἰδού he may attempt to regain the Corinthians' possibly flagging attention,⁵⁵⁵ or to emphasise the importance of what he is about to say.⁵⁵⁶ In itself, his first sentence is ambiguous. He could be saying, either that this is *the third time*⁵⁵⁷ *he has made preparations*⁵⁵⁸ to visit Corinth (and is now ready to do so), or that he is ready *to visit Corinth for the third time*. The word order could count in favour of the former alternative.⁵⁵⁹ The more substantial arguments, however, support the latter.⁵⁶⁰ The immediate context points to it, since Paul goes on to say that he will not be a (financial) burden to his readers. This is relevant only to an actual stay in Corinth, not to mere preparation for a visit.⁵⁶¹ Next, the comparable assertion in 13.1, τρίτον τοῦτο ἔρχομαι, suggests that in the present verse also the τρίτον modifies the verb ἐλθεῖν.⁵⁶² Lastly, Paul was unlikely to emphasise preparation to visit, since the Corinthians' complaint was that he was perpetually announcing plans to visit them, but the plans never materialised.⁵⁶³

When he visits, he will adhere to his policy of refusing maintenance. He wants the Corinthians themselves, not their financial assistance.⁵⁶⁴ This sounds as though he believed he was

---

⁵⁵³ The τοῦτο is omitted by some witnesses (K L P 614. 629. 945. 1241 *pm* b), probably by accidental error rather than intent. The word adds to the emphasis of the opening ἰδού and is certainly original.

⁵⁵⁴ A few witnesses (𝔓⁴⁶ 630. 1739. 1881 *pc*) place θησαυρίζειν before τοῖς γονεῦσιν. Again, this looks like a simple case of transcriptional error.

⁵⁵⁵ See BAGD s.v. ἰδού 1.a.: the word 'serves to enliven a narrative ... by arousing the attention of hearers or readers'.

⁵⁵⁶ See BAGD s.v. ἰδού 1.b.ε., where 2 Cor 12.14 is cited.

⁵⁵⁷ On τρίτον in the sense '[for] the third time', see BDF 154.

⁵⁵⁸ On ἑτοίμως ἔχω in the sense 'be ready' with a following infinitive see BAGD s.v. ἔχω II.1.; for this general use of ἔχω where English would use 'to be' see Moule, *Idiom Book*, p. 161; and on the adverb used predicatively see MHT, p. 226.

⁵⁵⁹ Belser, pp. 357–8.

⁵⁶⁰ See also Vol. I, p. 54.

⁵⁶¹ Meyer, p. 486; Bachmann, p. 405; Allo, pp. 326–7.

⁵⁶² Windisch, p. 399; Hughes, p. 460; Barrett, p. 323; Martin, p. 440.

⁵⁶³ Windisch, ibid.

⁵⁶⁴ Windisch, ibid., notes an example in Cicero, *Fin.* II 26.85, of the thought that it is the person, not his property, that counts: 'Me igitur ipsum ames oportet non mea, si veri amici futuri sumus' ('So you must love me myself, not my possessions, if we are to be genuine friends' LCL).

under criticism on the grounds that (like the sophists, or some of them) he was only after their money.[565] There may be some hint of this in v. 16. Perhaps the original sense of injury on account of his refusal of a proffered benefaction[566] had turned into suspicion that the rejection of Corinthian funding could not be wholly genuine. He must be getting money from them in some other, devious, way, i.e., by soliciting donations ostensibly for the collection but in actuality for himself. Repudiating any such intention, Paul insists that the Corinthians themselves are his concern. Several commentators claim that his ultimate objective in all this is to restore the relationship between the Corinthians and Christ.[567] The implication of such exegesis would seem to be that any criticism of Paul as their apostle is at the same time a form of alienation from Christ himself. But he does not precisely say this, and such a total identification of himself with Christ would surely suggest some degree of egocentricity on his part.[568] It may simply be that the Corinthians' suspicions of him are inimical to their acceptance of the pastoral guidance which they so clearly need (vv. 20–21) from him, and which he would wish to provide in an affectionate manner.

With the second half of the verse Paul seems both to substantiate his immediately previous disclaimer (that he is not *seeking* financial profit from his readers) and also to offer further justification for the alleged 'wrong' (v. 13) he had done the Corinthians (in not *accepting* financial help). Whilst his own attitude (*vis-à-vis* the Corinthians, at least) is consistent, it does look as though he is responding to disparate criticisms. However that may be, his response is seen to take the form of a statement of a natural law: the obligation of parents to support their children, and not the converse.[569] It is the converse which is stated first, and is the more important.[570] It is not the responsibility of the Corinthians to

---

[565] Windisch, ibid.; cf. Bultmann, p. 235.

[566] See above on 11.7, pp. 682–3.

[567] Barrett, p. 323; Furnish, p. 564; Martin, p. 440.

[568] This would be particularly the case if Furnish is correct when he suggests that (in Paul's view) it would be the Corinthians' 'gift of their lives to Christ' that would demonstrate Paul's *own* apostolic legitimacy. Nevertheless, this interpretation of the apostle's thinking is by no means impossible.

[569] Chrysostom, *PG* 61 col. 586 (NPNF XII, p. 405). Evidence that the obligation was seen in this way in Paul's day is provided by Philo, *Vit. Mos.* (*Life of Moses*) II 245 (cited by Windisch, p. 399): νόμος φύσεως ἐστι κληρονομεῖσθαι γονεῖς ὑπὸ παίδων ἀλλὰ μὴ τούτους κληρονομεῖν ('in the natural order of things, sons are the heirs of their fathers, and not fathers of their sons', LCL). Whilst this concerns inheritance, the basic motif would no doubt be seen as applicable also in respect of the general support of children by parents. Other commentators likewise see a concept of natural law as the basis for Paul's words here: Bultmann, p. 235; Furnish, p. 558; Martin, p. 441.

[570] See below, on v. 15, for a discussion of Paul's responsibility to make provision for his converts.

'store up', θησαυρίζειν, provision for him. The reference is obviously financial, but is there, in addition, some more specific significance in the use of this particular verb? It does suggest the saving up of money. Consequently, both Plummer and Martin think that what Paul is disallowing is the raising of some kind of standing fund for him, as distinct from day-to-day, or occasional, monetary help.[571] Martin suggests that some such fund might have been established for the rival missionaries.[572] The idea is interesting. But it is fairly clear from 11.7–8 that Paul's refusal of Corinthian financial help was not confined to the rejection of capital: his practice in Corinth is contrasted with his acceptance of 'wages', ὀψώνιον, from the Macedonians.

The force of the argument depends on the validity of the natural law to which Paul refers, and on the validity also of his understanding of his own role as the Corinthians' spiritual father and its consequent implications. Unfortunately, he perhaps has to overlook, consciously or unconsciously, some difficulties in his position. First, if he were consistent in this interpretation of spiritual fatherhood, he would accept nothing at all from *any* church of his own spiritual begetting. But he has admitted (11.8–9) that he has received financial help from other churches. Secondly, if he takes his stand here on this principle of natural law, he implies that the Lord's command to which he refers in 1 Cor 9.14 constitutes a contravention of the law of nature. Is this really likely, from his point of view? Thirdly, in 1 Cor 9.3–7 he not only had accepted the propriety of receiving maintenance but had also appealed to natural human custom in support of the practice.[573] These problems may be mitigated to some extent by Bultmann's suggestion that what we have here is a saying which, like a proverb, is conceived of as a general truth, applicable in suitable cases (as here), but not to be taken as a binding law in every instance.[574] In any case, the imagery in which the general principle is expressed is different here from that of 1 Cor 9.3–7, 13–14. In fact, if the Jesus-saying to which Paul refers in 1 Cor 9.14 is that of Luke 10.7 (= Mt 10.10), i.e., that the labourer is worthy of his wage (or sustenance), the difference is substantial, and Paul could well have argued, if challenged on the point, that he had two separate natural principles in mind. The first difficulty is more intractable, however. The Macedonians (11.9) were just as much his spiritual children as were the Corinthians.[575]

He is more concerned to press this point, however, in the case

---

[571] Plummer, p. 362; Martin, p. 441.
[572] Martin, ibid.
[573] These difficulties are noted by Windisch, pp. 399–400.
[574] Bultmann, p. 236.
[575] See Excursus XII, on apostolic maintenance, pp. 704, 706–7.

of the Corinthians, because this spiritual paternity sets him apart from the rival apostles and distinguishes his legitimate authority in the Corinthian church from what he regards as their spurious authority. And the distinctive mark of his paternity, in this church, is that, like a responsible parent, he does not expect, or allow, his spiritual children to provide his living expenses.[576] Hence, there could be here some implicit allusion to his opponents. But might there be some further reference to them, the financial difference apart? Georgi claims that this is so. These people saw themselves as 'divine men' who embodied the divine law (the νόμος ἔμψυχος), which brings order to the cosmos, is identical with the natural law, and binds together the community. Georgi continues: 'In his counterargument, Paul would be saying that true *lex naturae* was the principle of community expressed in continuous human relationships, not the self-confident will of the pneumatic projected into the cosmos.'[577] One has to say that this exegesis seems highly improbable. Although Paul bases his argument on a principle of life which could be, and was, regarded as a natural law, he is not here concerned with quasi-philosophical distinctions between true and false conceptions of natural law itself. The words νόμος and φύσις occur neither singly nor in combination.

15. ἐγὼ δὲ ἥδιστα δαπανήσω καὶ ἐκδαπανηθήσομαι ὑπὲρ τῶν ψυχῶν ὑμῶν. εἰ[578] περισσοτέρως ὑμᾶς ἀγαπῶ[ν], ἧσσον ἀγαπῶμαι; Paul intends that his own conduct should be seen as an intensified individual expression of the general rule he has just propounded.[579] He will 'very gladly'[580] 'spend and be (totally) spent' for the sake of his own spiritual children. The phrasing is rhetorical.[581] Does this mean that there is no difference in sense between the simple verb δαπανήσω and the compound ἐκδαπαν-ηθήσομαι, i.e., that the latter simply intensifies the force of the former? Or are we to understand that the compound possesses some further content? Windisch opts for the second possibility. The simple δαπανήσω refers to the fact that Paul will himself take financial responsibility for his support. The compound ἐκδαπαν-ηθήσομαι relates in a more general way to his life of complete

---

[576] See the exegesis of 11.12.

[577] Georgi, *Opponents*, p. 241.

[578] See below, pp. 848–9, on the complicated textual variant which concerns both the beginning of v. 15b and the ἀγαπῶ[ν].

[579] The ἐγώ is emphatic, by virtue both of its presence and of its initial position in the sentence. If in v. 14 there is some implicit allusion to the different status and practice of his opponents, the ἐγώ may serve also to mark the contrast, as Filson, p. 413, suggests.

[580] See BDF 60(2): ἥδιστα is an elative superlative, as in v. 9.

[581] Paul uses virtually the same verb in different forms, active and passive.

self-sacrifice; cf. Phil 2.17[582] Barrett, however, suggests that the simple δαπανήσω itself possesses a wider reference: it includes monetary sacrifice, but also the expenditure of 'time, energy, and love'.[583] Hence, the content of the two verbs is fundamentally the same, although the ἐκ of the compound will have perfective force.[584] Paul's self-sacrifice, that is, will continue to its completion.[585] This is preferable. It does justice both to the similarity and to the difference between the one verb and the other. Paul is concerned for the Corinthians' total welfare and is therefore talking throughout of self-expenditure in the widest sense. Indirectly, this has a financial aspect, but it is primarily spiritual resources that he labours to provide for them.[586]

Nevertheless, the financial question is implicitly to the fore in what follows. It was previously mentioned in connection with the matter of Paul's love for the Corinthians (11.7–11), and in v. 15 he returns to it more explicitly, asking a rhetorical question.[587] Does his own greater degree of love meet with less love from his readers?[588] In fact he believes it does. But by using the interrogatory form he avoids outright condemnation and leaves room for a change in their attitude.[589] Furthermore, he does not suggest that they have no love for him at all,[590] but speaks of degrees of love.[591] All the same, the question is a reproach. Windisch notes the view that it is natural for love to beget love, citing Plutarch to this effect.[592] The Corinthians then, in Paul's eyes, were behaving

---

[582] Windisch, p. 400; followed by Bultmann, p. 236.

[583] Barrett, p. 324; followed by Martin, p. 443.

[584] Barrett, ibid.

[585] BDF 318(5).

[586] This does not, however, mean that the term ψυχή in the phrase ὑπὲρ τῶν ψυχῶν ὑμῶν has the sense 'soul', 'human spirit'. According to Jewett, *Anthropological Terms*, p. 346, Paul does not use the word 'in the sense of the higher, God-related life'. It appears to function simply as a more emphatic equivalent of the personal pronoun 'you': see, e.g., NRSV, REB; Furnish, p. 557. It may be used here to balance the opening emphatic ἐγώ.

[587] Bultmann, p. 237.

[588] See below on the textual variants. The sense is basically the same whichever reading is preferred.

[589] Martin, p. 444.

[590] By contrast, it would seem that the Corinthians themselves had charged Paul with a total lack of love for them (11.11).

[591] It is best, with Plummer, p. 363, and Martin, p. 444, to see the περισσοτέρως as correlated simply with the ἧσσον, 'the more ... the less', so that no point of comparison external to the sentence itself needs to be understood. Lietzmann, p. 158, suggests 'more than others do', but this would require the addition of ἐγώ, according to Bultmann, pp. 236–7, who notes the possibility of 'more than other churches' (so also Windisch, p. 401); this is rejected by Plummer, p. 363, since ὑμᾶς does not possess the required emphasis.

[592] Windisch, p. 401. The citation runs: ποιεῖ γὰρ τὸ πιστεύειν δοκεῖν πιστεύεσθαι, καὶ τὸ φιλεῖν φιλεῖσθαι ('For seeming confidence begets confidence, and love, love', LCL); see Plut., *Mor.* 143C.

unnaturally. But of course they would have seen the situation differently. Whilst for Paul his refusal of their financial assistance was a sign of his affection for them, for them it would be his acceptance of their offer that would be the proof of love.[593]

15b: The Text

In v. 15b there are two interrelated variants:

(i) εἰ περισσοτέρως   𝔓⁴⁶ ℵ* A B F G 33. 81* pc co
    εἰ καὶ περισσοτέρως   ℵ² D¹ Ψ 0243 𝔐 f vg sy
    περισσοτέρως   D* a g r Ambst
(ii) ἀγαπῶ   ℵ* A 33. 104*. 1241. 2495 pc
    ἀγαπῶν   𝔓⁴⁶ ℵ² B D F G Ψ 0243 𝔐 latt

If, for the major witnesses, we amalgamate the two sets of evidence, there are four possible readings of v. 15b as a whole:

(a) εἰ περισσοτέρως ὑμᾶς ἀγαπῶν ἧσσον   𝔓⁴⁶ B F G
    ἀγαπῶμαι
(b) εἰ περισσοτέρως ὑμᾶς ἀγαπῶ, ἧσσον   ℵ* A 33
    ἀγαπῶμαι
(c) περισσοτέρως ὑμᾶς ἀγαπῶν ἧσσον ἀγαπῶμαι   D*
(d) εἰ καὶ περισσοτέρως ὑμᾶς ἀγαπῶν ἧσσον   ℵ² D¹ Ψ 0243
    ἀγαπῶμαι

Readings (a) and (d) demonstrate the problem that is in some way the basis of the variant: the combination of εἰ with the participle ἀγαπῶν is syntactically incorrect, or apparently so.

Of these four possibilities, reading (c) can be discarded as secondary. D* stands alone amongst the Greek MSS in its lack of introductory εἰ. It is almost certainly evidence of an attempt to amend the syntax of some exemplar containing reading (a). Reading (d) also looks secondary. It could be explained as an amendment of (a), understood as the protasis of v. 15a (see below). The basic choice is between readings (a) and (b). Reading (b) presents no difficulty of sense or syntax. In addition, it could well give rise to reading (a) through a simple scribal error, i.e., the careless addition of N to ΑΓΑΠΩ. But it is equally possible, of course, that (b) derives from (a) as a result of scribal correction, and that (a) should be accepted as the *lectio difficilior*. In view of this possibility, it may be useful to ask whether there are any ways of rescuing the apparently incorrect syntax of (a). There are two which have received mention. First, it could be that the whole of v. 15b functions as the protasis of a conditional sentence in which the apodosis, v. 15a, is placed first.[594] Paul will be saying that *if*,

---

[593] Georgi, *Opponents*, pp. 241–2.
[594] Meyer, p. 487.

loving the Corinthians, he is loved the less by them, *then* he will gladly spend and be spent on their behalf. This scarcely makes much sense. The apostle's self-sacrifice for his spiritual children would hardly be *conditioned* by their *lack* of love for him. He might, of course, express the determination so to sacrifice himself *even if* they themselves have the less love for him. But this would require us to accept reading (d),[595] where the καί looks like a scribal addition, made precisely to alleviate the difficulty of (a) when syntactically attached to v. 15a. Secondly, it might be that Paul has left the reader to supply the finite verb εἰμί with ἀγαπῶν, thus forming a periphrastic tense. This is rejected by Metzger, however, on the ground that 'nowhere else does Paul make this kind of demand'.[596] But there could be a third option. The introductory εἰ could be understood not as conditional but as interrogative. Although this idiom is not found elsewhere in Paul, it does occur in other NT writers, and in the LXX.[597] Paul could well have been familiar with it. At least this interpretation does not require either an unwieldy attachment of v. 15b to v. 15a or the assumption that Paul is using a periphrastic tense but has omitted the essential element of εἰμί.

Decision between (a) and (b) is difficult, and can be only tentative. But the extent of the evidence in support of the participle ἀγαπῶν is rather impressive. Certainly it occurs in the two readings, (c) and (d), that we have categorised as secondary. But it may have been the persistent presence of the participle in the textual tradition which in part was responsible for the other variations. With hesitation we might opt for reading (a), the *lectio difficilior*, and suggest that the opening εἰ should be understood as interrogative.

16. Ἔστω δέ, ἐγὼ οὐ κατεβάρησα ὑμᾶς· ἀλλὰ ὑπάρχων πανοῦργος δόλῳ ὑμᾶς ἔλαβον. Now Paul clearly alludes to the complaint that appears to lie (somewhat inconsistently) beneath his previous words in v. 14.[598] In some way or other he has taken financial advantage of the Corinthians, and in a cunning fashion. He assumes their agreement[599] that he

[595] With Allo, p. 327.
[596] Metzger, *Textual Commentary*[1], p. 586.
[597] See MHT, p. 333. Examples quoted are: Mt 12.10; 19.3; Lk 13.23; Acts 1.6; Gen 17.17; 1 Kgdms 10.24; 2 Macc 7.7.
[598] See above, p. 844.
[599] The third singular imperative of εἰμί is used here as an argumentative device. It enables Paul to proceed from a position on which he assumes his readers will be in general agreement (see Furnish, p. 558) to a point on which he detects possible disagreement. Windisch, p. 402 n. 1, notes parallels in Epictetus. See *Diss.* II 4.5: ἔστω γάρ, φίλου οὐ δύνασαι τόπον ἔχειν. δούλου δύνασαι; ('For, assuming that you cannot hold the place of a friend, can you hold that of a slave?', LCL); see also I 29.22. The δέ has an inceptive function, marking the transition to a further point (as in 1 Cor 7.1, 25; 8.1; 11.2; 12.1).

himself[600] has not directly burdened[601] them, i.e., by openly requiring monetary assistance. But since he is crafty by nature,[602] he will have managed to get funds from them by some other means. Perhaps he is quoting what his opponents are actually saying about him, claiming such conduct to be a past fact.[603] Alternatively, he may simply be aware that suspicions of his financial probity were at least latent, if not already emerging, and may aim to forestall specific criticisms by answering them in advance. This, though, is less probable (see below).[604]

What, then, is implied by the criticism, actual or anticipated, that Paul is πανοῦργος?[605] The word was used in a bad sense quite generally,[606] and could be employed against opponents of any kind.[607] But it occurs more particularly, according to Betz, in polemic against the sophists[608] and against religious superstition. These two targets went together, since there was a tendency to identify religious charlatans with those regarded as fake philosophers. The dividing line was fluid. Furthermore, the charge of avarice was brought against both groups.[609] When Paul uses the term πανοῦργος in a context where he is defending his financial integrity, it is surely very likely, Betz suggests, that there is some connection with the polemics of the philosophical and religious

---

[600] The ἐγώ is emphatic (so Furnish, p. 558), contrasting Paul himself with the associates he is about to mention.

[601] On the verb καταβαρέω, see BAGD s.v. Some witnesses (F G 81. [104]. 326. 629. [1881 pc].) read κατενάρκησα ὑμῶν (ὑμᾶς 104. 1881 pc), obviously by assimilation to v. 13. Two MSS (𝔓46 D*) read ἐβάρησα ὑμᾶς: the more familiar simple verb will have been substituted for the compound. The reading κατεβάρησα ὑμᾶς (A B D2 Ψ 0243 𝔐) is original.

[602] There is some agreement that the participle ὑπάρχων may be more than a somewhat colourless equivalent of ὤν, 'being'. Plummer, p. 363, suggests that it almost contains the connotation φύσει, 'by nature', and Hughes, p. 464 n. 150, renders it 'being by constitution'. In addition, it may have a causal function. See Moule, Idiom Book, pp. 102–3; Furnish, p. 559.

[603] Plummer, p. 363; Windisch, pp. 402–3, thinks this is posibible.

[604] It is even less likely, pace Betz, Tradition, p. 117, that Paul is implicitly characterising his opponents as swindlers. This seems over-elaborate.

[605] This is the only occurrence of the word in the NT, although the cognate noun πανουργία occurs in Lk 20.23; 1 Cor 3.19; 2 Cor 4.2; 11.3; Eph 4.14. On 2 Cor 4.2 see Vol. I, pp. 300–1, n. 772, where Windisch, p. 133, is cited as noting the use of the word πανουργία in the philosophical polemic against the sophists.

[606] See BAGD s.v. πανοῦργος. The primary use is pejorative in Plato and Philo, and it is always unfavourable in early Christian literature; the meanings given are 'clever', 'crafty', 'sly'. See also LSJ s.v.: the basic meaning is 'ready to do anything', 'wicked', 'knavish'; also, in a less pejorative sense, 'cunning', 'clever', 'smart'.

[607] Betz, Tradition, p. 104.

[608] The use in relation to the sophists starts with Plato. See Betz, Tradition, p. 105 nn. 440–1, who cites, e.g., Soph. 239C; Protag. 317B; Gorg. 499B; Phaedr. 271C; see also n. 447 for reference to Diog. Laert. IV 46f., 49, 52.

[609] Betz, Tradition, pp. 104–5. See also Winter, Sophists, p. 218 and n. 73, on the charge of avarice.

milieu in which the apostle worked.[610] This may be so, but it is not very easy to see exactly what this connection would be. If we suppose Paul himself to be engaging in some way in anti-sophistic polemic,[611] he would apply the word to the rival missionaries, not to himself. Conversely, if it is a term used by his critics, to denigrate him, what would be the connection with the polemic against sophists? Paul is not a sophist (and the Corinthians seem to have favoured sophists). It would be better to suppose that it was simply religious charlatanism that he believed himself (in danger of being) charged with. But again, how plausible is this? Far from engineering really impressive displays of fake miracles, he seems to have produced little that was very memorable in the way of apostolic signs (12.12). He would scarcely have made much money, if any, as a γόης—a sorcerer,[612] or a (religious) cheat[613] (pretending to powers he did not possess). All in all, *pace* Betz, it seems more probable that the term πανοῦργος is used here in a quite general pejorative sense: '(craftily) clever'.

Having this sort of character, then, according to his critics, Paul has exploited his correspondents, it is claimed, by means of trickery. He has 'caught' them.[614] The metaphorical expression[615] may be his own: he has used the verb λαμβάνω in a similar way in 11.20.[616] At the same time it is very probable that he is responding to an accusation that has actually been made.[617] Why should he take the risk of putting ideas into his readers' heads, or of bringing to the surface suspicions that were merely latent and might die away? The charge may have originated with the rival missionaries[618] or with the Corinthians themselves.[619] The distinction is a fine one, since in the state of affairs that apparently prevailed in Corinth any casual insinuation suggested in the one group would have been taken up readily by the other group as well. From what foliows in vv. 17–18 it is clear what the content of the insinuation was. Paul had exploited the Corinthians financially through the agency of those fellow-workers whom he had sent to Corinth as his envoys. The details, however, are lacking, and are not easy to

---

[610] Betz, *Tradition*, p. 115, and preceding pp. 105–14.
[611] As Betz appears to do.
[612] LSJ s.v. γόης 1.
[613] Ibid. 2. Here it is noted that γόης is connected with σοφιστής in Plato, *Symp.* (*Symposium*) 203D. Ἔρως (Love) is described as δεινὸς γόης ... καὶ σοφιστής ('a master of jugglery ... and artful speech' LCL).
[614] BAGD s.v. λαμβάνω 1.c.
[615] The metaphor is derived from the literal use in hunting and fishing: BAGD ibid.
[616] See above, pp. 716–17.
[617] Plummer, p. 364; Hughes, p. 464; Martin, p. 445.
[618] Hughes, ibid.; Martin, ibid.
[619] Furnish, p. 557.

supply. We shall return to this question after we have considered these two verses.

17. μή τινα ὧν ἀπέσταλκα πρὸς ὑμᾶς, δι' αὐτοῦ ἐπλεονέκτησα ὑμᾶς; Paul first issues a general denial. He had used none of his envoys to exploit the Corinthians. The sense is plain enough, but the syntax is confused. A literal rendering of the sentence would run: 'Surely it is not the case that [μή] anyone of those I have sent to you, I exploited you through him?' The simplest explanation, proposed by Plummer, is that Paul may originally have had in mind a sentence shaped differently, which would have run: 'Have I ever sent anyone to you through whom you were defrauded?'[620] No explanation of the transition to the present sentence is offered, however, except for a reference to Paul's 'eagerness' which has caused him to forget the construction he started with. It could be that, having begun with τινά as the intended object of ἀπέσταλκα[621] as the main verb of the sentence, he immediately realised that it was not the sending that was the important point but rather the alleged exploitation. He would then have altered the intended construction, making πλεονεκτέω the main verb and relegating ἀποστέλλω to the relative clause. If this is the explanation, we should still need to show that the resulting sentence is in some way tolerable. It may be that it combines two idioms found elsewhere in the NT. First, the τινα ... δι' αὐτοῦ is an example of a suspended noun or pronoun (i.e., a noun or pronoun unrelated grammatically to the main sentence) which is resumed (in effect repeated) by a pronoun in another case (correctly related to the main sentence).[622] Secondly, there are two (combined and highly compressed) instances of case attraction. The full form of the phrase preceding ἀπέσταλκα would be τινὰ τούτων οὕς:[623] the accusative case of τινά is due to the required accusative of the relative pronoun. But this pronoun has itself been attracted into the case of its implicit antecedent τούτων.[624]

The general question of the origin of the charges to which Paul

---

[620] Plummer, p. 364. See also Windisch, p. 403, who proposes that the existing sentence could be a complex variation of: μή τινα ἀπέσταλκα δι' οὗ ἐπλεονέκτησα ὑμᾶς;

[621] According to Moulton, *Prolegomena*, p. 144, this is an example of 'a perfect of broken ... continuity': 'those whom (from time to time) I have sent'; cf. Martin, pp. 446–7, who sees the verb as an 'iterative perfect'. Turner, MHT, p. 70, however, claims it is aoristic; cf. Furnish, p. 559, who refers to the aorist συναπέστειλα in v. 18a. But the latter clearly refers to one single mission. The more natural interpretation of the τινα ὧν ἀπέσταλκα in v. 17 is that Paul has in view an undetermined plurality of associates sent to Corinth at different times.

[622] BDF 466(1).

[623] Ibid.

[624] BDF 294(4).

is responding will be discussed in the exegesis of v. 18. Here it will be convenient to consider the form of his response, which is felt to present some difficulty. In both verses it consists simply of a rhetorical question, introduced by a negative particle (μή in the present verse, μήτι in v. 18) which thus indicates that a negative reply is expected:[625] Paul is *not* guilty of financial sharp practice, even via his envoys. According to Windisch, it is surprising that so detestable a suspicion should be disposed of in this somewhat cavalier way.[626] Lietzmann supposes that no one had actually voiced such a suspicion. Rather, Paul is suggesting a logical possibility, so as to produce a *reductio ad absurdum* argument.[627] But this is unlikely. Why, as we have said already, would he put ideas into the opponents' heads? Betz, rather differently, suggests that the questions are intended not to defend the apostle but to castigate the rival missionaries. The verb πλεονεκτέω was used as a pejorative term to describe the conduct of sophists and charlatans.[628] Paul's own rejection of financial assistance is evidence that he does not himself belong to this category, and neither do his assistants, who follow his own practice. But by means of his rhetorical disclaimer on his own (and their) behalf he aims to discredit his opponents as sophists. It is against them that the charge of exploitation is really directed.[629] One is bound to ask, however, how the Corinthians were expected to grasp a charge so indirectly expressed. Moreover, the emphatic ἐγώ of v. 16, in the context of vv. 16–18, does not point to a contrast between Paul and the rival missionaries. It indicates the distinction his readers were making between his open conduct in person and the conduct of the envoys through whom, as they supposed, he was deviously exploiting them. There may be different reasons for the rhetorical form of Paul's response to this suspicion. In the first place, he may not know the origin or at least the details of the accusation,[630] in which case he can reply to it only with plain denial, given more force by its rhetorical formulation. But, secondly, the rhetorical questions assume his readers' agreement. He might intend in this way to indicate cor.·.dence in their fundamental support for him, despite everytuing. The form of his response would tacitly demonstrate the affection he has spoken of in v. 15.

18. παρεκάλεσα Τίτον καὶ συναπέστειλα τὸν ἀδελφόν· μήτι

[625] See BDR 440.
[626] Windisch, p. 403.
[627] Lietzmann, p. 159.
[628] Betz, *Tradition*, p. 116, with reference, n. 536, to G. Delling, on πλεονεκτέω, in *TWNT* VI, pp. 266–74.
[629] Betz, *Tradition*, pp. 116–17.
[630] Cf. Furnish, p. 565.

ἐπλεονέκτησεν ὑμᾶς Τίτος; οὐ τῷ αὐτῷ πνεύματι περιεπατήσαμεν; οὐ τοῖς αὐτοῖς ἴχνεσιν; At this point Paul appears to suppose that the Corinthians' suspicions may have focused on one particular occasion when his delegates visited Corinth.⁶³¹ If, as we have just suggested, he knew no details about the reason for the charge of financial exploitation, we must assume that he mentions this visit as the one most likely, in his mind, to evoke it. The obvious conclusion would be that it was some visit concerned with the collection. Perhaps, then, Paul is looking back at the occasion to which he refers in 8.16–24: there he was making plans for Titus's visit to Corinth, whilst here he alludes to it as a past event.⁶³² In both passages Titus is not the sole envoy. But there are difficulties with this explanation. The major problem is that in 8.16–24 Titus is to be accompanied by two colleagues, but here by only one. The difficulty is not to be solved by the argument that only one of the two in chap. 8 is Paul's own delegate, so that the other, not open to suspicion, would not be mentioned in the present verse. For in 8.18, 22, both are sent by Paul.⁶³³ A secondary problem would relate to the fact that in the case of the mission of 8.16–24 Paul had clearly taken precautions to avoid any charge of malpractice.⁶³⁴ Hence, it may be correct to suppose that here he is referring to the earlier visit by Titus to which he has alluded in 8.6.⁶³⁵ It is true that there is no reference in that verse to any accompanying ἀδελφός, but the allusion is brief, confined to a subordinate clause, and there would be no reason at this point to provide details of the mission.

Did Paul, in the present verse, originally name Titus's colleague? The unqualified ἀδελφός is odder here than the ἀδελφοί has seemed to be in 8.18 and 22, for two reasons: first, because in the previous verses the two 'brothers' are to some extent described, even though they remain anonymous; secondly, because in chap. 8 Paul is referring to people not yet known personally to the Corinthians, whilst here, obviously, the 'brother' in question has made personal contact with them. In discussing chap. 8 we have adopted the suggestion proposed by Betz, i.e.,

---

⁶³¹ Windisch, p. 403, notes that παρεκάλεσα Τίτον has to be supplemented by some such phrase as ἵνα ἔρχηται πρὸς ὑμᾶς. The meaning of παρακαλέω here is more likely 'request' (see BAGD s.v. 3., with this reference), 'ask' (so Barrett, p. 318), than 'urge' (BAGD s.v. 2.; both Furnish, p. 557, and Martin, p. 425, favour 'urge'). Titus and his colleague are instanced as a specific example of those whom, in v. 17, Paul has *sent* to the city. And note the implication of συναπέστειλα here.
⁶³² So Barrett, p. 325; 'Titus', p. 127; also Bruce, pp. 168–9, 251; Furnish, p. 566.
⁶³³ Watson, 'Painful Letter', p. 333; see also Vol. I, p. 15, n. 90.
⁶³⁴ The ἀδελφοί are accountable to the churches as well as to Paul.
⁶³⁵ So Martin, p. 448. And see above on 8.6. Klauck, p. 98, likewise supposes Paul to refer here to Titus's first visit to Corinth, which was concerned exclusively with the collection.

that Paul deliberately left the two ἀδελφοί anonymous because he did not wish to give the impression of having authorised them as individuals.[636] This motivation scarcely seems applicable in the present instance. There would not, either, be any obvious reason for a later deletion of an original name. Perhaps this earlier ἀδελφός was simply so much of a subordinate to Titus that the Corinthians would not have supposed him capable of any independent financial trickery. Paul might have been aware of this, and so have seen no reason to mention him specifically by name: 'the (his) colleague' would do well enough. That it is Titus who is the predominantly significant figure in respect of the Corinthians' suspicions is obvious from the following rhetorical question which refers to him alone.

The outright denial that Titus had exploited the Corinthians is supported by two further rhetorical questions, which this time indicate that an affirmative answer is expected.[637] Surely his behaviour in Corinth and Paul's behaviour were identical. Figuratively, they 'walked in the same footsteps'.[638] There is obviously a reference to their practical conduct.[639] But does the τῷ αὐτῷ πνεύματι mean that, in respect of this behaviour, they were guided by the same (Holy) Spirit, or that they displayed the same (human) disposition? Windisch opts for the first alternative. Paul refers to the Spirit of Christ.[640] In favour of this interpretation we could cite Gal 5.16: πνεύματι περιπατεῖτε.[641] In the context, Paul is clearly speaking of the Holy Spirit. But in the present verse the parallelism with the last, elliptical, sentence, '(we walked) in the same footsteps', which refers to human behaviour, suggests that the πνεῦμα here is the human disposition.[642] The point is that Titus and Paul conducted themselves identically, in spirit and in practice.

What, then, could have been the origin of the charge that Paul had exploited the Corinthians financially via his envoys? Plummer suggests, as one reason for it, that some of these envoys had in fact received maintenance money whilst in Corinth, and that Paul was thought to have shared in it.[643] Were that the case, however, he could scarcely claim the direct opposite as he does

---

[636] See Excursus VIII, p. 558.
[637] See BDR 440.
[638] See BAGD s.v. ἴχνος 1.; s.v. περιπατέω 2.
[639] The verb περιπατέω indicates that this is the case, and the context requires it.
[640] Windisch, p. 404; cf. NEB, REB.
[641] Furnish, p. 560, though favouring the second alternative, notes that this instance supports Windisch. He draws attention also to the use of τὸ αὐτὸ πνεῦμα of the Holy Spirit in 1 Cor 12.8, 9, 11.
[642] Barrett, p. 326; Furnish, ibid.; Martin, p. 449.
[643] Plummer, p. 364.

here (v. 18).[644] It is much more likely that the accusation had something to do with monies donated for the collection.[645] The reference to Titus in v. 18 would suggest it.[646] Titus heads the collection mission for which detailed arrangements are set out in 8.16–24, and according to 8.6 he had made an earlier visit to Corinth on collection business.[647] Even so, it is not altogether easy to envisage the nature of the charge. The money contributed by the Corinthians would presumably have remained in Corinth until the final journey of the delegates to Jerusalem (1 Cor 16.1–4). And whilst Paul's associates are seemingly suspected of its misappropriation there is no indication that they were accused of outright theft. Strachan suggests that some of this money may have been set aside to provide the eventual travel expenses of the delegates, including Paul himself, who were to convey the collection proceeds to their destination, and that this could have been the basis of the charge of financial exploitation.[648] But Paul appears to be talking here of some accusation relating to the past conduct of his envoys. Nevertheless, the suggestion that it may have had something to do with travel expenses may be helpful.

Perhaps the situation might be reconstructed in the following way. The accusation of financial exploitation was based on Titus's first collection visit to Corinth (8.6). It cannot relate to the second such visit (8.16–24), since Paul had taken precautions against suspicion of fraud on this occasion. On the first visit, Titus (with his colleague) must have received money from the Corinthians, not for maintenance whilst in Corinth, but for some purpose which Paul could have been assumed to sanction. Travel expenses would come into this category. In particular, Paul was expecting that the Corinthians would provide for him in this way for his eventual journey to Jerusalem to deliver the collection proceeds (1.16). If the Corinthians, at this earlier stage very willing to co-operate, had offered Titus money to meet the cost of his travel on his first collection visit to Corinth, he could well have felt free to accept the offer. But when Corinthian opinion began to turn against Paul, this donation to Titus might be remembered to his, and Paul's, discredit. Ought not the apostle to have financed his

---

[644] We should have to suppose that his own associates, Titus in particular, had given him a dishonest report of their practice in Corinth.

[645] Plummer (as a second suggestion), ibid.; Hughes, p. 464; Barrett, p. 324; Bultmann, p. 237; Martin, p. 446; Windisch, p. 403.

[646] Furnish, p. 565.

[647] The specific mention of Titus may be sufficient, therefore, to indicate Paul's awareness that the Corinthians' accusations may have something to do with the collection (*pace* Prümm, *Diakonia Pneumatos* 1, p. 688, and Betz, *Tradition*, p. 116 n. 538).

[648] Strachan, p. 35, n. 1.

envoys' travel himself? Perhaps he had done so, by calling upon the resources of the church where he was for the time resident. And if so, he had exploited the Corinthians, indirectly obtaining money from them on false pretence, for travel already funded. The charge would then grow and become more general, and Paul, unaware of its origin, would be at a loss to know how to respond, other than by outright denial.

It would be what the Corinthians had begun to see as the apostle's fraudulence that would account for the apparently contradictory attitude noted by some commentators. On the one hand, it seems that they blame Paul for his refusal to accept money from them (vv. 13–15), whilst on the other hand they claim that he has been exploiting them financially (vv. 16–18). There is no indication that the two charges come from two different groups of people.[649] It could be that both accusations come from the rival missionaries, who simply want to make doubly sure that Paul is put in a bad light.[650] But since the charges relate to his past dealings with the Corinthians, it is more probable that they come in the first instance from the church members themselves. Their displeasure at Paul's refusal to allow them public status and consequent honour as his financial patrons would be exacerbated by the suspicion that privately he had been getting money from them indirectly via his assistants.

3. CONCLUSION OF THE LETTER: CHAPTERS 12–13 (12.19–13.13)

(i) *Anxiety about the Corinthians' moral state* (12.19–21)

[19]Have you been thinking for a long time that we are presenting our defence to you? It is before God, in Christ, that we speak. And all this, beloved, is for your edification. [20]For I fear lest perhaps, when I arrive, I might find you not such as I wish, and that I myself might be found, in your view, to be such as you do not wish: lest perhaps there might be discord, envy, outbursts of anger, factiousness, slander, whispered gossip, conceit, disorder. [21]I am anxious lest, when I arrive, my God may again humiliate me before you, and I should grieve over many of those who have previously sinned and did not repent of the immorality, fornication and debauchery which they practised.

Paul has not been speaking to obtain a judicial verdict from the Corinthians, but for the sake of their spiritual and moral welfare, and on account of his love for them. He expresses his anxiety lest

---

[649] *Pace* Windisch, p. 402, and Bultmann, p. 237.
[650] So Martin, p. 445.

he should find various kinds of sinful behaviour, new and old, prevalent in the congregation when he arrives.

12.19–21 as translatio. Sundermann sees in these verses a transference of Paul's angle of vision. Instead of demanding the Corinthians' judicial verdict on his defence, he now moves the proceedings, as it were, to another 'court'. He casts his readers in a new role as recipients of a 'love-letter', and it is now their own conduct, not Paul's, that becomes questionable.[651] Formally speaking, this seems a correct appraisal of the function of these three verses. Initially it might seem that v. 19 on its own would be adequate as a means of transition from Paul's defence of his own apostolicity to his concern for the moral welfare of the Corinthians. But since vv. 20–21 are grammatically attached to v. 19 (φοβοῦμαι γάρ ... μὴ πάλιν ...), whilst 13.1 has no such connection with 12.21, the present division of the text will be correct.

19. Πάλαι δοκεῖτε ὅτι ὑμῖν ἀπολογούμεθα; κατέναντι θεοῦ ἐν Χριστῷ λαλοῦμεν· τὰ δὲ πάντα, ἀγαπητοί, ὑπὲρ τῆς ὑμῶν οἰκοδομῆς. In view of the immediately preceding assertions of Paul's financial probity the reference here to self-defence is scarcely surprising. Indeed, the question is raised by the contents of the whole letter up to this point (i.e., chaps. 10–12), as Paul implicitly recognises in his introductory πάλαι, 'for a long time', 'all along'.[652] The Corinthians may well think that self-vindication is what he has been engaged in. But does he here state definitely that they do think this, or is he, more tentatively, asking whether this might be the way they have understood him? Is the sentence a statement or a question? Furnish opts for the former, arguing that, as a question, v. 19a 'would blunt the effect of the preceding series of questions (vv. 17, 18) to which it does not belong'.[653] But there is in any case a fairly obvious break between vv. 18 and 19: v. 19 does not continue the series of questions which begin with an

---

[651] Sundermann, *Kraft der Rede*, pp. 205–7, 210–11. See the exegesis of v. 19 below.

[652] BAGD s.v. πάλαι 2.a. There is a textual variant here. The reading πάλαι has good support (ℵ* A B F G 0243. 6. 33. 81. 365. 1175. 1739. 1881 *pc* lat sa), but πάλιν is read by some witnesses (ℵ² D Ψ 𝔐 g vg^mss sy bo), whilst 𝔓⁴⁶ has οὐ πάλαι. The reading πάλιν looks secondary, not only on account of the MS attestation but also because it is easier. The use of πάλαι in the sense 'for some time past' is rare in the NT, possibly non-existent with the exception of the present verse (see Plummer, p. 367, and BAGD in loc.), whilst πάλιν is exceptionally frequent, and would readily be substituted by a scribe, either unconsciously or as an intentional 'correction'. It could also be explained as an assimilation to 3.1 and 5.12 (Barrett, p. 326 n. 1). The interrogative οὐ of 𝔓⁴⁶ may be an assimilation to v. 18 (Hughes, p. 469 n. 156).

[653] Furnish, p. 560. See also Barrett, p. 326; JB; NEB and REB punctuate as a statement (though the form of words might indicate a question).

interrogative particle, and the opening πάλαι indicates a wider
reference to the whole of the preceding discourse. Furthermore,
the original bearer of the letter, who would read it to the congregation, would by his delivery give due force to the questions of v.
18. Hughes, arguing that v. 19 itself should be understood as a
question, observes that the reading οὐ πάλαι in 𝔓⁴⁶ 'indicates that
in our earliest document this sentence was understood as interrogative'.⁶⁵⁴ On balance this interpretation is preferable. The
sense of the verse as a whole (see below) seems to require that v.
19bc should stand in an adversative relation to v. 19a. But if v. 19a
is itself a definite statement, one would expect that v. 19bc would
be introduced by an adversative particle to make the contrast
clear. The lack of any such is marginally easier to understand if v.
19a is intended as a question.

Either way, Paul is expressing what he imagines will, or may,
be his correspondents' subjective reaction⁶⁵⁵ to what they have
been hearing. He regards it as erroneous, and wants to put
the record straight. But where does the emphasis lie? What
part of the Corinthians' presumed impression of his intention is
he concerned to deny? According to some commentators, the
emphasis lies on the ὑμῖν. Paul is guarding against the suggestion
that he considers his readers to be his judges.⁶⁵⁶ It is not to them
that he is making his defence. The following κατέναντι θεοῦ
would support this interpretation. It is to God that he is
accountable.⁶⁵⁷ Bachmann, however, prefers to see the verb ἀπολογούμεθα as carrying the emphasis, and other exegetes allow that
there may be stress on the verb as well as on the personal
pronoun.⁶⁵⁸ Bachmann draws attention to the τῆς ὑμῶν οἰκοδομῆς
which concludes the verse. It is in the stressed final position and
implies a contrast with something in v. 19a. The point of contrast
must be the verb. Hence, Paul denies that he has been conducting
an exercise in self-defence. Rather, what he has been saying has
been for the sake of building up the church.⁶⁵⁹ In fact it is

⁶⁵⁴ Hughes, p. 469 n. 156. See also Plummer, p. 367; KJV, RSV, NRSV.
⁶⁵⁵ See BAGD s.v. δοκέω 1. On the present tense following πάλαι, see Moulton,
Prolegomena, p. 119: the sense conveyed is that of the English perfect. 'The
durative present in such cases gathers up past and present time into one phrase.' In
the present instance Moulton translates: ' "have you been thinking all this time?" '
⁶⁵⁶ Meyer, pp. 489–90; Rückert, pp. 380–1.
⁶⁵⁷ Wendland, p. 253; see also Windisch, pp. 406–7, Barrett, p. 328, and
Bultmann, p. 239, all three of whom would also allow that there is emphasis on
ἀπολογούμεθα. On κατέναντι θεοῦ, see also Vol. I, p. 215, on 2.17. Some MSS (D
Ψ 𝔐) read κατενώπιον τοῦ before θεοῦ (*P has κατενώπιον without τοῦ). But κατέναντι has much stronger attestation (𝔓⁴⁶ ℵ A B F G 0243. 6. 33. 81. 365. 630. 1175.
1739. 1881. 2464 pc). The ἐν Χριστῷ is omitted in 𝔓⁴⁶ b d Ambst.
⁶⁵⁸ Bachmann, p. 409; see also n. 657 above.
⁶⁵⁹ Bachmann, ibid.

probable that in v. 19bc Paul is responding to both the implications inherent in v. 19a. It is not before a Corinthian jury that he has been making his defence, nor has he, in any case, engaged in the presentation of an *apologia*.[660] But how, in all conscience, can he take this line? Certainly, he believes that it is ultimately to God's scrutiny that his words are exposed and that he speaks with a sense of accountability to Christ.[661] But it is the Corinthians whom he is directly addressing. And, since they are at liberty to accept or reject his apostolic self-portrait, it is in one sense their favourable judgement that he is soliciting. Even more problematic is his implicit denial that he has been concerned with self-defence. As Barrett points out, he had, in chaps. 10–12, 'argued that he was innocent of corrupt practices, and that in all respects he was at least the equal of his rivals'.[662] If this is not an *apologia*, what is?[663] Attempts are made to meet the difficulty by means of reference to motive and to method. An *apologia* in the usual sense, it is said, is a self-seeking discourse, which aims to put one's own person in a favourable light.[664] This is not true of what Paul has written. He is not seeking to further his own interests.[665] Certainly this is what he believes himself about his motivation, and so, if the verb ἀπολογέομαι carries the connotation of self-serving, he can with honesty disclaim such an intention. According to Windisch, it would imply also the extenuation of one's conduct by means of sophistic methods,[666] and Betz, in agreement, suggests that it is the rhetorical type of apology, more particularly, that Paul rejects.[667] It has to be said, however, that the other Pauline instances of this language[668] do not appear to possess any such specialised sense. In fact, it is not clear either that they necessarily carry the pejorative connotation of self-interest. In particular, Paul talks in 1 Cor 9.3 of his own ἀπολογία with no apparent qualms of conscience. But it might be that it was precisely this presentation (i.e., 1 Cor 9.3–18) of his case which had caused in Corinth some degeneration in the connotations of the 'apologetic' vocabulary. It is obvious that the question of

---

[660] See Windisch, p. 407; Bultmann, p. 239.

[661] There is a similar use of ἐν Χριστῷ with a verb of saying in Rom 9.1. Cranfield, *Romans*, pp. 451–2, supposes Paul to be saying, in part, that he speaks 'with a due sense of his accountability to Christ'.

[662] Barrett, p. 328. See also Windisch, p. 406.

[663] Betz, *Tradition*, p. 14, sees in chaps. 10–13 a fragment of a very carefully composed 'apology'. Cf. also Rückert, p. 381.

[664] Bachmann, ibid., and exegetes cited in n. 665 below.

[665] Schlatter, *Paulus*, p. 672; Windisch, p. 406; Héring, p. 99; Furnish, p. 567.

[666] Windisch, ibid.

[667] Betz, *Tradition*, p. 39.

[668] The verb ἀπολογέομαι occurs in Rom 2.15; the noun ἀπολογία in 1 Cor 9.3; 2 Cor 7.11; Phil 1.7, 16.

Paul's refusal of maintenance had not been resolved by the *apologia* of 1 Cor 9: his defence had not proved acceptable. Perhaps this was because he seemed to have shown no appreciation of the Corinthians' viewpoint. In that case, his defence of his own practice would begin to appear simply egotistic. Along with his appraisal of the cool reception of the substance of his defence there may then have come also some intimation of the pejorative sense now attached to the language of apology. Hence, as various commentators have observed, it is this element of egotistic self-interest that he is denying.

Doubtless, he is perfectly honest in making this denial. From his viewpoint, his personal interest is so totally identified with his apostolic vocation that assertion and defence of his personal, exclusive, pastoral responsibility and authority in Corinth is his clear apostolic duty, in no way a manifestation of self-interest. The Corinthians, however, cultivated now by others who call themselves apostles, and aware, in any case, that Paul is by no means the only Christian apostle of note (1 Cor 9.5; 15.5, 7, 9), may be inclined to see his exclusive claim to their allegiance as egotistic. Aware, perhaps, of this possibility, he insists that 'all things' are directed towards his correspondents' moral and spiritual improvement[669] (and not, by implication, towards any selfish end of his own).

How widely, then, does he intend τὰ πάντα to be understood? Does it refer to the totality of his relationship with the Corinthians?[670] Does it at least include the Painful Letter and Paul's conduct in respect of the collection, as well as all that is explicitly said and to which reference is made in the present letter?[671] These are possible suggestions. If accepted they would require us to supply ἐστιν as the verb, with τὰ πάντα as its subject. But it may be more natural to understand a repetition of the immediately preceding λαλοῦμεν, with τὰ πάντα as the object.[672] Paul has in view simply the contents of chaps. 10–12.[673] It is to this that v. 19a refers. And since in these chapters he has felt it necessary at times to speak somewhat harshly, he seeks to counterbalance this severity by addressing his correspondents as ἀγαπητοί. Sundermann would attach rather more significance to this form of address. Paul intends the Corinthians to understand his communication as a 'love-letter' since the very fact of his writing a letter at all is an expression of love. He could (in his own

---

[669] Furnish, p. 561, with reference to MHT, p. 190, notes that the ὑμῶν of v. 19c is emphatic by position.
[670] Barrett, p. 328.
[671] Martin, p. 460.
[672] Plummer, p. 368.
[673] Plummer, pp. 367–8.

view) simply have punished them instead.[674] A letter allows the recipients time, and is an attempt to prevent unwelcome behaviour on both sides. This certainly could have been in Paul's mind. Whether it would have seemed that way to the Corinthians is more doubtful. Would it be consonant with their attitude as described in 10.10–11?

20. φοβοῦμαι γὰρ μή πως ἐλθὼν οὐχ οἵους θέλω εὕρω ὑμᾶς, κἀγὼ εὑρεθῶ ὑμῖν οἷον οὐ θέλετε, μή πως ἔρις, ζῆλος, θυμοί, ἐριθεῖαι, καταλαλιαί, ψιθυρισμοί, φυσιώσεις, ἀκαταστασίαι· He goes on to explain why the process of edification to which he has just referred is, or may be, necessary. He speaks with apparent hesitation. He *fears*, lest *perhaps* the Corinthian church will be in a bad state when he arrives. So does he genuinely hesitate to pass judgement until he sees for himself?[675] Or does he simply intend to mitigate the harshness of what he knows he has to say?[676] The second suggestion appears more probable. The catalogue of sins in vv. 20–21 is very comprehensive. It is unlikely that Paul would implicitly accuse his readers in advance of their commission unless he was fairly certain that they were behaving in this way. Nevertheless, he first expresses his anxiety in a comparatively mild form: their moral situation may not turn out to be such as he would wish. The complementary possibility, that Paul himself may then present to them a less than acceptable *persona*,[677] initially also sounds mild. But these impressions lose force somewhat when we see how each anxiety is given more precise definition: in vv. 20b–21 it seems that serious forms of sin may be prevalent in the Corinthian church, and in 13.1–2 Paul issues a severe threat of punishment.[678]

This verse, then, explains the need for the οἰκοδομή of v. 19. And it is for the sake of this edification that Paul has said 'all' (τὰ πάντα) that has gone before. But at this point a problem confronts us. It is not immediately evident that Paul's lengthy defence of his own apostolic authority over against the claims of the rival missionaries has any direct connection with the remedy of the vices listed in vv. 20–21. Plummer suggests that these opponents have been forgotten,[679] but in view of the logical sequence we have just outlined this is unlikely. It is more likely, as Barrett

674 Sundermann, *Kraft der Rede*, pp. 208, 211.
675 Hughes, pp. 470–1.
676 Chrysostom, *PG* 61 col. 591 (NPNF XII, p. 408); cf. Allo, p. 333.
677 Windisch, p. 408, draws attention to the chiastic formulation: θέλω ... εὕρω ... εὑρεθῶ ... θέλετε. The form gives some emphasis to the complementarity of the relationship between Paul and the Corinthians.
678 Meyer, p. 492; cf. Bultmann, pp. 239–40.
679 Plummer, p. 368.

notes, that there is in fact a connection between the intrusion of the rival apostles and the type of sinful behaviour itemised in the present list.[680] Perhaps there were quarrels between those in the congregation who had completely seceded to the alternative apostolate and those (few, perhaps) who were still attached to Paul himself. (He has spoken in 10.6 about the completion of the Corinthians' obedience. This suggests that he could still count on the loyalty of some of them.) In addition, the rival missionaries were themselves engaged in mutual competition.[681] On their part the competition may have been comparatively friendly, but if various Corinthians became partisan for the one or the other they may have been quarrelling amongst themselves. Disputes sparked off by these circumstances would readily spawn the various particular vices included in the list.[682] The moral situation, in Paul's view, can be remedied only by the re-establishment of his own apostolic authority.

The list contains eight items. The first four occur, in the identical order, in the midst of a longer catalogue in Gal 5.20.[683] The first of these, ἔρις, 'strife', 'discord', 'contention',[684] is confined, in the NT, to the Pauline corpus. The next, ζῆλος, must here have its second sense, 'jealousy', 'envy'.[685] The following six nouns are all in the plural, and must mean 'instances of', 'manifestations of' whatever vice is in view. The meaning of ἐριθεία requires discussion, but the other items are straightforward: θυμός, 'anger';[686] καταλαλιά, 'slander';[687] ψιθυρισμός,

---

[680] Barrett, pp. 329–30, with reference to 'Opponents', p. 75.

[681] 10.12.

[682] As regards syntax, the clause lacks a verb. Windisch, p. 408, would supply either ὦσιν (so Furnish, p. 561) or εὑρεθῶσιν (with ἐν ὑμῖν also to be understood). The second alternative, as Plummer, p. 369, observes, may be understood from the previous sentence, and on that account is preferable.

[683] It is unlikely, therefore, pace Plummer, p. 369, and Furnish, p. 567, that the whole list is of intention arranged in four pairs. In Gal 5.20 the first four of 2 Cor 12.20 constitute the second, third, fourth and fifth items in a group of eight. See Burton, Galatians, p. 304. In the present verse, moreover, it does not seem very apt to couple θυμοί with ἐριθεῖαι, nor φυσιώσεις with ἀκαταστασίαι.

[684] BAGD s.v. ἔρις. Some witnesses (B D F G Ψ 𝔐 latt syʰ co) read the plural ἔρεις, but this is due, according to Metzger, Textual Commentary¹, p. 587, to assimilation to the plurals which follow ζῆλος. The singular (𝔓⁴⁶ ℵ A 0243. 33. 326. 945. 1739. 1881. 2495 al syᵖ) is original.

[685] BAGD s.v. ζῆλος 2. As with ἔρις, the plural ζῆλοι is read by some witnesses (ℵ D¹ Ψ 0243 𝔐 latt syʰ co). Again, the singular (𝔓⁴⁶ A B D* F G 33. 326 pc syᵖ boᵐˢ) is correct.

[686] BAGD s.v. θυμός 2., with the meaning of the plural given as 'outbursts of anger'.

[687] BAGD s.v. καταλαλιά: the only other occurrence (also plural) in the NT is in 1 Pet 2.1, but the adjective κατάλαλος occurs in Rom 1.30, and the verb καταλαλέω in Jas 4.11 and 1 Pet 2.12; 3.16.

864   COMMENTARY ON II CORINTHIANS

'whispering', '(secret) gossip';[688] φυσίωσις, 'conceit';[689] ἀκαταστασία, 'disorder'.[690]
The word ἐριθεία occurs seven times in the NT (Rom 2.8; 2 Cor 12.20; Gal 5.20; Phil 1.17; 2.3; Jas 3.14, 16). Before the NT period it is found only in Aristotle, 'where it denotes a self-seeking pursuit of political office by unfair means'.[691] The meaning in the NT is debatable.

(i) Is it synonymous with ἔρις, as another term for 'strife'? Windisch thinks that the context would support this sense. He draws attention also to a phrase in Philo: ἀφιλόνεικος καὶ ἀνερίθευτος.[692] The first adjective means 'not fond of strife':[693] the second we may assume to be parallel, and therefore synonymous. Hence, when we have mentally deleted the negating ἀν-, the remainder would indicate that the cognate ἐριθεία is connected with the idea of strife.[694] This suggestion, however, has not found favour, for various reasons. Despite the identity of the first three letters of each word, there is no etymological connection between ἔρις and ἐριθεία.[695] In the phrase in Philo, according to LSJ, the word ἀνερίθευτος means 'not honeycombed by intrigues'.[696] And if ἔρις and ἐριθεία are identical in meaning, why should both occur in the same vice-list?[697]

(ii) Does the word mean 'self-seeking', 'selfishness',[698] 'selfish

---

[688] BAGD s.v. ψιθυρισμός: hapax legomenon in the NT; the noun ψιθυριστής occurs in Rom 1.30.
[689] BAGD s.v. φυσίωσις. In secular usage it appears to be predominantly a (? rare) technical term in medicine. Here it is metaphorical, 'being puffed up', 'pride', 'conceit'. This is the only NT occurrence. The verb φυσιόω, however, is frequent in 1 Corinthians: 4.6, 18, 19; 5.2; 8.1; 13.4. The first four examples are passive, the last two active. All have the sense 'be inflated/inflate with pride'.
[690] BAGD s.v. ἀκαταστασία 2.
[691] BAGD s.v. ἐριθεία, with reference to Arist., Pol. 1302b 4; 1303a 14. See also LSJ s.v. II.1. (with the same references), 'canvassing for public office', 'intriguing'.
[692] Philo, Leg. Gai. [555] X 68 ('free from disputes and factions' LCL).
[693] LSJ s.v. ἀφιλόνεικος.
[694] Windisch, p. 408. In BAGD s.v. ἐριθεία this interpretation is allowed to be possible, though it is not preferred.
[695] See Plummer, p. 369. We may note that since the genitive of ἔρις is ἔριδος, the ἐριθ-words constitute a different group. See LSJ s.vv.: ἔριθος I. 'day-labourer', 'hired servant', II. metaph. 'servant'; ἐριθεύομαι I 'serve, work for hire', II.1. (of public officers) 'canvass', 'intrigue for office'; ἐριθεία I 'labour for wages'; II. (see above, n. 691 and below); Burton, Galatians, p. 308, notes that the verb is found in Polyb. X 25.9 with the meaning 'to seek the political co-operation of', 'to inveigle into one's party'.
[696] LSJ s.v. ἀνερίθευτος.
[697] The point is made in BAGD s.v. ἐριθεία, with reference to the (hypothetical) sources from which Paul may have derived his vice-lists, but the same argument would surely apply in Paul's own case also.
[698] Burton, Galatians, p. 308; BAGD s.v. ἐριθεία. Burton would derive this sense from the original meaning 'working for wages'. Cranfield, however, Romans, p. 148, commenting on Rom 2.8, notes that the general sense 'selfishness' could be seen as an extension of the Aristotelian usage.

ambition'?[699] Burton opts for this interpretation in Gal 5.20, and claims that it is appropriate to all the NT instances.[700] (iii) A third option, also suggested by Burton, would be the sense 'factiousness', 'party spirit', which he sees as appropriate in some of the NT examples, including 2 Cor 12.20.[701] Of these three options, the first is to be rejected for the reasons given. Of the other two, the third is preferable. If the vice-list is used here to describe the situation created (or perhaps exacerbated) by the advent of the rival missionaries, 'instances of party spirit' would be more directly relevant than the more general 'instances of self-seeking'.

Paul uses vice-lists elsewhere (Rom 1.29–31; 13.13; 1 Cor 5.11; 6.9–10; Gal 5.20–21), following the diatribal style exemplified in Epictetus.[702] Whilst in all cases they are relevant to his argument, those in the Corinthian correspondence are perhaps most crucial to the well-being of the recipient church. In the present instance the following verses clearly indicate that this is so.

21. μὴ πάλιν ἐλθόντος μου ταπεινώσῃ με ὁ θεός μου πρὸς ὑμᾶς, καὶ πενθήσω πολλοὺς τῶν προημαρτηκότων καὶ μὴ μετανοησάντων ἐπὶ τῇ ἀκαθαρσίᾳ καὶ πορνείᾳ καὶ ἀσελγείᾳ ᾗ ἔπραξαν. Paul is anxious also lest, when he arrives,[703] he may again face personal humiliation.[704] What sort of humiliation does

---

[699] BAGD s.v. ἐριθεία (in addition to 'selfishness').

[700] Burton, *Galatians*, p. 308.

[701] Burton, ibid. This, he notes, could derive from ('is cognate' with) the Aristotelian sense 'office-seeking'. In LSJ s.v. ἐριθεία II.2. the meanings given are 'selfish' or 'factious ambition', with reference to Jas 3.14 and Phil 1.17, and, in the plural, 'intrigues', 'party squabbles', with reference to Gal 5.20. (Whilst this last might appear to equate the meaning of ἐριθεία with that of ἔρις, the difference would lie in the emphasis given by ἐριθεία to the notion of faction.)

[702] See Bultmann, *Stil*, p. 71; examples he cites, p. 19 n. 3, in Epictetus include *Diss.* II 16.45; 19.19; III 2.3.

[703] The genitive absolute ἐλθόντος μου is incorrect from the classical standpoint, since the subject (μου) of the participle is identical with the object of ταπεινώσῃ and so an integral part of the main clause. See BDR 423(2) and MHT, p. 322. In some witnesses the text has been 'corrected', either to ἐλθόντα με ταπεινώσῃ ὁ θεός μου πρὸς ὑμᾶς (ℵ² Ψ 0243 𝔐 lat?) or to ἐλθόντα με πρὸς ὑμᾶς ταπεινώσῃ με ὁ θεός μου (D⁽¹⁾ syᴾ Tert). The remaining witnesses read ἐλθόντος μου, but divide on the reading of the finite verb: some (𝔓⁴⁶ D F G L P 6. 33. 81. 104. 365. 1175. 1241. 2464. 2495 pm) read the future indicative ταπεινώσει, instead of the aorist subjunctive ταπεινώσῃ (ℵ* A B 326). The reading ταπεινώσει is either an accidental error or (as Windisch, p. 410 n. 1, suggests) an adaptation to the following πενθήσω, understood as future.

[704] The reference of πάλιν is ambiguous. Windisch, p. 409, argues that its position implies connection with the participle ἐλθόντος: see also, e.g., RSV, NRSV, NEB, BCN. Most commentators, however, connect it with ταπεινώσῃ. It is the possibility of humiliation that carries the emphasis (Plummer, p. 369). And emphasis on another *visit* would more probably have caused πάλιν to be attached to the previous ἐλθών of v. 20 (cf. Allo, p. 334). For this second view see also, e.g., Barrett, p. 326; Furnish, p. 562; REB.

he have in mind? It may be chiefly the prospect of finding the congregation in a state of moral dereliction. If a flourishing church is the apostle's pride (1 Cor 9.2; 2 Cor 1.14), then the converse situation would be cause for humiliation. Paul sees himself as pastorally responsible for the Corinthians, and their ethical deficiency would be a clear sign that his authority has not been thoroughly established.[705] If, moreover, he should now find that he would have to exercise this authority for punitive destructive purposes, this also would be humiliating, since it was given him not for destruction but for constructive ends (10.8).[706] He may in addition fear that the persistence of the sins castigated in 1 Corinthians would provide his opponents with a useful weapon against his whole concept of the Christian life, i.e., 'his reliance on the new life of the indwelling Spirit as the all-sufficient power to change his Gentile converts within and without, from pagan ways to Christian ways'.[707]

Were these anxieties to be realised, Paul's third visit to Corinth would prove to be a second occasion of humiliation for him face to face with the congregation.[708] On his arrival he would see that, despite the apparently favourable response to the Painful Letter and despite all that he had said in the letter of chaps. 1–8, to elucidate the nature of his apostleship and also (6.14–7.1) to insist on ethical purity, his pastoral authority had been disregarded and endangered. In view of what would be a disastrous state of affairs, it is then somewhat surprising to see ὁ θεός as the subject of ταπεινώσῃ. Would Paul really regard God as having engineered the individual offence which seriously marred his second visit, and the general state of moral laxity which he fears he may find when he arrives for the third time? Barrett draws a comparison with the bestowal of the 'angel of Satan' of v. 7;[709] the 'thorn' ἐδόθη, 'was given', i.e., by God. Nevertheless, whilst this handicap did, of course, affect Paul's missionary endeavours, and, in consequence, those to whom he was sent, such results are not quite in the same category as wholesale moral degeneracy in the Corinthian church. It would perhaps be more probable that he should think of God as making use of sinful situations for good ends, rather than as originating the situations themselves. Plummer suggests that Paul saw humiliation as something beneficial,[710] whatever the cause.

[705] Windisch, p. 410.
[706] Martin, p. 465; with reference to Bultmann, p. 241.
[707] Bruce, p. 252.
[708] This is the more probable sense of πρὸς ὑμᾶς. See Barrett, p. 326, who translates 'in your presence', and Martin, p. 451, who has 'before you'; see also Furnish, p. 562. Plummer, p. 370, however, prefers 'in reference to you', 'in relation to you'.
[709] Barrett, p. 331.
[710] Plummer, p. 369.

The particular cause he has in view now is his continuing failure to induce penitence in those who for some time have been guilty of sexual misconduct. He fears lest he may have to grieve[711] over these people. The implication may be that he would see them as spiritually dead.[712] It is possible also that he may have in mind the particular grief he would feel, were he compelled at last to excommunicate them.[713] Barrett argues against this suggestion: Paul would be sorrowful simply on account of their sinfulness and impenitence, and in particular because he believed that such sins excluded the sinner from God's future kingdom (1 Cor 6.9–10).[714] But it may be significant that the verb πενθέω occurs in Paul only here and in 1 Cor 5.2, where there is a specific reference to exclusion of an offender from the church and where also it is a matter of sexual misconduct. Furthermore, in 13.2 Paul does indicate that he intends action of some sort against sinners.

The people in question are described by two participles: the first is in the perfect tense, the second is aorist. It is possible that the difference in tense has some significance. The perfect προημαρτηκότων would then indicate persistence in sinful conduct,[715] during some earlier period[716] or perhaps even up to the time of the present letter.[717] The aorist (μὴ) μετανοησάντων would signify failure to repent when some particular opportunity presented itself, such as Paul's original call for conversion,[718] a letter from him,[719] or the occasion of his second visit.[720] It is likely that the προ- of προημαρτηκότων takes us back at least to the period of 1 Corinthians. The list of sins which follows is somewhat

---

[711] In form, the verb πενθήσω can be either the future indicative or the aorist subjunctive. It appears to be understood as future indicative in JB, but is fairly clearly taken as aorist subjunctive in NRSV, NEB, REB, and by Barrett, p. 326, and Furnish, p. 557. This is preferable. Paul surely still hopes that he may *not* have to grieve over impenitent sinners. The future indicative, expressing a definite intention, would suggest the contrary.

[712] So Estius, p. 655: 'Tristiciam vero suam *luctum* vocat, ut innuat eos qui peccaverunt, Deo mortuos esse.' ('In fact, he calls his sadness *mourning*, so as to intimate that those who have sinned have died to God.') See also Osiander, p. 506; Hughes, p. 472.

[713] Osiander, ibid.; Schlatter, *Paulus*, p. 673; Bruce, p. 252; Hughes, p. 472; Filson, p. 416.

[714] Barrett, pp. 331–2.

[715] Plummer, p. 370; Hughes, p. 473 n. 167.

[716] Hughes, ibid.

[717] Furnish, p. 557, suggests this in his translation: 'many who have continued in their former sinning'. In his comment, p. 568, he allows that Paul may be aware that the problems of 1 Corinthians are still present.

[718] See below.

[719] Hughes, ibid.

[720] Plummer, p. 370.

reminiscent of 1 Cor 5.1–11 and 6.12–20.[721] Possibly Paul is even thinking of the pre-Christian life of these people.[722] How large this group of 'previous sinners' was we do not know, but the πολλούς implies that Paul believed it to be fairly numerous. The further significance of the word is debatable. Some exegetes take it as co-extensive with τῶν προημαρτηκότων: it is an imprecise expression for 'the many previous sinners'.[723] Others, however, take more seriously the use of the partitive genitive: the πολλοί would constitute the majority, not the totality, of the προημαρτηκότες. Osiander supposes them to be the most heinous of the sinners, whom Paul might be obliged to excommunicate.[724] Meyer suggests that they are those specifically guilty of unchastity.[725] The first suggestion is a possibility. The second, however, can be ruled out on linguistic grounds. The 'previous sinners' i.e. the whole group, are grammatically co-ordinated with 'those not having repented of their immorality, fornication and debauchery': in Paul's Greek they share the one definite article required to give both participles the force of relative clauses. It may be best to follow the interpretation proposed by Windisch. He sees an implicit contrast between πολλούς and πάντας. Paul may be expressing a modest hope that not all will have remained impenitent by the time he arrives in person, although he fears that *many* may.[726]

The strong language here and in 13.1–2 suggests that the required repentance is of a radical nature. According to Windisch, followed by Georgi, Paul is making use of missionary terminology,[727] and, Georgi suggests, is indicating that these people had never really converted to the Christian faith at all.[728] This interpretation is not impossible, but the linguistic argument is perhaps rather weak. Certainly the verb μετανοέω is a mission term in Acts (2.38; 3.19; 17.30; 26.20), but the present occurrence is the only instance of it within the Pauline corpus. We cannot, therefore, deduce what connotations it carried for him. Moreover, when he uses the cognate noun μετάνοια in 2 Cor 7.9, 10 he is not talking of repentance of pre-Christian vices, although, admittedly, he does use it also in Rom 2.4, of God's intention for the unconverted. The verb προαμαρτάνω occurs only in this section of

---

[721] Windisch, p. 411. The only linguistic point of contact, however, is the reference to πορνεία.
[722] See below.
[723] Bultmann, p. 241; Furnish, p. 562.
[724] Osiander, p. 506.
[725] Meyer, p. 495.
[726] Windisch, p. 410.
[727] Windisch, pp. 410–11; Georgi, *Opponents*, p. 237.
[728] Georgi, ibid.

2 Corinthians (12.21 and 13.2) in the whole NT, and whilst the simple verb ἁμαρτάνω does, in Romans, refer to human existence apart from Christ (Rom 2.12; 3.23; 5.12, 14, 16), this is in the context of theological argument rather than missionary appeal. Nevertheless, since the vices specifically named here are all related to sexual misconduct, and since, in Paul's view, such behaviour was a prominent characteristic of the pagan habits renounced at conversion (1 Cor 6.9–11), he could here be thinking in the way Georgi suggests.

The three vices mentioned, i.e., ἀκαθαρσία ('immorality', 'viciousness', especially of sexual vice[729]), πορνεία ('prostitution', 'unchastity', 'fornication', used 'of every kind of unlawful sexual intercourse'[730]), and ἀσέλγεια ('licentiousness', 'debauchery', 'sensuality', with especial reference to 'sexual excesses'[731]), are also listed in Gal 5.19, at the beginning of the vice-catalogue, with ἀκαθαρσία and πορνεία in reverse order.[732] Paul's purpose in Galatians, however, is rather different. There, he mentions these (and other) 'deeds of the flesh', in contrast to the 'products of the Spirit', to emphasise that his gospel by no means entailed ethical degeneracy (5.13). Here, he is referring to sins actually committed by some of the Corinthians, of which, he fears, they may still need seriously to repent.[733]

If Paul's anxieties did reflect accurately the situation in Corinth at the time he wrote the present letter, what might have been the relationship between these 'previous sinners' and the quarrelling, factious and arrogant church members whose attitudes and behaviour are delineated in v. 20 and were generated by the advent of the rival missionaries? Perhaps they remained as two distinct groups,[734] although, as Paul saw the situation, both would be equally recalcitrant in respect of their attitude towards himself.[735] Alternatively they may have merged to some extent.

---

[729] BAGD s.v. ἀκαθαρσία 2.

[730] BAGD, s.v. πορνεία 1.

[731] BAGD, s.v. ἀσέλγεια. An example of the word's reference to sexual excess is noted in Philo, *Vit. Mos.* I 305.

[732] Two of these, πορνεία and ἀκαθαρσία, are listed also in Col 3.5 and Eph 5.3; the third, ἀσέλγεια, occurs in the plural in Rom 13.13 and 1 Pet 4.3.

[733] On μετανοέω followed by ἐπί with the dative, in the sense 'repent of', 'repent because of', see BAGD s.v. μετανοέω. Meyer, pp. 494–5, attaches the ἐπί-phrase to the preceding πενθήσω: Paul would mourn many of the previous impenitent sinners because of their licentious behaviour. Plummer, p. 370, rightly argues, however, that such a construction, on account of the word order, would prove too awkward. Most exegetes (e.g., Allo, p. 334; Barrett, p. 326; Furnish, p. 557; Martin, p. 451) attach the phrase to μετανοησάντων. On the attraction of the relative pronoun ἤ ἔπραξαν see BDR 294. The expected ἤν, as direct object of the verb, is assimilated in case to the preceding ἀσέλγεια.

[734] This appears to be the view of Barrett, 'Opponents', p. 76.

[735] Cf. Wendland, p. 254.

Whilst the people in view in v. 20 may not have indulged in the immoral conduct of the 'previous sinners' of v. 21, they had obviously tolerated such behaviour instead of acting in accordance with Paul's injunctions in 1 Cor 5.9–13. Martin observes that in 13.2 they are all grouped together.[736]

---

[736] Martin, pp. 468–9.

(ii) *Threat of punishment when Paul arrives; exhortation to reformed conduct* (13.1–10)

[1]This is the third time I am coming to you. 'On the evidence of two or three witnesses every charge shall be established.' [2]To the former sinners and to all the rest I have said beforehand and I do say beforehand—when present the second time and now absent, that when I come again I shall not spare, [3]since you demand proof that Christ speaks in me, Christ who in your experience is not weak, but is powerful in your midst. [4]For indeed he was crucified through weakness, but he lives through the power of God. For indeed we are weak, in unity with him, but we shall 'live' with him, through the power of God, in our dealings with you.

[5]Put yourselves to the test: test whether you exist in faith, examine yourselves. Or do you not surely recognise yourselves—recognise that Jesus Christ is in your midst and within[1] you, unless perhaps you are unauthentic. [6]And I hope that you will come to know that we, in turn, are not unauthentic. [7]And we pray to God that you may do no wrong. We pray, not that we may appear visibly authentic, but that you may do what is good, whilst we may seem as though lacking authentication. [8]For we can do nothing against the truth, nothing but on behalf of the truth. [9]For we rejoice whenever we are weak but you are strong. This is what we indeed pray for: your restoration. [10]On this account I am writing this while absent so that when present I may not take severe action, in accordance with the authority which the Lord gave me for constructive work and not for destruction.

Paul now gives explicit warning that on his third visit he will, if necessary, take punitive action against those who persist in their sinful behaviour despite his warnings. Such action would, indeed, provide the proof the Corinthians demand that Paul is the spokesman of Christ. He urges them, nevertheless, themselves to assess their condition as believers, and he assures them of his prayers for their spiritual and moral restoration. And while he hopes they will come to recognise his authenticity as an apostle, this is not his prime concern. His prime concern is their own authenticity as Christians. He hopes that the letter he has been writing will enable him, when he arrives, to engage in his proper apostolic work, and not its negative, punitive converse.

13.1–10 as peroratio. As we have already noted, Sundermann has drawn attention to the parallels between this passage and the first eleven verses of chap. 10. As the latter functions as the exordium to Paul's speech of defence, so the present passage constitutes its peroration.[2] In vv. 1–4 there is a recapitulation of the basic theme of the letter, i.e., strength through weakness.[3]

---

[1] Paul could intend his ἐν ὑμῖν to be read both corporately and individually.

[2] Sundermann, *Kraft der Rede*, pp. 47–8, 214.

[3] Sundermann, *Kraft der Rede*, p. 219.

13.1. Τρίτον τοῦτο ἔρχομαι[4] **πρὸς ὑμᾶς. Ἐπὶ στόματος δύο μαρτύρων καὶ τριῶν σταθήσεται πᾶν ῥῆμα.** Here, Paul clearly states that he will definitely come to Corinth. In 12.14 he had spoken only of readiness to come. In 12.20–21 he refers to his imminent arrival by means of participles within subjunctive clauses, which tends to suggest that he may still be somewhat indefinite about his plans. Now any doubt is removed. Some exegetes, it is true, understand him still to mean that he is now ready to visit Corinth, i.e., that he is repeating what he has said in 12.14.[5] The ἔρχομαι contains within itself a future significance, and can refer simply to intention.[6] In one sense, of course, this is true: Paul is not yet (obviously) in Corinth, and it is scarcely likely that he composed the letter of chaps. 10–13 whilst actually travelling. But the point of debate emerges to view when we note that the verb is qualified by the preceding τρίτον τοῦτο.[7] Is Paul saying that this is the third time that he has formed the intention, as yet unfulfilled, of making a (second) visit to Corinth? Or is he saying that, having actually visited the city twice already, he will now make a third visit? Support for the first alternative goes with rejection of the occurrence of an interim visit after the sending of 1 Corinthians, support for the second with acceptance of this theory. We have argued for its acceptance.[8] This was partly on the ground of what seems the more natural interpretation of the two verses 12.14 and 13.1 themselves. Hence, at this point in our exegesis the argument might appear circular. But we pointed in addition to the implication of 2.1, where Paul refers to a painful visit to the city: since it is not likely that he viewed the foundation visit (successful) as an occasion of sorrow, this must be an interim visit, prior to the writing of the present letter. And the ὡς παρὼν τὸ δεύτερον of v. 2 favours this view also.[9] In consequence, we agree with those exegetes who understand Paul to say definitely that he is about to visit Corinth for the third time.[10]

[4] The reading ἐτοίμως ἔχω ἐλθεῖν (A vgᵐˢ) is clearly an assimilation to 12.14 (Allo, p. 335).

[5] Grotius, p. 510: 'Id est, tertium me iam itineri paro.' ('That is, I am now for the third time preparing myself for the journey.') See also Estius, p. 656; Bengel, *Gnomon*, p. 817; Hyldahl, 'Einheit', p. 303.

[6] Heinrici (1883), p. 392; cf. Belser, p. 365, who draws attention to the future reference of διέρχομαι in 1 Cor 16.5.

[7] On τρίτον τοῦτο, see BAGD s.v. τρίτος 3. The simple τρίτον and τὸ τρίτον are used adverbially with the sense 'the (a) third time'. This is classical and hellenistic, and is found in the NT at Mk 14.41; Lk 23.22; Jn 21.17. With the addition of τοῦτο (as in the present instance and at 12.14) the meaning becomes 'now for the third time', 'this is the third time'; see also Jn 21.14 (τοῦτο ἤδη τρίτον ἐφανερώθη Ἰησοῦς τοῖς μαθηταῖς.); in the LXX Num 22.28; Judg 16.15 (noted by Meyer, p. 499).

[8] Vol. I, pp. 49–50, 53–6.

[9] See below, pp. 875–6.

[10] Meyer, p. 499; Plummer, p. 371; Windisch, pp. 412–13; Allo, p. 335; and others.

What, then, does he mean by what follows? His words are a virtual quotation of Deut 19.15: ἐπὶ στόματος δύο μαρτύρων καὶ ἐπὶ στόματος τριῶν μαρτύρων σταθήσεται πᾶν ῥῆμα. He has abbreviated the ruling by eliminating repetition, but has not changed it otherwise. In the context in Deuteronomy it is a legal regulation, requiring the testimony of more than one witness to secure a conviction.[11] In the NT it is cited in Mt 18.16 in a passage dealing with church discipline and there is an allusion to it in a similar context in 1 Tim 5.19. In Heb 10.28 the author may refer to this verse in Deuteronomy or perhaps to the identical precept in Deut 17.6, when he speaks of the punishment entailed by violation of the law of Moses. It may be that there was some general familiarity with the ruling in the early church. If so, this must have been due to the influence of Palestinian Judaism. The rejection of the testimony of a sole witness was not known in Roman law in NT times, nor in Greek law.[12] And hellenistic Jewish writers did not see Deut 19.15 'as one of the laws valid for humanity at large'.[13] It is in the rabbinic literature, within the sphere of Judaism, that we find specific references to the ruling. Their relevance to Paul's day could be open to some question, but it has been argued that the rabbinic rules of evidence may have been valid already in the time of Hillel and Shammai (10–80 C.E.).[14] We may note also that these rules were at some stage developed to include the requirement that the witnesses had warned the accused.[15] There may be additional evidence in the Qumran texts for the currency in Paul's time of the basic Deuteronomic ruling: see CD 9.17–23[16] and IQS 5.25–26.[17]

Paul's own use of it in the present context has received various interpretations, which fall into two basic categories.

1. He is speaking quite literally of some process equivalent to legal proceedings, which he will, if necessary, set in motion when he arrives in Corinth. Complaints will be heard and witnesses will give testimony on each matter at issue.[18] Delcor finds evidence in

---

[11] The future indicative σταθήσεται is used to express an imperative. See BDF 362. The idiom is used to render 'categorical injunctions and prohibitions' in the legal contexts of the OT.

[12] Van Vliet, *No Single Testimony*, pp. 11–25.

[13] Van Vliet, *No Single Testimony*, pp. 26–42; the quotation is on p. 42.

[14] Van Vliet, *No Single Testimony*, pp. 53–4, 60–2.

[15] Van Vliet, *No Single Testimony*, pp. 53–4.

[16] Noted by Van Vliet, *No Single Testimony*, pp. 58–9; see also Furnish, p. 569.

[17] Noted by Furnish, ibid.

[18] Meyer, p. 500. This general viewpoint is supported by Goudge, p. 128; Allo, p. 335; Filson, p. 417; Hughes, p. 475; and others. The translation of the word ῥῆμα as 'charge' in e.g., RSV, NRSV, REB would appear to count in its favour, but since here it follows the Hebrew idiom whereby *dabar* can mean 'thing' as well as 'word' (see BAGD s.v. ῥῆμα 2.), it would be equally permissible to render it 'matter'

1 Cor 6 that Paul intended the setting up of courts in the Corinthian church. He claims that the apostle's own role would be parallel to that of the Qumran *mebaqqer*, as described in the *Damascus Document*, where this official functions as 'supreme judge' over all the communities.[19] There are, however, several objections to the view that Paul is referring to disciplinary proceedings of a quasi-legal kind. First, we may note that the legal maxim in its original context in Deut 19.15 is designed for the support of the accused, whilst in the present verse it has the character of a threat.[20] Secondly, the offences Paul is proposing to deal with are already a matter of public knowledge, so that inquiry with the help of witnesses would seem superfluous.[21] Thirdly, the particular stress on numbers in the first two verses of the chapter makes it highly likely that the 'two or three witnesses', are more probably to be related to Paul's visits to Corinth, two in the past and one in prospect,[22] or, perhaps, to his second visit, the present letter, and the prospective third visit.[23] Fourthly, one has to ask whether it is at all likely that Paul would have asked the members of the Corinthian church to testify against each other.[24] This would surely have exacerbated the attitudes castigated in 12.20, rather than putting an end to them. Not all these difficulties are of equal weight. Paul might have given a different slant to the Deuteronomic rule. Moreover, even though the offences were publicly known, he would not wish to proceed only on the ground of hearsay.[25] And he would need to protect himself against the charge of making arbitrary use of his apostolic authority. But the third and the fourth objections still appear substantial.

2. Paul is using the motif of witnesses in a transferred sense and is in some way connecting it with his visits to Corinth, or with visits combined with letters. Chrysostom says that he substitutes 'his comings and his warnings' for actual witnesses.[26] Is this likely? Van Vliet suggests that the Deuteronomic text may not always,

---

(Barrett, p. 327; Martin, p. 451) or 'point' (Furnish, p. 568). On the use of στόμα with the sense 'what the mouth utters' (here, 'evidence'), see BAGD s.v. 1.a. For ἐπί in the sense 'on the basis of', see BAGD s.v. I.1.b.β. For καί with the meaning 'or', see BAGD s.v. I.1.b.; also Denniston, *Particles*, p. 292.

[19] M. Delcor, 'The courts of the Church of Corinth and the courts of Qumran', pp. 69–84 in *Paul and Qumran*, ed. J. Murphy-O'Connor, London, 1968; see pp. 69–70, 75–6.

[20] Bachmann, p. 412.

[21] Bachmann, ibid.; Lietzmann, p. 160; Windisch, p. 414; Bultmann, p. 243; Martin, p. 469.

[22] Bachmann, ibid.

[23] So Bultmann, ibid., and Furnish, p. 575.

[24] Plummer, p. 372.

[25] Allo, p. 335.

[26] Chrysostom, *PG* 61 col. 596 (NPNF XII, p. 411).

within Judaism, have been interpreted in the completely literal
sense, but may have been seen simply 'as requiring good evidence
before somebody was convicted'.[27] In Paul's case, differently, he
could have been aware of the development of the requirement of
prior warning, and conflated this, which he does take literally,
with a metaphorical interpretation of the numerical specification
concerning witnesses. It is any way clear from 1 Cor 9.8–10 that
he is ready to apply scriptural texts metaphorically, with relation
to the life of the Christian community. Hence, it is readily
conceivable that in the present instance he is in part speaking
metaphorically, i.e., that he does not have in view some actual
process of ecclesiastical law. If this is so, it is not relevant that his
quotation requires the evidence of two or three separate
witnesses, whilst he would be providing only one, himself.[28] Nor is
it relevant, either, that his occasions of witness are separated in
point of time, whilst the Deuteronomic ruling at least implies that
the witnesses should appear simultaneously.[29]

This second interpretation, then, may well be plausible. In its
simple form the three witnesses are equated with Paul's three
visits to Corinth, the two in the past and the third to come.[30] As
Barrett points out, the words 'third' and 'second' in vv. 1–2 are
clearly to be connected with the 'two' and 'three' in the
quotation.[31] The first two visits are to be regarded as occasions of
warning, the third as the time for decision.[32] The complete
equation of witnesses with visits, however, is said to be
problematic in the case of the first visit. Paul's foundation visit to
Corinth was devoted to converting the Corinthians to the
Christian gospel, not to inquiries about their moral conduct and
bearing witness to their offences.[33] Consequently, Bultmann,
followed by Furnish, supposes that the first witness is Paul's
interim visit, and the second the present letter.[34] But this would
cause some confusion, in that the τὸ δεύτερον of v. 2 would now
refer to the first of the witnesses in v. 1, i.e., the first of the δύο
μαρτύρων, whilst the second of this pair is not, as one might
suppose, the interim letter (the Painful Letter), but this somewhat
later communication. And, granted that Paul is speaking

[27] Van Vliet, No Single Testimony, p. 48.

[28] Pace Meyer, p. 501, who regards this as a problem; cf Windisch, p. 413.

[29] Pace Windisch, ibid., who finds this a difficulty, although he does accept that
Paul is referring to his visits to Corinth.

[30] Bachmann, p. 412; cf. Lietzmann, p. 160; Calvin, p. 169; Bruce, pp. 252–3.

[31] Barrett, p. 333.

[32] Barrett, ibid; van Vliet, No Single Testimony, p. 96 n. 8, to whom Barrett
refers.

[33] Allo, pp. 335–6.

[34] Bultmann, p. 243; Furnish, p. 575.

metaphorically, it is surely over-complicated to suppose that the metaphor bifurcates in this way, so that the image of the witness applies both to visits and to a letter. In fact, the equation of the first witness with the first visit is not really problematic. Paul may well have given his converts warning against slipping back into the heathen vices which he lists in 1 Cor 6.9–10.[35] We prefer, then, to accept the simpler form of the second interpretation. Paul's quotation from Deuteronomy refers to his two past visits to Corinth and to the third which is imminent. It is difficult to deny a connection between the τρίτον of v. 1a and the τριῶν of v. 1b, and since the first refers to a visit it is at least very likely that the second has identical reference. The point of referring to the two previous visits with the aid of the biblical quotation is to add force to the following claim that he has given, and is now giving, due warning that sinners will be punished when he finally arrives.

2. **προείρηκα καὶ προλέγω, ὡς παρὼν τὸ δεύτερον καὶ ἀπὼν νῦν,[36] τοῖς προημαρτηκόσιν καὶ τοῖς λοιποῖς πᾶσιν, ὅτι ἐὰν ἔλθω εἰς τὸ πάλιν οὐ φείσομαι,** Paul's previous warning remains in force (even if the Corinthians had supposed it forgotten). This is the significance of the perfect tense of προείρηκα.[37] Its occasion will have been the apostle's interim visit to Corinth, i.e., his second visit: as (ὡς), present on this earlier occasion, he has given (prior) warning, so, now absent, he is giving (renewed) warning. This reading of the verse is contested, however, by some exegetes. It is argued that the ὡς παρών should be attached to προλέγω and that ὡς should be taken to mean 'as if': Paul has given (prior) warning (i.e., in 1 Cor 4.21), now he gives (further warning) as though present for a second time, but (in fact) absent.[38] The basic reason for this interpretation is the conviction that Paul had paid no interim visit to Corinth. Were this firmly established, one would perhaps be compelled to accept this unnatural and awkward division of v. 2a. But it is not by any means so established.[39] Furthermore, to give the required sense to ὡς παρών renders the reference to absence totally unnecessary.[40] Lastly, the use of the definite article with δεύτερον shows that it is a question

[35] Cf. Wolff, p. 261.

[36] Some witnesses (D¹ Y 𝔐 vg^ms sy sa) read γράφω after νῦν. This is a clarifying addition. As Metzger, *Textual Commentary*¹, p. 587, points out, there would have been no reason for omission, had the word been original. The shorter text (𝔓⁴⁶ ℵ A B D* F G I 0243. 6. 33. 630. 1175. 1739. 1881 *pc* lat) is to be accepted.

[37] Furnish, p. 569. On προλέγω in the sense 'warn', see LSJ s.v. προλέγω II.3.

[38] Belser, p. 361; Hyldahl, 'Einheit', p. 304. See also Estius, p. 656; Bengel, *Gnomon*, pp. 817–18.

[39] See Vol. I, pp. 49–50, 53–6.

[40] Plummer, p. 373; Denney, pp. 374–5. Meyer, p. 502, similarly, comments that the νῦν would be superfluous.

of the actual second occasion of Paul's presence, not of some
second time that is merely imaginary.[41]

He speaks again to 'those who have previously sinned'. They
will be those whom he found in a sinful and impenitent state, and
cautioned, during this second visit,[42] and primarily those guilty
of the sexual vice mentioned in 12.21.[43] Perhaps they are the
people (or some of them) whose behaviour was castigated in
1 Corinthians,[44] But who are 'all the rest' who are likewise
warned? It is not altogether probable that they are the remainder
of the whole congregation.[45] In that case, we should have expected
ὑμῖν πᾶσιν. Perhaps, then, they are those whom Paul has in mind
in 12.20, whose overt sinful behaviour has been generated, or
possibly exacerbated, by the advent of the rival missionaries.[46] He
may, in fact, have detected signs of it during his second visit, when
he may himself have been the victim of slander and gossip, and
may have then warned the perpetrators, but to no lasting effect.

When[47] he visits again,[48] he will act decisively. Possibly he is
quoting his actual words on the occasion of his second visit when
he says ἐὰν ἔλθω εἰς τὸ πάλιν οὐ φείσομαι.[49] But what is he threatening to do? There are various suggestions. Perhaps he proposes
the excommunication of those sinners who refuse to repent.[50] We
should then have in prospect a disciplinary situation comparable
to that of 1 Cor 5.3–5, 11–13. There might, however, be a vital
difference, in that the church as a whole might not now support
the apostle.[51] He might be thinking of some punishment similar to
that of 2.6–11.[52] This would mean a temporary exclusion from
congregational activities, more especially the Eucharist.[53] But
again this would require majority support from the members of
the congregation.[54] A different suggestion is that he has in mind

[41] Allo, p. 336; Hughes, p. 475 n. 168; Furnish, p. 570.
[42] Cf. Plummer, ibid.
[43] Windisch, p. 415; Barrett, p. 333.
[44] Allo, p. 337.
[45] Pace Allo, ibid., and Furnish, p. 570.
[46] Barrett, p. 333.
[47] There is considerable agreement that ἐάν here means 'when': see e.g.,
Plummer, p. 373; Allo, p. 337; Martin, p. 472. For this use of ἐάν, see BAGD s.v. 1.d.
[48] The εἰς τό preceding πάλιν is omitted in 𝔓46 F G. Either the words seemed
superfluous, or else the omission is a simple scribal error. The phrase itself occurs
nowhere else in the NT. It is the equivalent of the simple πάλιν: see BAGD s.v. 2.
[49] The ὅτι would have a recitative function. See Plummer, p. 374; Allo, ibid.;
Furnish, p. 570; and Martin, pp. 471–2.
[50] Plummer, ibid., thinks this a possibility; cf. Windisch, p. 415.
[51] Barrett, p. 334, who adds that it might be Paul himself who was 'excommuni-
cated'.
[52] Martin, p. 472.
[53] See Vol. I, p. 174.
[54] Martin, ibid., sees this as a difficulty.

the employment of 'supernatural power to inflict bodily sickness and suffering'.[55] These three exegetical proposals, whatever their respective merits, envisage Paul as taking practical action, should the present warning fail of its effect. Barrett, by contrast, claims that the apostle 'had in fact no weapon at all except the truth, the Gospel applied to the situation'. All that he could do would be to declare that the unrepentant sinners had alienated themselves from God, 'and fallen back into the realm of Satan'.[56] It seems altogether likely, however, that more is meant than this. For what Paul is promising, or threatening, to do is to provide the Corinthians with the 'proof' of his apostolic representation of Christ for which they ask (v. 3). It is improbable that a mere declaration of the lost state of the offenders would meet the demand. The miraculous infliction of bodily suffering would fit both the implicit requirement of visible action and also the probability that Paul is prepared to act alone if necessary.[57]

3. ἐπεὶ[58] δοκιμὴν ζητεῖτε τοῦ ἐν ἐμοὶ λαλοῦντος Χριστοῦ, ὃς εἰς ὑμᾶς οὐκ ἀσθενεῖ ἀλλὰ δυνατεῖ ἐν ὑμῖν. The opening ἐπεί, 'since', shows that in Paul's view the 'proof' the Corinthians are demanding[59] will have something to do with his 'not sparing' the wrongdoers (v. 2) in the Corinthian Christian community. But what did the Corinthians themselves have in mind? How is the τοῦ ἐν ἐμοὶ λαλοῦντος Χριστοῦ to be interpreted? There are variations in translation, since some renderings have '(of) the Christ who speaks'[60] and others 'that Christ is speaking'.[61] This is not of any significance, since there is no real difference between 'proof of' and 'proof that'. The interpretation of ἐν ἐμοί, however, may be of more importance. Should it be translated as

---

[55] This is one of the suggestions offered by Plummer, p. 374.

[56] Barrett, p. 334.

[57] That an apostle was thought able to inflict, miraculously, some kind of physical suffering is attested in Acts 5.3–5, 9–10. See also Munck, *Salvation*, pp. 189–90, who thinks that some miraculous punishment is in view, although he supposes that it would be, if put into effect, the destruction of the whole Corinthian church. This is less probable.

[58] Most witnesses read ἐπεί. A few (6 *pc*) have ἐπειδή, with identical meaning. Several (F G b d r Ambst) read ὅτι, which involves no alteration in sense, but might be the result of too mechanical assimilation to the ὅτι of v. 2 (where it introduces direct or indirect speech, by contrast with its causal function in the variant in the present verse). Epiphanius has εἰ. This could be due to loose quotation, or to the purely accidental omission of the first two letters of ἐπεί. Alternatively, it might have been an intentional alteration, designed to soften the unqualified assertion οὐ φείσομαι. This is less likely, however, since patristic sympathies would lie with the apostle rather than with the Corinthians. The reading ἤ (a f vg Pel) perhaps derives from a Greek MS which had εἰ, identical or closely similar in pronunciation.

[59] See BAGD s.v. ζητέω 2.c. for the sense 'demand', adopted by Furnish, p. 568.

[60] See, e.g., NEB, REB, BCN ('o'r Crist sy'n llefaru'); Furnish, ibid.

[61] See, e.g., RSV, NRSV; Martin, p. 451.

'in me'[62] or, as instrumental in function, 'through me'?[63] The first alternative might suggest a deeper inward unity between Paul and Christ, of the nature described in Gal 2.20. The second, it is argued, aligns Paul with the prophets and others through whom God has chosen to speak. In the LXX, this divine action is frequently expressed by means of the verb λαλέω followed by the preposition ἐν.[64] In the present verse, the phrase would indicate authoritative apostolic utterance.[65] In favour of 'in me' there is the formal parallel with the concluding ἐν ὑμῖν.[66] The latter, however, may mean 'among you',[67] 'in your midst', rather than 'within you (as individuals)'. In favour of 'through me' there would appear to be the septuagintal evidence noted above. On examination however, this is less impressive. In the majority of cases the verb λαλέω is followed not by the simple ἐν but by the phrase ἐν χειρί, with the name of the prophet in the genitive case. Of the references given, there are three only where the verb is followed by ἐν with a personal pronoun in the dative.[68] Consequently, septuagintal usage is not decisive for Paul's meaning. Nevertheless, in one sense the ἐν must be instrumental.[69] Paul is not referring, and neither are the Corinthians, to a purely inward experience of verbal communion with Christ. The question is whether, through Paul's words to the Corinthians, the authentic voice of Christ himself is heard.

In what form did they expect, or require, this Christ-speech to be heard? Several commentators suppose that they were looking for charismatic demonstrations such as ecstatic speech, accompanied, perhaps, by miraculous signs.[70] They would look for outwardly perceptible signs of inspiration.[71] But would this be sufficient? Paul has claimed (12.12), surely truthfully, already to have produced the 'apostolic signs' in Corinth, and it seems unlikely that he would have referred to his abundant endowment with glossolalia (1 Cor 14.18), unless his readers had witnessed, to some small degree at least, his possession of the gift.[72] The

---

[62] So, e.g., RSV, NRSV, BCN ('ynof fi'); Barrett, p. 327.
[63] So, e.g., REB, NEB; Furnish, p. 568; Martin, ibid.
[64] Heckel, *Schwachheit*, p. 122. References given in nn. 6, 7 include 2 Kgdms 23.2; 3 Kgdms 8.53, 56; 12.15; 15.29; 16.7; 22.24, 28; Jer 26.13; Hag 2.1; Zech 7.7.
[65] Heckel, *Schwachheit*, ibid.
[66] There is no reason to suppose that ἐν ὑμῖν has an instrumental sense.
[67] REB.
[68] 2 Kgdms 23.2 (ἐν ἐμοί); 3 Kgdms 22.24 (ἐν σοί), 28 (ἐν ἐμοί).
[69] For ἐν used to designate a personal agent, see BDR 219(1), and the reference to 1 Cor 6.2 (ἐν ὑμῖν κρίνεται ὁ κόσμος).
[70] Furnish, p. 576; Martin, p. 473; cf. Bultmann, p. 244.
[71] Bultmann, ibid.; cf. Windisch, p. 417.
[72] It is true that he affirms his preference for rational discourse, but this would have rung hollow, had the Corinthians not had first-hand knowledge of his glosso-lalic ability.

Corinthians appear to want something more in the way of proof of his apostolic representation of Christ. It would not have seemed unreasonable to them to make such a request. After all, as the following relative clause shows,[73] they themselves, collectively, possessed all these spiritual gifts, as Paul himself had noted (1 Cor 12.7–10). Of an apostle something further was to be expected. Perhaps, then, this 'something more' was to be a practical demonstration that Paul had the power, acting in Christ's name (cf. 1 Cor 5.3–5), to inflict overt and spectacular punishment on blatant sinners. Windisch offers this as one suggestion amongst others.[74] What would be expected would be a miraculous form of punishment such as the blinding of Elymas in Acts 13.8–11. Might there be a possible connection with the sentence passed on the delinquent of 1 Cor 5? Had the sentence failed to take effect?[75] If the wrongdoer, excluded from the church and thus 'handed over to Satan', had nevertheless remained alive and healthy, Paul's claim to be Christ's spokesman might have begun to look a little thin, and in need of confirmation. It may be, then, that both for Paul and for the Corinthians the 'proof' would consist in his effective and immediately obvious punishment of sinners.[76]

Other suggestions are offered, however, in respect of Paul's own understanding of what the δοκιμή should be. According to Bultmann, it is the power of the word of Christ to build up the church. Paul will be enabled to give right decisions in ethical matters, and to find the right word to bring wrongdoers to repentance, or, in the worst case, to hand the congregation over to divine judgement.[77] How the 'worst case' suggestion fits the concept of building up the congregation ethically and spiritually is not made clear. Barrett, similarly, appears to see the proof as the fact of the power of Christ within the Christian community, whilst allowing that it might consist in the declaration that the unrepentant (the whole church?) had 'fallen back into the realm of Satan'.[78] This type of interpretation, however, is not wholly convincing. On the one hand, the references to the positive aspects of Paul's mediation of the power of Christ are scarcely congruent with the warning at the end of v. 2. (And Paul has surely said already everything that he can say in the way of ethical exhortation and the call to penitence.) And on the other hand, mere declaration, without practical evidence of its efficacy, would

---

[73] See below.
[74] Windisch, p. 417.
[75] Windisch suggests this connection, but does not accept it.
[76] See Meyer, pp. 503–5.
[77] Bultmann, pp. 244–5.
[78] Barrett, pp. 334–5.

not serve to convince the Corinthians that Paul is truly the spokesman of Christ.

For this Christ, in their experience, is essentially powerful.[79] The implicit contrast with what they believe they know of Paul's experience of Christ is heightened by the chiastic structure[80] of the relative clause, which brings the personal pronouns ὑμᾶς and ὑμῖν to emphatic positions at the beginning and the end of the clause, and thus, in the case of εἰς ὑμᾶς, provides a recognisable contrast with the preceding ἐν ἐμοί. This understanding of v. 3b assumes that Paul is quoting what the Corinthians themselves are saying. But before we proceed further along this line we need to take note of other interpretations. Perhaps he has in view, simply and solely, the power which he foresees Christ will exercise in a negative sense, for punishment, when he himself arrives for his third visit to Corinth.[81] The verb δυνατεῖ, however, is in the present tense, and would not naturally suggest such a future reference. Perhaps, then, Paul is speaking in a positive way, seriously, and of his own initiative, of the power of Christ that has resulted in the foundation of the Corinthian church, and the bestowal of so many spiritual gifts upon its members, and of the apostolic signs he himself had wrought.[82] But it is not clear how this would fit the context. The whole of v. 3 is grammatically dependent upon v. 2, which speaks of the sinners in Corinth and warns of prospective punishment. It is preferable, then, to revert to the view that v. 3b reflects what the Corinthians themselves were saying, and that by implication they intended an adverse comparison as far as Paul was concerned. If so, Paul's quotation will contain an ironical nuance.[83] The power of Christ they claim to possess (cf. 1 Cor 4.8) may indeed be exercised amongst them (ἐν ὑμῖν), but in more ways than one. They have in mind their past and present experience of Christ's power, the abundance of their χαρίσματα and the like, but in his mind this power, through his agency, may be exercised to their disadvantage when he arrives in person in Corinth.[84]

[79] On the verb δυνατέω, see BAGD s.v. It is rare, and, as Plummer, p. 374, notes, it is peculiar to Paul in biblical Greek. In Rom 14.4 and 2 Cor 9.8 (see above, p. 577) it is the equivalent of δύναμαι (cf. LSJ s.v. δυνατέω), but here means 'be strong' (LSJ s.v. 2). According to BDF 108(2), it is 'a back-formation from the older ἀδυνατεῖν'.

[80] The chiastic structure is noted by, e.g., Plummer, ibid.; Furnish, p. 570; Martin, p. 456.

[81] Meyer, p. 504; cf. Wendland, pp. 255–6; Héring, p. 101.

[82] Plummer, ibid.; cf. Barrett, p. 335.

[83] Filson, p. 418. See also Prümm, *Diakonia Pneumatos* I, p. 715, who draws attention to 1 Cor 4.10, where Paul ironically cites the Corinthians' self-description.

[84] Furnish, p. 576.

They were, of course, asking for a proof that he speaks for Christ, and we have argued that this δοκιμή would consist in his power to punish sinners. But were they in earnest? What he has said in 12.21 and 13.2 suggests that these sinners were numerous—in his eyes at any rate. In fact, it could well be that some of them, alienated from Paul by his earlier strictures and moral demands, were foremost amongst those who were demanding that he should prove his apostolic claim to speak for Christ. If so, they could scarcely have feared punishment themselves. So how genuine was the request for proof? Various answers are possible. On the part of those who still remained loyal to Paul it would be a genuine demand. But others, including those liable to punishment, may have supported the request in the expectation that it would not be met (Paul would not come, or, if he did, he would fail the test): the church would then finally be freed of the apostle's attempts at supervision. Yet others might have looked forward to the dramatic punishment of a few blatant evildoers, confident that their own less obvious sins would not attract attention. Their concern would have been for a demonstration of miraculous apostolic power, rather than for the rooting out of sin as such. They would see themselves as spectators rather than as victims.

4. καὶ γὰρ[85] **ἐσταυρώθη ἐξ ἀσθενείας, ἀλλὰ ζῇ ἐκ δυνάμεως θεοῦ. καὶ γὰρ ἡμεῖς ἀσθενοῦμεν ἐν αὐτῷ, ἀλλὰ ζήσομεν σὺν αὐτῷ ἐκ δυνάμεως θεοῦ εἰς ὑμᾶς.** This verse as a whole substantiates v. 3, which itself is explanatory of the οὐ φείσομαι at the end of v. 2. When Paul arrives in Corinth he will not spare the sinful, since the congregation is demanding proof that he speaks with the power of Christ. This they shall have. But because he is seen by the Corinthians as weak, and indeed has himself stressed his weakness (albeit as the context in which he is endowed with divine strength), he needs to affirm its christological basis quite clearly. The Christ of whose power in Paul his readers demand evidence has himself suffered weakness, but nevertheless is the recipient of divine power. As a consequence, the weakness of the apostle is no hindrance to his own exercise of the power of Christ. The opening καὶ γάρ, 'for indeed',[86] will then possess this general explanatory reference.

It was 'because of weakness', ἐξ[87] ἀσθενείας, that Christ was

---

[85] Some witnesses (א[2] A D[1] Ψ 𝔐 lat sy Ambst) read εἰ before ἐσταυρώθη. This reading is secondary. It weakens the force of the assertion of Christ's weakness, turning it into a concession only: cf. Barrett, p. 327 n. 1; Martin, p. 452. The omission of εἰ has substantial support (𝔓[46vid] א* B D* F G K P 0243. 33. 81. 104. 365. 1241. 1739 al co Eus), and is to be accepted.

[86] See, e.g., Lambrecht, *Studies*, p. 592.

[87] See BAGD s.v. ἐκ 3.f., where this reference is given.

crucified. Heckel observes that this assertion has caused problems from the beginning of the history of exegesis, and that various attempts have been made to mitigate it.[88] These he lists as follows.

(i) The insertion of εἰ following καὶ γάρ,[89] with the intention of giving Paul's plain statement a conditional or concessive sense, 'even if', 'although'. The point of Paul's argument is thereby lost. For him, the weakness which resulted in crucifixion is the christological key to his own weakness, and its strongest justification.[90]

(ii) Some patristic exegetes referred the ἀσθένεια to the human sinfulness which was remedied by Christ's death.[91] But the atonement concept is not in view here.[92]

(iii) Chrysostom, with reference to 1 Cor 1.18–25, claims that Paul expresses the viewpoint of unbelievers: the weakness is not a reality, although by worldly standards this is what the crucifixion of Christ looks like.[93] Bruce follows this general line of exegesis.[94] So also does Furnish. He claims that Paul appears to view Christ's death 'as a demonstration of that weakness in and through which God's power is operative for salvation', and cites 1 Cor 1.17–31 as relevant to the interpretation of the present verse. The ἐξ ἀσθενείας, he suggests, could mean ' "in accordance with" the apparent "weakness" of God'. He doubts that Paul would consider the death of Christ to result from his weakness.[95] This third interpretation is equally unconvincing. With reference to Chrysostom, Heckel reiterates the point made under (i). Christ's (genuine) weakness is the basis of Paul's argument.[96] In the second half of v. 4 the apostle's own weakness is set in parallel to that of Christ, and his own weak condition is certainly real. The comparison with 1 Cor 1.17–31, I suggest, is misleading. In the first place, this passage is chiefly concerned with wisdom. Secondly, Paul's words about power and weakness can readily be seen as a highly compressed expression in which the two-stage Christ-event of 2 Cor 13.4 is collapsed into the single concept of the crucified Christ as the power of God. (It may be simpler to interpret 1 Cor 1.17–31 by means of 2 Cor 13.4, rather than *vice versa*.)

(iv) The ἐκ, it is argued, does not possess causal force. According to Bultmann, the meaning is simply 'as a weak person'.

[88] Heckel, *Schwachheit*, p. 125.
[89] See above, p. 882 n. 85.
[90] Heckel, *Schwachheit*, pp. 125–6.
[91] Heckel, *Schwachheit*, p. 126, with reference (n. 34) to Ambrosiaster, Pelagius, Origen, and Epiphanius.
[92] Heckel, *Schwachheit*, p. 127.
[93] Chrysostom, *PG* 61 col. 599 (NPNF XII, p. 414).
[94] Bruce, p. 253.
[95] Furnish, p. 571.
[96] Heckel, *Schwachheit*, pp. 126, 128.

The ἐκ is used to provide a rhetorical correspondence with ἐκ δυνάμεως.[97] Heckel points out, however, that precisely this repetition of the preposition suggests a correspondence in content, and thus a causal function for ἐκ. It is Paul's habit to use identical prepositions in antitheses (so, e.g., κατὰ σάρκα, κατὰ πνεῦμα), and here it serves to sharpen the contrast between human weakness and divine power.[98] Bultmann argues against the causal force on the basis of Phil 2.7–8. The point seems to be that since Christ's weakness was inherent in his having been born as man (Phil 2.7), this weakness cannot have been the reason for his crucifixion.[99] This is scarcely compelling. Christ's death was still due to, or made possible by, the essential weakness of humanity's earthly-bodily existence.[100]

We conclude, then, that Paul is speaking of Christ's own weakness, not hypothetically, nor simply as seen by the eyes of unbelievers, but as an actuality, and as the cause of his death. It is the weakness essentially inherent in mortal human existence.[101] In the unique case of Christ, as Barrett observes, the weakness of his death by crucifixion was a demonstration of the grace by which he became poor (8.9),[102] that is, became man (Phil 2.7).

Conversely, it is by reason of the power of God that he lives eternally.[103] It is God who raised Jesus from the dead (Rom 8.11; 1 Cor 6.14; 2 Cor 4.14). And this risen life is not just a state of being but is also a form of activity, as the δυνατεῖ of v. 3 shows.[104] According to Windisch, the antithesis 'crucified through weakness—living out of the power of God' was a familiar christological formula, serving to do away with the offence of the cross for believers: see 1 Cor 1.23–25; Heb 2.9; Ign., Eph 7.2 (πρῶτον παθητὸς καὶ τότε ἀπαθής).[105] The evidence adduced, however, is weak. There is wide linguistic divergence amongst the references cited, and it is unlikely that Paul would have made use of a formula designed to remove the offence of the crucified Christ.

He proceeds to relate what he has said about Christ to his own

---

[97] Bultmann, p. 245; cited by Heckel, *Schwachheit*, pp. 128–9.
[98] Heckel, *Schwachheit*, p. 129.
[99] Bultmann, p. 245.
[100] See Heckel, *Schwachheit*, pp. 124–5, for this understanding of ἀσθένεια.
[101] All the interpretations discussed above, whatever their differences, understand ἀσθένεια as a human condition. Güttgemanns, by contrast, claims that Paul is referring to a Corinthian gnostic slogan which saw ἀσθένεια as a cosmic demonic power. See *Der leidende Apostel*, pp. 148–51. This is highly speculative. Moreover, it can scarcely be correlated (as Paul's argument requires) with the ἀσθενοῦμεν of v. 4b, which refers to Paul's own physical and psychological state.
[102] Barrett, pp. 335–6; cf. Meyer, p. 505.
[103] Windisch, p. 418.
[104] Bultmann, ibid. This holds good, whether or not Paul is quoting the Corinthians with a hint of irony.
[105] Windisch, p. 418.

apostolic condition, and, with his concluding sentence, comes finally to make the claim that will give substantiating force to his threat of punitive action at the end of v. 2 [106] The basic line of thought is clear enough. At the same time, the precise function of the καὶ γάρ which opens v. 4b is not immediately obvious. Taken at face value, and as related to v. 4a, the combined particles would imply that Paul's own experience of weakness and strength in unity with Christ confirms the fact that strength in weakness is true of Christ himself.[107] But this is not the point at issue. It is not the power of Christ that the Corinthians doubt, but the power of Paul. (To suppose, as Windisch seems to do,[108] that Paul is concerned to confirm the truth of a christological statement inverts the thrust of his argument.) As Bultmann observes, what one would expect would be an expression of consequence (as in Rom 6.4):[109] 'as a result ... we also shall "live"'. But it may be that Paul's concern to substantiate his promise or threat that the Corinthians will get the proof they have been asking for (vv. 2–3) has caused him to repeat the causal καὶ γάρ of v. 4a,[110] perhaps now with the sense 'for we also'[111] rather than 'for indeed'.

His reference to his own weakness may be quite general. He may have in view the persecution and suffering reflected in his description of apostolic life in 4.7–14, and also in 12.9–10 and 11.23–27.[112] With these experiences in the background, however, he may be thinking more particularly of the 'thorn' of 12.7, and also of his apparently 'weak' showing in Corinth. In this respect he would have in mind what to the Corinthians appeared to be his weak and unimpressive personal presence (10.10),[113] and also his former sparing of the wrongdoers amongst them.[114] This verse, as we have noted, provides the grounding, ultimately, for the οὐ φείσομαι of v. 2, which implicitly indicates that up to this point he had not personally inflicted punishment in Corinth.[115] It is ἐν

---

[106] Cf. Lambrecht, *Studies*, p. 591; Bachmann, p. 414.

[107] Meyer, pp. 505–6; Plummer, p. 375. This is not quite the same thing (*pace* Bachmann, ibid.) as saying that Christ's weakness and strength is grounded in that of Paul.

[108] Windisch, ibid.

[109] Bultmann, p. 246.

[110] Bultmann, ibid., sees the καὶ γάρ of v. 4b as parallel to that of v. 4a, and as grounding v. 3.

[111] See Lambrecht, *Studies*, pp. 592, 596.

[112] Allo, p. 338; Chrysostom, *PG* 61 col. 600 (NPNF XII, p. 414); Windisch, p. 419.

[113] Windisch, ibid.

[114] Meyer, p. 506.

[115] The logical link with vv. 2–3 indicates that the plural ἡμεῖς ἀσθενοῦμεν refers only to Paul himself, *pace* Furnish, p. 571, who suggests that his associates may be included. There is an equally noticeable change from singular to plural in 11.21a, and here it is clear from the following vv. 21b–23 that Paul alone is meant in v. 21a.

886 COMMENTARY ON II CORINTHIANS

αὐτῷ,[116] i.e., ἐν Χριστῷ, that Paul is weak. Here, this will probably mean something like 'participating in' Christ's own weakness, not by external imitation or similarity of fortune but by virtue of the internal unity described in Gal 2.20 and Rom 8.10. This is, for Paul, a true description of his apostolic existence. True as it is, however, it is not the main point in v. 4b.[117] This is expressed in the concluding sentence: ἀλλὰ ζήσομεν σὺν αὐτῷ[118] ἐκ δυνάμεως θεοῦ εἰς ὑμᾶς.[119] And here we have an exegetical problem. The whole context requires the assertion that, despite the weakness to which he has just referred, Paul will show himself powerful in his forthcoming dealings with the Corinthian congregation. But the expression ζήσομεν[120] σὺν αὐτῷ does not convey this claim with any clarity. More than that, it may seem positively to point in a quite different direction. The verb stands in parallel with the ζῇ of v. 4a, where ζάω refers to the resurrection life of Christ.[121] The following σὺν αὐτῷ moreover, taken in conjunction with the verb, is reminiscent of 4.14, καὶ ἡμᾶς σὺν Ἰησοῦ ἐγερεῖ, and 1 Th 4.14, ὁ θεὸς τοὺς κοιμηθέντας διὰ τοῦ Ἰησοῦ ἄξει σὺν αὐτῷ:[122] it is obvious that in both these passages Paul is speaking of the final resurrection. And it has been argued that whenever he uses expressions which convey the idea of being 'with' Christ the idea is exclusively eschatological.[123] Are we, then, compelled to conclude that there must be here a reference (at least additionally) to the eternal, future, life of the resurrection?[124] But what would be the point (even if we allow that such an allusion

---

[116] Some witnesses (ℵ A F G *pc* r syᵖ bo) read σὺν αὐτῷ at this point. The reading ἐν αὐτῷ (B D Ψ 0243 𝔐 vg syʰ sa Ambst) has good support, however, as Metzger, *Textual Commentary*¹, p. 588, observes, and the reading σύν is due, he suggests, p. 587, to the influence of the later σὺν αὐτῷ. At this later point the converse assimilation has occurred in a few MSS (𝔓⁴⁶ ᵛⁱᵈ D* 33. 326 *pc* (g)).

[117] See Lambrecht, *Studies*, pp. 593–5. With reference to Grosheide, he argues that in sentences introduced by (καὶ) γάρ and with a second clause introduced by δέ or ἀλλά it is this second clause which may contain the real point to which the initial γάρ makes reference.

[118] See above, n. 116: some witnesses read ἐν αὐτῷ.

[119] See n. 125 below.

[120] Some MSS (D² Ψ 𝔐) read the middle future ζησόμεθα. The majority (𝔓⁴⁶ ℵ A B D* F G 0243. 33. 81. 104. 365. 630. 1175. 1241. 1739. 1881. 2464 *al.*) have the active ζήσομεν. The latter, in view of its wide attestation, is correct.

[121] Heckel, *Schwachheit*, p. 133.

[122] Windisch, p. 419.

[123] A. Deissmann, *Die neutestamentliche Formel, in Christo Jesu*, Marburg, 1892, p. 126; as cited by Hoffmann, *Toten*, pp. 303, 308. See also Heckel, *Schwachheit*, ibid. Hoffmann argues that by no means all the Pauline σύν-formulations have an eschatological reference. But the examples he cites are all compound verbs, with the single exception of Rom 6.8, ἀπεθάνομεν σὺν Χριστῷ. This does allow the possibility that the σὺν αὐτῷ in the present verse is non-eschatological, but does not offer strong support for this view.

[124] So Heckel, *Schwachheit*, ibid.

would be only additional)? It is doubtful whether the Corinthians were concerned, the one way or the other, about Paul's individual eschatological prospects. Furthermore, the concluding εἰς ὑμᾶς¹²⁵ does suggest, as Lambrecht points out,¹²⁶ that what he is talking of is his imminent demonstration of apostolic power in Corinth.¹²⁷ Bultmann notes the correspondence with the εἰς ὑμᾶς of v. 3.¹²⁸ If, then, we accept this 'non-eschatological' interpretation, which the context seems to demand, how are we to account for Paul's use of language which in itself would more naturally refer to future resurrection? In part it may be due simply to a desire to stress the parallel between the weakness and power of Christ, seen in actual death and resurrection, and his own, derivative, power-despite-weakness, in which, however, suffering has not yet resulted in death and the life of the resurrection is still to come. In part, also, he does believe (4.10–11) that in some way the resurrection life of Jesus is revealed within his present mortal life. In relation to the situation in Corinth to which chap. 13 is addressed, he may understand this to mean, as Barrett suggests, that 'God will grant him such a measure of resurrection life as will suffice' for him to deal with this state of affairs.¹²⁹ What then, lastly, of the σὺν αὐτῷ, which contributes to the impression that Paul has the future life in mind? Prümm is helpful here. He suggests that we may gain access to the apostle's intention by noting his use of σύν in 1 Cor 5.4, where the community is (to be) gathered together, to condemn the sinner of v. 1, σὺν τῇ δυνάμει τοῦ κυρίου ἡμῶν Ἰησοῦ.¹³⁰ We have suggested above that Paul may be aware that his readers might have in mind this earlier occasion.¹³¹ If this is right, and if he recalls his words in 1 Corinthians, it is possible that the σὺν αὐτῷ of the present verse is a compressed version of the phrase in 1 Cor 5.4. In that case, it contains no reference to the future resurrection life of believers with Christ.

5. Ἑαυτοὺς πειράζετε εἰ ἐστὲ ἐν τῇ πίστει, ἑαυτοὺς δοκιμάζετε· ἢ οὐκ ἐπιγινώσκετε ἑαυτοὺς ὅτι Ἰησοῦς Χριστὸς ἐν ὑμῖν; εἰ μήτι ἀδόκιμοί ἐστε. Paul has responded to the Corinthians' demand that he authenticate himself as Christ's

¹²⁵ The εἰς will mean 'with respect to', 'with reference to', see BAGD s.v. εἰς 5. A few witnesses (B D² r) omit the phrase εἰς ὑμᾶς. This may be due to pure accident. Alternatively, it may have been an intentional scribal 'correction', to excise what seemed to be an awkward intrusion into an obvious allusion to the future life.
¹²⁶ Lambrecht, *Studies*, p. 598.
¹²⁷ So most commentators. See, e.g., Meyer, pp. 506–7; Bachmann, p. 415; Allo, p. 338; Strachan, p. 38; Hughes, p. 479.
¹²⁸ Bultmann, p. 246.
¹²⁹ Barrett, p. 337.
¹³⁰ Prümm, *Diakonia Pneumatos* I, p. 712.
¹³¹ See above, pp. 877, 879–80.

spokesman with the warning that such authentication may not be to their liking. Now, to obviate the need for harsh measures on his part, he urges them to test *their own* authenticity as Christians.[132] The initial position of the reflexive pronoun ἑαυτούς before both imperatives gives it emphasis,[133] and the duplication of the basic injunction[134] underlines its importance.

What Paul's readers are to test is whether[135] they are ἐν τῇ πίστει, literally, 'in (the) faith'. But what exactly does he mean by this phrase? The word πίστις can be used in various senses, with resulting differences of interpretation.

(i) Does it mean 'body of belief', or 'doctrine'?[136] Is Paul telling his readers to test their own orthodoxy? In the formal sense of such terms this seems unlikely. Martin, however, appears to include something like this nuance of meaning in his definition. The word here, he suggests, has 'particular allusion to a correct appreciation of the Pauline Gospel versus the rival kerygma (11:4)'.[137] But the general context (12.19–13.2; 13.7) has more to do with the practical moral conduct of the Corinthians than with kerygmatic beliefs as such.[138] Paul is not asking them to assess their state of doctrinal orthodoxy.

(ii) Wendland, followed by Barrett, relates v. 5a more closely to v. 5b: to exist ἐν τῇ πίστει is synonymous with the indwelling of Christ in believers.[139] But to say that faith 'is the life of Christ in the believer'[140] produces some confusion. Faith describes the attitude of the Christian to Christ, which is not the same thing, strictly speaking, as Christ's becoming present and active within the spirit of the Christian, however closely related and necessarily complementary the one may be to the other.

(iii) Faith is to be understood primarily as obedience: so Bultmann,[141] followed by Furnish.[142] This is Paul's basic conception of faith,[143] and it has appeared already in the

---

[132] Cf. Bultmann, p. 247.

[133] Bachmann, p. 415; Plummer, p. 375; Windisch, p. 420; Barrett, p. 337; Furnish, p. 571.

[134] As Wolff, p. 263, notes, the verbs πειράζω and δοκιμάζω are used synonymously. For πειράζω see BAGD s.v. 2. a, 'put (someone) to the test'; for δοκιμάζω followed by the reflexive pronoun, see BAGD s.v. δοκιμάζω 1., 'examine oneself'.

[135] For εἰ as an interrogative particle, 'whether', see BAGD s.v. V.2.

[136] See BAGD, s.v. πίστις 3.

[137] Martin, p. 478: he allows for a more general sense as well (see below).

[138] The occurrence of the article with πίστις does not mean that the word must have the sense 'the faith', i.e., 'the Christian religion', or 'Christian doctrine'. There are several examples elsewhere in which the article is found with the noun where πίστις clearly refers to the believer's attitude to God (Rom 3.30, 31; 4.20; 11.20).

[139] Wendland, p. 257; Barrett, p. 338.

[140] Wendland, ibid, translated by Barrett, ibid.

[141] Bultmann, p. 247.

[142] Furnish, p. 577.

[143] According to Bultmann, *Theol. of the NT* I, pp. 314–16.

present letter, at least by implication: in 10.6 he describes the state of affairs he hopes for in Corinth as one in which obedience will be completed, whilst in 10.15 he looks for the increase of faith. In the letter of chaps. 1–8, moreover, we find the explicit connection between obedience and testing: in 2.9 the 'tested character' (δοκιμή) of the readers consists in their being 'obedient' (ὑπήκοοι).[144] In consequence, it could be that the apostle's call to self-examination in respect of their faith might associate itself in their minds with the thought of obedience. As Bultmann notes, the result of the self-testing, Paul would hope, would be the attestation of a moral condition which would leave no future opening for vices of the kind mentioned in 12.20–21.[145] This interpretation is suited to the context, and may be right. And yet one has to ask whether this virtual equation of faith with obedience is altogether valid. Bultmann himself allows that faith is also confession and confidence.[146] Moreover, a glance at a concordance will show that the 'faith' vocabulary in the Pauline letters is very much more numerous than the vocabulary of 'obedience'. Possibly, then, Paul uses πίστις here in a wider sense.

(iv) In this wider sense, to 'exist in faith' means simply to live the Christian life, contrasted with the life of the unbeliever.[147] To Paul, the contrast would be a sharp one. Martin comments: 'Paul is speaking of a new situation and a new existence as Christian (5.17).' It will be inclusive of obedience and trust,[148] but according to this definition 'faith' will have a more extensive scope. This would accord with a similarly general use of πίστις in 1.24.[149] It appears to be the best exegetical option.

That what the Corinthians themselves need (at least in their present state) is authentication is emphasised, not only by the repetition of the reflexive pronoun in its prominent position, but also by the use of δοκιμάζω, which echoes the δοκιμή of v. 3, i.e., their own demand for authentication from Paul. His exhortation to them to engage in self-evaluation is in line with the Greek philosophical tradition.[150] Perhaps, for some of his readers, this

---

144 References cited by Bultmann, in his commentary, p. 247.

145 Bultmann, ibid.

146 Bultmann, *Theol. of the NT* I, pp. 317–19, 322–3.

147 Héring, p. 102; Martin, p. 478.

148 Martin, ibid.

149 As Furnish, p. 577, suggests, the apparent contradiction between the confidence of 1.24 and the questioning tone of the present verse will have resulted from the shaking of Paul's confidence in the interval between the letter of chaps. 1–8 and that of chaps. 10–13.

150 See Furnish, p. 572, with reference to H. D. Betz, *Galatians*, Hermeneia, Philadelphia, 1979, p. 302 nn. 90–4, and also to Windisch, p. 420 n. 1, as citing Marcus Aurelius X 37. Here the point is that consideration of another person's

might give more force to his words. According to Betz, we may note further, the use of the δοκιμή-language in these verses (3, 5–7) indicates that Paul has drawn the Corinthians into a dialogue on the question of authentication (in its application to Paul, his opponents, and the Corinthians themselves), and this dialogue is the theological centre of the letter. The imperatives in the present verse express its basic intention, since the decisive question concerns the Corinthians' own position. In the course of the letter, having begun with uncertainty about Paul, they then become uncertain about the rival missionaries and then about themselves.[151] This is certainly one way of reading chaps. 10–13. But perhaps it does not do sufficient justice to the prominence throughout of Paul's self-defence, which may well seem to be the predominant issue.

The motif of self-defence will recur in v. 6. First, however, Paul follows his exhortations with a question and an apparent qualification. The point of the question is not altogether easy to determine. Do they not know, he asks, that Jesus Christ[152] is 'within' them?[153] There are various ways of understanding this.

(i) The question really relates to the Corinthians' judgement of Paul himself. Chrysostom supposes that Paul is pointing out to the Corinthians that, since, through self-examination, they are able to verify that Christ is in *them*, it must be still more certainly true that Christ is in *him*, as their teacher.[154] Hughes takes the same line. If the Corinthians have experienced divine grace through receiving the gospel, this provides clear proof that it is Christ who

---

actions must be preceded by the consideration of one's own: ἄρχου δὲ ἀπὸ σαυτοῦ, καὶ σαυτὸν πρῶτον ἐξέταζε ('But begin with thyself, cross-examine thyself first', LCL). Furnish adds that Dio Chrysostom is following this tradition when he commends the Delphic pronouncement on self-knowledge (*Or.* IV 57). Dio's text runs: οὐδεὶς γὰρ τῶν ἀφρόνων καὶ πονηρῶν ἐπίσταται ἑαυτόν. οὐ γὰρ ἂν τοῦτο πρῶτον προσέταττεν ὁ Ἀπόλλων ὡς χαλεπώτατον ἑκάστῳ, γνῶναι ἑαυτόν ('For no foolish and evil man knows himself; else Apollo would not have given as the first commandment, "Know thyself!" regarding it as the most difficult thing for every man,' LCL; more literally, 'else Apollo would not command this first, to know oneself, as the most difficult thing for each man.').

[151] Betz, *Tradition*, pp. 133–4.

[152] There are variants here. The order Ἰησοῦς Χριστός (B D Ψ 𝔐 a vg^ms sy) is preferable to Χριστὸς Ἰησοῦς (א A F G P 0243. 326. 629. 630. 1175. 1241. 1739. 1881. 2464 al b vg Ambst). The reading of B conforms to Paul's general practice, and there would be no reason here for him to diverge from it. See Vol. I, pp. 81–2. The other variant concerns the omission or addition of ἐστιν after ὑμῖν. The verb is lacking in several witnesses (𝔓46 B D* 33 *pc*), present in others (א A D² F G Ψ 0243 𝔐). The omission is probably original. It creates an awkward ellipsis which would demand correction.

[153] For the grammatical construction following ἐπιγνώσκετε, see BAGD s.v. ἐπιγινώσκω 2.a; a parallel is noted in 1 Cor 14.37 (ἐπιγινώσκετε ἃ γράφω ὑμῖν ὅτι κυρίου ἐστιν ἐντολή).

[154] Chrysostom *PG* 61 col. 601 (NPNF XII, p. 414).

speaks through Paul since it was through his ministry that the gospel came to them.[155] Whilst, however, Paul could certainly have this thought in mind, the question of his own authentication does not occur explicitly until v. 6. There it is introduced as an additional point, and the emphatic ἡμεῖς suggests some contrast with those to whom v. 5 refers.

(ii) Windisch suggests that Paul may be reproducing the Corinthians' own self-conscious judgement: 'Jesus Christ is within us.' In quoting them he would wish to remind them that their self-examination must turn out well.[156] But this does not quite fit the way Paul uses this same formula ([ἢ] οὐ[κ] + verb of knowing) elsewhere. Windisch himself refers to 1 Cor 3.16: οὐκ οἴδατε ὅτι ναὸς θεοῦ ἐστε; But here the formula is used to remind the readers of what they appear to have forgotten, not to introduce an allusion to what they are themselves (rightly or wrongly) certain about. The same use occurs in 1 Cor 6.19.

(iii) According to Bultmann, the point is this. The Corinthians assume that Christ is 'in them' (cf. Windisch), but have failed to understand what this means. They have failed to realise that the indwelling Christ is the Lord, who critically assesses them and makes demands upon them.[157] Further, there is an implicit allusion to Paul's authentication. If the Corinthians are recalled to the realisation of the indwelling Christ as Lord, they will recognise that Christ demands what Paul is demanding, and should therefore conclude that he is Christ's spokesman.[158] Whether this further nuance of meaning is present is debatable, as we have noted under (i) above. But the basic point is valid. Paul expresses himself elliptically, but he seems to be saying something like this. His readers must remember that the presence of the indwelling Christ[159] requires that they should conform to the standards of behaviour that Christian faith demands, and therefore that they should themselves critically test the quality of their Christian life. This will be at the same time a test of the reality of their new Christian existence in the fullest sense.[160] The initial οὐκ of the question in v. 5b has indicated that an

---

[155] Hughes, pp. 480–1.
[156] Windisch, p. 420.
[157] Furnish, p. 577, follows Bultmann on this.
[158] Bultmann, p. 247.
[159] Is this indwelling seen as corporate, the presence of Christ in the community, or as individual, Christ's presence within the believer, or as both? Probably as both. The specific references elsewhere to the indwelling of Christ refer to the individual believer: Rom 8.9–10; Gal 2.10. Divine presence in the community is the presence of the Spirit, 1 Cor 3.16, or of God, 2 Cor 6.16. But since the Spirit is the Spirit of Christ, as well as the Spirit of God (Rom 8.9–10), the Spirit's indwelling in the community is also that of Christ.
[160] See above, on the meaning of πίστις.

affirmative answer is expected. Surely the Corinthians know that Christ is within, is amongst, them. But in v. 5c Paul adds a qualification: εἰ μήτι, unless, perhaps,[161] they are unauthentic as Christians. Why this qualification? Plummer and Windisch suppose that it expresses genuine fear lest the Corinthians might, after all, turn out not to be genuine.[162] Allo, however, thinks that Paul intends to stir them out of their indolence,[163] and Martin suggests that he is speaking ironically.[164] These two suggestions combined provide a more likely interpretation than the supposition that real doubt is intended. The irony would catch the hearers' attention and arouse a response. There is then a better connection with v. 6. Had Paul wished to say that he doubted the genuineness of his readers' Christian faith, but that he hoped for recognition of his own, we should expect a stronger adversative at the beginning of v. 6 than δέ.

6. ἐλπίζω δὲ ὅτι γνώσεσθε ὅτι ἡμεῖς οὐκ ἐσμὲν ἀδόκιμοι. It is at this point that Paul expresses the hope that his readers will recognise his own authenticity.[165] This must mean his authenticity as a Christian apostle. In what way, then, does he foresee that this recognition may come about? There are two sharply divergent views. One interpretation is represented by Chrysostom and Meyer. Chrysostom takes Paul's words as a threat. If the possibility of Corinthian unauthenticity mentioned in v. 5c should be realised, the readers will show that they wish to receive the proof of Christ's presence in Paul in the form of punishment, and he is threatening that this is what they will get.[166] Meyer takes a similar view, and comments that it is not until v. 7 that Paul expresses his affection for the Corinthians.[167] This is the less probable interpretation. In v. 5c we do not have any strong suggestion that the readers will very likely prove to be ἀδόκιμοι: the clause is probably ironical, and in any case the εἰ μήτι is hesitant.

---

[161] On εἰ μήτι see BAGD s.v. εἰ VI. 9.
[162] Plummer, p. 376; Windisch, p. 421.
[163] Allo, p. 339.
[164] Martin, p. 479.
[165] The main verb ἐλπίζω is singular, whilst in the ὅτι-clause we find the plural ἡμεῖς ... ἐσμέν. Furnish, p. 578, suggests that the plural may include Silvanus and Timothy (see 1.19), who had assisted in the founding of the Corinthian church. This is unlikely. It is clear that in the letter of chaps. 10–13 Paul uses first plurals on occasions when he is referring to himself alone: see, e.g., 10.7–11; 11.6. See Vol. I, p. 106. Conversely, the singular ἐλπίζω is not significant as marking any distinction between reference solely to Paul and reference to the apostle with his associates, since, as Windisch, p. 34, notes, he habitually uses the singular λέγω, γράφω, and ἐλπίζω, whether or not he employs the literary plural for other verbs. See also Carrez, 'Le "Nous" ', p. 483, who includes this verse in the category of first plurals which refer to Paul as an individual.
[166] Chrysostom, PG 61 col. 601 (NPNF XII, p. 415).
[167] Meyer, p. 508.

Furthermore, ἐλπίζω would be an odd verb for Paul to use by way
of introducing a threat. As Bultmann observes, we should expect
φοβοῦμαι.[168] The alternative explanation would find here the
expression of a genuine hope for positive recognition of Paul's
apostolate. If the Corinthians accede to his request that they test
themselves, this in itself will be proof of such recognition.[169] And
if, as a result, they are able to affirm their own Christian standing,
this also will vindicate Paul's authenticity, since it was through his
agency that they had come to faith.[170] Perhaps, as Furnish
maintains, this does not amount to an expression of actual confidence.[171] Had Paul been totally certain of the outcome he could
well have written οἶδα rather than ἐλπίζω. Nevertheless, it is a
positive rather than a negative attitude that is reflected here. We
prefer this alternative explanation: Paul's hope is real.

**7. εὐχόμεθα[172] δὲ πρὸς τὸν θεὸν μὴ ποιῆσαι ὑμᾶς κακὸν
μηδέν, οὐχ ἵνα ἡμεῖς δόκιμοι φανῶμεν, ἀλλ' ἵνα ὑμεῖς τὸ
καλὸν ποιῆτε, ἡμεῖς δὲ ὡς ἀδόκιμοι ὦμεν.** In v. 6 Paul had
momentarily turned back to the question of his own authentication. Now he comes back to the situation of his readers. The δέ
marks this slight contrast.[173] With the Corinthians again in view,
Paul then tells them of his prayer[174] for them. He intends to
communicate its content, but does so with some ambiguity. There
are three main difficulties. In v. 7a the grammatical function of
ὑμᾶς is not clear, nor is the sense to be given to ποιῆσαι κακόν. In
v. 7b–c the force of ἵνα requires discussion. And in 7d we shall
need to ask how and why the apostle can envisage himself as
ἀδόκιμος, disclaiming in 7c the intention to be seen as δόκιμος.

Taking these questions one by one, we come first (v. 7a) to the
ambiguous function of ὑμᾶς and ποιῆσαι … κακόν. Simply from
the grammatical viewpoint ὑμᾶς could serve either as the object of
ποιῆσαι κακὸν or as the subject. If the former alternative is
correct, the subject of the infinitival phrase remains implicit:
either we are to understand ἡμεῖς (from the main verb in the first

168 Bultmann, p. 249. We may note that the absence of a verb of apprehension
would count against Martin, p. 480, who supposes Paul fears lack of acknowledgement.
169 Bultmann, p. 248.
170 Barrett, p. 338.
171 Furnish, p. 572.
172 The reading εὐχόμεθα has substantial attestation (𝔓46 ℵ A B D* F G K P 33.
81. 104. 365. 1175. 1241. 2464. 2495 al lat syʰ co). The alternative εὔχομαι (D2 Ψ
0243 𝔐 a b vgᵐˢˢ syᵖ saᵐˢ Ambst) is probably an assimilation to the singular ἐλπίζω
of v. 6.
173 Windisch, p. 421.
174 See BAGD s.v. εὔχομαι 1. for parallels to the verb followed by πρὸς τὸν θεόν
(or some other word for deity): e.g., Xen., *Symp.* 4.55 (εὐχομένου πρὸς τοὺς θεούς);
2 Macc 15.27 (πρὸς τὸν θεὸν εὐχόμενοι).

plural) or else the implied subject is τὸν θεόν (consequent upon the preceding πρὸς τὸν θεόν). But which of the two basic alternatives has the better support? Is ὑμᾶς the object or subject of ποιῆσαι κακόν? Some degree of support can be recorded for the view that ὑμᾶς is the object. In the first edition (1961) of the New English Bible New Testament the translation runs: 'Our prayer to God is that we may not have to hurt you.' The implicit subject here is ἡμεῖς. Ewald had previously taken the same line.[175] Lietzmann also interprets ὑμᾶς as the object, but with τὸν θεόν as the implicit subject. The prayer is that God will not need to punish the Corinthians. Paul prays that his apprehension (v. 5c) lest they should be found ἀδόκιμοι may not be realised.[176] This line of interpretation, however, is generally felt to be unlikely. The phrase ποιῆσαι κακόν would be an unusual expression for the meting out of punishment.[177] There is an intentional parallel, moreover, between this clause and the following ἵνα ὑμεῖς τὸ καλὸν ποιῆτε, and this means that κακόν, as the opposite of τὸ καλόν (moral good),[178] must refer to moral evil.[179] Lastly, the expression κακὸν ποιεῖν does not take an accusative of the object.[180]

Hence, it is much more probable that ὑμᾶς is the subject of the infinitival clause. In the complete New English Bible (1970), in which there has been some minor revision of the first edition of the New Testament, the translation of v. 7a now runs: 'Our prayer to God is that you may do no wrong.' This interpretation has majority support.[181] The content of the κακόν is left vague. It may be that Paul's prayer bears some relation to v. 5c. The fulfilment of his petition that the Corinthians should do no evil at all[182] would obviate the possibility (however remote, or ironically expressed) that they might perhaps turn out not to be genuine Christians.[183]

Secondly, what is the function of the ἵνα in v. 7b and v. 7c–d? Does it introduce the purpose of Paul's prayer? Or does it indicate that the following clauses refer, negatively and positively, to the content of the prayer? Either is possible grammatically,[184]

---

[175] Ewald, p. 313. See also Grotius, p. 511: 'Ne cogar cuiquam poenam infligere.'
[176] Lietzmann, pp. 161–2.
[177] Meyer, p. 509; Windisch, p. 422; Barrett, p. 339; Bultmann, p. 249.
[178] For this sense of καλός, see BAGD s.v. 2.b.
[179] Allo, p. 339; cf. Barrett, ibid.; Bultmann, ibid.
[180] Kümmel, p. 214; Barrett, ibid.
[181] See, e.g., REB, RSV, NRSV, JB; Barrett, p. 327; Furnish, p. 569; Martin, p. 451.
[182] Note the additional emphatic μηδέν.
[183] Cf. Martin, p. 481.
[184] See BAGD s.v. ἵνα I.1.a. and II.1.a.γ. On the latter function, cf. Wiles, *Intercessory Prayers*, p. 173.

and as regards sense a decision is difficult. In favour of taking the ἵνα-clauses as final there is the preceding μὴ ποιῆσαι ὑμᾶς κακὸν μηδέν. Against this interpretation there is the question of whether Paul would really pray with the purposive intention that he might himself be unapproved (v. 7d). The suggestion is still there, of course, if the ἵνα-clauses amplify the content of the prayer, but it would be less pronounced. We take the ἵνα as referring to the prayer-content, though the decision is a fine one.[185]

The third problem relates to the sense to be given to the adjectives δόκιμος (v. 7c) and ἀδόκιμος (v. 7d). Clearly Paul is talking about his authenticity, or alleged unauthenticity, as an apostle. But his genuineness might be demonstrated in two quite opposite ways.[186] It might be seen as proved by his capacity for engendering Christian faith and building up Christian communities. But equally his apostolicity might be validated by his displaying remarkable powers of inflicting punishment on moral delinquents. Earlier in the Corinthian correspondence he has referred to the first criterion (1 Cor 9.1–2; 2 Cor 3.1–3), but in the present context, in vv. 2–3, it seems to be the second that is in view. If the first ἵνα-clause expands obliquely upon the μὴ ποιῆσαι ὑμᾶς κακὸν μηδέν, Paul could be praying that he may not receive validation through 'successful' visible punishment of recalcitrant sinners. Rather, in the second ἵνα-clause, he desires to remain in this sense unauthenticated. But there is a problem here. If this is the meaning of v. 7d, as we would maintain, the sense given to ἀδόκιμοι differs from its meaning in v. 6, i.e., not authenticated by success in positive, constructive Christian work. It may be, however, that the connotations of the word vary somewhat. The basic sense is 'unauthentic', 'unapproved', as an apostle. But different aspects of this hypothetical unauthenticity may be in view at different points.

Paul's positive prayer for his readers is that they may do what is morally good.[187] Plummer suggests the additional nuance of 'morally beautiful'.[188] Furnish observes that τὸ καλόν is 'a cardinal theme of Hellenistic ethics',[189] but goes on to note, with Windisch, that in the Pauline context the meaning of τὸ καλὸν ποιεῖν is to be obedient to the will of God: see Rom 7.21–22.[190]

8. οὐ γὰρ δυνάμεθά τι κατὰ τῆς ἀληθείας, ἀλλὰ ὑπὲρ τῆς ἀληθείας. Paul explains the reason for his prayer (v. 7) that the

---

[185] In support of purpose, see Meyer, p. 509; Plummer, p. 377. In support of content, see Allo, pp. 339, 341.
[186] Compare the note on v. 6 above.
[187] See above, p. 894 n. 178.
[188] Plummer, p. 377.
[189] Furnish, p. 573.
[190] Furnish, p. 578; Windisch, p. 422.

Corinthians may do what is good, whatever the consequence for himself: he is able to do nothing but what serves the truth. But what does he mean by ἀλήθεια? And why does he begin by negating the possibility of acting against the truth?[191] The second of these questions is perhaps easier to answer than the first. The same idiom has been employed in v. 7 and it may have seemed natural to repeat it. Or it could be that Paul is making use of some existing proverbial saying, perhaps slightly reshaped for his own purpose. Furnish comments that the verse 'sounds like a general maxim affirming the sovereign power of *the truth*'.[192] The negative aspect of the assertion may be due to the original maxim.

The sense to be attached to ἀλήθεια in the present context, however, is more debatable. Two basic interpretations have been suggested.

(i) The word refers to the real facts (or the potential real facts) of the Corinthian situation. This is the interpretation proposed by Chrysostom. Paul is envisaging the fulfilment of his prayer in v. 7, that the Corinthians may do no evil whatsoever but rather do good. If this is the truth about them, Paul will remain ἀδόκιμος: his punitive powers will remain untested because his readers will deserve no punishment. He cannot act in contravention of this state of affairs. Rather, he must promote it.[193] There are some objections, however, to this exegesis. Bultmann claims that ἀλήθεια in the sense 'the actual facts of the situation' is not found elsewhere in Paul.[194] And Meyer argues that the ὑπὲρ τῆς ἀληθείας demands a more comprehensive interpretation.[195]

(ii) Here ἀλήθεια is synonymous with the gospel. Meyer points to 4.2 and 6.7 where the word is used of the content of Paul's proclamation.[196] His activity on behalf of the gospel would include the concern for his converts' moral goodness which he has shown in v. 7.[197] This makes good sense of the positive aspect of the assertion. The negative aspect may have no very definite

---

[191] For δύναμαι followed by the accusative, see BAGD s.v. 3.: ποιεῖν is to be supplied.

[192] Furnish, p. 579. See also Windisch, p. 423, who notes similar sentiments in Ecclesiasticus: see e.g. 4.25 μὴ ἀντίλεγε τῇ ἀληθείᾳ, 28 ἕως θανάτου ἀγώνισαι περὶ τῆς ἀληθείας. From Plato he cites *Symp.* 201C : οὐ μὲν οὖν τῇ ἀληθείᾳ ... δύνασαι ἀντιλέγειν ('No, it is Truth ... whom you cannot contradict', LCL). He observes that Philo identifies 'the truth' with philosophy and reproaches the sophists with fighting 'against the truth': *Post. Caini*, 101–2. The present saying might have been coined by the philosophers and picked up by Paul from current speech.

[193] Chrysostom, *PG* 61 col. 602 (NPNF XII, p. 415).

[194] Bultmann, p. 250.

[195] Meyer, p. 510.

[196] Meyer, ibid. Other exegetes who interpret ἀλήθεια in this sense include Filson, p. 421; Tasker, p. 189; Bultmann, ibid; Furnish, p. 579.

[197] Cf. Tasker, ibid.

content.[198] Or it might express in strong terms, although obliquely, Paul's ultimate lack of concern for his own personal interests (v. 7d),[199] by contrast with his urgent desire that the truth of the gospel should be visibly demonstrated in the lives of the Corinthians. This second interpretation of ἀλήθεια may be preferable.

9. χαίρομεν γὰρ ὅταν ἡμεῖς ἀσθενῶμεν, ὑμεῖς δὲ δυνατοὶ ἦτε· τοῦτο καὶ εὐχόμεθα, τὴν ὑμῶν κατάρτισιν. Paul adds further confirmation of his claim in v. 7 that his concern is for the Corinthians, not for himself. As in v. 7, his assertion is underlined by the emphatic use of ἡμεῖς and ὑμεῖς. He rejoices whenever he himself is weak but his readers are strong. At the same time, the reversion to the language of strength and weakness points back to vv. 3–4.

How comprehensive is the state of weakness which Paul has in mind here? Some commentators restrict the sense of ἀσθενῶμεν to the content of v. 7d i.e., as synonymous with the ἀδόκιμοι, interpreted to mean 'untested in respect of punitive power'.[200] Barrett, however, takes it in a more general sense, as a reference to Paul's 'unremitting service and self-abasement'.[201] Furnish accepts the view that v. 9a amplifies the conclusion of v. 7 and understands the weakness envisaged as, in part, situations in which there is no call for the apostle to exercise punitive discipline. But he would broaden the concept as well, to include all those forms of weakness which serve as the means of disclosing the power of God (4.7; 12.9–10; 13.3–4); v. 9a is an extension of 12.9.[202] On various counts it seems probable that this broader view of the sense of ἀσθενῶμεν is correct. First, the ὅταν, 'whenever', generalises the statement. Secondly, Paul's previous allusion in v. 4 to his own weakness has connected this condition with his unity with the crucified Christ, i.e., with a relationship which determined his whole apostolic existence, not simply one facet of it in relation to one particular church.

Just as the reference to Paul's weakness directs his correspondents back to his words in v. 4, so his allusion to their strength is reminiscent of what he has said in v. 3 about Christ's being powerful (δυνατεῖ) amongst them. There, however, he was speaking ironically, we have argued, quoting the Corinthians' self-description with a hint that their experience of Christ's power might turn out not to their liking.[203] Here he must be speaking seriously. He does

[198] See above, p. 896.
[199] Filson, p. 421.
[200] Chrysostom, *PG* 61 cols 602–3 (NPNF XII, pp. 415–16); Meyer, p. 511; see also Plummer, p. 378; Hughes, p. 483; Bruce, p. 254.
[201] Barrett, p. 340.
[202] Furnish, pp. 579–80.
[203] See above, p. 881.

rejoice, should they be endowed with genuine spiritual strength. In view of v. 7, the sense must be 'morally strong'.[204] This is what Paul prays for.

The τοῦτο refers back to the hoped for moral and spiritual strength of his correspondents,[205] and the concluding τὴν ὑμῶν κατάρτισιν is a comprehensive term for the bringing about of this good moral condition. Plummer, differently, supposes τοῦτο to have a forward reference. The prayer is additional to what has gone before, and the κατάρτισις, similarly, must have some additional meaning, i.e., 'perfection'.[206] This is unlikely. Quite apart from the difficulty of determining the meaning of κατάρτισις, the formulation of the prayer does not allow for this interpretation. Reference to an extra prayer-content would require something like: εὐχόμεθα δὲ καὶ τοῦτο, 'and we pray for this also'.

The word κατάρτισις is hapax legomenon in the NT, and is only sparsely attested elsewhere.[207] Exegetes therefore look to its cognates for clues to its meaning here. In Eph 4.12 the noun καταρτισμός appears (again as hapax legomenon in the NT). This appears to be a medical term in origin, referring to the setting of a broken bone, and to mean, more generally, 'preparation'.[208] But the sense given for its use in Eph 4.12, in BAGD, is 'equipment', 'equipping', with the possible alternative 'training', 'discipline'.[209] This scarcely seems relevant to the present occurrence of κατάρτισις.[210] The verb καταρτίζω, however, is comparatively frequent. Hence, it would seem better to look to the use of the verb for assistance in determining the sense of the noun κατάρτισις. The relevant meanings of καταρτίζω cited in BAGD would be either (a) 'restore', 'put to rights',[211] or (b) 'make complete'.[212] It is the second sense that is favoured in BAGD as relevant to the sense of κατάρτισις,[213] and is preferred by Plummer[214] and by Windisch,[215] who both see Paul as having in

204 Barrett, p. 340; Prümm, *Diakonia Pneumatos* I, p. 727.
205 Meyer, p. 511, takes τοῦτο as a backward reference.
206 Plummer, p. 378.
207 BAGD s.v.
208 BAGD s.v. καταρτισμός.
209 Ibid.
210 Hughes, p. 484, however, takes up the medical sense of καταρτισμός and supposes that Paul has derived a metaphor from it. As a medical technical term it denotes the 'resetting of what has been broken and dislocated'. Hence, Paul is praying that the Corinthians may be 'fully integrated in the communion of the Church ... articulated as members together in the body of Christ'. This interpretation seems improbable. First, the medical sense appears sparsely attested. Would Paul have known it? Secondly, he does not seem to be thinking here of the relationship of the Corinthians to the wider church.
211 BAGD s.v. καταρτίζω 1.a.
212 Ibid. 1.b.
213 BAGD s.v. κατάρτισις.
214 Plummer, p. 378.
215 Windisch, p. 424.

mind religious and moral perfection. But this seems less likely than derivation from the first sense. Barrett points out that there was much in the Corinthian church that needed to be put to rights. Its members needed to be 'restored to a proper Christian life'.[216] It is probable that Paul had in view this need for spiritual and moral rectification.

10. διὰ τοῦτο ταῦτα ἀπὼν γράφω, ἵνα παρὼν μὴ ἀποτόμως χρήσωμαι κατὰ τὴν ἐξουσίαν ἣν ὁ κύριος ἔδωκέν μοι, εἰς οἰκοδομὴν καὶ οὐκ εἰς καθαίρεσιν. It is because of his concern for the Corinthians' moral and spiritual restoration (v. 9) that Paul writes the letter. The διὰ τοῦτο probably has a backward reference.[217] It is not impossible, however, to understand its reference, alternatively, as pointing forward, in anticipation of the following ἵνα-clause: Paul's reason for writing is his desire to avoid the need for the exercise of severe discipline when he arrives.[218] His use elsewhere of διὰ τοῦτο fails to provide clear evidence for either alternative.[219] Nevertheless, in favour of a backward reference in the present verse there is the fact that otherwise this sentence would stand as an isolated remark, since the λοιπόν of v. 11, 'Finally', introduces the letter closing. Ambiguity attaches also to the content of ταῦτα. What 'things' is Paul writing[220] about? A number of major commentators suppose him to have in view everything that has been said from 10.1 onwards.[221] Others see the ταῦτα as more limited in reference, i.e., to what follows 12.19,[222] or in particular to the threats of 12.19–13.4.[223] In view of the contents of the ἵνα-clause, there must be some allusion specifically to those parts of the letter which

[216] Barrett, p. 340; Martin, p. 484.
[217] Meyer, p. 511; Windisch, p. 425.
[218] Barrett, p. 327.
[219] The phrase does not occur in Galatians or Philippians. Of the 14 instances in Romans, Corinthians, 1 Thessalonians and Philemon, 9 have a clear backward reference (Rom 1.26; 5.12; 13.6; 1 Cor 11.10, 30; 2 Cor 4.1; 7.13; 1 Thess 3.5, 7): none, however, is followed by a ἵνα-clause. Of the remaining instances, one, in Philem 15, is followed by a ἵνα-clause and has a clear forward reference: τάχα γὰρ διὰ τοῦτο ἐχωρίσθη πρὸς ὥραν ἵνα αἰώνιον αὐτὸν ἀπέχῃς. Another (Rom 4.16), followed likewise by ἵνα, is ambiguous.
[220] Allo, p. 340, comments on the present tense of γράφω, remarking that the epistolary aorist was not an absolute rule with Paul. This might appear misleading. In the recognised letters there are five epistolary instances of ἔγραψα (1 Cor 5.11; 9.15; Gal 6.11; Philem 19, 21), and five instance of γράφω or γράφομεν (1 Cor 4.14; 14.37; 2 Cor 1.13; 13.10; Gal 1.20). Hence, the use of epistolary ἔγραψα would scarcely look like a 'rule' from which Paul deviates only occasionally. However, the four examples of γράφω (γραφόμεν) in 1–2 Corinthians may be due to the need to distinguish between present and past letters.
[221] Windisch, pp. 424–5; Furnish, p. 574; Barrett, p. 340; Martin, p. 485.
[222] Meyer, p. 512.
[223] Bultmann, p. 251.

criticise the Corinthians' attitudes and behaviour, but this does not preclude a wider reference to the letter as a whole.

The purpose of the entire communication, then, is the prevention of harsh action[224] on Paul's part, such as he has threatened in v. 2.[225] The general sense of the ἵνα-clause is obvious. But its elaboration by means of the prepositional phrase κατὰ τὴν ἐξουσίαν with its dependent relative clause is capable of two different interpretations.

(i) It relates to the ἀποτόμως χρήσωμαι. The sense is that, should such action nevertheless be necessary, it would be, despite appearances, a form of edification, not of destruction: this would be in accordance with the authority given to the apostle, which is for the former purpose, not for the latter.[226] This is somewhat complicated. And why should Paul speak of καθαίρεσις, at all, if harsh action is simply a form of οἰκοδομή?

(ii) The reference is to the μή of the previous clause. Paul's object is *not* to act harshly, and this purpose is in accordance with the authority given him. It was given with a view to the edification of his churches, not in order to destroy them.[227] This alternative is preferable.

(iii) The Letter-ending (13.11–13)

According to the most usual analyses, the last three verses of 2 Cor 13 (13.11–13) constitute the letter-ending either of the whole canonical letter (for those exegetes who maintain its unity) or of the letter contained in chaps. 10–13 (for those who regard these four chapters as a separate communication). Nevertheless, there are some commentators who diverge from this consensus in one or the other of two ways. First, some scholars would maintain that vv. 11–13 did not originally belong to 13.1–10. Secondly, others would allow this connection to be original, but would claim that the ending of the letter to which these verses belong extends further back into what would otherwise be considered as the letter-body. Both viewpoints have been already mentioned in the Introduction in Vol. I,[228] but merit further discussion. In

---

[224] See BAGD, s.v. ἀποτόμως, 'severely', 'rigorously'; and ibid s.v. χράομαι 2., 'act', 'proceed'.
[225] See above, pp. 877–8.
[226] This interpretation goes back to Chrysostom, *PG* 61, col. 605 (NPNF XII, p. 417). Amongst modern commentators it is supported by, e.g., Plummer, p. 379; and Martin, p. 486.
[227] Windisch, p. 425.
[228] See Vol. I, pp. 4, 9–10.

particular, the second has received consideration in some publications more recent than those taken into account originally.

(a) *The original context of 13.11–13.* According to Semler, these verses do not belong to their present context. In our own reading of Semler, we have followed Hausrath, who understands him to propose that 13.11–13 acts as the conclusion of the first of the letters contained in the canonical 2 Corinthians, i.e., chaps. 1–8 (plus Rom 16).[229] Martin, however, claims that Semler 'separated out 12:14–13:13 as a later codicil'.[230] This would presumably mean, first, that vv. 11–13 were originally attached to the rest of chap. 13, but, secondly, that these verses were part of what might be regarded as a much longer, and later, letter-ending. But is this a correct reading of Semler? Since Martin's comment follows his remark that it was Semler who first questioned the unity of 2 Corinthians, the implication is that the latter divided the epistle simply into two unequal parts, i.e., 1–12.13 and 12.14–13.13. This is not how Semler is usually understood.[231] It is true, however, that he himself is not very clear, but rather appears to be suggesting various possibilities. Schmiedel observes that it is only in n. 350 that he holds 10.1–13.10 to be a letter later than chaps. 1–8, whilst in nn. 353–5, 358, and 366 it is simply the section 12.19–13.10 that is so regarded; in his introduction, slightly differently again, Semler inclines to the view that the sections 12.14–21 and 13.1–10 may be one or two later letter(s).[232] Nevertheless, what does become apparent from Schmiedel's comments is that, *pace* the analysis implied by Martin, Semler did isolate 13.11–13 as separate from its present context. These verses, he thinks, are 'certain separate leaves, (which) have been less suitably added' to the conclusion of the letter.[233] At this point, he does not say where they came from. But in n. 350 he has spoken of chap. 10 and what follows as later 'inserted' into the letter of chaps. 1–8 (with Rom 16). This could give cause to suppose that, in Semler's view, 13.11–13 had originally constituted the conclusion of this earlier letter.

Whilst a few modern commentators likewise separate 13.11–13 from the present context,[234] the majority see them as following

229 See Vol. I, p. 4, and Hausrath, *Vier-Capitel-Brief*, p. 1.

230 Martin, p. xli.

231 The question of 13.11–13 apart, it is chaps. 10–13 that he is thought to have regarded as a separate letter. See, e.g., Kümmel, *Introd.*, p. 212; Furnish, p. 32.

232 Schmiedel, p. 74. He himself, p. 81, suggests that 13.11–13 originally came after 9.15.

233 Semler, p. 321 n. 366: 'quaedam separatae schedae, minus commode adiunctae fuerunt'.

234 Strachan, p. 145, follows Schmiedel (see above, n. 232). Bornkamm, *Vorgeschichte*, p. 187, attaches the verses to his Letter of Reconciliation (1.1–2.13; 7.5–16; 8).

upon 13.10. There are several reasons for this viewpoint. First, there are verbal contacts with the preceding verses: the καταρτίζεσθε recalls the κατάρτισιν of v. 9,[235] and the χαίρετε the χαίρομεν of the same verse.[236] Secondly, the exhortations to be of the same mind (τὸ αὐτὸ φρονεῖτε) and to be at peace (εἰρηνεύετε) may well refer to the fears Paul has expressed in 12.20, where he speaks of quarrelling, anger, disorder, and the like.[237] Thirdly, it is not likely that a section of some other letter would have been inserted into the letter to which 13.11–13 originally belonged immediately before these verses which concluded the first letter.[238] The more likely process of redaction would retain the beginning of the first letter of the combination and the ending of the last one.[239]

(b) *The extent of the letter-ending.* The last three verses of the epistle obviously contain Paul's final greeting and blessing. But would it be possible to regard some part of the preceding material as also belonging in some sense to the letter-ending? In Vol. I we considered and rejected the theory that chaps. 10–13 constituted the autograph subscription of the letter of chaps. 1–9, in part because this theory would not explain the change in the Corinthian situation apparent when chaps. 10–13 are compared with chaps. 1–9. But this objection would not apply in the same degree to the suggestion that chaps. 10–13 are to be seen as a postscript, written after the receipt of fresh news from Corinth. This possibility has now been explored by E. R. Richards,[240] in the light of the general use of epistolary postscripts in Paul's time.

Such postscripts, he finds, were used for various purposes: to add forgotten material, or to convey confidential material, or, crucially for our present discussion, to deal with material 'newly acquired since the letter body was finished'.[241] He claims that the last four chapters of 2 Corinthians might very well function as a postscript in this third way.[242] He observes that some time would be required for a secretary to draft the final copy of a letter, and points to a letter to Cicero from Cassius containing a postscript in which Cassius explains that since writing his original letter he has received further information.[243] Similarly, Cicero finishes a letter,

---

[235] Plummer, p. 379; Furnish, p. 585; Martin, p. 492.
[236] Furnish, ibid.; Martin, ibid.
[237] Plummer, pp. 379–80; Weima, *Endings*, p. 211.
[238] Plummer, p. 380.
[239] Furnish, p. 585; Martin, p. 492.
[240] Richards, *Secretary*.
[241] Richards, *Secretary*, pp. 83, 179; the phrase quoted is on p. 179.
[242] Richards, *Secretary*, pp. 180–1.
[243] Richards, *Secretary*, pp. 83–4.

but receives a letter himself 'with additional details that elicit more discussion' in a postscript.[244] Perhaps, then, Paul might have been apprised of a change in the Corinthian situation, after he had drafted 2 Cor 1–9 but before the letter had been sent off, and consequently added a postscript consisting of chaps. 10–13. This would explain the change of tone. Richards argues further that 'Paul tends to be more abrupt or stern in his personal postscripts'. See 1 Cor 16.22–24; Philem 20–25; possibly Gal 6.12–18.[245]

How is this suggestion to be evaluated? Weima sees it as 'a legitimate proposal', but points out that it lacks 'explicit support in the text'.[246] This is clearly true, and should perhaps be spelled out in detail. First, in the example given in which Cicero adds a postscript to deal with new information he indicates explicitly that this is so.[247] It is true that Richards can cite a further letter from Cicero where the addition of a postscript is not specifically mentioned.[248] But as Richards himself observes, the extra material follows after one of Cicero's customary closing formulae.[249] Hence, its nature as a postscript can be deduced from its placing. In both places we have the 'explicit support' for the presence of a postscript which Weima finds lacking in 2 Cor 10–13. Secondly, the postulated fresh information which would have evoked such a postscript would obviously have signified a change in Paul's personal relationship with the Corinthians. Would he not have made explicit mention of it, as he does in a similar (though not identical) situation in respect of the Galatians (Gal 4.14–16)? Would he not, that is, have drawn attention in so many words to the contrast between what he had previously heard of the Corinthians' affectionate longing for him (7.7, 11) and what he now hears, in the course of writing the same letter, about their complaints of lack of love on his part (11.11)? Thirdly, the further argument that Paul's change of tone in chaps. 10–13 may be explicable on the grounds of his sterner attitude in personal postscripts is not wholly convincing. It has to be said that such an attitude is less than obvious in Philemon, that if it is apparent in Gal 6.11–18 it is equally apparent in earlier sections of the letter (1.6; 3.1; 5.1–12), and that whilst the anathema of 1 Cor 16.22 may strike a harsh note it is not essentially more severe than the warnings

---

[244] Richards, *Secretary*, p. 85. The reference is to Cic. *Fam.* I 9.26, and the relevant sentence, cited by Richards, runs: 'Scripta iam epistola [Richards' 'epistolam' is a misprint] superiore, accepi tuas litteras de publicanis.' ('After the above letter was already written, I received your communication about the revenue-farmers.')

[245] Richards, *Secretary*, pp. 180–1.

[246] Weima, *Endings*, p. 209.

[247] See above, n. 244.

[248] Richards, *Secretary*, p. 85; with reference to Cic., *Fam.* XIX 9.2.

[249] Richards, ibid.

elsewhere, e.g., in 11.27–30. Finally, there is another consideration which would tell against the postscript theory. The letter of chaps. 1–8 concludes with Paul's recommendation of Titus and his two companions who are to travel to Corinth to assist the Corinthians to complete their contribution to the collection for Jerusalem. Paul is most anxious that this should be done without further delay. Would he, then, keep this delegation waiting whilst he composed such a lengthy addition to his original letter? Alternatively, if, in view of his new information, he decided it would be useless to send them to Corinth for this purpose, why did he not delete chap. 8 (and perhaps most of chap. 7)?

A different suggestion about the extent of the letter-ending may be mentioned more briefly. Schnider and Stenger argue that it begins at 12.14. With that verse there begins the 'apostolic parousia' which, they claim, belongs to the ending on account of its close connection with the concluding paraenesis: see Rom 15.14–29; 1 Cor 16.1–12.[250] But this structural argument fails to take account of the fact that the nature of Paul's personal presence and behaviour in Corinth was itself a matter of criticism and contention. In other words, the discussion of his 'parousia' must surely count as a major element of the letter-body. In 12.14–18 he is still defending his position in the matter of maintenance. Moreover, we have seen that the Fool's Speech most likely continues as far as v. 18. And if we are to look for a 'parousia' reference closely attached to what is clearly the ending of the letter, it is obviously available in 13.10.

We conclude, therefore, that the letter-ending of 2 Cor 10–13 consists of the section 13.11–13. Weima comments that these verses contain 'all four of the epistolary conventions regularly found in the closings of Paul's other letters'. These are:

11a Hortatory Section
11b Peace Benediction
12　Greetings
13　Grace Benediction[251]

(c) *Translation and exegesis*

[11]Finally, brothers, rejoice, co-operate in your restoration, accept admonition, be of the same mind, be at peace. And the God of love and peace shall be with you. [12]Greet each other with a holy kiss. All the members of the holy people greet you. [13]The grace of the Lord Jesus [Christ] and the love of God and communion with the Holy Spirit be with you all.

---

[250] Schnider and Stenger, *Briefformular*, pp. 73, 75.
[251] Weima, *Endings*, p. 209.

**11a. Λοιπόν, ἀδελφοί, χαίρετε, καταρτίζεσθε, παρακα-
λεῖσθε, τὸ αὐτὸ φρονεῖτε, εἰρηνεύετε,** That this is the point of
transition to the letter-ending is signified by the initial λοιπόν,
ἀδελφοί, an expression which 'typically serves in Paul's letters to
introduce a closing hortatory section'.[252] Some of these sections
are of a general nature. The present passage, however, as in Rom
16.17–20, has direct reference to what has been said in the letter-
body.[253] The initial τὸ λοιπόν means 'finally',[254] and simply serves
to mark the transition. But the ἀδελφοί as a form of address may
have more significance, as several exegetes remark. For Furnish,
it emphasises Paul's 'solidarity' with the Corinthians, and thus
serves 'to accentuate the following admonitions'.[255] Weima sees
the apostle as wishing to restore a good relationship with his
correspondents after the harsh things he has been saying to
them.[256] It is certainly interesting to observe that the vocative
ἀδελφοί is frequent in 1 Corinthians (19 instances), but rare in
2 Cor 1–9 (twice), and here only in 2 Cor 10–13.[257] Perhaps this is
simply because there is a greater proportion of direct ethical
exhortation in 1 Corinthians, although not all the instances of
ἀδελφοί are immediately so connected. But might the disparity
relate also to Paul's growing concern for the maintenance of his
apostolic authority in Corinth? The term ἀδελφοί may suggest
'solidarity', as Furnish supposes. But it implies also a fundamental
equality of status. If, at the time of writing of 1 Corinthians, Paul
felt reasonably confident that his pastoral authority was accepted

---

[252] Weima, *Endings*, p. 208. See also p. 146, where Weima give a list of these
passages and especially notes the introductory word or phrase of each, as follows:

Rom 16.17–18, 19b	ἀδελφοί
1 Cor 16.13–16, 22	ἀδελφοί
2 Cor 13.11a	λοιπόν, ἀδελφοί
Gal 6.17	τοῦ λοιποῦ
Phil 4.8–9a	τὸ λοιπόν, ἀδελφοί
1 Th 5.25, 27	ἀδελφοί
Philem 20–22	ναὶ ἀδελφέ

[253] Weima, *Endings*, p. 147. See the following exegesis for details. On the
passage in Romans he comments, p. 148: 'Paul's autograph warning in 16.17–20
against those who create dissension and division recalls his earlier appeals against
disunity in the Roman congregation stemming from tensions between the "weak"
and the "strong".'

[254] BAGD s.v. λοιπός 3.b. See also, e.g., Plummer, p. 380; Barrett, p. 341;
Furnish, p. 581; Martin, p. 490. On the use of (τὸ) λοιπόν see, in addition: Roller,
Formular, p. 66 and n. 308; also p. 67, where Roller comments that this is the only
occasion in Paul's letters where we have something resembling the τὰ δ'ἄλλα of the
secular letters; Thrall, Martin, *Particles*, p. 30.

[255] Furnish, p. 581.

[256] Weima, *Endings*, p. 210.

[257] Plummer, p. 380, notes the frequency of the address in 1 Corinthians and its
rarity in these two sections of 2 Corinthians.

in the Corinthian church, he would feel also free to write to the members of the congregation as to his Christian brothers, i.e. to those who, equally with himself, shared the status of sonship to God (Rom 8.14–17). But subsequent events (the incident during the Interim Visit, the Painful Letter, and the advent in force of the rival missionaries) had shaken this confidence and freedom. So it is only at the very end of the present letter in defence of his authority that Paul reverts to his original form of address, as a gesture of conciliation and in the hope that he may now be understood.

Is the χαίρετε likewise intended as a conciliatory gesture? If it has its usual meaning, 'rejoice', this could perhaps be so.[258] In several translations, however, it is understood to mean 'farewell'.[259] According to BAGD, it could have this sense in Phil 3.1 and 4.4.[260] It is supported in the present verse by Plummer on the ground that the meaning 'rejoice' would be somewhat incongruous after the threat of ruthless action in v. 2.[261] This certainly appears to be a difficulty. Nevertheless, most commentators take χαίρετε in the sense 'rejoice', for several reasons. First, it stands at the head of a list of four imperatives in the second person plural.[262] Secondly, in a similar passage in 1 Th 5.16, where χαίρετε is followed by a series of imperatives, 'rejoice' is the only meaning possible.[263] Thirdly, the verb means 'rejoice' in v. 9.[264]

What of the following imperatives? The first, καταρτίζεσθε, is ambiguous in two respects. Does καταρτίζω, here, have the sense 'restore', 'put to rights', or does it mean 'make complete'?[265] A few commentators opt for the second sense, finding here an allusion to the achievement of perfection.[266] Most, however, prefer the first,[267] and since it is this meaning we have favoured in discussing the cognate noun κατάρτισις in v. 9[268] we shall adopt it here. The other point of ambiguity concerns the voice of καταρτίζεσθε. In form, it could be either passive or middle in a reflexive sense. The linguistic possibility of the latter alternative is attested in Mt 21.16 in a quotation from Ps 8 (LXX).3: κατηρτίσω αἶνον, 'you have prepared praise for yourself' (NRSV).[269] Barrett

---

[258] See below.
[259] RSV, NRSV, NEB, REB, BCN; Barrett, p. 341.
[260] BAGD s.v. χαίρω 2. a.
[261] Plummer, p. 380.
[262] Bultmann, p. 252; Furnish, p. 581; Weima, *Endings*, p. 210 n. 2.
[263] Furnish, p. 581; Weima, ibid.
[264] Furnish, ibid.; Martin, p. 498; Weima, ibid.
[265] See BAGD s.v. καταρτίζω for these meanings.
[266] Plummer, p. 380; Filson, p. 423.
[267] See, e.g., Tasker, p. 190; Furnish, p. 581; Barrett, pp. 341–2; Martin, p. 490.
[268] See above, pp. 898–9.
[269] BAGD s.v. καταρτίζω 2.b.

takes it in this sense, translating, 'Pull yourselves together'.[270] Martin, similarly, has, 'aim for restoration'.[271] He comments that Paul would be 'lessening the burden on the Corinthians', had he intended the imperative to be understood as passive: this is not likely, since he is anxious for them to take action before he arrives in person.[272] Furnish, however, takes καταρτίζεσθε as passive, 'be restored', on the ground that it relates to the prayer for the Corinthians' restoration in v. 9.[273] If, in view of these differing interpretations, one looks to BAGD for guidance, the note on the verse appears at first sight less than helpful, since the imperative is classified as passive, but translated, 'mend your ways'.[274] But in fact this lexical entry may point to the resolution of the difficulty. The form of the imperative may be passive. But a passive *imperative*, in the logical nature of things, must have a kind of reflexive nuance, since it requires a response from the person addressed. In the present instance, the Corinthians will be restored by God in answer to prayer, but at the same time their co-operation is needed.[275]

The same question of voice arises in the case of the following παρακαλεῖσθε, which may be middle or passive. Barrett takes it as middle, 'exhort one another',[276] and Martin, similarly, translates, 'encourage one another'.[277] As Meyer points out, however, these injunctions would have been expressed by παρακαλεῖτε ἀλλήλους (cf. 1 Th 4.18; 5.11), or παρακαλεῖτε ἑαυτούς (cf. Heb 3.13).[278] It is better to take the imperative as passive, 'be admonished',[279] 'be exhorted'.[280] Paul is urging the Corinthians to respond to the entreaties, explicit or implicit, conveyed by his letter.[281] The following τὸ αὐτὸ φρονεῖτε, 'be of one mind',[282] is straightforward. It probably refers back to 12.20,[283] and urges the positive attitude which will counteract the sinful behaviour deplored there. The εἰρηνεύετε, 'be at peace', will likewise refer to this previous

---

[270] Barrett, p. 341.
[271] Martin, ibid.
[272] Martin, p. 499.
[273] Furnish, p. 581.
[274] BAGD s.v. καταρτίζω 1.a.
[275] See Cranfield, *Romans*, p. 607, for a similar understanding of μεταμορφοῦσθε in Rom 12.2.
[276] Barrett, p. 341.
[277] Martin, p. 490.
[278] Meyer, p. 513, with reference to de Wette, p. 261, who renders the verb, 'ermahnet euch unter einander'.
[279] Hughes, p. 487.
[280] Plummer, p. 380.
[281] Hughes, p. 487; see also Prümm, *Diakonia Pneumatos* I, p. 728, and Furnish, pp. 581–2.
[282] Furnish, p. 581.
[283] Windisch, p. 426.

warning.[284] Chrysostom supposes that there is some distinction between εἰρηνεύετε and the preceding τὸ αὐτὸ φρονεῖτε: people may 'be of one mind' as regards doctrine but at variance with each other on the personal level.[285] It is doubtful, however, whether Paul would have had this distinction in mind. The more likely connection between the two exhortations would be that of cause and effect, as suggested by Barrett, with reference to Calvin: εἰρηνεύετε 'expresses the result of being of the same mind'.[286] This concludes the string of imperatives. Their accumulation suggests to Martin 'that Paul is urgently (and passionately?) encouraging the Corinthians to remedy the situation in the church before he arrives'.[287] Perhaps this is so. But there is an even longer string of imperatives in 1 Th 5.16–22 (immediately, as in 2 Cor 13.11, preceding the peace benediction), addressed to a church which did not present Paul with the acute problems found in Corinth.

11b. καὶ ὁ θεὸς τῆς ἀγάπης καὶ εἰρήνης ἔσται μεθ' ὑμῶν. At this point we have the Pauline epistolary convention which Weima entitles the 'peace benediction', an element which is found in all the recognised epistles except 1 Corinthians and Philemon.[288] The usual form, however, refers to God as ὁ θεὸς τῆς εἰρήνης: it is only here that τῆς ἀγάπης is added.[289] But even the usual form is unusual, viewed in a wider context. Furnish notes that there is only one Jewish example of the phrase 'God of peace' to be found, i.e., in *T. Dan* 5.2.[290] Nevertheless, it is legitimate to ask whether, in broader terms, Paul is indebted to some aspect of Jewish tradition. Does his formula, perhaps, derive in some way from liturgical practice? Weima notes that a peace-petition would sometimes conclude a worship service, and, in particular, that the blessing of Num 6.24–26, which includes a peace-blessing as the final element, was used regularly in this way.[291] He claims, however, that there is a 'closer analogy' to be

---

[284] Windisch, ibid.; Furnish, p. 585.
[285] Chrysostom, *PG* 61 col. 606 (NPNF XII, p. 418).
[286] Barrett, p. 342; Calvin, p. 176.
[287] Martin, p. 493.
[288] Weima, *Endings*, p. 87; see the table on p. 89. The benediction consists of the following elements: (a) an introductory particle (δέ or καί); (b) the reference to the divine source of blessing; (c) the wish (variously expressed—the verb is ἔσται in Phil 4.9b as here in 2 Cor 13.11); (d) the reference to the recipient. This is the analysis in *Endings*, pp. 88–9. Whether the terms 'benediction' and 'wish' are strictly correct may be debatable (see below).
[289] Plummer, p. 381, and Furnish, p. 582, note that the phrase ὁ θεὸς τῆς ἀγάπης occurs nowhere else in the NT, and Furnish that it is not found in the OT either.
[290] Furnish, p. 582; cf. Weima, *Endings*, p. 91. The sentence runs: 'but be at peace, holding to the God of peace. Thus no conflict will overwhelm you.' (*OTP* I, p. 809).
[291] Weima, *Endings*, p. 98; he refers, p. 98 n. 1, to *m. Ber.* 5.4; *m. Meg.* 4.3, 5, 6, 7; *m. Sota.* 7.6.

found in Semitic letters of the first decades of the second century.[292] In these letters, 'the most common closing formula was the farewell wish, expressed in Aramaic and Hebrew letters by a wish for "peace"'.[293] The presence of a farewell wish, in turn, however, may derive from hellenistic epistolary practice.[294] Since Paul is in other respects indebted to the latter, it is more likely that it would be the epistolary rather than the liturgical convention that would be the immediate source of his 'peace benediction'.

Two further questions which require discussion relate to the form of v. 11b but also raise issues of meaning. The first is the unusual addition of τῆς ἀγάπης. This is easy to account for, since reference to love is relevant to the preceding exhortation to be of the same mind and at peace with each other,[295] and to the overcoming of the vices listed in 12.20.[296] Such amendment of the Corinthians' attitudes and behaviour will be consonant with the indwelling of God in their community to which Paul had referred in his earlier letter (2 Cor 6.16), since God is characterised by love.[297]

The second question, however, is more complex. What kind of sentence is v. 11b? Furnish uses the term 'blessing',[298] and Weima calls this element of the letter-ending a 'benediction', and regards its content as a 'wish'.[299] But the verb ἔσται is in the future indicative. Can this tense and mood be used to express a wish? One would expect the optative εἴη. Further, if the discussion should suggest that v. 11b is simply an assertion, one would then have to ask what its logical relationship is to v. 11a.

To begin with, what is the justification for treating v. 11b as a 'wish' or 'benediction'? Here we may refer to the work of Wiles.[300] In the course of his investigation of Paul's prayers he asks whether there are some 'wish-prayers' which have the verb in the future indicative instead of in the optative, or (to put the question the other way round), whether there are some apparent 'declarations' in the future indicative which may or should be understood as wish-prayers. The texts under consideration are: Rom 16.20a; 1 Cor 1.8; 2 Cor 13.11b; Phil 4.7, 9b, 19; 1 Th 5.24b. Wiles observes that in some instances (Rom 16.20a; Phil 4.19;

[292] See Weima, *Endings*, pp. 59–61. The majority of the letters studied belong to the period of the Bar Kokhba revolt (132–35 C.E.): a few are slightly earlier.
[293] Weima, *Endings*, p. 99.
[294] Weima, *Endings*, p. 65–6.
[295] Furnish, p. 586.
[296] Weima, *Endings*, pp. 92–3.
[297] Cf. Barrett, p. 343.
[298] Furnish, pp. 582, 586.
[299] Weima, *Endings*, p. 88 and throughout.
[300] Wiles, *Intercessory Prayers*.

1 Th 5.24b) the textual tradition alternates between the future indicative and the optative.[301] This could indicate that scribes understood the future indicative as the expression of a wish and substituted the optative, simply because 'the two forms could be used interchangeably in petitionary prayer'.[302] As further evidence of interchangeability Wiles draws attention to Ps 20 (LXX).9–11; in these verses there is an alternation between optative and future indicative, where the Hebrew text has imperfect jussive forms, 'which would imply a wish'.[303] Having considered the Pauline texts individually, he then concludes that Rom 16.20 is a wish-prayer, that 1 Th 5.24b is a declaration,[304] and that 2 Cor 13.11b and two of the Philippians texts are primarily statements, but could also be taken as 'surrogates for peace blessings or prayers near the end of the letter'.[305] In the case of 2 Cor 13.11b, Wiles comments further that its situation 'points to its being a surrogate for a peace-prayer in the closing liturgical pattern, in preparation for the holy kiss'.[306] This last point is of dubious value, since Wiles depends here on an article by J. A. T. Robinson which itself has come under criticism.[307] He is in any case cautious about his conclusions. Weima and Furnish appear more confident that v. 11b is a blessing, though Furnish uses the term 'promise' also, which perhaps confuses the issue somewhat.[308] In favour of the view that v. 11b constitutes a wish, we could refer to the possible influence on Paul of the Semitic peace-wish as an epistolary farewell.[309] Against this interpretation, however, there is still the ambiguity of the indicative verb, and the fact that this so-called 'peace benediction' does not, either, follow the pattern of Paul's grace benedictions. A comparable peace benediction would run: ὁ θεὸς τῆς (ἀγάπης καὶ) εἰρήνης μεθ᾽ ὑμῶν.

Hence, the alternative interpretation of v. 11b clearly requires

---

[301] Wiles, *Intercessory Prayers*, p. 33.

[302] Wiles, ibid.

[303] Wiles, *Intercessory Prayers*, pp. 33–4.

[304] Wiles, *Intercessory Prayers*, p. 35. This is surely obvious, since a wish would scarcely be introduced by a relative pronoun. This would be true also in the case of 1 Cor 1.8, although Wiles, p. 35, regards this verse as a wish-prayer.

[305] Wiles, *Intercessory Prayers*, p. 36, with reference to Phil 4.7, 9b; Phil 4.19 is 'primarily declarative'.

[306] Wiles, *Intercessory Prayers*, p. 107 n. 2.

[307] See Wiles, *Intercessory Prayers*, p. 66 n. 1, for the reference to J. A. T. Robinson, 'Traces of a Liturgical Sequence in 1 Cor. xvi: 20–24', *JTS* n.s. 4 (1953), pp. 38–41. For criticism, see C. F. D. Moule, *Essays in New Testament Interpretation*, Cambridge, 1982, pp. 222–6: 'A Reconsideration of the Context of *Maranatha*'. Other proponents of the basic idea are noted in Fee, *First Corinthians*, p. 834 n. 6.

[308] Furnish, p. 586.

[309] See above, pp. 908–9.

consideration. At face value this half-verse appears to be simply the declaration of a promise. It is what its form indicates: a statement. Why the elaborate argumentation designed to present it as a benediction? As we have briefly noted above, it is the logical relationship of 11b to 11a that is problematic. Although the connective is merely the comparatively neutral καί, this in itself allows space for conjecture as to the existence of some more specific logical link in Paul's mind. Is the relationship conditional? Windisch claims that v. 11b is an assurance that God will be with the Corinthians, provided that they pay attention to the exhortations of v. 11a. These imperatives function, logically, as the protasis of a conditional concept which has v. 11b as its apodosis. The notion is 'Pelagian'.[310] There is, of course, no explicit syntactical evidence for this interpretation. But it is probably rejected more because of its theological implications than on account of syntactical deficiency. Is God's presence (not a matter of grace but) something that has to be earned or deserved by amendment of conduct and attitudes? Another reading of the verse, supported by Barrett and Furnish, is that v. 11b gives the grounding for v. 11a. The fact that God is the supplier of love and peace will make it possible for the Corinthians to put Paul's exhortations into practice.[311] But this would surely require something like ὁ γὰρ θεός ... Or perhaps Paul is simply juxtaposing separate syntactical items, i.e., a string of imperatives followed by the assertion of a promise, without intending to suggest any organic relationship between them.[312] This is the simplest solution. It is obviously possible to promise, by implication, God's presence to help and support the Corinthians as they endeavour to respond to Paul's exhortations without making the support conditionally dependent upon the endeavour.[313]

A definite conclusion is difficult. On balance, however, we prefer to understand v. 11b as a promise, somewhat loosely connected in thought with v. 11a in the last of the various ways we have noted. The fact that the grace-benediction in v. 13 mentions God in addition to Christ (and the Spirit) might also tell against the interpretation of v. 11b as a benediction.

12. Ἀσπάσασθε ἀλλήλους ἐν ἁγίῳ φιλήματι. Ἀσπάζονται ὑμᾶς οἱ ἅγιοι πάντες. Here we have the closing greeting which

---

[310] Windisch, p. 426.

[311] Barrett, p. 343; Furnish, p. 586, with reference to Barrett.

[312] Barrett, p. 342, thinks this also is a possibility.

[313] See the somewhat similar comment by Bultmann, pp. 252–3. The thought, he says, is not Pelagian: 'Denn der Gedanke, daβ Gott als der Gott der Liebe und des Friedens nur bei denen weilt, die Liebe und Frieden wirken, schlieβt den Verdienstbegriff nicht notwendig ein' (see p. 253).

had become a regular convention in the endings of hellenistic letters, and which was nearly always expressed by means of the verb ἀσπάζομαι.[314] The identical formula ἀσπάσασθε ἀλλήλους ἐν φιλήματι ἁγίῳ occurs also in Rom 16.16 and 1 Cor 16.20; similarly, in 1 Th 5.26 we have ἀσπάσασθε τοὺς ἀδελφοὺς πάντας ἐν φιλήματι ἁγίῳ.[315] The specifically Christian element is the injunction to exchange the 'holy kiss'. The general custom of exchanging kisses was widespread in the ancient world, in various contexts and for various purposes.[316] Relatives and friends kissed each other, and a kiss could also function as a mark of respect.[317] Kisses were exchanged at greeting and parting, both in the ancient world in general[318] and also in Judaism.[319] A kiss could be a sign of reconciliation.[320] According to Stählin, it could function also in a religious context as 'a sign of brotherhood' when given to those who were received into a closed group; he notes: 'Those received into a religious fraternity by a kiss are called οἱ ἐντὸς τοῦ φιλήματος.'[321] Paul's description of the kiss as 'holy', however, is something new, it appears.[322] What is its significance? Weima observes that it could refer to the need for 'proper and holy motives'. There was later patristic concern in this respect.[323] But it served primarily to distinguish the greeting kiss of believers from the greetings of non-believers. The latter were certainly a symbol of 'friendship and goodwill', but the former was (also) a symbol of unity within the church.[324] In Paul's usage it challenges his readers to eliminate any mutual hostility that may remain in their midst.[325] The fellowship of the church, moreover, is grounded in the presence of the Holy Spirit, and this presence holds good for the exchange of the kiss[326] which is the outward sign of the fellowship of the ἅγιοι.[327]

---

[314] See Weima, *Endings*, pp. 39–45, 105.

[315] See also 1 Pet 5.14: ἀσπάσασθε ἀλλήλους ἐν φιλήματι ἀγάπης.

[316] See G. Stählin, on φιλέω, in *TWNT* IX, pp. 112–69. On the kiss, see pp. 118–22, 124–6, 136–44.

[317] Stählin, on φιλέω, pp. 118–19, 124.

[318] Stählin, on φιλέω, p. 120.

[319] Stählin, on φιλέω, p. 125.

[320] Stählin, on φιλέω, pp. 120, 125.

[321] Stählin, on φιλέω, p. 121; the quotations are from the ET in *TDNT* IX, p. 122.

[322] Weima, *Endings*, p. 113.

[323] Weima, ibid.; see n. 1 for references to Tertullian and Clement of Alexandria. Cranfield, *Romans*, p. 796, quotes Ambrosiaster as indicating such concern.

[324] Weima, ibid.

[325] Weima, *Endings*, p. 114.

[326] Karl-Martin Hofmann, *Philema Hagion*, BFCT 2nd ser. 38, Gütersloh, 1938, p. 91.

[327] Hofmann, *Philema Hagion*, p. 23. The greeting with the holy kiss is thus, p. 91: 'nämlich reale Mitteilung und tatsächlicher Austausch der Agape, die durch den heiligen Geist gewirkt ist, den heiligen innewohnt und von ihnen betätigt wird.'

These various considerations would seem to account satisfactorily for Paul's allusion to the holy kiss. There has been the further suggestion, however, that it reflects a fixed element within the embryonic liturgies in the Pauline churches. According to Lietzmann, the Pauline letter would be read in the assembly, then would follow the kiss of peace, and then the Lord's Supper, introduced by the triadic greeting of 2 Cor 13.13.[328] Stählin, with reference to the closing of 1 Corinthians, sees the greeting, with the kiss (1 Cor 16.20), and the anathema and *Maranatha* (1 Cor 16.22) as constituting the introduction to the supper.[329] The argument in favour of this viewpoint is threefold. First, Lietzmann points out that in the old liturgies the triadic greeting found in 2 Cor 13.13 always follows the kiss of peace. This suggests that the connection is ancient, and derives from the ritual of the Pauline churches.[330] Secondly, Justin refers to the kiss of greeting in connection with the eucharist,[331] and it is seen to come immediately before the offering of the bread and wine.[332] Thirdly, in 1 Cor 16.20, 22, as already noted, the kiss is associated with the *Maranatha*. In the *Didache* (10.6) the *Maranatha* concludes the final prayer in the eucharist.[333]

There are several objections, however, to this whole line of argument. First, if a connection exists between the epistolary convention and the liturgical usage, it is more likely that the latter was secondary, derived from the former.[334] Secondly, it is interesting that there is no mention of the eucharistic kiss in the Apostolic Fathers. Stählin, who draws attention to the fact, finds it odd.[335] But it is so, only if we start from the assumption that it was already part of the liturgy in the apostolic age. In that case, there might indeed be an unaccountable gap between Paul and Justin. Otherwise it is not odd at all. On the contrary, the existence of the gap tells against the correctness of the liturgical theory. Thirdly, it must be emphasised that the contexts of Paul's allusions to the kiss (to state the obvious) are epistolary, not liturgical. And this holds good for other items which are later found in a liturgical context. They are intermingled with other contents which are in no sense liturgical. In 2 Cor 13.12, the injunction to

---

[328] H. Lietzmann, *Messe und Herrenmahl*, Bonn, 1926, p. 229 (ET, D. H. G. Reeve, *Mass and Lord's Supper*, Leiden, 1979, p. 186).

[329] Stählin, on φιλέω, p. 138; cf. Martin, p. 501. Furnish, p. 583, allows that it is possible that the kiss had become part of the liturgy (although Paul's reference may simply relate to an ordinary kiss of greeting).

[330] Lietzmann, *Herrenmahl*, p. 229 (*Lord's Supper*, p. 186).

[331] Justin, *Apol.* I 65; *PG* 6 col. 428; cited by Windisch, p. 427, and others.

[332] Noted by Furnish, p. 583; cf. Weima, *Endings*, p. 85 n. 3.

[333] See Robinson, 'Liturgical Sequence', p. 39.

[334] Barrett, p. 343.

[335] Stählin, on φιλέω, p. 140.

exchange the kiss precedes the transmission of the greeting from 'all the saints'. In 1 Th 5.26 it is followed by an instruction about the reading of the letter. In Rom 16.16 the reference to the kiss is preceded by Paul's personal greetings to specific individuals and followed by the general greeting from 'all the churches of Christ'. This intermingling is most apparent in the very passage on which the liturgical theory is most commonly based, i.e. 1 Cor 16.19–24: the injunction to exchange the kiss is preceded by greetings from the churches of Asia, from Aquila and Prisca, and from 'all the Christian brothers'. It is followed by Paul's epistolary signature. Then comes the *Maranatha*, then the grace, and finally Paul's love to his readers.[336] It seems highly unlikely, therefore, that these letter-endings reflect a fixed liturgical pattern already in existence. Of course the 'holy kiss' could be termed 'liturgical' in a more general sense, in that it would be exchanged when the members of the church met for worship.[337] But that is all.

The greeting to the Corinthians from 'all the saints' is paralleled in Rom 16.16 by the reference to 'all the churches of Christ', by the reference in 1 Cor 16.19 to 'the churches of Asia' and in 16.20 to 'all the brothers', and by the 'all the saints' of Phil 4.22.[338] Weima sees in this second greeting of v. 12 a hidden allusion to Paul's apostolic authority since the greeting is of so broad a nature, and also a reminder to the Corinthians that they are accountable to the wider church, not only to themselves.[339]

Furnish notes that in some English versions (KJV, RV, NEB [also REB]) v. 12b is numbered as v. 13 and the closing grace as v. 14. This originated, apparently, with the second folio edition of the Bishops' Bible in 1572.[340]

13. Ἡ χάρις τοῦ κυρίου Ἰησοῦ [Χριστοῦ] καὶ ἡ ἀγάπη τοῦ θεοῦ καὶ ἡ κοινωνία τοῦ ἁγίου πνεύματος μετὰ πάντων ὑμῶν. As in all the other epistles of the Pauline corpus, this letter ends with a grace-benediction beginning with ἡ χάρις, and consisting of three items: wish(es), divine source(s), and recipients.[341] But whereas in the other letters the blessing consists simply of the

---

[336] On the oddity of this order, should the liturgical theory be accepted, see also Moule, 'Reconsideration' (see above, p. 910 n. 307) who asks why, if the letter was intended as 'the homily, leading on into the eucharist', the *Maranatha* comes before the grace and the apostle's love.

[337] Cf. Windisch, p. 427.

[338] On the greeting from 'all the saints', Furnish, p. 583, refers to T. Y. Mullins, 'Greeting as a New Testament Form', *JBL* 87 (1968), pp. 418–26, who cites P Oxy 530 as a secular example of a third person greeting: see p. 421. The greeting runs: ἀσπάζεταί σε Θεωνᾶς.

[339] Weima, *Endings*, pp. 212–13.

[340] Furnish, p. 583.

[341] Weima, *Endings*, pp. 78–83; see the table on p. 80. In the present instance there are textual variants which require discussion: see below, p. 921.

wish that the grace of Christ should be with the recipients, here the benediction is expanded with reference to the love of God and the κοινωνία of the Holy Spirit. This could look like an embryonic trinitarian formula, and, since it is unique within the Pauline literature, the question arises as to whether it might be post-Pauline in origin.[342] As we shall see,[343] however, the term 'trinitarian' may be in some respects misleading. Furthermore, there is nothing in this longer formula which would be alien to Paul's own theological outlook.

If, then, we accept the whole verse as originally Pauline, there are four main questions to be considered. First, can anything be said about background influences which may have played some part in the construction of Paul's expanded formula? Secondly, what is the meaning of the various elements of the triadic blessing? Thirdly, how and why did the expansion come about? And fourthly, how 'trinitarian' is the formula?

(i) Windisch claims that the Christian formulation must have been influenced by external religious tendencies, such as the invocation of three gods in prayer, and philosophical motifs such as the Philonic triad of God, Sophia and Logos. For apostolic Christianity was primarily aware only of a duality of divine persons, i.e., God and Christ, or Father and Son.[344] Bultmann, however, points out that the order of mention in the Pauline triad counts against this. In these other threefold motifs and practices the Father God would be named first.[345] In any case, Windisch's suggestion is more than a little implausible. Would Paul, having mentioned what to him were such experiential realities as divine grace and love, then proceed to complete his formulation with a third element derived from some extraneous cultic or religio-philosophical milieu? In fact, Windisch comes near to contradicting himself. For he suggests that in Paul's discussion of spiritual gifts in 1 Cor 12 we may have the beginning of a conception of the Spirit as a personal power with a personal will.[346] In that case, the concept of threefold personal divine being originates within Christian experience. Elsewhere in the NT it becomes explicit only in the baptismal formula in Mt 28.19: βαπτί-ζοντες αὐτοὺς εἰς τὸ ὄνομα τοῦ πατρὸς καὶ τοῦ υἱοῦ καὶ τοῦ ἁγίου πνεύματος. It is unlikely that Paul was aware of this tradition. Had this been so, we should have expected a nearer approach to it.[347]

---

[342] Barrett, p. 343, suggests the possibility, although in his comments, pp. 344–5, he does not appear to treat the formula as post-Pauline.
[343] See below, pp. 920–1.
[344] Windisch, pp. 429–30.
[345] Bultmann, p. 254.
[346] Windisch, p. 429.
[347] Plummer, p. 384.

The order of the divine entities is different from the order in the present verse, and two of their titles also differ from those of the Pauline formula. It is not likely, either, that there is any link with the Johannine tradition concerning the Spirit as Paraclete. Windisch notes that there is a parallel of sorts here, in that, as ἄλλος παράκλητος (Jn 14.16, 26), the Spirit is very nearly raised to personal status (cf. 1 Jn 2.1, where Christ himself is παράκλητος).[348] Again, however, the terminology is quite different. It seems, then, that what we have here is a development within the Pauline tradition itself, unaffected by external influences.

(ii) Turning now to the question of meaning, we have to begin by asking whether Paul's formula is, in fact, a blessing, or whether he is making a declaration. Does he pray that divine grace, love, and fellowship (may) be with his correspondents, or does he assert that these gifts are (will be) with them? The verb is omitted. Obviously we are to supply some part of εἰμί, but which? Should it be εἴη (optative) or perhaps ἔστω (imperative), to express the first of our alternatives? Or are we to supply ἐστίν or ἔσται (indicative), to express the second?[349] In support of this second possibility it could be argued that it would express a certainty that the alternative lacks.[350] But the alternative rests on better evidence. In favour of the optative, there is its use in other Pauline blessings and wishes: see Rom 15.5; 15.13; 1 Th 3.11; 3.12–13; 5.23. And the imperative would find support in Graeco-Roman letters, since it would correspond with 'the common hellenistic farewell wish ἔρρωσο that is always expressed in the imperative mood'.[351] Paul is uttering a blessing, leaving either the optative or the imperative of εἰμί to be understood.[352]

The main point for discussion under the present heading can also be expressed in grammatical terms, but in one instance opens out into a wider debate. The grammatical question concerns the force of the genitives of the divine names. In the first phrase, 'the grace of the Lord Jesus [Christ]', the genitive τοῦ κυρίου Ἰησοῦ [Χριστοῦ] is clearly subjective, expressing the origin of grace. Paul prays that Christ will bestow upon the Corinthians the blessing of his gracious favour.[353] Similarly, in the second phrase,

---

[348] Windisch, pp. 429–30.
[349] See Weima, *Endings*, p. 83, for this formulation of the problem, and pp. 83–4 for discussion of it.
[350] The argument is noted by Weima, *Endings*, p. 83.
[351] Weima, *Endings*, pp. 83–4; see p. 84 for the words quoted.
[352] Weima, *Endings*, p. 84.
[353] On Paul's understanding of grace, see the comment on 1.2, in Vol. I, p. 97. On the subjective force of the genitive, see Furnish, p. 583, who draws attention to the parallels in 8.9 and 12.9.

'the love of God', the τοῦ θεοῦ is usually understood as subjective, i.e., as denoting God's love for man rather than man's love for God.[354] This is the more natural sense in the context of a blessing. It is the third phrase, the κοινωνία τοῦ ἁγίου πνεύματος, that is ambiguous. Is the genitive, (a), subjective, indicating origin? This would mean that the κοινωνία is the fellowship within the Christian community engendered by the action of the Spirit. Or is the genitive, (b), objective? In that case κοινωνία will refer to the participation of believers in the life and power of the Spirit. In the one instance, (a), what is in view is the relationship of believers with each other, in the other, (b), the direct relationship with the third of the divine entities as with the other two.

There is some support for the first alternative, (a): the genitive is subjective, and the intention of the blessing is that the Spirit may create fellowship within the Christian community. Two reasons are given. (1) The first genitive in the verse is subjective (Christ is the source of grace), and it is likely that the other two genitives are to be understood in the same way.[355] (2) The general context would support this interpretation. Party spirit has damaged church life in Corinth, and in consequence a prayer for renewed fellowship within the community would be felt by Paul to be appropriate.[356] Against this viewpoint, however, it could be argued that elsewhere in the NT a genitive following κοινωνία is usually objective, indicating what it is that participants share in.[357] This is most obvious in 1 Cor 10.16: κοινωνία ... τοῦ αἵματος τοῦ Χριστοῦ, κοινωνία τοῦ σώματος τοῦ Χριστοῦ.[358] See also 1 Cor 1.9: κοινωνίαν τοῦ υἱοῦ αὐτοῦ;[359] Phil 3.10: κοινωνίαν τῶν παθημάτων αὐτοῦ;[360] and possibly Phil 2.1: κοινωνία πνεύματος.[361] In addition, one has to ask whether party spirit *within* the Corinthian church has really been a prime concern in the letter of chaps. 10–13 (or, indeed, within the canonical 2 Corinthians as a whole).

This brings us to the consideration of alternative (b): the genitive is objective, and Paul is thus praying that his readers may experience personal communion with the Holy Spirit. In favour of this interpretation there are various considerations.

(1) It would be supported by the NT instances cited above as

354 See, e.g., Windisch, p. 428; Bruce, p. 255; Barrett, p. 344; Furnish, p. 583; Martin, p. 504.
355 Tasker, p. 191; cf. Bruce, p. 255.
356 Bruce, p. 255; cf. Martin, p. 505.
357 Meyer, p. 514 n. 2.
358 Windisch, p. 428; Lietzmann, p. 162; Meyer, p. 514 n. 2.
359 Meyer, ibid.; Windisch, ibid.
360 Windisch, ibid.
361 Meyer, ibid.

918   COMMENTARY ON II CORINTHIANS

counting against alternative (a),[362] with the possible exception of Phil 2.1.[363]

(2) Chrysostom appears to support the objective interpretation. He comments that whilst Paul speaks here of the κοινωνία of the Spirit, elsewhere (1 Cor 1.9) he refers to the κοινωνία of the Son.[364] Thus Chrysostom understands the πνεύματος of the present verse in the same way as the υἱοῦ of the other passage, i.e., as objective.[365] There is no Greek patristic evidence for the subjective interpretation.[366]

(3) What, then, of the argument under (a) (1) that all three genitives should be understood in the same way, and hence as subjective? This is scarcely decisive. In 2 Th 2.13, we have genitival phrases similarly related, but the functions of the genitives differ. In ἐν ἁγιασμῷ πνεύματος καὶ πίστει ἀληθείας, the first genitive must be subjective, the second objective.[367]

(4) The argument under (a) (1) relates to grammatical congruity. But congruity of sense would favour alternative (b). When Paul speaks of the grace of Christ and the love of God he has in mind a personal relationship between Christ and the Corinthians and between God and the Corinthians. The third phrase would then most probably refer to personal relationship between the Corinthians and the Spirit, not to relationships between various church members. There is a good case for the view that τοῦ ἁγίου πνεύματος is an objective genitive. Nevertheless, we still need to look at two possible counterarguments. The phrase κοινωνία πνεύματος in Phil 2.1 is clearly important, since it is the only NT example cited in which the dependent genitive, as in 2 Cor 13.13, is πνεύματος. And here the sense of the expression is ambiguous. The following verse speaks of mutual love and unity of mind within the community, which could suggest that the genitive might have a subjective function. Furthermore, the evidence of Chrysostom may be ambiguous likewise. He sees κοινωνία as the Spirit's gift to the church,[368] and this could likewise imply that πνεύματος is seen as subjective.

---

[362] See above.
[363] See below.
[364] Seesemann, *KOINΩNIA*, p. 56, with reference to Chrysostom, *PG* 61, col. 608 (NPNF XII, p. 419).
[365] Seesemann, ibid.
[366] Seesemann, *KOINΩNIA*, p. 70. He cites, p. 72, Oecumenius and Theophylact as using μετοχή and μετάληψις as synonyms for κοινωνία.
[367] Seesemann, ibid.
[368] See, G. V. Jourdan, 'KOINΩNIA in 1 Corinthians 10:16', *JBL* 67 (1948), pp. 111–24; see pp. 116–17. He claims that Chrysostom makes it clear that 'he regarded κοινωνία, χάρις and ἀγάπη to be gifts from the three Divine Persons equally'. This is so, but in the context the point is the equality of divine status, not the precise nature of each gift.

It seems that the arguments on each side may be somewhat finely balanced. Perhaps it is on this account that some commentators suggest that both ideas are implicit in the phrase κοινωνία τοῦ ἁγίου πνεύματος: fellowship within the community engendered by the Spirit, by virtue of participation in the Spirit's power. Prümm supposes that we may have a genitive with a dual function, indicating both origin (subjective) and participation (objective).[369] This solution is not wholly convincing. Certainly the Greek genitive is multifunctional. But does this also mean that in some one particular instance it can possess more than one function?[370] It is better to make a choice. In our view, the second alternative, (b), is preferable. The genitive is objective, and Paul wishes the Corinthians personal fellowship with the Spirit, in addition to experience of the grace of Christ and of the love of God. In each case what he has in mind is relationship with divine being. In adopting this interpretation we follow Kümmel,[371] Barrett,[372] Furnish,[373] and Seesemann.[374]

(iii) How and why did this expansion of the usual Pauline grace benediction come about? It is likely that Paul began with his usual blessing which refers only to the grace of Jesus Christ.[375] Deciding then to expand it, he would naturally, we might suppose, refer next to the love of God, since Christ and God are regularly associated in his opening epistolary greetings, and last would come the mention of participation in the Spirit. Whether this means that we find here an intentional trinitarian formula we shall discuss below, but reference to Lord, God, and Spirit is not in itself an innovation at this late point in the Corinthian correspondence: see 1 Cor 12.4–6. The question of why Paul on this occasion expanded his usual epistolary conclusion is more difficult. Plummer offers two suggestions. Perhaps a longer blessing might have seemed suitable to a church which had been so divided by faction.[376] But Paul has already addressed this situation in v. 11, and in any case the problem of factionalism is not a main concern in chaps. 10–13. Alternatively, he may have wished to assure his readers of his affection, after what will have

---

[369] Prümm, *Diakonia Pneumatos* I, p. 732; Martin, p. 505 (with some hesitation). Prümm is followed by M. McDermott, 'The Biblical Doctrine of KOINΩNIA', *BZ* 19 (1975), pp. 64–77, 219–33. Martin, ibid., cites J. Hainz, *Koinonia: Kirche als Gemeinschaft bei Paulus*, BU 16, Regensburg, 1982, p. 61. Furnish, p. 584, notes others in favour of assigning a dual function to the genitive.
[370] See also Seesemann, *KOINΩNIA*, pp. 40–1.
[371] Kümmel, p. 214.
[372] Barrett, p. 341.
[373] Furnish, p. 584.
[374] Seesemann, *KOINΩNIA*, throughout.
[375] Plummer, p. 383.
[376] Plummer, ibid.

seemed his harsh treatment of them.[377] If so, however, why did he not explicitly send them his own love (as he had done in 1 Cor 16.24)? Plummer may have a point here, nevertheless. Weima notes that the word πάντων is also an addition to Paul's usual formula. In itself this is a common epistolary convention. But the fact that he makes use of it may be intended to indicate that he wishes his benediction to include those whom he had censured at an earlier stage in the letter.[378] If so, we should have to reject the rather different explanation which Martin proposes to account for the addition of the reference to the Spirit to the more usual binitarian formula, i.e., that it has a polemical connotation, with an oblique allusion to the 'other spirit' of 11.4.[379] This would be inappropriate, if the expanded conclusion is to be understood as in some sense a conciliatory gesture. Such a gesture might be especially appropriate, also, if Paul were to regard this letter as the conclusion of his correspondence with the Corinthian church, and the fuller form of the benediction would likewise appear fitting in such circumstances. In 10.16 he has spoken of his hope of evangelistic mission in areas 'beyond' Corinth, and in Rom 15.22–24 he plans to visit Rome and Spain, observing that he has 'no further scope' in his present locale. Whilst his imminent third visit would enable him to make his farewells in person, he might have thought it profitable to leave the church also with a full benediction in written form, praying that its members might be endowed with all the blessings which derive from the threefold personal divine agency of Christ, God, and Spirit.

(iv) To what extent might the benediction be termed 'trinitarian'? Obviously, in comparison with the later doctrine, it is not explicitly so. Nothing is said or implied about the mutual relationship of the divine entities,[380] the terms 'Father' and 'Son' are not used,[381] and the sequence in which each is mentioned should caution against finding here a reflection of the developed concept.[382] At the same time it would be possible to see in the Pauline formula one of the starting points of trinitarian development. This is denied by Kümmel, who sees it, rather, as a way of expressing belief in the eschatological saving act of God in history, in sending Christ and bestowing the Spirit.[383] Barrett,

---

[377] Plummer, ibid.

[378] Weima, *Endings*, p. 82. He comments: 'In ancient letters, the adjective πᾶς in a prepositional phrase was commonly added to expand the scope of a farewell wish or greeting.' See p. 32 for examples of the elaboration of farewell wishes by means of such phrases as μετὰ τῶν σῶν πάντων, σὺν τοῖς σοῖς πᾶσιν.

[379] Martin, p. 497.

[380] Strachan, p. 145; cf. Furnish, p. 587.

[381] Furnish, ibid.

[382] Furnish, ibid.; cf. Weima, *Endings*, p. 81.

[383] Kümmel, p. 214.

however, regards Kümmel as mistaken. He points out that, in Paul's benediction, 'Christ, God, the Spirit, appearing in balanced clauses in one sentence, must stand on one divine level'. This will eventually raise the question of their mutual relationship, as will what Paul says or implies elsewhere about Christ as God's Son, and about the Spirit as the Spirit of Christ.[384] Barrett's view is preferable.

Textual variants in verse 13
1. Whilst most witnesses read Ἰησοῦ Χριστοῦ, a few (B Ψ 323. 1881 *pc*) have simply Ἰησοῦ. The arguments on either side tend to balance one another out. First, each reading might be plausibly explained as arising out of the other. If the longer text should be original, accidental scribal omission of Χριστοῦ could be due to homoioteleuton; the scribe's eye would have skipped from the οὗ of Ἰησοῦ to the identical ending of Χριστοῦ. But if the shorter text should be original, the longer reading could be the result of the general scribal tendency to expand the divine names. Secondly, both readings could find support in Pauline usage. The longer version occurs in Gal 6.18; Phil 4.23; 1 Th 5.28; Philem 25: the shorter in 1 Cor 16.23. In relation to this second point, however, it is worth noting that the four instances attesting the longer version occur without variants, whilst at 1 Cor 16.23 some witnesses also have the longer form. This brings us to a third line of argument. Initially these textual facts would seem to count in favour of the longer reading, as consonant with the better attested usage in Paul's letters. But in 1 Cor 16.23, according to Metzger, *Textual Commentary*[1], p. 570, the longer reading is secondary. And a further fact is that the original shorter text is supported by the two main witnesses, i.e., B Ψ, which attest the shorter reading in 2 Cor 13.13. This certainly could mean that in our present verse the scribes of B Ψ changed an original longer reading so as to create conformity with 1 Cor 16.23. Alternatively, however, it could well suggest that in both cases these two witnesses have preserved the original shorter reading, in face of a widespread tendency to conform the grace benedictions of the Corinthian letters to Pauline usage elsewhere. Such a tendency, moreover, would go hand in hand with the scribal habit of expanding the divine titles. Certainty is impossible, but the shorter reading has more to be said in its favour than might at first appear.
2. The omission of ἁγίου in 𝔓⁴⁶ is an obvious scribal error.
3. The concluding ἀμήν (ℵ² D Ψ 𝔐 lat sy bo) is secondary: see Metzger, *Textual Commentary*[1], p. 588. Its omission (𝔓⁴⁶ ℵ* A B F G 0243. 6. 33. 630. 1175. 1241. 1739. 1881 pc sa bo^ms Ambst) is correct.

---

[384] Barrett, p. 345.

The Subscription.[385] For detailed information, see Metzger, *Textual Commentary*[1], p. 588, [2] p. 519. The original form is πρὸς Κορινθίους β (𝔓[46] ℵ* A B* 33). Later witnesses add the information that the letter was written from Philippi (B[c] K L P 201. 205. 209. 328. 337. 642), and that Titus and Luke were the scribes (K L), to whom some witnesses add Barnabas (201. 205. 209. 328. 337). That the letter was written from Philippi will be an intelligent guess on the basis of the references to Macedonia in chaps. 2, 8–9 and on the assumption of the unity of the canonical epistle. That Titus was one of the amanuenses will have been deduced from the allusions to him in chaps. 7–8. That Luke was the other must depend on Acts 20.6. The addition of Barnabas may come from 1 Cor 9, but takes no account of the separation recorded in Acts 15.36–41.

EXCURSUS XVI

2 Cor 10–13: some rhetorical perspectives

As we have seen, renewed interest in the rhetorical characteristics of the Pauline letters has produced several studies of these chapters. It may be of interest to make some assessment of the two more recent monographs to which we have drawn attention in the exegesis, and to consider their possible implications, should their arguments prove acceptable.

Sundermann, we have observed, analyses the structure of the letter in detail, finding in it a complex of separate units which correspond to the classical divisions of a speech, together with some freedom of organisation.[386] As we have worked through the exegesis, we have found the analysis in general to be plausible. It has not caused any change in exegetical decisions. Nevertheless, it has provided an interesting perspective on the structure of chaps. 10–13, and has given additional support to the view that in these chapters we have a separate letter from

---

[385] The term 'subscription' is used here, as in both editions of Metzger's *Textual Commentary* in the sense given to it in his book *The Text of the New Testament* (Oxford, 1968), pp. 205–6, i.e., of 'scribal additions ... appended to the Pauline Epistles, giving information regarding the traditional place from which each was sent, as well as in some cases what was believed to be the name of the amanuensis or of the messenger who was to carry the Epistle'. Other scholars employ the same term with reference to postscripts which were always part of the original letter, summarising its contents; see, e.g., Richards, *Secretary*, pp. 81–3, and his references to the work of G. J. Bahr. Roller, *Formular*, pp. 73–7, differently again, uses subscriptio of the final greeting written in a different hand. In a letter sent by the Emperor Justinian the term itself occurs: 'Divina subscriptio'. It precedes the final good wish and indicates the Emperor as the sender. Cranfield, *Romans*, pp. 803–4, follows Roller. Within the conclusion of the letter, the greeting of 16.20b, ἡ χάρις τοῦ κυρίου ἡμῶν Ἰησοῦ μεθ' ὑμῶν, functions as Paul's subscription.

[386] Sundermann, *Kraft der Rede*, throughout.

Paul to Corinth.[387] DiCicco takes a different approach, demonstrating Paul's use of the three methods of persuasion: proof of the orator's moral character, the arousal of appropriate emotion, and logical argument.[388] This, in our view, is a helpful way of looking at the text. It is rejected, however, by Winter, who comments,

> If it is correct that Paul rejects these persuasive techniques in his evangelism in Corinth (1 Cor. 2:1–5) as has been argued here, it is inexplicable why he would make such full use of them in a later letter to the Corinthians without again calling into question his integrity.[389]

This objection could also well apply, *mutatis mutandis*, to the rhetorical analysis proposed by Sundermann. But in face of the detailed argumentation adduced by both authors in favour of their rhetorical theories, the objection can scarcely be upheld with any confidence, unless supported by equally detailed considerations. We may add three further points. First, by claiming to speak 'as a fool' in 11.1–12.18, Paul has covered himself to some extent against a possible charge of lack of integrity. Secondly, in 1 Corinthians itself Paul can be seen to be in two minds about the appropriate style of evangelism. Was it to be wholly reflective of the content of the gospel (1 Cor 2.1–5)? Or was he to adapt his approach to various types of audience (1 Cor 9.20–22)? Thirdly, in his correspondence with the Corinthians Paul was not, in any case, concerned with primary evangelism of either type. The passage cited by Winter is of doubtful relevance.

If, then, these chapters do show some evidence of Paul's use of rhetorical technique, what are the implications? Most obviously, it would look as though he possessed a considerable degree of rhetorical training. He knows, and can make use of, the conventional divisions of a speech. He is sufficiently confident, according to Sundermann's analysis, to fit smaller units, each with its separate pattern, into the larger structure, and to reverse the more usual order of proof and refutation.[390] He keeps track of all these complexities. Moreover, since this letter is a response to a crisis situation, it must have been composed fairly rapidly. Sundermann, however, claims indifference to the question of Paul's rhetorical education. The use of rhetoric as an instrument of analysis is independent of whether or not the author, in the production of the text, is consciously guided by the rules methodically formulated by means of the rhetorical system. Sundermann is concerned with the rhetorical stamp of the Pauline text, whether this is conscious or unconscious, deliberate or unintentional.[391] It is possible for authors to write in accordance with

---

[387] See above, pp. 595–6, and throughout.

[388] DiCicco, *Ethos, Pathos and Logos*; see above, pp. 698–9 (πάθος), p. 706, pp. 797–8 (ἦθος), and pp. 831–2 (λόγος).

[389] Winter, *Sophists*, p. 229 n. 114.

[390] According to Sundermann, (*Kraft der Rede*, p. 45), the refutation precedes the proof. Cicero has the reverse order in his discussions of the parts of a speech: see *Inv.* I 14.19; *Part. Or.* 9.33. This, of course, could be regarded as a major objection to the theory proposed.

[391] Sundermann, *Kraft der Rede*, p. 13.

theory without knowledge of it.[392] As a generalisation this may be true. But we are offered no firm evidence. Neither Sundermann nor Classen, to whom he refers, provides a specific example of an ancient text whose author is known to have been wholly uneducated in rhetoric but who nevertheless has produced a work that conforms in some detail to the rules of rhetoric. In the case of the Pauline letters some qualification is certainly necessary. As Classen points out, Paul's command of Greek gave him access to Greek literature, which was itself impregnated with the rhetorical conventions.[393] And had he never, during his formal education or in the course of his travels in the Mediterranean world, heard speeches which conformed to these conventions? We may remind ourselves that listening to speeches was itself one of the ways of learning to speak (or write) rhetorically.[394] Hence, it seems improbable that Paul completely lacked rhetorical education. Sundermann claims to be neutral on this question. But it cannot be regarded as irrelevant if one is concerned with understanding Paul's relationship with the Corinthians, who had a low view of his oral proficiency (10.11; 11.6).

It is not possible fully to investigate the question here. We may conclude, however, by taking note of two recent views. First, Murphy-O'Connor argues forcefully that Paul would certainly have been educated in rhetoric. After all, the Corinthians had to allow that his letters were impressive, despite his poor showing as an orator. Moreover, in 1 Cor 2.2. it is significant that he presents his style of preaching as 'a matter of choice'. He could, realistically, have chosen the other alternative.[395] His letters, according to Forbes, display the mastery of rhetoric that comes of 'long practice, and possibly long study as well'.[396] In striking contrast, the second of the two authors, R. Dean Anderson, thinks it unlikely that Paul had received any formal education in rhetoric. He refers to 2 Cor 10.10 and 11.6, and to what Paul says in Phil 3.5 about his Jewish upbringing.[397] Chiefly, however, his view is based on his examination of Rom 1–11, Gal 1–5.12 and 1 Corinthians. The sections investigated fit neither the conventional rhetorical genres nor a rhetorical scheme of the parts into which an oration may be divided. Any connection that may be observed, Anderson claims, may depend simply on 'the fact that most literary productions have a beginning, middle and an end'.[398] Since he does not deal with 2 Cor 10–13 (or with any other

---

[392] Ibid., n. 18, with reference to C. J. Classen, 'Paulus und die antike Rhetorik', *ZNW* 82 (1991), pp. 1–33, p. 31.

[393] Classen, 'Rhetorik', pp. 3–4.

[394] Winter, *Sophists*, pp. 30–1, 33–4.

[395] Murphy-O'Connor, *Paul*, pp. 50–1, with reference, n. 129, to P. Marshall, *Enmity in Corinth*, p. 390.

[396] Forbes, 'Comparison', p. 23; cited by Murphy-O'Connor, *Paul*, p. 51 n. 131.

[397] R. Dean Anderson Jr, *Ancient Rhetorical Theory and Paul*, Contributions to Biblical Exegesis and Theology 17, Kampen, 1996, pp. 249–50.

[398] Anderson, *Ancient Rhetorical Theory and Paul*, pp. 251–2; the quotation is on p. 252. Rather similarly, Professor Cranfield, in a note referring to 2 Cor 10.1–11, suggests to me that the use of an *insinuatio* to evoke interest and gain agreement would be a natural way of approaching one's audience, as would a *probatio*, and that such strategies would come about without the aid of rhetorical theory. The rhetoricians may simply formalise actual practice.

part of the epistle), we do not know whether the same conclusions would result from a similar study of these four chapters. If this should be so, they would appear to clash with the specific and detailed analysis proposed by Sundermann, on the on the one hand, and with Murphy-O'Connor's view of Paul's education on the other. All three works share 1996 as their year of publication. Hence, no one author can respond to either or both of the others. The questions raised remain open.

ESSAY I

PAUL'S OPPONENTS IN CORINTH: THE EVIDENCE OF 2 CORINTHIANS

A full exposition and critique of the numerous suggestions concerning the identity of these opponents would require a separate monograph. All that can be done here is, first (I), to summarise and comment on the main lines of approach to the problem, and, secondly (II), to ask what light may be thrown upon the question by the exegesis developed in this commentary. We are concerned to identify in some way those rivals and critics of Paul whose presence is apparent in 2 Cor 10–13 and to whom there seems to be a preliminary reference in 2.17–3.1. It is clear that these people have come to Corinth from elsewhere: in chaps. 10–13 they are spoken of in the third person, whilst Paul addresses the church itself, as a whole, in the second person;[1] in 10.12–18 he refers to certain people who are intruding on his missionary territory;[2] the expression ὁ ἐρχόμενος (11.4) points in the same direction;[3] lastly, these opponents claim to be ἀπόστολοι (11.13), i.e., missionaries,[4] or administrative agents,[5] and thus sent to Corinth from some other Christian centre.

This marks a difference between 2 Corinthians and the first canonical epistle. There is nothing in 1 Corinthians to show that Paul's critics in Corinth were anything other than indigenous members of the Corinthian church. It follows that, as a preliminary step, we can rule out the theory proposed by Baur, in which evidence from 1 Corinthians is used to form a composite picture. Baur started from the description in 1 Cor 1.11–12 of the rival parties (as he saw them) in the church, and posited the existence of a Petrine faction, over against Paul's followers, which was connected with the Christ-group and thereby with the opponents of 2 Cor 10–13 who claimed (10.7) to be 'Christ's'. The originators of the Petrine faction were outsiders, i.e., Jewish Christians, Judaizers of the Galatian type, who had penetrated into the

---

[1] In this connection, see also Barrett, pp. 253–4, on 10.6.
[2] Cf. Plummer, p. 289.
[3] Windisch, p. 326.
[4] Barrett, *Signs*, p. 70.
[5] Barrett, 'Shaliah:', p. 100.

Corinthian congregation.[6] We should also rule out Schmithals' suggestion that, since the opponents in all the Corinthian letters were identical, Paul's rivals are to be seen as Jewish Christian gnostics acting as missionary apostles: a fairly substantial part of the evidence for the gnostic element comes from 1 Corinthians, as interpreted by Schmithals. The claim of the opponents in 2 Cor 10.7 to be 'Christ's' is said to reflect 1 Cor 1.12, which expresses the gnostic claim to be a part of the cosmic Christ. Similarly, the reference in 2 Cor 11.4 to 'another Jesus' is seen as gnostic. It is interpreted in terms of 1 Cor 12.1–3, which speaks of Christian ecstatics who, in their inspired state, would curse Jesus. In Corinth, Schmithals claims, the ἄλλος Ἰησοῦς signified the accursed fleshly dwelling of the heavenly spirit.[7] The theories proposed by Baur and Schmithals, therefore, will be disregarded, in view of their reliance on evidence deriving from 1 Corinthians.

In addition, in what follows we shall proceed in accordance with the critical position for which we have argued in Vol. I: chaps. 10–13 are a separate and later letter.[8] This means that we shall not begin with the assumption that aspects of Paul's apostolic defence which appear in chaps. 1–9 must necessarily refer directly to the opposition he faced when writing chaps. 10–13. On this account, and in view of the situational difference between the two canonical epistles, described above, it is the last four chapters of 2 Corinthians that must provide the primary evidence for the character and intentions of the rival mission.

In a third and final section (III) of this essay we shall attempt to understand the Corinthian controversy both from Paul's standpoint and from the point of view of the Corinthians themselves.

I THE MAIN THEORIES

These are numerous and varied, but most may be roughly divided into two categories: those which sponsor some type of Judaizing theory, and others which see the opponents as claiming some elevated 'spiritual' status. In addition there are some theories which combine these two viewpoints.

---

[6] Baur, *Paulus* I, pp. 287–343, on the Corinthian epistles; see especially pp. 288–90, 294–5, 297, 300, 309, 313, 318.

[7] Schmithals, *Gnosticism*, pp. 197–9, 124–35.

[8] Vol. I, pp. 5–20.

1. *Opponents as Judaizers*

Although the specific Judaizing interpretation proposed by Baur met with later criticism,[9] the basic thesis that the opponents in Corinth promoted the policies and interests of Jewish Christianity was developed by succeeding scholars in various ways. We note here some representative examples.

(i) *Plummer: the opponents insist on the importance of the law.* These people claimed to be 'ministers of righteousness' (11.15), concerned with the keeping of the law of Moses. When they came to Corinth, they found some of Paul's Gentile converts still practising heathen vices (12.21), a situation which either generated or intensified their opposition to Paul himself. As 'ministers of Christ' (11.23), 'they claimed that their teaching was much nearer to that of Christ, who had kept the law, than was St. Paul's'.[10] Plummer finds support for this interpretation in chap. 3, where, he argues, Paul implicitly condemns Judaizing insistence on the keeping of the law, by showing the 'inferiority of the Law to the Gospel'.[11] If the condemnation is expressed only indirectly, this is because the Corinthians already knew what these people taught.[12] Perhaps so. But the arguments Plummer offers are either weak or mistaken. If the law was the prime concern of these opponents, it is very strange that the actual word νόμος occurs nowhere at all in 2 Corinthians.[13] And in the case of Galatians, the fact that there also Paul's correspondents knew what his opponents were teaching in no way prevented his explicit reference to the matters in dispute. More importantly, as our exegesis has shown,[14] the argument in chap. 3 is not designed to *prove* the inferiority of the law to the Gospel. This is taken for granted as the basis for the claim that the ministry of the new covenant must itself possess glory, a glory greater than that of Moses.

(ii) *Käsemann: the opponents attack Paul's apostolic authority.* The opponents claim the authorisation of Jerusalem, and contend that Paul's apostolicity is questionable because he lacks such

---

[9] Georgi, *Opponents*, p. 3, observes that Baur's critics were able to disregard his analysis of the history of the early church by charging him with 'dogmatism' of the Hegelian kind. No doubt as a result of this sort of attitude, Plummer, p. 298, was able to claim that the hypothesis of 'the conflict between Petrine and Pauline tendencies' had by his time (1915) been abandoned.

[10] Plummer, p. xxxvii.

[11] Plummer, p. 89.

[12] Plummer, pp. xl–xli.

[13] Martin, p. 336.

[14] See Vol. I, pp. 240–1.

authorisation. Their letters of recommendation are official documents deriving from the Jerusalem church. Letters with no such guarantee would not have occasioned the extensive exposition of the apostolic office found in chap. 3. And only the authority of Jerusalem would have been sufficient to weaken Paul's hold on his congregation. The references to the ὑπερλίαν ἀπόστολοι are not references to the opponents in Corinth (accused of satanic deceit[15]), but to the Jerusalem apostles, despite the apparent run of the argument in 11.4–6. (Paul is fighting on two fronts, hence he refers to opponents in vv. 4, 6, but to the Jerusalem apostles in v. 5.) Paul must, cautiously, assert his equality with the Jerusalem leaders. A group in the Jerusalem church (see Gal 2.4) aims to subordinate Paul to that church, and the rival missionaries are their emissaries. Paul lacks the criterion of apostolicity possessed by the original apostles (see Paul's assertion of his own criterion in 10.12–16). The latter were commissioned by Jesus himself—and perform the apostolic 'signs'. Paul is deficient in the latter, and, having no connection with the original apostles, has no connection with Jesus.[16]

This understanding of the opponents was criticised by Bultmann. Käsemann has misunderstood the purport of the discussion of the μέτρον τοῦ κανόνος, the criterion of apostolic authority in Corinth, in 10.12–16. According to Käsemann, it is the opponents who accuse Paul of failing to measure up to this standard. But this is wrong. It is Paul who accuses them, by implication, of falsely claiming, i.e., boasting of, conformity to the criterion. Moreover, the letters of 3.1 do not necessarily come from Jerusalem: they are on a par with letters which the Corinthian church might furnish (ἐξ ὑμῶν). It is quite possible, further, for Paul both to refer to his opponents as servants of Satan and also, nevertheless, to assert his equality with them, since to do the latter is essential: the Corinthians must realise that his powers are equal to those of his rivals. And Käsemann's exegesis of 11.4–6 is not convincing. If v. 6 refers to the rival missionaries, then so must v. 5, since v. 6 explains v. 5 more fully. In any case, the ὑπερλίαν ἀπόστολοι in 12.11 must be the visiting missionaries, since the allusion here is to the apostolic signs performed in Corinth, by the 'super-apostles' and by Paul.[17] Bultmann has the better of the argument, in respect of the exegesis of the relevant verses of the text. It is true that there is the difficulty of reconciling Paul's assertion of equality with his opponents and his castigation of them as servants of Satan. But

15 Paul would not assert *equality* with such people.
16 Käsemann, 'Legitimität'; see especially pp. 41–2, 44–7, 50–1, 56–7.
17 Bultmann, *Probleme*, pp. 20–30.

we have a similar problem in 11.18–23, where Paul must be talking about his rivals in Corinth, but yet must allow that they are διάκονοι Χριστοῦ.

(iii) *Oostendorp: the opponents assert the primacy of Israel.* The opponents are linked with the Palestinian church, and see themselves as living in the end-time when the promises of the establishment of God's kingdom in Zion are to be fulfilled. This is deduced from the reference in 11.4 to the εὐαγγέλιον ἕτερον, seen as an allusion to the evangelical (εὐαγγελιζόμενος) messenger of God's reign in Isa 52.7, which the opponents apply to themselves as the heralds of the kingdom.[18] Further, they style themselves Ἰσραηλῖται and σπέρμα Ἀβραάμ, and these titles serve to distinguish them from the Gentile Christians of Corinth, indicating their superior position as members of the nation of Israel.[19] Their acceptance of support from the Corinthians fits in with this self-understanding. According to the OT promises, the nations were to have a place in God's kingdom by attaching themselves to Israel (Zech 2.11), and Israel was to enjoy the wealth of the nations (Isa 61.6). Paul's opponents combined the two themes. Gentile support for the Jewish missionaries secured their attachment to Israel. And Paul's refusal of support might be seen as robbing the Corinthians of their place in the kingdom.[20] In addition, they regard the law as the means by which the Spirit is received. Whilst in chap. 3 Paul himself distinguishes between the covenant of the letter, i.e. the law, and the covenant of the Spirit, the opponents would not do so. According to Ezek 36.26–37 the gift of the Spirit is associated with the keeping of the written statutes. Furthermore, insistence on the keeping of the Mosaic law leads to their criticism of Paul for his failure to punish sinfulness and root it out. He lacks the power to do so because he lacks the Spirit (10.2).[21]

How convincing is this portrait of the opponents? Some of its components, while feasible, are not totally compelling. The word εὐαγγέλιον is Paul's own term for his message,[22] and in 11.4 the emphasis lies not on the word itself but on its qualification as ἕτερον. Whilst it may have some echoes of the OT promises, as Oostendorp suggests, it would resonate in this way in wider Christian circles, and would not, therefore, in itself offer specific information which would serve to characterise the opponents in Corinth more precisely. Again, Paul's refusal of financial support

---

[18] Oostendorp, *Another Jesus*, pp. 9–10, and see above, pp. 667–8.
[19] Oostendorp, *Another Jesus*, pp. 12–13.
[20] Oostendorp, *Another Jesus*, pp. 77–8.
[21] Oostendorp, *Another Jesus*, pp. 17–18, 35–6, 80.
[22] See above, p. 668.

was a cause of disaffection in Corinth prior to the arrival of the visiting missionaries of 2 Corinthians, and for other reasons. Oostendorp's most telling argument might be the opponents' insistence on their Jewishness, as Israelites, descendants of Abraham, and Hebrews. Why was this insistence necessary? And therefore necessary for Paul as well? The suggestion that they promoted the superiority of Israel would provide an answer to the question. But it is not the only possible answer. In our own exegesis of 11.22 we have suggested a different reason for these claims on the part of Paul's opponents. Jewish members of the congregation may have been ridiculed by fellow Jews for succumbing to the message of a new covenant preached by one whose own Judaism was in doubt, and the newcomers could have insisted on their own Jewish credentials in order to reassure these Corinthian Jewish Christians and enhance their own influence in the church. And possibly, as Aramaic speakers with Palestinian connections, some of them may have impressed all the Corinthians on account of their likely more direct link with the original disciples. Furthermore, if their message was the primacy of Israel, one might ask why it was apparently so congenial to the Gentile, as well as to the Jewish, members of the Corinthian church. The Corinthians' dilatoriness in respect of the collection for Jerusalem scarcely suggests that such a message would be especially welcome.

(iv) *Barnett: revival of the traditional view.* The rival missionaries probably come from Judaea, since in 10.12–16 there is an allusion to the Jerusalem agreement on spheres of missionary activity. They intend to promote the righteousness 'associated with Moses and the law' (11.15). Hence, they are to be seen as Judaizers in the traditional sense, who persuade Gentile Christians to adopt the Jewish way of life. The fact that the term 'righteousness' occurs only once in 1 Corinthians (1.30) suggests that the issues it raises had not been discussed in Corinth until the writing of 2 Corinthians. In Romans, however, written after the close of the Corinthian correspondence and probably in Corinth, the topic has become a main theme. Romans, then, may reflect Paul's struggle with his rivals in that city, and the legal righteousness which he attacks may represent their viewpoint. The Mosaic covenant, for them, remains in force. In Jewish tradition the glory of Moses remained undiminished, and Paul's opponents see this as 'a sign of the continuing applicability' of the Mosaic law.[23]

This characterisation of the opponents is vulnerable to the same basic criticism as has been directed at the theory adopted by

---

[23] Barnett, pp. 33–9; the quoted phrases are on pp. 35, 37.

Plummer some eight decades previously. Why does the term νόμος occur nowhere at all in 2 Corinthians, if fidelity to the Mosaic law was a key feature of the opponents' message? And there is the same difficulty in respect of the exegesis of chap. 3, now enhanced by the suggestion that the issues discussed in Romans mirror the new topics of controversy, recently introduced into Corinth by the rival missionaries, hence indicating the substance of their message. In our exegesis of chap. 3 we have argued that Paul takes for granted, and therefore assumes Corinthian knowledge of, the proposition that the Mosaic law is an instrument of death and condemnation. In other words, he must already have taught his converts some earlier version of the arguments he develops at length in Romans. He did not develop them in conflict with the newcomers. And if not, then we cannot conclude that the positions he controverts in Romans reflect the outlook and policy of the rival missionaries of 2 Cor 10–13.

2. Opponents as possessing special 'spiritual' status

This is a somewhat amorphous category. We shall consider a few theories which define the opponents in one way or another as 'spirit-people',[24] and shall then give more attention to Georgi's extensive presentation of them as θεῖοι ἄνδρες, 'divine men'.

(i) 'Spirit-people'. The first notable presentation of this viewpoint comes from Lütgert in 1908.[25] It follows his rejection of the Judaizing theory, on the grounds that there is no mention of circumcision. The opponents, he points out, claim to give the Corinthians a different Spirit (11.4). They themselves possess Spirit, and will bestow it to a greater extent than Paul does. They work miracles, and attach importance to visions and revelations. They also offer a deeper understanding of Jesus (11.4), and claim superiority to Paul in the matter of γνῶσις (11.6). Hence, they are gnostics. Lütgert is criticised by Käsemann, on this last point, on the ground that there is no evidence of their having promoted a speculative salvation-doctrine,[26] and by Georgi because he did not do justice to the Jewish (and Palestinian) origin of these people.[27] Bultmann, however, agrees with Lütgert that the opponents were gnostics. Paul agreed with them in respect of

---

[24] The term is borrowed from Murphy-O'Connor, *Paul*, p. 294, and elsewhere, as a better English equivalent of 'Pneumatiker' than, e.g., 'pneumatics'.

[25] W. Lütgert, *Freiheitspredigt*; see especially pp. 49, 67–71, 75, 79.

[26] Käsemann, 'Legitimität', p. 40.

[27] Georgi, *Opponents*, p. 5.

their Christ-myth, and would have no ground for polemic on this score. (Hence, there would be no need to refer to it.)[28]

We have already observed that the gnostic theory is adopted by Schmithals, and have initially queried his presentation of it on the ground that some essential evidence for it comes from 1 Corinthians.[29] But perhaps it might be useful here briefly to consider some of his further supporting arguments, which are based on 2 Cor 10–13. In 11.4–6, he claims it is γνῶσις which appears by implication to be the governing concept of the opponents' preaching. This γνῶσις would be a hellenistic form of knowledge, Schmithals suggests, which claimed to enable a person to become aware of his divine nature, to achieve certainty of immortality, and to find the way to heaven, freed from the fetters of the demonic powers. The πνεῦμα ἕτερον in 11.4 is the spirit within man which constitutes his true self. Further, it is possible to detect two items of indirect polemic against gnostics in Paul's account of his rapture to paradise. He uses the third person to indicate that the paradisal, heavenly state is not already his present possession, as gnostics would suppose it to be. And for the true gnostic the experience of rapture would be of necessity non-bodily, whereas Paul allows the alternative possibility.[30] But there are other explanations, as we have seen, of both the third person style and also of the mention of both types of rapture.[31] Moreover, gnostics would not proclaim, as a gospel message, another Jesus, since, as Schmithals himself claims,[32] they cursed 'Jesus' as the earthly dwelling of the spiritual Christ. And if the 'other spirit' is the gnostic's true self, it is not clear how it could be spoken of as 'received'. If there are hints here and there in 2 Corinthians that Paul may be incidentally combating gnostic ways of thinking, this could be due to the fact that, as Barrett remarks, 'the circumstances presupposed by 1 Corinthians cannot have completely ceased to exist'.[33]

Lastly, under this first heading, we need to consider the theory proposed by Friedrich.[34] He claims that the opponents are hellenistic Jewish Christians, miracle-workers and gifted with inspired speech, who see Moses as the type of the Messiah. Moses, as well as Christ, possesses divine glory, and Christians are followers of both. These people belong to the circle of hellenists originally associated with Stephen. Stephen was a charismatic

[28] Bultmann, *Probleme*, p. 23.
[29] He is criticised on this score by Friedrich, 'Gegner', pp. 193–4.
[30] Schmithals, *Gnosticism*, pp. 135–8, 145, 149–50, 167–8 n. 1, 211–12.
[31] See above, pp. 781–2, 786–7.
[32] Schmithals, *Gnosticism*, p. 134.
[33] Barrett, p. 30.
[34] Friedrich, 'Gegner'; his view is briefly noted in Vol. I, p. 238.

preacher and miracle-worker, and according to his speech in Acts 7 he saw Moses as the forerunner of Christ. It is this form of the Christian message that Paul is controverting in 2 Cor 3.[35] Friedrich's reconstruction does base itself on the NT text. But we should argue that as regards 2 Cor 3 it is a mistaken understanding. In this chapter the contrast is not between the transient glory of Moses and the permanent glory of Christ, as would be required by Friedrich's understanding of the opponents whose influence Paul is contesting. The contrast lies between Moses as agent of the Sinai covenant and the Christian apostles as ministers of the new covenant.[36] Moreover, it is significant that in those parts of Stephen's speech where he is speaking of Moses and the law the term δόξα, so crucial in 2 Cor 3, nowhere occurs. Consequently, there seems to be no very compelling evidence in support of Friedrich's theory.

(ii) θεῖοι ἄνδρες ('divine men'). (a) Georgi argues that the religious and cultural background of the opponents is the thought-world of hellenistic Judaism and its missionary apologetic.[37] The titles they use (11.22) indicate the superiority of Judaism and of its representatives.[38] Of relevance, in respect of this background, is the fact that the medium of Jewish propaganda was the exegesis of the law that took place in the synagogue.[39] The exegetes were the interpreters of divinely-inspired texts. These texts spoke of the inspired individuals of Israel's past, men who could be termed ἔνθεοι, 'inspired by God'. And the supreme example was Moses, who could be described as a θεῖος ἀνήρ, a 'divine man' (Jos., Ant. III. 180).[40] Moreover, the written text possessed its own holy power.[41] Scriptural exegesis was an encounter with this divine power and transformed the exegete himself. 'The intensive observation of the θεῖοι ἄνδρες in the tradition transformed the observers into θεῖοι ἄνδρες themselves.'[42]

(b) What, then, has this type of Jewish missionary apologetic to do with Paul's opponents in Corinth? Georgi finds evidence of a connection in 2 Cor 3. Whilst this chapter belongs to a separate letter, earlier than that of chaps. 10–13, he thinks that it is the same group of opponents whom Paul is dealing with in both, so

[35] Friedrich, 'Gegner'; see especially pp. 182–5, 195–201, 203–4, 212–15.
[36] See the exegesis of 3.7–18: Vol. I, pp. 237–97.
[37] Opponents, pp. 83–151.
[38] Opponents, pp. 41–60.
[39] Opponents, pp. 84–9.
[40] Opponents, pp. 124, 126.
[41] Opponents, p. 137.
[42] Opponents, p. 148.

that evidence from the earlier communication can be used to elucidate the later one.[43] It is clear from chap. 3 that the opponents were concerned with the figure of Moses, as the representative of the law, and indeed identified with it.[44] They see Moses's ministry in a positive light, not as an agency of death but as a representation of divine power, the ministry of a θεῖος ἀνήρ, as in the apologetic of hellenistic Judaism.[45] It is this glorification of Moses that Paul is contesting. For the opponents, moreover, since Moses's divine power remains inherent in the law, they are themselves transformed into 'divine men' by their engagement with it.[46] We see from 12.12 that they performed miracles, which will have resembled those of the hellenistic and hellenistic-Jewish figures who were regarded as 'divine men' by virtue of their miraculous powers.[47] The opponents' gospel will have presented Jesus, the miracle-worker, as the most outstanding θεῖος ἀνήρ of all.[48] Their aim, in coming to Corinth, appears to have been simply the urge to indulge in competition with Paul, since missionary competition was a prevalent feature of the age in its religious aspect.[49]

(c) This exposition of the nature of the opposition Paul was contesting has been highly influential. Nevertheless, it is possible to query its validity in various ways. First, it may be that Georgi relies too heavily on the opponents' titles in 11.22 as indications of their background in hellenistic Judaism. Whilst the word 'Εβραῖος may have a number of different connotations in various contexts, we should not necessarily suppose, as Georgi appears to do, that all, or at least most, are present on any particular occasion of its use. More particularly, it may well be significant that the phrase σπέρμα 'Αβραάμ occurs nowhere at all in the hellenistic Jewish literature Georgi has examined. In 4 Macc 18.1 we do, certainly, find the similar expression τῶν 'Αβραμιαίων σπερμάτων ἀπόγονοι. But in the context it appears to support the exclusiveness of Judaism rather than its hellenistic outreach. Georgi allows this, but argues that such an interpretation would be contrary to the outlook and intention of the book as a whole.[50] Nevertheless, its isolated occurrence and somewhat ambiguous purport do not inspire confidence in the phrase's significance for 2 Cor 11.22, as an indication of the opponents' connection with

---

[43] *Opponents*, pp. 229–30.
[44] *Opponents*, p. 250.
[45] *Opponents*, p. 254.
[46] *Opponents*, pp. 258–64, especially pp. 259, 263.
[47] *Opponents*, pp. 236, 275 and p. 308 n. 283.
[48] *Opponents*, p. 274.
[49] *Opponents*, pp. 236–8.
[50] *Opponents*, pp. 49–50.

hellenistic Jewish apologetic. This is particularly so, in view of the fact that in Gal 3.29 Paul uses the term τοῦ 'Αβραὰμ σπέρμα when confronting opposition which has some connection with the church of Jerusalem. Secondly, it is argued that the term θεῖος ἀνήρ is too general and fluid in usage to assist in clarifying the identity of the opponents. More particularly, it should not be seen as equivalent to 'miracle-worker'. In addition, it is questionable 'whether the *sources* are adequate enough to construct the picture of Hellenistic-Jewish missionary activity that Georgi does'.[51] Thirdly, the run of the argument in 2 Cor 3 is not what would be required as a response to the type of opposition postulated by Georgi. Paul defends a position, the glory of the Christian ministry, on which such opponents would have agreed, and takes for granted without argument a view of the Mosaic law, as the instrument of condemnation and death, with which they would profoundly have disagreed.[52] Fourthly, the reference to miracle-working in 12.12, which obliquely indicates that the opponents claim to be thus authenticated, may serve just as well to connect them with the Jerusalem church[53] as to ally them with the hellenistic Jewish apologetic hypothesised by Georgi.

3. Opponents as combining Judaizing and 'spiritual' characteristics

Under this head two theories will be considered, i.e., that of Barrett (1971)[54] and that of Murphy-O'Connor (1996).[55]

(i) *Barrett.* Discussion of the theories in sections 1. and 2. has indicated that 2 Corinthians appears to provide two contradictory sets of data: evidence which suggests that the opponents were Judaizing Christians, probably connected with Jerusalem, and other evidence which implies that they were 'spirit-people' of one sort or another, to be seen against a hellenistic background.[56] The resolution of the contradiction proposed by Barrett is that the opponents themselves belonged to the former category, but that they may have adopted some characteristics of the latter in order to impress the Corinthians, who employed hellenistic criteria to

---

[51] C. R. Holladay, *Theios Aner*, pp. 236–7, 239; the quotation is on p. 239.
[52] See Vol. I, pp. 296–7, and the exegesis of 3.7–18.
[53] See, e.g., Acts 3.1–10; 9.32–42; 2.43.
[54] 'Opponents', pp. 60–86.
[55] *Paul*, pp. 280–322.
[56] 'Opponents', pp. 78–9.

distinguish true apostles from false.[57] The main points in the argument are as follows.

(a) Paul calls his opponents ψευδαπόστολοι (11.13). This is a term which belongs within the setting of Judaism.[58] There are other ψευδο-words in the NT which have a Jewish background. In Gal 2.4, for example, the ψευδάδελφοι must be Jewish Christians. Barrett suggests that Paul, in his turn, was regarded by Jewish Christians as himself a ψευδαπόστολος, and that what was at issue was the question of the fulfilment of Judaism.[59]

(b) The text shows that the Corinthian situation was complex, and that there were two groups with whom Paul had to deal in addition to the Corinthians themselves. The people whom he allows to be διάκονοι Χριστοῦ (11.23) must surely be different from those castigated as servants of Satan (11.13–15). And Käsemann is correct in maintaining that these 'servants of Satan' cannot be the same as the ὑπερλίαν ἀπόστολοι (11.5; 12.11), since of this latter group Paul simply says that he is not inferior to them—an 'intolerable' comment if they are identical with the former. The difficulty presented by the close connection between 11.5 and 11.6, where v. 5 refers to the ὑπερλίαν ἀπόστολοι and v. 6 obliquely to the rival missionaries in Corinth, is met with the suggestion that in v. 6 the primary reference is not actually to these opponents but to the criteria the Corinthians used to evaluate the quality of such visiting missionaries. Hence, the false apostles are to be distinguished from the ὑπερλίαν ἀπόστολοι.[60]

(c) The latter, in all probability, are the Jerusalem apostles. The term is mildly ironical, and thus reminiscent of the way Paul speaks of the 'pillar-apostles' in Gal 2.6, 9, i.e., of James, Cephas, and John. Moreover, in 10.12–18 the question as to who has apostolic rights in Corinth recalls the division of labour referred to in Gal 2.7–10. Paul blames his opponents for failing to observe it. This implies that those whom they claim to represent are the authorities with whom Paul had made the agreement.[61]

(d) In 12.6 the allusion to the τις who might think too highly of Paul on the basis of his visionary experiences, should he wish to boast of them at greater extent, hints at the kind of criteria the Corinthians would apply in their evaluation of apostles. What they looked for was a display of overt spiritual power, defined in a hellenistic sense.[62]

How is this theory to be assessed? On the one hand, the claims

[57] 'Opponents', p. 80.
[58] 'Opponents', p. 65.
[59] See 'ΨΕΥΔΑΠΟΣΤΟΛΟΙ (2 Cor 11.13)', pp. 87–107.
[60] 'Opponents', pp. 64, 70–1.
[61] 'Opponents', pp. 65, 70, 79.
[62] 'Opponents', pp. 72–3.

that the opponents may have some connection with the Jerusalem church and that in chap. 10 the Jerusalem agreement on spheres of missionary activity lies somewhere in the background carry conviction. On the other hand, the understanding of the ὑπερλίαν ἀπόστολοι as the Jerusalem apostles is untenable, as we have shown in our exegesis of the relevant passages. The super-apostles are the rival missionaries present in Corinth. But we may still accept Barrett's case for some connection with Jerusalem. As we have seen, miracle-working was characteristic of the Jerusalem church, and may have characterised its associates elsewhere.[63] In fact, Barrett's way of explaining the 'pneumatic' element in the profile of the opponents in Corinth may simply prove unnecessary. In addition to miraculous healings Luke credits the nascent church with glossolalia, and Stephen and Peter with visions.

(ii) *Murphy-O'Connor*. This theory of the opposition to Paul in Corinth begins with a consideration of the influence of Apollos, the eloquent and learned Christian Jew from Alexandria (Acts 18.24–25), who could well himself have been influenced by the philosophy of Philo. Murphy-O'Connor suggests that Apollos will have met needs in the Christian community which had been disregarded by Paul, i.e., the desire for a rhetorical presentation of the gospel and the need for 'intellectual fulfilment'. Hence the formation of the Apollos group and the Paul group was inevitable.[64] Moreover, the influence of Apollos is to be seen in the emergence of a group of 'spirit-people' (1 Cor 2.6, 15; also 4.8, 10). With reference to R. A. Horsley, Murphy-O'Connor claims that the language used by this group suggests the influence of Philonic philosophy, obviously mediated by Apollos.[65]

It is these 'spirit-people', the πνευματικοί, who then give hospitality to a group of Judaizers. They derive from Antioch, and, having caused trouble in Galatia, have crossed over to Europe to continue their campaign in the Pauline churches there.[66] In Corinth they claim to be 'servants of the new covenant', and in this capacity insist on the continuing validity of the law. In opposition to Paul, they form an alliance with the spirit-people. What the two groups have in common is their belief in the importance of Moses:

> For the Judaizers he was the great Lawgiver, whose words had enduring value. For the spirit-people nourished on a

---

[63] See above, p. 841.
[64] *Paul*, pp. 274–7.
[65] *Paul*, pp. 280–2.
[66] *Paul*, pp. 293–4.

form of Philonism, he was much more. Philo regularly presents Moses as 'the perfect wise man' (*Leg. All.* I 395), who epitomized all Hellenistic virtue as 'king and lawgiver and high priest and prophet' (*Vita Mosis* 2.3; cf. *Praem.* 53–6).

Since Philo magnifies the law of Moses, the 'Philonic' tendencies of the πνευματικοί could be exploited by the Judaizers.[67] In response, in the letter of 2 Cor 1–9, Paul attempts to separate these two groups, so as to deprive the Judaizers of a base in Corinth. In chap. 3 he engages in denigration of Moses, as lacking openness and as the agent of a dispensation associated with spiritual blindness. And he takes advantage of the fact that the Judaizers had introduced the idea of a new covenant, which enabled Paul himself to designate the law 'as the old covenant'. This would destroy its attraction for the 'spirit-people' who saw themselves as forward-looking.[68] Murphy-O'Connor supposes that this letter was effective in that it deprived the Judaizers of the possibility of turning the πνευματικοί 'into Law-observant Christians'. Hence they resorted to vicious criticism of Paul himself. It is to this criticism that he responds in the letter of 2 Cor 10–13.[69]

How is this understanding of the opposition to be evaluated? In its favour it can be said that the suggestions concerning Apollos's influence in Corinth are certainly plausible. The attraction of his teaching for some of the church members may well have generated or increased dissatisfaction with Paul's own teaching and personal characteristics. The difficulty arises when we consider the tenability of the Judaizing aspect of the theory. There are several objections to the scenario proposed by Murphy-O'Connor:

(a) The claim that it is intruding Judaizers who have introduced the theme of the new covenant is surely incorrect. In 1 Cor 11.25 Paul refers to the καινὴ διαθήκη as part of an earlier tradition which he received and passed on to the Corinthians.

(b) In 2 Cor 3 there may be, perhaps, some denigration of Moses. But this has nothing directly to do with Judaizing opponents of the Galatian type. As we have several times noted, in this chapter Paul takes for granted agreement on the negative aspects of the Mosaic law: he does not argue for them. Indeed, the somewhat unfavourable picture of Moses is not itself the main point. The thrust of the argument is to insist on the glory of the ministry of the new covenant despite appearances to the contrary.

(c) The total absence of any reference to circumcision throughout 2 Corinthians makes the identification of the opponents

---

[67] *Paul*, pp. 302–4; the quotation is on p. 303.
[68] *Paul*, pp. 309–11.
[69] *Paul*, pp. 317–19.

as troublemakers of the Galatian type highly problematic. Perhaps such people had penetrated to Philippi, but in Paul's response to that situation we do have such a reference (Phil 3.2–3).

(d) Whilst it is in 2 Cor 10–13 that the presence and influence of external opponents is most obvious, in this presentation little or no evidence is produced from these chapters to identify them.

II RESULTS OF EXEGESIS

Since we have found none of the theories surveyed above entirely satisfactory as an explanation of the opponents whom Paul is combating in the letter of chaps. 10–13, it may seem hazardous to produce yet another such. At the same time, our own exegesis may have provided a few clues to the identity of these people, which it might be useful to collect together. We confine our attention to the last four chapters of the canonical epistle. As we have seen in Part I of this essay, most commentators suppose that chap. 3 is also relevant to the identification of the rival missionaries. We do not ourselves share this view, since we have argued that the criticism of Paul's claim to be the agent of a new covenant comes initially from the synagogue, not from other Christian missionaries. If we work on the basis of chaps. 10–13, there seem to be three areas in which the exegesis may throw light on the identity of Paul's rivals and the nature of their mission: their assumption of the right to work in Corinth; the content of their message; and their personal characteristics.

1. In 10.12–18 Paul queries the right of his opponents to conduct a mission in Corinth. This is the territory God had allotted to Paul himself. These others have simply taken over illicitly, and they are boasting of their success in an area where he has done all the groundwork. In the background, in all probability, there is the agreement on the division of missionary responsibilities reached with the Jerusalem apostles. We have suggested, however, that this would have left Corinth as ambiguous, and hence disputed, territory. If, then, the opponents claimed some right to it, they will have belonged in some way to the Petrine mission. And it may well have seemed to them that it was Paul who had trespassed on their preserves. According to Acts 18.4 he had initially preached to the Corinthian Jews, and he himself refers to such preaching in 1 Cor 9.20.

2. Paul implicitly charges his rivals with preaching another Jesus and a different gospel. We have interpreted the first as a splendid figure of post-resurrection glory by contrast with the Pauline gospel of the crucified Christ. The second we have understood as

a message stressing obedience to the teaching of the earthly Jesus, including some measure of Torah-observance. In view of the glory traditionally ascribed to Moses, the original law-giver, there is no necessary conflict between these two aspects of the opponents' message.

3. As regards personal characteristics, these people stress their full Jewish credentials. In addition, the term Ἑβραῖοι may indicate Palestinian connections and competence in Aramaic. This could suggest that they might claim a close link with Jesus's original disciples and with the original tradition of his Aramaic teaching. They claim apostolic status. They are miracle-workers, and it is highly probable also that they are visionaries who boast of their visions. As missionaries, they accept as a matter of principle material support from the congregations amongst whom they work. This last characteristic, together with the likelihood of their connection with the Jerusalem apostles who had been Jesus's first followers, suggests that they are part of the Petrine mission to the Jews (cf. 1 Cor 9.5). In view of the Petrine traditions in the early chapters of Acts, their miracles and visions would fit this hypothesis well enough. We have already noted that membership of the Petrine mission is a conclusion that may be drawn from their apparent assumption of a right to work in Corinth.

There is one characteristic, however, that may seem to run counter to this description of Paul's rivals. This is their apparent competence in Greek rhetoric. They have impressed the Corinthians, it seems, by their oratorical eloquence (11.6). Does this fit their Palestinian connections, and their probable connection with the Jerusalem apostles? Barrett, who sees these people as 'Jerusalem Jews', recognises this need to explain the hellenistic element in the picture we get of the opponents. His solution is that they have accepted the Corinthians' criteria of apostleship and have adopted 'a measure of hellenization'. But is this sufficient? It is by no means clear how, without any previous training or practice, they could have presented themselves successfully in this *ad hoc* manner to an audience at least superficially versed (as any Greek audience would be) in the critical assessment of public speakers. So does this difficulty cast doubt on the profile we have adumbrated? Not necessarily. The Petrine mission, if it was to progress successfully westwards beyond Palestine, must surely have been served by some reasonably fluent Greek-speakers. And Greek-speakers in the Mediterranean world may well have had opportunity gradually to acquire some degree of sophistic style and presence, in view of the sophists' ubiquity, attested by Philo. It is important, moreover, to remember that these opponents are portrayed as a group. It would not have been necessary for each member of the group to have been equally endowed with every advantage the Corinthians may have found desirable. The Greek-speaker capable of rhetorical flourishes may have known little Aramaic. Conversely, the native Aramaic-speaker, valued for his first-hand familiarity with Jesus's Aramaic teaching, might not have required a degree of bilingualism substantially higher than that possessed by most Jews in the hellenistic world. The recruitment of agents in the first category, moreover, would have been facilitated by the establishment of the Petrine headquarters in Jerusalem. Of the many Jews from the Diaspora who came to the city some will have become followers of Christ, and of these some may have possessed rhetorical skills.

Finally, in our discussion of 11.4, we have suggested that this missionary group, fundamentally part of the Petrine mission to the Jews, may represent an early form of the evangelistic enterprise which later comes to view in the mission charge at the conclusion of the Gospel of Matthew. This is not in any way to suggest that these people shared Matthew's fully-developed theology or, more especially, christology, nor is it to imply that the evangelist was later directly dependent on them or their successors. But it is not impossible that in the early fifties there was some common ground between this missionary group and a proto-Matthean circle, and that the latter may have had some influence on the former.

III THE CORINTHIANS' VIEWPOINT AND PAUL'S

1. *Viewpoint of the Corinthians*

Paul is clearly angry with the Corinthians for their ready acceptance of the rival missionaries. But the Corinthians themselves may have welcomed these people in all good faith, and might be able to defend themselves in various ways.

First, if these missionaries in some way represent the Jerusalem church, it might not seem disloyal to Paul to receive them and offer them scope for their work. Paul himself, by insistently promoting the collection, had surely given recognition to the special status of the Jerusalem Christians. Indeed, in the letter containing chap. 8 he had suggested (8.14) that this church might supply some deficiencies amongst the Corinthians themselves. And secondly, in an earlier letter (1 Cor 3.5–9) Paul had allowed for 'team work' in the case of Apollos, who was not working under his direction as one of his own assistants. Why should the situation be different in respect of these new missionaries? Thirdly, if their teaching was not identical with Paul's, their hearers might well have regarded it as supplementary to his rather than opposed to it. In any case, if their 'other Jesus' emphasised the glorious Christ exclusively, this one-sidedness could have been seen by the Corinthians as a necessary counterweight to Paul's concentration on the crucified Jesus. Moreover, if the rival missionaries were agents of the Petrine mission, they could claim that their gospel was based on the experience of the apostle who was the first (as Paul tells us in 1 Cor 15.5) to be granted a manifestation of the risen Christ. In addition, these people will be seen as closer than Paul to Jesus's original teaching.

Fourthly, the Corinthians would probably have regarded the opponents' use of rhetoric as a useful evangelistic technique. In their city it might have favourable results for the spread of the gospel. In 1 Corinthians Paul had certainly explained (1 Cor 2.1–3) that he had of set intent rejected a quasi-sophistic approach when he first came to Corinth. But it is not clear how this fits in with his later assertion (1 Cor 9.23) that he has 'become all things to all men', so as to save some of them by whatever means possible. Might the Corinthians not conclude that this principle allowed the evangelist to become a sophist to the sophists?

Fifthly, it is clear from 2 Cor 11.7–12 that Paul's refusal of maintenance was still a point of contention in Corinth. To some in the church his policy may have continued to arouse doubts about his apostolic status, and doubts also, therefore, about their own Christian standing. Extra validation from representatives of the Petrine mission might not be unwelcome. It may be that social considerations also come into the picture. The influential Corinthians will have preferred those who accepted their patronage, and thus conformed to their own class-based system.[70] Even if they did not go so far as to regard Paul's rejection of their offer as an insult (though some may have done), it did put something of a question mark against their social system and its values. And yet they could have pointed out that their social rank enabled them to host the Lord's Supper, to contribute generously to the collection, and perhaps to persuade others of their class to join the Christian movement. Moreover, they were the natural administrative leaders of the congregation. Might they not have felt unappreciated, perhaps aggrieved?

2. *Paul's viewpoint*

This is expressed, of course, throughout the letter of chaps. 10–13, and we shall take up the topic in the following essay. Here we make a few general suggestions.

[70] Horrell, *Social Ethos*, pp. 220–5.

First, the aggressive tone and the totally unyielding self-defence of chaps. 10–13 may be due in part to the Corinthians' negative response to Paul's letter of chaps. 1–8. He might well have felt both sorrow and anger at the apparent failure of his readers to appreciate its force. He had explained in depth the meaning of his inglorious lifestyle (4.7–11), his suffering (1.3–6), and his apostolic ministry (5.11–6.10). All this , it seems, had been either ignored or met with complete incomprehension. What sticks in the Corinthians' memory is his feeble personal presence and his contemptible oratory.

Secondly, Paul was concerned about wider evangelistic issues. He will have regarded it as vitally important that the Jerusalem agreement in respect of missionary work (Gal 2.1–10) should be maintained. He himself, he would insist, had so maintained it. By founding the Corinthian church in a major city of the Gentile world he had kept his side of the agreement. It was not he who was trespassing on the territory of other apostles, but the rival missionaries at present in Corinth. We have seen that the latter could dispute this interpretation of the Jerusalem concordat. Nevertheless, Paul's own understanding of it would be tenable. If it was breached in an important city such as Corinth there would be little hope of its maintenance elsewhere. Corinth would be likely to influence both the further dissemination of the Christian message and also the contacts between existing churches.

Thirdly, it is important to remember that this is not the end of the story of the interaction between Paul and the Corinthians, although it is the latest episode we can document from Paul's own hand. It may well be that when Paul eventually arrived in Corinth for the winter of 56–57 C.E. some better understanding was reached between the apostle and the church. Even in the age of the fax-machine, immediate face to face encounter may often prove the better way to resolve differences. How much more would this be true when views and letters were carried over long distances, possibly by travellers on foot. Perhaps, during Paul's final stay in Corinth, such a resolution did occur: most of his correspondence, after all, was preserved. We have suggested that Paul, on his part, may have mitigated his determination to accept no maintenance from the church.[71] Perhaps he might have achieved some success in explaining his attitude towards the matter of social status. In this respect, whilst it is possible to sympathise with the Corinthians, it does seem that Paul's insight was the more profound. It was based on the example of Christ (8.9), and Paul lived up to it.

[71] See Excursus XII, pp. 707–8.

Postscript
What had happened to the rival missionaries? Presumably they had moved on elsewhere, perhaps because Paul's letter of chaps. 10–13 had changed the Corinthians' attitude towards them. Did Paul suspect (or even know) that they were on their way to Rome? If so, this might have given further impetus to his intention to write to the church there and have helped to condition the content of his letter. He would have wanted, in any case, to introduce himself in advance to the Christians of Rome,[72] and he would have in mind the nature of this church, a Jewish Christian foundation which was now a mixed community of Jews and Gentiles. What better way of introduction than for Paul to expound at length his understanding of the basic Christian gospel and its relationship and relevance to both Jews and Gentiles? If he now suspected that his rivals in Corinth might have moved on to Rome, such a letter would be even more imperative. Their scornful denigration of Paul in Corinth and their ability to influence adversely even a church of his own foundation would bode ill for his own reception by the Roman Christians. In part he could be writing to counteract such an eventuality.

[72] Murphy-O'Connor, *Paul*, pp. 331–2.

ESSAY II

PAUL THE APOSTLE

1. General background

Under this heading we shall discuss the origin and meaning of the term ἀπόστολος and its use in the NT, possible parallels to the Christian institution, and the Christian apostolate itself.

(i) *Origin and meaning of ἀπόστολος.* The word occurs 79 or 80 times in the NT. It is frequently found in the plural, with the definite article and without further qualification, with the implication that the people concerned hold a particular office or perform a particular function familiar to the readers (e.g., Acts 2.42; 9.27; Gal 1.17; Eph 2.20). There is the same implication when the noun is used predicatively without the article (e.g., οὐκ εἰμὶ ἀπόστολος; 1 Cor 9.1; cf. 1 Cor 12.29). Familiarity with the NT might therefore suggest that the word ἀπόστολος, with reference to a person, was generally current, either in the biblical Greek of the LXX, or in secular usage, or in both. This is not so. There is one example only in the LXX (ἐγώ εἰμι ἀπόστολος πρός σε σκληρός, 3 Kgdms 14.6) and one in Symmachus (Isa 18.2).[1] There are a few instances in non-biblical Greek with the meaning 'messenger', 'ambassador', 'delegate' (e.g. ἀπόστολος ἐς τὴν Μίλητον, Hdt 1.21; cf. 5.38).[2] Otherwise, there is a wide range of meanings ('naval expedition', 'colony', 'export licence', for example).[3] Clearly some explanation is required to account for the frequent use of ἀπόστολος in the NT to denote a person. Before considering the various suggestions, however, it will be useful to note the range of those whom the NT writers term ἀπόστολοι.

Chronologically the earliest attested use of the word in the NT is in the Pauline letters. Paul speaks of himself as ἀπόστολος (Rom 1.1; 1 Cor 9.1; Gal 1.1) or as ἀπόστολος Χριστοῦ Ἰησοῦ (1 Cor 1.1;

---

[1] Barrett, '*Shaliaḥ*', p. 96.
[2] LSJ s.v. I.1.
[3] LSJ s.v. II.

2 Cor 1.1). It is connected in his mind with his direct divine calling (Gal 1.1) and the commission to preach the gospel (Rom 1.1), and with the revelation of the risen Christ which he had experienced (οὐκ εἰμὶ ἀπόστολος; οὐχὶ Ἰησοῦν τὸν κύριον ἡμῶν ἑόρακα; 1 Cor 9.1). He refers also to others as ἀπόστολοι (οἱ λοιποὶ ἀπόστολοι, 1 Cor 9.5; τοῖς ἀποστόλοις πᾶσιν, 1 Cor 15.7; τοὺς πρὸ ἐμοῦ ἀποστόλους, Gal 1.17). Who are these people? In view of the Lucan identification of the Twelve with the apostles, it is natural to suppose that Jesus's eleven original disciples, together with Matthias as the replacement for Judas Iscariot, formed at least the nucleus of the group Paul refers to in 1 Cor 9.5 and Gal 1.17. That there were others in addition is indicated in 1 Cor 15.7, since the Twelve have already received separate mention in v. 5.[4] In Rom 16.7 Andronicus and Junia(s) are so designated,[5] and Barnabas, in all probability, should also be included in the apostolic group, since in 1 Cor 9.6 Paul couples him with himself as having the right to apostolic maintenance.[6] Finally, in addition to those whose apostolic status he recognised, Paul refers also to people who claimed the title but whom he himself regarded as impostors and so stigmatised as 'false apostles' (2 Cor 11.13). Barrett points out that this substantiates the other evidence that there was a recognisable category of 'apostles of Christ'. If there are spurious apostles there must be real ones.[7]

In view of the substantial nature of this Pauline evidence, are we, then, to conclude that the use of ἀπόστολος as a Christian technical term was the creation of Paul himself? This is improbable. Had it been so, it is unlikely that he would have referred to the Jerusalem authorities as 'those who were apostles before me', or that opponents would have arrived in Corinth with the claim that they too were 'apostles of Christ'. The term, with its Aramaic or Hebrew equivalent, would appear to go back to the earliest days of the Jerusalem church. This then raises the question as to whether the usage might have originated in the language and practice of Jesus himself. In all three synoptic gospels the word ἀπόστολος is used of his twelve disciples. According to Lk 6.13, he himself gave them this title, and in Mt 10.2–7 these ἀπόστολοι are sent out on a preaching mission (see also Mk 6.7–13, 30). We thus have at least two, possibly three, historical contexts in which the term 'apostle' became current: the Pauline mission, the church of Jerusalem and its dependent churches, and perhaps the mission of Jesus himself. As regards

[4] Barrett, *First Corinthians*, p. 343.
[5] Cranfield, *Romans*, pp. 788–9.
[6] Schmithals, *Office of Apostle*, pp. 63–4.
[7] Barrett, *Signs*, p. 36.

the function to which the word pointed, there appears to be one common factor. In each case the preaching of a message played some part. This is most obvious in Paul's case (1 Cor 1.17; Gal 1.15–16), but he saw it as a function of the Jerusalem 'pillars' also (Gal 2.7–9), and it is a feature of the synoptic passages. Further discussion of function depends on consideration of the degree to which Christian usage was dependent upon existing Jewish models. Linguistically, the nearest non-biblical Greek use would bε that of 'messenger'.

(ii) *Parallels to the Christian institution?* Are there any biblical, Jewish, or hellenistic models which might throw light on the Christian concept(s) of apostleship? There have been four suggestions, two of which we shall discuss.[8] The first of these is proposed by Hahn, who sees a relationship between the Christian apostle and the OT prophet. The verb 'to send', *šălaḥ* plays an important part in the call-narratives in Isa 6.8, Jer 1.7, and Ezek 2.3, which refer to a mission deriving from God, and this way of speaking is reflected in the NT where the Greek verbs ἀποστέλλω and πέμπω are similarly used with reference to the prophets and to the prophetic figure of John the Baptist, in Lk 11.49 and in Mk 1.2, Mt 11.10, and Jn 1.6, 3.28.[9] The relevant allusions are rather few, however, and these verbs are used quite frequently of ordinary, 'non-theological' sending. Hahn is on firmer ground when he notes, as others have done, the connection in Paul's thinking between the prophetic calling and his own apostolic vocation, as shown in the parallels between Gal 1.15 and Jer 1.5, Isa 49.1.[10] Moreover, the unity of Christophany and mission in the case of the apostles of Christ corresponds with the unity of theophany and mission in the case of the OT prophets.[11] But how do these considerations assist us to understand the Christian adoption of the actual term ἀπόστολος? The explanation would presumably depend (a) on the connection between the verb 'to

---

[8] The other two are the Cynic-Stoic emissary and the gnostic apostle. The Cynic knows himself to be sent as a messenger from Zeus. K. H. Rengstorf, on ἀπόστολος, in *TWNT* I, pp. 406–48, rejects this possibility. The word is not used of this figure, and the deity is pantheistic (pp. 408–9, 411–12). We might ask also if Cynic sages would have been so numerous in Jerusalem as to provide models for the nascent church. Even less likely is the claim by W. Schmithals, *Office of Apostle*, pp. 198–230, that the Christian apostolate derives from a gnostic apostolate in Syria. This would require us to suppose that the Christian movement, within five or six years, had spread to Antioch, become synthesised with some form of gnosticism, moved back to Jerusalem, and then lost some of its distinguishing characteristics to the extent that Paul, in total ignorance, was able to align himself with it.

[9] Hahn, 'Apostolat', pp. 66–7.

[10] Hahn, 'Apostolat', p. 68; see also Vol. I, p. 80 n. 10.

[11] Hahn, ibid.

send' and the calling of the prophets, and (b) on the parallelism between the prophetic calling and the apostolic vocation. When these two connections are themselves brought together, we could see how the comparatively rare word ἀπόστολος (cognate of ἀποστέλλω) might have been brought into service to designate the Christian figure who is called and sent. How tenable is this line of argument? It may well have force in the case of Paul, from whom much of the significant evidence is derived. But the term ἀπόστολος does not appear to have been his creation. One then has to ask whether his own understanding of his apostolic calling would necessarily have occurred to the Jerusalem apostles. The Christian message, after all, was that the present time was the time of the fulfilment of scriptural prophecy, rather than an era of fresh prophetic activity.

The second suggestion for discussion relates to the Jewish institution of the šāliaḥ.[12] Rengstorf claims that here we have the closest parallel to the ἀπόστολος of the NT. The šāliaḥ is a commissioned representative with full powers, authorised, e.g., to conclude a betrothal or to convey a writ of divorce, to lead public prayers or to act as the delegate of a court. Whilst the institution is basically a legal one, it was employed also in the religious sphere: for example, rabbis were sent out by the central authorities to appoint teachers of the Scriptures and of the Mishnah. Rengstorf has to allow, however, that the term was never applied to Jewish missionaries. Turning to the NT, he notes the Synoptic references to the mission of the Twelve: Mt 10.15; Mk 6.7; Lk 9.1–2. As endowed by Jesus with ἐξουσία, these disciples are his authorised representatives, and correspond with the Jewish šĕliḥim. During Jesus's historical lifetime, however, this authorisation was not permanent, but was for a limited period only. The post-Easter apostolate was thus something new. Through their Easter experiences, Rengstorf claims, the Twelve believed themselves commissioned, first, to act as Christ's representatives within the Christian community, and, secondly, to become missionaries (see Mt 28.19–20; Lk 24.46–9; Acts 1.6). This second element distinguishes the Christian institution from its Jewish counterpart.[13]

Various criticisms may be brought against this explanation. The developed Jewish institution whereby the central authorities regularly sent out emissaries to the Diaspora did not exist before 70 C.E.[14] Moreover, there are difficulties even if we think in more general terms of the legal principle which allowed one man to act

---

[12] Cognate of šālah, send.
[13] Rengstorf, on ἀπόστολος, in *TWNT* I, pp. 414–38.
[14] Hahn, 'Apostolat', pp. 62–3; Schmithals, *Office of Apostle*, pp. 100–1.

as plenipotentiary for another. This is a juristic concept, and the plenipotentiary's commission is temporary: the apostle has a religious function, and a permanent commission.[15] The message of the Jewish delegate is accepted on the ground of his authorisation, whilst the apostle's authority depends on his message.[16] But some of these objections lack force. It is not entirely true that the authority of the apostle is wholly dependent on his message. Were that so, Paul would probably not have used the term ἀπόστολος at the beginning of letters to reinforce the authority of the epistolary message he is about to convey. And it is perhaps a mistake to draw too strong a contrast between the temporary commission of the Jewish delegate and the permanent commission of the Christian apostle. In the very early days, if the return of Christ was believed to be imminent, the distinction between 'temporary' and 'permanent' would not be so clear. This could be true also of the difference between 'religious' and 'juristic'. The messianic king would be regarded as possessing both types of function, and both would devolve upon his authorised representatives.[17] The date of origin of the Jewish institution is more problematic, but Barrett can point to a few items of evidence which could suggest its existence in some form prior to 70 C.E.[18] More importantly, he argues that it is precisely the NT evidence which may be adduced to support this conclusion. What we are concerned with is 'an institution that first-century Jews and Christians had in common', despite some differences.[19] This would explain the adoption of the term ἀπόστολος by the first Christians, since we may suppose that it was already in use by Greek-speaking Jews 'as an established rendering of שׁלִיחַ'.[20] Of the various suggestions as regards parallels to the Christian apostolate, this seems the most plausible.

(iii) *The Christian apostolate.* The synoptic writers see the Christian apostolate as beginning, in some sense, during the historical lifetime of Jesus.[21] This may not be wholly anachronistic. Barrett suggests that Jesus would have used his disciples as his agents, sending them to carry out tasks such as finding lodgings, and that, whilst not primarily commissioned to preach the Kingdom of God, they might well have communicated

---

[15] Schmithals, *Office of Apostle*, p. 106; see the extended discussion on pp. 100–10.
[16] Schmithals, *Office of Apostle*, p. 106.
[17] This may be illustrated in Acts 5.1–11.
[18] Barrett, 'Shaliah', p. 95.
[19] Barrett, 'Shaliah', pp. 98–9.
[20] Barrett, 'Shaliah', p. 98.
[21] Lk 6.13; Mk 3.14; 6.30; Mt 10.2; Lk 9.10; 17.5; 22.14.

their own belief to those whom they encountered.[22] Perhaps we might say a little more than this. Mark's claim (6.12) that the disciples were sent to preach repentance is, again, not necessarily an anachronism. Jesus had originally identified himself with the mission of John the Baptist, who had preached repentance to Israel. Jesus's own proclamation began similarly (Mk 1.15), but its high point was the message of the imminence of the Kingdom of God. It is not historically improbable that he might have sent some of his disciples to go ahead of him (cf. Lk 10.1), to issue a preliminary summons to penitence as preparation for the reception of his own climactic message.

If, then, some of Jesus's authorised agents had been involved during his historical lifetime with the preparation of Israel for the coming of the Kingdom of God, they would surely see this task as even more urgent in the post-Easter period, when, as they believed, Jesus had been installed through resurrection as himself the promised messianic king. The account in Acts of the apostolic preaching in Jerusalem must correspond to some degree with historical fact. It provides the explanation of the existence of the Jerusalem church, and it would be consonant with what we might suppose to have been the disciples' interpretation of their Easter experiences. With the establishment and growth of the church, however, to the initial proclamation of the gospel there was gradually added a different function with which the šĕlîḥîm of Jesus believed themselves entrusted. Barrett draws attention to Mt 19.28, where Jesus promises his disciples that in the new age they shall sit on twelve thrones, judging the twelve tribes of Israel. The Jerusalem apostles, on behalf of the Messiah, are to act 'as officials and administrators' of the new community, 'the eschatological Israel' which has now been inaugurated.[23] In all probability, it was this understanding of the apostolate which was in part responsible for the difference which arose between the Jerusalem church and Paul.

2. *Paul's apostolate*

There are four topics for discussion: Paul's experience of vocation; his relationship with the Jerusalem apostles; his relationship with the Corinthians as reflected in 2 Corinthians; lastly, the extension of his apostolic authority when 2 Corinthians becomes part of canonical scripture.

---

[22] Barrett, 'Shaliaḥ', pp. 101–2.
[23] Barrett, 'Shaliaḥ', p. 101.

(i) *Paul's experience of vocation.* As we have seen already, and as is frequently noted, when Paul briefly speaks about his original calling he does so in terms which echo accounts in the OT which describe the experiences of the prophets. The appearance of the risen Christ (1 Cor 9.1; 15.8) corresponds with the theophanies in which the divine call was mediated to Isaiah and Ezekiel (Isa 6.15; Ezek 1), and Paul's conviction that he was sent to preach the gospel to the Gentiles (Gal 1.15–16) is reminiscent of Jeremiah's call to be a prophet 'to the nations' (Jer 1.5).[24] At the risk of stating the obvious, we may add that the Christophany must therefore have contained verbal elements (as in Acts 9.4–5; 22.7–8; 26.14–18), not only to identify the nature of the divine presence but also to specify the task to which the recipient of the revelation was summoned, as in the prophetic experiences. Knowledge of the claims of those Paul had been persecuting would have given content to the message he now believed himself to have been entrusted with: the rejected and crucified Jesus of Nazareth had been vindicated as God's Messiah and God's Son. In addition, his words in 2 Cor 4.4 and 6 may be based on his conversion vision. If so, he will have seen Christ as the image of God, as reflecting God's glory.[25] Furthermore, in our exegesis of 12.1–4 we have agreed with the suggestion that the rapture to the third heaven may have confirmed his initial belief in his divine calling.

But how, exactly, did Paul then come to apply to himself the term ἀπόστολος? Perhaps there was a combination of factors. He knew that the major representatives of the Jesus-movement in Jerusalem were so styled in Greek-speaking Christian groups, and what he had seen or heard of them in his persecuting period would have related to their public appearances, and so to their proclamation of the message he was now to preach himself. The use of ἀποστέλλω in Isa 6.8 and of ἐξαποστέλλω in Jer 1.7 and Ezek 2.3 may have played a part. Even, perhaps, the term may have been part of the verbal content of the Christophany.

Clearly this revelation experience gave Paul the immense confidence which powered his mission in Asia Minor, Macedonia, and Greece. His authority as an apostle came directly, he believed, from the risen Christ, just as the authority of the prophets had come directly from God. This prophetic background would also have encouraged him, in the light of the call of Jeremiah, to accept continuing responsibility for the moral and spiritual building-up of the Christian communities he had founded (cf. Jer 1.10). And just as the prophets of the OT proclaimed the word of

---

[24] See above, pp. 948–9.
[25] See Vol. I, pp. 309–11, 318–19.

the Lord, so Paul is convinced 'that when he preaches it is God who really is the speaker'.[26] The negative aspect of this consciousness of divinely given authority is that he believes he has the power to destroy as well as to construct (13.10).[27] Whether this was ever put to the test remains obscure. The Corinthian church he constructed, which he implicitly threatens in 2 Cor 10–13, both remained in existence and also preserved his letters. This probably suggests that his apostolic power was not finally challenged. In his other foundations it seems that no such fundamental challenge arose. According to Holmberg, the last four chapters of 2 Corinthians are the only occasion in the Pauline letters 'where the apostle does not take it for granted that he will be obeyed'.[28] Moreover, in his work of building up Christian communities, Paul prefers to think of his authority as paternal in character. This he has in common with contemporary philosophers concerned with moral teaching.[29] Although such a role might sometimes demand harsh criticism it could still be seen as constructive, and could be regarded as such by his churches as well as by Paul himself.

Fundamentally, he is confident of his apostolic calling. At the same time there are occasional hints that he may have felt the need of some 'external' validation of his vocation. Twice in the Corinthian letters he appeals to the existence of the Corinthian church as providing such validation (1 Cor 9.1–2; 2 Cor 3.1–3). It is probable, however, that this apparent sense of need for confirmation was evoked by questioning, explicit or implicit, on the part of others, deriving from their encounters with other missionaries. In the first instance cited, acquaintance with the practice of Cephas on the part of Paul's critics may have influenced the situation. This brings us to the second topic for discussion.

(ii) *Paul's relationship with the Jerusalem apostles.* Our only firsthand evidence comes from Galatians. There, in response to the situation in Galatia, Paul is concerned to emphasise his independence of Jerusalem and his comparative lack of contact with the apostles resident in the city. Within the space of almost two decades he had visited Jerusalem only twice. Once was simply to visit Cephas (Gal 1.18–19). The second time was to secure the agreement of the major apostles on his policy for the evangelisation of the Gentiles (Gal 2.1–10). Thus, it appears that for a

---

[26] Holmberg, *Paul and Power*, p. 76.
[27] Holmberg, *Paul and Power*, p. 79.
[28] Holmberg, *Paul and Power*, p. 81.
[29] A. J. Malherbe, 'Exhortation in First Thessalonians', *NovT* 25 (1983), pp. 238–56, comments, p. 244: 'it had become common by Paul's time for the sage to exhort his listeners as their father, and to think of them as his children.'

long time he had been operating independently of Jerusalem. To quote Bruce, commenting on Gal 1.24: 'during the years which followed Paul's brief visit to Jerusalem, as in the shorter interval which preceded it, he was actively engaged in preaching the gospel, without requiring or receiving any authorization to do so from the leaders of the mother-church.'[30] But this may be something of an oversimplification. According to Acts 13–14, Paul had belonged at some stage, together with Barnabas, to the church in Antioch. The two of them had been sent out on mission by this church, with Barnabas, it would appear, as the senior partner.[31] And Antioch had connections with the Jerusalem church. Nevertheless, by the time Paul arrived in Macedonia he and Barnabas have separated, and Paul himself is apparently in charge, with Silvanus/Silas and Timothy as his assistants.[32] His independence of the Antioch-Jerusalem axis certainly seems absolute as regards the foundation of the Corinthian church. During this later period of the European mission and Paul's prior work in Galatia, he must have regarded himself as operating on the basis of the agreement recorded in Gal 2.7–9. But what, precisely, was the arrangement that had been sanctioned? As Paul saw it, it gave him independent control, not only over the initial process of evangelisation but also over the growth and nurture of the churches he had founded. The authority given him covered, he believed, the spiritual and moral building-up of the life of these churches (2 Cor 10.8), and also the power of discipline in a negative sense (1 Cor 5.3–5; 2 Cor 13.10). Now pastoral guidance may begin to verge on administrative control. This would be true of Paul's other churches, as well as of Corinth. The founding apostle keeps in touch by letters, and by visits when practicable. From the angle of vision of the authorities in Jerusalem, it would look as though Paul is creating an independent ecclesiastical empire. This may well have been a basic point of contention. Paul would be seen as wanting to have it both ways. On the one hand, he insisted that Gentile Christians were as much a part of the people of God as Jewish Christians. But on the other hand, he wanted to keep control of these groups himself. He seemed unwilling that they should come under the direct jurisdiction of the apostles originally appointed by Jesus as the administrators of the community of the Messiah, the nucleus of the restored Israel of the end-time. Paul himself may indeed have intended the collection, in part, as a means of establishing some formal relationship between his Gentile churches and

[30] Bruce, *Galatians*, p. 105.
[31] Murphy-O'Connor, *Paul*, pp. 95–6.
[32] 1 Thess 1.1; 3.2; cf. Acts 15.39–40.

Jerusalem. But from the point of view of Jerusalem this would have been a project they had not authorised, to promote an association on terms Paul alone had drawn up.

(iii) *Paul's relationship with the Corinthians.* Paul's relationship with the Corinthian congregation had not been entirely smooth during the period prior to the first of the letters contained in the canonical 2 Corinthians (i.e., chaps. 1–8/9). Initially he had had to deal with the various problems reflected in 1 Corinthians. Then had come the unhappy interim visit, and the mysterious offence, committed by some member of the church, which had occasioned Paul's Painful Letter. The letter of 2 Cor 1–8/9 is in part an acknowledgement that the Corinthians had put matters to rights as far as that incident was concerned, together with an explanation of Paul's failure to visit and a plea to resume the collection. But the main theme of the letter, stretching from 2.14 to 7.4, consists of a defence and explanation of his service as an apostle. And this accounts for the predominant emphasis on his suffering. He speaks of participation in the sufferings of Christ (1.5), and refers allusively to tribulation he experienced in Asia (1.8–10). He constructs a hardships-list in 4.8–9. This is introduced by a general image in v. 7 of his inglorious lifestyle, the earthenware container of the treasure of the gospel, which indicates that the point of the hardships is the display of divine power which ensues as their consequence. In v. 10, furthermore, apostolic suffering has a revelational function, in that it presents a visual image of the death of Jesus. In 4.17, suffering is the prelude to glory. The further passage in 6.3–10 can also be seen as a hardships-list, and in 7.5 Paul refers to affliction suffered in Macedonia. In all this he sees his suffering as christologically or theologically grounded, and as essential to his apostolic service. His defence is necessitated by Corinthian criticism of his inglorious personal presence, deriving from adverse comparison with the glorious figure of Moses in Jewish tradition and from the general influence of the secular ethos of the city.[33]

It seems that this letter did not have the effect Paul hoped for, and the crisis intensified, evoking the letter of 2 Cor 10–13. Rival claimants to apostolic authority were present in force, and gaining influence over the Corinthians. It would seem that they displayed the kind of personal glory attractive to the church, and were aiming to supplant Paul. What was he to do?

His response is to write a fresh letter devoted almost entirely to self-defence. It contains two hardships-lists: a lengthy and specific

---

[33] On the Moses question, see the exegesis of chap. 3 in Vol. I. On the Corinthian ethos in general, see Savage, *Power through Weakness*, pp. 35–53.

one in 11.23–9, and a much shorter, general one in 12.10. The first has some affinity with similar catalogues placed in the mouths of secular heroes such as Alexander, and may serve in part to show Paul's leadership qualities, powers of endurance, and the like. The second is in complete contrast. Following upon the account of his prayer to be relieved of the 'thorn', it vividly emphasises his recognition that his human weakness is the necessary context for the display of the power of Christ. Other aspects of apologetic include Paul's insistence that, if necessary, he can act powerfully (10.4–6, 11; 13.2, 4; cf. 12.12); his claim that Corinth is his missionary territory (10.13–16); his insistence that his aides have not exploited the church financially (12.16–18); and his castigation of the rival missionaries (10.12; 11.4, 12–15, 20). There is a difference in tone and outlook between this letter and the previous one. In the letter of chaps. 1–8 Paul had in part put his case in comparatively detached terms, arguing theologically in chap. 3 for the necessary glory of the ministry of the new covenant. And even when, as in chaps. 4 and 6, the personal reference may be nearer the surface, what is said there about engagement in ministry can readily be understood in a more general and inclusive sense. This is not so in chaps. 10–13. Here it is Paul in person, Paul as an individual, who is insisting on his exclusive apostolic claim to pastoral control over the Corinthian church. He writes, moreover, in a style which may well appear aggressive. All this can easily give the impression of egocentricity, as might his apparent failure to consider whether the Corinthians might have a tenable point of view.[34] Was Paul an egotist, then? The question at least requires discussion.

The thesis of an egotistic Paul is put most forcefully by Graham Shaw in his book *The Cost of Authority*. The chapter on 2 Corinthians offers useful material for its evaluation, since it provides a substantial part of the argument. We select some of the key points for discussion. In the earlier part of the epistle, it is apparent, Shaw claims, that Paul is determined to win either way, whether his gospel is accepted or whether it is rejected. See the 'arrogant and divisive' assertion in 2.15–16. For the apostle, 'welcome and hostility both strengthen his image of himself'.[35] His inglorious and precarious lifestyle might seem to urge caution towards the acceptance of his claims. He argues, however, that the discrepancy serves as 'proof of total dependence upon God': see 4.1–14.[36] And the way he handles the Corinthians' eventual response to the affair of the offender is designed to show that his

---

[34] See above, pp. 942–3.
[35] *Cost of Authority*, p. 103.
[36] *Cost of Authority*, p. 104.

own honour has in the end achieved vindication.[37] With reference to 5.13–6.1, Shaw argues that whilst Paul sees his own life as immediately directed by Christ, he regards the Christ-direction of his converts as requiring his own mediation. This means that Paul himself submits to 'a Christ who is largely the creation of his own projections', whilst the believer has to submit to the real personal will of the apostle.[38] Further evidence of egocentricity is to be found in chaps. 10–13. In 10.10 we see that Paul's critics note a contrast between his letters and his personal presence. This suggests that 'much of the assertion and self-importance of the letters is compensation for a man whose personal impact was unremarkable'.[39] And commenting on 11.12–15, Shaw says of the apostle: 'The elevation of his own authority is such that he can tolerate no independent source of power in the communities which he has founded.'[40] Lastly, he argues that all Paul has said about his weakness in chaps. 11–12 is to be seen simply as 'preparation for the most aggressive assertion of power'.[41] In 13.2–4, the point is that 'Christ is today vindicated by the discipline of the refractory Corinthians, as he was in the past by being raised from the dead.'[42]

How is this portrait of Paul to be assessed? To begin with, two general points may be in order. In the first place, Shaw writes from a non-theistic philosophical standpoint: 'the only reality of God lies in the use of that word by human beings'.[43] It follows also that the only reality of Christ, after the death of the human Jesus, lies, in Paul's case, in an image produced by his own psyche. In neither case would there be reference to any transcendent reality. Apparent experience of contact with divine being would simply be the self talking to the self. In one sense this would indeed constitute egocentricity, if not of the conscious, culpable type. But granted the possible truth of the theistic alternative, the matter becomes more complicated. Whilst there remains the possibility that, in any one instance, the apparent contact with God or Christ may be an egocentric delusion, there exists the alternative possibility that the experience is a reality. Theophany or Christophany would not automatically be ruled out of consideration as a genuine divine manifestation, and the prophetic or apostolic apprehension of the divine might contain truth that such a person would be obligated to communicate. That it would be a message

---

[37] *Cost of Authority*, pp. 108–10.
[38] *Cost of Authority*, pp. 114–15; the quotation is on p. 115.
[39] *Cost of Authority*, pp. 119–20.
[40] *Cost of Authority*, p. 121.
[41] *Cost of Authority*, p. 123.
[42] Ibid.
[43] *Cost of Authority*, p. 282.

apprehended by a particular prophet or apostle could give the impression of egotism on the part of the messenger. But such ambiguity is inherent in such a situation. Paul believed himself entrusted with an overwhelmingly important divine message. His efforts to propagate it and to guide its recipients in working out its implications may have involved him in the appearance, perhaps indeed the reality, of egocentricity. But this might have been the inevitable hazard of a calling to which, overall, he devoted himself with great self-sacrifice.

The second general point is that Shaw fails to take into consideration Paul's historical background. The apostle's intolerance of any 'independent source of power' could well have had some justification. By asserting his independence of Jerusalem he was protecting, so he believed, the interests of the Gentile mission against a claim to control which could ultimately have reduced its scope to Jewish proselytism, and diminished its success. Another instance of the disregard, or more probably unawareness, of Paul's historical context concerns what to a modern reader sometimes appears to be his aggressive attitude or his harsh treatment of his correspondents, characteristics which can certainly give the impression of egotism. They may be due, however, to Paul's employment of the contemporary convention of frank speech, παρρησία.[44] In the Graeco-Roman world, frank speech was used by friends or teachers to benefit some other person or group by correcting their conduct.[45] It might vary in degree from harsh, undiluted criticism to gentle correction mixed with praise.[46] Paul's use of παρρησία in his letters reflects this variety.[47] In the Corinthian correspondence the letter containing chaps. 1–7 may be placed between the two extremes.[48] That of chaps. 10–13, however, stands at the harsh end of the scale, as undiluted criticism. Also, it contains a considerable amount of 'ethos augmentation'. According to the convention, the character of the one meting out frank speech was important. Weakness of character was ineffective. So Paul has to insist on his consistency (11.12), and on his love for his converts (11.11; 12.15, 19), and he tells them about the extraordinary privilege of his rapture to heaven (12.2–4). He speaks harshly to his readers and he talks

---

[44] I am indebted for what follows to a seminar paper, 'Frank Speech in the Pauline Correspondence', by J. Paul Sampley, delivered at the SNTS meeting in Birmingham, August 1997.

[45] 'Frank Speech', pp. 1–5.

[46] 'Frank Speech', p. 3.

[47] The remainder of the paper, pp. 5–19, is devoted to the Pauline use, summed up in the diagram on p. 16.

[48] 'Frank Speech', pp. 11–12.

about himself.[49] All this appears egocentric, but could be seen as acceptable (just) within the conventions of his day.

Turning to more particular issues, we might consider Shaw's interpretation of 2.15–16. Presumably his main objection is to the categorisation of those who reject Paul's preaching as the ones destined for destruction and, in 4.3–4, as blinded by 'the god of this world'. This is seen as enhancing Paul's self-image. But there is other, or at least additional, motivation to be taken into account. Paul was deeply concerned about Jewish rejection of the Christian message (Rom 9.1–5)—a rejection to which he refers in 2 Cor 3.14–15. Some explanation was needed, whether or not egotism on his part came into the picture. Whether his claim of dependence on God is egotistic, as Shaw claims also, is in one sense a non-question. Since Paul obviously believed in God, there is no reason a priori to regard the claim of dependence as self-serving. To the non-theist, of course, it might well seem to be a form of covert or unconscious self-aggrandisement, since it could not, ex hypothesi, be anything else. Of Shaw's other arguments for Paul's egocentricity, we should agree, in part, with one but reject the two others we have mentioned. We should allow that there is a degree of egotism in the way the apostle handles the Corinthians' eventual response to the affair of the offender. Chiefly on the basis of suggestions made some considerable time ago by Windisch, we have ourselves drawn attention to egocentric elements in 2.1–11 and 7.5–16.[50] We disagree, however, with the suggestion that Paul's epistolary self-assertion is compensation for personal ineffectiveness. Whilst this does have some basis in 10.10, to regard him in general as personally ineffectual makes nonsense of his missionary achievements. And the contention that all that is said about weakness in chaps. 11–12 is simply preparation for 13.2–4 does scant justice to the contents of these chapters.

Shaw's presentation is obviously very one-sided. Nevertheless, it does seem that there is some element in Paul's character that might be termed egocentricity. We need to ask, however, whether this might not be the negative converse of positive qualities vitally necessary for the exercise of his calling as apostle to the Gentiles. He travelled the length and breadth of the eastern Mediterranean, sometimes alone, without the facilities which official or upper-class travellers might be able to command. He would need to be a man of robust personality and with a strong sense of identity. Otherwise he would not have survived the hazards of his journeys, nor would he have made much impact in the towns and

[49] 'Frank Speech', pp. 12–14, 16.
[50] See Vol. I, pp. 169, 496.

cities he visited with the gospel message. Murphy-O'Connor, who gives a vivid description of the dangers faced by travellers, suggests, moreover, that whilst Paul's ideal would have been the 'totally other-directed mode of existence' exemplified by Jesus, his travel difficulties would militate against its adoption. He would be compelled to worry about his own safety, and to make sure, for example, that his leather-working tools were not stolen if he put up for the night in some inn. Circumstances forced him to consider himself, and to struggle against the danger of egotism.[51] He did not always prevail, according to Murphy-O'Connor, who finds in Phil 2 an example of the apostle's concern for his own interests and his identification of these interests with those of Christ.[52]

In some respects, then, Paul could be seen as egocentric. But perhaps 'self-absorbed' might be a better term. He did not pursue his own advantage in the sense of seeking fame or financial gain. His letters are not written as literary products for publication, to impress an educated audience. But he is certainly absorbed in his own individual calling, perhaps to the exclusion of accepting other people as genuinely other. His deep conviction of vocation and of the consequent authority bestowed on him will have resulted in a mental and emotional outlook focused on his own understanding of the gospel and on his own methods of pastoral guidance. This means that whilst he wants his converts to become mature in faith and practice, they are expected to show a maturity consonant with his own understanding of Christian truth and life. Consequently, he may become uneasy and authoritarian (perhaps aggressively so) when members of his churches become attracted to other missionaries. And yet, in the case of the situation reflected in 2 Cor 10–13, he may well have been more far-sighted than the Corinthians in his grasp of the implications, should his rivals succeed in their takeover bid.[53] In any case, his absorption in his own understanding of the gospel can be seen as the negative side of the positive qualities of conviction and commitment essential for the successful accomplishment of his mission. We should not forget, either, that Paul's response to his critics and rivals in Corinth has given future generations a picture of Christian ministry possessed of considerable theological depth and spiritual insight. This brings us to our final topic.

(iv) *2 Corinthians as canonical.* To regard the epistle as valuable to the Church for the understanding it offers of Christian ministry

51 Murphy-O'Connor, *Paul*, pp. 96–101.
52 Murphy-O'Connor, *Paul*, pp. 223–4.
53 See above, p. 944.

is not, necessarily, to go so far as to treat it as canonical. We may read other such discussions which appear equally valuable, and possibly more appropriate to the present day. To see 2 Corinthians as canonical, that is, as part of Scripture, is to attribute to the epistle some higher degree of inspiration and authority than pertains to other religious literature. Barnett terms this 'dominical authority', and relates it to Paul's 'unique place' as 'apostle to the Gentiles, authorized ... to edify the churches (10:8; 12:19; 13:10)'.[54] The implicit basis of this viewpoint is twofold: acceptance of Paul's interpretation of his Christophanic experience, and the complementary attribution of special authority to the NT writings, extending over the centuries and reaching to the present. For Barnett, it seems, all this is acceptable. Paul's words to the Corinthians may readily be seen as applicable to the churches of the present day, and readers can be urged to put themselves in the place of the original recipients.

The matter, however, may not be quite so straightforward. Complexities begin to emerge. First, there is the picture of the apostle's personal character which emerges from his interaction with the Corinthian church. Secondly, there is the question as to whether the canonicity of 2 Corinthians has been to some degree responsible for the anti-Judaism of the post-Pauline Christian Church.

(1) Was Paul an egocentric authoritarian? If so, can he possibly be regarded as an authoritative, scriptural model for later Christian ministry? We have argued that he does give the impression of self-absorption and seems unable imaginatively to envisage the Corinthian situation from the Corinthians' own point of view. We have suggested further, however, that these aspects of his character may emerge as the shadow-side of the positive qualities necessary for his mission. And despite the harshness of the letter of chaps. 10–13 there may well have been some final rapprochement.[55] The probability, however, that both sides in the previous conflict had made up their differences did not necessarily mean that the Corinthians now saw Paul as exemplifying the apostolic ideal *par excellence*.

This comes with canonicity and the consequent tendency to disregard any negative traits in Paul's character. After Jesus, he becomes the supreme model of Christian ministry. His readers, Barnett claims, are to be edified by the passages in which he explicates 'the *non*-triumphalist, "slave"-like character of his ministry ... (e.g., 2.14–16; 4.1–15; 6.3–13)'. His visions might have engendered pride, but he had been taught humility by his experience of

54 Barnett, pp. 47–8.
55 See above, p. 944.

the 'thorn'.[56] The difficulty, of course, is that it is Paul himself who tells us all this. This is not, *ipso facto*, a reason to discount it. But it does need to be correlated with the indications of self-absorption to which we have drawn attention. Paul was a highly complex character. The positive aspects of his apostolic *persona*, whilst surely preponderant, were nevertheless balanced, to some degree, by more negative traits. This does not, however, make him any the less of a model or an ideal for those appointed to Christian ministry today. For what, in any case, is required of such a model? A person with no flaws may be unreal, or at least unhelpful to those to whom he is presented as an ideal—perhaps, even, psychologically damaging. A bishop who expects of his or her clerics total, perfect, and perpetual commitment to endurance, patience, service, sacrifice and love may soon have few clergy left who are not undergoing treatment for stress. A more realistically human Paul, psychological warts and all, could well prove to be the genuine 'canonical' figure: prone, on occasion, to authoritarian behaviour and lapses from selflessness, but nevertheless to be admired for his achievements, for his faith and courage, and for his theological and spiritual insight. And if, in 2 Corinthians, he might seem to speak rather too often of himself, who else was there to speak knowledgeably of him, in respect of his experience of the divine power which overcame, but did not remove, his personal weakness, the hindrance of the σκόλοψ, and the hazards, such as the trouble in Asia, which imperilled his life? Within the Christian tradition, these elements of autobiography, preserved with the authority of canonical Scripture, must have served as sources of hope and encouragement to many subsequent generations of believers caught in like circumstances, and may still do so.

(2) The other difficulty does not arise from the character or conduct of Paul himself, but from the use made of the epistle in later centuries to support anti-Judaism. In chap. 3 we find a negative picture of contemporary Judaism (vv. 14–18): minds are hardened and hearts are veiled. This picture is evoked by criticism of the apostle on the part of non-Christian Jews,[57] not by gratuitous anti-Judaism on Paul's part. Paul himself, as a Jew, was deeply concerned for his own people, and struggled to find reasons, within God's providence, for their rejection, for the most part, of the Christian gospel.[58] In later Christian history, however, Church and Synagogue become radically separated, and this passage in 2 Corinthians, now canonical Scripture, is used in the

---

[56] Barnett, p. 48.
[57] See Vol. I, p. 297.
[58] Rom 9.1–5; 11.

service of anti-Jewish propaganda. Chrysostom, commenting on 2 Cor 3.14, in the light of the OT and of historical event, claims that God has demonstrated the abolition of the old covenant, 'first indeed by shutting up its sacrifices and its whole ritual in one place, the Temple, and afterwards destroying this'.[59] In one sense, the argument could stand on the twin bases of the OT and of the destruction of the Temple in 70 C.E. But it is very likely the scriptural reference in 2 Cor 3 that indicates to Chrysostom that the historical event was indeed the work of God. It is clear also from what follows in the course of his exegesis that Paul's words, in his view, sanction virulent anti-Judaism. He speaks of 'the senseless Jews', and claims that Paul proves 'their grossness and groveling nature', and 'takes down' their 'inflation'.[60] It seems likely, furthermore, that the influence of 2 Cor 3–4 was more widespread. It is to be seen in the sculpture and stained glass of medieval Europe where images of the Church and the Synagogue stand side by side, in sharp contrast the one with the other. The woman personifying the Church stands crowned, erect and triumphant, with open eyes. The Synagogue is a drooping, depressed figure with blindfolded eyes and a broken staff, on occasion with falling books in her hand, symbolising the five books of the law: 'The sculptures graphically depict the centuries-long Christian belief that God's covenant with the Jews had been broken and was now replaced by a "new covenant" exclusively with the church.'[61] The canonicity of 2 Corinthians has in this respect had undesirable consequences, in that it must surely have reinforced anti-Jewish attitudes. The solution to the problem, however, is not to reject canonicity as such, but to remind ourselves that Rom 9–11 is also canonical, and presents a somewhat different outlook: 'Paul's attitude to non-Christian Israel remains a positive one. He does not give up his hope for them, nor his love. He does not deny to the majority of the Jews the use of the name Israel, with all the theological values attached to it.'[62] The one canonical letter needs to be complemented by the other, and account taken of the fact that 2 Cor 3 was written in a conflict situation, whereas Romans was not.

[59] NPNF XII, p. 312.
[60] NPNF XII, p. 311.
[61] G. A. Zinn, 'History and Interpretation', page following p. 126 in *Jews and Christians*, ed. J. H. Charlesworth, New York, 1990, pp. 100–26. See the illustrations on the following unnumbered pages.
[62] Fraikin, 'The Rhetorical Function of the Jews in Romans', pp. 104–5. See, however, R. W. Wall, in *The New Testament as Canon*, JSNTSS 76, Sheffield, 1992, p. 264. He observes that the tensions and separation between the Church and the Synagogue 'were in large measure the result of Paul's preaching and his Gentile mission'. This appears to suggest that the popular view of Paul as 'anti-Judaic' might not be altogether mistaken.

In at least one respect, then, the canonicity of 2 Corinthians might be seen as a somewhat ambivalent legacy to the Church of later ages. But we could end on a more positive note, in relation to the relevance of the canonical epistle to contemporary theological concerns. During the second half of the twentieth century, there has been considerable preoccupation with christology. In Britain there has been popular as well as academic interest, kindled initially by the publication of John Robinson's *Honest to God* in 1963,[63] and increased in 1977 by the collection of essays in *The Myth of God Incarnate*.[64] This is not the place to engage in the debate as such. I wish simply to draw attention to three facts and then to consider their implication. The facts are these: that the canonicity of 2 Corinthians has preserved the epistle for our own attention at the present day; that it contains various indications of Paul's christological beliefs; and that these beliefs, developed very early in the history of the Christian movement, begin to point in substance to the definitions of the later creeds. This then may have some relevance for assessment of the truth of the credal assertions.

The first fact speaks for itself. The second needs substantiation. If we look carefully, we find that the epistle contains a number of allusions to the major elements of the Christ-event, mentioned as though they should be familiar to Paul's readers. Christ was rich in his pre-existent state, but became poor through incarnation (8.9). He is the image, εἰκών, of God, the embodiment of divine Wisdom, who reveals God's glory, God's nature (4.4, 6). Sinless in himself, he became identified with sinful humanity and died on their behalf (5.21). On their behalf also he was raised from the dead (5.15). In his own right, moreover, this Christ hears and responds to prayer, and bestows divine power upon Paul to counteract his weakness (12.8–9). He is God's son (1.19), and the bestower of divine grace (13.13). The third fact, consequently, is that, within a space of between twenty and twenty-five years after the crucifixion of Jesus,[65] Paul had developed and taught a comparatively 'high' christology in which the divinity and the humanity of Christ are fully attested. This is not yet the language of the Nicene Creed, but it points clearly in that direction. If we then go on to ask how Paul came to hold these beliefs, the most likely answer would be that his understanding of Christ derived in large part from his personal experience. The Christophany which effected his conversion showed him Christ as the image of God,

---

[63] John A. T. Robinson, *Honest to God*, London, 1963.

[64] *The Myth of God Incarnate*, ed. John Hick, London, 1977.

[65] Jewett, *Dating Paul's Life*, end-graph, gives 33 C.E. as the more probable date of the crucifixion, and 30 C.E. as the less probable. We have dated the contents of 2 Corinthians in 56 C.E.: see Vol. I, p. 77.

the manifestation of God's glory. This initial perception of the nature of Christ could then have been enhanced by the experience of heavenly rapture, which may have included a vision of the glorified Christ enthroned in heaven. And he has experienced the power of Christ, in answer to prayer, in the same way as he had experienced, in Asia, the power of the God who raises the dead.

What, then, might be the significance of this Pauline christology and its probable origin for the contemporary debate? When the christological content of the creeds is under discussion, it is more often John's Gospel which is seen as the chief, if not the only, scriptural influence on credal development. But if we are concerned with the truth, as well as the history, of this development, emphasis on the Fourth Gospel has two drawbacks. First, whilst on the surface it is Jesus himself who speaks of his full divinity (10.30; 14.9–10), this contrasts sharply with the sayings and manner of discourse attributed to Jesus in the Synoptic tradition, and it is the latter which is seen as the more historical, in the ordinary sense of the word. Secondly, a presentation of this kind gives us no hint as to how the Johannine christology originated, if we cannot suppose that Jesus himself spoke in this way. The Pauline christology that makes its indirect appearance in 2 Corinthians (and in other letters) does not suffer from these drawbacks. It would not be open to direct contradiction by any other of the NT writings. And more importantly we do have indications as to how Paul's beliefs may have originated and developed.

How, then, would this Pauline evidence relate to the question of the truth or otherwise of traditional christology? We have to begin (logically, if not experientially) where Paul himself began prior to his experience of Christophany. We begin, that is, with belief in the living God of monotheistic faith. In fact, the majority of scholars engaged in the christological debate during the last few decades have accepted this belief, whatever their particular understanding of it. Given its acceptance, we can then consider its implications for our present question. This basic faith in God allows the possibility of genuine contact with divine being. It allows, therefore, that Paul's christophanic experience may have been a genuine occasion of such contact, and, in consequence, that his interpretation of it was true. It allows also that he may have known the bestowal of actual divine power in response to his prayers to Christ. That this was so may well be attested by the success of his missionary endeavours despite the human weaknesses seen by the Corinthians as inimical to his apostolic status. If the second Corinthian epistle contributes in some small way to acceptance of the belief in Christ as God the Son incarnate, this may be the most important effect of its preservation as part of canonical Scripture.

INDEX I

AUTHORS OF THE MODERN PERIOD
(from the beginning of the sixteenth century)

Whilst the indexing aims to be as comprehensive as possible, there are three qualifications. First, the index does not include the authors of the articles in *TWNT* (cf. Vol. I, p. xv). Secondly, whilst it does include the names of the commentators whose work has been gratefully used in the preparation of the present commentary, it lacks the relevant page references (unmanageably numerous in many cases), which are replaced by *passim*. In these circumstances the term covers the use of other works by the same scholar. Thirdly, *passim* is used occasionally in the case of other authors who have written extensively on the epistle as a whole, or on substantial sections of it (indicated by the relevant page numbers), or whose work in other respects has been mentioned frequently.

INDEX II
CLASSICAL AND HELLENISTIC WRITERS

INDEX III

BIBLICAL AND PSEUDEPIGRAPHIC TEXTS

INDEX IV

SUBJECTS

INDEX V
PAPYRI, QUMRAN TEXTS, RABBINIC WRITINGS